Communications in Computer and Information Science 865

Commenced Publication in 2007
Founding and Former Series Editors:
Phoebe Chen, Alfredo Cuzzocrea, Xiaoyong Du, Orhun Kara, Ting Liu, Dominik Ślęzak, and Xiaokang Yang

More information about this series at http://www.springer.com/series/7899

Paula Escudeiro · Gennaro Costagliola
Susan Zvacek · James Uhomoibhi
Bruce M. McLaren (Eds.)

Computers Supported Education

9th International Conference, CSEDU 2017 Porto, Portugal, April 21–23, 2017 Revised Selected Papers

Springer

Editors
Paula Escudeiro
Instituto Superior de Engenharia do Porto
Porto
Portugal

Gennaro Costagliola
University of Salerno
Fisciano
Italy

Susan Zvacek
University of Denver
Denver, CO
USA

James Uhomoibhi
School of Engineering
University of Ulster
Newtownabbey
UK

Bruce M. McLaren
Carnegie Mellon University
Pittsburgh, PA
USA

ISSN 1865-0929 ISSN 1865-0937 (electronic)
Communications in Computer and Information Science
ISBN 978-3-319-94639-9 ISBN 978-3-319-94640-5 (eBook)
https://doi.org/10.1007/978-3-319-94640-5

Library of Congress Control Number: 2018947445

Printed on acid-free paper

This Springer imprint is published by the registered company Springer International Publishing AG part of Springer Nature
The registered company address is: Gewerbestrasse 11, 6330 Cham, Switzerland

Preface

The present book includes extended and revised versions of a set of selected papers from the 9th International Conference on Computer Supported Education (CSEDU 2017), held in Porto, Portugal, during April 21–23, 2017.

CSEDU 2017 received 179 paper submissions from 50 countries, of which 12% are included in this book. The papers were selected by the event chairs and their selection is based on a number of criteria that include the classifications and comments provided by the Program Committee members, the session chairs' assessment, and also the program chairs' global view of all papers included in the technical program. The authors of selected papers were then invited to submit a revised and extended version of their papers having at least 30% innovative material.

CSEDU aims at becoming a yearly meeting place for presenting and discussing new educational environments, best practices, and case studies on innovative technology-based learning strategies and institutional policies on computer-supported education including open and distance education, using computers. In particular, the Web is currently a preferred medium for distance learning and the learning practice in this context is usually referred to as e-learning. CSEDU 2017 gave an overview of the state of the art as well as upcoming trends, and promoted discussion about the pedagogical potential of new learning and educational technologies in the academic and corporate world.

The papers selected for this book contribute to the understanding of current research on computer-supported education, including the integration of digital resources in teaching and learning, design and development of technologies for instruction, management of educational data, use of educational data for decision-making, game- and simulation-based learning, and use of online environments to support community-building. These contributions reflect the wide range of topics presented at the conference where authors had the opportunity to discuss their ideas with peers and explore related issues.

We would like to thank all the authors for their contributions and also the reviewers who helped ensure the quality of this publication.

April 2017

Paula Escudeiro
Gennaro Costagliola
Susan Zvacek
James Uhomoibhi
Bruce M. McLaren

Organization

Conference Chair

Bruce M. McLaren	Carnegie Mellon University, USA

Program Co-chairs

Paula Escudeiro	Instituto Superior de Engenharia do Porto, Portugal
Gennaro Costagliola	Università di Salerno, Italy
Susan Zvacek	NA, USA
James Uhomoibhi	Ulster University, UK

Program Committee

Dor Abrahamson	University of California, Berkeley, USA
Mehdi Adda	Université du Québec à Rimouski, Canada
Shirley Agostinho	University of Wollongong, Australia
Jan Aidemark	Linnaeus University, Sweden
Nelma Albuquerque	Concepts and Insights, The Netherlands
Efthimios Alepis	University of Piraeus, Greece
Eleftheria Alexandri	University of Patras, Greece
Zehra Altinay	Near East University, Cyprus
António Andrade	Universidade Católica Portuguesa, Portugal
Galia Angelova	Institute of Information and Communication Technologies, Bulgarian Academy of Sciences, Bulgaria
Francisco Arcega	Universidad de Zaragoza, Spain
Inmaculada Arnedillo-Sanchez	Trinity College Dublin, Ireland
Ivon Arroyo	Worcester Polytechnic Institute, USA
Juan Ignacio Asensio	University of Valladolid, Spain
Anders Avdic	Dalarna University, Sweden
Breno Fabrício Terra Azevedo	Instituto Federal de Educação, Ciência e Tecnologia Fluminense, Brazil
Adriano Baratè	Università degli Studi di Milano, Italy
Jorge Barbosa	UNISINOS, Brazil
Patrícia Brandalise Scherer Bassani	Universidade Feevale, Brazil
Emad Bataineh	Zayed University, UAE
Clemens Bechter	TBS, Thailand
Lilia Cheniti Belcadhi	University of Sousse, Tunisia

Kay Berkling	Cooperative State University Baden-Württemberg, Karlsruhe, Germany
Pavol Bistak	Slovak University of Technology, Slovak Republic
Marlies Bitter-Rijpkema	Open University, The Netherlands
Lars Bollen	Universiteit Twente, The Netherlands
Andreas Bollin	Klagenfurt University, Austria
Katrin Borcea-Pfitzmann	Technische Universität Dresden, Germany
Elmar-Laurent Borgmann	Hochschule Koblenz, University of Applied Sciences, Germany
Ivana Bosnic	University of Zagreb, Croatia
Federico Botella	Miguel Hernandez University of Elche, Spain
Jesús G. Boticario	aDeNu Research Group, UNED, Spain
François Bouchet	Laboratoire d'Informatique de Paris 6, France
Benedict du Boulay	University of Sussex, UK
Ghizlane El Boussaidi	École de Technologie Supérieure, Canada
Tharrenos Bratitsis	University of Western Macedonia, Greece
Krysia Broda	Imperial College London, UK
Dumitru Burdescu	University of Craiova, Romania
Egle Butkeviciene	Kaunas University of Technology, Lithuania
Santi Caballé	Open University of Catalonia, Spain
Pasquina Campanella	University of Bari Aldo Moro, Italy
Chris Campbell	Griffith University, Australia
Martin Cápay	Constantine the Philosopher University in Nitra, Slovak Republic
Alberto Cardoso	University of Coimbra, Portugal
Thibault Carron	Pierre and Marie Curie University, France
Carlos Vaz de Carvalho	ISEP, Portugal
Vítor Carvalho	IPCA and Algoritmi Research Centre, UM, Portugal
Isabel Chagas	Universidade de Lisboa, Portugal
Ben Chang	National Central University, Taiwan
Amitava Chatterjee	Jadavpur University, India
Mohamed Amine Chatti	University of Duisburg-Essen, Germany
Lukas Chrpa	University of Huddersfield, UK
Alison Clark-Wilson	University College London, UK
Jo Coldwell-Neilson	Deakin University, Australia
Marc Conrad	University of Bedfordshire, UK
Fernando Albuquerque Costa	Universidade de Lisboa, Portugal
Gennaro Costagliola	Università degli Studi di Salerno, Italy
Gennaro Costagliola	Università di Salerno, Italy
Manuel Perez Cota	Universidade de Vigo, Spain
Caroline M. Crawford	University of Houston-Clear Lake, USA
John Philip Cuthell	Virtual Learning, UK
Thanasis Daradoumis	University of the Aegean/Open University of Catalonia, Greece/Spain
Sergiu Dascalu	University of Nevada, Reno, USA

Claudia Deco	Universidad Nacional de Rosario, Argentina
Stavros N. Demetriadis	Aristotle University of Thessaloniki, Greece
Giuliana Dettori	Istituto per le Tecnologie Didattiche, Italy
Darina Dicheva	Winston-Salem State University, USA
Yannis Dimitriadis	University of Valladolid, Spain
Lars Dittmann	Technical University of Denmark, Denmark
Danail Dochev	Institute of Information and Communication Technologies, Bulgarian Academy of Sciences, Bulgaria
Toby Dragon	Ithaca College, USA
Manuel Palomo Duarte	Universidad de Cádiz, Spain
Amalia Duch	Polytechnical University of Catalonia, Spain
Ishbel Duncan	University of St. Andrews, UK
Martin Ebner	Technische Universität Graz, Austria
Joseph Ekstrom	Brigham Young University, USA
Paula Escudeiro	Instituto Superior de Engenharia do Porto, Portugal
João Sena Esteves	University of Minho, Portugal
Si Fan	University of Tasmania, Australia
Mingyu Feng	SRI International, USA
Richard E. Ferdig	Kent State University, USA
Rosa M. Fernandez-Alcala	University of Jaen, Spain
Davide Fossati	Emory University, USA
Rita Francese	Università degli Studi di Salerno, Italy
Gabriele Frankl	Alpen-Adria-Universität Klagenfurt, Austria
Vittorio Fuccella	Università di Salerno, Italy
Judith Gal-Ezer	The Open University of Israel, Israel
Mikuláš Gangur	University of West Bohemia, Czech Republic
Iván García-Magariño	Universidad de Zaragoza, Spain
Serge Garlatti	TELECOM Bretagne, France
Isabela Gasparini	UDESC, Brazil
Xun Ge	University of Oklahoma, USA
Sébastien George	Université du Maine, France
Ramon Fabregat Gesa	Universitat de Girona, Spain
Biswadip Ghosh	Metropolitan State University of Denver, USA
David Gibson	Curtin University, Australia
Henrique Gil	Escola Superior de Educação do Instituto Politécnico de Castelo Branco, Portugal
Manuel Castro Gil	National University for Distance Education, Spain
Mercè Gisbert	Universitat Rovira i Virgili, Spain
Anabela Gomes	Polytechnic Institute of Coimbra, Portugal
Maria João Gomes	Universidade do Minho, Portugal
Nuno Pina Gonçalves	Superior School of Technology, Polytechnical Institute of Setúbal, Portugal
Anandha Gopalan	Imperial College London, UK
Christian Guetl	Graz University of Technology, Austria
Nathalie Guin	Université Claude Bernard, Lyon 1, France

Jean-Marc Labat	Université Pierre et Marie Curie, France
H. Chad Lane	University of Illinois, Urbana-Champaign, USA
Teresa Larkin	American University, USA
Rynson Lau	City University of Hong Kong, Hong Kong, SAR China
Tobias Lauer	Offenburg University of Applied Sciences, Germany
José Paulo Leal	University of Porto, Portugal
Celina Leão	University of Minho, Portugal
Dominique Leclet	UPJV, France
Mark Lee	Charles Sturt University, Australia
Newton Lee	Newton Lee Laboratories LLC and Institute for Education Research and Scholarships, USA
Marie Lefevre	Claude Bernard University of Lyon 1, France
Andrew Lian	Suranaree University of Technology, Thailand
Veronica Liesaputra	Unitec Institute of Technology, New Zealand
Cheng-Min Lin	Nan Kai University of Technology, Taiwan
Chiu Pin Lin	National Tsing Hua University, Taiwan
Andreas Lingnau	Humboldt-Universität zu Berlin, Germany
Martin Llamas-Nistal	University of Vigo, Spain
Luca Andrea Ludovico	Università degli Studi di Milano, Italy
Heide Lukosch	Delft University of Technology, The Netherlands
Krystina Madej	Georgia Tech, USA
Veronika Makarova	University of Saskatchewan, Canada
Maria Marcelino	UC, Portugal
Jacek Marciniak	Adam Mickiewicz University, Poland
Ana González Marcos	Universidad de la Rioja, Spain
Ivana Marenzi	Leibniz University Hannover, Germany
José Couto Marques	FEUP, Portugal
Lindsay Marshall	Newcastle University, UK
Scheila Martins	Pontificia Universidade Católica de Minas Gerais, Brazil
Tania Di Mascio	University of L'Aquila, Italy
Manolis Mavrikis	London Knowledge Lab, UK
Bruce Maxim	University of Michigan-Dearborn, USA
Elvis Mazzoni	University of Bologna, Italy
António José Mendes	Universidade de Coimbra, Portugal
Robert Meolic	University of Maribor, Slovenia
José Carlos Metrôlho	Instituto Politécnico de Castelo Branco, Portugal
Louise Mifsud	Oslo and Akershus University College of Applied Sciences, Norway
Bakhtiar Mikhak	Harvard University, USA
Peter Mikulecky	University of Hradec Kralove, Czech Republic
Michihiko Minoh	Kyoto University, Japan
Riichiro Mizoguchi	Japan Advanced Institute of Science and Technology, Japan

Leo van Moergestel	HU Utrecht University of Applied Sciences, The Netherlands
Gyöngyvér Molnár	University of Szeged, Hungary
António Moreira	Universidade de Aveiro, Portugal
Leonel Morgado	Universidade Aberta, Portugal
Maria Morras	Universitat Pompeu Fabra, Barcelona, Spain
Jerzy Moscinski	Silesian University of Technology, Poland
Maria Moundridou	School of Pedagogical and Technological Education (ASPETE), Greece
Antao Moura	Federal Universisty of Campina Grande (UFCG), Brazil
Wolfgang Mueller	Weingarten University of Education, Germany
Jogesh K. Muppala	Hong Kong University of Science and Technology, Hong Kong, SAR China
Yuko Murakami	Tohoku University, Japan
Antoanela Naaji	Vasile Goldis Western University, Romania
Hiroyuki Nagataki	Okayama University, Japan
Ryohei Nakatsu	National University of Singapore, Singapore
Minoru Nakayama	Tokyo Institute of Technology, Japan
Sotiris Nikolopoulos	Technological Educational Institute of Larissa, Greece
Kazunori Nozawa	Ritsumeikan University, Japan
Fátima L. S. Nunes	Universidade de São Paulo, Brazil
Ebba Ossiannilsson	The Swedish Association for Distance Education (SADE), Sweden
Kuo-liang Ou	National TsingHua University, Taiwan
Alessandro Pagano	University of Bari, Italy
George Palaigeorgiou	University of Western Macedonia, Greece
José Palma	Escola Superior de Tecnologia de Setúbal, Portugal
Stamatis Papadakis	University of Crete, Greece
Pantelis Papadopoulos	Aarhus University, Denmark
George Papadourakis	School of Applied Technology, Greece
Iraklis Paraskakis	South East European Research Centre, Greece
Pramod Pathak	National College of Ireland, Ireland
Paul Peachey	University of South Wales, UK
Francisco García Peñalvo	Salamanca University, Spain
Isidoros Perikos	University of Patras, Greece
Donatella Persico	CNR, Italian National Research Council, Italy
Antonio Ramón Bartolomé Pina	Universitat de Barcelona, Spain
Niels Pinkwart	Humboldt University, Germany
Mário Paulo Teixeira Pinto	Polytechnic of Porto, Portugal
Leonard A. Plugge	Cooperative SURF, The Netherlands
Petra Poulová	University of Hradec Králové, Czech Republic
Alexandra Poulovassilis	Birkbeck College, University of London, UK
Tamara Powell	Kennesaw State University, USA
Francesca Pozzi	CNR, Italian National Research Council, Italy

Augustin Prodan	Iuliu Hatieganu University, Romania
Yannis P. Psaromiligkos	Piraeus University of Applied Sciences, Greece
Ricardo Queirós	DI/ESEIG and CRACS, Portugal
Clark Quinn	Quinnovation, USA
Khalid Rabayah	Arab American University, Palestinian Territory, Occupied
Altina Ramos	Universidade do Minho, Portugal
Fernando Ramos	University of Aveiro, Portugal
Liana Razmerita	Copenhagen Business School, Denmark
Eliseo Reategui	Universidade Federal do Rio Grande do Sul, Brazil
Petrea Redmond	University of Southern Queensland, Australia
Manuel José Cabral Dos Santos Reis	University of Trás-os-montes e Alto Douro, Portugal
Fernando Reinaldo Ribeiro	Instituto Politécnico de Castelo Branco, Portugal
Anna Riccioni	University of Bologna, Italy
Martin Rich	Cass Business School, UK
Chiara Rossitto	Stockholms University, Sweden
Rebecca Rutherfoord	Kennesaw State University, Georgia
Libuse Samkova	University of South Bohemia, Czech Republic
Demetrios Sampson	Curtin University, Australia
Albert Sangra	Open University of Catalonia, Spain
Juan M. Santos	University of Vigo, Spain
Georg J. Schneider	University of Applied Sciences Trier, Germany
Wolfgang Schreiner	Johannes Kepler University, Austria
Ulrik Schroeder	RWTH Aachen University, Germany
Abhishek Shukla	R. D. Engineering College, India
Pei Hwa Siew	Universiti Tunku Abdul Rahman, Malaysia
Jane Sinclair	University of Warwick, UK
Ole Smørdal	University of Oslo, Norway
Zacharoula Smyrnaiou	University of Athens, Greece
Filomena Soares	Algoritmi Research Centre, UM, Portugal
Michael Sonntag	Johannes Kepler University, Austria
Eliza Stefanova	Sofia University, Bulgaria
Claudia Steinberger	University of Klagenfurt, Austria
Craig Stewart	Indiana University, USA
Jun-Ming Su	National University of Tainan, Taiwan
Masanori Sugimoto	Hokkaido University, Japan
Jarkko Suhonen	University of Eastern Finland, Finland
Tamara Sumner	University of Colorado Boulder, USA
Katsuaki Suzuki	Kumamoto University, Japan
Bénédicte Talon	ULCO, Université Lille Nord de France, France
Qing Tan	Athabasca University, Canada
Brendan Tangney	Trinity College Dublin, The University of Dublin, Ireland
Luca Tateo	Aalborg University, Denmark
Marco Temperini	Sapienza University of Rome, Italy

Uwe Terton	University of the Sunshine Coast, Australia
A. Min Tjoa	Vienna University of Technology, Austria
Stephan Trahasch	University of Applied Sciences Offenburg, Germany
Maria Uther	University of Winchester, UK
Mario Vacca	Italian Ministry of Education, Italy
Luis de la Fuente Valentín	Universidad Internacional de la Rioja, Spain
Ioannis Vardiambasis	Technological Educational Institute (TEI) of Crete, Greece
Kostas Vassilakis	TEI of Crete, Greece
Norman Vaughan	Mount Royal University, Canada
Andreas Veglis	Aristotle University of Thessaloniki, Greece
Ioanna Vekiri	Independent Researcher, Greece
Francisco L. Gutiérrez Vela	University of Granada, Spain
J. Ángel Velázquez-Iturbide	Universidad Rey Juan Carlos, Spain
Giuliano Vivanet	University of Cagliari, Italy
Harald Vranken	Open Universiteit, The Netherlands
Pieter de Vries	Delft University of Technology, The Netherlands
Erin Walker	Arizona State University, USA
Alf Inge Wang	Norwegian University of Science and Technology, Norway
Xinli Wang	Michigan Technological University, USA
Christopher Wells	McGraw-Hill Education, USA
Martin Wessner	Darmstadt University of Applied Sciences, Germany
Leandro Krug Wives	Universidade Federal do Rio Grande do Sul, Brazil
Jie Chi Yang	National Central University, Taiwan
Amel Yessad	Laboratoire d'Informatique de Paris 6, France
Katarina Zakova	Slovak University of Technology in Bratislava, Slovak Republic
Diego Zapata-Rivera	Educational Testing Service, USA
Mark Zarb	Robert Gordon University, UK
Thomas Zarouchas	Computer Technology Institute and Press Diophantus, Greece
Iveta Zolotova	Technical University in Kosice, Slovak Republic
Javier García Zubía	Universidad de Deusto, Spain
Susan Zvacek	NA, USA

Additional Reviewers

Alya Itani	IMT Atlantique Bretagne-Pays de la Loire, France
Atsushi Ito	Utsunomiya University, Japan
Antonis Natsis	Aarhus University, Denmark
Andrés Paz	École de Technologie Supérieure, Canada
Issam Rebai	IMT Atlantique, France

Invited Speakers

Nikol Rummel	Bochum University, Germany
Manolis Mavrikis	London Knowledge Lab, UK
Martin Bush	London South Bank University, UK
David Guralnick	Kaleidoscope Learning, USA

Contents

Information Technologies Supporting Learning

Effectively Using Classroom Response Systems for Improving Student Content Retention

Robert Collier[1(✉)] and Jalal Kawash[2]

[1] Department of Computer Science, Carleton University, 1125 Colonel by Dr., Ottawa, Ontario, Canada
robert.collier@scs.carleton.ca

[2] Department of Computer Science, University of Calgary, 2500 University Dr. NW, Calgary, Alberta, Canada
jalal.kawash@ucalgary.ca

Abstract. Classroom response systems are widely recognized as an effective tool for providing formative feedback and engaging students, but our research supports the hypothesis that these systems also provide opportunities for improving content retention. This is evidenced by an experiment we conducted on two distinct sections of an introductory course in computer science, wherein large collections of classroom response system questions were presented to different sections at different stages. Questions that were offered immediately after the corresponding material had the express purpose of providing an opportunity for formative feedback, while questions that were presented later were expected to improve content retention. The performance of participants on the corresponding questions of the final examination was then reviewed, and statistical analyses indicate that participants performed better on those questions that corresponded to the classroom response system questions provided for content retention.

1 Introduction

The modern pervasiveness of the smartphone and laptop computer has changed the habits of this generation of postsecondary students, and there are many opportunities to integrate these technologies into the classroom. Classroom response systems represent one such opportunity. These systems are exemplified by the practice of presenting a question to an entire class that can be answered anonymously via laptop, smartphone, or "clicker". This activity provides valuable and immediate feedback for both instructors and participants - instructors can quickly examine the performance distribution of the class on the question presented (and adjust the pace or revisit topics as required) and students can self-evaluate their understanding, relative to the rest of the participants. Classroom response systems are also widely recognized as a valuable tool for improving engagement, by transforming students from a passive recipient to an active participant.

P. Escudeiro et al. (Eds.): CSEDU 2017, CCIS 865, pp. 3–21, 2018.
https://doi.org/10.1007/978-3-319-94640-5_1

Student engagement and formative feedback opportunities are both a crucial part of an effective classroom. That said, the possibility that there are other applications of a classroom response system (for improving the features of a course) definitely warrants further investigation. With this paper we examine an experiment that we conducted as part of an investigation into the potential use of classroom response systems for improving student content retention by using the system to allow the class to revisit content that had been a part of a previous lecture. This paper revisits and expands on the conference paper originally presented by Robert Collier at Computer Supported Education (CSEDU) 2017 [1].

The remainder of this paper is organized as follows. Section 2 discusses related work in the context of the use of classroom response systems. The course in which our experiment takes place is discussed in Sect. 3. The experiment design is presented in Sect. 4, and the results are given in Sects. 5 and 6. Finally, the ongoing efforts of the authors in using classroom response systems in their most recent courses is briefly discussed in Sect. 7 before a concluding summary is presented in Sect. 8.

2 Classroom Response System

For many instructors, the decision to include classroom response system activities in a course is made to improve student engagement. That said, it is widely recognized that the formative and typically immediate feedback that can be provided by a classroom response system can aid both students and instructors. A question on which a particular student under-performs relative to the other students in the class can indicate an area of weakness or an opportunity for growth, and thus students can use classroom response system questions to self-assess their own understanding (of the current topic). Furthermore, the immediate and specific nature of the feedback provided by a classroom response system can be contrasted against traditional assessment tools (e.g., quizzes, assignments, etc.) where several topics are often assessed simultaneously and feedback is not immediately available. Additionally, and perhaps more importantly, the feedback provided to instructors allows instructors to adjust the pace of the lecture (or revisit previous topics) to match the immediate learning needs of the participating students.

Numerous studies [2–6] have reported that the use of classroom response systems in the classroom can improve student engagement (to the benefit of student learning) and (as noted previously) provide an opportunity for both students and instructors to receive important feedback. Although virtually all surveyed materials reinforce that students are satisfied with the classroom response system activities from the studies, on more than one occasion [7,8] it has been noted that the studies that report learning improvements might be observing an effect associated with improved interactivity in the classroom. This would indicate that those studies cannot conclusively demonstrate that the classroom response system is actually required to achieve the observed improvements in learning. This reasonable consideration notwithstanding, the use of classroom response system as a tool to engage students remains largely undisputed. Classroom response systems have also been used to successfully identify students that are struggling [9], and Porter et al. showed that performance in classroom response system early in the term was a good predictor of students' outcomes at the end of the term [10].

Unfortunately it must also be acknowledged that there is evidence that the adoption of a classroom response system could present a hindrance to students and could negatively interfere with content retention. Draper and Brown [11] reported that some students believed the classroom response system activities to be little more than a distraction from their learning objectives. Furthermore the review by Kay and Lesage [4] cited works that discussed the potential for in-class discussions to actually confuse students by exposing students to differing approaches/perspectives. Although these are both legitimate concerns, these issues are not inherent to classroom response systems and could conceivably arise after any activity that prompts in-class discussion. Given the numerous studies of the potential advantages that are associated with classroom response systems, we definitely feel that there is sufficient evidence to motivate the investigation of these systems as a tool for improving content retention.

It should be noted that a number of reviews [2,4,12] have noted that much of the research into the benefits and drawbacks associated with the use of classroom response systems has been qualitative and/or anecdotal, and that there are relatively few studies using control groups and quantitative analyses. The authors believe the experiment presented in this paper to be among the first to offer a quantitative assessment of the use of classroom responses systems as a tool to improve content retention (as opposed to a tool explicitly used for improving student engagement or providing feedback opportunities). It should, however, be specifically noted that the approach described by Brewer [13] is somewhat similar in that the solutions to the classroom response system questions would not be provided to the students until the following class. Although this practice could conceivably improve retention as well, the express purpose of using the response system was described in that study to be feedback (for both the instructors and students), not an improvement to content retention. Similarly, although Caldwell [14] does not mention retention specifically, she does describe a "review at the end of a lecture." This could also conceivably improve retention if these questions pertained to the beginning of a particularly lengthy lecture.

It should also be emphasized that our paper is concerned only with the potential applications of classroom response systems to the problem of content retention; although several other studies have looked at classroom response systems for the retention of students in computer science programs, this is not directly related to the problem of content retention. Porter, Simon, Kinnunen, and Zazkis [15,16], for instance, indicated that they used clickers as one of the best practices for student retention (i.e., in the program), but it is not clear how this class response system is used and how it is affecting content retention. Furthermore, unlike Tew and Dorn [17], we do not aim to develop general instruments for assessment. Our approach is ad-hoc with the specific objective of determining if there is measurable evidence that a class response system can help improve retention of content and knowledge by students.

Finally, a related issue for which there have been several studies (albeit with conflicting results) concerns whether or not the use of classroom response systems can improve student performances on final exams. Diana Cukierman suggested that studying the effect of a classroom response system on outcomes such as final exam scores may be infeasible [18] and an experiment by Robert Vinaja that used recorded lectures, videos, electronic material, and a classroom response system did not demonstrate an impact of these practices on grade performance [19]. This is contrary to the finding of Simon et al. that peer instructed subjects (in a CS0 course specifically) outperformed those who are traditionally instructed [20]. Daniel Zingaro confirmed this finding in a CS1 context [21] and Zingaro and Porter went further to show that students who learn in the class environment retain the knowledge better than students who did not [22]. Huss-Lederman similarly reported on a 2-year experiment in which first year students showed better learning gains as a result of using a classroom response system, but there was a drop in these gains in the second year [23]. In comparison, our work starts from the thesis that classroom response system possibly have an effect on knowledge retention (and, by extension, on final exam scores). Our aim was to quantify this observation in a first-year computer science course and in contrast with the aforementioned studies, the driving question of our research is when and how classroom response questions can be effective in improving learning outcomes.

3 Course Details and Objectives

The course within which this experiment was conducted was CPSC 203, Introduction to Problem Solving Using Application Software. This was a first year computer literacy course at the University of Calgary designed specifically for students that were not working towards a major in computer science. As a result, although a basic level of familiarity with personal computers was assumed of the students, the course was designed such that it did not assume incoming students would have any significant foundation of computer science knowledge upon which to build. Most of the students in attendance are undergraduate students from the schools of business, management, and/or social science, but students from the natural sciences, communications, and other disciplines would also register for this course on a regular basis. The course was taught in a traditional lecture-style format, with content delivered over 13 weeks through a combination of lectures (75 min, twice a week) and tutorials (100 min weekly).

The principle learning outcome for this course is to impart an introduction to many of the fundamental areas of the computer science discipline. As a result the course features a particularly broad range of topics. After the initial weeks of the course, during which some very basic introductory materials are presented alongside a discussion of research design fundamentals, the remainder of the course could be logically divided into three "modules". Figure 1 is a diagrammatic representation of the topics of the course, presented to students during the first (i.e., introductory) lecture to demonstrate the interconnectedness and dependencies of the topics to follow (with arrows to indicate topic dependencies).

The first of these modules introduces both set theory and graph theory before discussing the application of these principles to problem-solving (e.g. traffic light scheduling). During some previous offerings of this course these topics are followed by several short introductory computer programming lectures, but these lectures were not presented as part of the course offerings discussed in this paper.

The second module introduces both propositional and predicate logic before exploring the fundamentals of relational database management systems. These topics (i.e., classical logic and database management) are then brought together for the introduction of Structured Query Language (SQL).

The final module provides a brief introduction to the principles of computer networking and security (e.g., encryption and authentication with public-key cryptography). Although these topics are somewhat independent of the previous materials, they do broaden the knowledge base to ensure that students are able to remember, understand, and apply many core computer science topics.

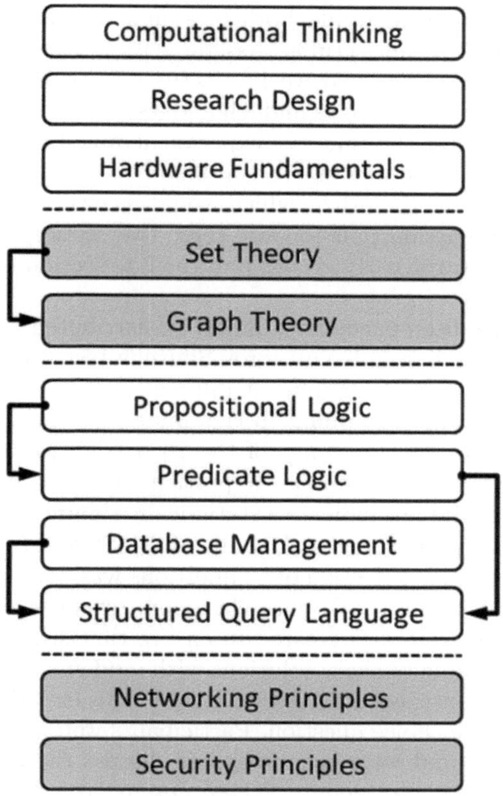

Fig. 1. Topics and dependencies [1].

4 Experimental Design

At the time of this investigation, classroom response systems have been used in CPSC 203 since 2010. As previously noted, these systems are widely recognized to encourage student engagement, provide formative feedback for students, and grant an opportunity for instructors to assess the degree to which the current material is being absorbed. It was our hypothesis that, without sacrificing all of these benefits it might be possible to adapt the activity into one that would allow students to revisit and reinforce content discussed in a prior lecture. Notwithstanding the fact that it is necessary to ask students about the content that has been presented over the last few minutes to determine if they have absorbed the material and/or created adequate study notes, asking questions pertaining to content that is still fresh in the minds of the students (i.e., in either working or intermediate-term memory) might do very little to aid students in storing the material into long-term memory.

The fall semester of 2014 afforded a unique opportunity for a controlled experiment on the effectiveness of a classroom response system for improving content retention. The expected enrollment was sufficiently large to justify the creation of two distinct sections that would both be taught by the same instructor, in (nearly) synchronous 75 min lectures. Assignments, quizzes, and examinations would all be shared and the two weekly lectures for each section would also taught on the same days (Tuesdays and Thursdays). In fact, the most significant observable differences (at the time the experiment was designed) were that one section would receive its lectures starting at 9:30 AM and would contain roughly half as many students as the other, which would receive its lectures starting at 12:30 PM. In the discussion that follows, these two sections will be referred to as the early section (or the early group) and the late section (or the late group), respectively.

The performance discrepancy that might be attributed to the differing lecture times notwithstanding, a Kolmogorov-Smirnov test was used to determine if there were any statistically significant differences between the scores on the portion of the final exam pertaining to this investigation. This nonparametric test, applied to the final exam scores of the 26 participants that made up the sample from the early section and the 46 participants that made up the sample from the late section, did not indicate a statistically significant difference in their respective final exam performances (D-value of 0.1378 and p-value of 0.898).

For this experiment, a collection of 54 questions was developed for the period of 14 lectures during which the Tophat classroom response system would be in use. Minor variations were also created to ensure that students from the early section would not be able to share solutions with students from the late section. Every classroom response system question used in this experiment was designed as a four-item multiple choice question. Participants were always provided 150 s to submit a response and were encouraged to discuss the question with other students in their immediate vicinity. These design decisions were made in an attempt to ensure that the question format was kept as consistent as possible throughout the semester, and as a result the principle differences that might exist between the questions themselves was the content of the corresponding lecture topic. That said, it is worth explicitly noting that the tasks associated with each question were not necessarily at the same level of difficulty. Using the terminology associated with the cognitive domain of Bloom's hierarchical taxonomy of educational objectives [24], the tasks associated with answering each question ranged from "lower-level" tasks such as simply remembering or understanding basic facts (i.e., knowledge or comprehension questions) and "higher-level" tasks such as writing a source code fragment (i.e., a synthesis question).

The course was designed such that four questions would be posed to each section during each lecture (except during the first lecture, which would feature only two). The four questions associated with each lecture would be divided (at random) into complementary sets A and B (of two questions each)—the early sample would be asked the questions from set A immediately after the material

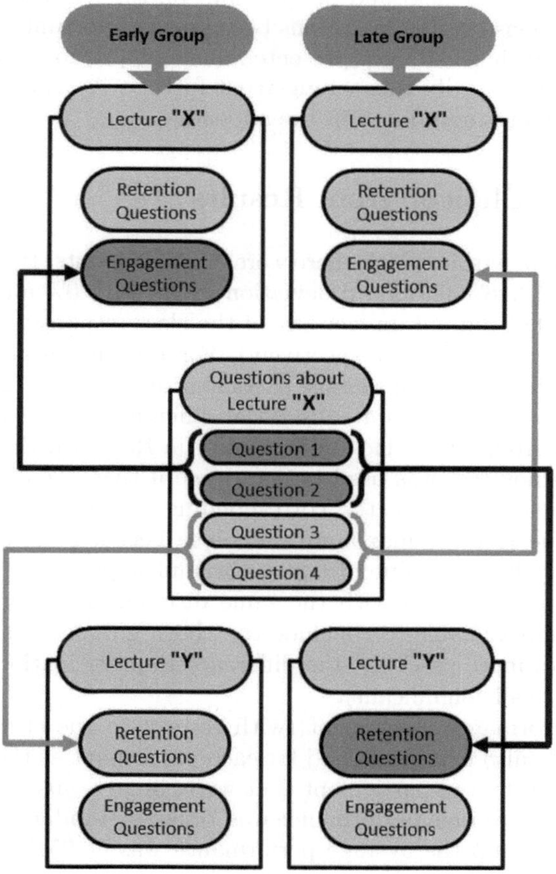

Fig. 2. Experimental design.

was presented and the questions from set B at the beginning of the following class, while the late section would be assigned the reverse.

As a clarifying example, if the four questions associated with the lecture on topic “X” of the course were designated questions 1, 2, 3, and 4, respectively, the early section could be asked questions 1 and 2 immediately after the material had been presented (i.e., during the lecture on topic “X”) and these questions would (from a design perspective) be principally concerned with engagement and feedback. The two variants on questions 1 and 2 would be presented to the late section at the beginning of the following lecture (i.e., the lecture on the next topic, “Y”) and would here be principally concerned with improving content retention. Similarly, questions 3 and 4 would be retention questions to the early section and engagement and feedback questions to the late section. In this way, both classes answered 27 questions immediately after the material was presented (allowing for the traditional role of the classroom response system as an engagement and feedback) and 27 questions on the following class (wherein the classroom response system questions become an opportunity for students to revisit the material that had been presented during a previous lecture). Figure 2 has been included to clarify this arrangement further. Actual sample questions used in this study are reproduced in the appendix.

5 “Multiple Choice” Item Results

For the early group, within which there were 26 participants, the average participation level was 73.18% (standard deviation 27.16; with 0% and 100% indicating participants that did not answer any of the class response system questions and answered every question, respectively). For the late group, within which there were 46 participants, the average participation level was 72.48% (standard deviation 24.85). As there was a substantial difference between the number of students in each group and a lack of normality in the data, the nonparametric Kolmogorov-Smirnov test was used to determine if there were any statistically significant differences between the corresponding participation levels. With a calculated D-value (for the maximum difference between the distributions) of 0.1288 and a very large p-value of 0.929, the null hypothesis (that both samples come from a population with the same distribution) cannot be rejected. It is, thus, not unreasonable to conclude that both groups were equally willing to participate (or, more precisely, the difference in participation levels was not considered statistically significant).

A simple performance assessment (with respect to the classroom response system questions only) can be derived for each participant as the fraction of the questions answered by the participant that were, in fact, answered correctly. In the early group the average performance was 70.66% (standard deviation 13.74) while in the late group the average performance was 66.95% (standard deviation 13.54). Once again the Kolmogorov-Smirnov test was used to determine if there were any statistically significant differences (since the data sets were not normally distributed) but with a D-value of 0.2533 and a p-value of 0.218, the null hypothesis that both samples came from the same distribution cannot be rejected. It is not unreasonable to interpret, from this, that neither of the participant groups was able to outperform the other. This is a welcome result considering that both groups received exactly the same number of questions for both the engagement and retention questions.

Having established that it would not be unreasonable to compare each of the groups on specific questions (to assess the degree to which specific questions can improve retention), four of the twenty multiple choice questions and one of the eight short answer questions from the final exams were designed such that they would both reflect and resemble classroom response system questions encountered by the class. Although this is unarguably a rather small sample from which to draw conclusions, it is important to recognize that the typical classroom response system question (i.e., designed to improve student engagement and provide an opportunity for feedback) is not necessarily a suitable question for a summative assessment tool like a final exam.

It should be noted that virtually all of the material from the final exam was accompanied by at least one related classroom response system question (with the exception of one multiple choice question and one short answer question that addressed material covered in the first three weeks, before the classroom response system came into use). Nevertheless it must also be noted that most of the corresponding final exam questions did not resemble their classroom response system counterparts. Consequently the authors feel that the most generalizable conclusions will be drawn from the observed performance differences (between students that encountered the corresponding classroom response question during the same lecture as the material vs. the following lecture) for those exam questions where the parallels to the corresponding classroom response questions were undeniable.

Two of the four multiple choice final exam questions pertained directly to structured query language (SQL). The former (denoted MCQ1) requested that the students select the correct "where" clause to produce a specific result, while the latter (denoted MCQ2) presented a SQL query and requested the students provide the number of rows that would be returned. Of the group of students that encountered MCQ1 during the same lecture as the corresponding material (i.e., the lecture on the construction of "Where" clauses), 38.5% answered the classroom response system question correctly and 57.7% answered the corresponding final exam question correctly. If this is contrasted against the group of students that encountered MCQ1 during the following lecture (i.e., at least 48 hours later), only 32.6% answered the classroom response system question correctly but 60.9% answered the final exam question correctly. A simple summary of these results would observe that the group of students that received the classroom response system question in the following lecture did "better" on the final exam question, even though their performance on the classroom response question was worse than the other group. This result is depicted in Fig. 3.

Of the group of students that encountered MCQ2 during the same lecture as the corresponding material (i.e., the lecture on Cartesian products and join

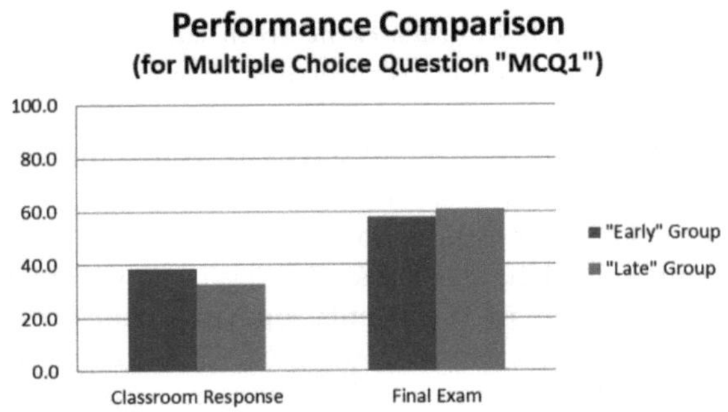

Fig. 3. Performance on an application level question [1].

operations), 58.7% answered the classroom response system question correctly and 41.3% answered the corresponding final exam question correctly. Of the other group, on the other hand, 69.2% answered the classroom response system question correctly and 61.5% answered the final exam question correctly. As with MCQ1, the students that received the classroom response system question in the following lecture did "better" on the final exam. It may, however, be worth noting that this same group performed "better" on the classroom response system question as well. This result is depicted in Fig. 4.

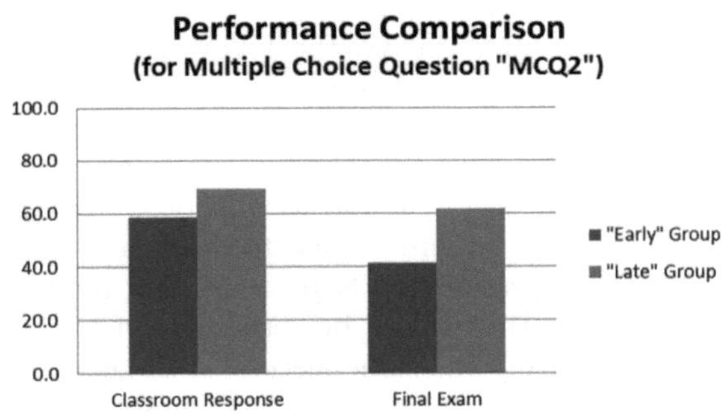

Fig. 4. Performance on an application level question [1].

The other two of the four multiple choice final exam questions considered for this investigation pertained to networking. Using the terminology from the cognitive domain of Bloom's taxonomy [24], where the structured query language questions discussed previously could be said to assess at the application level, these networking questions would be best categorized as assessment tools for the knowledge and comprehension levels (respectively). The former (denoted MCQ3) pertained to the differences between user datagram protocol (UDP) and transmission control protocol (TCP) and the latter (denoted MCQ4) pertained to the POST and GET operations of the hypertext transfer protocol (HTTP). Of the group of students that encountered MCQ3 during the same lecture as the corresponding material, 53.8% answered the classroom response system question correctly and 84.6% answered the corresponding final exam question correctly. For the sample that encountered the classroom response question during the following lecture, 26.1% answered the classroom response system question correctly and 93.5% answered the corresponding final exam question correctly. In spite of the very significant difference in performance on the classroom response question itself (with only 26.1% of the late sample answered the classroom response question correctly), once again the final exam question results indicate that the group of students that received the classroom response system question in the following lecture did "better" on the final exam. This result is depicted in Fig. 5.

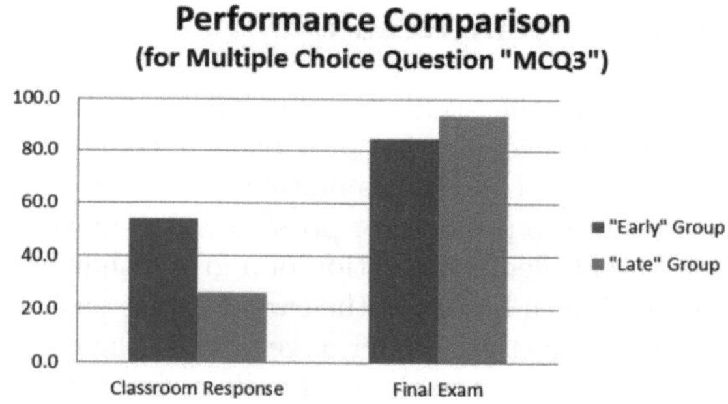

Fig. 5. Performance on a knowledge level question [1].

Of the group of students that encountered MCQ4 during the same lecture as the corresponding material, 53.8% answered the classroom response system question correctly and 88.5% answered the corresponding final exam question correctly. When this is contrasted against the results from the late group, the familiar pattern was evident; 37.0% of the late group answered the classroom response question correctly but 91.3% answered the final exam question correctly. This result is depicted in Fig. 6.

It is worthy to note at this point that these results are very intuitive; a classroom response question posed to the class at the beginning of the lecture, but pertaining to content from a previous lecture, is not being used to provide feedback about the immediate learning needs of the classroom. It does, however, stand to reason that such a question is an opportunity to reinforce (and bridge the current lecture with) content from a previous lecture, thereby improving student retention. This would, naturally, be evidenced by a relative performance improvement on the corresponding questions of the final exam.

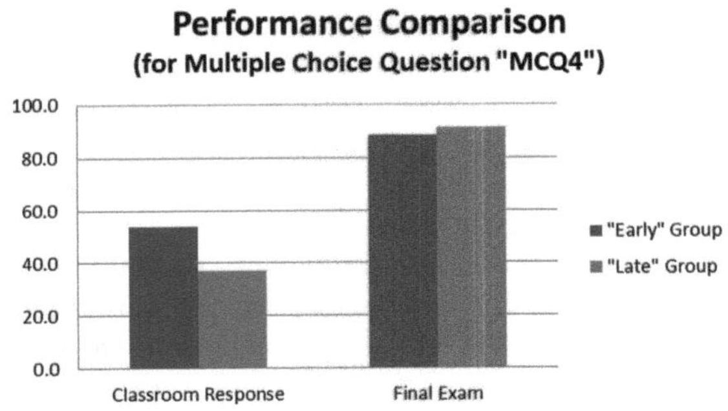

Fig. 6. Performance on a comprehension level question [1].

6 "Short Answer" Item Results

The final question posed to the students on the final exam that corresponded directly to a classroom response question previously encountered by the students used the short answer format (i.e., it was neither a multiple-choice question nor was it any other format where prompts or possible answers were provided to the student). This question entailed the creation of a graph that, when subjected to a graph colouring algorithm (n.b., one of the earlier topics on the course) requires the same number of colours as the number of vertices in the graph. Consequently it could be argued that according to the terminology from the cognitive domain of Bloom's taxonomy [24] this question was a synthesis level question.

Both the early and late participate samples (i.e., those that encountered the classroom response question immediately after the material was presented in lecture or at the beginning of the following lecture, respectively) achieved the same performance level (i.e., 50%) on the classroom response question. Nevertheless, the results of the experimental analysis indicated that the average mark achieved (on the corresponding short answer question of the final exam) by the late sample was greater than the average mark achieved by the early sample (78.0% and 73.3%, respectively). Although this is consistent with the previous results, the conclusion must be tempered by the fact that this difference was not found to be statistically significant (according to an unpaired student t-test). The distributions of students (from the early and late samples) that achieved full marks, partial marks, or no marks on the corresponding final exam question is depicted in Fig. 7.

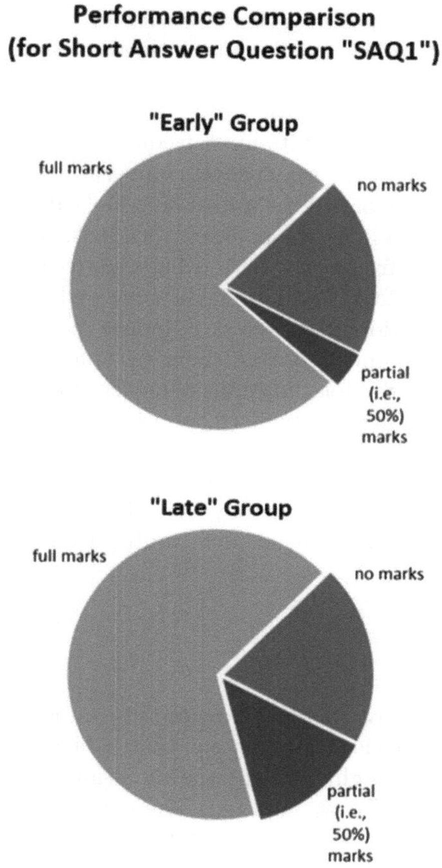

Fig. 7. Performance on a synthesis level question [1].

7 Ongoing Efforts

The authors remain committed to the use of classroom response systems in their own classes. In the most recent academic year (beginning September 2016 and ending April 2017), the authors employed the Poll Everywhere classroom response system on four large first-year courses (two sections of an introductory programming course of 271 and 243 students, respectively, and two sections of a discrete mathematics course of 325 and 291 students, respectively) and the Tophat classroom response system on four upper-year courses (two sections each of courses on the principles of operating systems and computer architecture). All of these courses were targeted at students pursuing an undergraduate degree in computer science, and the reaction to the classroom response system activities has always been very positive. Mid-semester feedback was collected for both of the introductory programming courses, and only 7.8% of the participants indicated that they did not like using Poll Everywhere (257 responses were received, with 68.5% and 23.7% of the participants indicating that they either liked the use of Poll Everywhere or had no opinion, respectively). Some students even provided additional feedback later on, explicitly noting their appreciation of the use of the system and requesting its more frequent use in future courses.

For the Tophat usage in the upper-level courses, the students completed end-of-semester surveys, where one of the questions was "what did the course instructor do to help your learning in the course?" Students' answers to this question mentioned Tophat more frequently than other classroom practices. Specifically, in the winter semester of 2017, 76.47% of the surveyed students in the computer architecture course mentioned the class response system Tophat as an effective practice that helped and improved their learning. In the operating systems course, this figure is 77.78% for the same semester. The number of valid instruments received for these courses are 85 (response rate of 73.91%) in the computer architecture course and 45 (response rate of 52.32%) in the operating systems course. The survey also included questions on what needs to be changed in the course in order to improve their learning. Out of the total 130 surveys that were received in both courses, only one student stated that dropping Tophat would be an improvement.

8 Conclusions

Since there are now many classroom response system options available that require only the ubiquitous smart phone with which to interact, the largest remaining obstacle that might prevent the inclusion of such an activity is the considerable investment of time required. The development of suitable items is certainly a significant undertaking (not unlike the development of any other item bank) but it should also be explicitly noted that presenting each item, allowing students time to formulate and submit a response, reviewing the distribution, and discussing the results is a considerable investment as well. Even with an instructor-imposed time limit (as in the investigation discussed in this paper), a small set of questions each class can consume a significant amount of time and may require an adjustment to the pace as well, depending on the distribution. Nevertheless, the benefits to the class if these costs can be incurred are well-established. As previously noted, classroom response system activities present an excellent opportunity for improving student engagement (and, if the questions are a source of marks for the student, motivation) and providing immediate formative feedback.

The results of the experiment discussed in this paper support the hypothesis that the very same activity can be easily adapted to improve student content retention (by simply varying the interval between the time when the content was presented and the time of the classroom response system activity). Questions posed to the students at the beginning of a following lecture are an opportunity for students and instructors to briefly revisit material in a structured activity, and this, in turn, presents an opportunity for students to reinforce knowledge that has passed into long-term memory. Although this approach does entail sacrificing the utility of the classroom response question as an approach for acquiring immediate feedback, it does not preclude some of the other more typical application of these questions as a way of motivating or engaging students.

The final examination items used in this experiment were designed such that they would assess (as much as possible) knowledge at several different levels of Bloom's taxonomy [24] while at the same time having a clear and apparent connection to a previously encountered classroom response system question (and corresponding lecture). Every student in attendance of the lecture (regardless of whether or not they participated in that specific classroom response activity) would have encountered the question (and subsequent discussion), with the only difference being whether they encountered it in the same lecture as the corresponding content or in the lecture that followed. In all cases, the student sample that encountered the classroom response item in the following lecture exhibited better performance than the student sample that encountered the item immediately after the material had been presented. As noted previously, this is an intuitive (and not particularly surprising) result, since items that do not immediately follow the corresponding lecture content cannot be said to provide immediate formative feedback. Contrarily, these items, though structurally identical to a traditional classroom response question, were used to improve content retention and it is encouraging that the use of these content retention questions would appear to be correlated with measurable improvements in performance.

It is, however, noteworthy that the results would also seem to suggest (albeit with less certainty) that students do not perform as well on the classroom response system questions themselves when delivered in the following lecture. This is also a relatively unsurprising result, but the impact was measurable and should be considered if classroom response activities are used in part to determine a student's final grade. Regardless, and although the amount of in-class time that must be dedicated to the activity is certainly not insignificant, student reaction to these activities is predominantly positive and the empirical evidence presented here supports the claim that the use of classroom response systems can aid students with content retention while keeping them engaged and motivated.

Appendix: Questions Used in the Study

This appendix contains each of the final exam questions (i.e., the stem and alternatives, where applicable) associated with this investigation (i.e., multiple choice questions designated MCQ1, MCQ2, MCQ3, and MCQ4) and the corresponding classroom response system questions. As previously noted, participants would have 150 min to submit a response and then the results would be analyzed, the alternatives would each be discussed, and the solution would be presented.

MCQ1

Multiple Choice Question 1 [MCQ1] from the Final Exam. The EMPLOYEE table has the following columns: EmployeeID, FirstName, LastName, Job, and Salary. Which of the following WHERE clauses would be used to retrieve data for all the salespersons that have a salary less than 35000 and everyone who is not a salesperson and whose salary is above 35000? (n.b., the data should all appear in the same table.)

(a) WHERE (Job = 'Sales' OR Salary < 35000)
AND (Job != 'Sales' OR Salary > 35000)
(b) WHERE (Job = 'Sales' OR Salary < 35000)
OR (Job != 'Sales' OR Salary > 35000)
(c) WHERE (Job = 'Sales' AND Salary < 35000)
AND (Job != 'Sales' OR Salary > 35000)
(d) WHERE (Job = 'Sales' AND Salary < 35000)
OR (Job != 'Sales' OR Salary > 35000)

The Corresponding Classroom Response System Question. What Where clause should you use if you want to retrieve all the male employees from the marketing department with all the female employees from the research department?

(a) WHERE (GENDER = 'Male' AND DEPT = 'Marketing')
AND (GENDER = 'Female' AND DEPT = 'Research')
(b) WHERE (GENDER = 'Male' AND DEPT = 'Marketing')
OR (GENDER = 'Female' AND DEPT = 'Research')
(c) WHERE (GENDER = 'Male' OR DEPT = 'Marketing')
AND (GENDER = 'Female' OR DEPT = 'Research')
(d) WHERE (GENDER = 'Male' OR DEPT = 'Marketing')
OR (GENDER = 'Female' OR DEPT = 'Research')

MCQ2

Multiple Choice Question 2 [MCQ2] from the Final Exam. If table EMPLOYEE has 250 rows of data and table DEPARTMENT has 10 rows of data, how much data (i.e., how many rows) is retrieved by: SELECT * FROM EMPLOYEE, DEPARTMENT?

(a) 10
(b) 250
(c) 260
(d) 2500

The Corresponding Classroom Response System Question. If the DEPARTMENT table has 5 rows and the EMPLOYEE table has 100 rows, how many rows does the following query return: SELECT * FROM DEPARTMENT, EMPLOYEE?

(a) 5
(b) 20
(c) 500
(d) 2000

MCQ3

Multiple Choice Question 3 [MCQ3] from the Final Exam. Which of the following benefits does UDP offer relative to TCP?

(a) UDP consumes fewer computer resources by not managing connections.
(b) UDP guarantees that packets of a transmission arrive in the same order they were sent.
(c) UDP does not divide a message into packets.
(d) UDP guarantees that all packets successfully arrive at the destination.

The Corresponding Classroom Response System Question. Which of the following statements is true?

(a) UDP is a connection-oriented protocol.
(b) TCP is analogous to the postal system.
(c) TCP and UDP are based on packet-switching.
(d) None of the above.

MCQ4

Multiple Choice Question 4 [MCQ4] from the Final Exam. Suppose that you have opened the webpage at “my.ucalgary.ca”. Which of the following statements is true?

(a) POST is generated when you click the “Sign In” button.
(b) GET is generated when you lick the “Disclaimer” hyperlink.
(c) GET is generated when you click the “About CAS” hyperlink.
(d) All of the above.

The Corresponding Classroom Response System Question. Under the Hypertext transfer protocol...

(a) POST is generated when clicking a hyperlink.
(b) GET is generated when clicking a hyperlink.
(c) GET is generated when you press the button to login to D2L.
(d) POST is generated when a URL is entered in the browser’s address field.

SAQ1

Short Answer Question 1 [SAQ1] from the Final Exam. Give an example of a graph that has five (5) vertices and the minimum number of colours to legally colour it is also five (5). To clarify, if the minimum number of colours to legally colour the graph is five, then you cannot legally colour it with four or fewer colours. Recall that a legal colouring requires that no two adjacent vertices have the same colour.

The Corresponding Classroom Response System Question. What is the minimum number of colours necessary for colouring the following graph such that no two adjacent vertices have the same colour?

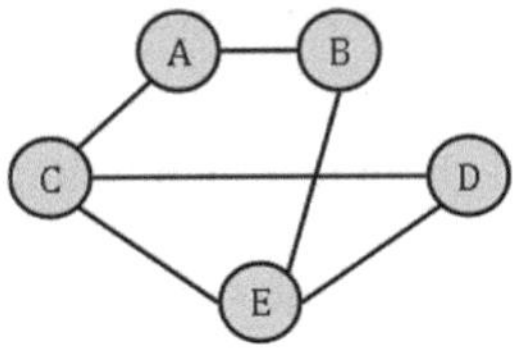

(a) 1
(b) 3
(c) 4
(d) 5

References

1. Collier, R.D., Kawash, J.: Improving student content retention using a classroom response system. In: CSEDU 2017 - Proceedings of the 9th International Conference on Computer Supported Education, Porto, Portugal, 21–23 April 2017, vol. 1, pp. 17–24 (2017)
2. Boscardin, C., Penuel, W.: Exploring benefits of audience-response systems on learning: a review of the literature. Acad. Psychiatry **36**, 401–407 (2012)
3. Moss, K., Crowley, M.: Effective learning in science: the use of personal response systems with a wide range of audiences. Comput. Educ. **56**, 36–43 (2011)
4. Kay, R.H., LeSage, A.: Examining the benefits and challenges of using audience response systems: a review of the literature. Comput. Educ. **53**, 819–827 (2009)
5. Bruff, D.: Teaching with Classroom Response Systems: Creating Active Learning Environments. Jossey-Bass, San Francisco (2009)
6. Moredich, C., Moore, E.: Engaging students through the use of classroom response systems. Nurse Educ. **32**, 113–116 (2007)
7. Blasco-Arcas, L., Buil, I., Hernandez-Ortega, B., Sese, F.J.: Using clickers in class. The role of interactivity, active collaborative learning and engagement in learning performance. Comput. Educ. **62**, 102–110 (2013)
8. Webb, A., Carnaghan, C.: Investigating the effects of group response systems on student satisfaction, learning and engagement in accounting education. Issues Acc. Educ. **22**, 391–409 (2006)

9. Liao, S.N., Zingaro, D., Laurenzano, M.A., Griswold, W.G., Porter, L.: Lightweight, early identification of at-risk CS1 students. In: Proceedings of the 2016 ACM Conference on International Computing Education Research, ICER 2016, pp. 123–131. ACM, New York (2016)
10. Porter, L., Zingaro, D., Lister, R.: Predicting student success using fine grain clicker data. In: Proceedings of the Tenth Annual Conference on International Computing Education Research, ICER 2014, pp. 51–58. ACM, New York (2014)
11. Draper, S.W., Brown, I.M.: Increasing interactivity in lectures using an electronic voting system. J. Comput. Assist. Learn. **20**, 81–94 (2004)
12. Judson, E., Sawada, D.: Learning from past and present: electronic response systems in college lecture halls. J. Comput. Math. Sci. Teach. **21**, 167–181 (2002)
13. Brewer, C.A.: Near real-time assessment of student learning and understanding in biology courses. BioScience **54**, 1034–1039 (2004)
14. Caldwell, J.E.: Clickers in the large classroom: current research and best-practice tips. CBE Life Sci. Educ. **6**, 9–20 (2007)
15. Simon, B., Kinnunen, P., Porter, L., Zazkis, D.: Experience report: CS1 for majors with media computation. In: Proceedings of the Fifteenth Annual Conference on Innovation and Technology in Computer Science Education, ITiCSE 2010, pp. 214–218. ACM, New York (2010)
16. Porter, L., Simon, B.: Retaining nearly one-third more majors with a trio of instructional best practices in CS1. In: Proceeding of the 44th ACM Technical Symposium on Computer Science Education, SIGCSE 2013, pp. 165–170. ACM, New York (2013)
17. Tew, A.E., Dorn, B.: The case for validated tools in computer science education research. Computer **46**, 60–66 (2013)
18. Cukierman, D.: Predicting success in university first year computing science courses: the role of student participation in reflective learning activities and in i-clicker activities. In: Proceedings of the 2015 ACM Conference on Innovation and Technology in Computer Science Education, ITiCSE 2015, pp. 248–253. ACM, New York (2015)
19. Vinaja, R.: The use of lecture videos, ebooks, and clickers in computer courses. J. Comput. Sci. Coll. **30**, 23–32 (2014)
20. Simon, B., Parris, J., Spacco, J.: How we teach impacts student learning: peer instruction vs. lecture in CS0. In: Proceeding of the 44th ACM Technical Symposium on Computer Science Education, SIGCSE 2013, pp. 41–46. ACM, New York (2013)
21. Zingaro, D.: Peer instruction contributes to self-efficacy in CS1. In: Proceedings of the 45th ACM Technical Symposium on Computer Science Education, SIGCSE 2014, pp. 373–378. ACM, New York (2014)
22. Zingaro, D., Porter, L.: Tracking student learning from class to exam using isomorphic questions. In: Proceedings of the 46th ACM Technical Symposium on Computer Science Education, SIGCSE 2015, pp. 356–361. ACM, New York (2015)
23. Huss-Lederman, S.: The impact on student learning and satisfaction when a CS2 course became interactive (abstract only). In: Proceedings of the 47th ACM Technical Symposium on Computing Science Education, SIGCSE 2016, p. 687. ACM, New York (2016)
24. Bloom, B.S.: Taxonomy of Educational Objectives: The Classification of Educational Goals. Longmans, Green (1956)

Design of a Learning Space Management System for Open and Adaptable School Facilities

Ari Tuhkala[1(✉)], Hannakaisa Isomäki[1], Markus Hartikainen[1], Alexandra Cristea[2], and Andrea Alessandrini[3]

[1] Faculty of Information Technology, University of Jyväskylä, Jyväskylä, Finland
ari.tuhkala@gmail.com
[2] Department of Computer Science, University of Warwick, Coventry, UK
[3] Duncan of Jordanstone College of Art and Design, University of Dundee, Dundee, Scotland

Abstract. In this design-based research project, a learning space management system was developed for the Valteri School Onerva in Central-Finland. The school represents a modern educational environment with open and adaptable learning spaces. The goal was to develop a software to support the stakeholders in organising flexible pedagogical activities and sharing pedagogical practices. To reach this goal, we utilised value-focused thinking as a requirements elicitation method, to identify the objectives that the stakeholders associate with the new environment. In the implementation phase, we organised participatory design workshops, to involve the stakeholders in decision-making, to ensure that the prototype development was proceeding according to their needs. As a result, we elaborate how we utilised value-focused thinking, what were the objectives that were identified, and how they were transformed into system requirements. Finally, we describe the first prototype of the learning space management system, which was developed using these requirements.

Keywords: Classroom management · Learning spaces
Educational technology · Special education · Value-focused thinking
Participatory design

1 Introduction

The traditional classroom setting of children sitting on benches and patiently listening to a teacher is not easily applicable in special education. The classrooms are often considered less inspiring, and an activity-driven approach is more appropriate [1]. For example, children with hearing and vision problems can benefit from visual and physical stimulations and moving between different spaces, and children with autism disorders benefit from the use of technologies

P. Escudeiro et al. (Eds.): CSEDU 2017, CCIS 865, pp. 22–43, 2018.
https://doi.org/10.1007/978-3-319-94640-5_2

and digital artefacts that promote collaborative educational activities and attentional exercises [2]. To overcome these issues, a new school was recently created in Finland, the Valteri School Onerva, which was just finished in early 2016. Its stated goal was to enable functionality, physical activity, and the application of new technologies. The idea of an open and adaptable school was a focus from the planning and construction stages of the school. Under this concept, all physical spaces are understood as potential spaces for learning, not just the classroom, and the environment is dynamically adapted to the needs of the practised pedagogy. A simple example is using stairways as an active learning space: children might physically move from one stairway step to another, while learning the number line, months, or weekdays (Ikkelä-Koski, personal communication, May 5, 2014).

However, the activities in the modern school environment of the Valteri School Onerva must be supported with modern technology. In the stairway example, in a regular educational setting, with the current level of support, it would not be possible to know if the stairway was already in use, as the stairway is a non-traditional learning space and would not be considered by any scheduling tool. The lack of such critical information prevents teachers from implementing such new pedagogical ideas, even simple ones, due to the time costs if the targeted space is not available and the whole class must return to the classroom. Moreover, not all teachers have the time and resources to develop new ideas and surely are not aware of all the available possibilities. Unfortunately, we find the current facility (or classroom) management systems not suitable for use in this dynamic environment. The systems for commercial or non-commercial organisations seem to be developed mainly for standard administrative needs. Instead of traditional facility management features, teachers need a tool that supports them in organising flexible pedagogical activities and sharing pedagogical practices. To successfully develop a learning space management system, we need to carefully examine the objectives that teachers associate with the open and adaptable environment.

As a result, the requirements for a learning space management system were produced in the ONSPACE research project between May 1 and December 5, 2014, before the building construction even started [3]. Requirements elicitation is one of the most critical activities of software development and is known to be a major reason for project failures [4]. We grounded our research in two assumptions: First, to have a better understanding of teachers' work, we needed to involve our stakeholders and arrange user-centred workshops, based on participatory design principles. Participatory design emphasises shared decision-making, which is crucial when different stakeholders are involved [5]. Second, traditional requirements elicitation concentrates on identifying system's goals, functionality, and limitations [4]. While this is fundamental, we argue that the stakeholders' objectives need to be defined more holistically than just considering the actual system. Therefore, we applied a method developed by Professor Ralph Keeney and proposed in the book *Value-focused Thinking: A Path to Creative Decision*

Making [6]. The method offers systematic guidelines, which are described in a later section, for identifying objectives for the defined decision problem.

This study has both methodological and practical contributions. Value-focused thinking has been applied in multiple domains, but less in the context of requirements elicitation, especially as they relate to education. Learning space management systems are currently gaining attention as modern schools increasingly adjust to the idea of open and adaptable learning environments [7]. The identified objectives were used during the implementation of the learning space management prototype. To fulfill our goals, we framed the following research questions:

- *How can value-focused thinking be implemented and applied to the requirements elicitation context?*
- *What are the objectives associated with an open and adaptable school environment?*

For the first question, we describe in detail how we applied the method, and for the second, we interpret recordings from the workshops and present the identified objectives, with the help of teachers, administrative personnel and rehabilitation instructors. The original requirements specification document is in Finnish and consists of 32 pages; therefore, its full inclusion is beyond the scope of this paper. Instead, we highlight and discuss the process of extracting the objectives, followed by a discussion of the objectives. The prototype of the system was developed in 2015, in the sequel project called ONSPACE2, and the objectives were used as guiding evaluation principles by software engineers during development of the learning space management system.

2 Towards Novel School Facilities

Facility management considers assets that are not the primary activity for the organisation, but essential to function [8]. These assets are typically buildings and properties, while information systems, human resources, and finance are understood as separate areas. In education context, assets may include school buildings, accessories, vehicles, and permissions to certain services, like a health-care specialist or a school psychiatrist. While efficient management of these assets can make a significant difference regarding financial cost and value in any organisation, the physical environment itself, like the school building, can have an enormous impact on facilitating learning [8–10]. A good physical environment gives resources, inspiration, and motivation for learning. Moreover, the physical environment can be enhanced with virtual properties, by using information technology [11]. The virtual resources can extend the social action, by allowing distant interactions and enabling learning activities for students with perception problems. In addition to physical and virtual aspects, there is a social dimension: how interactions are made possible between people within organisation culture.

Lievonen and Kinnunen [12] point out how information technology extends learning situations beyond school buildings. Therefore, spatial navigation, spatial control, interpersonal communication and collaboration need to be considered. Kumpulainen and Mikkola [13] even argue that learning 21st-century skills, like critical thinking, problem-solving or media literacy, are challenging to promote in an educational environment that is restricted to a particular space and time. They call for learning environments that reconfigure spaces for learning, because there is an increasing number of students who feel disengaged and disconnected from formal education.

The principal stakeholder of this study, the Valteri School Onerva, has utilised modern ideas based on Kuuskorpi's [14] Doctoral Thesis in the construction of their new building. Kuuskorpi defines the dimensions for a physical learning environment as: societal orientation, individual orientation, informal learning processes and formal teaching (Fig. 1), and learning spaces can be positioned according to these dimensions. In the Valteri School Onerva, this means that the physical space and its furniture can be adapted to different purposes and the common spaces are made available to various functions.

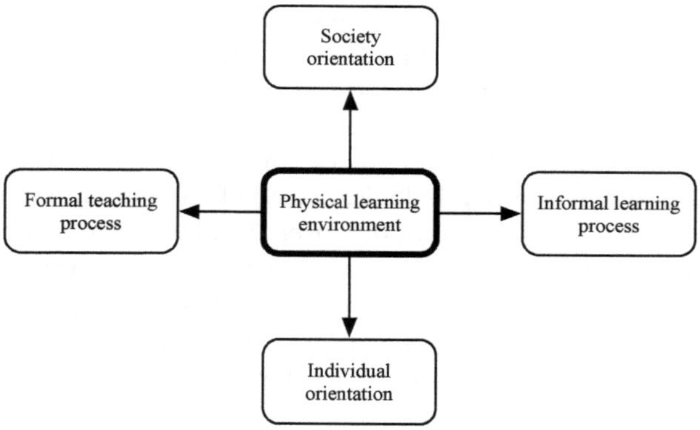

Fig. 1. Dimensions for a physical learning environment [14].

Nevari [15] has designed the concept for the new building, illustrated in Fig. 2. The areas are called *parks*, *fountains*, and *dens*. A park is an open space, which can be easily modified for group work, presentations and physical activities. A fountain is a partially open space for collaborative learning, which can be divided into different areas, to suit both formal and informal learning situations. A quiet, individual and closed space is called a den, and it can be used for focusing on a task, individually or in small groups. In addition to the novel concept of physical space, there are no prearranged spaces for teachers or students. The idea is that the learning and working activities will happen in the space that is most suitable at the current moment, instead of staying in classrooms or offices. This idea is the underlying motivation for our study, to develop technology that could give the best support for organising activities in this unique environment.

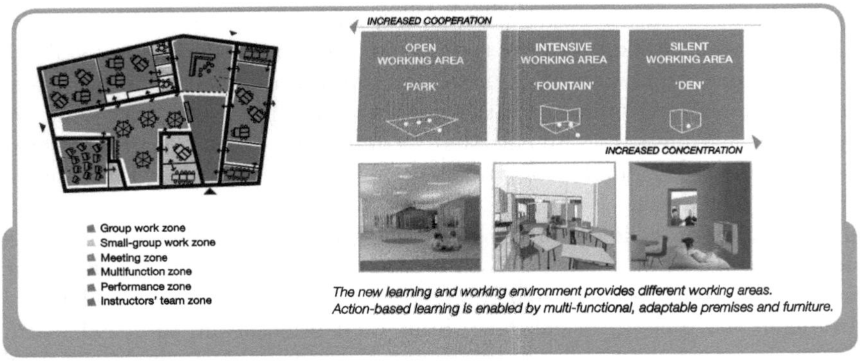

Fig. 2. Concept of the Valteri School Onerva [15].

3 Approaches for User Participation and Involvement

User participation and involvement are considered essential for success in system development [16–18], as they improve the quality of the system, by generating more precise requirements [19] and tend to lead to a positive attitude and perceived usefulness among users [20, 21]. Participation refers to assignments, activities and behaviours that users engage in during the system development process and involvement is a psychological state of the individual, defined as the importance and relevance of a system to a user [16]. User involvement can also be seen as a broader concept, in which users are somehow involved in the system's development process, whereas user participation refers to more active and intentional involvement [22]. Kujala [23] has presented methodological approaches to achieving participation and involvement (Table 1).

Table 1. Methodological approaches to achieve participation and involvement [23].

Participatory design	User-centered design	Ethnography	Contextual design
Democratic participation	Usability	Social aspects of work	Context of work
Workshops, prototyping	Task analysis, prototyping, usability evaluations	Observation, video analysis	Contextual inquiry, prototyping

In user-centred design, ethnology, and contextual design, participation can be characterised as an approach by the designer to gain information from participants. The fundamental difference in participatory design is that it encourages participants to actively take part in the decision making and creative processing of the solution [5]. The goal of participatory design is not just to empirically understand the design activity (or users, as in user-centred design), but to simultaneously envision, shape, and transcend it to benefit the participants [24].

The ideological grounding of participatory design emerged from Scandinavian workplace democracy, to ensure that people who are affected by technology can also participate in making decisions about it [25–28]. In participatory design, the following statements are understood as guiding principles: participants from diverse backgrounds are seen as experts in how they live their lives and design in collaboration with other professionals [29,30], participants have the right to influence technological decisions affecting their private and professional lives [31], and especially, participatory design is seen as appropriate in the context of special needs [32–35]. Thus, we have based our workshops on participatory design, to adopt these principles, and we have implemented value-focused thinking as a requirements elicitation technique.

4 Value-Focused Thinking

Value-focused thinking (VFT) comes from the operational research field and has been applied to decision problems in multiple domains, such as defence, environment, energy, government, corporations, and intelligence [36]. The underlying principle of VFT is that, when faced with a decision problem, participants should first examine their *values*. In general, values are core concepts within individuals and society [37]. Values are desirable and trans-situational goals that serve as principles that guide one's lives [38,39]. Keeney [6,40] employs values as principles for evaluation of actual or potential consequences of action or inaction, of proposed alternatives, and of made decisions. In VFT, decision makers reflect what they want to achieve, instead of immediately comparing alternative solutions. Values, moreover, can be made explicit for examination, by associating them with a specific statement of objectives, which are in the form of a verb, followed by an objective [6,41].

The basic steps of the VFT process are as follows: develop a list of values, convert values to objectives, and classify them, as a means-ends objective network [42,43]. The starting point is the statement of the problem to be solved. The definition of the problem must be made carefully, to ensure a shared understanding of the situation. Participants are asked to make a list of anything that they hope to achieve, by solving the problem being addressed. This is done without any restrictions or constraints in reflection, to reach the different dimensions that participants find valuable. After generating the initial list, participants are encouraged to extend the list, by using different mind-probing techniques (Table 3 in [40]). For example, participants can be asked to review each item and articulate why they care about it, which in turn might lead to new items. This phase of producing a comprehensive list requires intensive thinking and discussion, and it will most likely take several iterations.

The list is considered as completed, when participants cannot find any new information about the problem. Then, each list item is translated into the format of objectives (Keeney defines this phase as converting values into a common form). For example, if the participants expressed that the school day is too busy, the item might be *"rush"*, and the objective would be *"reduce rush"*. This might raise a discussion, for instance, on why there is rush and how it could be reduced. This, in turn, may generate new items and objectives. Finally, the list needs to be examined for possible redundancies, which have to be eliminated.

The next phase is to classify objectives as *fundamental* - or *means objectives.* Fundamental objectives characterise the essential interests in the decision situation, representing the goals that participants value. Means objectives are of interest due to their implications for the degree to which fundamental objectives can be achieved. For example, if reducing rush is a fundamental objective, the respective means objectives could be about having the needed accessories available. Finally, the structure of these objectives is illustrated, by building a *means-ends network*, which demonstrates how the different objectives are related to each other. The process of structuring objectives results in a deeper and more accurate understanding of what one cares about and helps to clarify the decision context and enhances the quality of decisions [40].

5 Methodology

5.1 Stakeholder Organisation

The Valteri School Onerva is one of the six learning and consulting centres for Valteri schools that operate under the Finnish National Board of Education. The school provides services that support learning and school attendance, in order to implement general, intensified, and special support. In the school, education is combined with rehabilitation and guidance that support learning, to form a seamless whole. The school has expertise particularly in supporting needs relating to vision, hearing, language, and interaction. The school's mission is to increase the accessibility of support services and promote the neighbourhood school principle. The school aims to realise this, by making their operations more effective, creating new action models and innovations, and utilising new technology. The aim is to develop solutions for learning and rehabilitation that support learning for individuals. The school's activities are guided by a development-oriented approach and the utilisation of research and networking.

5.2 Data Gathering Process

To gather the data for the extraction of our requirements rooted in the theory as explained above, we have organised four workshops (Table 2) in collaboration with the school's staff. The data was collected by recording the workshops with a video camera or mobile phone; the researchers also took notes. The participants were special education teachers, occupational therapists, visual sense specialists, and researchers. The researchers who participated in the workshops were all from the University of Jyväskylä, Faculty of Information Technology. There was some variation between workshops: in the first workshop there was one person from the technical staff, and in the last workshop, there were two members of the instructional staff, but otherwise, the membership stayed constant. All of the workshops were held in the old school's facilities, to help researchers understand the context at the given time and provide teachers and staff members with familiar surroundings.

Table 2. Value-focused thinking workshops [3].

1	14.5.2014	8 teachers, 1 technical staff, 3 researchers	Video
2	24.8.2014	6 teachers, 4 researchers	Video
3	27.9.2014	6 teachers, 3 researchers	Audio
4	12.12.2014	6 teachers, 2 instructors, 3 researchers	Video

The first workshop acquainted the participants with one another and familiarised everyone with the context of our study. Informal group discussions were conducted, during which we asked questions about the plans for the new school building, elicited their ideas of an open and adaptable environment, and discussed the initial needs for the learning space management system. The technical staff member presented a three-dimensional (3D) model of the new school building, and researchers analysed it, together with the participants. The researchers produced conceptual maps of the building, to gain a better understanding of the new environment. Finally, the participants discussed the initial desired functions and the possible users of the system.

In the second workshop, the participants were asked to provide ideas that they considered important for the open and adaptable environment. This triggered intensive discussions, which resulted in a list of words (items) which described anything that the participants perceived as valuable in the school context. The list was reviewed and discussed again, and the participants were asked to classify these 'raw' words, by defining higher level categories to encompass all of them. Finally, the participants transformed the items into objectives, which represented their shared understanding of how each item could be achieved. Next, the objectives were examined as a whole, with the goal of removing redundancy and disentangling abstract objectives, transforming them into more concrete ones. The emerging objectives were scrutinised again, by asking the participants *"why is this item important?"*. The goal of this iterative, cyclical process was to encourage more elaboration of the objectives, as well as good grounding and justification for each emerging objective, and finally, good placement in the overall context. Because time was limited during the workshop itself, the participants were asked to finish the task by themselves afterwards, and they sent the final document by email to the researchers.

5.3 Extracting Functional Requirements

The analysis of the first two workshops was based on the VFT methodology. First, the recordings were checked, to ensure that there was no missing data, and to verify the notes the researchers took during the discussion. The resulting document then included a full list of objectives. When analysing the objectives, we found that some of them were directly related to the actual system, whilst others related to the whole organisation. Therefore, the objectives were divided into two categories: system objectives and organisational objectives. From the system objectives, we derived the requirements that defined the initial functions of the system and illustrated them as a use case diagram. Every use case was then described in use case scenarios, which detailed how the user interacts with the system.

In the third workshop, the researchers described to participants how the use case diagram were constructed and how the system would be used, by describing the use case scenarios. Furthermore, the researchers presented initial user profiles, system architecture, and non-functional requirements. The participants then discussed the requirements and gave feedback on how they could be enhanced. After the workshop, the requirements were updated, based on the feedback from the participants. The final version of the document was sent to the participants two weeks before the final meeting, in December 2014. In the last meeting, participants evaluated the outcomes and validated the produced requirements. The participants appreciated the transparency of the design process and how researchers were able to communicate using language they understood. Finally, researchers thanked the participants for their collaboration and discussed future plans for the prototype development.

5.4 Identifying Objectives

The recordings of the four workshops were transcribed completely, in order to gain an overall view of the data, which were then exported into the ATLAS-ti software, for a more detailed interpretation. Data was analysed through a process of open coding [44], to develop a list of utterances that are related to the objectives of the group, that is, what the group considered important, or the way they thought that the desired situation could be achieved. All 153 utterances were examined one by one and assigned at least one code. The coding process was overlapping: a single utterance could be connected to many different codes and vice-versa. If it was impossible to connect an utterance with any of the previous codes or imagine a new code, the utterance was removed as an irrelevant phrase. Finally, 133 utterance remained that had been assigned at least one code. The rejected utterances were examined again, to ensure that no relevant data was removed by chance or mistake.

The utterances inside the codes were refined, to ascertain that the codes had a coherent structure. The codes, including the assigned utterances, were analysed, to differentiate between fundamental objectives and means objectives. If the assigned utterance expressed an essential objective, it became a candidate for a fundamental objective. If the assigned utterance expressed something that was important because of its implications for some other objective, it was a candidate for a means objective. Finally, the transcriptions were read through again, to validate the structure of the objectives.

6 Resulted Objectives

The fundamental objectives regarding an open and adaptable environment were identified as follows: improving communication, strengthening the community, increasing efficiency, enabling functionality, taking special needs into account, and ensuring privacy (Table 3). These are further discussed one by one. Each of these fundamental objectives were allocated means objectives, in order to bring these objectives closer to the actual implementation. Moreover, means objectives were further classifed into *organisational means* and *technological means*. Organisational level means represent the social actions that contribute towards the fundamental objective. System level means were defined as those features of the system that could possibly contribute to an associated fundamental objective.

6.1 Improved Communication

The first fundamental objective regarded improved communication. The hope was that teachers, staff, and students would not be isolated in the classrooms and this would encourage more communication between people. We thus interpreted communication as a central objective, even though it often appeared implicitly in the data, because it is strongly connected to other objectives. For example, the connection with privacy appears as a need to have spaces available for private conversations between teachers, students, and other stakeholders. Participants emphasised that, regardless of the features or possibilities of the system, there is a need for a culture of open communication. It is unavoidable that conflicts will occur when adjusting to a new environment. Participants agreed that the responsibility for solving conflicts cannot be outsourced entirely to technology. Even when a mechanism for automatically resolving reservation-related conflict would exist, the prioritisations policy must be determined by the people.

Communication can be improved in many ways at the system level. The primary feature required was that the system could be accessed by mobile devices. The participants stressed that they do not have time to look for a desktop computer during the day. One proposition was that there could be tablet devices ported near the learning spaces, making it easy to check the status of the space and make a reservation. The participants brought up the issue that information related to reservations needed to be easily accessed and needed to contain some mandatory fields: contact information of the person who made the reservation and the purpose of the reservation. From a pedagogical perspective, there should also be features allowing for commenting, rating and sharing knowledge about the learning possibilities of spaces.

6.2 Strengthened Community

A strong community was conceptualised as a situation wherein the whole school community is able to negotiate shared goals among stakeholders and work together towards them. As discussed before, the participants emphasised the need for a culture of open communication. The participants concluded that they

Table 3. Summary of identified objectives: fundamental objectives and means objectives (organisational and technological).

Fundamental objectives	Organisational means	Technological means
Improve communication	Communication culture; Discuss conflicting reservations	Access with mobile devices; Automatic conflict handling; Information about reserved spaces; Purpose for reservations; Owner of a reservation
Strengthen community	Responsible use of resources; Negotiated rules and norms; Open discussion	A "right of way" feature; Reservation status
Increase efficiency	Planned behaviour	Visual information; Real-time information; Usability; Mobile use
Enable functionality	Think differently; Functional pedagogy; Creative use of spaces	Recommends suitable spaces; Shows accessories; Shows the purpose of a space; Shows size of a space; Accessible from different locations and with different devices
Pedagogical use	Empower students; Guide to responsive use of ICT	Authentication policy; Generic student accounts; Take account of special needs; Accesible user interface
Ensure privacy and security	Respect privacy of others	Critical information on dedicated servers

needed to learn ways to co-operate in an open and adaptable environment: the actions are less confined to classrooms, and possible conflicting encounters need to be negotiated. It is not just the policies and rules that need to be negotiated with the school staff, the whole operational culture of the school needs shifting.

The participants proposed an interesting feature for the system, which was named *"right of way"*. The idea was that the system could understand if someone had privileges to certain spaces and automatically reorganise the reservations, based on these privileges. This raised an intense discussion about what constituted privileges and whether this idea conflicted with the open and adaptable environment. Moreover, this feature would be rather complicated to implement, technically.

An essential method of strengthening the community was found to be the possibility of marking reservations with open or closed status. An open reservation means that the space is reserved for certain people, but others are still welcome to use it at the same time. Some spaces are divided into smaller rooms or areas, which could be used in parallel. For example, two classes of deaf children, communicating via sign language, could share the same room, as long as they would use the separating curtains available in the room. This feature was appreciated by the participants, because it further supported the idea of collaboration and more efficient use of facilities.

6.3 Increased Efficiency

The participants extensively discussed how everyday life would be organised in the new environment. The idea of not having their own classrooms was both fascinating and frightening. The main expectation from the technological tool was that it would help to organise the school activities. This is a crucial issue and affects the whole work community, as one teacher commented: *"I think, it [the system] would help to sort things out, without unnecessary hassle. It is something that would have a great impact on our work atmosphere"*. We interpret that time is the most limited resource the participants have, and it is extremely important that using the developed technology does not waste it. The participants also emphasised how the ability to plan activities beforehand will make the working day more tranquil.

When considering the actual system, the participants described that efficiency was about getting real-time information that could be used everywhere and that was easy to use. They also noted the possibility of having visual information. A concrete example of the relationship between ease of use and efficiency being discussed was based on their previous experiences with a facility management system which had a complicated function for removing reservations and resulted in too many *"no-show"* reservations. A visual view (visual interface) of the building was important for the participants. They were used to perceiving the dimensions of the new building on the map. The possibility of making reservations with a visual picture was thought to be more accessible than, for example, a list of available spaces. Mobile access was again mentioned, because it supported the idea of an open and adaptable environment, by encouraging people to move around.

6.4 Enabling Functionality

The participants shared the view that action-based learning has a very important role in special education; therefore, enabling functionality is one of the main goals of the open and adaptive environment, and so, it seemed rather self-evidently to qualift as a functional objective. Functionality was conceptualised as a vision where activities are always happening in the space that is most suitable for the intended pedagogical practice and that is available at the current moment. The participants hoped that a more functional environment would lead to more creative pedagogy, due to the possibilities the new learning spaces are offering. However, creativity was seen as a challenge: how to question the old practices (and think differently) and pedagogically combine the needs of the students and new learning spaces?

The main question at a system level was what spaces are made available for reservation. There seemed to be contradictory views between the new way of understanding all spaces as *"open learning spaces"* and the need for individual and private spaces for certain tasks. This discussion resulted in interesting observations; for instance: if there is a room with several workstations, does the reservation apply to the whole room, or is it possible to reserve only a single workstation? Solving these issues led to a clearer understanding of the level on which the decisions are made: between people, pre-programmed in technological systems, or as institutional policies. According to the participants, the following features of the system would enable functionality: the system is able to recommend the most suitable spaces based on certain criteria, it is easy to see important information in the system, and the system can be accessed from any location in the school, with most used devices.

6.5 Pedagogical Use

The students of the school have a wide range of special needs. Different perceptional abilities present a challenge between the creative and dynamic use of learning spaces and the need for structure and formality. For example, it is essential for blind students to learn how to navigate through the building and find the necessary accessories inside the learning spaces on their own. The school introduced several guides for this, including typical tracks for blind people, but also innovative uniquely textured walls, which helped identify the respective spaces, as well as a novel sound-based guidance system (specific intersections emitting different little tunes, to be uniquely identifiable).

The participants, however, discussed that the world itself is not structured for the needs of blind people, and an important aim is to teach students to act independently outside the school. This reflects the idea that using the system should be one way to facilitate the students' independence. The system was seen as an opportunity to enhance responsibility, by empowering students to reserve learning spaces for themselves and by guiding students towards responsible use of information and communication technology (ICT). The participants noted that permitting students to use the system could result in accidental or intentional misuse, but they seemed to agree that, despite the possible unwanted scenarios, it is important to accustom students to ICT.

An important issue was to decide on user policies and authentication within the system. One possibility was to create user accounts for every student, but this would raise challenges related to security and technical implementation. Information related to students has high-security classification, which would mean tight restrictions in the system. The participants proposed the possibility of making generic user accounts for students, so their personal information could not be revealed. Special needs were to be taken into account in system development, to make pedagogical use of the system possible.

6.6 Ensuring Privacy and Security

An important matter of discussion was how privacy could be ensured in the open and adaptable environment. The participants emphasised the need for private spaces, to have conversations with stakeholders and how this privacy needs to be respected. They also commented that visual positioning information about staff or students could be very useful, but that it raises many privacy-related problems. However, participants explained that they have actually had emergency situations during which a student has been completely lost.

From a technical perspective, the discussion focused around how the current technological infrastructure is connected to the system and what security vulnerabilities it might cause. The participants concluded that critical student information is stored in dedicated servers and that access to the system should be restricted.

7 Learning Space Management System Prototype

In order to implement the objectives that resulted from the VFT workshops, firstly, the researchers created a use-case diagram. This use case diagram of the prototype is presented in Fig. 3. The functions within *Onspace mobile* are optimised for mobile devices (responding to the fundamental objective of increased efficiency, via the technological means of 'mobile use', as well as the fundamental objective of enabling functionality, via the technological means of accessibility from different locations and via different devices). The administration functions *Onspace web* are only available from the administrative interface (responding to the fundamental objective of ensuring privacy and security, viathe technological means of having critical information on dedicated servers).

These two different interfaces reflect the fact that the prototype allows for two user roles: user and admin(istrator). In addition to the user functions, the administrator can edit all reservations, user information, and learning spaces. The server functionality is developed with the Django Web framework, the PostgreSQL open source database, and HTTP servers Nginx and Gunicorn. The user interface is built on a variety of open source Javascript libraries.

The main use scenario, user logging in and making a reservation with the map-based interface, is presented in Fig. 4: (1) The user logs in with his credentials. (2) The prototype automatically assigns the current date and the next rounded half hour as the starting time for a reservation and displays the first floor of the building. If the user changes the parameters, the map under the search view is immediately updated. (3) The map shows the areas in the single floor of the building and how many free learning spaces the area has. (4) The user chooses the area C from the first floor and can now see the map of the area, which has currently four available learning spaces. (5) The user clicks on

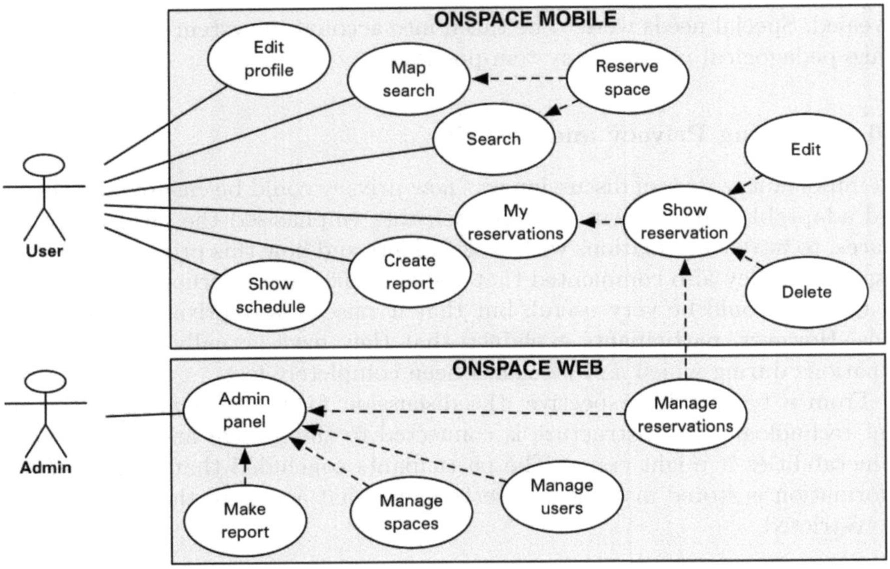

Fig. 3. Use case diagram.

Table 4. Participatory design workshops during the implementation stage.

Initiation	17. June, 2015
1. Workshop	27. August, 2015
2. Workshop	17. September, 2015
3. Workshop	21. October, 2015
4. Workshop	19. November, 2015
Final meeting	17. December, 2015

the desired learning space, and the reservation model opens. The learning space information includes a description and the accessories it has. The user can write the purpose of the reservation and needs to choose whether the reservation is open or closed for other people. (6) The user can see all the reservations as a list or on a calendar. The reservations can be edited and removed, by clicking.

7.1 Prototype Development Through Participatory Design

The prototype implementation was carried out by the first author and a project researcher during May - December 2015. During the development phase, we organised another set of monthly participatory design workshops (Table 4). The first meeting included mainly decision-making stakeholders, such as the Head of the School, and was focused more on project practicalities, such as timetables, responsibilities, and contracts. The school's ICT staff manager was also

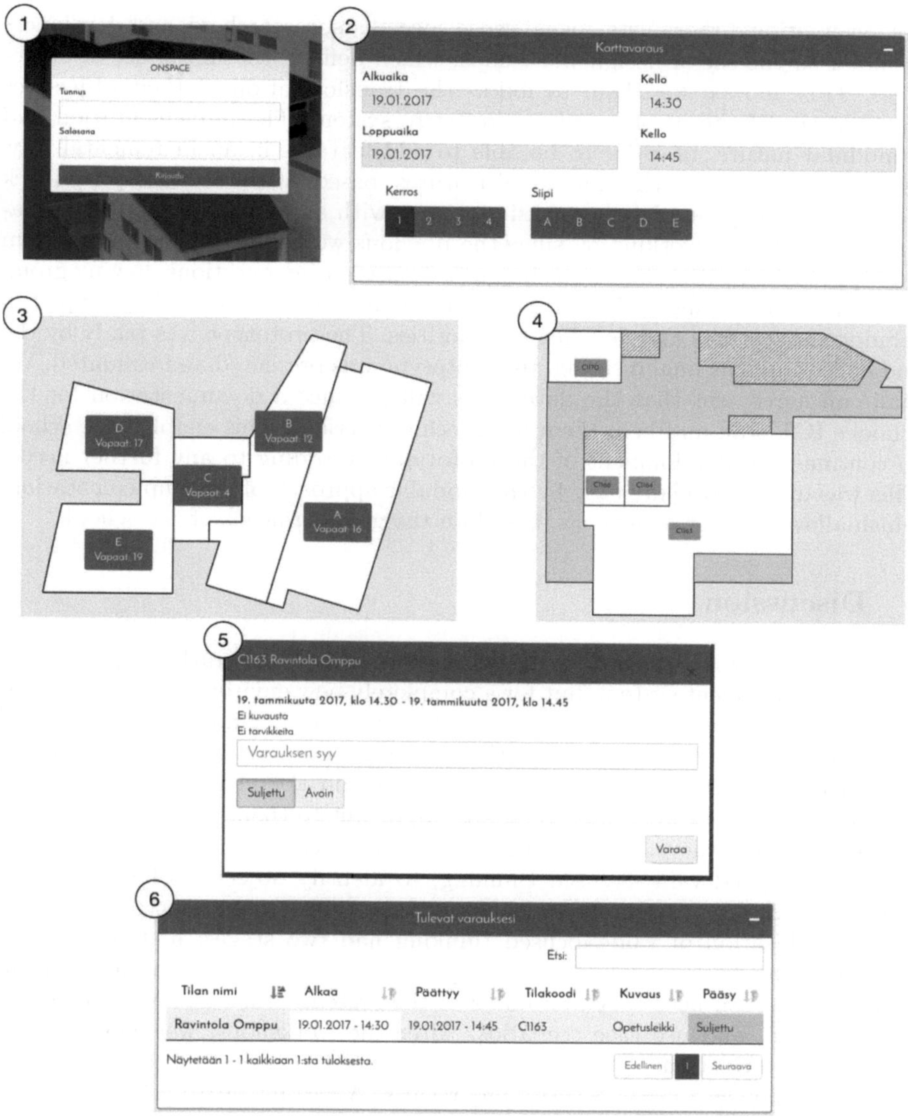

Fig. 4. Use case of logging in and making a reservation.

present, to describe the current technical infrastructure. We agreed to develop a responsive web application that could be used by different computers and mobile devices, due to the fact that the school staff uses a broad range of mobile devices, from different manufacturers.

The workshops represented iterative cycles of negotiation, development, and demonstration. The participants of the workshops were: special education teachers, occupational therapists, visual sense specialists, researchers, and developers - similar to the set of design workshops, which defined the initial set of objectives. This allowed for them to follow the transformation of their objectives into practical features of a running software system. The implementation had a modular nature, in order to be able to add features in an incremental way, as well as to easily rectify individual features, based on the workshop feedback from the participants. Every workshop began with an explanation on what features we had been working on since the previous workshop. Then, the problem was approached with different techniques: by presenting questions, having group discussions, and using a sketching tool. Feedback from the workshop helped in refining the features and deciding on priorities. The prototype was ready by the end of 2015. In the final meeting, the prototype was presented and validated. We made an agreement that the developers will produce a documentation for the school's ICT staff and help them with technical issues. This enabled the school to continue the development of the prototype, according to any further needs. This was made especially easy by the modular approach of our implementation, which allows further extensions, based on the growing needs of the school.

8 Discussion

The design process described is an example of re-imagining a rather typical information management system, but for a completely new environment, represented by the open and adaptable school. It was clear from the beginning that we needed to reinvent the characteristics of facility management systems. In practice, we needed to encourage the participants to reflect on the new surroundings and their everyday work, to frame what was important to them and to clarify what they wanted to achieve. To reach this goal, we organised four workshops, during which we applied value-focused thinking, to identify objectives for a learning space management system for an open and adaptable environment.

Our utilisation of value-focused thinking had two stages: first, we needed to analyse the workshops from the perspective of requirements specification, in order to establish necessary attributes of the system - that is, functions, a use case diagram, and use case scenarios. After the workshops, we made a more in-depth investigation of the data, using an open coding analysis. This two-staged analysis was used to verify our results. As Morse et al. [45] state, data may demand to be treated in different ways, so the analytic procedure should match the research questions. The first analysis stage was more practical and straightforward, while the second stage required a more reflective strategy and critical discussions about the project, between the authors of this paper.

The fundamental objectives identified were, as described above: improving communication, strengthening community, increasing efficiency, enabling functionality, pedagogical use of the system, and ensuring privacy and security. These fundamental objectives, as well as the means to achieve them, are described at a system - as well as at an organisational level. We argue that this approach helped and will help developers, in general, to take a more holistic view in the development phase. The functions and features of the system need to be considered together with organisational level means, and they should be in line with approved fundamental objectives. The results render a more in-depth representation about the context, people, and environment for which the system is developed.

We implemented a prototype of the system and involved our stakeholders in monthly participatory design workshops. The participants had a real opportunity to influence the prototype development and there was strong collaboration between researchers and participants. Researchers were able to learn about the work and the new environment of the participants and the researchers were able to share knowledge about technical possibilities, as well as restrictions. The workshops were advantageous, because the stakeholders continuously discussed the underlying philosophy of the new school and how the prototype should support it. The concept of the *"old way"* was used to describe the traditional school, where teachers have their own classrooms and learning activities are pre-programmed in timetables. The prototype that supports the *"new way"* would enable the dynamic and creative use of learning spaces and prevent teachers from returning to the habit of reserving a single space for extensive periods of time. This method additionally helped the developers to understand the most important objectives and optimise their resources to meet then.

We also collided with various issues during the design process. VFT does not put emphasis on the complex power relationships participants may have. The method assumes that people are able to communicate their thoughts, regardless of the social hierarchies that may constrain the discussion. Furthermore, VFT examines the identified objectives as a whole, while the objectives between different stakeholders might be very conflicting. The question is, whose objectives are we supposed to meet? As an example, the requirements did not include a feature to make recurring reservations. However, when the implementation phase was ending, the administrative staff was disappointed, because of the lack of that feature. They need to rent certain assets for other organisations and the contracts are made for long time periods, and manually inputting and updating these reservations with the prototype would be an arduous task.

Furthermore, the rationale of VFT is that decision-making is based on the values of decision makers, rather than just comparing possible alternatives. The concept of value is very challenging, because of the different definitions of value in different research fields and even among individuals. Keeney's [6,40] definition is very general, and the difference between the concepts of value and objective is not completely clarified. To underline the point, for some people, value is about currency or efficiency and for others it is about ethical questions. As an anecdote, Cockton [46,47] changed the name of the concept from value to worth after struggling with the same issue. It may seem appealing to use a pre-defined set of values, as in Schwartz's [48] theory of basic values, which provides more depth to the contents and structure of values, but as Isomursu et al. [49] discussed, using a pre-defined framework to analyse and interpret the findings can lead to confirmation bias.

Even if we embrace Keeney's definition, the question arises of how to reach abstract constructions that may be difficult to form as statements. For example, Iversen et al. [50] pointed out that values are not static entities that are waiting for researchers and developers to collect them, but more like changing, complex and abstract ways of being and thinking. Keeney seems to take it for granted that decision makers are automatically people who are able to express what is important to them. For example, when designing with children, there should be more appropriate methods than just asking *"what it is that one cares for"*. People's values tend to emerge, change and even conflict, and researchers should carefully consider who is answering these questions and what they mean.

9 Conclusion

In this paper we have described how the objectives for a learning space management system for a very special type of adaptive school were identified with the value-focused thinking method and how the system prototype was developed. We find it of utmost importance to understand the participants as a human agents, with intentions, feelings, and attitudes, instead of contenting ourselves with a generic definition of users with shared goals [22,51]. Different stakeholders consider the confronted design problems from their own perspectives and it needs to be acknowledged that the goals of the stakeholders can conflict. Concludingly, we found value-focused thinking as an applicable method, allowing for a holistic approach to requirements elicitation. However, at the same time, we found that more focus on the different stakeholder roles is needed. We have implemented a system prototype which instantiates the identified objectives. However, more data is needed to investigate the outcomes of the developed system prototype and the impact of using value-focused thinking.

Acknowledgements. We would like to express our gratitude to the Valteri School Onerva's personnel for participating in the research project. We also thank Kirsi Heinonen, M.Sc., for assisting in the data collection. This research has been funded by the Valteri School Onerva and the University of Jyvaskyla, Faculty of Information Technology, under the projects entitled ONSPACE and ONSPACE2. The research did not receive any specific grant from funding agencies in the public, commercial, or not-for-profit sectors.

References

1. Özen, A., Ergenekon, Y.: Activity-based intervention practices in special education. Educ. Sci.: Theor. Prac. **11**, 359–362 (2011)
2. Alessandrini, A., Cappelletti, A., Zancanaro, M.: Audio-augmented paper for therapy and educational intervention for children with autistic spectrum disorder. Int. J. Hum.-Comput. Stud. **72**, 422–430 (2014)

3. Tuhkala, A., Isomäki, H., Hartikainen, M., Cristea, A., Alessandrini, A.: Identifying objectives for a learning space management system with value-focused thinking. In: Escudeiro, P., Costagliola, G., Zvacek, S., Uhomoibhi, J., McLaren, B. (eds.) Proceedings of the 9th International Conference on Computer Supported Education (CSEDU). SCITEPRESS - Science and Technology Publications, Porto (2016)
4. Pacheco, C., Garcia, I.: A systematic literature review of stakeholder identification methods in requirements elicitation. J. Syst. Softw. **85**, 2171–2181 (2012)
5. Frauenberger, C., Good, J., Fitzpatrick, G., Iversen, O.S.: In pursuit of rigour and accountability in participatory design. Int. J. Hum.-Comput. Stud. **74**, 93–106 (2015)
6. Keeney, R.L.: Value-Focused Thinking: a Path to Creative Decision Making. Harvard University Press, Cambridge, Massachusetts (1992)
7. Sanoff, H., Walden, R.: School environments. In: The Oxford Handbook of Environmental and Conservation Psychology, pp. 276–294 (2012)
8. Kok, H.B., Mobach, M.P., Omta, O.S.: The added value of facility management in the educational environment. J. Facil. Manag. **9**, 249–265 (2011)
9. Kumpulainen, K., Rajala, A.: Negotiating time-space contexts in students' technology-mediated interaction during a collaborative learning activity. Int. J. Educ. Res. **84**, 55–57 (2015)
10. Todhunter, B.J.: An examination of the views of key stakeholders on the development of learning spaces at a regional university. J. Facil. Manag. **13**, 204–222 (2015)
11. Keppell, M., Riddle, M.: Distributed learning spaces: physical, blended and virtual learning spaces in higher education. In: Physical and Virtual Learning Spaces in Higher Education, pp. 1–20. IGI Global (2012)
12. Lievonen, M., Kinnunen, P.: Main features of an ideal learning space: a user-based description. In: Proceedings of the 6th Annual Architectural Research Symposium in Finland, p. 8 (2014)
13. Kumpulainen, K., Mikkola, A.: Researching learning across space and time in extended learning environments. In: PersPectives from Finland - Towards New Learning Environments, pp. 9–22. Juvenes Print - Suomen Yliopistopaino Oy (2014)
14. Kuuskorpi, M.: Future physical learning environment. User oriented flexible and changeable teaching spaces. Dissertation, University of Turku (2012)
15. Nevari, J.: Oivaltamo: avautuva oppimistila. Ph.D. thesis, Lahti University of Applied Sciences (2013)
16. Barki, H., Hartwick, J.: Measuring user participation, user involvement, and user attitude. MIS Q. **18**, 59–82 (1994)
17. He, J., King, W.R.: The role of user participation in information systems development: implications from a meta-analysis. J. Manag. Inf. Syst. **25**, 301–331 (2008)
18. Mahmood, A.M., Burn, J., Gemoets, L., Jacquez, C.: Variables affecting information technology end-user satisfaction: a meta-analysis of the empirical literature. Int. J. Hum.-Comput. Stud. **52**, 751–771 (2000)
19. Harris, M.A., Weistroffer, H.R.: A new look at the relationship between user involvement in systems development and system success. Commun. Assoc. Inf. Syst. **24**, 739–756 (2009). Article 42
20. Abelein, U., Paech, B.: Understanding the influence of user participation and involvement on system success - a systematic mapping study. Empirical Softw. Eng. **20**, 28–81 (2015)
21. McGill, T., Klobas, J.: User developed application success: sources and effects of involvement. Behav. Inf. Technol. **27**, 407–422 (2008)

22. Iivari, J., Isomäki, H., Pekkola, S.: The user - the great unknown of systems development: reasons, forms, challenges, experiences and intellectual contributions of user involvement. Inf. Syst. J. **20**, 109–117 (2010)
23. Kujala, S.: User involvement: a review of the benefits and challenges. Behav. Inf. Technol. **22**, 1–16 (2003)
24. Spinuzzi, C.: The methodology of participatory design. Tech. Commun. **52**, 163–174 (2005)
25. Bjerknes, G., Bratteteig, T.: User participation and democracy: a discussion of Scandinavian research on system development. Scand. J. Inf. Syst. **7**, 73–98 (1995)
26. Ehn, P.: Work-oriented design of computer artifacts. Ph.D. thesis, Umeå Universitat (1988)
27. Halskov, K., Hansen, N.B.: The diversity of participatory design research practice at PDC 2002–2012. Int. J. Hum.-Comput. Stud. **74**, 81–92 (2015)
28. Muller, M.J., Kuhn, S.: Participatory design. Commun. ACM **36**, 24–28 (1993)
29. Sanders, E.B.N., Brandt, E., Binder, T.: A framework for organizing the tools and techniques of participatory design. In: Proceedings of the 11th Biennial Participatory Design Conference, PDC 2010, p. 195. ACM Press, New York (2010)
30. Sanoff, H.: Special issue on participatory design. Des. Stud. **28**, 213–215 (2007)
31. Bergvall-Kåreborn, B., Ståhlbrost, A.: Participatory design: one step back or two steps forward? In: Proceedings of the Tenth Anniversary Conference on Participatory Design, vol. 2008, pp. 102–111 (2008)
32. Benton, L., Vasalou, A., Khaled, R., Johnson, H., Gooch, D.: Diversity for design. In: Proceedings of the 32nd Annual ACM Conference on Human Factors in Computing Systems - CHI 2014, pp. 3747–3756. ACM Press, New York (2014)
33. Frauenberger, C., Good, J., Keay-Bright, W.: Designing technology for children with special needs: bridging perspectives through participatory design. CoDesign **7**, 1–28 (2011)
34. Guha, M.L., Druin, A., Fails, J.A.: Designing with and for children with special needs. In: Proceedings of the 7th International Conference on Interaction Design and Children - IDC 2008, p. 61. ACM Press, New York (2008)
35. Malinverni, L., MoraGuiard, J., Padillo, V., Mairena, M.a., Hervás, A., Pares, N.: Participatory design strategies to enhance the creative contribution of children with special needs. In: Proceedings of the 2014 Conference on Interaction Design and Children - IDC 2014, pp. 85–94. ACM Press, New York (2014)
36. Parnell, G.S., Hughes, D.W., Burk, R.C., Driscoll, P.J., Kucik, P.D., Morales, B.L., Nunn, L.R.: Invited review-survey of value-focused thinking: applications, research developments and areas for future research. J. Multi-Criteria Decis. Anal. **20**, 49–60 (2013)
37. Williams, R.M.: Change and stability in values and value systems: a sociological perspective. Underst. Hum. Values: Individ. Societal Values **1**, 5–46 (1979)
38. Friedman, B.: Value-sensitive design. Interactions **3**, 16–23 (1996)
39. Schwartz, S.H.: Universals in the content and structure of values: theoretical advances and empirical tests in 20 countries. Adv. Exp. Soc. Psychol. **25**, 1–65 (1992)
40. Keeney, R.L.: Value-focused thinking: identifying decision opportunities and creating alternatives. Eur. J. Oper. Res. **92**, 537–549 (1996)
41. Keeney, R.L.: Identifying, prioritizing, and using multiple objectives. EURO J. Decis. Process. **1**, 45–67 (2013)
42. Sheng, H., Nah, F., Siau, K.: Strategic implications of mobile technology: a case study using value-focused thinking. J. Strateg. Inf. Syst. **14**, 269–290 (2005)

43. Sheng, H., Siau, K., Nah, F.F.H.: Understanding the values of mobile technology in education. ACM SIGMIS Database **41**, 25 (2010)
44. Corbin, J.M., Strauss, A.: Grounded theory research: procedures, canons, and evaluative criteria. Qual. Sociol. **13**, 3–21 (1990)
45. Morse, J.M., Barrett, M., Mayan, M., Olson, K., Spiers, J.: Verification strategies for establishing reliability and validity in qualitative research. Int. J. Qual. Methods **1**, 13–22 (2002)
46. Cockton, G.: Value-centred HCI. In: Proceedings of the Third Nordic Conference on Human-Computer Interaction - NordiCHI 2004, pp. 149–160. ACM Press, New York (2004)
47. Cockton, G.: Designing worth is worth designing. In: Proceedings of the 4th Nordic Conference on Human-Computer Interaction Changing Roles - NordiCHI 2006, Number October, pp. 165–174. ACM Press, New York (2006)
48. Schwartz, S.H.: An overview of the Schwartz theory of basic values. Online Readings Psychol. Culture **2**, 1–20 (2012)
49. Isomursu, M., Ervasti, M., Kinnula, M., Isomursu, P.: Understanding human values in adopting new technology - a case study and methodological discussion. Int. J. Hum.-Comput. Stud. **69**, 183–200 (2011)
50. Iversen, O.S., Halskov, K., Leong, T.W.: Values-led participatory design. CoDesign **8**, 87–103 (2012)
51. Isomäki, H.: The human modes of being in investigating user experience. In: Isomäki, H., Saariluoma, P. (eds.) Future Interaction Design II, pp. 191–207. Springer, London (2009). https://doi.org/10.1007/978-1-84800-385-9_10

Towards Evidence-Based Academic Advising Using Learning Analytics

Mariia Gavriushenko(✉), Mirka Saarela, and Tommi Kärkkäinen

Faculty of Information Technology, University of Jyväskylä,
P.O. Box 35, 40014 Jyväskylä, Finland
magavriu@student.jyu.fi, {mirka.saarela,tommi.karkkainen}@jyu.fi

Abstract. Academic advising is a process between the advisee, adviser and the academic institution which provides the degree requirements and courses contained in it. Content-wise planning and management of the student' study path, guidance on studies and academic career support is the main joint activity of advising. The purpose of this article is to propose the use of learning analytics methods, more precisely robust clustering, for creation of groups of actual study profiles of students. This allows academic advisers to provide evidence-based information on the study paths that have actually happened similarly to individual students. Moreover, academic institutions can focus on management and updates of course schedule having an effect of clearly characterized and recognized group of students. Using this approach a model of automated academic advising process, which can determine the study profiles, is presented. The presented model shows the whole automated process, where the learners will be profiled regularly, and where the proper study path will be suggested.

Keywords: Academic advising · Learning analytics
Robust clustering

1 Introduction

To monitor progress of students in their studies is the core measuring activity of an educational institution. The learning goals can be given in a general way, as a list of courses to be passed, or through the credit-based system, which is most commonly used to characterize the study requirements in many learning environments. Credit-based information can be utilized under various student granularities: for an individual student, at the same time enrolled group of students, students with the same major subject, students in one department, or faculty, or university, or country etc. Evidently, aggregated study progress profiles of different groups of students can then be linked to comparisons and assessments, e.g., between different departments, faculties, universities, or national higher education institutions, for the purpose to identify and indicate differently performing educational units.

P. Escudeiro et al. (Eds.): CSEDU 2017, CCIS 865, pp. 44–65, 2018.
https://doi.org/10.1007/978-3-319-94640-5_3

On the level of an individual student, availability of personalized support is very important constituent of a learner's success [41]. When a learner receives punctual personalized advises, the current status of studies and the remaining learning path should be consulted. For this purpose, academic advising (AA) is an iterative collaboration process between student, academic adviser, and academic institution, to tackle especially the student retention. Advisers provide versatile assistance to the students during their studies, making the educational experience relevant and supported.

AA is based on cooperation between adviser, student and institution. It consists of intentional interactions with a curriculum, a pedagogy, and set of students' learning outcomes. AA process is based on relationships between adviser and advisee respectful of the student's concerns. AA activity has been known since 1870 [59]. AA normally starts when a students begin their education in university.

AA normally starts when a student begins his education at the university, and stops when his degree has been completed. Adviser has to make sure that the student is making required studies in time for graduation, that is why academic adviser has to support learner's study path, especially at the beginning of his academic life. Academic adviser should provide for the student his relevant study possibilities and make sure that predefined study plan is being followed. It could depend on organizational culture, especially the stability or dynamicity of the course schedule.

Usually, academic adviser connects with the students through email, social media, web, wikipages etc. for sharing necessary information. However, regular meetings also take place, especially at the beginning of the learning semester or by student's/ adviser's request. For more personalized support, adviser should know the status of the student's studies and when the student is in need of a study advise.

Departments at the universities provide preliminary recommendations to do certain, especially compulsory courses, to proceed normally with the major subject studies. For example, an electronic personal study plan should be prepared with academic adviser at the University of Jyväskylä (JYU). Advising is organized according to the *satellite model* referring to the distributed responsibility of academic units [59]. The *engagement model* between advisee and adviser characterize the principal spirit of counseling [20].

The starting point for a study plan assessment discussion at the JYU is a study plan itself and the completed studies. The actual number of studies that have been made during the academic year is less than recommended. It has been seen especially in computer science. Advising intervention is needed in this situation, because it became common when actual study path deviates from the plans. It might be that student is struggling with something or and he or she needs help. But how does an individual student and especially an individual study adviser know, what is the relation between students' realized study path and that of the peer students? Thus, could we, instead of comparing against the predefined plans, advise students based on evidence from the actual study paths of other similar students?

Therefore, the purpose of this article is to propose an automated AA system based on a learning analytics method [9]. While generally concerned with student models to improve learning, learning analytics methods have shifted from the traditional statistical techniques to the more sophisticated data mining techniques that can also cope with a large amount of unstructured data [21,26,45,50,52]. Here, we propose to use one of these techniques, more precisely robust clustering [6,47], to create groups of actual profiles of students concerning their studies. Such profiles summarize the different typical accumulations of completed studies, increasing the general awareness of the common study flows. That means that individual students can explicitly be linked to their student peers who have a similar study path profile in the same institutional environment. This allows an adviser to plan a possible intervention adaptively for a larger pool of students instead of following each student individually.

Creating general study profiles of students can help departments in their assessment and planning of when (and how) they provide the courses, especially the compulsory ones [47]. By automating general student profiling it is possible to provide essential support for adaptive on-line advising along the lines suggested, for example, in [25,41]. Individual student's perspective, from self-regulated learning and study planning point of view without AA interface, was thoroughly addressed in [4] (see also [5]). By utilizing general student profiles of a higher educational institution we also follow the current trend in learning analytics of not only tackling learning problems of students within a single class- or school-level but to learning analytics problems on an educational organizational level [52]. Such a focus was, for example, recently also addressed by de Freitas et al. [22] and Daniel [16].

The contents of this paper is as follows: after the introduction, we provide a short background on academic advising, we provide a short background on AA in general. Then, in Sect. 3, we describe the robust clustering method and explain how it has been applied in the student data. Also, we present the student profiles and their interpretation. After in Sect. 4 we propose a system model for automated AA with described functions, as well as present a comparison of automated and manual AA.

2 Background

AA is a collaborative process in which adviser and advisee enter a dynamic relationship where adviser helps advisee to enhance the learning experience by helping in making academic decisions [25]. The decision support could be made by analysis of student's records, as well as some external factors like interests, goals, academic capabilities, schedules etc. [42]. Developmental Advising means helping students to define and explore academic and career goals and pathways, as well as to develop problem-solving and decision-making skills; Prescriptive Advising, which is the more traditional advising model, is mainly concentrated on providing the information to the students according to their academic program, progress, academic policies, course selection, etc.; Intrusive Advising refers to contacting with student in critical periods like first year of study before the declaring major, graduation period, or when students are at-risk or they are high-achieving students [42].

Next we briefly summarize a pool of directly AA related work that was identified through a non-systematic search. Our main concern here is to illustrate the strong link between the needs and practices of AA and the general utility of student profiling.

2.1 On AA

Student voices on AA were raised in only some articles. Al-Ansari et al. [2] used questionnaire to study student satisfaction and support-seeking patterns among dental students in Saudi-Arabia. Very low (only 7.6%) primary utility help rate of advisers in the academic matters was encountered. Even if the advisers were available when needed, they were not able to provide the most relevant information, e.g., on important dates and courses. Hence, up-to-date course and timetable information seems to be a prerequisite for AA, which is handled by the in-house developed, integrated study information system *Korppi*[1].

The pedagogical side of AA was also focused rarely. In the work [19] author studied academic advisers through the lens of transformational leadership, i.e. how advisers can create a connection to students that positively influence their study paths (by increasing and inspiring study motivation and engagement/commitment in studies through individual and intellectual consideration). A questionnaire for undergraduate students strengthened the importance of transformational leadership activities in adviser-student communication and collaboration, independently from the student's characteristics. The lack of time for individual counselling efforts that was visible in most of the reviewed articles here was not emphasized in [19]. Dougherty [17] studied academic advisers from those students' perspective who are doing very well in their studies. These students are called high-achieving students. Authors address the need for the investigation of unique characteristics of these students.

Technical support for AA has been considered in many articles. The availability of extensive information on courses to support automatization of AA was emphasized in [7]. The authors proposed course outline data extractor application, which helps in recognizing similar or comparable courses between different institutions, also helping both students and academic advisers to keep track of the variety of topics that (i) have been covered in the completed studies, (ii) should be covered to complete minor or major subject modules or the actual degree. The authors in [41] proposed an integrated knowledge-based framework based on semantic technology that supports computer-based (automatic) e-Advising on the suitable courses for the students. Naturally individual learning history data provide the starting point for the system and, for this purpose, the authors implemented and tested a data integration tool.

[1] https://www.jyu.fi/itp/en/korppi-guide.

The high workload of academic advisers, especially due to individual but many times recurrent handling of basic issues with multiple students in a hurry, was addressed in [25], with the proposition of an intelligent, semantic, web-based application to assist decision making and automatization of repetitive counselling tasks. Core of the system consisted of rule-based inference engine, which mapped student profile with the study program profile and organizational rules, to provide automatic suggestions on the courses to be enrolled in the upcoming semester. In the preliminary evaluation, a positive feedback of the system was obtained, although the main limitation of suitability to only study programs which follow a clear, predefined study path of courses, was recognized. With very similar aims and functionality, another web-based on-line adviser was described in [20]. This system was also evaluated positively when compared to the current advising system. The authors emphasized that such a tool only supports and does not replace a human academic adviser.

Conversational, fully autonomous agent supporting AA dialogs using natural language processing (NLP) were suggested in [35]. The proposed system contained an extensible knowledge base of information and rules on academic programs and policies, course schedules, and a general FAQ. NLP performance of the proposed system was evaluated positively. Also, the similar multi-agent approach was suggested in [61] for AA. This approach helps tackling a dynamic and complex individualized study planning and scheduling problem. As well as in [3] was proposed a decision tree model for AA affairs based on the algorithm C4.5. The output is evaluated based on Kappa measure and ROC area. The main conclusion was made that the difference between the registered and gained credit hours by a student was the main attribute that academic advisers can rely on [2].

As can be concluded, earlier studies have mostly concentrated on research prototypes which focus only on few main components or tool support for existing learning management systems. Taking into account that user modeling is one of the key factors for including personalization into the learning system, many researchers used ontologies for learners' models, because ontologies have many advantages for creation of user models [7,11,25,30,37,41].

Data-mining techniques have also been applied to the learning environments in order to track users' activities, extract their behavior profiles and patterns, and analyze the data for future improvement of the learning results, as well as for identifying types of learners [39]. Mostly, for developing personalized learning plan, researchers used decision tree search, heuristic algorithms, genetic algorithms, item response theory and association rules. Also, many studies used semantic web technologies, neural networks and multi-agent approach. Most of the previous studies on personalized learning path generation schemes have mainly focused on guiding the students to learn in the digital world; i.e. each learning path represents a set of digitalized learning objects that are linked together based on some rules or constraints [38]. While determining such digitalized learning paths, the learning achievements, on-line behaviors or personalized features (such as learning style) of individual students are usually taken into consideration [10,12–14,54].

2.2 On Personalization of Student Support

In general, many researchers have paid attention to developing *e-learning systems with personalization*, and the most common aspect in these system is the *creation of the personalized learning path* for each individual student or group of students. Most of personalized systems consider learner preferences, interests and browsing behaviors, because it will help to provide personalized curriculum sequencing service [27]. In the study [13] authors proposed a personalized e-learning system which is based on Item Response Theory (PEL-IRT). This system is considering course material difficulty and learner ability, to provide individual learning path for learners. Learner's ability estimation was based on an explicit learner's feedback (the answers of learners to the assigned questionnaires). The system appeared mostly like a recommendation system of the courses for the learners. Authors in [27] proposed a genetic-based curriculum sequencing approach and used case-based reasoning to develop a summative assessment. The empirical part indicated that the proposed approach can generate appropriate course materials for learners taking into account their individual requirements. Later, in [11], the authors developed a personalized web-based learning system grounded on curriculum sequencing based on a generated ontology-based concept map, which was constructed by the pre-test result of the learners. Optimization problem for modeling criteria and objectives for automatic determination of personalized context-aware ubiquitous learning path was suggested in [29]. This learning model not only supports learners with alternative ways to solve problems in real-world situations, but also proposes more active interaction with the learners. Authors in [62] proposed Decision Support System for student advising based on decision tree for an automated program planning and scheduling. The proposed approach takes into account prerequisite rules, the minimum time (minimum number of terms), and the academic recommendations. The adaptive course sequencing for personalization of learning objectives was suggested in [30] using neural networks, self organizing maps and the back-propagation algorithm.

A very closely related work to ours was reported in [53]. Authors proposed a case-based reasoning paradigm which is based on the assumption that similar students will have similar course histories. The system used the experience and history of graduated students in order to propose potential courses for the students. Unfortunately, this approach required matching between students' histories. Also, similar case-based reasoning was used by [40] for developing a recommendation system for a suitable major to students based on comparison of the student information and similar historical cases.

As reviewed, many suggestions for intelligent software and information system support of AA have been given. Many studies describe the creation of intelligent learning systems that can make a curriculum sequencing more flexible for providing students with personalized and adaptive study support services

[8,23,36,36,43,57]. Universities are more and more looking into developing self-service systems with intelligent agents as an addition or replacement for the labor-intensive services like AA. For example, The Open University of Hong Kong has developed an intelligent on-line system that instantly responds to enquiries about career development, learning modes, program/course choices, study plans, and graduation checks [37].

However, the institutional starting point concerning available digital information, especially for the web-based systems that have been proposed, seems to vary a lot. Some systems start and focus on providing easy access to course and degree requirements information whose availability is to be assured first. On the other hand, we might start from the situation where we can readily access most of the relevant data: (i) course information with basic contents, learning goals, assessment methods, acceptance criteria, schedule and location, teachers and lecturers etc.; (ii) individual, anonymous study records on passed courses and completed studies. (Note that reliable information on student admission is currently not directly available in the organization under consideration).

3 Creation of Study Path Profiles Using Robust Clustering

3.1 Data

To illustrate the proposed approach, we utilized the real study records of the Bachelor (B.Sc.) and Master (M.Sc.) students majoring in Mathematical Information Technology at the University of Jyväskylä (JYU/MIT). The MIT programs at JYU are comparable to a major in Computer Science at other universities. The information technology administration at JYU has recently created a data warehouse of passed courses from all the students. On one hand, these data can be utilized by the departments. On the other hand, the electronic study plan system does not provide a direct interface for larger student groups. That means that both from accessibility and evidence-basedness points of view, we focused on analyzing the real study log of the passed courses covering the four calendar years 2012–2015. The log was anonymized by keeping the student IDs as keys. It should be noted that students can start their studies either in the beginning of September (autumn term) or January (spring term). Hence, the original study registry log included a heterogeneous set of B.Sc. and M.Sc. students who had started their studies either before 2012 or in the beginning of spring or autumn terms during 2012–2015.

The whole study log contained 15370 passed courses by 1163 different students on 1176 different course IDs. Altogether, there were 942 male students (81%) in the data, who on average completed 59.9 ECTS. Only 221 female students (19%) of the students were female and they had completed on average 57.0 ECTS. Since at least 180 ECTS are needed for a B.Sc. and an additional 120 ECTS for a M.Sc. degree, we conclude that most of the students in the log were either in the beginning of their studies or—as already reported for the previous student data in [47]—progressing very passively and slowly. Both, the gender distribution as well as the slow progression, assemble rather typical situations in Computer Science programs [15,34,44,58].

Figure 1 shows the discrete density distribution of the size of the passed courses. According to the figure, 5 ECTS and 3 ECTS are the two most common sizes of the courses, the former covering around 30% of the studies. Moreover, there are a lot of small courses (1–6 ECTS) with the exception of the M.Sc. thesis, which is worth 30 ECTS. Teaching in JYU is organized into four periods during one academic year (plus the summer semester) in such a way that a course of circa 5 ECTS can fit to one period. Since the passed courses represent both major and minor subject studies, we argue here that the division of the overall learning objects as courses is not optimal. During the course of writing this article, we also discovered that the instructions of JYU for preparing the next curriculum for 2017–2019 include a strong recommendation to decrease the number of courses with only a few credits. Thus, this observation already provides an example on how summarization of study log data produces visibility and feedback to the organization.

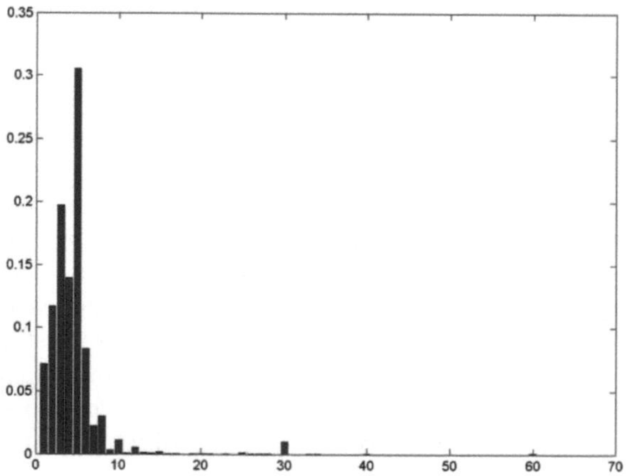

Fig. 1. Probability of size of a course [24].

In a next step, we aggregated how many credits per semester each student completed. This was performed similarly as in [47]: each calendar year was divided into two semesters, the spring term (from January to June) and the autumn term (from July to December). As explained above, there are three academic semesters, spring, summer (June–August), and autumn, where spring and autumn are further divided into two periods. However, since usually only a few courses are completed during the summer (this is illustrated in [47]), it was reasonable to divide the calendar year into only two parts for further analysis.

The semesterwise study accumulation represents the overall study activity: how many credits were made by a student per semester. Our second main concern, directly related to AA, is to study how effectively (i.e., when) the compulsory part of the B.Sc. major studies has been made. In our case, during 2012–2015, there were ten different compulsory courses of interest, for which both autumn and spring term starters had their separate study recommendations. Some, but not all, compulsory courses were provided more than once in an academic year. Hence, as the second transformation of the study log, we created a student-wise indication of that semester when one of the ten compulsory bachelor courses was passed. Naturally, the counting of semesters started from that one when the student was enrolled to the studies. This yields to 10 integer variables of range $[1, 8]$.

In what follows, we profile, analyze and compare two students cohorts: those who started their studies in the beginning of the autumn term 2012 (A2012) or 2013 (A2013). Hence, for A2012 we end up with 8 and for A2013 with 6 integer variables representing the aggregated amount of credits on half-a-year scale. Since the students have progressed in their studies very differently and many of them have not been active during all the semesters of interest, both of the data sets are very sparse containing a lot of missing values [47]. This is the key property that is taken into account in the profiling approach that is described next.

3.2 Robust Clustering Method

As already explained, our goal is to assist the academic advisers by recommending suitable courses for students based on passed courses of (possibly more advanced) students with similar study path. For this, we need to identify general profiles of similar students and this is, precisely, the purpose of clustering. Partitional (or representative-based [63]) clustering seems to be the right family of clustering methods to choose from because it assigns each observation to exactly one cluster, which is represented by its most characteristic point, the cluster centroid, which represents the common profile. Within a cluster, distances of observations to the prototype determine the most typical or representative members of a cluster. Thus, instead of following many different student profiles, the academic adviser can just follow the most common profiles to get an overview of the whole cohort.

Generally, partitional based clustering algorithms consist of an initialization step, in which the initial centroids of each cluster are generated, and iterations of two steps where (i) each observation is assigned to its closest centroid, and (ii) the centroid of each cluster is recomputed by utilizing all observations assigned to it. The algorithm stops when the centroids remain the same over two iterations. The most popular and most applied partitional clustering algorithm is the *k-means* [31], also in learning analytics studies [52]. This algorithm works very well for full and approximately normally distributed data since the sample mean is the most efficient estimator for samples that are drawn from the normal distribution. However, the sample mean is highly sensible to all kinds of outliers [28] as well as missing values, which can be characterized as special types of outliers. Since our data is—as explained in Sect. 3.1–very sparse, this clustering approach would not be suitable here. Furthermore, for a non-symmetric (skewed) distribution, the sample mean is not necessarily the most efficient estimator and other location estimates might be preferable [50,55]. Moreover, as more thoroughly explained in [47], the quantization error for the integer-type variables like here has uniform not Gaussian distribution.

The spatial/geometric median is a robust nonparametric location estimate, which remains reliable even if half of the data is contaminated [33,55]. Mathematically, the spatial median is the Weber point that minimizes the (nonsquared) sum of the Euclidean distances to a group of given points $\{\mathbf{x}_i\}, i = 1, 2, \dots n$:

$$\arg\min_{\mathbf{c}} \sum_{i=1}^{n} \|\mathbf{x}_i - \mathbf{c}\|. \tag{1}$$

Although the basic concept is easily understood and has been extensively discussed in the literature (albeit under various names, see [18]), its computation is known to be difficult.

In [6], the difficulty of computing the spatial median during partitional clustering was solved with the SOR (Sequential Overrelaxation) algorithm (see [6] for details). Moreover, in the implementation of the resulting *k-spatial-medians* clustering algorithm, only the available (i.e., the not-missing) data is taken into account when the centroid is recomputed.

To sum up, all of these above discussed properties—most importantly, the robustness to missing data and the fact that every cluster is represented by a centroid—make the *k-spatial-medians* clustering very suitable for creating student's general study profiles. The fact that such a clustering approach works very well for sparse educational data has been previously shown in [46,48,49,51]. The initialization of the robust clustering method was realized similarly as in [49]: We started with multiple repetitions of *k-means* for the complete data – without missing values – and then, applied *k-spatial-medians* to the best of those results.

Concerning the second representation of the study log, we note that the information whether a mandatory course was passed by a particular student in a certain semester is a binary one. This means that to find the semester-wise co-occurrences one could apply association rule mining, especially the famous Apriori-algorithm [1]. Hence, we note that use of *k-spatial-medians* clustering with the proposed encoding provides a scalable and—since we do not need to binarize variables—also an easier and faster alternative to association rule mining with very similar support for the educational knowledge discovery.

3.3 Clustered Student Profiles

Similarly to the earlier work in [46–48,60], we apply four different internal cluster validation indices to determine the number of clusters: Knee Point (KP) of the clustering error, Ray-Turi (RT), Davies-Bouldin (DB), and Davies-Bouldin∗ (DB∗). All the computations here were carried out in the Matlab-environment, using own implementations of all the algorithms.

From the two student groups A2012 and A2013, we include in clustering only still active students, i.e. those who have made credits during the autumn term 2015 (the last one analyzed). Furthermore, we restrict ourselves to those students for whom over half of the variables are available [55]. This means that the 47 analyzed students in A2012 have made studies during at least four out of the seven possible semesters (including the last one) and the 76 students in A2013 at least in three out of the five semesters. Because of the anonymity, we obtained further assistance in relation to the metadata and interpretation of the clusters from the Study Amanuensis of the Department [56].

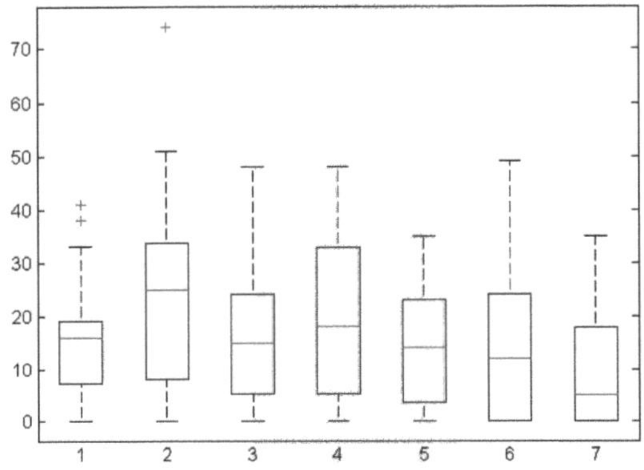

Fig. 2. Boxplot for A2012 [24].

A2012. The boxplot in Fig. 2 shows the large variability in the study accumulations both within semesters and between semesters. We see the larger accumulations in the spring terms during the first two years, and a slightly decreasing overall trend after that. There are always exceptional students who have made much more studies than their peers.

KP, DP, and DP∗ indicated four clusters and RT had also local minimum there, so we choose to analyze four different general study progress profiles. The profiles for A2012 are depicted in Fig. 3, where the size of the cluster is given in the top-right corner. The profiles are sorted in the ascending order with respect to the total number of credits.

The main group of 21 students in the first cluster illustrate a potential start of the studies in the first year, with strong passivation after that. They have obtained prototypically 65 ECTS until the end of 2015. Based on [56], by a closer look on the 8 students from the cluster closest to the centroid, these are all older B.Sc. and M.Sc. male students (born before 1990). They are either distant students studying while working or have completely chosen to change their orientation from an earlier occupation and already finished degree. The difficulties in studies and reasons of such a behavior, for a similar adult student profile, were thoroughly discussed in the earlier work [32] from the same context (department) than here.

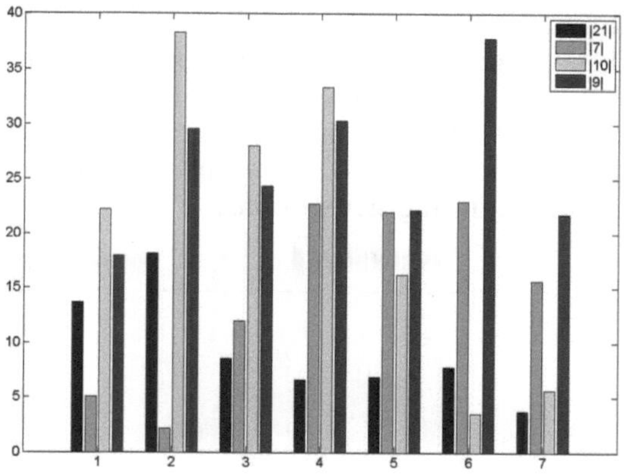

Fig. 3. Credit accumulation prototypes for A2012 [24].

The second group of only 7 students, who generally obtained 103 ECTS, shows opposite behavior: very slow start in the first year, activating to an appropriate level then. Three most characteristic students here were young males, who were involved in the military service during the first study year. This complete explains the observed behavior.

The third group of 10 students, who generally obtained 147 ECTS, did their studies very actively for the first 4–5 semesters. Analysis of the three most characteristics students revealed two young and one older male students who either took job or became active in student organizations during the third year of the studies.

The fourth profile with 9 students, altogether 184 ECTS in general, illustrates that a good start on the study activity carries over the semesters. Three mostly characteristics students were again all males, one M.Sc. student and two B.Sc. students. Note that similar finding on the importance of active start in an individual course level was given in [47].

Students who are mostly in need of AA are the ones in the first cluster. They can be identified either in the beginning of their studies or after the second semester, because even if still making studies, their accumulation is much less than in the third and fourth cluster. Their characterization also suggests the department to rethink the study entrance criteria.

A2013. For A2013 all cluster indices suggested three profiles, which are illustrated in Fig. 5. This and the fact that there are now one profile less than in A2012 suggests more stable organization of the curriculum. Also the boxplot in Fig. 4 supports such finding, especially showing smaller variability in the obtained credits between the autumn and spring terms compared to A2012 in Fig. 2.

Student group in the need of intrusive AA consists of those 23 students with smallest accumulation of credits. These students start and continue very slowly in their studies, although the level of activity was increasing in the fourth and fifth semesters. Their general ECTS accumulation after five semesters was 44 ECTS. Analysis of the five most representative students revealed two older male students (birth year before 1990), two males with indications of military service, and a female student. According to [56], especially the younger students showed signs of low self-regulation during AA sessions.

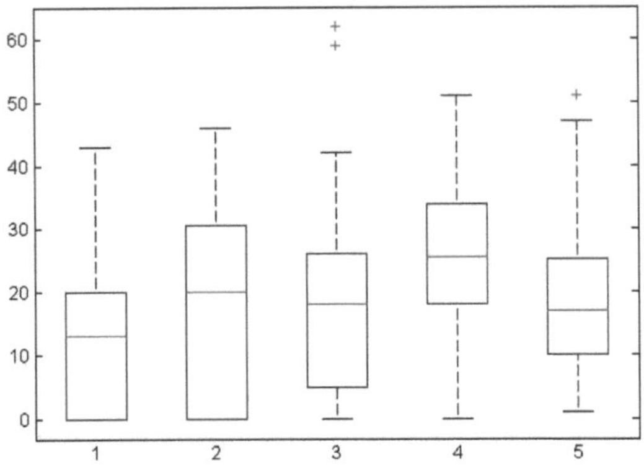

Fig. 4. Boxplot for A2013 [24].

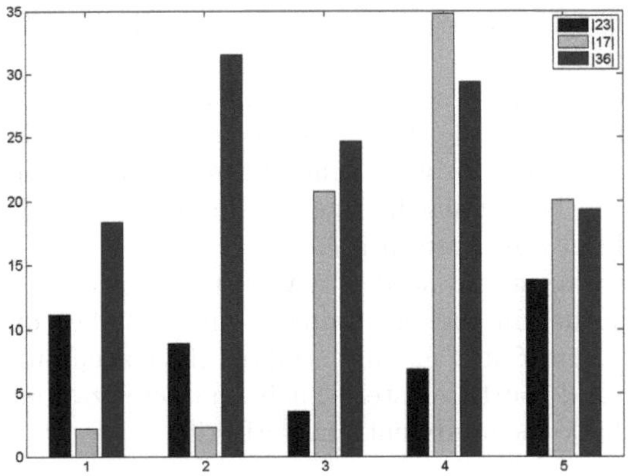

Fig. 5. Credit accumulation prototypes for A2013 [24].

The second profile of 17 students, completing typically 80 ECTS, showed similar behavior to the second profile in A2012: the minimal first year is raised to a good level of study activity later. A closer look on the five most representative students showed young, two female and three male students. Four of these had identified themselves as a non-active student during the first study year, again mostly due to the military service of the young male students.

The third profile of 36 most active students, accomplishing 123 ECTS typically, showed similar overall behavior than the fourth profile in A2012. The first semester is slightly smaller but then the study path proceeds in the desired way. Recapitulation of the meta data of five most representative students showed five male students, of whom three were oriented towards game programming and development - the most recent study line of the department.

We note that even if the boxplot in Fig. 4 indicated more stable study path with respect to autumn and spring semesters, the two profiles of truly active students still illustrated larger study accumulations in the spring than in the autumn. These findings are, however, mostly explained by the longer calender time for the two periods in the spring term compared to the autumn term – a general peculiarity of the Finnish higher education system.

The similarities and differences between the two sets of profiles just discussed emphasize the importance of the use of evidence-based information in AA. On one hand, there are repetitive profiles of students proceeding in their studies well or slowly. The latter ones needs to be detected and supported in an intrusive manner in AA. The home department responsible for major subject studies and the other departments providing minor subject studies should be informed about the found hindrances of the study paths. In the case analyzed here, there is a clear change of study accumulation profiles from A2012 to A2013, which suggests that the organization of courses, the capabilities of students, and/or their support through AA have improved in the educational organization under study.

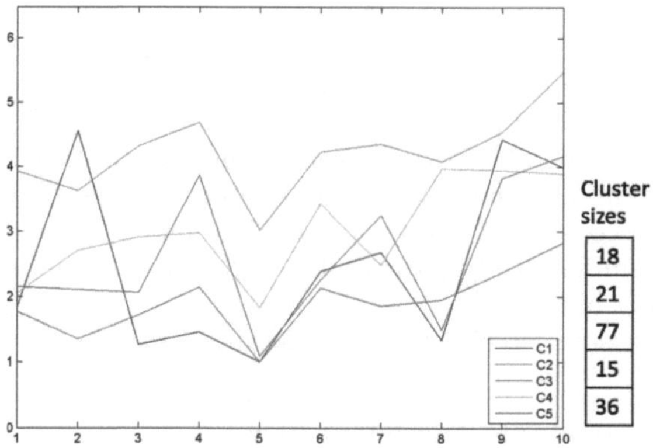

Fig. 6. Mandatory B.Sc. course prototypes for active MIT students 2012–2014.

The third clustering result related to pass semester of the mandatory courses is given in Fig. 6. By far the largest cluster C3 with 77 students presents a favorable pattern where all mandatory courses are made during the early study semesters. This suggests that the organizational arrangements to offer equal study possibilities for the students starting either in autumn or spring semester are working as planned for most of the students. However, cluster C4 with 15 students shows a kind of one-semester-delayed pattern of passing the courses. Similarly to the previous two profiles, also this clustering result encapsulates the cluster C2 with 21 students, who start slow/late but then proceed desirably. For a group of 18 students in C1, the second mandatory course is postponed very late, and for a group of 36 students in cluster C5, the fourth mandatory course is passed later than usual. Altogether, patterns in clusters C2, C4, and C5 indicate need of further efforts in both course offerings or arrangements and AA.

4 Proposition of a System Model

As shown, it is important to follow the actual progress of the students in their studies. There might be no need for an advising intervention, but if so, one should automatically notify the students and the study counselling on the deviations in the study path. The problems of not passing courses and not following suggested study plans usually also call for organizational considerations whether learner ability and the difficulty level of the recommended curriculum are matched to each other properly [27].

4.1 Proposed System Architecture

This subsection describes the novel system architecture for AA and automatic feedback based on recognized student group profiles which are obtained by using clustering. We also present an overview of the AA process as both manual and automated process.

The architecture of the proposed system's model for the AA is presented in Fig. 7. The system has two main databases: learner profile database and curriculum database. Learner profile database stores learner's data about studies, assessment results, timetables of completed studies, etc. Curriculum database stores information about compulsory courses, other courses, timetables, etc. The AA system's part consists of several blocks like linking individual students to their peers with similar study path profile together with the recommendation block and planning block.

Based on the system architecture, the details of system's main functionality read as follows:

1. Collection of learner's personal information.
2. Collection of information about the courses and completed studies.
3. Creation of study progress profiles along the lines of Sect. 3.
4. Linking the individual student to student peers with similar study profile in the institutional environment.
5. Student's progress check. If student is linked to a profile requiring intrusive advising, inform the adviser and the student by providing the interpreted study profile to support the communication and problem solving.

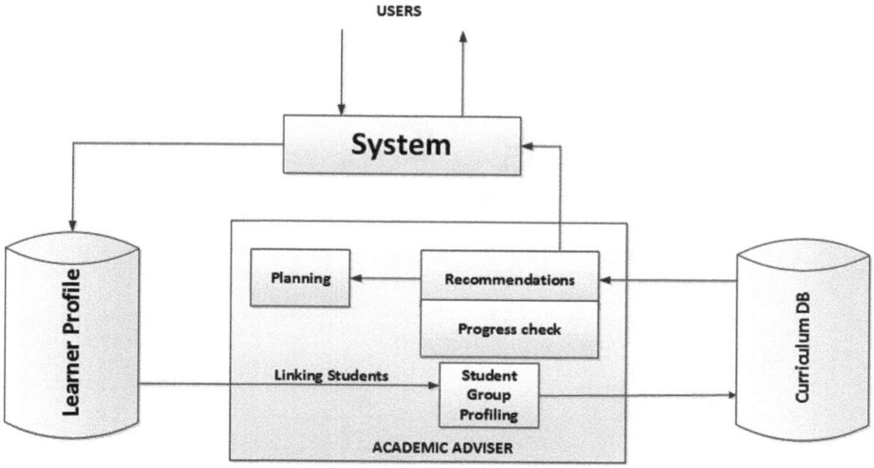

Fig. 7. Architecture of the academic adviser [24].

6. Modification of the study plan on recommended courses and their timetables by taking into account the evidence related to the identified study profile.
7. Planning and realization of an intrusive profile intervention adaptively for a larger pool of students.

Data collection related to the system is, naturally, all the time active. The evidence-based study profiles can and should be recomputed on regular basis. A natural suggestion would be to do this after the studies made during the previous semester have been stored and become available for clustering.

4.2 Automated Academic Advising Process

The automated process of AA, related to the system's architecture and main functionality as described above, is presented in Fig. 8. The given proposition allows manual control of the continuous advising activity for every learner individually, or the more automated process where the role of the advisers is shifted to the higher level of abstraction. The difference on the level of learner's life cycle between these two use cases is depicted in Fig. 9. The automated process is highlighted with the red color in the figure. In the automated scenario, the responsible persons of the study organization only provide policies, planning and regulations. This can reduce the responsibility for the daily routine work and could help to provide recommendations for a larger pool of students rather than for the each individual learner.

The work-flow related to Fig. 8 reads as follows: The learner is choosing the study program of an educational institution. After that he or she chooses with AA the proper courses which are related to the chosen program and creates a study plan. Information about the student, the required courses and progress

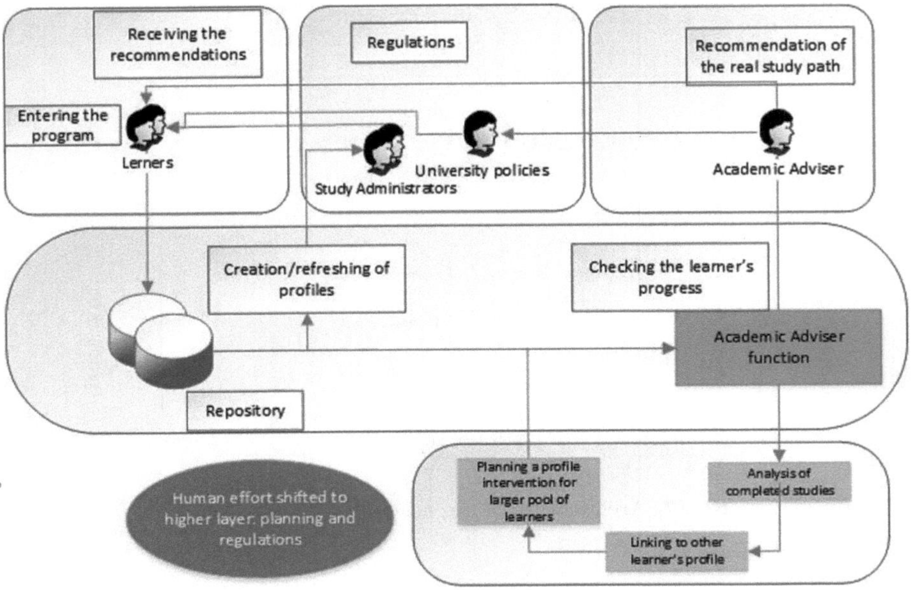

Fig. 8. Automated academic advising process [24].

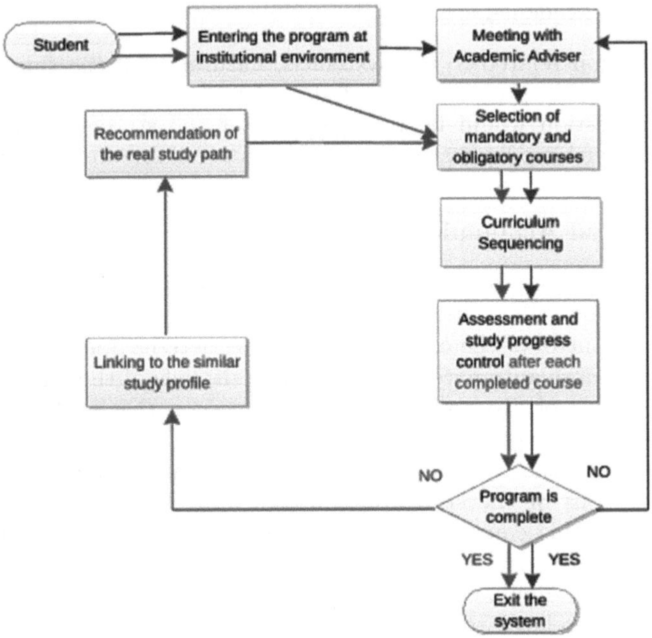

Fig. 9. Comparison of the manual and automated processes of learner's study life cycle [24]. (Color figure online)

in them is stored in the database and is automatically changed/refreshed after each passed course. After passing several courses, system can attach a student to a group of students with similar, actual study path. If learners are doing well, evidence-based determination and communication of this during advising encourages them to continue like that. If they are attached to a profile which does not progress with the studies as expected, the system can identify this early and provide intrusive AA support for both the advisor and the students in question.

The proposed automated mechanism solve an important problem of improving and providing academic advising, because more and more students should receive guidance with their study plans before graduating. This system will help to plan when and how to provide the courses, especially the compulsory ones, as well as to plan a profile intervention adaptively for a larger pool of students, which will reduce the human effort of academic advising.

The proposed architecture and model of the system are intended for a development phase to prototype the whole automated process, where the learners will be profiled regularly, and where the proper study path will be presented, as well as deviating learners detected. The model of the AA system will have automated process of study path recommendation. This system will help to plan when and how to provide the courses, especially the compulsory ones, as well as to plan a profile intervention adaptively for a larger pool of students, which will reduce the human effort of AA.

5 Conclusions

The topic of AA has been the subject of many research efforts, but in academic practice, more often than not, AA is still not reaching the desired level of effectiveness and efficiency. There is a need for a proper personalized AA, and it is very important in academic life. It is decisive that learner should receive proper advising – poor or no advising is known to have a negative effect on the progress in studies [2].

In this work a compact literature review about AA, mostly focusing on Automated Academic Advising and Intelligent Academic Advising was presented. This paper aims at improving the practice of AA by proposing a model of an automated AA system. The key component of this model is based on learning analytics, more precisely robust clustering, which is especially suitable for data with missing values. This method helps in detecting student groups (clusters) based on the shared study paths. Study path is considered to be a sequence of courses a student has taken and completed during his/her studies.

A system architecture towards the development of an automated system for the academic advising process was presented. The system is in the development stage. However, the discussion and comparison of the steps of the manual and the proposed automated academic advising process was shown. The system will recommend a proper study path according to profiled learners, as well as deviating learners will be detected and will be supported by academic advisers. This automated process will help to plan interventions for a larger pool of students and that will reduce human effort of AA. Moreover, academic institutions can focus on management and updates on course schedule knowing the a clearly characterized groups of students. Note that even if the sample groups of students that were profiled here were very small, the used method is scalable to hundreds of thousands of students [48].

The identified student groups and the corresponding study trajectories are based now only on the students' progress – the number of credits they are earning, but not on any other information that would characterize the courses that form the trajectory. e.g. subject matter of the course, student's achievement, if it is obligatory or elective etc. That is why by continuing the development of this work, we could take into account analysis which is not only based on the number of credits, but also on student's majors, minors, subject matter interests to consider the study paths with higher granularity than per semester. Moreover, future work should include in the main functionality of the proposed system an automated notification for the academic advisers about students and their progress, with the interpretation of needs to modify and re-plan the study path. Furthermore, the proposed system should be properly evaluated. A number of users will evaluate it: whereas interviews can help to qualitatively estimate the results or questionnaires to find out if the system architecture was designed suitably, according to users needs, and if the recommended learning path was appropriate for the student.

References

1. Agrawal, R., Srikant, R.: Mining sequential patterns. In: 1995 Proceedings of the Eleventh International Conference on Data Engineering, pp. 3–14. IEEE (1995)
2. Al-Ansari, A., El Tantawi, M., AbdelSalam, M., Al-Harbi, F.: Academic advising and student support: help-seeking behaviors among Saudi dental undergraduate students. Saudi Dental J. **27**(2), 57–62 (2015)
3. Al-Sarem, M.: Building a decision tree model for academic advising affairs based on the algorithm C 4–5. arXiv preprint arXiv:1511.04026 (2015)
4. Auvinen, T.: Educational technologies for supporting self-regulated learning in online learning environments. Aalto University (2015)
5. Auvinen, T., Paavola, J., Hartikainen, J.: STOPS: a graph-based study planning and curriculum development tool. In: Proceedings of the 14th Koli Calling International Conference on Computing Education Research, pp. 25–34. ACM (2014)
6. Äyrämö, S.: Knowledge Mining Using Robust Clustering. Jyväskylä Studies in Computing, vol. 63. University of Jyväskylä, Jyväskylä (2006)
7. Biletskiy, Y., Brown, J.A., Ranganathan, G.: Information extraction from syllabi for academic e-Advising. Expert Syst. Appl. **36**(3), 4508–4516 (2009)
8. Brusilovsky, P.: Adaptive educational systems on the world-wide-web: a review of available technologies. In: Proceedings of Workshop "WWW-Based Tutoring" at 4th International Conference on Intelligent Tutoring Systems (ITS 1998), San Antonio, TX (1998)
9. Chatti, M.A., Dyckhoff, A.L., Schroeder, U., Thüs, H.: A reference model for learning analytics. Int. J. Technol. Enhanc. Learn. **4**(5–6), 318–331 (2012)

10. Chen, C.M.: Intelligent web-based learning system with personalized learning path guidance. Comput. Educ. **51**(2), 787–814 (2008)
11. Chen, C.M.: Ontology-based concept map for planning a personalised learning path. Br. J. Educ. Technol. **40**(6), 1028–1058 (2009)
12. Chen, C.M.: Personalized e-learning system with self-regulated learning assisted mechanisms for promoting learning performance. Expert Syst. Appl. **36**(5), 8816–8829 (2009)
13. Chen, C.M., Lee, H.M., Chen, Y.H.: Personalized e-learning system using item response theory. Comput. Educ. **44**(3), 237–255 (2005)
14. Chen, C.M., et al.: Ontology-based concept map for planning personalized learning path. In: IEEE International Conferences on Cybernetics & Intelligent Systems (2008)
15. Cohoon, J.M., Aspray, W.: Women and Information Technology: Research on Underrepresentation, vol. 1. The MIT Press, Cambridge (2006)
16. Daniel, B.: Big data and analytics in higher education: opportunities and challenges. Br. J. Educ. Technol. **46**(5), 904–920 (2015)
17. Dougherty, S.B.: Academic advising for high-achieving college students. High. Educ. Rev. **4**, 63–82 (2007)
18. Drezner, Z., Hamacher, H.W.: Facility Location: Applications and Theory. Springer, Heidelberg (2001). https://doi.org/10.1007/978-3-642-56082-8
19. Drozd, D.S.: Student preferences for academic advisors as transformational leaders. Ph.D. thesis, Texas A&M University (2010)
20. Feghali, T., Zbib, I., Hallal, S.: A web-based decision support tool for academic advising. Educ. Technol. Soc. **14**(1), 82–94 (2011)
21. Ferguson, R.: Learning analytics: drivers, developments and challenges. Int. J. Technol. Enhanc. Learn. **4**(5–6), 304–317 (2012)
22. de Freitas, S., Gibson, D., Du Plessis, C., Halloran, P., Williams, E., Ambrose, M., Dunwell, I., Arnab, S.: Foundations of dynamic learning analytics: using university student data to increase retention. Br. J. Educ. Technol. **46**(6), 1175–1188 (2015)
23. Fung, A., Yeung, J.: An object model for a web-based adaptive educational system. In: Proceedings of the IFIP International Conference on Educational Use of Technologies (ICEUT 2000) (2000)
24. Gavriushenko, M., Saarela, M., Kärkkäinen, T.: Supporting institutional awareness and academic advising using clustered study profiles. In: Proceedings of the 9th International Conference on Computer Supported Education: CSEDU, vol. 1, pp. 35–46. INSTICC, ScitePress (2017)
25. Henderson, L.K., Goodridge, W.: AdviseMe: an intelligent web-based application for academic advising. Int. J. Adv. Comput. Sci. Appl. **6**(8), 233–243 (2015)
26. Hershkovitz, A., Knight, S., Dawson, S., Jovanović, J., Gašević, D.: About "learning" and "analytics". J. Learn. Anal. **3**(2), 1–5 (2016)
27. Huang, M.J., Huang, H.S., Chen, M.Y.: Constructing a personalized e-learning system based on genetic algorithm and case-based reasoning approach. Expert Syst. Appl. **33**(3), 551–564 (2007)
28. Huber, P.J.: Robust Statistics. Springer, Heidelberg (2011)
29. Hwang, G.J., Kuo, F.R., Yin, P.Y., Chuang, K.H.: A heuristic algorithm for planning personalized learning paths for context-aware ubiquitous learning. Comput. Educ. **54**(2), 404–415 (2010)
30. Idris, N., Yusof, N., Saad, P., et al.: Adaptive course sequencing for personalization of learning path using neural network. Int. J. Adv. Soft Comput. Appl. **1**(1), 49–61 (2009)

31. Jain, A.K.: Data clustering: 50 years beyond K-means. Pattern Recogn. Lett. **31**(8), 651–666 (2010)
32. Kaihlavirta, A., Isomöttönen, V., Kärkkäinen, T.: A self-ethnographic investigation of continuing education program in engineering arising from economic structural change. Stud. Contin. Educ. **37**(1), 99–114 (2015)
33. Kärkkäinen, T., Saarela, M.: Robust principal component analysis of data with missing values. In: Perner, P. (ed.) MLDM 2015. LNCS (LNAI), vol. 9166, pp. 140–154. Springer, Cham (2015). https://doi.org/10.1007/978-3-319-21024-7_10
34. Kinnunen, P., Marttila-Kontio, M., Pesonen, E.: Getting to know computer science freshmen. In: Proceedings of the 13th Koli Calling International Conference on Computing Education Research, Koli Calling 2013, pp. 59–66. ACM, New York (2013). https://doi.org/10.1145/2526968.2526975
35. Latorre-Navarro, E.M., Harris, J.G.: An intelligent natural language conversational system for academic advising. Editor. Preface **6**(1) (2015)
36. Lee, M.G.: Profiling students' adaptation styles in web-based learning. Comput. Educ. **36**(2), 121–132 (2001)
37. Leung, C.M., Tsang, E.Y., Lam, S., Pang, D.C.: Intelligent counseling system: a 24 x 7 academic advisor. Educause Q. **33**(4), n4 (2010)
38. Liu, C.L., Wu, S., Chang, M., Heh, J.: Guiding students to do remedial learning in school campus with learning objects' spatial relations. In: 16th International Conference on Computers in Education Conference, pp. 249–256. Citeseer (2008)
39. Minaei-Bidgoli, B.: Data mining for a web-based educational system. Ph.D. thesis, Michigan State University (2004)
40. Mostafa, L., Oately, G., Khalifa, N., Rabie, W.: A case based reasoning system for academic advising in Egyptian educational institutions. In: 2nd International Conference on Research in Science, Engineering and Technology (ICRSET 2014), pp. 21–22, March 2014
41. Nguyen, T.B., Nguyen, D.N., Nguyen, H.S., Tran, H., Hoang, T.A.D.: An integrated approach for an academic advising system in adaptive credit-based learning environment. J. Sci. Nat. Sci. Technol. **24**, 110–121 (2008)
42. Noaman, A.Y., Ahmed, F.F.: A new framework for e academic advising. Procedia Comput. Sci. **65**, 358–367 (2015)
43. Papanikolaou, K.A., Grigoriadou, M., Magoulas, G.D., Kornilakis, H.: Towards new forms of knowledge communication: the adaptive dimension of a web-based learning environment. Comput. Educ. **39**(4), 333–360 (2002)
44. Papastergiou, M.: Are computer science and information technology still masculine fields? High school students' perceptions and career choices. Comput. Educ. **51**(2), 594–608 (2008)
45. Rogers, T.: Critical realism and learning analytics research: epistemological implications of an ontological foundation. In: Proceedings of the 5th International Conference on Learning Analytics and Knowledge, pp. 223–230. ACM, New York (2015). https://doi.org/10.1145/2723576.2723631
46. Saarela, M., Kärkkäinen, T.: Discovering gender-specific knowledge from Finnish basic education using PISA scale indices. In: Proceedings of the 7th International Conference on Educational Data Mining, pp. 60–68 (2014)
47. Saarela, M., Kärkkäinen, T.: Analysing student performance using sparse data of core bachelor courses. JEDM-J. Educ. Data Min. **7**(1), 3–32 (2015). http://www.educationaldatamining.org/JEDM/index.php/JEDM/article/view/JEDM056
48. Saarela, M., Kärkkäinen, T.: Do country stereotypes exist in PISA? A clustering approach for large, sparse, and weighted data. In: Proceedings of the 8th International Conference on Educational Data Mining, pp. 156–163 (2015)

49. Saarela, M., Kärkkäinen, T.: Weighted clustering of sparse educational data. In: Proceedings of the 23rd European Symposium on Artificial Neural Networks, Computational Intelligence and Machine Learning (ESANN 2015), pp. 337–342 (2015)
50. Saarela, M.: Automatic Knowledge Discovery from Sparse and Large-scale Educational Data: Case Finland. Jyväskylä Studies in Computing, vol. 262. University of Jyväskylä, Jyväskylä(2017)
51. Saarela, M., Hämäläinen, J., Kärkkäinen, T.: Feature ranking of large, robust, and weighted clustering result. In: Kim, J., et al. (eds.) PAKDD 2017. LNCS, vol. 10234, pp. 96–109. Springer, Cham (2017). https://doi.org/10.1007/978-3-319-57454-7_8
52. Saarela, M., Kärkkäinen, T.: Knowledge discovery from the programme for international student assessment. In: Peña-Ayala, A. (ed.) Learning Analytics: Fundaments, Applications, and Trends. SSDC, vol. 94, pp. 229–267. Springer, Cham (2017). https://doi.org/10.1007/978-3-319-52977-6_8
53. Sandvig, J., Burke, R.: AACORN: a CBR recommender for academic advising. Technical report TR05-015, DePaul University (2005)
54. Schiaffino, S., Garcia, P., Amandi, A.: eTeacher: providing personalized assistance to e-learning students. Comput. Educ. **51**(4), 1744–1754 (2008)
55. Sprent, P., Smeeton, N.C.: Applied Nonparametric Statistical Methods. CRC Press, Boca Raton (2016)
56. Study Amanuensis: Private Communication, 2 November 2016
57. Tang, T.Y., McCalla, G.: Smart recommendation for an evolving e-learning system: architecture and experiment. Int. J. eLearning **4**(1), 105 (2005)
58. The Daily Telegraph: University degree subjects with the highest dropout rates (2017). http://www.telegraph.co.uk/education/educationpicturegalleries/11002595/University-degree-subjects-with-the-highest-dropout-rates.html?frame=2824912. Accessed 01 Mar 2017
59. Tuttle, K.N.: Academic advising. New Dir. High. Educ. **2000**(111), 15–24 (2000)
60. Wallden, L.J.: Kansainvälisten koulutusarvioiden vertailu koulutuksellisen tiedonlouhinnan keinoin. University of Jyväskylä, Jyväskylä Studies in Computing (2016)
61. Wen, F.L.S.L.D., McGreal, F.Z.K.R.: e-Advisor: a multi-agent system for academic advising. Int. J. Adv. Comput. Sci. Appl. **6**(8) (2015)
62. Werghi, N., Kamoun, F.K.: A decision-tree-based system for student academic advising and planning in information systems programmes. Int. J. Bus. Inf. Syst. **5**(1), 1–18 (2009)
63. Zaki, M.J., Meira Jr., W.: Data Mining and Analysis: Fundamental Concepts and Algorithms. Cambridge University Press, Cambridge (2014)

Code ABC MOOC for Math Teachers

Pia Niemelä[1(✉)], Tiina Partanen[2], Linda Mannila[3,4], Timo Poranen[5], and Hannu-Matti Järvinen[1]

[1] Pervasive Computing, Tampere University of Technology, Tampere, Finland
pia.niemela@tut.fi
[2] City of Tampere, Tampere, Finland
[3] Aalto University, Espoo, Finland
[4] Linköping University, Linköping, Sweden
[5] Computer Science, University of Tampere, Tampere, Finland

Abstract. Computing is the latest add-on to enhance the K-12 curricula of many countries, with the purpose of closing the digital skills gap. The revised Finnish Curriculum 2014 integrates computing mainly into math. Consequently, Finland needs to train math teachers to teach computing at elementary level. This study describes the Python and Racket tracks of the Code ABC MOOC that introduce programming basics for math teachers. Their suitability for math is compared based on the course content and feedback. The results show that conceptually the functional paradigm of Racket approaches math more closely, in particular algebra. In addition, Racket is generally regarded as more challenging in terms of syntax and e.g. for utilizing recursion as an iteration mechanism. Math teachers also rank its suitability higher because the content and exercises of the track are specifically tailored for their subject.

Keywords: Curriculum research · Computer science education
K-12 education · In-service teacher training · MOOC
Computational thinking · Math-integrated computer science · Python
Racket · Programming paradigms · Imperative · Functional

1 Introduction

Our society is becoming increasingly digitalized, which has therefore given rise to a global discussion on the role of computer science (CS) in K-12 education. As a consequence, a number of countries all over the world have introduced computational thinking, computing or CS (or aspects thereof) into their K-12 curricula. Since 2014, for instance, students in England have had Computing on their schedule from the age of five. In Finland, aspects of CS were included in the national curriculum in fall 2016, when the 2014 national curriculum came into force. Programming was introduced as part of the cross-curricular theme of digital competence, and also specifically integrated into the syllabi of crafts (Y3-9) and mathematics (Y1-9). In Y1-2, math teachers now need to help students learn how to create and test simple programs (unplugged, step-by-step instructions),

P. Escudeiro et al. (Eds.): CSEDU 2017, CCIS 865, pp. 66–96, 2018.
https://doi.org/10.1007/978-3-319-94640-5_4

while students in Y3-6 should learn how to program in a visual programming language. The new learning objectives for mathematics in Y7-9 intend to develop students' algorithmic thinking skills and applying programming in problem solving. The target is reached when "*a student can apply the principles of algorithmic thinking and is capable of implementing simple programs*" [15].

Integrating programming into comprehensive education is a remarkable change: both pre- and in-service teachers need to learn to program and to understand the core elements of computational thinking. Such curriculum enhancements change the job description of a teacher retrospectively. Consequently, employers are responsible for the need to train teachers and for providing time for sufficient professional development. Although this training need is recognized by the government, in-service training resources are insufficient as Finnish teacher training departments have not yet fully responded to the new requirements and the growing need.

Against this background, all voluntary training initiatives have been warmly welcomed by schools, principals and teachers. In this paper, we present the Code ABC MOOC, a project initiated informally by a group of volunteer educators to respond to the gap in teachers' formal training and preparedness for teaching programming. The initiative was later sponsored by the Technology Industries of Finland Centennial Foundation and the Finnish National Board of Education. The Code ABC MOOC offers four tracks targeted at teachers working at different school levels: ScratchJr (Y1-2), Scratch (Y3-6), Racket (Y7-9) and Python (Y7-9). In addition to supporting elementary school teachers in learning the basics of programming, the Code ABC MOOC also serves as a tool for highlighting best practices for teaching programming. This paper concentrates on the two tracks targeted at teachers of Y7-9, namely the Python and Racket tracks.

In this study we extract the key concepts and aspects of programming and computational thinking from the examined tracks of the Code ABC MOOC in an effort to strengthen the conceptual basis of the programming syllabus. The teacher feedback illustrates how these concepts have been adopted and evaluates the suitability of the material for supporting teachers in adopting the new curriculum. In addition, our study attempts to link these CS concepts to appropriate mathematics topics. In this regard, the differences between the programming languages used in the two tracks are noted and explained based on the underlying programming paradigms. Our goal is to answer three main questions:

- What CS concepts and computational thinking skills do these Code ABC tracks introduce?
- What topics did the teachers find challenging, inspiring, or suitable for math?
- Which programming paradigms do the tracks align with and how do they support math?

The paper is organized as follows. First we discuss previous work in fields related to our study, after which we describe our research context. Next we present and discuss the results, before concluding the paper with some final remarks.

2 Related Work

2.1 CS in K-9 Education

As noted in the introduction, introducing aspects of CS in K-9 education is an international trend. This is, however, not a new trend. As long ago as 1967, Papert developed the LOGO language [35], specifically aimed at teaching children how to program. His goal was to use programming as a tool to let children be creative with technology and to support their learning in other domains such as mathematics, the arts, languages and science. As computers became increasingly popular, accessible and easy to use, the focus in the school debate shifted from CS and learning how to program to IT and learning how to use computers and software. In the last five years, the trend has once again shifted, as the digital transformation has shown the need for understanding the digital world. Consequently, there has been an active debate on the need to shift the focus away from our future citizens being mere passive consumers of technology, and towards them becoming active producers.

Internationally, we now see an increasing trend for integrating aspects of CS into K-9 education. For instance, in Europe the majority (17 out of 21) of countries participating in a survey conducted by the European Schoolnet in 2015 reported doing so [4]. The way in which this is accomplished varies. Some countries focus on K-12 as a whole, whereas others primarily address either K-9 or grades 10–12. Some countries have introduced CS as a subject on its own (e.g. Computing in England) while others have decided to integrate it with other subjects, by, for instance, making programming a cross-curricular element (such as in Finland). Instead of computing and programming, some countries also use the term computational thinking.

Computational thinking (CT) has gained prominence, particularly in conjunction with the discussion on integrating aspects of CS as part of K-9 education. However, Papert had already set the course for CT much earlier, in 1996 [34]:

"Computer science develops students' computational and critical thinking skills and shows them how to create, not simply use, new technologies. This fundamental knowledge is needed to prepare students for the 21st century, regardless of their ultimate field of study or occupation". Not simply using computers but also creating digital artifacts is a valid stance – helping pupils to identify themselves as potential creators fosters their sense of empowerment.

In her seminal article, Wing [58] renewed this emphasis by establishing the term 'computational thinking' as an essential part of the recent CS education discourse, yet its comprehensive definition was omitted. To date, several definitions and operational descriptions of CT have been suggested. Even if no consensus on the definition has been reached, many of the suggestions build on the core of Wing's later description (2010, [59]): *The thought processes involved in formulating problems and their solutions so that the solutions are represented in a form that can be carried out by an information-processing agent.*

When operationalizing the term, it is commonly presented as a set of concepts and approaches. For instance, the support organization Computing at School (CAS) in England, describes CT as "the processes and approaches we draw on when thinking about problems or systems in such a way that a computer can help us with these." (CAS, p. 1) They define CT in terms of six concepts (logic, algorithms, decomposition, patterns, abstraction and evaluation) and five approaches (tinkering, creating, debugging, persevering and collaborating).

Relevance for Our Study. In the Finnish curriculum programming is to be taught as part of math [15]. Compared to programming, math already has a well-established syllabus that has evolved into its current state since the dawn of the educational system. Apart from a few minor syllabus areas being dropped from or reintroduced into the curriculum, the core content of the math syllabus has remained more or less the same for decades. In order to facilitate a smooth transition, there is a need to build on the well-established math core in order to introduce the analogous and logically progressive steps for CS. It is tentatively assumed that integrating CS into math will move the center of gravity of the syllabus towards CT.

2.2 Bidirectional Transfer: $math \leftrightarrow CS$

Math is at the very core of programming, which requires algebraic, logic and problem-solving skills. Synergy implies mutual benefit between two entities, and although the benefits that a good understanding of math and perceived self-efficacy confer on the learning of computational skills are clear [45,62], the transfer in the other direction, from programming to math, may not be that obvious. In a successful transfer, however, a student should be capable of finding the common underlying conceptual bases of different topics [23]. Finding such analogies not only requires a certain level of intellectual maturity, but also that a student has elaborated on the learning material conceptually in order to reach a deeper understanding of the topic.

Transfer may happen either laterally or vertically [17], near or far, or by the low road or the high road [41] implying a certain hierarchy of learning. In addition, one of the two complementary subjects tends to be interpreted in the learners' minds in a more abstract manner, while the other focuses on its application [44]. In the case of math and CS, math is more abstract, while CS can be understood as applied math [8]. In math, educators have long talked about conceptual and procedural knowledge [18]: conceptual knowledge comprises a full possession of the appropriate concepts and the ability to link them together, i.e., the high road to knowledge transfer, while procedural knowledge (the low road) consists of well-internalized mathematical routines.

Relevance for Our Study. Based on previous research, one potential assumption is that practicing math routines will provide an appropriate resource for programming exercises. To achieve this, the current math syllabus needs to be bridged with the corresponding programming topics. It seems reasonable to assume that this could be valuable not only to students, but also for in-service teachers, who might find similarities between math and programming motivating when learning to program themselves.

2.3 Programming Metaphors, Languages and Paradigms

When attempting to determine the role of CS in education, various metaphors are used, e.g. thinking of programming as literacy, as a driver for the maker culture and a maker mind-set, or grounded math [7]. If the literacy metaphor is used, then programming as digital literacy emphasizes the same logical skills as are applied when constructing linguistically correct sentences, such as using and/or/not in order to express the internal logic of a sentence. From a 'maker mindset', the programming language should be as productive as possible, easy to learn ("low floor"), usable in a wide range of potential application areas and types ("wide walls") and facilitate the creation of both basic and advanced programs ("high ceiling"). In such contexts, scripting languages and visual programming languages such as Scratch (scratch.mit.edu) can be particularly useful.

The question of what programming language to use has been heavily debated throughout the years, in particular when discussing novice programming. At university level, most discussion has surrounded textual languages, such as Java, C, Python and Scala. Languages have been compared based on, for instance, how easy they are to learn, how many errors students make when using them, how verbal the languages are and potential syntactical overload. However, at the K-9 level this question has not been as actively discussed, for a number of reasons. First, programming at school level is still rather new, and thus still evolving into its final form. The goal of learning the basics of programming at school is not to educate future programmers, but rather to give them a basic understanding of the digital world. In addition, at the moment, educators seemed to reach a consensus about the programming progression at school, starting with unplugged activities, followed by visual programming languages with a textual language being introduced in the later grades (7–9). Nevertheless, there are some studies on programming languages at K-9 level as well. Despite the popularity of Scratch and other block-based languages, some studies have questioned the benefits of these in enhancing problem-solving skills and good programming practices [22,33] as these are claimed to lead to bottom-up development and fine-grained programming without coherence [33]. In sum, the problems relate to abstraction skills, i.e., "not seeing the forest for the trees" and designing the program in advance. On the other hand, other studies have found that visual programming languages such as Scratch make it easier for novices to learn some concepts, for instance, construct of conditions [27,31] and to switch to textual programming later on. Another consequence of using block-based languages is the tight integration with the development environment (IDE), whether on-line or stand-alone. Such powerful IDEs become a new norm along with visual programming.

In addition to metaphors and languages, programming paradigms are essential for defining the angle of approach to teaching programming. Each paradigm provides its own basic concepts with paradigm-specific restrictions, which leads to different kinds of implementations and programming styles. Some tasks are more easily implemented in one paradigm, whereas other paradigms are more appropriate for other applications (e.g. due to their efficiency or flexibility). Consequently, there is not only a discussion around what programming language to use, but there are also recurring arguments about "the right paradigm for the job". To be able to make well-informed language and paradigm choices, decision-makers and educators should have an adequate understanding of the alternatives available.

The division of programming languages into different paradigms is not easy, and is further blurred by multi-paradigm languages. Wegner (1989) simply divided languages into two fundamental categories: imperative and declarative [55]. In this division, the imperative paradigm comprises procedural, object-oriented, and distributed (parallel) languages, whereas the declarative one consists of functional, logic, and database languages. However, a parallel paradigm is not commensurate with, for instance, an object-oriented paradigm, which provides for parallel implementations as well. This problem can be circumvented by separating the programming model (sequential/parallel) from paradigms altogether, thus enabling new combinations. This change was proposed by Bal and Grune [3], who also raised the previous sub-paradigms of procedural, object-oriented, functional and logic to main categories.

Constantly increasing in number, multi-paradigm languages challenge this categorization. For instance, Scratch puts paradigm categorization to the test. Some of the features of Scratch comply with an object-oriented paradigm. According to Van Roy's taxonomy, having a cell and a thread, i.e. assignment and concurrency, categorizes Scratch as an object-oriented paradigm [54]. However, the lack of data abstraction (inheritance) and functions makes the data encapsulation model of Scratch oxymoronic in regard to object-orientedness. Since Scratch targets only GUI applications reactive to user-generated events and inter-sprite messages, an event-loop [54] or event-driven paradigm [14] would seem to be a more accurate categorization. A few sources refer to Scratch as agent-based programming, where each sprite acts as an independent agent according to the defined rules. The interplay of such agents, for instance, facilitates easy STEM simulations [52].

Relevance for Our Study. Since our study compares two tracks of the Code ABC MOOC, one using a functional language and the other an imperative one, this discussion of paradigms is important. In this section we look more closely at the paradigms most relevant to our study: imperative and functional programming, exemplified by Python and Racket respectively.

Imperative Paradigm and Python. Some argue that the imperative paradigm is appropriate for introducing programming as it makes it quite straightforward to translate algorithms into code, for instance. There are a wide range of imperative languages which can be used as general purpose languages and for particular application areas. Python (python.org) was originally designed with education in mind. The developer, Guido van Rossum, even suggested that everybody could master programming using Python back in 1999 [46]. The language had already aroused interest as a programming language for novices in the early 2000s, due to, for instance, its clear and readable syntax, strong introspection capabilities, natural expression of procedural code, high level dynamic data types and its extensive standard library and third party modules providing functionality for a wide range of tasks. Python is one of the most commonly used languages in general use today (number 5 on the TIOBE programming index list in August 2017) and is widely used in education [9,10,21, etc.].

Guzdial and Ericson [21] has a clear vision of the importance of web programming and sees Python as a viable tool for this, describing it as "one of the best web languages". However, he does not object to mixing paradigms and languages, exemplified by the Jython environment for students (JES) project, which combines Python with Java [5]. Nevertheless, Python is object-oriented even without Java by virtue of its own class model that provides e.g. polymorphism and multiple inheritance. Python easily interweaves multiple paradigms, although at the basic level it does fall into the imperative paradigm. Recently, Python was endowed with functional features as well, such as maps, comprehensions, and generators [28].

The Python material of the Code ABC track has been translated and modified based on the project outcomes of AP Computer Science Principles [19]. Already in 2003, Guzdial and Soloway [20] championed the 'CS for all' ideology and the potential of CS over specific syllabus areas of math, such as calculus. He argues that teaching CS for all – not just for mathematically oriented students – should involve "sampling" instead of sorting. It is essential to allow space for students' authentic interests, such as arts, crafts, and music in the hunt for intrinsic motivation. Incorporating the maker mindset with tinkering, and creative and socially meaningful activities is especially beneficial for reaching less motivated student groups, including girls [6].

Functional Paradigm and Racket. In contrast to the multi-faceted nature of Python, the subset of Racket used in the Code ABC MOOC is more constrained and the closest metaphor would be "grounded math", where the pure functional programming language may be regarded as a realization of lambda calculus. Transfer between math and CS is claimed to be closest to the functional programming paradigm [26,50]. For example, functions in algebra can be practiced using functional programming languages. Combining functional programming with math is not new. Historically, attempts range from the early use of LOGO [16,25] to recent experiments employing Racket and Haskell [1]. While the results from the LOGO initiatives have varied [25], the Racket evaluations have been positive and stable [12,13,49,50].

The Racket programming language (http://racket-lang.org) is a multi-paradigm language, and thus also supports functional programming. Racket includes a programming IDE, DrRacket, designed especially for teaching purposes [13]. In contexts where DrRacket cannot be installed, the web-based environment WeScheme [61] steps into the breach, also enabling online sharing and remixes. DrRacket has built-in support for so-called 'Student Languages' starting with Beginning Student and ending with Advanced Student Language. Each of these Student Languages gradually introduces new programming primitives and concepts. Simplified syntax and semantics aim at helping beginners grasp the core concepts of function design, such as composition and function calls. Tool creators have also defined more precise error messages in order to assist novices in debugging and analyzing their code [30].

For the sake of the purity of the functional paradigm, the imperative features of Racket are held back. For instance, the assignment operation (set!) and functions causing side effects (display, read) are not introduced until the Advanced Student Language level. Felleisen et al. wrote the guide 'How to Design Programs' for high school and college level students [12], and in its most recent version the imperative features are done away with altogether to introduce appropriate coding practices.

The guide systematizes problem solving with Design Recipe, which teaches how to divide a problem into smaller solvable steps in the process of designing functions with a test-driven approach [12]. The use of Design Recipe has been shown to foster the right order of operations and the composition of nested functions. Thus, Felleisen and Krishnamurthi suggest that functional programming provides the strongest evidence for the favorable effects of programming on math skills [13].

A number of articles promote Racket's Beginning Student Language as a prominent way of learning algebra [26,50], especially with well-designed instructions. These should include purposefully planned exercises and pedagogical models, such as the Cycle of Evaluation [50], which visualizes expressions and the use of parentheses. The algebraic approach of functional programming has been shown to improve the understanding of math concepts such as variables and functions [49,50,60].

Comparison and Summary of the Paradigms of the Code ABC. In summary, Fig. 1 illustrates the Code ABC, which is comprised of functional, event-driven, and imperative paradigms. In line with the paradigms, the figure also illustrates the corresponding language used in the MOOC and the closest metaphors. Obviously, these metaphors are speculative. Different "paradigm camps" tend to adhere to their own discourse: Scratch promoters, led by Resnick, highlight sharing and the unimpeded creation of one's own artifacts with the analogy of virtual LEGO construction, i.e. block snapping [32,43]. The founder of the Python language, Van Rossum, emphasizes the readability and efficiency of code [47], whereas the Racket camp regards functional computing as being rooted in lambda calculus, thus inherently connected with math, in particular algebra [13,49,50].

Van Roy categorizes languages based on their declarativeness and expressiveness [48,54]. In his fine-grained paradigm taxonomy, Van Roy defines a horizontal

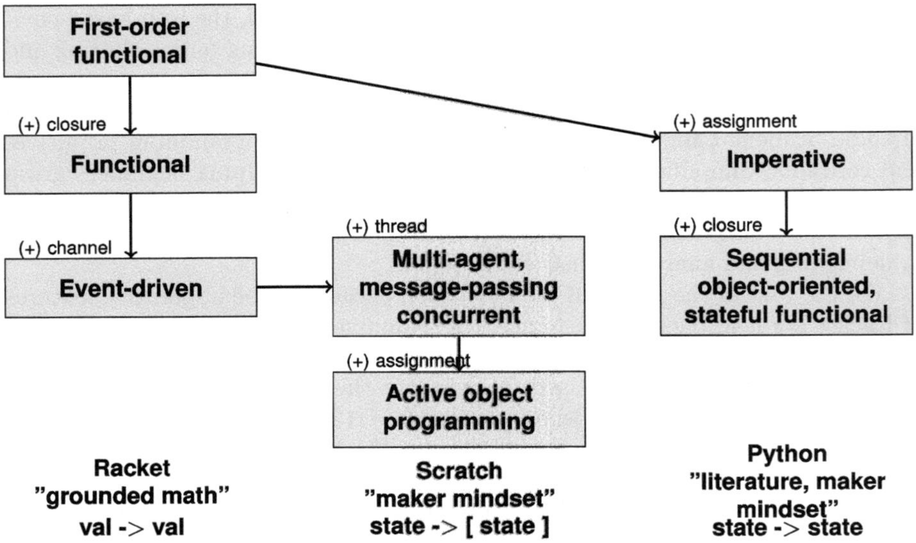

Fig. 1. The Code ABC paradigm taxonomy complying with [54].

axis of declarativeness based on whether a state is unnamed or named, and adds expressiveness step-by-step (for instance, assignment, closure, channel, and thread) in order to evolve the paradigm taxonomy from simple to more complex concepts. In distinguishing between functional and imperative paradigms, the diagnostic question is: can you assign a variable, i.e. have a named state? The answer divides paradigms into either imperative or functional. An imperative paradigm is statement-centric, the assignment being a statement as well. Each statement changes the state of the system, hence, imperative computation may be understood as state transformations in a sequence, i.e., $state \rightarrow state$. This is in contrast to the functional paradigm, which may be described as sequential value transformations, $val \rightarrow val$ without states. A named state enables modularity and the storage and management of updatable memory, which moves the paradigm in a less declarative direction.

A closure establishes a new variable scope in the context of a function. It 'closes' both a pointer to code and an environment for free variables. In the functional paradigm, closures are a central concept because they enable nested and higher-order functions that can access data from the outer scope, i.e. variables of the previous frames in the stack. Higher-order functions are a powerful substitute for e.g. for/while iterations without incrementable counters. Otherwise, control structures would be cumbersome to implement.

The event-driven paradigm leans on events that trigger execution, e.g. at the user's initiative. An event may trigger a message to be broadcast through a channel (or a port). In Scratch, several loosely-coupled receivers may listen to the same message [29]. Because the order of receivers is not determined, the concurrency model comprises explicit sending and implicit receiving, which implies a non-deterministic final state, i.e., *state* → [*state*]. Infinite forever loops are implemented as threads that enable concurrency.

3 The Code ABC

The initial idea for the Code ABC MOOC was introduced in spring 2015 by Tarmo Toikkanen and Tero Toivanen. The original concept was to help teachers learn programming using material that has been prepared especially for them by their peers, for instance, more experienced teachers. The first course, the so called Code ABC beta, was held in Autumn 2015 with three tracks: ScratchJr, Scratch and Racket. The Python track was added for the spring 2016 version of the MOOC. So far (fall 2017) 3649 participants have studied programming in the Code ABC MOOCs.

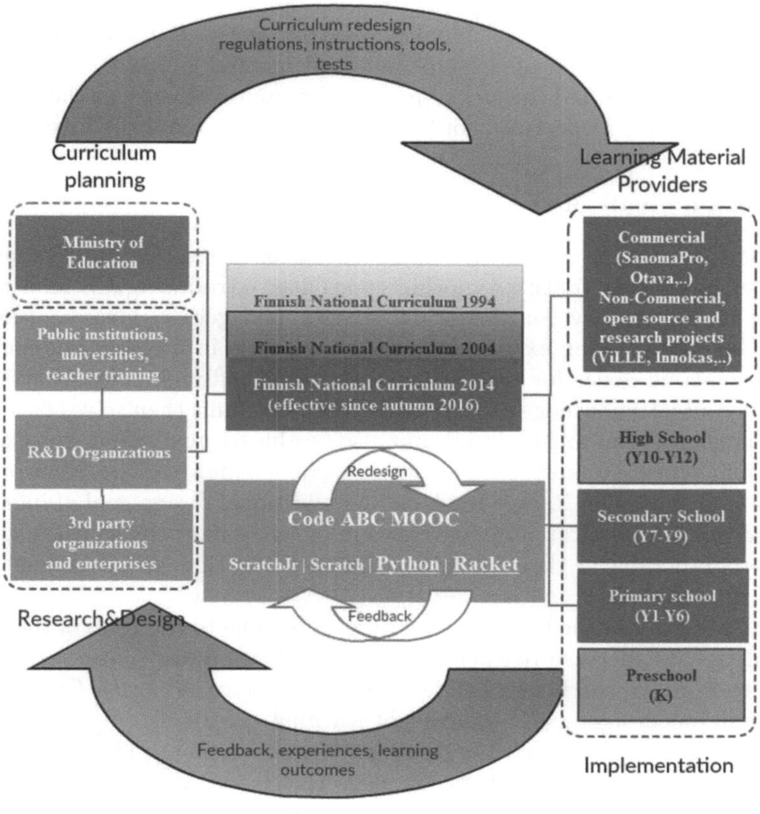

Fig. 2. Nested DBR cycles of curriculum updates (update/10 years) and Code ABC tracks (2 updates/year) [40].

The initial three tracks of the Code ABC beta (ScratchJr, Scratch, and Racket) were developed by a group of Finnish teachers and were improved incrementally based on the feedback from several iterations. The continuous development followed the principles of design based research (DBR), aiming at linking theory and practice in the discipline of education [42]. DBR stipulates the use of several iterations and redesigns of an educational artifact based on feedback and experience. Figure 2 illustrates the process of two nested design cycles.

The outer cycle is the curriculum planning cycle that takes place once a decade, while the inner is the iterative process of developing the Code ABC tracks twice a year. Development proceeds in cycles, taking into account the feedback given by different stakeholders, especially the customers, which in this context are in-service teachers. The artifact is then redesigned together with course instructors and researchers, whose research interests lie in integrating CT into elementary education.

The original material for the Python track was developed in the USA in similar cycles by Guzdial and Ericson [11]. This material was translated and adapted for the Code ABC MOOC in a project funded by the Finnish National Board of Education, coordinated by the Innokas Network at the Faculty of Educational Sciences at the University of Helsinki and implemented jointly by the Faculty of Educational Sciences and the Department of Computer Science at the University of Helsinki and the Department of Computer Science at Aalto University.

3.1 Design Goals of the Code ABC Tracks

The first three tracks of the Code ABC (ScratchJr, Scratch, and Racket) had a number of general goals: promoting creativity; introducing CS as a tool for creating something new and inspiring; sharing pedagogical ideas and artifacts during the course; using exercises directly applicable in a classroom context in order to make it easier for teachers to get started; offering course participants sufficient content knowledge so that they would not limit themselves to applying ready-made programming materials but also be able to create their own exercises; and enabling peer-support by encouraging participants to help each other on discussion forums. The Racket track had an additional design goal of integrating mathematics into programming exercises in order to motivate math teachers to adopt programming in their teaching, and to prove that programming lessons are not time wasted.

The main goals of the Python track were, according to the goals of the original material [10], to increase teachers' knowledge of computer science concepts as well as to improve teachers' confidence in their ability to teach CS principles. The course was designed as a lightweight learning experience [11], allowing busy teachers to participate when they had 20–60 min to spare. The exercises were designed to be small and feature low cognitive loads, which was achieved by placing relevant examples just before the exercises. The course did not focus on any individual subject such as mathematics – on the contrary, the material was aimed at anyone interested in teaching programming and CS.

3.2 Course Implementation

The Code ABC MOOC was implemented using the A+ learning platform developed by Aalto University (https://plus.cs.hut.fi/). Piazza was utilized as the discussion platform and Rubyric for showcasing and peer reviewing returned artifacts [2]. Both the Python and the Racket tracks grouped learning objects into entities; termed modules in Python, and topics in Racket. For the sake of consistency, we will use 'topic' for both in this paper. At the end of each topic, feedback was collected with Grader, an on-line survey tool developed at Aalto University. Grader was also used to collect pre- and post-course surveys. The feedback was collected in order to further develop the courses. Teachers attended the Code ABC MOOC tracks free of charge. Both tracks spanned several months from February to May, 2016. No compensation was granted for course participants except for 2–3 credit points from the Open University of Helsinki after course completion (2 cp for Python (P), 3 cp for Racket (R)).

4 Study Design and Data Collection

Our study is based on the Spring 2016 course implementation consisting of the second iteration of the Racket track and the Finnish translation of version 2 of the Python material. We conducted a pre-course survey to get background information about the participants (Python N = 320, Racket N = 137).

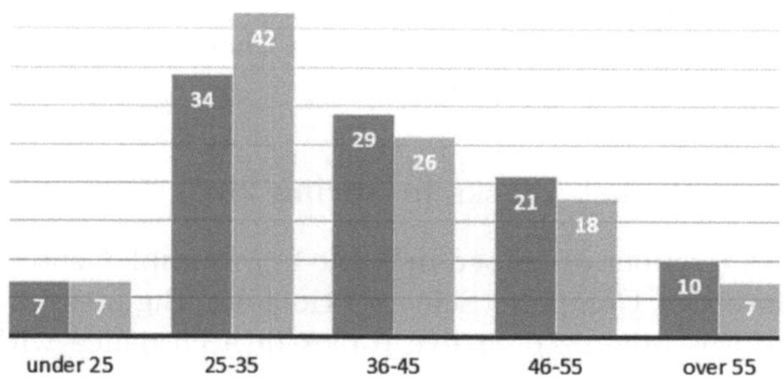

Fig. 3. Age distribution of course participants in % (P blue, R green). (Color figure online)

The largest participant group represented 25 to 35 year-olds (Fig. 4) the majority of whom were female (Python track 65%, Racket track 78%). Math teachers formed the largest groups (Fig. 3) in both tracks (Python track 48%, Racket track 88%). The next largest groups were science and CS teachers. The majority of the participants represented the original target group, i.e., K-9 teachers (Python track 72%, Racket track 91%).

Based on the survey, most participants had some previous experience in programming (Python track 78%, Racket track 74%). Quite a few had already used

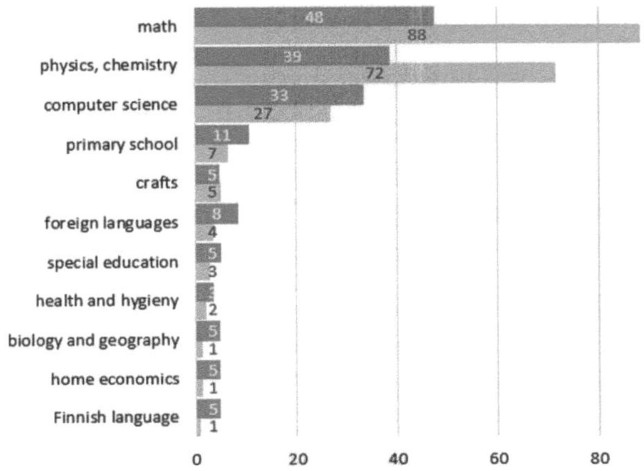

Fig. 4. Subjects taught by the teachers (P blue, R green; a subject omitted if P and R less than 5%). (Color figure online)

programming in their teaching (Python track 48%, Racket track 38%). In order of popularity, the languages previously used by the Python track participants were Scratch 34%, Java 32%, Basic 28%, Pascal 25%, C++ 23%, JavaScript 21%, C 18%, Python 17%, Visual Basic 17%, FORTRAN 12%, LOGO 11%, C# 6% and Perl 5%. In Racket, the order of popularity was Scratch, 34%, Java 26%, C++ 23%, Pascal 22%, Basic 20%, Python 15%, Visual Basic 14%, JavaScript 10%, FORTRAN 9%, LOGO 8%, and C 7%. Other languages were only mentioned by 5% of the participants or less.

4.1 Python and Racket Tracks in Spring 2016

The Python track (content described in Table 1) was implemented as a localized translation of the ebook Computer Science Principles: Big Ideas in Programming [10]. The course was organized in five topics in accordance with the original material: introduction to computing, naming, repetition, decision making, and data manipulation. Participants concluded the course by writing an essay on the pedagogical aspects of programming.

The original material is arranged in a book format, and should thus be read in a sequential manner. All the exercises are embedded in the ebook's browser environment and they are automatically assessed and graded. The material has been designed to follow an example-exercise format to facilitate learning [10]. Multiple exercise types are used: multiple choice and fill-in-the-blanks test conceptual understanding, Parson's problems are used for teaching basic programming constructs, and exercises consisting of modifying active code segments in the on-line programming environment provide wider opportunities to try out the concepts learned [36]. In addition, the material utilizes the code lens concept to demonstrate program execution [11].

As the original material did not specifically focus on how programming should be taught in Finnish schools, the Code ABC MOOC had an additional course project, during which the teachers designed a 2-h lesson on any subject of their choice. The course projects were reviewed by both peers and course staff. The lessons that the teachers had designed typically reflected the subjects that they taught in schools, ranging from learning languages to applying CS in crafts. The participants had to complete 85% of the automated exercises and the final essay in order to pass the course.

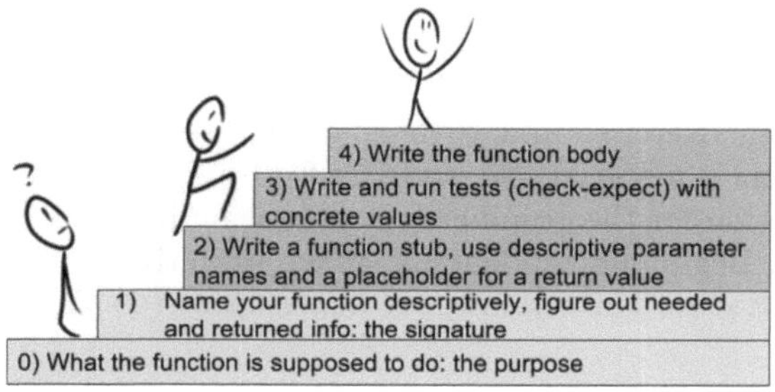

Fig. 5. The design recipe [12] presented as a staircase fostering a step-by-step design [37].

The Racket track was designed so that different aspects of algorithmic thinking (abstraction, logic, repetition) were introduced side by side, starting from easier ideas and progressing to more advanced topics [39]. Altogether, the course content comprised seven topics: introduction to programming, control structures, functions and design recipe for functions, recursion, user interactions, lists, and higher-order functions with Turtle graphics (content described in Table 1). The very core of the Code ABC Racket track material is to reveal the nature of programming as a sort of applied mathematics, and to show how mathematics can be taught through programming. Hence most programming exercises are in a math context. The implementation of the Racket track was inspired by the Systematic Program Design online course offered by edx.org [24] and the material was constructed following the same procedure:

1. Short motivational video, in which the lecturer introduced the contents and the purpose of the exercises. A few videos also responded to questions from the previous week.
2. Tutorial videos introduced the core concepts as screen captures. The lecturer demonstrated the concepts to be learned with DrRacket. Its stepper tool was extensively employed in explaining the evaluation rules. Concise lecture notes were available on-line as well, but the majority of the course content was provided as videos. The course participants were expected to test the programming examples themselves while watching the videos.

3. The Design Recipe was used to demonstrate the principles of function design, see Fig. 5. By using the recipe, a user can solve one detail at a time and proceed step-by-step until the whole function is ready. The implicit intent is to solidify writing test cases before implementing the actual function body, which complies with the test-driven development.
4. The exercises and their solutions were delivered as both DrRacket and WeScheme files and used as self-tests of the course content presented in the video tutorials.
5. Hands-on exercises differed from the Systematic Program Design exercises as self-review for code and multiple choice quizzes were not used. Also, the final course project was an essay about the pedagogical aspects instead of a programming project as in Systematic Program Design.

The programming exercises and their solutions were taken from the Coding for schools student's material [38] and the Coder's handbook [37], which contains documentation for the graphics and animation libraries (2htdp/image and 2htdp/universe), Beginning Student Language primitives, and new libraries for turtle graphics (Racket Turtle) and user interactions (display-read).

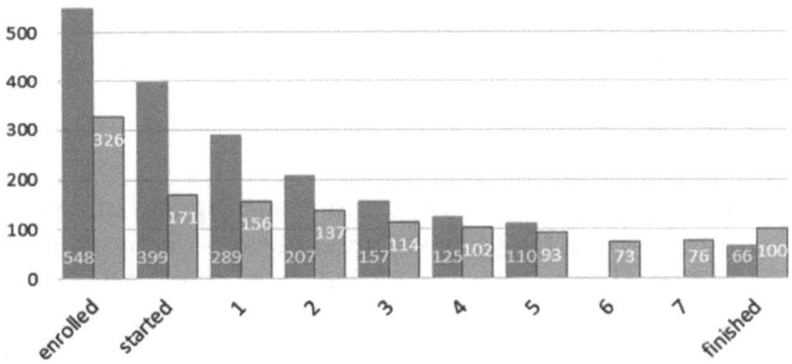

Fig. 6. Number of participants/topic (P blue, R green). (Color figure online)

Participation and Course Completion Levels. Figure 6 shows the number of participants per topic. By "enrolled" we mean participants who registered to the MOOC, whereas "started" refers to participants who showed some activity in the first topic (completed one exercise or gave feedback). The numbers 1–7 refer in Racket case to participants who completed the corresponding topic. The numbers 1–5 in Python case refer to participants who completed the feedback form at the of each topic. The Racket track was started by fewer participants (N = 171) than the newly introduced Python track (N = 399). Both courses lost participants during the course period, but in the end more participants completed the Racket track (N = 100, 58% of the started participants) than the Python track (N = 66, 17% of the started participants). If the percentages are calculated per enrolled participants we get lower values for completion rates: Python 12% and Racket 31%. Only 80% of the course work was required to pass in Racket track, which allowed skipping one topic. This explains the lower numbers for topics 5, 6 or 7 in Fig. 6.

4.2 Research Methods

The methods of the study are curriculum research and content analysis of the participants' feedback. Curriculum research examines the most central concepts of the curriculum, which in our context correspond to CS concepts in the Code ABC MOOC. In deriving the main concepts, we counted their frequency in content, that is, how often they occurred. We also asked participants what they had learned after each topic, and their responses were similarly analyzed by counting the occurrence frequencies. After extracting the most central CS concepts, the paradigm-oriented differences were examined more thoroughly. The goal of the review was to check how good a match the respective paradigms were for teaching math.

5 Results

5.1 What CS Concepts and CT Skills Do the Python and Racket Tracks Introduce?

Figure 7 illustrates the topics taught vs. the topics learned for each course. The brighter-colored bars to the left correspond with the relative word frequencies in the course content. The most frequent word has a value of 100%, and other frequencies are compared to this maximum. The lighter-colored bars to the right represent the course content based on participants' responses to the question "What did I learn?".

In the figure, the blue Python tornado lies above the green Racket tornado. From the shape of the tornados we can conclude that the wider Python tornado covers a larger range of concepts with about equal intensity. In contrast, the Racket course focused on functions and a handful of other concepts. The relative similarity of the mirrored right side indicates that the participants in both tracks seemed to learn the intended concepts.

The Python topics in the upper blue tornado indicate that the main concepts of the Python track were control structures (selection and iteration). Boolean operators (and, or, not) were widely exploited in the program examples, including conditions for iterations, such as for and while loops. All selection and iteration-related topics appear in the list: boolean ops (1st), for (4th), loop (7th), if (8th), index (11th), range (12th), iteration (14th), condition (17th), while (18th).

Naming and variables (2nd) were the second most central concepts, reflecting the stateful and assignment-oriented nature of Python as an imperative language. We also group statements (10th) here, as a superclass, including functions (9th), procedures (16th) and assignments. By comparing functions and procedures the material highlighted the difference of functions returning a value and procedures lacking return values.

The third topic group were applications, exemplified by turtle (3rd) and pixel-level image editing (15th). Concept-wise, these applications do not bring anything new, but rather give students the opportunity to put the pieces together while working on engaging problems. The last group consists of data types and

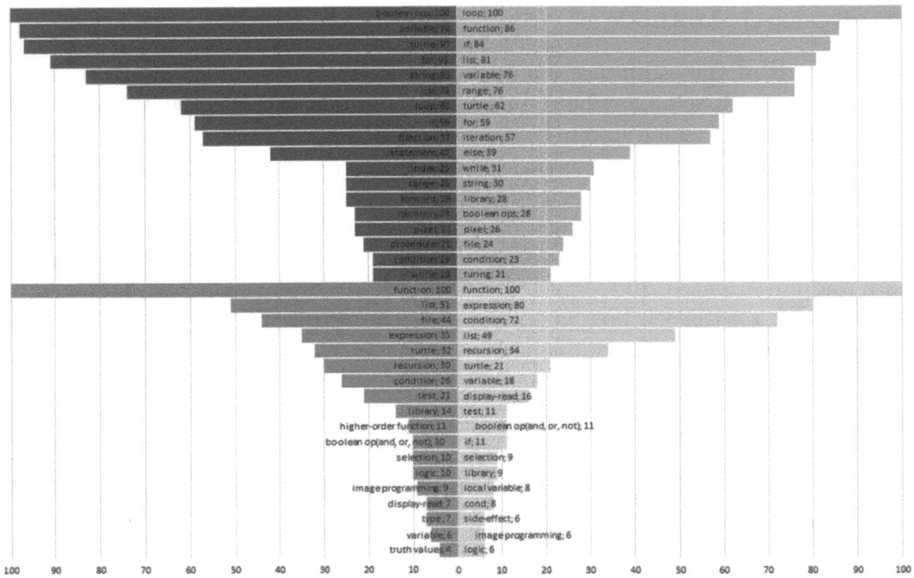

Fig. 7. To the left the relative word frequencies of the MOOC material (P blue, R green); to the right teachers' feedback to the question "What did I learn?" (Color figure online)

structures of string (5th) and list (6th); in the course, strings are named (used as variables) and lists are iterated. So, list would fit in the iteration of the first group as well.

The participants echoed these emphasis areas, apart from the Turing machine and file areas, which received more emphasis than they had in the text. The Turing machine, completeness and halting problems, were used to explain the history and most prominent ideas of CS. Files were introduced in the last topic (Data handling) simultaneously with related functions such as `open` and `close`. Statements and index were not mentioned.

The analysis of the Racket course concepts is only partial for technical limitations; we were not able to analyze video material since it was not transcribed into textual format. The analysis is based on the lecture notes and textual material in the course platform, so the analysis might be missing some concepts that were taught but are not showing in Fig. 7.

In the green Racket tornado functions, expressions, conditions, lists, recursion and Turtles form the top 6 concepts mentioned on both taught and learned sides. Testing, boolean operators and library usage are mentioned next. The high frequency of the 'file' concept on the lecture side is explained by the fact that the term appeared frequently throughout the course instructions ("Save your code in a file", "Send your file for peer-review", etc.) even though file handling was not explicitly taught. The participants reflected, quite faithfully, the same concepts except higher-order functions and type, which were missing from the list of concepts mentioned by the participants.

5.2 What Topics Did the Teachers Find Challenging, Inspiring, or Suitable for Math?

The participants evaluated each topic after completion using 5-point Likert-scales. The evaluation was based on a set of criteria such as difficulty level, enthusiasm, and suitability for their teaching. The following subsections present the results of these evaluations.

Table 1. Fundamental concepts and CT related aspects of the Python and Racket tracks with regard to the underlying paradigm.

<table>
<tr><th></th><th>Python (imperative)</th><th>Racket (functional)</th></tr>
<tr><td>1</td><td>Basic operations, computing.
What is a computer, program (Python vs. Java)?
Background, Turing machine (completeness).</td><td>Introduction to Racket programming,
global constants.
CT: problem decomposition using functions</td></tr>
<tr><td>2</td><td>Naming (including variables) applied to numbers, strings, objects such as turtles and images, as well as functions
string: substrings, indexing.
Functions ($f(x)$, $g(x)$) vs. procedures ($p(x)$).
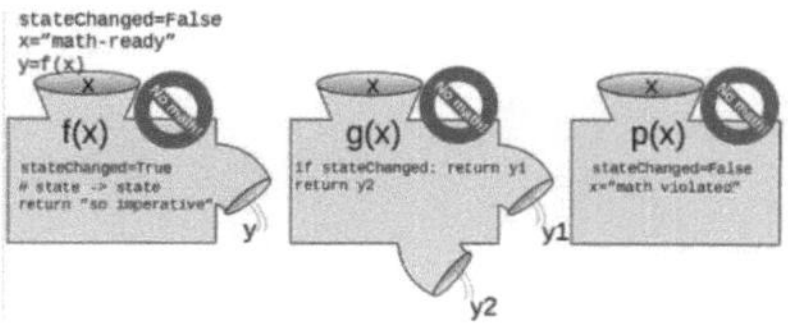
</td><td>Control structures: selection (<code>if</code>), truth values, comparisons.
Function definition: purpose, signature.
Unit tests using <code>check-expect</code>
*)The $k()$
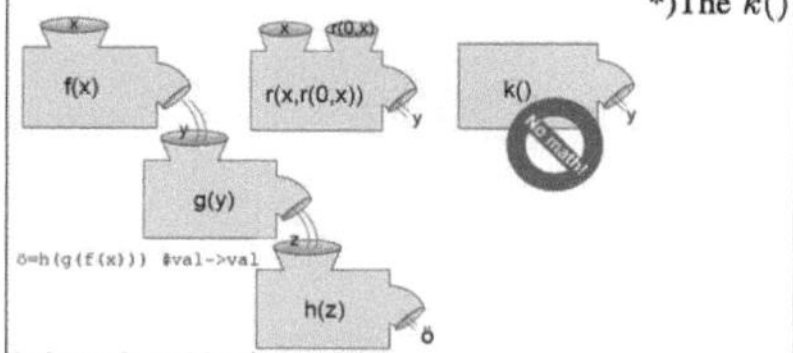

is introduced in the topic 4.</td></tr>
<tr><td>3</td><td>Control structures: iteration (<code>for</code> and <code>while</code>).
Iteration based on list or counter condition, e.g.,
a list [1,2,3] iterated based on range:
<code>for item in list: block</code>
<code>while (condition): block</code>
Block: indentation-grouped commands
CT: becoming aware of iterative patterns.</td><td>The Design Recipe[12]: test-driven development.
Selection (<code>cond</code>): comparisons, predicates.
Logical ops for combinations: <code>and</code>, <code>or</code>, <code>not</code>.
Interactive applications: animations, mouse events
CT-abstraction: Design Recipe.</td></tr>
<tr><td>4</td><td>Blocks by indentation.
Control structures, also nested, selection: <code>if</code>, <code>elif</code>, and <code>else</code>.
Decision making:
– condition (logical expression) in iteration or selection
– logical operators for combinations.
<code>if condition: block</code>
<code>else: print("condition false")</code>

CT abstraction: flowchart illustrating the control flow.
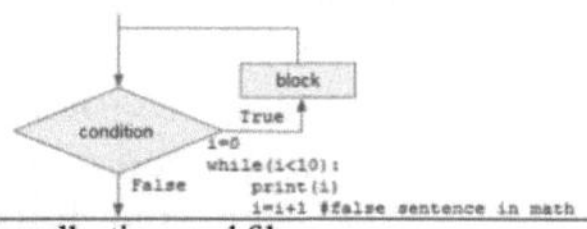
</td><td>Reading user input with <code>display-read</code> (user interaction causes side-effects);
the user input stored into a local variable.
Recursion, here factorial $n!$ as an example:
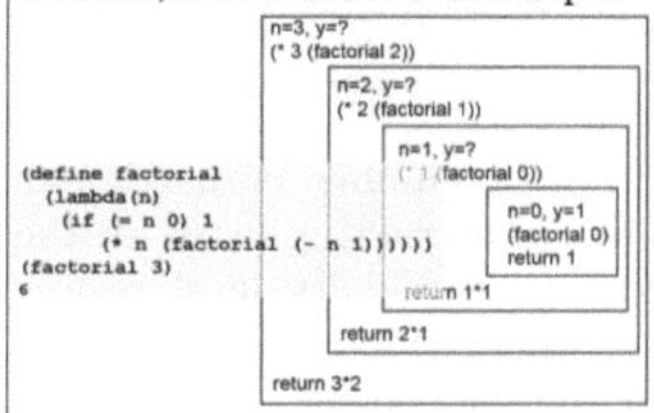
</td></tr>
<tr><td>5</td><td>Data handling: collections and files.
Collection operations:
1. indexing
2. string: <code>split</code>, <code>find</code>, <code>substring</code>
3. list: <code>len</code>, <code>range</code>, <code>for-each</code>.
Reading files: <code>open</code>, <code>close</code>, <code>readlines</code>.
Conventions: commenting.</td><td>Iterating lists recursively, producing new lists or one accumulated value.
Image files.</td></tr>
<tr><td>6</td><td>Revision, extra material.</td><td>Iterations cont.
Higher-order functions: <code>map</code> and <code>apply</code>, lists.</td></tr>
<tr><td>7</td><td colspan="2">Finnish curriculum reflections in regard to CT/CS, and how to integrate computing with own teaching subject.</td></tr>
</table>

Challenging Topics. The average level of difficulty experienced for each topic is given in Fig. 8 (1 = not challenging enough, 5 = far too challenging). For both tracks, the difficulty level increased during the first four topics. After the fourth topic in the Racket track, the difficulty level decreased, whereas it continued to increase in the Python track. Topic 4 in the Racket track (recursion) was considered most challenging. Animations (topic 3) and lists (topic 5) are the next most challenging. Starting from topic 5 the challenge level in Racket starts to decrease. Explanation might be that there were less exercises in topic 5 than in the previous topics. Also topic 6 covered Turtle graphics programming, which is conceptually simpler than functions and recursion.

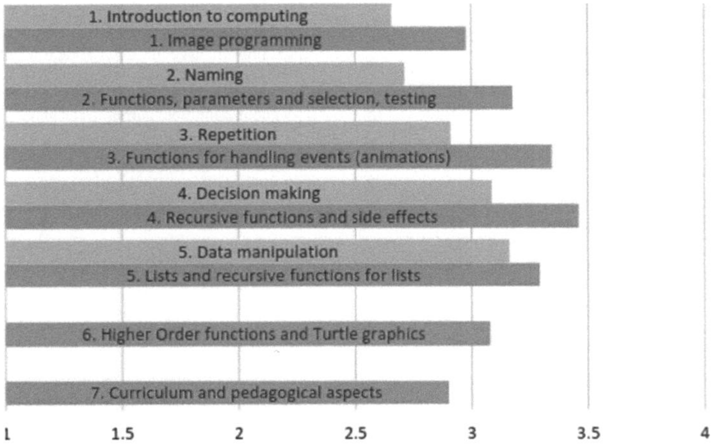

Fig. 8. Difficulty level/topic (P blue, R green). (Color figure online)

The list below provides a few free-text feedback snippets describing challenging topics:

Python

- Repetition: a number of participants were not capable of constructing loops on their own
- Decision: the difficulty level rose sharply compared to the previous modules; too much information and challenge
- Image processing: exercises felt hard and difficult to understand for beginners, and did not foster learning repetition
- Data manipulation: A few exercises were too difficult, e.g. in searching data from a file, one really needs to know what each function returns

Racket

- The most challenging topics included recursion, animation, lists, and loops
- Recursion: content of topic 4 was clearly too much. It should have been split into two separate topics
- Lists: topic 5 also challenged a number of participants

Inspiring Topics. The average enthusiasm score for each topic is shown in Fig. 9 (1 = not inspiring at all, 5 = extremely inspiring). The highest levels of enthusiasm were reported in Racket for Turtle graphics (topic 6) and Image Programming (topic 1). This is in line with Toikkanen's [53] findings of the mesmerizing effect of Turtle throughout all the Code ABC MOOC tracks. Young students immediately start drawing Logo-like figures after discovering the `pen.down` function. In addition, animation (topic 3) inspired a good number of participants.

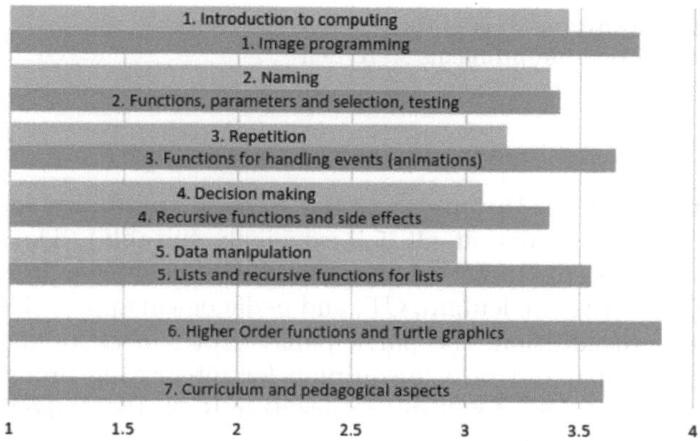

Fig. 9. Level of enthusiasm/topic (P blue, R green). (Color figure online)

For the Python track, the difficulty level (Fig. 8) and the level of enthusiasm seem to go hand in hand, i.e. the more difficult the material, the less enthusiasm experienced. In Racket, this trend is less visible. For example, animations (topic 3) are considered to be both challenging and inspiring at the same time. The lower levels of enthusiasm for the Python material could also be due to the fact that the material was originally meant for a different audience, whereas the Racket material was specifically designed for in-service math teachers. For instance, the math teachers did not find Python's image processing particularly fit for their purposes. After the second module, the clamour for hands-on programming in order to learn became louder; yet during the first module, the Parson's problems were regarded as both easy and motivating. Overall, the participants questioned the usefulness of some exercises because they lacked ready-made student material that could be utilized in a school context, which is probably also is reflected in the enthusiasm scores. Below we summarize the most inspiring aspects of the courses in order. We also provide some excerpts from teachers' responses (translated from Finnish).

Python

- Turtle images were fun and inspiring. *I was proud to be able to modify the Turtle code so that it formed a house*
- Image processing was inspiring as well. *As an art teacher it was easier to understand (than math)*
- Data Manipulation: Working with the Small Particles Data example (looking for values in the list, calculating averages), and the possibility to investigate real-life problems were beneficial

Racket

- Image programming: drawing and designing own images. Possibility to see code, games and images drawn by other participants gave new ideas for teaching, i.e., sharing artifacts promoted creativity and increased enthusiasm

Suitable Topics. Figure 10 represents the average suitability scores for each course topic (1 = not suitable at all, 5 = extremely suitable). The highest suitability score was given to Racket's last topic, which includes material about CS as a new addition to the curriculum, CT, and pedagogical approaches to teaching the new content. In addition, the participants wrote an essay on ideas stimulated during the course and/or a lesson plan for integrating programming into their teaching. The next most suitable topics were Racket's Image Programming (topic 1) and Turtle Graphics (topic 6). Topic 5 scored high as well, featuring a quiz that utilized recursive function and lists in implementation. The least suitable was topic 4, which employed recursion and user interaction.

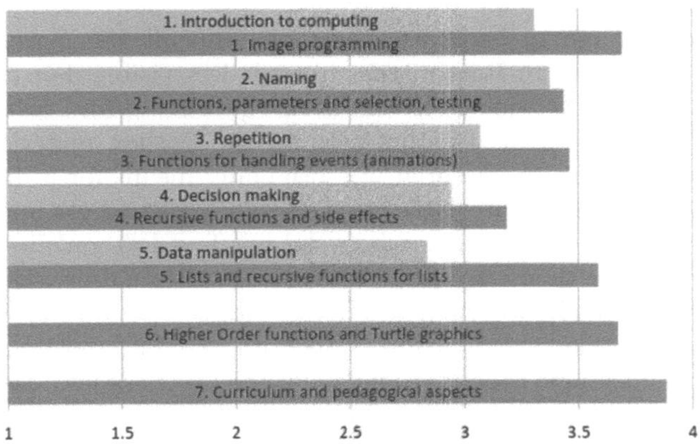

Fig. 10. Suitability of the course topics (P blue, R green). (Color figure online)

Python scored notably lower in suitability. As mentioned, the material was not originally designed for math teachers, although these made up half of the participants (48 %). Hence, the generic material did not meet the teachers' needs.

Surprisingly in this regard, the Data Manipulation topic (number 5) averaged as the least suitable topic, even though it included real-life applications from, for instance, the statistics domain. Nevertheless, some teachers noted its value:

Python

- Turtle graphics could be used to teach geometry (focuses on angles and side lengths)
- Repetition, Decisions: using numbers, strings, turtles and images consistently within all topics was perceived positively
- Data manipulation (Statistics):
  - *In data analysis, real world problems made me understand what programming can be used for (environmental science and geography, analyzing air pollution in USA) and its usefulness in analyzing big amounts of data*
  - *Easy access to online data made me think I could use this in my teaching*
  - *Using statistics in mathematics could be useful (if I were a math teacher)*

Racket

- Possibility to utilize exercises in the school context
- Functions (Algebra): content was designed specifically for math teachers (including the exercises and utilizing the functional paradigm), thus the material and tools were useful for teaching

5.3 Which Paradigms Do the Tracks Align with and How Do They Support Math?

Neither of the Code ABC tracks pronounced explicit paradigm considerations, nor were they present when the participants evaluated the topics. More experienced programmers compared languages – not paradigms – focusing mainly on the learning threshold (the lower the better) and differences in syntax, e.g. confusion with the excessive amount of parentheses and the prefix notation of Racket. However, several topics inherently implied paradigm-related issues. In the Python track, the Naming topic introduced data mutability and immutability, variable assignments, and in accordance with variables the most common misconceptions as well. The Python material highlighted the difference between functions and procedures, and introduced code division in the form of reusable modules and libraries. Python contains a class structure and an option for object-orientation but, in this context, Python was classified as imperative even though a few objects, such as turtles, were extensively utilized throughout the MOOC (in effect requiring the introduction of dot notation).

Similarly, the Racket material does not explicitly emphasize the underlying paradigm and hardly mentions the term 'functional' at all. However, the built-in principles of Felleisen's 'How to design a program' [12] recommend avoiding imperative features and re-assignment of global variables. These principles aim at a purely functional programming style. However, the enhancement of `display-read` indicates the need for pointing out side-effects contradicting this purity: `display-read` interacts with a user. With regard to the variables in Racket, it is possible to define constants and `let` allows local variables to be assigned. These can still not be re-assigned without the `set!` command, forbidden by functional paradigm purists.

Having no re-assignable variables – thus no loop counters – has its implications for iterations as well. Although looping lists with the command of `foreach` is still possible, missing a re-assignable counter leads towards recursion and higher-order functions, where recursion calls "fake" mutability with expressions as function arguments and by returning partial results. Higher-order functions, such as `map`, `apply` or `filter`, creates new lists or accumulates values, based on given lists and functions. Later, these functional list-handling mechanisms were introduced in the Python language as well, along with lambda calculus and list comprehensions. In Python, however, there are "imperative" ways of looping (such as `for` and `while`), leaving a minimal need for recursion compared to Racket. In both tracks, the paradigm-influenced alternatives for implementing iteration and selection structures were the core content of the whole course.

As the paradigms reside implicitly in the material, it is no surprise that the teachers do not pay much attention to them. As with learning to drive a car, all attention is first drawn to the main aspects of driving – not to comparing the features of various car models. Nevertheless, teachers with previous programming experience compared the features of the course language to their previously learned languages. For instance, teachers in the Python track stated that *I learned that Python is simpler than Java (lists and their handling), I learned `for` and `foreach` loops and list modifications*, and *In my experience, Python requires less lines of code. Another nice thing was that when defining variables you don't need to think as much as in Java.*

In Racket, on the other hand, the teachers' first impressions in particular were as follows: *I learned Racket's syntax. Writing mathematical expressions is cumbersome compared to Python, Java, Pascal, Ruby, and Visual Basic* and *If you consider using Racket at school, it is relatively complex compared to, for instance, Java.* On a more positive note, Racket teachers also noted some benefits: *Racket is really engaging! The first exercise was well selected: it is nice to immediately achieve some colorful shapes instead of the traditional "Hello World". I did not know that programming can be this much fun!*

Algebra lies at the core in terms of math focus. It includes fundamentals such as functions, variables, statements and expressions, which are fundamental not only in math, but also in CS. In CS, functions and variables all encompass implementation mechanisms. However, the differences between concepts in these two disciplines may cause misconceptions and programming errors that are difficult to detect. In Table 1, module 2 compares the differences between functions in both tracks. Compared with Racket, Python allows remarkable freedom of implementation, which becomes particularly visible with functions.

In math, the function definition dictates at least one function parameter as input, and one and only one as output. It is possible to write a function without parameters in both languages, such as *k()* (the rightmost figure in the 2nd row), which is not valid in math. In Python, a procedure $p(x)$ may return no value explicitly (in which case Python implicitly returns *None*), which is not acceptable in math, if x is in domain. Neither may a function return multiple values with the same input, as does the function $g(x)$, which returns either $y1$ or $y2$ based on the state.

What is wrong with the $f(x)$ on the Python side then? On the face of it, nothing: it gets at least one input as a parameter (in this case x) and returns only one output (y), as specified. However, the function body changes the global state of the outer program by re-assigning the global variable `stateChanged`, i.e., it causes a side-effect. Functions causing side-effects are not allowed in math. The idea of functional purity in the Racket track prevents side-effects, and in Python, no side-effects arise if the programmer is aware of the pitfalls and is capable of avoiding them. In accordance with a pure functional paradigm, immutable data and having no side-effects makes, for instance, parallel execution possible: different threads handling the same data can rely on the validity of the data.

In Racket, variables are essentially constants. In math, variables are also constants in the context of evaluating the value of an expression. The variables do not change during the evaluation, but between evaluations. For example, in the case of function $y = f(x)$, x changes when the position moves on the x-axis. Thus, in math, the term *variable* can be deceptive, because variable does not actually vary. Instead, the terms *a symbol* or *a representative* might give a more authentic view of the true meaning of the concept.

In the imperative paradigm, the situation with variables becomes even more obscure with the counter-type behavior. As an example, see the fourth row in Table 1, where the `while` loop exploits the value of i to decide when to stop. In the loop body, i is incremented with the assignment of $i = i + 1$. In math, this statement makes no sense. In CS, the statement is split by the equal sign to enable the left and the right value to be referred to separately. The left value opens a gaping rabbit hole to the underlying world of hardware specifics and constraints that are normally carefully guarded. In essence, it represents the memory address to which the right side – still a normal expression – is assigned.

Re-assignment is a dangerous operation and provides an endless source of error; for instance, if types are mixed in assignment. Thus, typing relates closely to variables. In static typing, a type must be given when a variable is defined and it is checked during the compilation. In dynamic typing, variables need not be assigned a specific type, but it may change assignment-by-assignment in runtime: now an integer, after the next assignment maybe a string. The operations allowed for integers differ remarkably from those allowed for strings. Strong typing prevents operations on invalid types [51], while prevention leads to compile and runtime errors when these are detected. Both Racket and Python are dynamically and strongly typed languages.

In Arithmetics, types of integer and decimal numbers provide more in-depth affordances. Typing relates to number sets in math, such as integers, and rational and irrational numbers. In math, gradual progression from simple to more complex operations results in changes in the respective number sets as well. With addition and multiplication, a student remains in the comfort zone of integers. With subtraction, the student may move into negative numbers. A substantial paradigm shift happens when division is introduced, which along with fractions transfers a student into the zone of rational numbers, represented as decimals in code.

The ultimate challenge at elementary level is irrational numbers, which are met when a ratio is never-ending and non-repeating. Irrational numbers result e.g. from square root operations, and surds, such as $\sqrt{2}$, are never-ending. In a computer context, the limits of the physical memory allocated to each variable complicate the handling of such irrationalities. Historically in CS, selecting the right type has been important due to the constraints of memory size: a number has to be cut when the allocated bytes are used up resulting in the cut part being lost. The type implies the number of bytes in use, which influences the preciseness of a number.

Preciseness is also a consideration in many scientific calculations, for instance when rounding and defining significant numbers. In math, $\sqrt{2}$ or trigonometric expressions such as *sin(60)* are exact. However, when represented in decimal format they are not, irrespective of the length of the type of `float`. All in all, in Arithmetics, when calculating basic and advanced operations, a computer can be compared to a calculator, with which students practice new arithmetic functions such as `abs`, `sqrt`, or `exp`, and drill the right order of calculations.

In the Python material, math equations, such as speed-distance-time calculations, exemplify the use of a newly introduced mathematical functions. The Racket material is more geometry-oriented, placing greater emphasis on calculating areas, angles, and perimeters. Even if extensively used in examples, Geometry is not central to understanding the concepts of CS. Our study, however, notes its value as an area providing visually appealing applications.

Logic and logical operations (`and`, `or`, `not`) combine conditions into more complex conditions. Conditions – or logical expressions – fall into the area of logic. However, in the current math syllabus, logic does not have a prominent position. As logical expressions prompt control structures, the natural progression would be to learn logic first. Consequently, control structures and the use of conditions might fit within both Logic and Arithmetics.

Selections, or decisions as the Python track calls them, correspond to inequalities in math: 1D inequalities, such as $x > 0$, are represented on a number line. Whether the line is open-ended or close-ended depends on the comparison operator: $<$ and $>$ result in open-ended lines, while $\leq$ and $\geq$ result in close-ended ones. In 2D inequalities, such as $y > x$, the line divides the coordinate plane into two halves, one of which is shaded. An open-ended condition is represented as a dashed line, a closed condition as a solid one. Consequently, inequalities can be expanded to 3D as well.

Conditions can also be combined. When multiple inequalities hold simultaneously, the number-line is cut into segments, and lines define geometric shapes in a coordinate plane, most often triangles. In 3D, conditions may result in solid geometry shapes, such as prisms. In addition, conditions apply to piecewise defined functions, which, for instance, have discontinuity points or behave differently depending on the range of x.

Iterations or recursive structures are relatively rare in elementary math. The accumulator pattern introduced in both tracks can be used in Statistics, e.g., when calculating mean values, or when looking for *min* or *max* values. Later, Σ and $\prod$ operations are applied iteratively to the defined number domain and these new notations abbreviate e.g. the previous calculation of the mean. In Pre-Algebra, recognizing growing patterns prepares for sequences, abstracted later as functions in Algebra [56,57]. It is axiomatic that sequences and their sums and series are iterative. In inductive problem solving, a student determines the nth term in a sequence. Instead of the iterative `for` and `while` loops favoured by Python, Racket favours recursions. In contrast to induction, which starts from the first and aims at finding the nth term, recursion starts from the nth term and aims at reaching the first. The recursive calculation of factorial ($n!$) illustrates the product type iteration; see topic 4 in Table 1. Basic operations of Probability, combinations and permutations, make extensive use of factorials.

6 Conclusions

We have studied two approaches to teaching programming to in-service elementary school teachers in Finland. The majority of the participating teachers were mathematics teachers, which is understandable, given that programming has been added to the math syllabus in the new curriculum. Below we summarize our findings.

What CS Concepts and CT Skills Do These Code ABC Tracks Introduce? Both tracks covered a substantial amount of basic programming concepts in their respective programming languages, such as subprograms (functions or procedures), conditional structures, boolean logic, data types, and lists. The Python track provided a generic synopsis of programming basics. As a primer, Python provided a history and some general knowledge about computers and CS. After this history review, the track focused on imperative programming fundamentals, such as assignment and for/while loops. Each new concept was demonstrated using numbers, strings, images, and Turtles. The Racket track, on the other hand, presented programming as yet another way of learning math rather than as a generic tool. Programming appeared as a new means of problem solving by exploiting functions. In addition to functions, control structures of selection and iteration were introduced. Iterations consisted of recursion and higher-order functions that manipulated lists.

CT links math and CS. When solving a problem, dividing the problem into smaller subproblems is essential (decomposition). In the context of programming, subproblems are subprograms, i.e. functions. Functions were discussed substantially more in Racket than in Python. As a recipe for a well-planned function, the Racket track introduced Design Recipe by Felleisen [12]. This Recipe promotes test-driven development: unit tests are implemented before a function body. Both courses emphasized the importance of using descriptive names for functions and variables, and the need for clear comments in order to improve readability; these coding conventions may be considered to be part of CT as well.

What Topics Did the Teachers Find Challenging, Inspiring, or Suitable for Math?

- Challenging:
  - The most challenging topics in the Python track were data and image processing, evidently due to the extensive exploitation of Repetition and Decision structures. Furthermore, the difficulty level suddenly rose when moving from Repetition to Decision.
  - In Racket, the most challenging topics included recursion (loops), animation, and lists, by far the most challenging of which was recursion.
  - The Racket track required a significant amount of effort because of the hands-on exercises and complex topics. Frequently, the exercises took more time than expected. This was experienced as a challenge by the participants, who had to take care of their normal work duties during the course.
- Inspiring (enthusiasm in the survey):
  - Turtle graphics were considered inspiring in both tracks. In Python, Turtle moves exemplified both Repetition and Decision topics, while in Racket, Turtle was linked with higher-order functions, which also rank high in the list of most challenging CS topics.
  - In Python, the participants were interested in learning more about the history of CS, and the prominent and influential persons behind it. The Image Processing exercises divided opinion, some considered it interesting while others found it difficult, tedious, and a rather useless topic for the target group, (math teachers). Data processing was also received with mixed feelings. Some appreciated the real-life applications but a number of participants regarded it as too difficult.
  - The Racket participants valued highly creative and playful open-ended exercises allowing them to create their own 'art', even though this was not considered to be "traditional math" or central to conceptual learning. Sharing artifacts with others was one significant factor in creating enthusiasm and promoting creativity.
- Suitable for teaching:
  - In Python, suitability ranked significantly lower than in Racket. Even when the Racket track was challenging, it scored higher. The difference in suitability scores indicates that the course content should be tailored to better suit the target group, in this case math (and science) teachers.
  - In the Racket track, the participants regarded the pedagogical essay, image programming, Turtle graphics, animation and quiz as the most suitable and interesting.
  - Suitability and enthusiasm seem to correlate.

Which Paradigms Do the Tracks Align with and How Do They Support Math? Conceptually, the functional paradigm is closer to math, in particular in its representation of functions and variables. The imperative paradigm comprises more elements that are foreign to pure math. As imperative, Python might call for less effort in its approach, but it contains built-in hazards that may cause misconceptions and programming errors. For instance, re-assigning a global variable changes the state and function outcome, thus conflicting with the mathematical definition of a function. In these paradigms, the meaning and importance of a variable varies as well. A variable's visibility is defined by its scope (local/global). In functional Racket, global variables are constant and re-assigning local variables is not advisable either. In Python, global variables can be re-assigned anywhere and types will change accordingly, which is indefensible from the viewpoint of math. Without having become used to re-assignable variables and the possibility of comparing, a novice programmer will learn the functional programming smoother and regard it more suitable and inspiring. In contrast, an experienced imperative programmer lacks his normal means of exploiting variables, which causes frustration.

The Finnish curriculum integrates CS into math without allocating more time to teach it. This necessitates making the CS syllabus as close as possible to math: no time can be wasted on learning irrelevancies or concepts causing unnecessary confusion. The curriculum, however, should determine the targeted CS concepts more precisely. Languages should be categorized based on those concepts and their math-suitability in order to make justified tool selections. Systematic research and various learning experiments will enable determination of the concepts, computational thinking skills, and teaching practices best suited to closing the digital skills gap, as stipulated by the Finnish Curriculum 2014.

Acknowledgments. We gratefully acknowledge the grant support of the Finnish National Board of Education and Technology Industries of the Finland Centennial Foundation that enabled the development of the Code ABC MOOC during the research period of Spring 2016. In addition to the funders, we thank the Aalto University A+ and Rubyric teams for their efforts to continuously improve the MOOC platform. Last but not least, thanks to Tarmo Toikkanen, Tiina Korhonen, Otto Seppälä, and Arto Hellas for providing Code ABC MOOC material and corrections for this paper.

References

1. Alegre, F., Moreno, J.: Haskell in middle and high school mathematics. In: TFPIE, vol. 1. EPTCS, Sophia-Antipolis (2015)
2. Auvinen, T., Karavirta, V., Ahoniemi, T.: Rubyric: an online assessment tool for effortless authoring of personalized feedback. ACM, Workingpaper (2009)
3. Bal, H.E., Grune, D.: Programming Language Essentials. Addison-Wesley, Boston (1994)
4. Balanskat, A., Engelhardt, K.: Computing our future: computer programming and coding-priorities, school curricula and initiatives across Europe. European Schoolnet (2014). http://www.eun.org/resources/detail?publicationID=661

5. Barr, V., Guzdial, M.: Introducing CS to newcomers, and JES as a teaching tool. Commun. ACM **59**(11), 10–11 (2016)
6. Brady, C., Orton, K., Weintrop, D., Anton, G., Rodriguez, S., Wilensky, U.: All roads lead to computing: making, participatory simulations, and social computing as pathways to computer science. IEEE Trans. Educ. **60**(1), 59–66 (2017)
7. Burke, Q., Burke, Q.: Mind the metaphor: charting the rhetoric about introductory programming in K-12 schools. Horizon **24**(3), 210–220 (2016)
8. Dijkstra, E.W.: How do we tell truths that might hurt? In: Dijkstra, E.W. (ed.) Selected Writings on Computing: A Personal Perspective, pp. 129–131. Springer, New York (1982). https://doi.org/10.1007/978-1-4612-5695-3_22
9. Ericson, B., Adrion, W.R., Fall, R., Guzdial, M.: State-based progress towards computer science for all. ACM Inroads **7**(4), 57–60 (2016)
10. Ericson, B., Guzdial, M., Morrison, B., Parker, M., Moldavan, M., Surasani, L.: An eBook for teachers learning CS principles. ACM Inroads **6**(4), 84–86 (2015)
11. Ericson, B.J., Rogers, K., Parker, M., Morrison, B., Guzdial, M.: Identifying design principles for CS teacher ebooks through design-based research. In: Proceedings of the 2016 ACM Conference on International Computing Education Research, ICER 2016, pp. 191–200. ACM, New York (2016). https://doi.org/10.1145/2960310.2960335
12. Felleisen, M., Findler, R., Flatt, M., Krishnamurthi, S.: How to Design Programs, 2nd edn. MIT-Press, Cambridge (2014). http://www.ccs.neu.edu/home/matthias/HtDP2e/
13. Felleisen, M., Krishnamurthi, S.: Viewpoint Why computer science doesn't matter. Commun. ACM **52**(7), 37–40 (2009)
14. Fesakis, G., Serafeim, K.: Influence of the familiarization with scratch on future teachers' opinions and attitudes about programming and ICT in education. In: ACM SIGCSE Bulletin, vol. 41, pp. 258–262. ACM (2009)
15. Finnish National Board of Education: National core curriculum for basic education 2014. In: National Core Curriculum for Basic Education 2014. Publications, Finnish National Board of Education (2016). https://www.ellibs.com/fi/book/9789521362590/national-core-curriculum-for-basic-education-2014
16. Futschek, G.: Algorithmic thinking: the key for understanding computer science. In: Mittermeir, R.T. (ed.) ISSEP 2006. LNCS, vol. 4226, pp. 159–168. Springer, Heidelberg (2006). https://doi.org/10.1007/11915355_15
17. Gagné, R.M.: The Conditions of Learning. Holt, Rinehart and Winston, New York (1965)
18. Gray, E.M., Tall, D.O.: Duality, ambiguity, and flexibility: a proceptual view of simple arithmetic. J. Res. Math. Educ. **25**, 116–140 (1994)
19. Guzdial, M.: Drumming up support for AP CS principles. Commun. ACM **59**(2), 12–13 (2016)
20. Guzdial, M., Soloway, E.: Computer science is more important than calculus: the challenge of living up to our potential. SIGCSE Bull. **35**(2), 5–8 (2003)
21. Guzdial, M.J., Ericson, B.: Introduction to Computing and Programming in Python, a Multimedia Approach. Prentice Hall Press, Upper Saddle River (2009)
22. Gülbahar, Y., Kalelioglu, F.: The effects of teaching programming via Scratch on problem solving skills: a discussion from learners' perspective. Inform. Educ. Int. J. **13**(1), 33–50 (2014)
23. Jarvis, S., Pavlenko, A.: Crosslinguistic Influence in Language and Cognition. Routledge, Abingdon (2008)
24. Kiczales, G.: UBCx: SPD1x Systematic Program Design - Part 1 (version 1) (2015). https://www.edx.org/xseries/how-code-systematic-program-design

25. Kulik, J.A.: Meta-analytic studies of findings on computer-based instruction. In: Technology Assessment in Education and Training, vol. 1, pp. 9–34. Psychology Press (1994)
26. Lee, I., Martin, F., Denner, J., Coulter, B., Allan, W., Erickson, J., Malyn-Smith, J., Werner, L.: Computational thinking for youth in practice. ACM Inroads **2**(1), 32–37 (2011)
27. Lewis, C.M.: How programming environment shapes perception, learning and goals: Logo vs. Scratch. In: Proceedings of the 41st ACM Technical Symposium on Computer Science Education, pp. 346–350. ACM (2010)
28. Lutz, M.: Learning Python: Powerful Object-Oriented Programming. Safari Books Online, O'Reilly Media (2013). https://books.google.fi/books?id=ePyeNz2Eoy8C
29. Maloney, J., Resnick, M., Rusk, N., Silverman, B., Eastmond, E.: The Scratch programming language and environment. ACM Trans. Comput. Educ. (TOCE) **10**(4), 16 (2010)
30. Marceau, G., Fisler, K., Krishnamurthi, S.: Measuring the effectiveness of error messages designed for novice programmers. In: Proceedings of the 42nd ACM Technical Symposium on Computer Science Education, pp. 499–504. ACM (2011)
31. Meerbaum-Salant, O., Armoni, M., Ben-Ari, M.: Learning computer science concepts with Scratch. Comput. Sci. Educ. **23**(3), 239–264 (2013)
32. Monroy-Hernández, A., Resnick, M.: FEATURE empowering kids to create and share programmable media. Interactions **15**(2), 50–53 (2008)
33. Meerbaum-Salant, O., Armoni, M., Ben-Ari, M.: Habits of programming in scratch. In: Proceedings of the 16th Annual Joint Conference on Innovation and Technology in Computer Science Education, pp. 168–172. ACM (2011)
34. Papert, S.: An exploration in the space of mathematics educations. Int. J. Comput. Math. Learn. **1**(1), 95–123 (1996)
35. Papert, S., et al.: Logo Philosophy and Implementation. Logo Computer Systems Inc., Highgate (1999)
36. Parsons, D., Haden, P.: Parson's programming puzzles: a fun and effective learning tool for first programming courses. In: Proceedings of the 8th Australasian Conference on Computing Education, vol. 52. pp. 157–163. Australian Computer Society, Inc. (2006)
37. Partanen, T.: Coding for Schools: Coder's Handbook (in Finnish) (2016). http://racket.koodiaapinen.fi/manuaali/
38. Partanen, T.: Coding for Schools: Student Exercises (in Finnish) (2016). http://racket.koodiaapinen.fi/tehtavat/
39. Partanen, T., Mannila, L., Poranen, T.: Learning programming online: a Racket-course for elementary school teachers in Finland. In: Proceedings of the 16th Koli Calling International Conference on Computing Education Research, pp. 178–179. ACM (2016)
40. Partanen, T., Niemelä, P., Mannila, L., Poranen, T.: Educating computer science educators online: a Racket MOOC for elementary math teachers of Finland. In: 9th International Conference on Computer Supported Education, CSEDU 2017. SciTePress (2017)
41. Perkins, D.N., Salomon, G.: Teaching for transfer. Educ. Leadersh. **46**(1), 22–32 (1988)
42. Reimann, P.: Design-based research. In: Markauskaite, L., Freebody, P., Irwin, J. (eds.) Methodological Choice and Design, pp. 37–50. Springer, Dordrecht (2011). https://doi.org/10.1007/978-90-481-8933-5_3

43. Resnick, M., Maloney, J., Monroy-Hernández, A., Rusk, N., Eastmond, E., Brennan, K., Millner, A., Rosenbaum, E., Silver, J., Silverman, B.: Scratch: programming for all. Commun. ACM **52**(11), 60–67 (2009)
44. Rich, P.J., Leatham, K.R., Wright, G.A.: Convergent cognition. Instr. Sci. **41**(2), 431–453 (2013)
45. Lent, R.W., Lopez, F.G., Bieschke, K.J.: Mathematics self-efficacy: sources and relation to science-based career choice. J. Couns. Psychol. **38**(4), 424 (1991)
46. van Rossum, G., et al.: Computer programming for everybody. Proposal to the Corporation for National Research Initiatives (1999)
47. Rossum, G.V.: Python programming language. In: USENIX Annual Technical Conference, vol. 41, p. 36 (2007)
48. Van Roy, P.: Programming paradigms for dummies: what every programmer should know. In: New Computational Paradigms for Computer Music, vol. 104 (2009)
49. Schanzer, E., Fisler, K., Krishnamurthi, S., Felleisen, M.: Transferring skills at solving word problems from computing to algebra through Bootstrap. In: Proceedings of the 46th ACM Technical Symposium on Computer Science Education, pp. 616–621. ACM (2015)
50. Schanzer, E.T.: Algebraic Functions, Computer Programming, and the Challenge of Transfer (2015). https://dash.harvard.edu/handle/1/16461037?show=full
51. Scott, M.L.: Programming Language Pragmatics. Morgan Kaufmann, Burlington (2000)
52. Sengupta, P., Kinnebrew, J.S., Basu, S., Biswas, G., Clark, D.: Integrating computational thinking with K-12 science education using agent-based computation: a theoretical framework. Educ. Inf. Technol. **18**(2), 351–380 (2013)
53. Toikkanen, T., Leinonen, T.: The code ABC MOOC: experiences from a coding and computational thinking MOOC for finnish primary school teachers. In: Rich, P.J., Hodges, C.B. (eds.) Emerging Research, Practice, and Policy on Computational Thinking. ECTII, pp. 239–248. Springer, Cham (2017). https://doi.org/10.1007/978-3-319-52691-1_15
54. Van-Roy, P., Haridi, S.: Concepts, Techniques, and Models of Computer Programming. MIT Press, Cambridge (2004)
55. Wegner, P.: Guest editor's introduction to special issue of computing surveys. ACM Comput. Surv. **21**, 253–258 (1989)
56. Wilkie, K.J.: Students' use of variables and multiple representations in generalizing functional relationships prior to secondary school. Educ. Stud. Math. **93**(3), 333–361 (2016)
57. Wilkie, K.J., Clarke, D.M.: Developing students' functional thinking in algebra through different visualisations of a growing pattern's structure. Math. Educ. Res. J. **28**(2), 223–243 (2015, 2016)
58. Wing, J.M.: Computational thinking. Commun. ACM **49**(3), 33–35 (2006)
59. Wing, J.M.: Computational Thinking: What and Why? Link Magazine (2010)
60. Wright, G., Rich, P., Lee, R.: The influence of teaching programming on learning mathematics. In: Society for Information Technology and Teacher Education International Conference, vol. 2013, pp. 4612–4615. editlib.org (2013)
61. Yoo, D., Schanzer, E., Krishnamurthi, S., Fisler, K.: WeScheme: the browser is your programming environment. In: Proceedings of the 16th Annual Joint Conference on Innovation and Technology in Computer Science Education, pp. 163–167. ACM (2011)
62. Zeldin, A.L., Pajares, F.: Against the odds: self-efficacy beliefs of women in mathematical, scientific, and technological careers. Am. Educ. Res. J. **37**(1), 215–246 (2000)

Using the Students' Levels of Preparation and Confidence as Feedback Information in Quiz-Based Learning Activities

Pantelis M. Papadopoulos[1], Antonis Natsis[1(✉)], and Nikolaus Obwegeser[2]

[1] Centre for Teaching Development and Digital Media, Aarhus University, Aarhus, Denmark
{pmpapad, anatsis}@tdm.au.dk

[2] Department of Management, Aarhus University, Aarhus, Denmark
nikolaus@mgmt.au.dk

Abstract. This paper examines ways to enrich the feedback information students receive in closed-type quiz activities that include a revision phase (i.e., students are allowed to change their initial answers after they receive information from their peers, teacher, or system). Typically, in such activities, the information students receive is based on the percentage of students under each possible question choice. The conducted study analyzes the potential of two additional variables, namely the students' level of preparation and confidence. Both variables are self-reported and, therefore, subjective. During the Fall semester 2016, 91 sophomore students enrolled in an Information Systems course participated in the study for five weeks. The activity was taking place during the first 20 min of each class. Students had to go through three phases and (a) answer a multiple-choice quiz with 8 questions and 4 options for each question, (b) receive feedback based on the whole classroom population, and (c) see the correct answer and discuss them with the teacher in the lecture that follows. The students were randomly grouped into four conditions, based on the feedback they received. The control group only received information on the percentage of students that selected each choice, the Confidence group received feedback on the percentage and the average level of confidence of students that selected each choice, the Preparation group received feedback on the percentage and the average level of preparation of students that selected each choice, and finally the Both group received feedback on the percentage and both the average level of confidence and preparation of students that selected each choice. Result analysis showed that in the most challenging questions (i.e., the ones where students' answers were diverging) the students in the Confidence, Preparation, and Both groups significantly outperformed the students in the Control group. In addition, both confidence and preparation variables were significantly correlated to students' performance during the initial phase, suggesting that students were accurate and sincere in describing their preparation and confidence levels. This paper is an extended version of [1], presented at the 9th International Conference on Computer Supported Education.

Keywords: Feedback · Group awareness · Formative assessment Quiz · Confidence · Preparation

P. Escudeiro et al. (Eds.): CSEDU 2017, CCIS 865, pp. 97–115, 2018.
https://doi.org/10.1007/978-3-319-94640-5_5

1 Introduction

The multiple-choice quiz is a versatile tool that can be used in many different educational contexts for a range of learning purposes. For example, a quiz activity can be used as an assessment tool by the teacher or can be offered as a self-assessment tool to the students. It can be mandatory or optional, taken once or several times. It can be held at any point during a class, or even outside the classroom. A quiz activity in the beginning of the class could provide a useful reference on students' knowledge and this reference can be later used by the teacher in identifying and addressing misconceptions that could affect the lectures to come. On the other hand, short quiz activities during the lecture can maintain students' engagement and attention while assuring the teacher that the lesson taught is indeed understood by the audience [2]. Finally, a quiz near the end of the lecture would allow students to review the day's class and increase their retention.

While pen-and-paper quiz activities are common and easily administered, computer-supported quiz activities significantly increase the learning benefits, by providing personalized and customizable information in real-time [3]. Timely feedback and the ability to repeat the quiz activity multiple times may offer additional opportunities for self-reflection and self-assessment to the students [4–6].

The interested teacher can find a range of freely available tools that support the design and implementation of quiz activities in different educational contexts. Even though the functionalities offered by these tools may differ significantly, the underline remains the same, specifically to ask the student to find the correct answer(s) out of a set of possible answers to a question. A typical example of such a tool is Socrative[1]. Apart from offering an easy way to use menus to create and use quizzes, Socrative also supports tracking students' progress through a series of quiz activities, allowing the teacher to assess the progress made during a semester. Following a different approach, PeerWise[2] is based on student-generated questions. In other words, the students have to author interesting, challenging, and well-phrased questions. At the same time, they can answer and review the quality and difficulty of questions submitted by their peers. PeerWise is a widely used tool, and part of its success is arguably based on the fact that it incorporates gamification in the form of leaderboards and badges [7]. Similarly, Kahoot[3] offers a variety of quiz types, apart from multiple-choice questions, such as fill-in-the-blanks, matching words, etc. The design of Kahoot is significantly based on game elements, enhancing also competition between the students.

The present study aims at exploring the potential of multiple-choice quiz activities in formative assessment, in conjunction with the inclusion of both objective and subjective metrics in the feedback information the quiz tool provides to the students. Finally, this paper is an extended version of [1], presented at the 9th International Conference on Computer Supported Education.

---

[1] http://www.socrative.com/.

[2] https://peerwise.cs.auckland.ac.nz/.

[3] http://getkahoot.com.

2 Background

2.1 Quiz and Group Awareness

One element that Socrative, Kahoot, and Peerwise have in common is that students can receive feedback information from both the teacher and fellow students. For example, feedback coming from the teacher can appear as pre-entered hints pointing to the correct choice, or as explanations on why a choice may be wrong/correct. Feedback based on fellow students usually presents information about peers' activity, including average scores of a group of people (e.g., the whole class), distribution of class population into the different choices, etc. Providing feedback information based on peers' activity allows the students to compare their own knowledge to their peers'. According to Bodemer [8], these comparisons support group awareness and are beneficial to students' learning. Yet, the student-based feedback the user receives in all three quiz tools provides information solely on the percentage of students that selected each question choice. We argue that although the percentage metric is widely used, easy to understand, and to a great degree useful for the students, it provides information only on a surface level, without being able to include qualitative information on the groups of people that selected each choice. Metrics that could further describe relevant characteristics of fellow peers could be essential for students, in terms of comparison and self-assessment.

Group awareness has already been identified as an important design aspect for educational technology tools, with several studies describing the learning benefits that emerge when students are able to compare and analyze peer activity (e.g., [9, 10], for a review). One can find two different definitions of the term in the literature. Cognitive group awareness refers to information that allows the students to understand the level of knowledge their peers have attained, while social group awareness refers to information that depicts peers' activity in the group [11]. In the context of the current study, the focus is on cognitive group awareness with the feedback metrics used aiming at providing an aggregated picture of the group knowledge, with the term "group" referring to the whole class population.

The present study combines objective and subjective metrics in an effort to present peer characteristics and support group awareness. Thus, in addition to the objective percentage metric, the feedback that the students receive includes subjective, self-reported, information on peers' level of confidence and preparation. Previous studies highlight the learning gains that such a combination of objective and subjective metrics offers to the students (e.g., [12, 13]). For example, previous research shows that asking students to denote how confident they feel about their answers to a quiz can significantly improve their metacognition [5].

We maintain that the inclusion of both objective and subjective metrics in the feedback information provided to the students could offer a better picture on peers' knowledge. We expect that this, in turn, could increase knowledge group awareness and, eventually, students' performance.

2.2 Student Learning and Engagement

Literature abounds with research evidence on the ways the students' engagement and performance are positively affected by quiz activities. For example, Méndez-Coca and Slisko [14] reported that the use of Socrative made students more engaged in the learning activity. In addition, students explicitly expressed positive attitudes towards the approach, underlining that Socrative increased their motivation to actively participate in the class and enhanced their communication with their fellow students. The beneficial impact of quizzes on peer interaction could be linked to the learning gains students reap by externalizing their knowledge. Of course, the process of answering closed-type, multiple-choice, questions does not provide the same opportunities for knowledge externalization as a written task that engages the students into formulating and structuring valid arguments. Nevertheless, the process of making one's opinions explicit can still offer the basis for meaningful peer interaction [15]. To promote dialogue between students, Méndez-Coca and Slisko [14] formed groups of students with different opinions, thus creating the opportunities for meaningful discourse.

Arguably, one of the main advantages of quiz activities is the overall positive attitudes students show towards them. In their study, DiBattista et al. [16] focused on students' attitudes by comparing two multiple-choice testing settings. In the first one, students were receiving immediate system feedback, while in the second the multiple-choice testing was conducted with pen-and-paper. Research data provided overwhelming evidence that students preferred the first setting, even though further data analysis showed that the performance and personal characteristics of students in the two settings were comparable.

Another important advantage of quiz activities is their ability to incorporate game elements in their design. It is common for quiz activities that are administered inside the classroom to showcase aspects of gamification [17]. Typical examples of gamification are complex grading systems (e.g., positive/negative/weighted grades), tier or karma points (that can be used to unlock functionalities or other rewards), badges (that denote significant achievements, such as a streak of correct answers), leaderboard (that show the high-achievers in a group), and so on. It is important to note that these game elements are not linked to the learning process itself. In other words, receiving a badge does not provide additional scaffolding to the student, nor changes the studying conditions. Nevertheless, the positive impact of game elements on student engagement has been reported multiple times in the literature (e.g., [7, 18]). It is also worth noting that in order to retain students' engagement in a quiz, the design should extended beyond game elements, since, as Wang [6] suggested, the engagement that is based on the novelty effect of superficial awards should be expected to decrease over time. A rigorous instructional design will discourage students from "gaming the system" [19] or disengaging because of the injection of unproductive peer competition in the learning process [20].

2.3 Study Motivation

The motivation for this study was our effort to improve the feedback information the students receive in closed-type, multiple-choice quizzes that allow for a revision phase.

In this study, the feedback information based on the objective percentage metrics is enriched with two self-reported (thus, subjective) metrics that could paint a more detailed picture on the class knowledge. The preparation metric shows students' opinions on how prepared they feel just *before* they participate in the quiz. The confidence metric on the other hand shows how certain students are that they have selected the correct choice *after* answering each question. Thus, the preparation metric is based on a single question answered before the quiz is administered, while the confidence metric is the average of the confidence scores submitted by the student after answering each of the eight questions of the weekly quiz.

It is important to note here that this study is a part of a larger research effort that explores the potential of closed-type formative assessment tools in increasing student engagement and performance in different educational contexts. A necessary requirement for the successful implementation of such an approach is to keep the overhead for the teacher at a minimum level. Furthermore, another aspect of the long-term research effort is to evaluate how a series of quiz activities could eventually provide enough information for the compilation of knowledge profiles for the students and how these profiles could positively affect knowledge group awareness in collaborative learning activities (e.g., group assignments). However, the discussion of the long-term research plan extends outside the scope of the present paper.

3 Method

3.1 Participants and Domain

The subject domain of our study was the "Business Development with Information Systems – BDIS" course. Usually, undergraduate students during their second year (third semester) of studies are enrolled in BDIS. The course offers five credit units (i.e., ECTS) to participants and is part of the "Bachelor's Degree Programme in Economics and Business Administration" in the Department of Management. The course is taught in parallel in both Danish and English. For the purpose of this study, we focused only on the English version. The intended learning objectives of the course are to engage students in the analysis, evaluation, and application of models based on Information Systems, Decision Making, and Business Management domains in a challenging case-study that usually lasts throughout the academic semester. As a common practice in the university the study was conducted in, the lecture material (i.e., relevant literature, lecture notes, external links) was available online to the students, a week prior the respective lecture. Studying the course material beforehand is not mandatory, but encouraged, with students spending time preparing for the upcoming lecture at different degrees. The assessment process of the course includes a case-study group assignment with a written case report as an outcome, and individual final oral examination in which students are required to elaborate on the case analysis and conceptual knowledge of the domain.

The course duration is 14 weeks and includes weekly 2 h lectures in an auditorium. The average number of enrolled students each year is approximately 180. The actual number of students present during lectures, though, fluctuates significantly each week, since attendance is not mandatory. Even though all students were invited to participate in the study, we only used data collected from students that attended all lectures during the study period. Students that were present in only some of the lecture during the study period were still able to participate, but their data were excluded from the analysis. At the end, the findings of the study were based on a sample of 91 sophomore students. The students were distributed randomly into one of four treatment groups (see next Section) by the system at the time of their first login. Student distribution into the four groups was:

- Control: 27 students;
- Confidence: 22 students;
- Preparation: 22 students;
- Both: 20 students.

Students' participation was voluntary, and the activity was not part of students' formal assessment in the course.

3.2 The Saga System

The study was conducted on the "Self-Assessment/Group Awareness – SAGA" online quiz system that was designed and developed by the research team of this study. SAGA has a long-term scope, being the platform we are going to use to explore the different aspects of quiz activities in a series of studies. Despite the variety of available online quiz tools, no system was able to support the research design of the current study. By creating our own system we were able to tailor its functionality to our research goals and achieve higher degrees of flexibility and customization, using different feedback metrics for different groups and monitoring student activity.

Students in SAGA start their activity by logging in and answering a question regarding the amount of time they spend during the week studying the material of the lecture they are currently attending. The preparation question was stated as follows:

Some of the teaching material for today's class became available during the last week.

Using a scale from '1: Not at all' to '5: I have read it thoroughly', how much time did you spent preparing for today's class?

Students' answer in this question was the only entry point for the preparation metric that was used later in the revision phase. It was not possible to test whether students' answers in the preparation question were accurate. Nevertheless, this metric could provide an estimate on how students self-assess their preparation. In addition, this metric was used later to analyze whether the level of preparation, as self-reported by the students, was correlated with their actual performance in the quiz.

Next, students moved on to the initial part of the quiz activity, answering a series of eight multiple-choice questions. Each question and the accompanying four choices had been previously inserted in the system by the course instructor. In all questions, there was only one correct answer.

For each question, students had to select one of the available choices and denote their level of confidence, before they would be allowed to continue to the next question. The confidence question appearing under each question was stated as follows:

> *Using a scale from '1: Not at all' to '5: Very confident', note how confident you are that you have selected the correct answer.*

Similarly to preparation, the question regarding confidence was self-reported and as such we were not able to assess its accuracy. However, we were able to analyze whether students' self-assessment was correlated to their performance. The confidence metric was calculated for each student as the mean value of the 8 answers the student provided in the confidence question in the eight quiz questions.

Students had to answer all 8 questions of the quiz to move to the next phase, revision. During the revision phase, the students were able to browse once again all the questions and decide whether or not to revise their initial answers. To assist students in their decisions, the system was providing feedback based on the class activity during the initial phase. The feedback information was different for each group in the study, compiled with a different combination of the percentage, preparation, and confidence metrics (Fig. 1):

- Control: the percentage of student in the class that selected each option;
- Confidence: the percentage and the average confidence score of students that selected each option;
- Preparation: the percentage and the average preparation score of students that selected each option;
- Both: the percentage, the average confidence, and the average preparation scores of students that selected each option.

Each metric was calculated against the whole classroom population. Thus, the value of a feedback metric that was appearing in different groups was the same. During revision, the students were also able to change their initial answers to the respective confidence questions. Thus, even in the case where students choose not to revise an initial answer, they can still change their self-reported confidence level. This could be useful, for example, in cases where feedback reinforced (or challenged) a student's perspective on which the correct answer was. After finishing the revision phase, the students were able to see their scores and the correct answers.

This was the end of the quiz activity. Next, the teacher was able to decide whether to discuss the correct answers with the students right away or revisit them at a later stage during the lecture that was about to start. It is worth noting at this point that throughout the quiz activity, the teacher was able to monitor students' activity in real time and initiate the next phase of the process. In addition, the teacher had access to an aggregated view of the class performance in each phase and could share this view while discussing the correct answers after the quiz had finished.

3.3 Process and Study Conditions

The study took place during the Fall semester of 2016 and lasted five weeks in total, with the first four weeks being used for typical weekly quizzes related to the respective

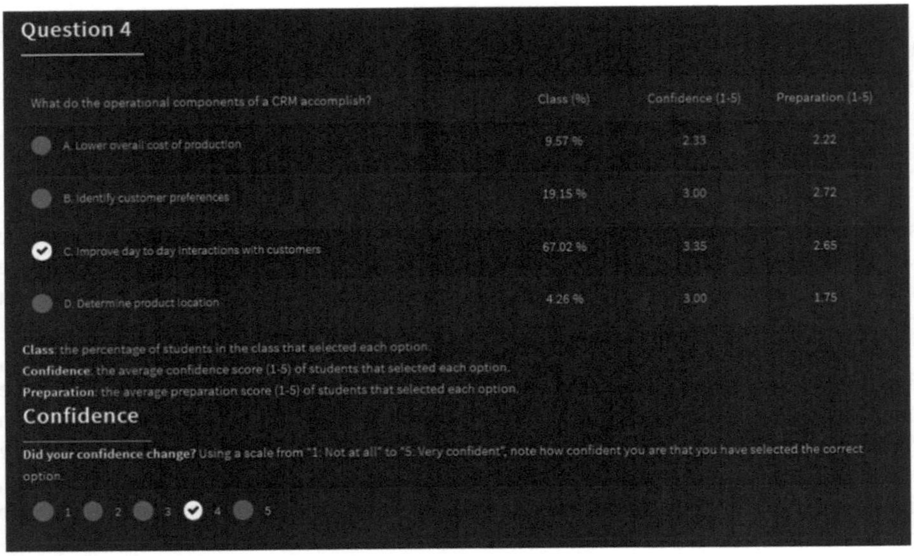

Fig. 1. Screenshot of the SAGA system during the revision phase for students in the both group – all metrics (percentage, confidence, and preparation) are available [1].

lectures, and the last week used for a retention quiz and the survey questionnaire of the whole activity.

In a typical weekly quiz, the students had to login to the SAGA tool and go through the three phases of the process, namely provide initial answers to the eight multiple-choice questions, revise their initial answers based on the feedback they receive, see the correct answers and discuss them with the teacher. We informed participating students of the research scope of the activity, clarifying that their placement into a study group is random, that their performance will not have an impact on their assessment in the course (this was also guaranteed by the course formal regulations), and that they may receive different information by the SAGA tool during the activity.

The weekly quiz was administered during the first 20 min of the 2 h lecture session. Keeping the quiz activity short was an important requirement in our design, since the goal was not to disrupt the teacher's lecture plan. In addition, the quiz activity should support students' learning and engagement in the course, without requiring significant additional effort or resources from the teacher (e.g., preparation and administration of the quiz). The 20 min used for the quiz activity were allocated to the three phases of the process as such: ten minutes for the initial phase, five minutes to reflect on the received feedback and perform the revision, and five minutes to check the correct answers and discuss them with the teacher. All students were at the same phase at any point during the activity, while the next phase could be activated earlier than planned, in case all students had finished the current activity.

The retention quiz took place during the fifth week of the activity and was not previously announced to the students. On the contrary, the students were expecting the typical weekly quiz for the lecture that was about to start. The retention quiz included a selection of 16 questions that had been previously used in the weekly quizzes. The quiz was followed by a questionnaire that included both open and closed-type questions, asking students to share their opinions regarding the usefulness of the different feedback metrics, the impact of the quiz activities on the amount of effort they put in preparing for the lectures, and the overall improvement of the SAGA tool and the quiz process. Lastly, the students were asked to fill in the Scale for Social Comparison Orientation (SSCO) [21, 22]. The SSCO instrument contains 11 statements focused on how often students compare themselves with others. Comparison could refer to students' feelings, opinions, abilities, etc. and it is not characterized as "good" or "bad" by the instrument. Since the research goal during the fifth week of the activity was to measure students' retention, opinions, and SSCO profile, the quiz phase did not have the revision phase. Instead, students submitted their initial answers to the retention quiz, then filled in the survey and the SSCO instrument, and saw their scores and the correct answers at the end of the activity.

The students participated in every aspect of the activity individually. Participation was anonymous and no personal information was recorded on maintained by SAGA or the research team. Finally, the study conditions were identical for all students in the study, apart from the different feedback information the four groups received during the revision phase.

3.4 Research Design

The study followed a between-subjects 2 × 2 factorial design with the combination of feedback metrics in each group being the independent variable of the study (Table 1).

The dependent variables of the study were students' performance on the quizzes (i.e., initial and revision scores for weekly, and initial score for retention) and their responses on the survey questionnaire and on the SSCO instrument.

3.5 Data Collection and Analysis

For all the statistical tests performed in the study, the level of significance was chosen at 0.05. For the analysis of students' performance in the quizzes (weekly and retention) and their responses in the SSCO instrument, we used parametric tests. On the contrary, non-parametric tests were used for the analysis of students' responses in the survey questionnaire. The reason for this was that test assumption analysis showed that the normal distribution criterion was violated for that dataset.

Table 1. Levels of independent variables and student groups [1].

		Confidence feedback	
		No	Yes
Preparation feedback	No	Control	Confidence
	Yes	Preparation	Both

Each week, we compared students' performance in the four groups, analyzing both the dataset of each week and the aggregated dataset of all weeks up to that point. Thus, at the end of the fourth week, our dataset included information on all 32 questions used. The retention quiz dataset was analyzed separately from the weekly quizzes, since the research goals and the study design was different. In addition, at the end of the fourth week, another analysis took place, taking into account only a subset of the total 32 weekly questions. This subset included only questions that students found challenging. In other words, we were not able to know at the beginning of the study which of the questions submitted by the teacher would be difficult for the students. As expected, there were some questions in which the vast majority of the students got the correct answer even during the initial phase of the quiz. This meant that the additional feedback provided in the revision phase (i.e., confidence and preparation metrics) had little effect on students' decision, since the percentage metric was showing clearly that there was a strong consensus in the classroom on the correct answer. So, the subset analysis focused only on the questions in which the percentage information alone was not able to direct the students to the correct answer. To phrase it differently, the challenging questions subset included the questions where there was a somewhat balanced distribution of students into the four question choices.

We mentioned earlier that the percentage metric is widely used in quiz tools. We expected that the students in this study would rely primarily on this percentage information before checking how confident or prepared the students under each question choice were. Thus, we argue that the impact of the two newly introduced metrics could be visible in cases in which the percentage information alone could not "clearly" point to the correct choice.

To maintain a level of objectivity, we agreed on a definition of what constitutes a "clear" case and we examined our dataset after the fourth week to identify the challenging questions. Our definition for "clear" cases for the percentage metric included two mandatory conditions:

- The correct choice was selected by at least 50% of the students;
- The correct choice had a least 20 points difference from the second most selected choice.

These two conditions ensured that the majority of the students selected the correct choice during the initial phase and that there was no clear alternative. For example, if in a question the choice A was selected by 55% of the students and choice B was selected by 40% of the students, then the question would be identified as challenging, since student population appeared split. As such, the subset included questions in which the percentage metric was either pointing to a wrong choice (e.g., the most favorite choice was wrong) or the distribution of selected answers was ambiguous (e.g., students were divided between two or more choices).

Using this definition, we identified 13 challenging questions. Since we did not anticipate which of the questions might be challenging during the design phase, the distribution of these questions in the four weekly quizzes was unbalanced: four challenging questions in the first week, five in the second, one from the third, and three from the fourth. Eventually, the impact of the confidence and preparation metrics on student performance was analyzed using this subset.

We used these 13 challenging questions and we added three more that were close to be categorized as challenging to compile the list of the 16 questions used in the retention quiz. Adding these three questions allowed us to create a longer and somewhat balanced quiz that included four questions from the first week, five from the second, three from the third, and four from the fourth.

4 Results

4.1 Weekly Quizzes

Table 2 presents students' performance in the four weekly quizzes.

Table 2. Students' performance in the four weekly quizzes [1].

	Control			Confidence			Preparation			Both		
	M	*SD*	n	M	*SD*	n	M	*SD*	n	M	*SD*	n
Week 1												
Initial	4.58	*(1.53)*	27	4.48	*(1.19)*	22	4.15	*(2.34)*	22	4.85	*(1.73)*	20
Revision	6.25	*(1.32)*	27	6.40	*(1.29)*	22	5.62	*(2.22)*	22	6.46	*(1.39)*	20
Week 2												
Initial	3.50	*(1.27)*	27	3.64	*(1.17)*	22	4.13	*(1.14)*	22	4.06	*(1.43)*	20
Revision	4.35	*(0.87)*	27	4.01	*(1.34)*	22	4.69	*(0.94)*	22	4.50	*(1.04)*	20
Week 3												
Initial	5.52	*(1.64)*	27	5.19	*(1.74)*	22	5.43	*(1.59)*	22	5.09	*(1.63)*	20
Revision	6.87	*(1.10)*	27	7.08	*(1.38)*	22	7.00	*(1.00)*	22	7.05	*(1.25)*	20
Week 4												
Initial	3.73	*(1.98)*	27	3.52	*(1.37)*	22	4.14	*(1.83)*	22	4.05	*(1.43)*	20
Revision	5.76	*(1.04)*	27	5.26	*(1.05)*	22	6.14	*(1.15)*	22	6.06	*(1.21)*	20

It is obvious that there is no apparent pattern in students' performance. On the contrary, the differences observed on the initial scores of a group in different weeks indicate different levels of difficulty for the weekly test, or different levels of preparation. Despite our effort to have quizzes of similar difficulty each week, it is possible that students' understanding of the topics covered in the associated reading material available to them during the week differed. Similarly, students' preparation level refers to their perceived readiness to answer questions on the lecture's topics. The question about preparation refers to the amount of effort spent by the students, but not on whether this effort was spent effectively on understanding the learning material.

According to the two-way analysis of variance (two-way ANOVA) we performed, the four groups were comparable in the initial phase of the quiz in all four weekly quizzes ($p > 0.05$). Similarly, the results of the two-way analysis of covariance (two-way ANCOVA), when using students' initial phase scores as covariate, showed that the four groups also performed the same in the revision phase, over all four weeks ($p > 0.05$). Regarding revision, the paired-samples t-test showed that all student groups improved significantly from the initial to the revision phase, in all four quizzes.

4.2 Subset Performance

Table 3 presents students' performance in the subset of the 13 challenging questions.

Table 3. Students' performance in the 13 challenging questions.

Challenging	Control			Confidence			Preparation			Both		
	M	*SD*	n	M	*SD*	n	M	*SD*	n	M	*SD*	n
Initial	4.44	*(4.34)*	27	3.82	*(3.59)*	22	5.27	*(3.98)*	22	4.40	*(2.87)*	20
Revision	4.00	*(4.29)*	27	4.90	*(3.00)*	22	6.36	*(4.22)*	22	6.60	*(3.73)*	20

*$p < 0.05$

Performing a question-by-question qualitative analysis, we found out that students relied first and foremost on the percentage metric. Specifically, the percentage of the most popular choice during the initial phase of the quiz was increasing during the revision phase. Notably, this was happening even in cases in which the most popular choice during the initial phase was wrong. By using our definition of "clear" cases, we found out that the percentage metric was pointing to a specific correct choice in 24 out of the 32 questions available in the four weekly quizzes. However, in five cases, the percentage metric was pointing at a wrong choice. Thus, the eight questions in which students' distribution in the four question choices was split, and the five questions in which the percentage metric was pointing at a wrong choice, formed the subset of the 13 challenging questions we mentioned earlier.

We argue that the additional feedback metrics would be more useful to the students for this subset of questions. By transferring the "clear" case definition to the confidence and preparation metrics, we discovered that the confidence metric was pointing at the correct choice in eight of the challenging questions, while the preparation metric was doing the same for seven of the challenging questions.

We analyzed groups' improvement from the initial to the revision phase of the study, using paired-samples t-test. Results showed that only the Control group did not manage to improve its performance. On the contrary, Confidence ($t [21] = 2.324$, $p = 0.030$, $d = 0.720$), Preparation ($t[24] = 2.027$, $p = 0.046$, $d = 0.630$), and Both ($t [19] = 2.979$, $p = 0.008$, $d = 0.970$) groups improved significantly. Two-way ANCOVA, using initial phase scores as a covariate, showed a significant main effect for the confidence ($F(1,86) = 4.115$, $p = 0.046$, $\eta^2 = 0.046$) and preparation ($F(1,86) = 7.153$, $p = 0.009$, $\eta^2 = 0.077$) metrics, but not for their interaction ($p > 0.05$).

4.3 Retention Test

Table 4 presents students' performance in the retention quiz. The results of the two-way ANOVA revealed no significant difference in performance of the four groups in the retention test ($p > 0.05$).

Table 4. Students' performance in the retention quiz.

Retention	Control			Confidence			Preparation			Both		
	M	*SD*	n	M	*SD*	n	M	*SD*	n	M	*SD*	n
Initial	10.00	*(3.23)*	27	10.86	*(2.14)*	22	10.68	*(3.24)*	22	10.80	*(3.2)*	20

4.4 Student Opinions and Behavior

Analysis of the internal consistency of the SSCO instrument used to record students' social comparison treats showed that the reliability of the instrument was mediocre (Cronbach's $\alpha = 0.635$) and lower than it is usually reported in the literature. Students' SSCO score in all groups were comparable. In addition, the SSCO score was not correlated to the total number of revisions performed, the total number of correct/wrong revisions performed, the initial/revised performance, nor the initial/revised confidence values.

Table 5 shows students' opinions on the most important questions of the survey questionnaire administered at the end of the study. The results of the Kruskal-Wallis and Mann-Whitney tests revealed no significant differences between the four groups ($p > 0.05$). Corroborating our question-by-question analysis, students stated that the percentage metric was the most useful metric for them during the revision phase of the study (M = 3.62, SD = 1.01). The second most useful feedback metric, according to students, was the level of confidence (M = 3.32, SD = 1.20), and the third was the level of preparation (M = 2.64, SD = 1.43).

We also asked students to suggest additional feedback metrics that could have been useful for them. Students mentioned past performance (M = 3.20, SD = 1.14), argumentation (M = 3.15, SD = 1.15), and peer communication (M = 2.87, SD = 1.19). The level of confidence (M = 3.35, SD = 1.11) and preparation (M = 3.15, SD = 1.19) were also included in the list, by students that did not have access to these metrics during the current study. Regarding the three new metrics suggested by the students, past performance refers to the average score a student received in previous weekly quizzes, argumentation refers to students' ability to read/write anonymous justifications for the choices, and peer communication refers to chatting anonymously with peers online for a brief period of time.

Students were asked to estimate whether their participation in the weekly quizzes motivated them to increase the amount of time they spent preparing each week for the upcoming lecture (Q1). Result analysis showed no significant different between the four groups ($p > 0.05$), with students having diverging opinions (M = 2.49, SD = 1.28). Nevertheless, students' answers in the preparation question in the four weekly quizzes and the retention test revealed a significant increase of the preparation time during the study. The results of the analysis of variance, with repeated measures with a Greenhouse-Geisser correction (sphericity assumption was violated), showed that the mean value for the preparation level were statistically significantly different ($F(3.306, 247.966) = 44.128$, $p = 0.00$, $\eta^2 = 0.370$). Figure 2 presents the average preparation score for 91 participating students in each week of the study.

Table 5. Students' responses in the questionnaire. Scale – 1: Not at all; 5: Very much [1].

Control *n* = 27		Confidence *n* = 22		Preparation *n* = 22		Both *n* = 20		Total *n* = 91	
M	*SD*	M	*SD*	M	*SD*	M	*SD*	M	*SD*
Q1. Has the quiz made you spend more time preparing during the week for each lecture?									
2.17	*(1.04)*	2.90	*(1.17)*	2.68	*(1.39)*	2.17	*(1.37)*	2.49	*(1.28)*
Q2. Do you find the percentage values you see useful in choosing your final responses?									
3.72	*(0.89)*	3.43	*(0.87)*	3.73	*(1.12)*	3.61	*(1.15)*	3.62	*(1.01)*
Q3. Do find the confidence values you see useful in choosing your final responses?									
–	–	3.33	*(1.19)*	–	–	3.30	*(1.25)*	3.32	*(1.21)*
Q4. Do find the preparation values you see useful in choosing your final responses?									
–	–	–	–	2.59	*(1.53)*	2.70	*(1.39)*	2.64	*(1.44)*
Q5. How useful do you think the confidence level (confidence level of fellow students that selected each option) would be for you in choosing your final answers?									
3.61	*(0.85)*	–	–	3.14	*(1.28)*	–	–	3.35	*(1.12)*
Q6. How useful do you think the preparation level (average preparation level of fellow students that selected each option) would be for you in choosing your final answers?									
3.28	*(1.22)*	3.05	*(1.20)*	–	–	–	–	3.15	*(1.20)*
Q7. How useful do you think the past performance (average past scores – based on previous weeks – of fellow students that selected each option) would be for you in choosing your final answers?									
3.83	*(0.85)*	2.95	*(1.28)*	3.14	*(1.28)*	2.00	*(0.95)*	3.20	*(1.14)*
Q8. How useful do you think argumentation (a short argument for each option, written by a fellow student – anonymity remains) would be for you in choosing your final answers?									
2.72	*(1.36)*	3.05	*(0.97)*	3.18	*(1.25)*	3.22	*(1.04)*	3.06	*(1.15)*
Q9. How useful do you think peer communication (opportunity to briefly text anonymously with fellow students) would be for you in choosing your final answers?									
2.78	*(1.06)*	2.95	*(1.16)*	2.95	*(1.49)*	2.78	*(1.08)*	2.87	*(1.20)*

As expected, students' confidence increased significantly from the initial to the revision phase in all four weeks, for all four study groups ($p < 0.05$). In addition, correlation analysis showed that confidence, preparation, and initial performance scores were all significantly correlated (Pearson's bivariate correlation coefficient) ($p < 0.01$). This indicates that the students were accurate in estimating their levels of preparation and confidence, since the most prepared were also the most confident students, in addition to having higher initial phase scores.

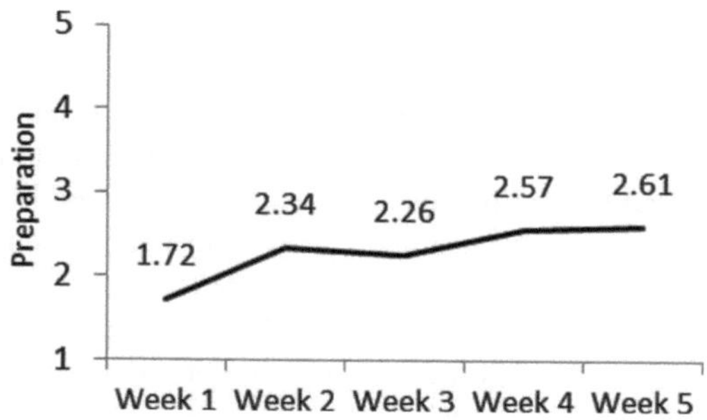

Fig. 2. Student preparation [1].

Student statements in the open-ended questions of the survey painted a strongly positive picture, regarding students' attitudes towards the activity. Some of the statements recorded are the following:

Nice program design, well-put questions.

The quiz is a good starting point for the lectures. However it should be kept short.

I really like that you asked us about these things. I am a huge fan of giving feedback and striving for improvement. I am a highly competitive person and the quizzes are compelling to me.

Regarding suggestions for improvement in future versions of the SAGA tool, students suggested (student's statement in quotation marks):

- Gamification: "Maybe a leaderboard/high score list".
- Information on the wrong answers: "It might be nice to know which answers we already got wrong".
- Additional information on peers: "How many lectures the persons have participated in".
- Feedback from a specific group of people: "I would like to see my study-group's feedback".
- Splitting the two phases of the quiz before and after the lecture: "Reading the actual curriculum before the class OR repeat the second phase [i.e., revision] of the quiz at the end of the class to actually see if we are taking something out of the lecture".

Finally, analysis of the SAGA log files showed that although the total allocated time for a weekly quiz was 20 min (i.e., 10 min for the initial phase, five minutes for the revision, and five minutes for the discussion), the actual time students needed on average was significantly lower. Specifically, students used approximately six minutes for the initial phase and four minutes for the revision. This finding is important, since one of the activity requirements was to keep it short and avoid disrupting the lecture plan. In addition, this allowed more time to the teacher to discuss the questions and students' performance.

5 Discussion

The weekly quiz analysis showed that the four student groups were comparable throughout the activity. As we have already mentioned, this should have been expected up to a point, since the additional feedback information provided by the confidence and preparation metrics becomes more useful in cases where the percentage metric alone is not enough to guide the students. A certain challenge for designing the current activity was to predict the number of cases where the additional feedback would be important. Despite the effort to have weekly quizzes of similar difficulty, factors such as the complexity of the topics covered each week, students' preparation, etc. affected students' scores in the initial phase, thus determining to a great degree the need for additional feedback. As such, the low number of challenging questions identified each week was not enough to create a significant difference between student groups in the weekly quizzes.

At first glance, one could expect that the difference observed in the subset performance would also be evident in the retention quiz. However, the lack of any significant difference in the retention test can be easily explained. The last phase of the activity each week was the discussion between the teacher and the students on the correct answers and students' performance. In other words, the teacher had plenty of time during the lecture to revisit the questions used in the weekly quiz and provide further explanations to students about the correct choice. The weekly quizzes are a snapshot of students' knowledge just before the day's lecture. We expect that this picture was significantly different at the end of the two-hour lecture that followed our activity. Thus, it makes sense that by the fifth week of the activity, all students had acquired the same level of knowledge. Groups' performance in the retention test was not just comparable; it was overwhelmingly satisfactory, with more than 10% of the student population achieving a perfect score (i.e. 16/16).

By analyzing each question separately, it was easy to figure out that students relied primarily on the percentage metric during the revision phase. It was clear that students changed their initial answers to the most popular question choice, in cases where the percentage metric was pointing to a specific choice. Students' trust on the percentage metric was so strong that in several cases, students that had selected the correct choice during the initial phase, revised their answers to the most popular, but incorrect, choice during the revision phase. However, despite some misleading cases, the percentage metric is still a very useful way to provide feedback on class knowledge. In our study, the percentage feedback was pointing at the correct choice in 19 out of the 32 total questions of the weekly quizzes. Additional benefits of using the percentage metric are the fact that it is objective and commonly used – thus familiar and easily understood by the students. However, our argument is that the percentage metric cannot provide any qualitative information on the student population under each question choice.

This qualitative information could be offered by metrics such as the level of confidence and preparation. The shortcoming of these two metrics is that they are self-reported (thus subjective) and their validity is affected by students' metacognitive ability to self-assess their level of confidence and preparation. In the current study, preparation, confidence, and initial performance were correlated, suggesting that our students were accurate in their assessment. This may not be the case in a different context, in which student metacognition or their engagement (i.e., time spent on preparation) in the course is low. One question that arises is how students view these two metrics. In our survey, students expressed a positive opinion about the percentage and confidence metrics, while they had diverging views on the usefulness of the preparation metric. A possible explanation could be that students relied more on confidence because it depicted students' understanding after answering a question, while the preparation question was answered before the quiz had started.

Statistical analysis showed clearly that students that received any combination of the two additional feedback metrics were able to significantly outperform the Control group that received only percentage feedback. Thus, the current study provides empirical evidence on the potential of integrating simple subjective metrics, such as the levels of confidence and preparation, in quiz activity, in order to provide a more detailed picture on class knowledge.

Regarding students' attitudes towards the activity, analysis of the SSCO instrument showed that social comparison was not an issue in this study, since no correlation was found between the SSCO score and any other major study variable (e.g., number of revisions performed, initial/revised performance, etc.). However, the low recorded reliability of the tool (i.e., Cronbach's $\alpha = 0.635$) may also be the reason for this. It can only be hypothesized that, in a different context, students' social comparison traits could also affect their behavior in an activity that engages them in comparing their knowledge with that of the whole class.

A very encouraging finding, in favor of the quiz activity, is that despite students' responses in the survey, it seems that their engagement increased significantly during the study. This finding is linked to the learning benefits quiz activities may have on a course in general and it is not attributed to a certain study condition, since it is evident in all four groups.

Overall, students expressed a positive opinion towards the activity, offering also useful suggestions for improvement. Out of these suggestions, students in the Control and Preparation groups asked for the inclusion of the confidence metric in the feedback. Past performance metric was also a popular suggestion, indicating that students are in favor of objective metrics. Finally, it is worth noting that, although they were the least desirable, reading/writing anonymous arguments for each question choice and direct anonymous peer texting were both evaluated positively.

6 Conclusions

This study provided empirical evidence on the potential of combining subjective metrics with widely used objective metrics, such as the percentage, in order to support students in closed-type quiz activities that include a revision phase. The implication for designers and teachers is that subjective metrics can be used effectively to get a better picture of class knowledge and assist students in improving their performance. The three feedback metrics used in this study provide information on three different questions a student may ask in a quiz activity: What do the others say (percentage)?

How much have they studied (preparation)? How confident are they of their answers (confidence)?

Future research will focus on including additional metrics and addressing some of the limitations of this study. As such, future studies are planned with larger audiences, different subject matters, and multimodality in representation of the metric information (e.g., combination of text with graphs and color schemes). Finally, as we have repeatedly mentioned, another goal of this series of studies is to analyze the effect of short quizzes on student engagement and performance. As such, the goal of a future study will be to compare classes with and without the quiz activities.

Acknowledgements. This work has been partially funded by a Starting Grant from AUFF (Aarhus Universitets Forskningsfond), titled "Innovative and Emerging Technologies in Education".

References

1. Papadopoulos, P.M., Natsis, A., Obwegeser, A.: Improving the quiz: student preparation and confidence as feedback metrics. In: The Proceedings of the 9th International Conference on Computer Supported Education – CSEDU 2017, Porto, Portugal (2017, in press)
2. Buil, I., Catalán, S., Martínez, E.: Do clickers enhance learning? A control-value theory approach. Comput. Educ. **103**, 170–182 (2016)
3. Sosa, G.W., Berger, D.E., Saw, A.T., Mary, J.C.: Effectiveness of computer-assisted instruction in statistics: a meta-analysis. Rev. Educ. Res. **81**(1), 97–128 (2011)
4. Bransford, J.D., Brown, A., Cocking, R.: How People Learn: Mind, Brain, Experience and School. National Academy Press, Washington (2000)
5. Kleitman, S., Costa, D.S.J.: The role of a novel formative assessment tool (Stats-mIQ) and individual differences in real-life academic performance. Learn. Individ. Diff. **29**, 150–161 (2014)
6. Wang, T.-H.: Web-based quiz-game-like formative assessment: development and evaluation. Comput. Educ. **51**(3), 1247–1263 (2008)
7. Denny, P.: The effect of virtual achievements on student engagement. In: Proceedings of the SIGCHI Conference on Human Factors in Computing Systems (CHI 2013), pp. 763–772. ACM, New York (2013)
8. Bodemer, D.: Tacit guidance for collaborative multimedia learning. Comput. Hum. Behav. **27**(3), 1079–1086 (2011)
9. Janssen, J., Bodemer, D.: Coordinated computer-supported collaborative learning: awareness and awareness tools. Educ. Psychol. **48**(1), 40–55 (2013)
10. Lin, J.-W., Mai, L.-J., Lai, Y.-C.: Peer interaction and social network analysis of online communities with the support of awareness of different contexts. Int. J. Comput. Supp. Collab. Learn. **10**(2), 139–159 (2015)
11. Buder, J.: Group awareness tools for learning: current and future directions. Comput. Hum. Behav. **27**(3), 1114–1117 (2011)
12. Erkens, M., Schlottbom, P., Bodemer, D.: Qualitative and quantitative information in cognitive group awareness tools: impact on collaborative learning. In: Looi, C.-K., Polman, J., Cress, U., Reimann, P. (eds.) Transforming Learning, Empowering Learners: 12th International Conference of the Learning Sciences, pp. 458–465. International Society of the Learning Sciences, Singapore (2016)

13. Schnaubert, L., Bodemer, D.: Subjective validity ratings to support shared knowledge construction in CSCL. In: Lindwall, O., Häkkinen, P., Koschmann, T., Tchounikine, P., Ludvigsen, S. (eds.) Exploring the Material Conditions of Learning: The Computer Supported Collaborative Learning (CSCL) Conference 2015, vol. 2, pp. 933–934. International Society of the Learning Sciences, Gothenburg (2015)
14. Méndez-Coca, D., Slisko, J.: Software Socrative and smartphones as tools for implementation of basic processes of active physics learning in classroom: an initial feasibility study with prospective teachers. Eur. J. Phys. Educ. **4**(2), 17–24 (2013)
15. Papadopoulos, P.M., Demetriadis, S.N., Weinberger, A.: "Make it explicit!": improving collaboration through increase of script coercion. J. Comput. Assist. Learn. **29**(4), 383–398 (2013)
16. DiBattista, D., Mitterer, J.O., Gosse, L.: Acceptance by undergraduates of the immediate feedback assessment technique for multiple-choice testing. Teach. High. Educ. **9**(1), 17–28 (2004)
17. Deterding, S., Dixon, D., Khaled, R., Nacke, L.: From game design elements to gamefulness: defining "gamification". In: Proceedings of the 15th International Academic MindTrek Conference: Envisioning Future Media Environments, pp. 9–15. ACM, New York (2011)
18. Wang, A.I.: The wear out effect of a game-based student response system. Comput. Educ. **82**, 217–227 (2015)
19. Baker, R., Walonoski, J., Heffernan, N., Roll, I., Corbett, A., Koedinger, K.: Why students engage in "gaming the system" behavior in interactive learning environments. J. Interact. Learn. Res. **19**(2), 185–224 (2008)
20. Papadopoulos, P.M., Lagkas, T., Demetriadis, S.N.: How revealing rankings affects student attitude and performance in a peer review learning environment. In: Zvacek, S., Restivo, M. T., Uhomoibhi, J., Helfert, M. (eds.) CSEDU 2015. CCIS, vol. 583, pp. 225–240. Springer, Cham (2016). https://doi.org/10.1007/978-3-319-29585-5_13
21. Gibbons, F.X., Buunk, B.P.: Individual differences in social comparison: the development of a scale of social comparison orientation. J. Pers. Soc. Psychol. **76**(1), 129–142 (1999)
22. Buunk, A.P., Gibbons, F.X.: Social comparison orientation: a new perspective on those who do and those who don't compare with others. In: Guimond, S. (ed.) Social Comparison and Social Psychology: Understanding Cognition, Intergroup Relations and Culture, pp. 15–33. Cambridge University Press, Cambridge (2006)

Preliminary Evaluations of AMBRE-KB, an Authoring Tool to Elicit Knowledge to Be Taught Without Programming

Awa Diattara[1,2(✉)], Nathalie Guin[1], Vanda Luengo[3,4], and Amélie Cordier[1]

[1] Université de Lyon, CNRS, Université Lyon 1, LIRIS, UMR 5205, 69622 Lyon, France
{awa.diattara,nathalie.guin, amelie.cordier}@liris.cnrs.fr
[2] Univ. Grenoble Alpes, LIG, 38000 Grenoble, France
[3] Sorbonne Université, UPMC Université Paris 6, 75005 Paris, France
[4] CNRS, UMR 7606, LIP6, 75005 Paris, France
vanda.luengo@lip6.fr

Abstract. This paper describes the design and preliminary evaluations of AMBRE-KB. The goal of this authoring tool is to assist authors to elicit knowledge needed to design AMBRE ITSs without any programming. Such ITS enable learners to acquire a specific method in problem-solving. AMBRE-KB is based on meta-models of knowledge to be acquired. It supports the acquisition of knowledge to be taught, and the description of problems to be solved. At the end of the knowledge elicitation process, it enables the author to have a feedback about the process by testing the resolution of problems described. We present the authoring process and the evaluations made in four domains: resolution of equations (1st and 2nd degree), the calculation of areas of geometric shapes, the plural of French nouns and the formation of French adverbs ending with '*ment*'.

Keywords: Authoring tool · Knowledge acquisition
Problem solving methods · Intelligent Tutoring Systems

1 Introduction

This paper describes a work conducted in the context of AMBRE [1]. The purpose of this project is to design Intelligent Tutoring Systems (ITSs) for teaching problem solving methods [2, 3]. ITSs designed within this project enable the learner to acquire a specific method in problem-solving. In each application domain, a method is based on classification of problems and solving tools.

To help the learner in building his/her own classification, the AMBRE project proposes a learning process based on reasoning by analogy, called the AMBRE cycle [1]. The AMBRE cycle consists in showing first solved problems (serving as cases-base initialization) to the learner and then encouraging him/her to apply analogical reasoning to solve other problems.

P. Escudeiro et al. (Eds.): CSEDU 2017, CCIS 865, pp. 116–137, 2018.
https://doi.org/10.1007/978-3-319-94640-5_6

AMBRE ITSs are based on a knowledge-based system coded in Prolog, a programming language for knowledge representation. This knowledge-based system relies on a problem solver and uses two main types of knowledge: knowledge about the method to be taught and knowledge to guide the learner when he/she solves problems, providing assistance and diagnosing his/her answers. However, building an AMBRE ITS, like any other ITS, is a labor-intensive process that requires expertise in the domain application and in programming [4, 5]. To reduce the effort of making AMBRE ITS and enable authors with no Prolog programming expertise to build their own ITS in the domain they are interested in, we propose to design an authoring tool for AMBRE project. The goal of this tool is to assist the author in knowledge elicitation process and to generate the domain models. This tool should also provide feedback to the author about the process enabling him/her to test the resolution of problems.

Many authoring tools have been proposed in the literature [4, 6, 7], but as far as we know, none of these tools meet our need, because either they do not match to AMBRE principle, or do not allow to represent all knowledge needed for the design of an AMBRE ITS. This is why we propose to design AMBRE-KB, an authoring tool for AMBRE project. This tool supports the acquisition of knowledge to be taught for a given domain, and the description of problems to be solved. It provides also assistance to the author during the knowledge elicitation process and enable him/her to have feedback at the end of the process by testing the resolution of problems and correcting his/her errors when the resolution fails.

This paper starts with a brief introduction related to knowledge acquisition methods and techniques within ITS authoring tool. Section 3 presents the approach adopted for the design of AMBRE-KB and illustrates the process of creating an ITS using this tool. Section 4 details the evaluations we made. The last section presents conclusion and directions of future work.

2 Related Work

In the literature, ITS authoring tools have been classified into two main groups: pedagogy-oriented and performance-oriented [4]. Pedagogy-oriented systems are those that focus on instructional planning and teach relatively fixed content. On the other hand, performance-oriented tools focus on providing rich learning environments in which students can learn skills by practicing them and receiving feedback.

REDEEM [8, 9], ISD-Expert [10] and DNA [11] are examples of the first category of authoring tool. To acquire knowledge, these systems use an interactive dialogue box. But, one of the notorious limits of these systems is that generally, experts feel constrained by the fixed sequence of data entry.

Further work focused on the acquisition of procedural knowledge. Several systems have been developed. We may mention for example DISCIPLE [12], DEMONSTR8 [13]. In DEMONSTR8, for example, the system infers production rules using programming-by-demonstration techniques, coupled with methods to further abstract the generated production. But, these systems are limited to domains where the knowledge can be represented step by step.

ASPIRE [7], an authoring tool that enables the design of constraint-based tutors, belongs to the category of performance-oriented tools. To acquire knowledge in this system, the authors use ontologies: (1) construction of the domain ontology, (2) acquisition of syntactic constraints directly from the ontology, and (3) use of a dialog box with the expert in order to infer semantic constraints. But this tool is limited to models based on constraints.

CREAM-Tools [14] also belongs to the category of performance-oriented tools since it allows the connection between skills and how to acquire them. For example, specific learning materials are linked to specific skills to support their learning. But approach adopted with this tool does not match to AMBRE principle.

Another authoring tool in this category is CTAT (The Cognitive Tutor Authoring Tools). CTAT assists in the creation and the delivery of two kinds of tutors: cognitive tutors [15] and example-tracing tutors [16, 17]. Cognitive tutors are based on a cognitive model with rules of production, and concern generally tasks of resolution of problems. The resolution is led step by step, and the behavior of the student at each stage is analyzed and corrected if it deviated from the planned procedure. However, cognitive tutors are limited to domain were the task of resolution of problems is made step by step and where all the knowledge of the domain can be represented in the form of production rules. Moreover, the design of such tutors required programming skills. Example-tracing tutors, the second type of tutors built by CTAT, have the advantage to be quickly developed without programming. To build an example-tracing tutor, the author builds at first the interface teaching by means of graphic tools, then he defines a graph of resolution of the strategies of resolution of the learners and their misconceptions. Example-tracing tutors present the same inconvenient as model-tracing tutors concerning the resolution of problems which is led step by step.

ITSs designing within AMBRE project belongs also to the category of performance-oriented tools, since they provide a learning environment in which students can learn how to solve problems in various domains and receive feedback about his/her answers. In particular, AMBRE ITSs are based on knowledge-based systems coded in Prolog. This Knowledge base relies on a solver which uses two categories of knowledge: knowledge about the method to be taught and knowledge to guide the learner providing him/her assistance and diagnosis of its answers. The knowledge to be taught are constituted by three types of knowledge: classification knowledge, reformulation knowledge and resolution knowledge. Problems are given in the form as a model we call descriptive model (presented in Sect. 3.1). To solve a problem for a given domain of learning, the solver uses the classification knowledge and the reformulation knowledge to (i) determine the class of the problem and (ii) to build a new model of the problem called operation model. Then, the resolution itself consists in applying to the operational model the solving technique associated with the class, to find the solution of the problem (see. Fig. 1.).

Classification knowledge is in the form of a classification tree of problems to be solved. Reformulation knowledge is constituted by a set of rules. These rules enable, from the statement of the problem, to identify the most specific class of classification tree to which the problem belongs. Resolution knowledge is constituted by solving techniques associated to each specific class of the classification tree. We considered existing authoring tools defined below, but they do not match to AMBRE principle or because techniques used do not enable to represent all knowledge needed by an AMBRE ITS. That is why we propose to define AMBRE-KB.

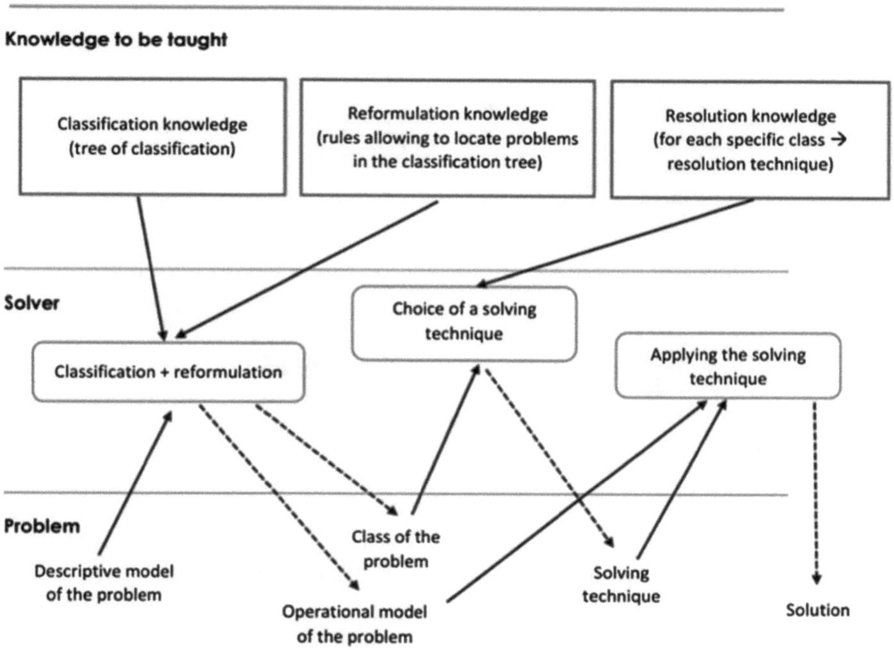

Fig. 1. Functioning of AMBRE solver [18].

3 AMBRE-KB Authoring Tool

The goal of AMBRE-KB (AMBRE-Knowledge Builder) is to assist authors in the creation of ITSs teaching problem-solving methods in the domain they are interesting in. Our intention is specially to allow the description of knowledge needed by the system without any Prolog programming expertise. For that, we propose an interactive knowledge acquisition process based on meta-models of knowledge to be acquired. We first present the approach adopted for the design of AMBRE-KB. We then describe the authoring process and finally the feedback provided at the end of the process.

3.1 Approach Adopted for the Design of AMBRE-KB

Figure *2* resumes the approach adopted for the design of AMBRE-KB. We defined a meta-model for each type of knowledge to be acquired [19]. For a given domain (see domain D Fig. 2), these meta-models define the form of knowledge to be acquired and constrain the interfaces proposed to the author to do so. At the end of the knowledge elicitation process, AMBRE-KB generated a Prolog version of these knowledge which constitute the knowledge base of the ITS.

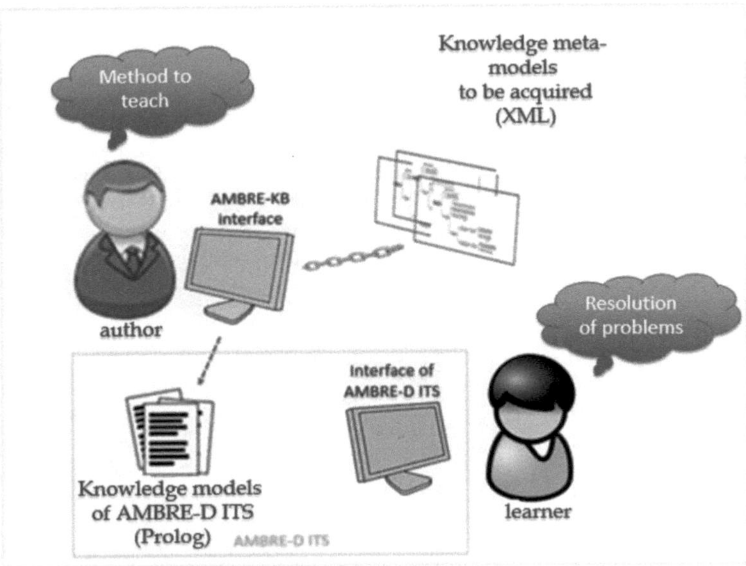

Fig. 2. Approach adopted for the design of AMBRE-KB.

3.2 Authoring Process

The authoring process in AMBRE-KB consists of nine steps summarized on Fig. 3.

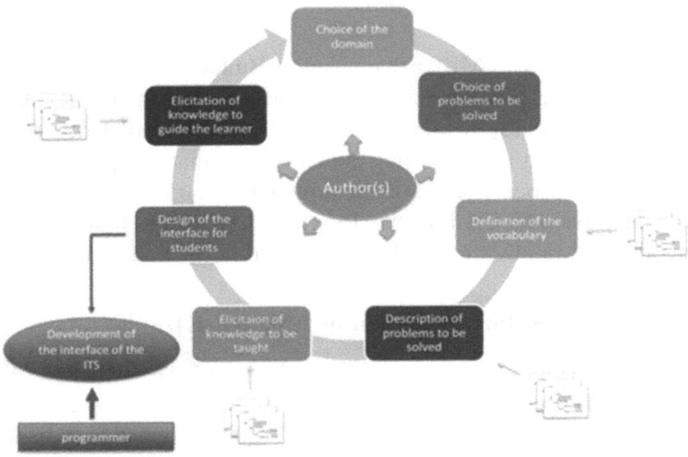

Fig. 3. AMBRE-KB authoring process.

Phase 1: Choice of a Domain of Learning. The first task to do when designing an AMBRE ITS is to choose the domain application. AMBRE ITSs are based on a classification of problems to be solved and the solving techniques. Thus, the author has to choose a domain in which he can establish a classification of problems and the solving techniques. Figure 4 shows an example of classification tree for the domain: plural of French nouns with the ending "*al*", "*ail*", "*ou*", "*eu*", "*au*".

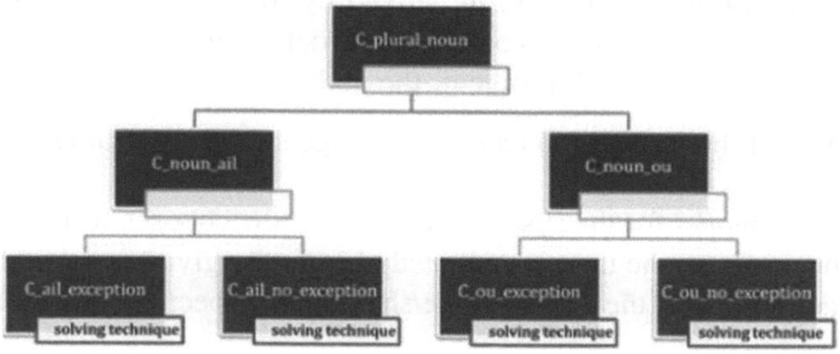

Fig. 4. A part of the classification tree for the plural of French nouns.

Phase 2: Choice of Type of Problems to be Solved. It is important before commencing the knowledge elicitation process that the author thinks about the type of problems to propose to the learners. This second step will help him/her to define the vocabulary (phase 3) - which plays a central role in definition of knowledge - and the classification tree (phase 4). The author has to define different types of problems that belong to each specific class of the classification tree.

Problems 1, 2, 3 and 4 are examples of problem for the plural of French nouns:

Problem 1: *Find the plural form of "bail".*
Problem 2: *Find the plural form of "detail".*
Problem 3: *Find the plural form of "bijou".*
Problem 4: *Find the plural form of "journal".*

Phase 3: Definition of the Vocabulary of the Chosen Domain. The third step consists in the definition of the vocabulary using AMBRE-KB. We need a vocabulary because, in AMBRE Project, problems are given to the system as a model we call descriptive model. This model describes a concrete situation which is the one represented in the statement of the problem. Objects that appear in the statement are concrete elements that constitute the contextual aspect of the problem. For example, in geometry, the objects can concern the characteristics of the geometric figure (dimensions of the segments, angles, and so on).

The objects are connected by relations to form a concrete situation. There are properties and relations on those objects. Each object is characterized by an identifier and a set of characteristics. The vocabulary is constituted by all objects needed to design all problems and the question to be answered. For example, to describe problems for the plural of French nouns, the following object can be defined:

Table 1. Example of vocabulary for the plural of French nouns.

Objects	Characteristics of objects
Noun	identifier → string ending_of_noun → string plural_of_noun → string

Phase 4: Description of Problems to be Solved by the System and the Learner. In the fourth step, the author uses the vocabulary to define problems to be solved by the system and the learner. For each problem, the author has to define:

- The *statement* of the problem in natural language so that the learner can understand what to do.
- The *descriptive model* for the system. For that, he/she chooses from the vocabulary, objects concerned, he/she then instantiated objects (by giving a name and a type for each characteristic of the object). He/she finally specifies the question to be answered.

For example, by using the vocabulary (see Table 1), the problem 1 above can be described as follow (see Fig. 5). The question mark is used to specify to the system the question to be answered. I this case the question concerns the plural of the noun.

Phase 5: Elicitation of Knowledge to be Taught. Using AMBRE-KB, the author defines the knowledge to be taught: *classification knowledge*, *reformulation knowledge* and *resolution knowledge*.

Classification knowledge is in the form of a classification tree where a class C2 is subclass of a class C1 if any problem of C2 is also a problem of C1. The root class is defined as the most general class, and the leaves, the most specific ones. For each class, a *discriminating attribute* is defined. This attribute must have different values in each subclass. Non-discriminating attributes - called *problem attributes* – can also be defined if they make sense for problems of the class. Problem attributes are useful for the resolution and their values depend on the problem to solve. Classes that are specific enough so that we can assign them a resolution technique are called *operational classes*. Figure 6, for example, shows a part of the classification graph for geometry defined with AMBRE-KB. *C_PLURAL_NOUN* is class root and its discriminating attribute is *ending*, "*ail*" '*ou*' and "*al*" are values of this attribute. Classes colored in yellow are operational classes, and the others are non-operational classes.

To define the classification tree, AMBRE-KB offers assistance to the author such as *flexibility* about the order of definition, *guidance* and *knowledge control*. For example, the expert can choose to build the tree from the root to the leaves or vice-versa. He/she has the possibility to define all classes, and then organize them as a hierarchy. He/she can also organize the classes into a hierarchy as the definition of classes progresses. Some classes can be defined adapting other classes. The system colors operational

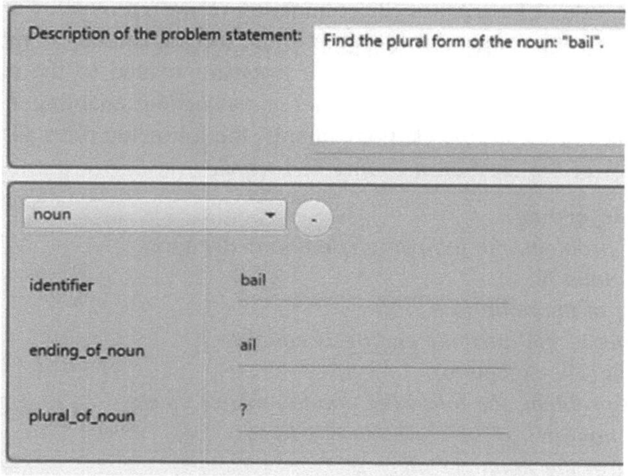

Fig. 5. Description of the problem P1 using AMBRE-KB.

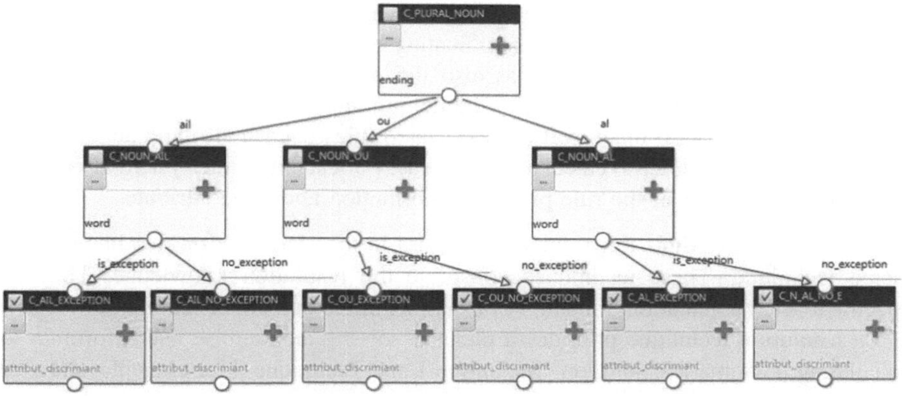

Fig. 6. A part of the classification tree for the plural of French noun defined with AMBRE-KB.

classes to guide the author. It checks if all non-operational classes have at least one subclass. Operational classes can have subclasses which are more specific or not. When two classes have the same discriminating attribute, the system suggests to the expert to define the attribute at the level of their lowest common ancestor class.

Reformulation Knowledge. In order to solve a given problem, the solver needs first to determine the class this problem belongs to. For that, the solver needs rules allowing to calculate the value of attributes (discriminating or not), thus allowing to locate the problem in classification tree. All rules constitute the reformulation knowledge.

A rule is defined by its *name*, a *set of premises* related to the elements of the statement (objects of the problems), and a *set of conclusions* enabling to calculate or to modify the values of the attributes. For example, the following rules allow to conclude about the values of the attributes: *ending* and *word.*

Rule 1: (rule_ending):
If for a given problem, the following conditions are meet:
- *there is a noun N*
- *the ending of the noun is E*

Then, the value of the attribute <u>*ending*</u> *is equal to* <u>*E*</u>.

Rule 2: (rule_ail_exception):
If for a given problem, the following conditions are meet:
- *there is a noun N*
- *the ending of the noun is "ail"*
- *L is the list of nouns ending by "ail" which are exceptions*
- *N belongs to L*

Then, the value of the attribute <u>*word*</u> *is equal to* <u>*is_exception*</u>.

To define rules with AMBRE-KB, the expert can choose, for example, to define rules as the definition of the classes progresses. In this case, for each class defined in the tree, he/she has to define the attributes (discriminating or not), and then the rules that enable to determine their values. He/she has also the possibility to first define the whole classification tree, and then, process to the definition of rules.

The system checks if the expert has associated rules to each attribute defined in the classification tree in order to calculate their value. For each rule, the system also checks if the conclusion part of the rule provides information about the attribute.

Resolution Knowledge. Each operational class in the classification tree has an associated technique. These techniques constitute the resolution knowledge. They are specific to each application domain. For example, in the domain of arithmetic problems [1], a resolution technique provides a plan for solving an exercise and a formula for calculating its numerical solution. Technique 1 and Technique 2 for example, show the resolution techniques associated respectively to classes: C_AIL_EXCEPTION and C_AIL_NO_EXCEPTION.

Technique 1.

- *Let N the noun of the problem*
- *Determine the radical of the noun N by removing the ending of the noun "ail"*
- *The plural of N is obtained by adding the ending "aux" to the radical of N*

Technique 2.

- *Let N the noun of the problem*
- *The plural of N is obtained by adding the ending "s" to N*

To explicit resolution knowledge using AMBRE-KB, the author has two possibilities: he/she can directly associate to each operational class of the classification tree the corresponding resolution technique or, he/she can define all classes first, and then define all resolution techniques, and finally connect each resolution technique to corresponding operational class (or classes). Figure 7 for example, shows the representation of technique 2 using AMBRE-KB.

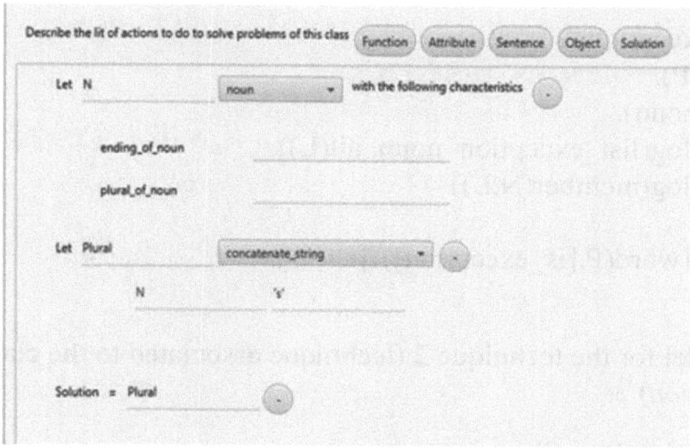

Fig. 7. Description of the technique 2 using AMBRE-KB.

Phase 6: Design of the Interface for Students. The seventh step consists in designing the interface of the ITS, and especially the tasks the student must perform to solve problems, based on the AMBRE cycle. But, as AMBRE-KB does not yet support the design of the interface, the development of this interface must be implemented by an IT specialist.

Phase 7: Elicitation of Knowledge to Guide the Learner. Using AMBRE-KB, and based on knowledge to be taught defined in phase 5, and the steps on resolution defined in phase 6, the author defines the knowledge to guide the learner.

Phase 8: Generation of Knowledge Models by AMBRE-KB. For each type of knowledge, AMBRE-KB generates a knowledge model in Prolog. All the knowledge models generated constitute the knowledge base of the ITS that the solver can uses to solve problems. For example, the Tables 2, 3 and 4 show the knowledge models generated by AMBRE-KB in Prolog to represent respectively *Problem 1*, R*ule 2* and the *Technique 2*.

Knowledge model for the problem 1 (plural_of_bail)

```
fait(probleme(plural_of_bail)). /*name of the problem*/
fait(enonce_naturel(plural_of_bail,'Find the plural
form of the noun: (bail).')). /*statement of the problem*/
fait(est_un(bail,noun)). /* the identifier of the noun*/
fait(plural_of_noun(bail,Question)). /* let Question is the plural of the noun*/
fait(inconnu(plural_of_bail,Question)). /* the question to be answered is to find the
value of Question*/
```

Knowledge model for the rule 2 (rule_ail_exception)

```
regle(rule_ail_exception):-
   si([probleme(P), /*let P the given problem*/
      est_un(N,noun), /*let N the noun of the problem*/
       eval_prolog(list_exception_noun_ail(L)), /*let L the list of exception*/
       eval_prolog(member(N,L)) /*N belongs to the list L*/
      ]),
   alors([ajouter(word(P,[is_exception]))]). /*the value of the attribute word is equal
to is_exception*/
```

Knowledge model for the technique 2 (technique associated to the class *c_ail_no_exception*)

```
appliquer_resolution(P,c_ail_no_exception):- /*technique associated to the class
c_ail_no_exception*/
  eval_prem(est_un(N,noun)), /* let N the noun of the problem*/
   concatenate_string(N,"s",Plural),:/* let Plural the result of the concatenation of N
and ''s'' */
  ajouter_bf(solution(P,Plural)). /*Plural is the solution of the problem*/
```

3.3 Feedback After the Authoring Process

Once the knowledge models are generated, the system enables the author to have feedback about the knowledge elicitation enabling him/her to test the resolution of problems he/she described for his/her domain. For example, when the resolution of a problem succeeds the system shows the solution of the problem and a lot of informations about the steps of its resolution such as the class of the problem, the attributes calculated and for each of them the rules tried, the rule executed and the resolution technique applied. In the same way, when the resolution of a problem fails, the system shows an error message enabling the author to understand what did not work in order to correct it. For example, when the resolution fails because of the solver did not find a rule allowing him to conclude about the value of an attribute, the system shows a message enabling the author to know what attribute is concerned. Figure 8, for example, shows the feedback when the author tests the resolution of *problem 1*.

4 Preliminary Evaluations

We conducted a first experiment to verify if AMBRE-KB is apt to encode correctly knowledge to be taught (classification knowledge, reformulation knowledge and resolution knowledge) so that the solver can use it to solve problems.

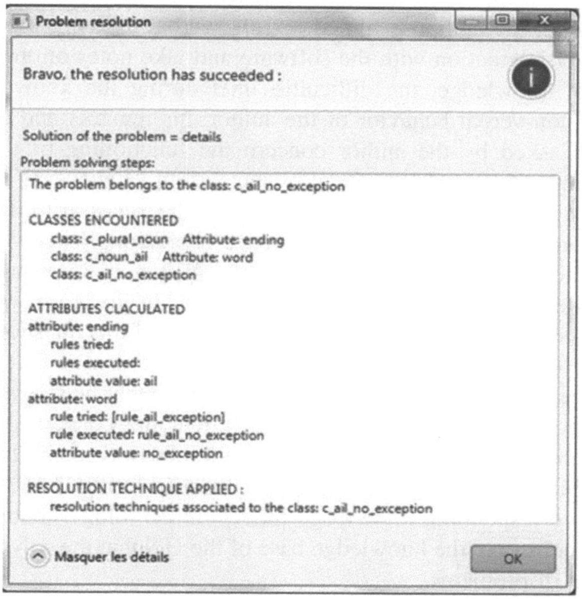

Fig. 8. Example of feedback when the resolution has succeeded.

4.1 Evaluation Protocol

The experiment procedure consisted in four stages:

- **1st Step.** This step consisted in presenting to the author the principle of AMBRE ITS, the form and the role of knowledge to be acquired. The functioning of AMBRE-KB is also presented to the author. At the end of this step, the author is invited to start thinking about a domain in which he/she is going to test AMBRE-KB.
- **2nd step.** During this step, the author has to choose a domain he has interested in to test AMBRE-KB. He/she has next to think about the type of exercises to propose to the learners. This step helps him/he to define the vocabulary of the chosen domain. Once the vocabulary is defined, he has also to think about the rules and the resolution techniques he has to define to solve problems. This task is as important as the previous one because it allows us to anticipate the test phase of generated files. Indeed, since the solver of AMBRE is coded in prolog, all knowledge must be generated in Prolog, as well as all functions used by the solver when trying to solve a problem. Usually, to défine a resolution technique, authors needs specific functions such as: for the calculations of sum of numbers (in geometry for example), calculation

of square of a number (for the equations for example). Most of these functions are specific to domain. For each domain, the solver needs to have the Prolog version of all function needed. So, it is important before using AMBRE-KB that the author defines the description of all functions he needs so that we can develop a Prolog version of them for the solver. At the end of this step, the author is ready to use AMBRE-KB to elicit knowledge needed to teach a method in his domain.

- **3rd step.** In this step, the author uses AMBRE-KB to explicit knowledge needed. During this step, the author is filmed and the verbal exchanges are recorded. We observe his/her interaction with the software and take notes on the time passed on every type of knowledge, the difficulties met during the knowledge elicitation, gestures and non-verbal behavior of the author, his remarks and questions. When the questions asked by the author concern the functioning of the tool, we first oriented him/her on the help proposed by the system. However, if the aid proposed by the system is not sufficient, we give him/her the necessary information so that he/she can continue the process of knowledge elicitation. When we notice that the author does nor move forward in knowledge elicitation, we consider that he/she feels difficulties about the functioning of the tool. In this case, we ask him/her a question to know what he wants to do. If the answer of this question corresponds to a feature taken into account by the tool, we guide him/her so that he can continue the knowledge elicitation process. Otherwise, when what he/she wants to do is not taken into account be the tool, we consider that the concerned task cannot be finished, and he/she continue the elicitation with others types of knowledge. When the author finishes eliciting all knowledge needed using AMBRE-KB, he can generate the corresponding knowledge models in a Prolog version. These knowledge models constitute the knowledge base of the ITS that the solver will use to test the resolution of problems.
- **4th step.** Using AMBRE-KB the authors test the résolution of the different problems he has defined. Two cases are possibles:
  - Either the solver is able to solve the problem. In this case the system shows to the author the solution of a problem. He/She can also see the different steps of the resolution such as: the class of the problem, the attributes calculated and for each of them, the rules tried, the rule executed, the values of attributes, and the resolution technique applied.
  - Either the resolution fails. In this case the system shows to the author an error message enabling him to understand what was wrong and how to correct it.

The experiment ends when the author finishes testing all problems. He/she completes a questionnaire composed of many sections about the functioning of AMBRE-KB, the proposed interfaces, the assistance proposed during knowledge elicitation, the feedback of the solver, and their profile (if they are programmers or not for example). The questionnaire we present them contains 31 questions divided in 4 categories:

- The *profile of the author and the domain application* (2 questions)
- The *elicitation of the different knowledge* (17 questions): definition of the vocabulary, description of problems, elicitation of classification knowledge, elicitation of reformulation knowledge, elicitation of resolution knowledge. The authors have 10 questions with 3 degrees of understanding to give their impression: "*I understood*

from the beginning", "I understood towards the end", "I did not understand"; 2 questions with direct answers: "*yes*" or "*no*"; 5 open questions enabling them to express themselves about the interfaces of AMBRE-KB and to propose suggestions for improvement if they want.

- The *principles of the interactive process* implemented through AMBRE-KB. The authors have 7 questions to judge the assistance proposed with AMBRE-KB: 4 multiple-choice questions and 3 questions allowing them to express themselves about the utility and efficiency of the assistance proposed. They have also the possibility to give suggestions for improvements.
- *General evaluation of AMBRE-KB*. The authors have 5 questions to estimate the general functioning of AMBRE-KB: 2 multiple-choice questions and 3 open questions allowing them to express themselves and to give suggestions.

4.2 Protocol Evaluation Criteria

Is AMBRE-KB able to acquire knowledge to be taught for a given domain?
Our objective in this part is to test if AMBRE-KB enable the author to elicit all knowledge needed for his domain. To do that this we have identified the following facets to evaluate: *definition of the vocabulary*, *description of problems, elicitation of classification knowledge*, *elicitation of reformulation knowledge*, *elicitation of resolution knowledge*. For each of them, we considered the following criteria:

Point to Evaluate: does AMBRE-KB enable the author to elicit all knowledge needed for each facet for the domain he/she has chosen?
Methodology Used: elicitation of knowledge with AMBRE-KB by author and then test of resolution of problems
Validation Condition: our hypothesis is that AMBRE-KB enables to elicit all knowledge needed for each facet to be evaluated.

The Table 2 for example, shows the criteria to evaluate the definition of the vocabulary.

Table 2. Criteria to evaluate the definition of vocabulary for a given domain.

Facet to evaluate	Definition of the vocabulary for the chosen domain
Point to analyze	Does AMBRE-KB enable the author to define the vocabulary for his/her domain?
Methodology	Using AMBRE-KB to define the vocabulary of the chosen domain and answering the corresponding questions in the questionnaire
Validation condition	AMBRE-KB enable the authors to define all knowledge needed to define the vocabulary for the domain

Does the assistance proposed by AMBRE-KB useful?
In order to evaluate the assistance proposed with AMBRE-KB, we identify the following facets to evaluate: *flexibility* offered by the system, the *guidance* and the possibility to *control knowledge elicited* during the process. For each of them, we considered the following criteria:

Point to Evaluate: is AMBRE-KB assistance useful for the author?
Methodology Used: elicitation of knowledge with AMBRE-KB by author and then analysis of answers to the questions concerning the assistance in the questionnaire
Validation Condition: the assistance proposed is useful and helps the author during the process.

Table 3 shows an example of criteria to evaluate the flexibility provided during the knowledge elicitation.

Table 3. Criteria to evaluate the flexibility provided during the knowledge elicitation.

Facet to evaluate	Flexibility during knowledge elicitation
Point to analyze	Is the flexibility in AMBRE-KB useful for the author?
Methodology	Using AMBRE-KB to define the vocabulary of the chosen domain and answering the corresponding questions in the questionnaire
Validation condition	The flexibility provided during the knowledge elicitation is useful and help the author during the process

Are the Interfaces Proposed with AMBRE-KB Intuitive Enough?
Our objective in this part is to test the satisfactory of the author about the interfaces proposed to elicit knowledge. To do that we opt for an empirical evaluation which consists in observing the author during the use of AMBRE-KB, and then to collect it impressions through a questionnaire. We have identified the following facets to evaluate: *interface for the vocabulary, interface for the problems, interface for classification knowledge, interface for reformulation knowledge, and interface for resolution knowledge*. For each of them, we considered the following criteria:

Point to Analyze: ergonomics of the proposed interfaces
Methodology Used: elicitation of knowledge with AMBRE-KB by author and then test of resolution pf problems
Validation Condition: our hypothesis is that AMBRE-KB enables the author to elicit knowledge without external help.

Table 4 shows an example of criteria to evaluate the interface allowing to define the vocabulary for a given domain.

Table 4. Criteria to evaluate the interface allowing to define the vocabulary for a given domain.

Facet to evaluate	Definition of the vocabulary for the chosen domain
Point to evaluate	Ergonomics of the interface
Methodology	Definition of the vocabulary and judgment of the author (answering the corresponding questions in the questionnaire)
Validation condition	The author was able to define the vocabulary of his/her domain without external help

4.3 Results and Discussion

The experiment was performed with five authors. Four domains were tested, two of them were tested each other by two authors, and the two others are tested by the same author (see Table 5).

Table 5. Domains tested and the authors.

Resolution of equations (1st and 2nd degree)	Application domains			
	The calculation of area in geometry	Plural of French nouns	French adverbs formation with "*ment*"	Resolution of equations (1st and 2nd degree)
2	2	1	1	2

The Table 6 resumes knowledge defined by both authors for the domain of equations.

Table 6. Comparison of results for the domain Equations for two authors.

	Number of knowledge defined for each category						
	Objects	Classes	Rules	Techniques	Problems	% resolution of problems without feedback	% resolution of problems with feedback
Author 1	5	6	5	4	20	75%	100%
Author 2	3	7	5	4	12	41%	100%

The authors defined different knowledge: they proposed different classification tree, and different vocabularies. The problems defined, rules and techniques are also different. Tables 7 and 8 for example, show the vocabulary defined by each of them.

Table 7. Vocabulary defined by the author 1 for equations.

Objects	Characteristics of objects
equation	unknown_variable → string unknown_value → number list_term → type enumerated {two_term, three_term}
two_terms	first_term → unknown_term second_term → constant_term
three_term	first_term → unknown_term second_term → constant_term third_term → unknown_term
unknown_term	coefficient → number
constant_term	value_of_constant → number

Table 8. Vocabulary defined by the author 2.

Objects	Characteristics of objects
equation	first_term → type enumerated {unknown_term, constant_term} second_term → type enumerated {unknown_term, constant_term} third_term → type enumerated {unknown_term, constant_term}
unknown_term	unknown_variable → string unknown_value → number coefficient → number degree → number
constant_term	value_of_constant → number

Figure 9 shows the classification tree define by the author 1.

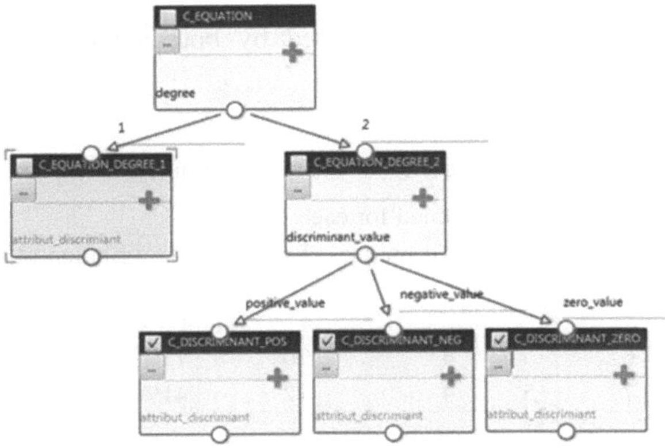

Fig. 9. Classification tree for equations defined by the author 1.

For the author 1, the system was able to solve 75% of problems without using the feedback. For the author 2, the system was able to solve 41% of problems without using the feedback. But, once they use the feedback, and to correct their errors, the system was able to solve the remaining problems.

The Table 9 resumes knowledge defined by both authors for the domain of geometry.

Table 9. Comparison of results for the domain of geometry for two authors.

	Objects	Classes	Rules	Techniques	Problems	% resolution of problems without feedback	% resolution of problems with feedback
Author 1	5	12	11	7	28	57%	85%
Author 2	8	12	11	7	18	61%	89%

As for the domain of equation, the two authors defined different knowledge. For the author 1, the system was able to solve 57% of the problems without the feedback and 85% with the feedback. The 15% remaining problems belong to the same class. The author was not able to test their resolution because he defined at the last moment a new function he needed to describe the technique associated with this class. Because the resolver did not have the Prolog version of these functions at his time, the resolution of these problems failed. As a reminder, during the second step of the experiment, the author is asked to define the description of all the functions he/she needs for the domain so that we can develop a Prolog version of them in order to allow the resolver to use them when solving problems.

For the author 2, the system was able solve 61% of the problems without the feedback, and 89% with the feedback. The resolution of the 11% remained problems fails because the system was not able to find a rule allowing him to conclude about the value of a discriminating attribute, but since the author did not correct the error, the resolution of these Problems have succeeded.

The plural of French nouns and the formation of French adverbs with the ending "*ment*" were tested successively by the same author. Table 10 for example, resumes the knowledge he defined for the two domains.

For the adverbs, the system was able to solve 45% of problems without the feedback, and 87% of problems with the feedback. For the 13% remaining problems, the resolution failed. Indeed, the author looked for the errors messages, and understood what to do to correct errors, but he did not attempt it. So, the system was not able to solve these problems.

For the plural of nouns, the system was able to solve 65% of problems without feedback. But once he used the feedback, he was able to solve the remaining problems. The author declared that using AMBRE-KB to elicit knowledge for two domains helped him/her a lot to more understand the functioning of AMBRE-kB.

Table 10. Knowledge defined by the same author for the plural of French nouns and the formation of French adverbs with the ending "*ment*".

	Objects	Classes	Rules	Techniques	Problems	% resolution of problems without feedback	% resolution of problems with feedback
Adverbs	1	17	16	11	22	45%	87%
Plural of nouns	1	13	9	8	24	65%	100%

In summary, for the four domains, 124 problems were defined. The resolver was able to solve 60% of them without the feedback and 91, 8% with the feedback. The 8.2% could not be solved either because the author understood his error but did not correct it, or because the author defined at the last moment new functions for which the solver didn't have a Prolog version to solve them. For all domains, the difference between the percentage of resolution without feedback and with feedback is more than

20%. This shows that the feedback proposed by AMBRE-KB is useful. When the resolution of a problem fails, the author must either add new knowledge or modify existing ones to correct the error. Then, it must generate again the knowledge models in order to take into account the modifications. The fact that the system can solve the problem again also shows that the system is interactive.

The analysis of the questionnaires shows the following results:

- **Elicitation of Knowledge.** Two of the author are programmers, and the other are non-programmers. The first had less difficulties to understand the principles implemented in this tool, but all of them one was able to elicit knowledge needed for their domain. Three of them observed a difference between the vocabulary they defined on paper at the beginning of the experiment, and the vocabulary they finally define when using AMBRE-KB. This is due to the fact that the interfaces proposed by AMBRE-KB did not allow them to represent the knowledge as they were defined. Nevertheless, with a small modification of their version on paper, they were able to define a vocabulary for their domain with the functionalities already implemented in AMBRE-KB.
- **Ergonomic of Interfaces.** For the evaluation of interfaces, we obtain the following results:
  - The five authors judge that the interface proposed for the definition of classification knowledge is the simplest and easiest to understand. They also say that they had no difficulty in understanding the functioning of the proposed interfaces for the vocabulary and the resolution techniques.
  - Concerning the interface or the definition of rules, 4 of them affirmed that the interface was not very intuitive at the beginning. They affirmed also that without our help they would not know how to proceed to define the rules. But once they understood how the interface works, they were able to define the rest of the rules on their own.
  - For the description of problems, the authors also encountered difficulties to indicating the question to be answered when describing problems because the interface was not very intuitive. Two of the authors say that they would like to have an explicit menu to do so. They benefited to our help to complete this task. The three other authors asserted that a simple posted message to be displayed by the system somewhere in the problem description interface would allowed them to understand what to do. Despite these remarks and suggestions, they all judged that the interfaces were fairly intuitive and easy to understand.
- **Assistance Proposed with AMBRE-KB.** Four of the authors reported that they have used the assistance proposed with AMBRE-KB. They particularly appreciated the feedback provided by the tool and affirmed that it helped them to better understand the functioning of the tool. Nevertheless, one of them said that this assistance can be enriched by increasing the interactivity of the system with more frequent pop-ups during the process. Two of them also stated that they would also like to have feedback directly at the level of the knowledge concerned. For example, when the resolution fails because of a blocked classification (because the system cannot find rules to conclude), to report the error directly in the classification level (classification knowledge definition interface), etc.

5 Conclusions

In this paper, we presented AMBRE-KB an authoring tool to elicit knowledge to be taught without programming. In particular, AMBRE-KB enables the description of problems to be solved and the elicitation of knowledge about the method to teach (classification knowledge, reformulation knowledge and resolution knowledge). This Tool is based on an interactive process constrained by the meta-models of knowledge to be acquired, which defined the form of these knowledge. To facilitate the process, AMBRE-KB helps the author during the knowledge elicitation providing flexibility especially about the order of definition of knowledge, guidance and control of knowledge as the knowledge elicitation progresses. At the end of the process, it enables also the author to have a feedback about the process by testing the resolution of problems. When the resolution succeeds, it enables authors to have the solution of the problems and a lot of information about the resolution steps such as the class of the problem, the attributes calculated and their values, the rules tried, the rules executed, and the resolution technique applied. When the resolution fails, the system sends an error message enabling the author to understand his/her error and to correct it.

We conducted an experiment with five authors to evaluate the knowledge acquisition process and its implementation through AMBRE-KB. Fours domains were tested: equation (by two authors), geometry (by two authors). The plural of French nouns and the formation of French adverbs with the ending "*ment*'. The last two domains were tested by the same author. This experiment permits to highlight the week points and the strengths of AMBRE-KB:

- For a given domain, AMBRE-KB is apt to generate knowledge models so that the solver can use them to solve problems of the domain.
- The interfaces proposed are intuitive enough and easy to use, but the interface for the rules and the description of problems can be improved.
- The authors appreciated assistance provided by the system, particularly the feedback
- For all domains, at least 40% of the problems have been solving without using the feedback, and at least 80% using the feedback (see Table 11).
- The feedback helps author to more understanding the functioning of AMBRE-KB and can be improved to make the elicitation easier.

This work focused on the acquisition of knowledge about the method to be taught. The next stage will concern the acquisition of knowledge intended to guide the learner during his/her learning. This knowledge will enable to propose to the learner help and explanations of various natures according to the step of its resolution or committed errors.

Table 11. Domain tested.

	Domains tested					
	Equations		Geometry		Plural	Adverbs
	Author 1	Author 2	Author 1	Author 2	Author	Author
Without feedback	75%	41%	57%	61%	66%	87%
With feedback	100%	100%	85%	89%	90%	100%

In addition, a relevant track in the continuation of our work is the integration of features of generalization of knowledge from cases. This feature will enable users to define an example, rather than an abstract knowledge, the system proposing them a generalization of the knowledge that they can validate or modify. The SimStudent [20] approach which is based on learning abstract knowledge from examples would be appropriate in the context of this work.

Acknowledgements. All thanks to Auvergne-Rhône Alpes region for supporting this thesis work.

References

1. Nogry, S., Guin, N., Jean-Daubias, S.: AMBRE-add: an ITS to teach solving arithmetic word problems. Technol. Instr. Cogn. Learn. **6**, 53–61 (2008)
2. Schoenfeld, A.H.: Problem solving in context. In: Charles, R.I., Silver, E.A. (eds.) The Teaching and Assessing of Mathematical Problem Solving, pp. 82–92. The National Council of Teachers of Mathematics, Reston (1988)
3. Schoenfeld, A.H.: Mathematical Problem Solving. Academic Press, Cambridge (1985)
4. Murray, T.: An overview of intelligent tutoring system authoring tools: updated analysis of the state of the art. In: Murray, T., Blessing, S.B., Ainsworth, S. (eds.) Authoring Tools for Advanced Technology Learning Environments: Toward Cost-Effective Adaptive, Interactive and Intelligent Educational Software, pp. 491–544. Springer, Dordrecht (2003). https://doi.org/10.1007/978-94-017-0819-7_17
5. Woolf, B., Cunningham, P.A.: Multiple knowledge sources in intelligent teaching systems. IEEE Expert **2**, 41–54 (1987). https://doi.org/10.1109/MEX.1987.4307063
6. Blessing, S.B., Gilbert, S., Ourada, S., Ritter, S.: Authoring model-tracing cognitive tutors. Int. Artif. Intell. Educ. Soc. **19**(2), 189–210 (2007)
7. Mitrovic, A., et al.: Authoring constraint-based tutors in ASPIRE. In: Ikeda, M., Ashley, K. D., Chan, T.-W. (eds.) ITS 2006. LNCS, vol. 4053, pp. 41–50. Springer, Heidelberg (2006). https://doi.org/10.1007/11774303_5
8. Ainsworth, S., Major, N., Grimshaw, S., Hayes, M., Underwood, J., Williams, B., Wood, D.: REDEEM: simple intelligent tutoring systems from usable tools. In: Murray, T., Blessing, S. B., Ainsworth, S. (eds.) Authoring Tools for Advanced Technology Learning Environments: Toward Cost-Effective Adaptive, Interactive and Intelligent Educational Software, pp. 205–232. Kluwer Academic, Dordrecht (2003)
9. Ainsworth, S.E., Grimshaw, S.: Evaluating the REDEEM authoring tool: can teachers create effective learning environments? Int. J. Artif. Intell. Educ. **14**, 279–312 (2003)
10. Tennyson, R., Breuer, K.: ISD EXPERT: an automated approach to instructional design. In: Tennyson, R. (ed.) Automating Instructional Design, Development, and Delivery SE - 9, vol. 119, pp. 139–161. Springer, Heidelberg (1994). https://doi.org/10.1007/978-3-642-78389-0_9
11. Shute, V.J., Torreano, L.A., Willis, R.E.: DNA—uncorking the bottleneck in knowledge elicitation and organization. In: Goettl, B.P., Halff, H.M., Redfield, C.L., Shute, V.J. (eds.) ITS 1998. LNCS, vol. 1452, pp. 146–155. Springer, Heidelberg (1998). https://doi.org/10.1007/3-540-68716-5_20
12. Tecuci, G., Keeling, H.: Developping an intelligent educational agent with disciple. Int. J. Artif. Intell. Educ. **10**, 221–237 (1999)

13. Murray, T.: Authoring intelligent tutoring systems: an analysis of the state of the art. Int. J. Artif. Intell. Educ. **10**, 98–129 (1999). (Ed. by, T. Murray, B. Stephen, A. Shaaron)
14. Nkambou, R., Frasson, C., Gauthier, G.: CREAMTools: an authoring environment for knowledge engineering in intelligent tutoring systems. In: Murray, T., Blessing, S.B., Ainsworth, S. (eds.) Authoring Tools for Advanced Technology Learning Environnements, pp. 269–308. Springer, Dordrecht (2003). https://doi.org/10.1007/978-94-017-0819-7_10
15. Koedinger, K.R., Corbett, A.T.: Cognitive tutors: technology bringing learning science to the classroom. In: Sawyer, R.K. (ed.) The Cambridge Handbook of the Learning Sciences, pp. 61–77. Cambridge University Press, Cambridge (2006)
16. Aleven, V., Mclaren, B.M., Sewall, J., Koedinger, K.R.: A new paradigm for intelligent tutoring systems: example-tracing tutors. Int. J. Artif. Intell. Educ. **19**, 105–154 (2009)
17. Aleven, V., McLaren, B.M., Sewall, J., van Velsen, M., Popescu, O., Demi, S., Ringenberg, M., Koedinger, K.R.: Example-tracing tutors: intelligent tutor development for non-programmers. Int. J. Artif. Intell. Educ. **26**, 224–269 (2016). https://doi.org/10.1007/s40593-015-0088-2
18. Diattara, A., Guin, N., Luengo, V., Cordier, A.: An authoring tool to elicit knowledge to be taught without programming. In: Escudeiro, P., Costagliola, G., Zvacek, S., Uhomoibhi, J., McLaren, B.M. (ed.) International Conference on Computer Supported Education, Porto, Portugal, pp. 82–91 (2017)
19. Diattara, A., Guin, N., Luengo, V., Cordier, A.: Towards an authoring tool to acquire knowledge for ITS teaching problem solving methods. In: Verbert, K., Sharples, M., Klobučar, T. (eds.) EC-TEL 2016. LNCS, vol. 9891, pp. 575–578. Springer, Cham (2016). https://doi.org/10.1007/978-3-319-45153-4_66
20. Matsuda, N., et al.: Learning by teaching SimStudent: technical accomplishments and an initial use with students. In: Aleven, V., Kay, J., Mostow, J. (eds.) ITS 2010. LNCS, vol. 6094, pp. 317–326. Springer, Heidelberg (2010). https://doi.org/10.1007/978-3-642-13388-6_36

Determining the Cognitive Value of Online Interactive Multimedia in Statistics Education

Natalya Koehler[1(✉)], Ana-Paula Correia[2], Nimet Alpay[1], and Carolyn LeVally[1]

[1] International Institute of Innovative Instruction, Franklin University, 236 E Town Street, Columbus, OH, USA
{natalya.koehler,nimet.alpay, carolyn.levally}@franklin.edu

[2] Educational Studies Department, The Ohio State University, 29 W Woodruff Ave, Columbus, OH, USA
correia.12@osu.edu

Abstract. Pursuing online degrees and taking online courses, especially in complex subjects, can be challenging to many adult learners who have to juggle work, family responsibilities, and financial commitments. To better address the needs of these students, a series of online interactive learning modules informed by multimedia theory for teaching declarative and procedural knowledge were created and integrated in an online statistics course. Design and development was followed by evaluative efforts, which were conducted over a period of nine months with a total of 167 undergraduate students and six instructors. Students' perceptions on the modules' usability features (e.g., pace of audio presentations, ease of navigation, and layout) as well as on cognitive support and effectiveness of the modules to teach statistics were analyzed. Students and instructors' reflections on their experiences with the modules were also gathered and analyzed. Both set of participants were overwhelmingly positive about their online learning and teaching experiences of statistics. Online courses and interactive multimedia firmly grounded in learning theories provide effective learning experiences and rich interaction with the course content. This is particularly important when teaching complex content as mathematics and statistics.

Keywords: Evaluation · Multimedia · Statistics

1 Introduction

Teaching and learning mathematics has often been identified as challenging and a barrier to students' graduation in higher education [1]. A likely contributor to this issue is that gateway courses such as basic statistics traditionally have low success and retention rates. In particular, online basic statistics courses can be troublesome because

Electronic supplementary material The online version of this chapter (https://doi.org/10.1007/978-3-319-94640-5_7) contains supplementary material, which is available to authorized users.

P. Escudeiro et al. (Eds.): CSEDU 2017, CCIS 865, pp. 138–153, 2018.
https://doi.org/10.1007/978-3-319-94640-5_7

of the inherent nature of the online environment, including the increased transactional distance within the course, as well as an increased need to support learner cognitive processing of the complex materials. "National statistics show that exit rates from many introductory courses are not what they should be at most institutions, yet few are changing how they teach; and even fewer are measuring the impact of any changes they try to implement" [2].

In face of these challenges, a course re-design was done to a statistics course offered at a large non-profit private university with a large selection of online courses and programs, named Franklin University. The needs assessment prior to the re-design revealed that there was a need to better support the needs of online students taking the course. This conclusion was made based on faculty members' interviews and student course evaluations. Most of students were adult learners who had to juggle work, family responsibilities, and financial commitments along with their academic programs. The majority of the students who took the statistics course as an online section was not even able to attend the live synchronous sessions because of schedule conflicts. To better address the needs of these students, a series of online interactive multimedia modules (refereed here as Software) was created. It consisted of weekly multimedia modules and aimed to help students synthesize the statistical knowledge and check their understanding of terminology, concepts, and procedures and ultimately increase student retention and the number of students receiving passing grades (letters grades A, B or C). It was therefore critical to investigate appropriate pedagogies for teaching statistics online to foster positive attitudes towards the learning of mathematics and support student conceptual understanding of the content. A study was initially reported [3], but this chapter focuses on the evaluative efforts to judge the cognitive value of the Software. It describes the two rounds of evaluation efforts conducted between August 2015 and April 2016. The following research questions guided the study:

1. What were the students' perceptions of how the Software supported their cognitive processing of the target concepts?
2. What was the overall student experience with the Software?
3. What unanticipated problems have students and instructors experienced with the Software?
4. Which features and instructional strategies implemented in the Software were the most helpful to students and instructors? And the least helpful?
5. What were the instructors' perceptions of student use of the Software?
6. What was the instructor's overall experience with the use of the Software in the online course?
7. What effect did Software have on the role of the instructor and the effectiveness of instruction in the course?

2 Statistics Education and Computer Assisted Learning

Repetitive practice through carefully selected and managed examples is considered an important way of learning statistics. It allows students to construct generalizations and see patterns [4]. The efficient way of engaging students in repetitive practice is using auto-graded assignments that can be provided by a textbook publisher or an in-house system, such as the Software.

In a meta-analysis study [5] found that Computer Assisted Instruction (CAI) has a moderate impact on student achievement. Some researchers emphasized that technology needs to be used not only for computing numbers, but also for concept exploration [6, 7]. Others stated that technology has the potential to expand the range of visualization techniques that can help learners understanding of concepts [8].

Support for a phenomenon referred to as the testing effect by [9]. If learners are asked comprehension questions requiring information recall after the training episode and during the training episode, learners will be able to remember the target material better. In addition, explanation of the correct answers after student attempt to answer a question, allows learners to correct their misconceptions about the material, which facilitates student comprehension of complex content. One of the benefits of CAI is the possibility of including embedded questions between clearly partitioned scenes that introduce statistical concepts. The questions allow students to check their comprehension of statistical concepts and animated presentations of statistical concepts help non-statistics major students to learn this subject [10]. Also, animated presentations of statistical concepts can help non-statistical majors learn statistics [10]. It was found that computer-animated graphics were more effective than static images in teaching statistics and the use of computer-animated graphics resulted in better students understanding of statistical concepts and retention of the material [11].

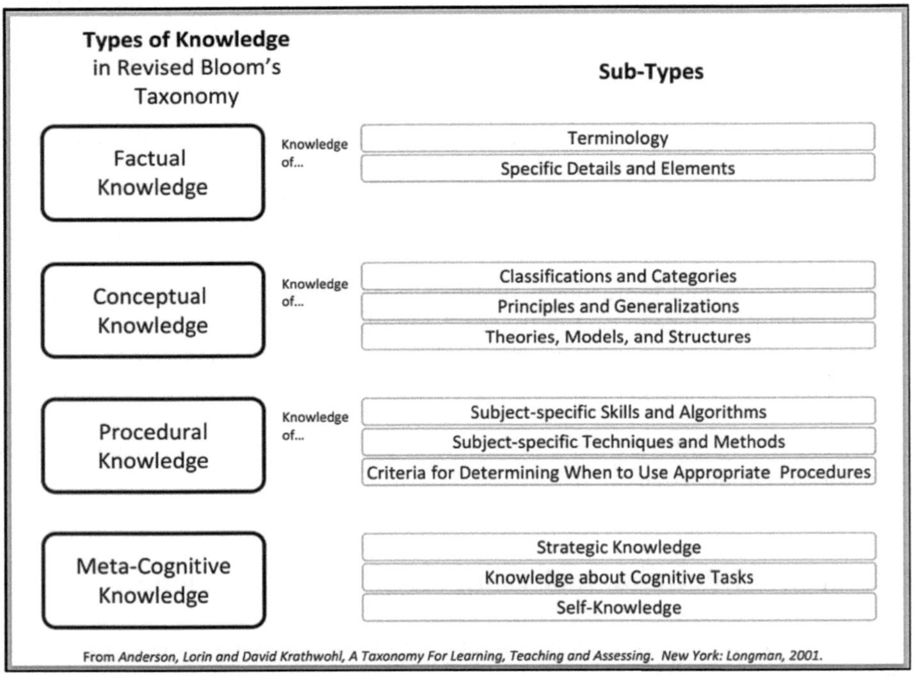

Fig. 1. Types and subtypes of knowledge described in the revised Bloom's Taxonomy [13].

Learning outcomes can be achieved if learners build factual, conceptual, procedural, and strategic knowledge of the subject matter learned in the course [12]. These types of knowledge are described in the revised Bloom's Taxonomy [13] as factual, conceptual, procedural and meta-cognitive knowledge. Figure 1 shows types and subtypes of knowledge described in the revised Bloom's Taxonomy.

A strong emphasis on guidance of the student learning process is advocated by [14]. The cognitive theory of multimedia learning describes the cognitive process that occur when exposed to multimedia learning [15]. Using both of the auditory and visual channels, student learning through multimedia instruction can be enhanced as information is presented using sound and images. Keller's attention, relevance, confidence, and satisfaction (ARCS) model features enhancing and sustaining motivation strategies. Instructional designers can build into the software interface a menu-driven program structure, which enhances learners' confidence by providing control access to different parts of courseware [16].

3 Methods

3.1 The Participants

According to the report from [1], for part-time students, the chances of graduation with a 4-year bachelor's degree within 8 years is 24.3%. This same report indicates that graduation rates are particularly low for lower socioeconomic status and older students. Since Franklin University undergraduate students largely fall into the above categories, it was important to make success possible for every student. Most Franklin University students are first generation college students who work part-time and balance work, classes and family responsibilities. The majority of them are financial aid recipients. Student average age is 33.27 years. Table 1 summarizes the demographics of undergraduate student population at Franklin University.

Table 1. Statistics of undergraduate student population at Franklin University [3].

Category	Percentage
Race	Caucasians – 66.7%
	African Americans – 21.6%
	Asians – 3.2%
	Hispanic – 3.2%
	Others – 5.3%
Student status	Full time – 33.6%
	Part time – 66.4%
Financial aid recipients	70%
Gender	Males – 43.5%
	Females – 56.5%

All students of Franklin University who were enrolled in the statistics course were eligible to participate in the study. The evaluation of the Software was conducted over a period of two semesters (August to December 2015 and January to April 2016) with 167 students. Eighty-six of the enrolled students (36%) agreed to participate in the first semester and 81 students (39%) agreed to participate in the second round of the second semester.

Six instructors out of 13 (46%) participated in the study between August and December of 2015, with two of them teaching face-to-face sections and another four teaching online sections. Six instructors out of 13 (46%) participated in the study between January and April of 2016. Three of them taught face to face sections and another three taught online sections.

3.2 The Software and Online Course

Twenty-eight online interactive multimedia modules were created in order to target the weekly learning outcomes. The explanations in the modules were augmented with animated and narrated real-life application examples, comprehension questions with immediate explanatory feedback, and interactive practice [17].

The Software were not only designed to provide additional information but rather to increase students' understanding of key concepts through the use of multimedia

Table 2. The Software main design decisions made based on theoretical underpinnings.

Software design decisions	Theoretical underpinnings
1. Use of animated real-life examples for illustrating statistical concepts	Stimulation of information recall through making associations and constructing generalizations [4]
2. Use of narrated animation for presenting new statistical concepts	Dual coding of information through auditory and visual channels increases efficiency and effectiveness of learning [18]
3. Presenting information in small segments	Segmenting principle [18]
4. Provide examples for demonstrating statistical procedures	Learning from worked-out examples is very effective during the initial stages of cognitive skill acquisition; it reduces cognitive load for novice students [19, 20]
5. Use of comprehension questions augmented with explanatory program feedback after each segment of statistical information	Comprehension questions allow students to check their comprehension of concepts and correct misconceptions [10]
6. Offer dynamic summaries that allow students to review, organize, and freely navigate target content in one slide	Reviewing and summarizing provides additional information recall and stimuli to see patterns in the target material [21]
7. Have supplemental content (for example, tips how to use calculators, thematic videos, audio transcripts) at hand as just in time help	Cognitive learning theory; additional resources offered when the learner needs them for accomplishing a task in order to reduce extraneous cognitive load [20–22]

instruction and periodic checks of student comprehension. Another goal in mind was to decrease student level of anxiety in an online statistics course by providing a solid instruction that students could use at their own pace and convenience. An example can be viewed at http://video.franklin.edu/Franklin/statistics/1a/story.html.

Table 2 shows the design decisions made and the theories that drove these decisions in order to support student cognitive processing of complex information.

The online course followed the requirements of the Ohio Department of Higher Education for a college level general education statistics course and the recommendations of the American Statistical Society's Guidelines for Assessment and Instruction in Statistics Education. The guidelines are, as follows:

1. Emphasize statistical literacy and develop statistical thinking;
2. Use real data;
3. Stress conceptual understanding, rather than mere knowledge of procedures;
4. Foster active learning the in classroom;
5. Use technology for developing conceptual understanding and analyzing data;
6. And use assessments to improve and evaluate student learning.

As a result, the course topics included sampling, types of data, graphs, variance and standard deviation, percentiles, rules of probabilities, confidence intervals, hypothesis testing, tests with qualitative data, correlation coefficient and least-squares regression. The Software was integrated in an undergraduate 4-credit online statistics course. The course was offered in both online and face-to-face formats. The duration of the course was 15 weeks. The course required a student to have an overall grade of 70% or higher for successful completion. All students who took the course had access to the following academic support services:

- Online and on-campus tutoring (scheduled by request)
- Walk-in tutoring
- Test preparation workshops
- Structural Learning assistance (group online sessions offered once a week to review the weekly course content and answer students' questions).

Training sessions for new instructors were offered, both face-to-face and online, to inform the teaching faculty about the new course design, products, and other changes in the course. Moreover, periodic teaching observations were conducted to provide the instructors with constructive feedback.

3.3 Study Design

This study explores students' and instructor perceptions of the benefit and cognitive value of the Software. The focus of the first semester evaluation was to collect preliminary information on the Software effectiveness and usability. It took place between August and December of 2015. The instrument for collecting student data consisted of four parts, as follows:

- Part 1: A log reporting any bugs that students encountered while interacting with the Software features.

- Part 2: Fourteen items (see Table 4) on the rating scale of 5 (5-strongly agree; 1-strongly disagree) about the Software used for its review. Students were asked to evaluate:
  - three usability features, such as pace of the audio presentations, ease of navigation, and layout of the Software;
  - overall learning experience with the Software;
  - amount of cognitive support provided by the Software;
  - helpfulness of Software features, such as:

    (1) explanations
    (2) real-life examples
    (3) summary slides
    (4) transcript of lectures
    (5) self-assessment questions
    (6) supplemental content (for example, tips how to use calculators, thematic videos, audio transcripts)
    (7) feedback to self-assessment questions.

- Part 3: Students answered two open-ended questions about what they liked about the Software and what changes they would like to make to it, if any.
- Part 4: Students were asked to write a paragraph about their learning experience using the Software as part of their online course in statistics and to provide examples to illustrate specific features and/or instructional strategies that have helped or have not help them to learn the course content.

The second round of evaluation from January to April 2016 evaluated the Software after minor bugs were fixed. For example, a few buttons on some screens did not work the way they were expected to and were fixed; a few pop-up windows did not show up and were also fixed. Since no major problems with software design were found in the first round, the data collection instruments to seek additional student feedback on the cognitive value of the Software remained the same in the second round.

On both rounds of evaluation, instructors' feedback was collected through an anonymous online survey. The instructors answered six open-ended questions focused on how the Software was used in the course by students and instructors.

3.4 Data Collection and Analysis Process

The data was collected from four sources: (1) students' responses to two open-ended questions, (2) 14-item survey ratings the Software features, (3) student reflections on their experiences on the online course and, (4) instructors' responses to six open-ended questions via online survey. The data collection instruments corresponding to the research questions are presented in Table 3.

Thematic content analysis was used for summarizing themes from student reflections on their learning experiences with the Software. *Composite* responses that reflect the content of all the responses in each category were created and tabulated. The most frequent themes were identified. Positive and negative student comments on their

Table 3. Research questions and data collection instruments [3].

Research questions	Data collection instruments
1. What were the students' perceptions of how the Software supported their cognitive processing of the target concepts? 2. What was the overall student experience with the Software? 3. What unanticipated problems have students and instructors experienced with the Software? 4. Which features and instructional strategies implemented in the Software were the most helpful to students and instructors? And the least helpful?	Online survey consisting of 14 statements, two open-ended questions and a reflection summary. Students could take the survey at their convenience within the allocated time for response. Students rated their experience with the Software using a rating scale of 5 (5-strongly agree, 1-strongly disagree)
5. What were the instructors' perceptions of student use of the Software? 6. What was the instructor's overall experience with the use of the Software in the online course? 7. What effect did Software have on the role of the instructor and the effectiveness of instruction in the course?	Online survey consisting of six open-ended questions

overall learning experience with the Software and its helpfulness in reducing mathematics anxiety were also examined.

Franklin University Institutional Review Board approved this study. An informed consent was obtained from instructors before they completed an anonymous online survey. Students who participated in the study were given bonus credits. Students who did not participated were given alternative course activities to gain equivalent number of credits. After reviewing the Software, students who participated in the study filled out the 14-item survey.

4 Results

Results from this study indicate learner satisfaction with the Software structure and activities. For example, explanations of new content, summary slides, worked out examples, and comprehension questions augmented with program feedback led to greater satisfaction with perceived knowledge gained and increased learner autonomy. The following sections provide a summary of the main results obtained.

4.1 Summary of Students' Quantitative Data

As reflected in Table 4, students' experiences with the Software were overwhelmingly positive.

Table 4. Students' experiences with the Software: survey questions (5-strongly agree; 1-strongly disagree).

Survey question #	Aug–Dec 2015 Mean (SD)	Jan–Apr 2016 Mean (SD)
1. I liked the layout of the sections in the lecture	4.7 (0.83)	4.7 (0.59)
2. I liked the navigation in the sections in the lecture	4.7 (0.73)	4.7 (0.53)
3. I liked the explanation and the examples used in the informational slides of the lecture sections	4.6 (1.2)	4.7 (0.67)
4. I liked the summary slides used throughout the sections	4.5 (0.94)	4.5 (0.76)
5. I found the transcript option useful	4.1 (1.06)	4.3 (0.89)
6. The sections helped me understand this week's material	4.6 (0.79)	4.7 (0.55)
7. The section design helped me retain the new information	4.4 (0.79)	4.5 (0.71)
8. The section design helped me maintain my attention	4.5 (0.85)	4.4 (0.69)
9. I found the self-assessment feature (Check Your Learning questions) helpful	4.5 (1.35)	4.5 (0.78)
10. The answer feedback to the Check Your Learning questions (explanations of the correct answers) were helpful	4.5 (0.72)	4.6 (0.73)
11. The answer feedback to the Check Your Learning questions was sufficient	4.3 (0.79)	4.4 (0.91)
12. I liked the supplemental content (if any), such as calculator tips and topic videos	4.3 (0.96)	4.4 (0.84)
13. The pace of the content was good	4.6 (0.72)	4.7 (0.62)
14. I enjoyed my experience using the lectures	4.5 (0.84)	4.6 (0.61)

Students rated the usability of the Software very high. The majority of students strongly agreed that they liked the layout, navigation, and pace of the instruction as indicated by the scores obtained in items 1, 2 and 9 in Table 4. Most participants strongly agreed that the Software supported their cognitive processing of the new information as shown by items 6, 7 and 8 scores.

The vast majority of the students found the Check Your Learning questions embedded in the Software helpful. Also, they highly valued the program feedback that provided the explanation of correct answers, and they found the feedback sufficient as shown by items 10 and 11 scores.

Such features as access to audio transcripts and supplemental materials (for example, help on how to use the calculator for accomplishing specific tasks) were highly valued by some students, but not by all of them (See items 5 and 12 in Table 4). This can be attributed to the difference in student prior knowledge of the topics. Transcripts allowed students with high prior knowledge to briefly go over familiar material. For example, the calculator help was used only by those students who needed it. The overwhelming majority of the study participants enjoyed their learning experience with the Software as item 14 score shows.

4.2 Summary of Students' Qualitative Data

Thematic content analysis was used for summarizing themes from student reflections on their learning experiences with the Software supported by illustrative examples. The themes fell under four categories:

(1) Effectiveness of multimedia design – software usability and visual design
(2) Effectiveness of multimedia instructional design – helpfulness of software features
(3) Effectiveness of support for cognitive processing of information provided by the Software
(4) Overall satisfaction with the Software.

Composite responses that reflected the content of all the responses in each category were created and tabulated. The most frequent themes are presented at the top of the table. Eighty-six students provided their comments. Some students commented on more than one theme. The results are presented in Tables 5, 6, 7 and 8.

Table 5. The themes from students' comments about effectiveness of multimedia design [3].

Theme	Aug–Dec 2015 # comments	Jan–Apr 2016 # comments
Supports well self-paced learning	25	30
The pace is appropriate	17	26
The quality of narration is appropriate	14	12
Easy to navigate	44	39
Colors are visually appealing	10	24
Color coding supports the information processing	7	10
The length of mini lectures was appropriate	16	25

Table 6. The themes from students' comments about effectiveness of multimedia instructional design – helpfulness of the Software features [3].

Theme	Aug–Dec 2015 # comments	Jan–Apr 2016 # comments
Summary slides are helpful	25	36
Real-life examples are helpful	23	17
Explanations are helpful to guide student learning	34	32
Self-assessments at the end of each chapter reinforce student learning	39	44
Program feedback on student answers to quiz questions is helpful and sufficient	46	50
Supplemental materials were helpful	24	21
The calculator tutorial was helpful	19	25
Inclusion of audio transcripts is helpful	20	21
Graphics and tables were helpful	18	12
Animated examples helped understand concepts	20	11

Table 7. The themes from students' comments about effectiveness of support for cognitive processing of information provided by the multimedia lectures [3].

Theme	Aug–Dec 2015 # comments	Jan–Apr 2016 # comments
Helped students understand the material	32	34
Helped students remember the material	37	23
Helped students maintain their attention	24	37
Helped students organize information for encoding into long-term memory	13	6

Table 8. The themes from students' comments about overall satisfaction [3].

Theme	Aug–Dec 2015 # comments	Jan–Apr 2016 # comments
Satisfaction with the software	25	32
Recommendation to build similar modules for other courses	10	12
Reduces phobia of mathematics	7	6

Overall, there were no negative comments. Students were satisfied with all aspects of the Software. They thought that the lectures gave a classroom feel to a non-classroom approach to learning. Students found that the lectures were very user-friendly and supported cognitive processing of the new content effectively. Following are examples of students' direct comments about the effectiveness of multimedia design:

- *The overall appeal of the lecture keeps the student visually entertained while providing the necessary information.*
- *Very user-friendly and easy to understand how to use it.*
- *The pictures also help to keep the viewer engaged in the topic.*
- *The use of different colors for each individual step can help the viewer 'code' the information that is being taught.*
- *The layout of each slide and the transitions allowed the majority of the information to remain visible with the exception of the Summary slides.*
- *I believe this video and the rest of the video lectures have been extremely useful for myself during this course. They are extremely user friendly and are done in an organized manner.*

Students used the Software as preparation for doing homework assignments (27 comments) and preparation for exams (9 comments). Also, students highly recommended building similar modules for other courses in which complex concepts are taught. Below students' direct quotes can be found on the effectiveness of multimedia instructional design and on the helpfulness of software features:

- *In the randomized experiment section, the colors of the coupons and the colors of flyers were color coordinated to make the student (me) visualize how to think about the percentages of the different groups of people. This demonstration was a real-world scenario that I could relate to and therefore made the material easy to understand and increased me chances of retaining the information.*

- *Having a structured design helps to understand the expectations and makes learning the information easier.*
- *The Summary is also important because it reiterates the key elements, which can also help the viewer retain the information.*
- *I actually have created notebooks throughout this course to help in reference and to help me learn and I actually printed many of the slides and put them in my notebook.*
- *I feel like the more I test myself on the subject material the more comfortable I get with determining the correct answer and confirming my understanding.*
- *I think that the feedback or each question is great because it gives explanations as to why or why not the answer to the question was right.*

Students were prolific in offering comments on how the Software helped them to both understand and remember concepts related with statistics. Some students wrote:

- *Useful tool to use for learning, definitely helped understand the material.*
- *The explanations break the material down in terms I can understand and relate to therefore making it easier to retain the information.*
- *By using this as a review I feel I was able to better retain the information.*
- *Each section was detailed enough but also not to lengthy so it held your attention.*
- *It was also helpful having the tutorial to be long enough to explain the information, but not too long to lose interest.*
- *It broke out the various data collection methods, specifically how to gather data as well as the strengths and weakness that may be associated.*

More comments on the satisfaction with the Software were obtained on the second round of evaluation. Based on the bugs report, students' suggestions for corrections were collected, tabulated and addressed and fixed. Such might have increased the level of students' satisfaction. There were also a few comments regarding the impact of the Software in reducing the phobia of mathematics.

There were also a few suggestions for improvement. Twenty students asked that more self-assessment questions be included in the Software. Nine students recommended three tries instead of two tries on the self-assessment questions. Four students would like to have a section containing all the videos teaching how to use calculators in one single place. Four students would like to have a reference to the specific page in the textbook. This last suggestion would help students go to the textbook, if extra study is required, without spending time searching it.

During the second semester (January to April 2016), most of the themes that came from students' comments remained the same compared to the first semester (August to December 2015). The major new theme that emerged was about having student experiences with the Software graded. One of the students, wrote the following comment:

Because these interactive lectures were not mandatory, I did not complete them for every section. When I felt like I was stuck on a problem or having a hard time remembering the material, I would use these lectures. I wish I had gone about the class differently and used these lectures each week. My reasoning was that because the amount of work in this class is so large, on top of the other classes I was taking, and my personal life, I did not have time to complete something if it was not part of the grade. It would be nice if these lectures counted for a portion of our grade.

4.3 Instructors' Feedback

Two face-to-face instructors and four online instructors were surveyed in the first semester, while three face-to-face instructors and three online instructors answered the survey in the second semester. All instructors provided favorable comments about the Software. Most of them recommended that their students should use the Software before they come to class or during synchronous online sessions. All the instructors believed that the Software was a good resource for helping students understand complex statistical concepts. Half of the instructors considered the Software as a tool that provided helpful ideas for teaching statistical concepts. *Composite* responses that reflected the content of all the instructor responses in each category were created and tabulated can be seen on Table 9.

Table 9. Instructor comments about their perceived effectiveness of the Software.

Areas of inquiry based on research questions	*Composite* responses	# instructors comments
The use of the software by the instructor for teaching the course	The online multimedia modules were highly recommended for students to watch before class	6
Effect of the software on the instructor role, if any	It freed instructor time for discussing and clarifying complex concepts in class and during synchronous online sessions. Good addition to the course	6
The use of the software during online synchronous sessions or in class, if any	(a) Some screens in the Software were used during the synchronous online sessions to help students visualize complex concepts	5
	(b) Played the videos in the Software instead of lecturing. This was not a very successful experience because the instructor lost students' interest	1
Perceived student reactions to the Software	Positive comments from students because it helps clarify the weekly content	6
Perceived effect of the software on student understanding of the topics	Excellent resource, supports understanding of the content because it is chunked down into easy to understand sections	6
The use of the Software for professional development, if any	(a) The software provides helpful suggestions to the instructor on how to help students understand the concepts	3
	(b) The Software did not have any impact on professional development	3

5 Discussion and Conclusions

Most of the students who participated in the evaluation of the Software found it highly valuable for their learning. The online interactive multimedia modules provided invaluable instructional support for online students, as well as face to face students. Students favored self-paced instruction, dual coding of information supported by multimedia lectures, systematic instruction of complex subject matter for online students, the opportunity to review the material at a later time, clear, concise and effective instruction, multiple examples, comprehension questions with explanatory program feedback and many other aspects of the Software.

Interestingly, students used the Software in additional ways that their instructors did not anticipate. It was not only used as initial learning before classroom instruction, but also served for reviewing the course material and for test preparation.

Surprisingly, one of the most valuable features in the Software appeared to be comprehension questions augmented with explanatory feedback. Also, several students mentioned that they would like to have similar instruction in other courses. Others regretted that student experience with the software was not part of their course grade. They thought that if the Software experience were graded, more students would be using it for their benefit.

One of the unanticipated consequences of the formative evaluation study was that by exposing students to the Software, the number of students who started using it on a regular basis increased because they realized that this was a more effective and efficient way of learning statistics. The following comments were chosen as the best representations of student experience with the Software. They are:

- *I have done much with online classes and various interactive programs such as Pearson Math XL, Webassign, and McGrawHill Math connect. The interactive lectures on the Franklin course site are far better than any of the others I have used.*
- *I really enjoy the interactive lectures. I think it gives a classroom feel to a non-classroom approach to learning.*
- *At the beginning of this course, I didn't look at the interactive lecture and opted to read the book and assist the [...] meetings on Thursdays. One day I decided to listen to the interactive lecture to see if it was helpful. I really liked it because I was able to hear someone explain the course and give concrete examples I could relate to. It really helped me understand the idea behind each chapter and what each formula and equation was used for.*

Table 10 shows Students performance and attrition rates over the intervention. It can be concluded that the Software accomplished its ultimate goal of increasing student retention and the number of students receiving passing grades (letters grades A, B or C). The attrition rates represent the percentage of students who drop the course. There was a 11% decrease from *before using the Software* to *January to April 2016 while using the Software*.

Design and develop online courses and interactive multimedia features firmly grounded in learning theories provide effective learning experiences to online learners that often lack a rich interaction with the course content. This is particularly important

Table 10. Percentages of students receiving passing grades and attrition rates for the semester before and after the use of the Software.

	Before using the Software	August to December 2015 while using the Software	January to April 2016 while using the Software
% students receiving passing grades	49.8%	66%	64%
Attrition rates	26%	17%	15%

when teaching complex content as mathematics and statistics. Therefore, it is critical to investigate appropriate pedagogies for teaching statistics online to foster learners' positive attitudes towards the learning of mathematics and support their conceptual understanding of the content.

5.1 Suggestions for Improvement

The major suggestions for improvement were about building additional interactive multimedia lectures for this course and similar resources for other statistics and mathematics courses. Some students wanted to have more multimedia presentation of the new material, more examples, more calculator tutorials, and more comprehension questions in the Software.

5.2 Study Strengths and Limitations

Only 36% and 39% of the students enrolled in the course between August 2015 and April 2016 participated in the evaluation. Thus, it is likely that the respondents were those who potentially might benefit from the Software use. Although not representative of the entire cohort of students, this evaluation provides useful information for the design and development of multimedia educational materials to teach statistics and support the needs of online students. The results of the study demonstrated that students valued the principles of sound educational practices applied to both online and face to face instruction. Also, student comments provided preliminary evidence of the effectiveness of the Software. This study benefits the field of multimedia instructional design by reporting on specific strategies employed to produce effective instructional solutions.

References

1. Complete College America: Time is the Enemy of Graduation (2011). http://completecollege.org/resources/
2. National Center for Academic Transformation: How to Redesign a College Course Using NCAT's Methodology (2014). http://www.thencat.org/Guides/AllDisciplines/ADChapterI.html

3. Koehler, N., Correia, A.-P., Alpay, N., LeVally, C.: Formative evaluation of a web-based multimedia intervention to support learning of statistics. In: Escudeiro, P., Costagliola, G., Zvacek, S., Uhomoibhi, J., McLaren, B.M. (eds.) Proceedings of the 9th International Conference on Computer Supported Education (CSEDU 2017), vol. 1, Science and Technology Publications, Porto, pp. 92–99 (2017)
4. Petty, N.W.: Drill and Rote in Teaching LP and Hypothesis Testing [Web log post] (2012). https://learnandteachstatistics.wordpress.com/2012/02/
5. Larwin, K., Larwin, D.: A meta-analysis examining the impact of computer-assisted instruction on postsecondary statistics education: 40 years of research. J. Res. Technol. Educ. **43**, 253–278 (2011)
6. Moore, D.S.: New pedagogy and new content: the case of statistics. Int. Stat. Rev. **65**, 123–165 (1997)
7. Garfield, J., Chance, B., Snell, J.L.: Technology in college statistics courses. In: Holton, D., et al. (eds.) The Teaching and Learning of Mathematics at University Level. New ICMI Study Series, vol. 7. Springer, Dordrecht (2001). https://doi.org/10.1007/0-306-47231-7_32
8. Chance, B., Ben-Zvi, D., Garfield, J., Medina, E.: The role of technology in improving student learning of statistics. Technol. Innov. Stat. Educ. **1**, 1–23 (2007)
9. Karpicke, J.D., Roediger, H.L.: The critical importance of retrieval for learning. Science **319**, 966–968 (2008). https://doi.org/10.1126/science.1152408
10. Sklar, J.C., Zwick, R.: Multimedia presentations in educational measurement and statistics: design considerations and instructional approaches. J. Stat. Educ. **17** (2009)
11. Wender, K.F., Muehlboeck, J.S.: Animated diagrams in teaching statistics. Behav. Res. Methods Instrum. Comput. **35**, 255–258 (2003)
12. Phye, G.D.: Academic learning and remembering. In: Phye, G.D. (ed.) Handbook of Academic Learning: The Construction of knowledge, pp. 47–64. Academic Press, San Diego (1997)
13. Anderson, L., Krathwohl, D.A.: Taxonomy for Learning, Teaching and Assessing: A Revision of Bloom's Taxonomy of Educational Objectives. Longman, New York (2001)
14. Kirschner, P.A., Sweller, J., Clark, R.: Why minimal guidance during instruction does not work: an analysis of the failure of constructivist, discovery, problem-based, experiential and inquiry-based teaching. Educ. Psychol. **41**, 75–86 (2006)
15. Moreno, R., Mayer, R.E.: A learner-centered approach to multimedia explanations: deriving instructional design principles from cognitive theory. Interact. Multimed. Electron. J. Comput. Enhanc. Learn. **2**, 12–20 (2000)
16. Song, S.H., Keller, J.M.: Effectiveness of motivationally adaptive computer-assisted instruction on the dynamic aspects of motivation. ETR&D **49**, 5–22 (2001)
17. Alpay, N., Ratvatsky, P., Koehler, N., LeVally, C.: Redesigning a statistical concepts course to improve retention, satisfaction, and success rates of non-traditional undergraduate students. J. Educ. Multimed. Hypermedia **26**, 5–27 (2017)
18. Mayer, R.E.: Multimedia Learning. Cambridge University Press, Cambridge (2009)
19. Stark, R., Mandl, H., Gruber, H., Renkl, A.: Conditions and effects of example elaboration. Learn. Instr. **12**, 39–60 (2002)
20. Sweller, J.: Cognitive load during problem solving: effects on learning. Cogn. Sci. **12**, 257–285 (1988)
21. Mayer, R.E., Moreno, R.: Nine ways to reduce cognitive load in multimedia learning. Educ. Psychol. **38**, 43–52 (2003)
22. Mayer, R.E., Moreno, R.: Aids to computer-based multimedia learning. Learn. Instr. **12**, 107–119 (2002)

Creating Virtual Enterprises to Strengthen IT Architects's Training

Lina Casas(✉), Mario Sánchez(✉), and Jorge Villalobos(✉)

Systems and Computing Engineering Department, Universidad de los Andes, Bogotá, Colombia
{lg.casas766,mar-san1,jvillalo}@uniandes.edu.co
http://www.uniandes.edu.co

Abstract. Due to the increasing importance of IT technologies in the organizations' operation, IT related jobs have become highly demanded. That is the case of IT architects, who are responsible for aligning the business needs and motivations with the technology solutions that support company functions. However, the offer of qualified IT architects is not enough to cover the demand. This happens mainly because the training needed to acquire the technology, business, communications, and management skills required for the role is long and difficult to get. This paper describes the creation of virtual enterprises as a tool for facilitating the training of IT architects. These virtual enterprises imitate the real challenges that an IT architect may confront in real life projects, thus helping the trainees acquire the desired experience and expertise.

Keywords: IT architecture · Project based learning
Virtual enterprises

1 Introduction

IT Architecture is the discipline that focuses on designing and delivering valuable technology strategies to companies [2]. It differs from Enterprise Architecture because IT Architecture not only comprises the design and planning of the IT solution that complies with the business's needs, but also includes the implementation of that solution. IT architecture has taken on great importance in recent years because of the potential it has to positively impact companies. However, it is not easy to find professionals with the required profile: An IT architect must have theoretical foundations of business and technology, but must also have soft skills and expertise that come with experience.

Due to the popularity of IT architecture, different training programs have been created for architects. Said programs range from seminars or short courses to extensive and long programs. Programs such as The Open Group TOGAF Certification Program [3], Certified IT Architect (CITA) [4], and IEEE Computer Society's Certified Software Development Professional Program [5] are quite

P. Escudeiro et al. (Eds.): CSEDU 2017, CCIS 865, pp. 154–178, 2018.
https://doi.org/10.1007/978-3-319-94640-5_8

popular and aim to produce highly adaptable professionals, with deep industry comprehension, high business insight, and profound technology knowledge.

However, coaching IT architects is not easy: they are expected to quickly become ready to face the complexity, inconsistency, and uncertainty of real projects. The above implies that IT architecture trainees must acquire concepts and knowledge but must know how to put them into practice. This requires them to solve challenges and complex cases in real like scenarios. One would think then that the best thing is that they practice in real companies but this could cause problems to the company. Therefore, an appropriate alternative is to use cases that simulate real problems.

With the purpose of providing these cases, we created an IT laboratory which consists of a set of simulation scenarios based on fictional organizations. These scenarios resemble a complete organization with strategic and operational components and real technology implementation supporting it. Furthermore, they illustrate different industries in order to teach students about different markets. They also recreate the complexity and imperfection of a real company. Taking those scenarios as a base, the students can have an environment to practice, reinforce, and integrate all the concepts concerning analysis, design, and implementation of IT architectures.

The scenarios are used on several academic projects focusing on different phases of IT architecture projects. The focus in each phase is determined according to the course and program level, and the set of skills the students should acquire or improve. At the end of the projects, the achievement of those competences can be evaluated. With the purpose of giving the students interesting projects to work on, the objective and scope of the projects should be carefully defined and the evaluation schemes adjusted and validated.

The paper is structured as follows. Section 2 describes what an IT architecture project is. Section 3 explains what a project based learning approach is. Section 4 details the proposed definition of an IT laboratory used to train undergraduate and graduate students. Section 5 details the construction of a conceptual scenario and Sect. 6 of an operational scenario. Then, Sect. 7 shows a case study of the IT laboratory use and evaluation in an academic program. Finally, Sect. 8 presents the conclusions regarding the benefits of the IT laboratory.

2 IT Architecture Projects

An IT Architecture (ITA) Project is typically distributed in non-linear phases or cycles. Each cycle has an internal set of activities whose purpose is to obtain a product or deliverable once it is finished. Also, at the end of each cycle there is a stakeholder's validation in order to get feedback and do the necessary adjustments.

We created a model with the common cycles in an IT architecture project process and its activities. This model, as shown in Fig. 1, is based on different frameworks and methodologies such as (Team Software Process) TSP [12],

(Rational Unified Process) RUP [11] and TOGAF's ADM [10]. The proposed process includes activities that go from planning to executing and deploying the solution, distributed through six major phases: (PP1) Planning, (PP2) Information Gathering, (PP3) Analysis, (PP4) Design, (PP5) Roadmap, and (PP6) Implementation. Each phase and its deliverables (such a document with the models or a code part) composes a portion of the final product to be delivered to the final users. This incremental approach assures quality and reliability of the product through continuous refining and adjustment. Because of this, in a typical IT Architecture project it is not strange to find redesign steps in subsequent phases.

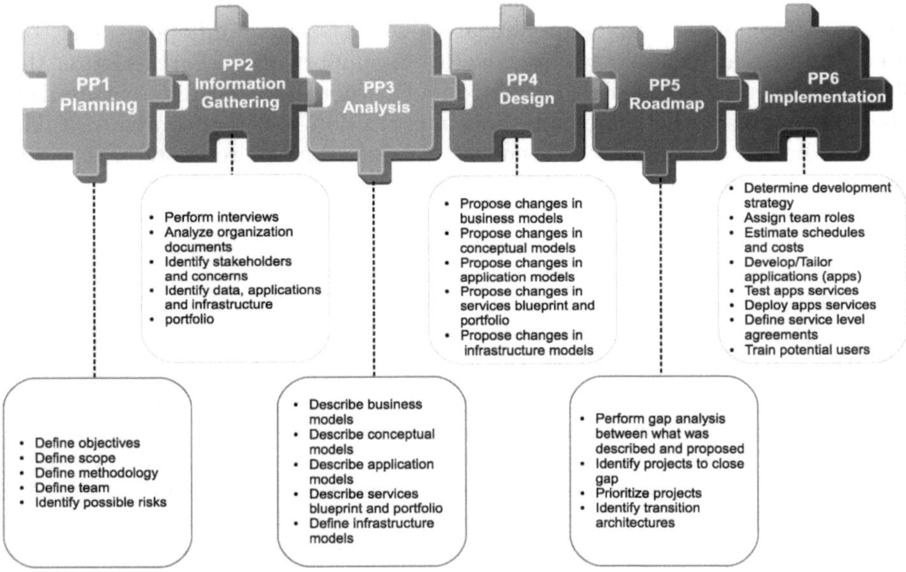

Fig. 1. IT architecture project process.

It is important to note that some frameworks and methodologies do not consider the final phase (PP6) Implementation as a part of an IT Architecture Process but more as a part of the Development Process. Nonetheless, we firmly believe that an IT Architecture is not complete until the final product is released. Moreover, the IT architect must be involved in all the phases even if the final step is performed by a development team. The reason for that is twofold: the architect's insight is truly important on the development tasks and a qualified architect must have profound knowledge of the development stages in order to get the expertise to execute ITA projects correctly.

In order to train architects that can adequately perform an ITA project, they should have skills concerning technology knowledge and personal abilities. To define these set of skills we performed a literature review and enhanced them through surveys and interviews with instructors and IT experts, as recommended by Kalampokis [14]. In the review we took into account the different roles of an IT architect and the competences each role needs to have in order to successfully contribute to an ITA project according to TOGAF [16], IASA [15], TSP [12], and RUP [11]. We also included the Accreditation Board for Engineering and Technology [13] which defines a series of abilities, called student outcomes, that represent what students from any discipline are expected to know and be able to do. Making a match between the consulted sources and the expert's validation, the list was completed and edited. The list is presented on Table 1. Using this list as a baseline, we calculated skills required in every phase of an architectural project, as shown in Fig. 2.

Table 1. Skills required by an IT architect. (Extended version of Table 1 on [1]).

ID	Skill	Type
SK1	Analyze and understand problems, requirements and constraints	Hard skill
SK2	Design, document and justify proposed solutions	Hard skill
SK3	Build, implement, operate and manage designs	Hard skill
SK4	Manage IT projects	Hard skill
SK5	Work in multidisciplinary teams	Soft skill
SK6	Work with other IT roles	Soft skill
SK7	Recommend implementation projects prioritization	Hard skill
SK8	Guarantee quality in IT	Hard skill
SK9	Lead work teams	Soft skill
SK10	Communicate business and IT concepts	Soft skill
SK11	Give value to business through IT	Hard skill
SK12	Understand the organizations business	Hard skill
SK13	Align business and IT	Hard skill
SK14	Define business projects scope	Hard skill
SK15	Manage software	Hard skill
SK16	Design software	Hard skill
SK17	Develop business strategies	Hard skill
SK18	Define the IT architecture	Hard skill
SK19	Optimize business capabilities	Hard skill
SK20	Manage the integration and reuse of existing elements of the EA	Hard skill
SK21	Design solution architecture	Hard skill
SK22	Integrate technologies	Hard skill
SK23	Give recommendations regarding to the appropriate solutions for specific problems	Hard skill

	PP1	PP2	PP3	PP4	PP5	PP6
SK1	●		●		●	●
SK2				●	●	
SK3				●	●	●
SK4	●	●			●	●
SK5	●	●				
SK6	●	●		●	●	●
SK7					●	●
SK8	●				●	●
SK9	●	●			●	●
SK10						●
SK11				●	●	
SK12		●				
SK13				●		
SK14	●					
SK15		●	●	●		
SK16			●	●		
SK17		●	●	●	●	
SK18				●		
SK19		●	●	●		
SK20			●	●	●	
SK21					●	
SK22				●		
SK23				●		
Total	7	8	6	13	12	8

Fig. 2. Skills required in each phase of an IT project.

3 Project Based Learning

Project Based Learning (PBL) is a pedagogical approach which aims to confront the students with problems and challenges similar to those found in the real world. It is mainly based on giving the students the opportunity to not only memorize concepts but also put them in practice on different projects and activities. PBL integrates knowing and doing and students take advantage of digital tools to produce high quality, collaborative products. Students acquire knowledge and learn elements of the core curriculum, but also apply what they know to solve authentic problems and produce results that matter. PBL refocuses education on the student, and not the curriculum – a shift demanded by the global world, which rewards intangible assets such as drive, passion, creativity, empathy, and resiliency. These can not be taught out of a textbook, but must be activated through experience [6]. More information about PBL work scheme and advantages can be found on [7,9].

Additionally, there has been research on the use of IT in the PBL approach. The use of IT technologies can be extremely helpful when defining projects because they can simulate real environments where students can practice. This is the case of Hypercase, an interactive system's analysis and design simulation tool which is used on different courses and books. More about Hypercase can be consulted on [8].

In order to correctly apply the project based approach, students must be confronted with reality simulated situations that help them gain the necessary expertise to act in each case. To be truly useful, the case studies must also meet some requirements. First, the cases must be coherent and resemble a real situation: they have to make sense and provide correct input for the students to practice with. Second, the cases have to present a complex context to the students. If they are confronted with an ideal and simplified situation they are not going to be ready to face a difficult one. Finally, they have to evolve in time as real enterprises do in response to regulations, market and technology changes.

In order to provide cases that cover all the requirements cited above, we created the IT Laboratory as a set of reality simulated scenarios in different business verticals. This laboratory has been used for six years as the main tool in more than ten graduate and undergraduate courses and for hundreds of students. The next two sections present the processes for creating and using scenarios in the laboratory.

4 IT Laboratory

The IT Laboratory is based on a solid and flexible infrastructure capable of supporting a set of virtual companies belonging to different business verticals, which pose architectural challenges that students must understand, analyse, and solve. The laboratory was created with the purpose of giving the students of different IT programs the opportunity to interact with reality simulated cases in a controlled environment. In this environment, training is complemented from the experience, in addition to the theoretical knowledge acquired. This approach can be used in undergraduate, graduate or business education, changing the size and difficulty of the assignments accordingly. These virtual companies or cases are called *scenarios* and they are divided in two groups: *conceptual scenarios* and *operational scenarios*.

Conceptual scenarios are composed by business, information, application, and technology models but without a real implementation to simulate its operation. *Operational scenarios* have a real technology solution in which students can work and implement IT architecture projects. An operational scenario implementation consists on a set of virtual servers supporting enterprise components like Enterprise Service Bus (ESB), Enterprise Resource Planning (ERP), Customer Relationship Management (CRM), and Business Process Management Suites (BPMS), as well as other custom made software applications. The underlying infrastructure recreates the software and hardware capabilities of a big or medium company. This infrastructure is composed by virtual machines with varying technology capabilities. Those virtual machines are hosted in a medium available datacenter.

Currently, the IT laboratory has more than thirty virtual machines, 1.5 TB of storage, 228 GB of memory and 2.8 GHz of processing power. It also has web pages describing the scenarios and has served as an experimentation environment for more than ten different students cohorts in three different programs. A model describing the deployment of one particular scenario is shown in Fig. 3. This model shows the supporting servers for an IT implementation, divided into front-end and back-end. The first group represents the servers's hosting components that are directly accessed by the users. The second one represents all the servers in charge of different functions and operations that do not have direct contact with the users. Additionally, there are components that do not belong in either group, since they are servers responsible for hosting auxiliary services such as load balancing and redirection.

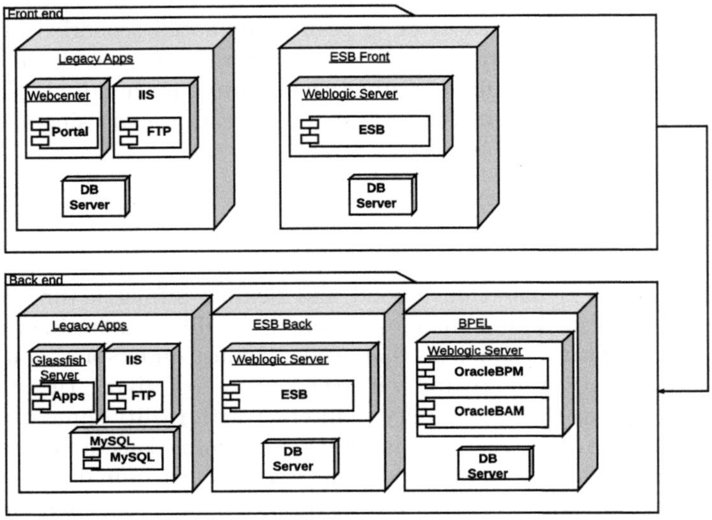

Fig. 3. Scenario deployment model.

Presently, our laboratory has 11 conceptual scenarios and 3 operational scenarios in diverse industries and with different contexts. Figure 4 shows the distribution of the different conceptual and operational scenarios. As it was previously exposed, there is a clear difference between the components in conceptual and operational scenarios. That defines the type of students that use the scenario and likewise the projects they have to face. Conceptual scenarios do have an architectural documentation the undergraduate students can review, use and change in order to develop the first five phases of an IT architecture project. However, because of the courses's level and objective, they do not implement or modify any solution. On the other hand, graduate students can use the operational scenarios to face complex and complete IT projects in order to complement their education.

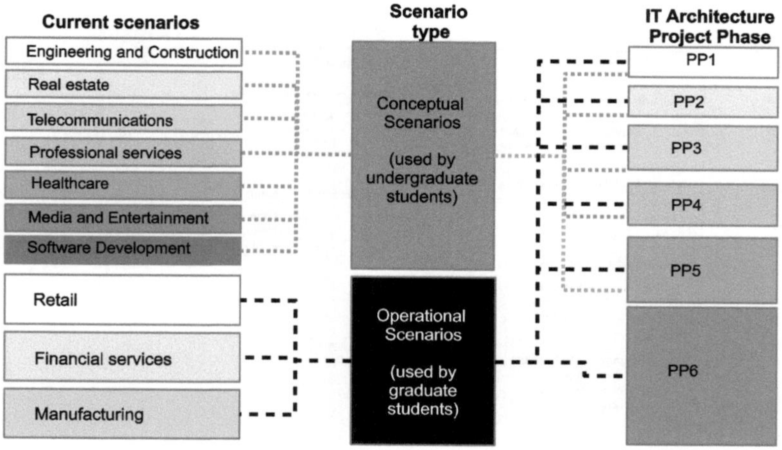

Fig. 4. IT laboratory distribution.

5 Conceptual Scenarios

A conceptual scenario (as shown in Fig. 5) is a virtual company which contains business, applications, data and infrastructure definitions but no real implementation or hardware representing said definitions. A conceptual scenario is conceived as the descriptions of the main elements of a company presented through the typical media that can be found in real companies. This media includes, but it is not limited to, web sites, brochures, internal reports, word an excel documents and financial sheets.

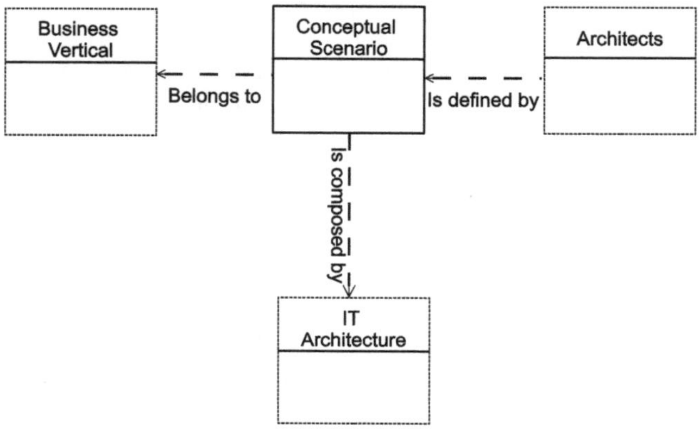

Fig. 5. Conceptual scenario definition.

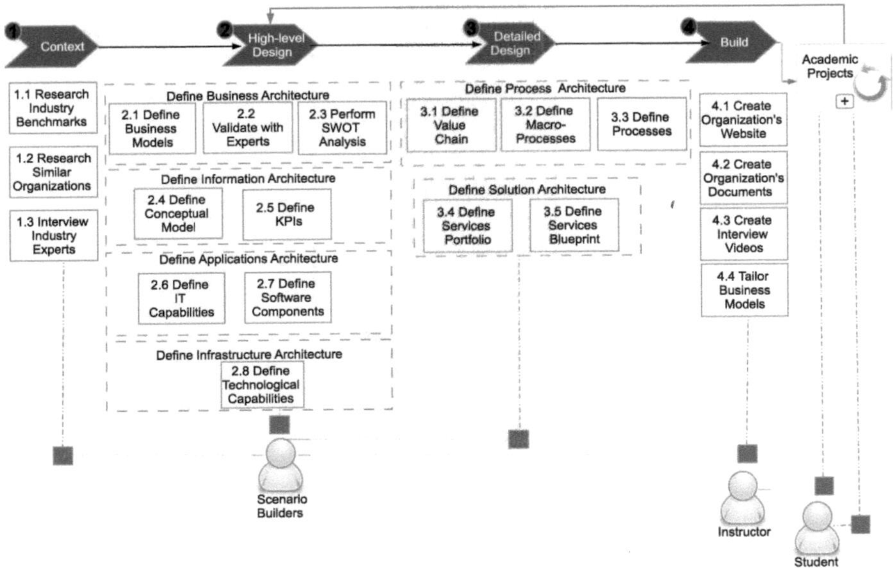

Fig. 6. Conceptual scenario's creation methodology.

A conceptual scenario is developed by a group of *scenario builders* with the help of industry experts who help by gathering information and validating conformance with the market and industry. The process for creating a conceptual scenario follows a specific methodology which is shown in Fig. 6 and explained step by step in the following subsections.

Some steps in this methodology are performed by the scenario builders that have to define and create all the artifacts of the scenario. Other steps for creating activities and generating rubrics are carried out by the instructors. Finally, there are steps for the students to take during the development of the activities associated with a project as part of their studies.

5.1 Context

Once the industry for the scenario is selected, the first step consists in acquiring background information about the industry. Scenario builders thus research the business vertical, and in particular, they look for industry's benchmarks which consists of key indicators, drivers, and comparisons of how companies perform relative to their competitors. This information gives them a solid foundation about the vertical and the most important indicators, motivators and challenges a company on that industry has to endure. Moreover, they look for similar organizations to learn more about their typical operation, resources and customers. Lastly, they have interviews with industry experts. All this information helps

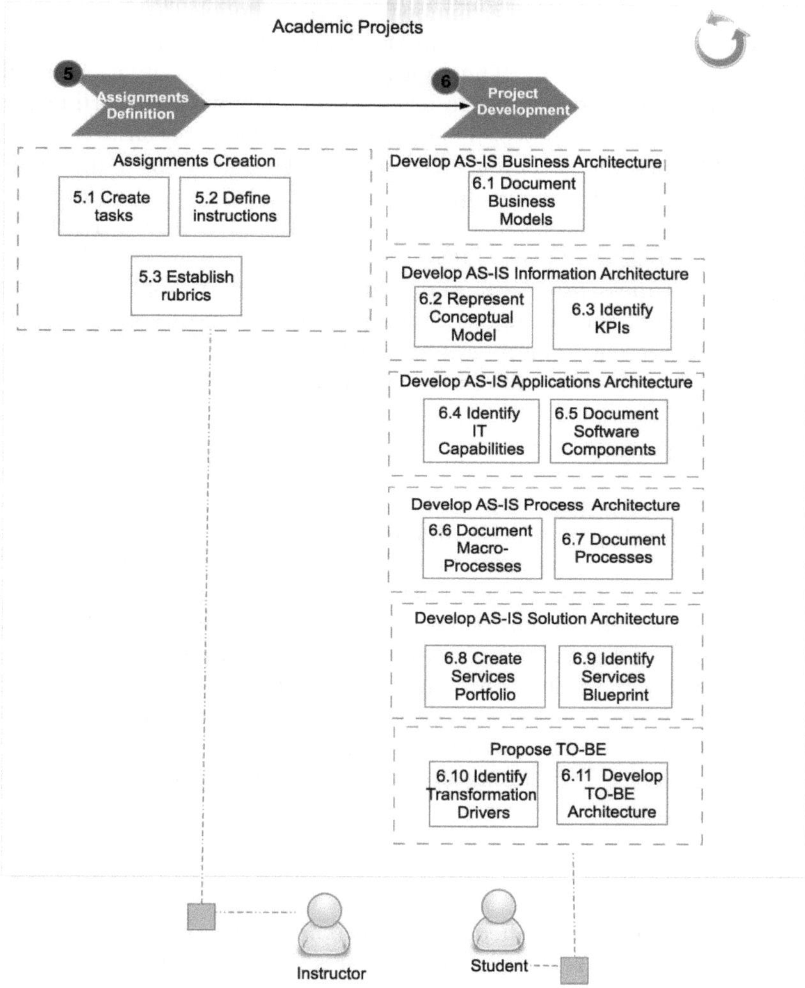

Fig. 7. Conceptual scenario's academic project phase.

scenario builders get a deeper understanding about the typical processes, infrastructure and day to day operation of that industry.

5.2 High-Level Design

With a more profound knowledge about the business vertical, scenario builders start a high level design of the four domains of IT architecture: Business Architecture, Information Architecture, Application Architecture, and Infrastructure Architecture.

In each domain, they design a number of critical models. After they are completed, there is a checkpoint with industry experts to validate if the architects work is correct and accurate. The typical step after the validation is adjusting and refining the models, and assuring compliance with the prime requirement of a utile case: coherence. Then, scenario builders perform a Strengths, Weaknesses, Opportunities, Threats (SWOT) Analysis in order to identify future transformation-drivers for the company.

During these steps, scenario builders also have to assure that the design shows a high complexity level. Thus, the scenarios require complex business models, many business processes, and a great number of applications, among others. Furthermore, the simulated company may have to be imperfect as any real company is, presenting problems and inefficiencies. This makes the scenario compliant with the second requirement of useful case studies.

5.3 Detailed Design

Taking the high level design as a base, scenario builders can start constructing more specific architectures: process architectures and solution architectures. The first one, starts with the previous business models and delves into the macroprocesses of the value chain. For each macroprocess, scenario builders design and model the processes and subprocesses that support or facilitate the company's operation. The second architecture, accommodates the application, information, and technology layers of the company including the service portfolio and the integration blueprint. The services portfolio organizes all the services the IT solution has to offer in order to support the business and the integration blueprint shows the interactions and the nature of these interactions in between the IT solution components.

5.4 Build

Once the definitions are finished, validated and fixed, the creation of media to represent them in a real like manner starts. Then, scenario builders tailor the models and medias in order for them to be consistent with the activities the students are going to perform. For example, if the students need to reconstruct a balance sheet, then the media must have some missing parts. With the tailored models, scenario builders create the company's website, writing information about the company objectives, motivation and the products/services it offers. Then, they construct internal documents such as brochures, financial and accountability sheets, reports, politics and manuals. Also, in order to correctly simulate the reality, the processes are not presented as documents with graphical representations or explicit sequence of activities but rather as pieces of stakeholder's interviews. This guarantees that the students will need to reconstruct the processes by themselves.

Also, the information presented is always updated to be compliant with current legal and market regulations. This makes the scenario meet the requirement of evolution over time.

When the scenario is finished, the Academic Project Phase shown in Fig. 7 starts.

5.5 Assignments Definition

During the assignments definition phase, the instructors create the tasks that students must work on. These tasks are divided in two categories: AS-IS architecture design and TO-BE architecture design. In each category there are different tasks related to the virtual enterprises analysis. For example the task can be the business model canvas definition. Once the tasks are defined, the instructor writes down the instructions in separated documents. Each document contains several tasks that complete a workshop and will have an associated grade within the course evaluations. Then, for each workshop, the instructor may define a rubric with detailed qualification criteria.

5.6 Project Development

During academic projects development, students must define the four domains of IT architecture for the company in its current state. In the business domain, they define the business, strategic and financial models. In the information domain, they identify all business entities, their relationships, and the main key business metrics. In terms of application domain, they should establish what technological capabilities the company supports and what software components are used.

Then, they continue analysing the company's operation through its business processes. For that, the students use the scenario's given information (interviews, brochures, reports or documents). Finally, the students must define and classify the services provided by the previously identified applications.

The four domains definition is defined for the current state of the organization. But, it must be defined for the future or desired state of the organization as well. The desired state is guided by the transformation drivers identified by the company. In addition, there must be a roadmap that explains in detail how to reach that desired state, through projects and transitions.

6 Operational Scenarios

An operational scenario (as shown in Fig. 8) is defined as a company in a specific industry vertical. It is developed by a group of *scenario builders* with the help of industry experts who help by gathering information and validating some of the subsequent steps. An operational scenario is mainly composed by two elements: an IT Architecture documentation and an IT solution. The first one consists mainly on the artifacts (models and documentation) related to the four IT architecture domains (business, information, application and technology). The IT solution refers to the software and hardware components needed to support the defined ITA. The process for creating an operational scenario follows a

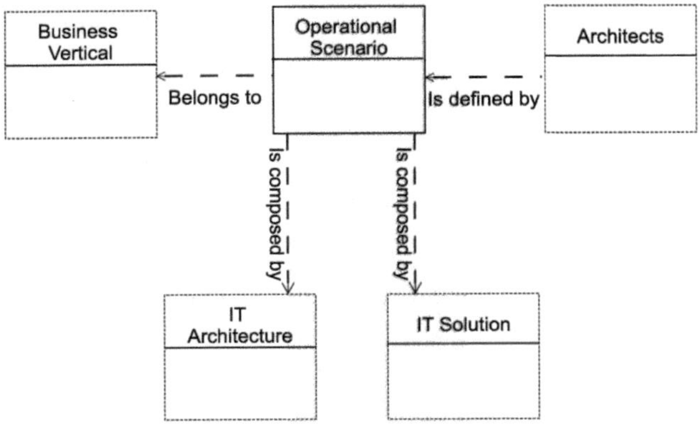

Fig. 8. Operational scenario's definition.

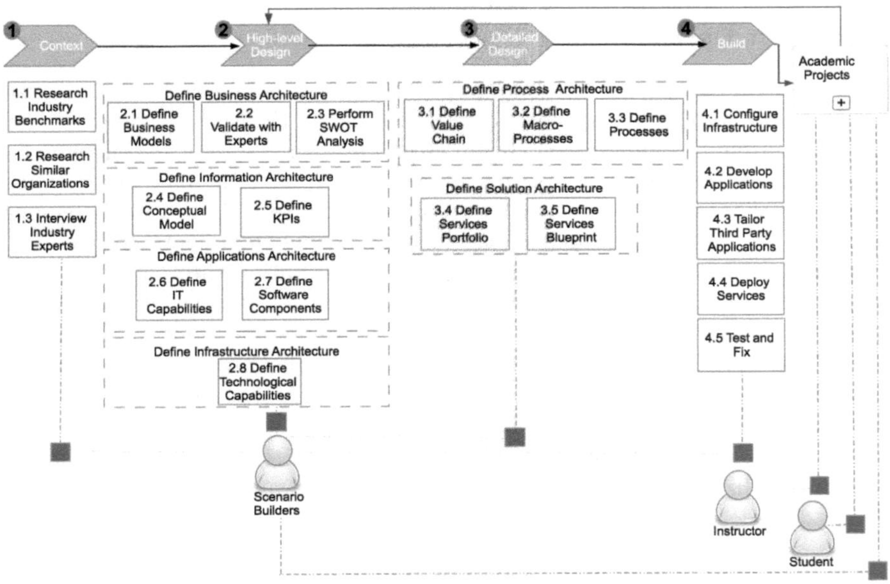

Fig. 9. Operational scenario's creation methodology. (Source: [1]).

specific methodology which is showed in Fig. 9 and explained step by step in the following subsections.

The first three steps (Context, High-level Design and Detailed Design) of the operational scenario's creation methodology are the same as those of the conceptual scenarios since they include the conceptualization of the company and the design of its IT architecture.

6.1 Build

With all the previous definitions, scenario builders start building code for each software component, expose the services, test them and, once finished, install and deploy the components on the infrastructure acquired for the scenario. When scenarios are completed they become useful for different courses and following their completion the Academic Projects phase showed in Fig. 9 begins. This phase is expanded in Fig. 10.

6.2 Initiative Definition

We define an *initiative* as a business transformation driver the student must materialize into real changes in the company business and IT components through a project. Choosing the initiatives is a complex task because they have to be consistent with the company's environment and assure that during their development students integrate the knowledge acquired on theoretical classes and develop correct skills. Therefore, the instructor has to do several activities before selecting a good initiative.

In order to identify possible initiatives, the instructor uses the SWOT analysis and looks for possible actions to exploit an opportunity, eliminate a weakness or mitigate the impact of a threat. Moreover, the instructor analyzes the company as a whole, taking into account external and internal forces that may affect its operation. This leads to other possible initiatives. Once the possible initiatives are written down, it is necessary to perform an evaluation to prioritize and select the best ones. For the evaluation there are two main criteria: the architectural effort, including skills involved, and the estimated time to develop the initiative. For the former one, the definition of the skills required in each IT project phase that was introduced in Sect. 2 is used.

The instructor estimates the effort points by measuring how much dedication each candidate initiative requires in the different phases of an architectural project. By dedication we refer to the time and level of expertise expected to complete the tasks of each phase. Then, the instructor calculates the weight of each initiative by multiplying the effort points in each phase of the project with the skills needed in that phase. Each of the final values from the different phases are finally summed to get the final architectural effort required to complete the initiative. These operations can be appreciated on Fig. 11.

After that, the instructor contacts a group of instructors and experienced IT architects to perform an expert's judgement to judge the approximate time that each initiative would take to be completed. Candidate initiatives are then prioritized: the most eligible ones are those with a high architectural effort but with a 4 month or less time frame, as it is the period in which the projects will take place. The instructor then selects one which meets the stated criteria.

Once the initiative is selected, rubrics with the evaluation criteria are refined, detailing which of the project phases are the most important and therefore deserve a greater weight on the student overall marks. Additionally, instructors

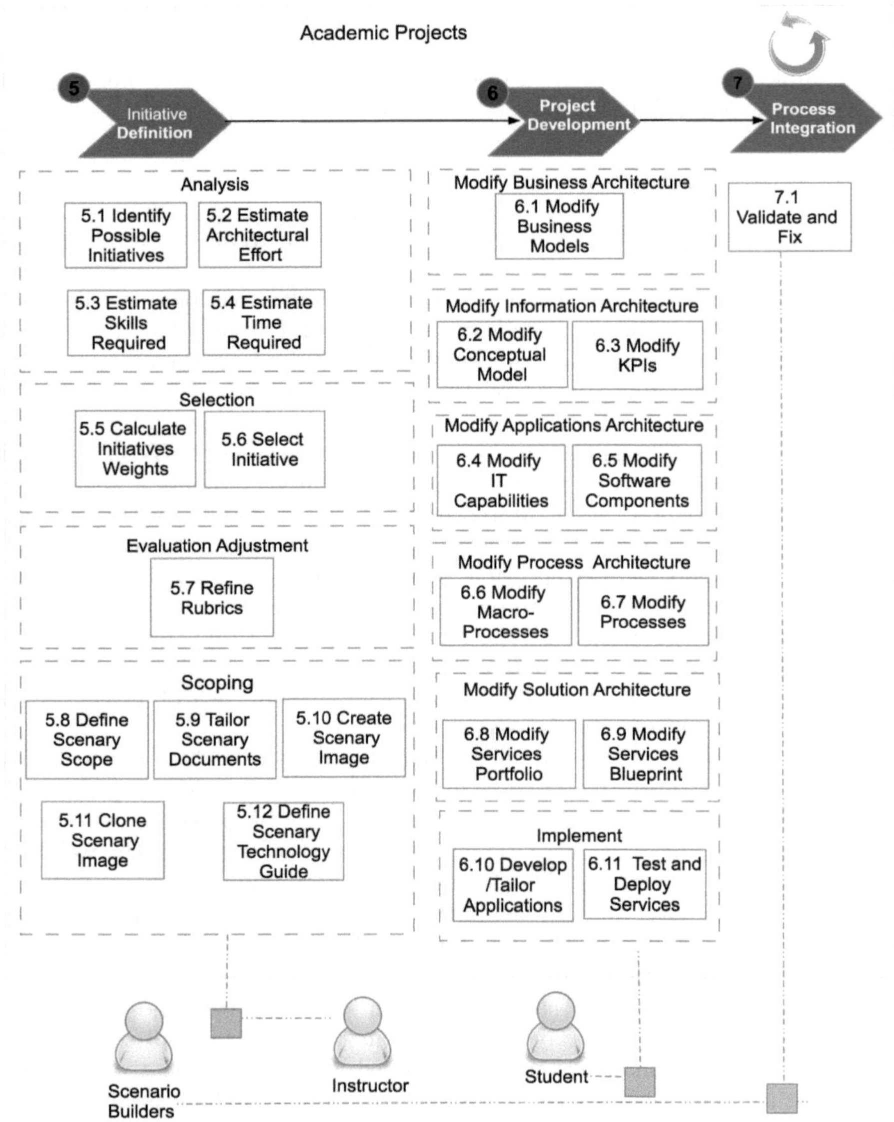

Fig. 10. Operational scenario's academic projects phase. (Source: [1]).

	Skills ponderation	I1	Points	I2	Points
PP1	3	3	9	5	15
PP2	2	1	2	1	2
PP3	1	3	3	1	1
PP4	1	1	1	5	5
PP5	2	3	6	3	6
PP6	6	5	30	5	30
Total	N/A	N/A	**51**	N/A	**59**

Fig. 11. Architectural effort calculation.

select the documentation that students need in order to understand the company and make the initiative real. Also, copies are made of the virtual machines hosting the scenario implementation. There has to be a copy for every team of students working on the project course, including a deployment guide and information about the technologies in which the scenario is based on.

6.3 Project Development

During the project development stage, the students have to go through the phases of an IT project in order to design and build the business an technology capabilities required to materialize the initiative. Depending on the initiative, changes will be required in the different architectural domain models. For example, if students are creating a whole new sales channel, there could be more modifications to the models than if they were altering some processes. Then, in order to correctly construct the initiative, students must follow some or all the stages of the process for an IT architecture project as stated in Sect. 2.

6.4 Project Integration

The key to having a reliable and self-sustainable scenario lies in this step because scenario builders can take the work done by the students, revise, adjust and add it to the scenario. Basically, scenario builders study the works done by the students and select the best ones. Then, after some modifications or adjustments, they integrate the new components to the scenario. This process assures the last requirement of a useful case: evolving in time as the scenario is always changing and improving.

7 Case Study: ECOS

The Software Construction Specialization (ECOS) is a postgraduate program at Universidad de los Andes oriented towards information technology professionals who want to acquire an architect profile. The program combines seven theoretical courses and three integrator projects (see Fig. 12). The first ones give students the foundation and concepts of the best practices in enterprise software construction. The projects provide a space in which students can apply their knowledge in the development of different stages of an IT architecture project process.

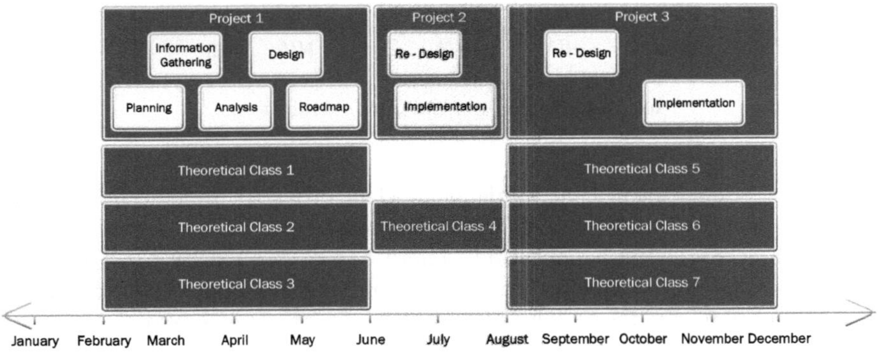

Fig. 12. ECOS structure.

In ECOS' projects, the IT laboratory is a key tool as it provides scenarios for the students to work. The scenario which has been used for the last six years is the Marketplace of the Alps (MPLA), a fictional scenario representing a marketplace between common goods retailers and manufacturers. The rest of this section shows a brief description of the MPLA scenario, the way ECOS used it during the past four years, and an evaluation of the laboratory.

7.1 The Scenario: MPLA

MarketPlace of the Alps is a company which provides a virtual system where different retailers can acquire products from a variety of options given by manufacturers or suppliers. Manufacturers offer their products, retailers specify what they want to buy and MPLA manages the transactions between them. The operation of MPLA revolves around four types of transactions:

PRICAT: Replicate product catalog (commercial supply) of a particular manufacturer to all retailers registered in MarketPlace that are interested in buying the product.

PO (Purchase order): Receive orders from a particular retailer and direct it to a specific set of manufacturers. The purchase order should only consider products for which the retailer has expressed interest in acquiring.

DA (Dispatching Advice): Receive notification of release, in response to a purchase order. This notice is sent from the manufacturer and is routed to the retailer which generated the PO.

RMA (Return Material Advice): Receive messages of merchandise return from the retailer and direct it to the manufacturer who made the delivery of the products (DA) to that entity.

The business model that supports the MarketPlace today is quite simple: Retailers generate a purchase order (PO) to the MarketPlace. The order includes: the desired product, maximum delivery date and maximum date associated auction duration. Then, the MarketPlace routes the order to all manufacturers who offer products that can fill the order. A reverse auction associated with the PO is created in order for the manufacturers to bid on. In the reverse auction, the manufacturers make their offers and the bid with the lowest price that meets the delivery date requested by the retailer is selected as the winner. Then, both the winning manufacturer and the retailer are notified and the manufacturer proceeds to generate a dispatch to the retailer.

MPLA's operation is totally based on different technology solutions. These solutions are mainly provided by Oracle Technologies and its integration is made through web services.

7.2 Usage

In ECOS, projects start with the definition of initiatives. As it is a graduated program, initiatives must present hard challenges and may involve the development of all the IT architecture project steps. The steps the students have to perform in the project are divided into three courses throughout a year (Project 1, 2, and 3) as shown in Fig. 12.

To exemplify the initiatives selection, Fig. 13 represents MPLA's SWOT analysis and Table 2 presents the candidate initiatives identified by ECOS instructors in 2014. In the analysis we can observe how the MarketPlace, by fully basing its operation on a technological platform, has as its strength the low operational costs, the possibility of doing business anywhere, and the speed and effectiveness of its service. On the other hand, there are also weaknesses in its business model: the inflexibility of transactions as they are defined in a single way on the platform, over dependence on technology, low margins and lack of control over the behavior of retailers and manufacturers.

On the other hand, there are some opportunities for improvement such as the creation of a mobile application to facilitate access to the platform, the creation of marketing campaigns to attract customers and the possibility of strengthening the relationship with current customers. Also, there are some threats that could affect the company. For example, changes in regulations could have a direct impact on the operation and the likelihood that businesses would create their own platforms would have a direct impact on their revenues.

This SWOT analysis helped instructors define the initiatives. All of them were evaluated to determine the effort needed to materialize each one. This evaluation was made by 4 ECOS instructors and then summarized. Then, taking those results and the skills required by each phase calculation, the architectural effort was determined, as it is shown in Fig. 14.

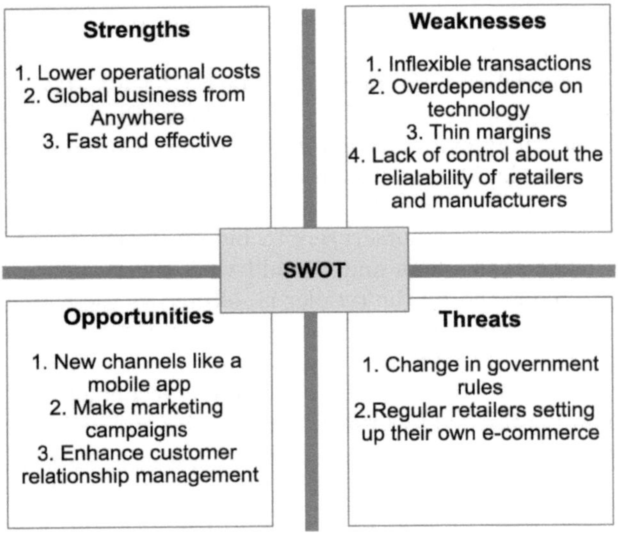

Fig. 13. MPLA'S SWOT analysis.

Table 2. Candidate initiatives.

ID	Initiative	Source
I1	Customer knowledge improvement	SWOT opportunity
I2	Reputation based selection	SWOT weakness
I3	New mobile app	SWOT opportunity
I4	Marketing campaigns	SWOT opportunity

	Skills ponderation	I1	Points	I2	Points	I3	Points	I4	Points
PP1	7	3	21	1	7	5	35	1	7
PP2	8	5	40	5	40	5	40	3	24
PP3	6	3	18	3	18	5	30	5	30
PP4	13	5	65	3	39	5	65	3	39
PP5	12	5	60	3	36	5	60	3	36
PP6	8	5	40	3	24	5	40	3	24
Total	N/A	N/A	**244**	N/A	**164**	N/A	**270**	N/A	**160**

Fig. 14. Architectural effort.

After that, the instructors performed the expert's judgement with the purpose of making an estimate of the time the students will need to complete the initiative. Then, taking the architectural effort and the average time determined by the instructors, the best initiative was selected, as seen in Fig. 15.

Then, the documentation and virtual machine copies were given to the thirty students divided in six groups. They started Project 1 reviewing and gathering additional information of MPLA in order to start making the analysis, design and roadmap phases correctly. Parallel to the time of Project 1 the students were also acquiring knowledge and useful concepts in their other courses which could be applied to the stages of the project. During Project 2 they were faced with the scenario implementation which has the components presented on Fig. 9. During this, a tutorial was provided to the students in order to familiarize them with the scenario's technologies. They were also allowed to refine the design and roadmap defined in Project 1. Finally, in Project 3 the students made the modifications to the legacy applications and enterprise systems in order to develop their designed customer knowledge improvements.

Initiative	I1	I2	I3	I4
Architectural Effort	244	164	270	160
Estimated Time	6 months	5 months	4 months	8,5 months

Fig. 15. Initiatives selection.

7.3 Evaluation

The evaluation of the IT laboratory was made in two ways. The first one was the continuous evaluation with the experts to validate coherence and pertinence of the built scenarios. This first evaluation was executed regularly as the IT laboratory was modified regularly. The second one was the IT laboratory impact on ECOS students. As we stated that the IT laboratory may facilitate the IT architects training and provide an environment in which students can get closer to an ITA project real experience, it is therefore necessary to measure students improvement on the academic and professional fields. For measuring this, we took three different indicators: the improvement of their marks along the courses; the program satisfaction surveys, and alumni surveys. We made our assessments in four different cohorts of the students of our program.

Marks Improvement. In this indicator we measured progress across the stages of the project, using the three integrator projects as check points. On each checkpoint, students must be faced with a stakeholder meeting and present their results as they would do in front of the customer. This stakeholder meeting is composed by industry experts and instructors who give the students feedback and state needed modifications. We found that the first check point is usually hard on the students as it is composed by the analysis and design steps and they usually have a great deal to modify and improve. The second one is a refinement of the previous step and a first approach to the implementation so they usually have a rough start on it too.

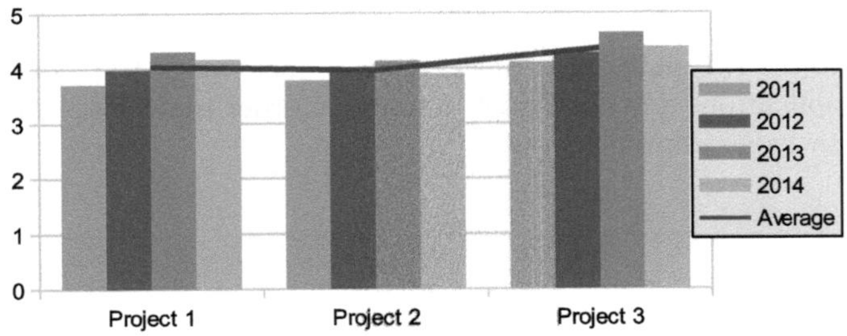

Fig. 16. Marks improvement.

Finally in the last integrator project they have to finish the refinement of the design and complete the implementation. It is clearly the hardest iteration of the project but as they have previously worked on the design and implementation, and at that point they have learned more concepts from theoretical courses in the program, they usually improve their results at the end of this phase. Results of this evaluation performed yearly during four years of the program with student groups of about forty people are shown in Fig. 16. We can see a growing model through the results of the first checkpoint and the last. These results help us understand if the continuous practice benefits the students performance on an ITA projects development according to the experts opinion.

Satisfaction Surveys. Another relevant indicator we considered was the student's perception of the entire specialization program. For that we sent students satisfaction surveys at the end of each individual course during the same four years of the previous indicator. Measuring each course gave us the possibility to adjust courses individually and also made an average in order to know the student's opinion on the program.

In the surveys we asked students to give a qualification from 1 to 5 according to how satisfied they were with the different courses; measuring contents, instructors, materials and the IT laboratory as the main course's support. We found that the general perception was undoubtedly good as the results from the four year period were high (See Fig. 17).

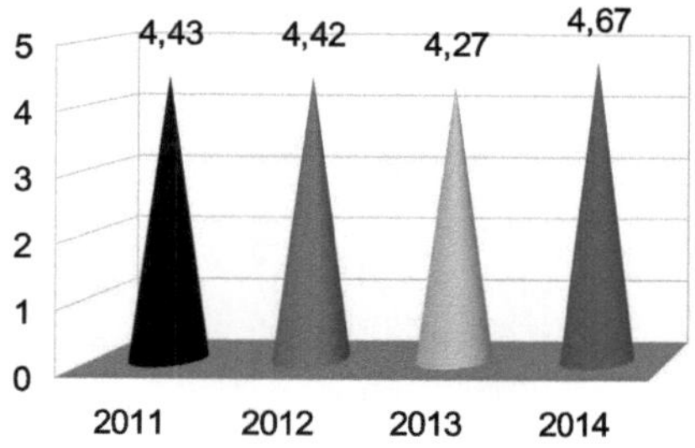

Fig. 17. Average qualification satisfaction surveys.

Alumni Surveys. As exposed previously, our intention is to generate professionals well suited for the real life projects. So, in order to find out if we were really making a change in our students's professional life, we questioned our alumni. Figures 18, 19 and 20 show the results of the most important questions as answered by 35 ECOS alumni students. As we can see, the surveys show a positive impact and a high development of the desired skills, proving the pertinence of the approach. Nonetheless, we are going to continue improving it in order to get even better results, have more reality simulated cases and help train more students.

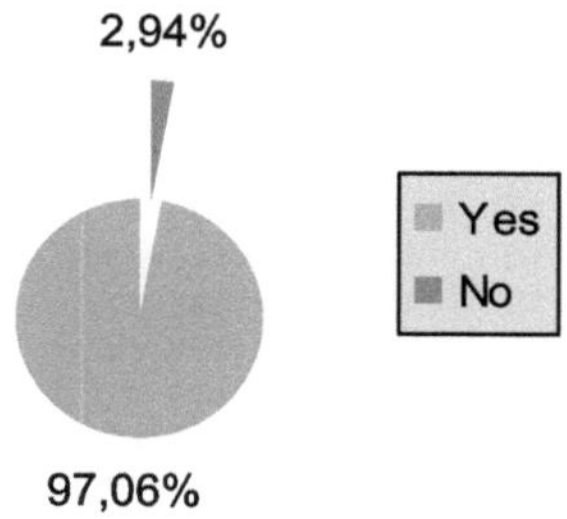

Fig. 18. Answer to question: do you think that during the courses Project 1, Project 2 and Project 3 you applied the concepts acquired in the other program's courses?

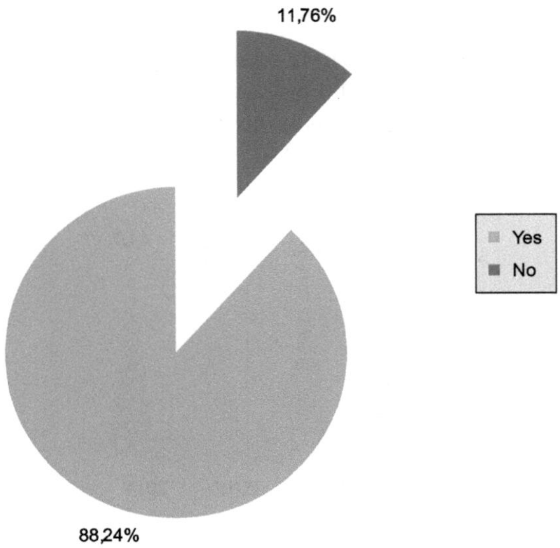

Fig. 19. Answer to question: do you think that the use of a tool like the IT laboratory was useful for your education?

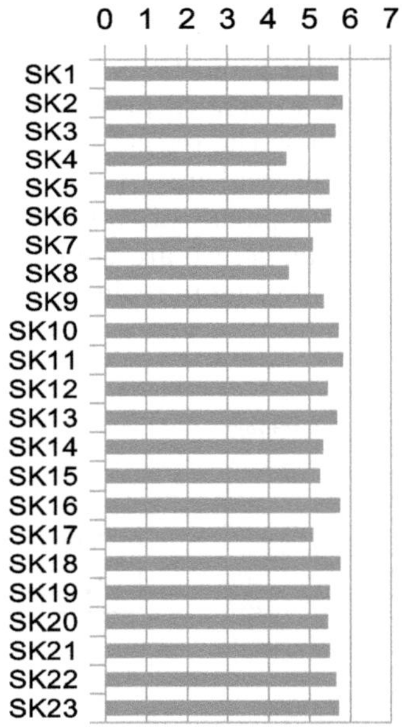

Fig. 20. Answer to question: indicate from 1 to 7 how much the following skills strengthened during your passing through the program, where 1 implies that you did not develop the skill and 7 that you developed it completely.

8 Conclusions

This article proposes the use of a technological tool in the application of PBL approaches to solve a particular problem: the poor supply of qualified IT architects to direct projects of technological transformation in companies. This tool consists of a series of virtual companies with clear organizational definition and in some cases real technology platforms. These companies are called scenarios and are divided into two types: conceptual and operational.

The first ones are focused on representing a real company through documentation similar to that found in real companies (website, brochures, information bulletins, spreadsheets, among others) and seek to have students who use it to develop competencies of analysis and design through the analysis of the information delivered, problem diagnosis, and proposal of technological solutions.

The latter scenarios extend conventional organizational definitions with a complete technological platform that recreates actual processes and operations. These are oriented not only to the analysis and design competencies but also to the development and implementation of the designed software.

The two types of scenarios have in common that they favor the three requirements of a case useful for PBL approach: coherence, complexity and evolution over time. Both guarantee these requirements during its construction, by involving several steps in their construction methodology. These steps include validation, and intrusion of errors and imperfections. It also includes updating steps where the scenario definitions are changed to comply with new trends and regulations.

The use of these scenarios and their efficiency has been validated in several courses of the Universidad de los Andes. In particular, the approach was evaluated in a postgraduate program called ECOS. The evaluation consisted of analyzing the usefulness of the scenarios through three fundamental axes: grade improvement, student satisfaction, and impact on graduates. In general, positive results were obtained: grades were improved as students gained more experience in developing projects on the virtual company assigned, they were satisfied with the program and its tools, and the alumni perceived an improvement in their professional skills.

This proves that the tool is of high value and that it can have a positive effect on the training of IT architects. It can help in complementing the theoretical training, thus favoring the development of skills critical to the development of IT architecture projects.

References

1. Casas, L., Sánchez, M., Villalobos, J.: Using an IT laboratory for training IT architects. In: Proceedings of the 9th International Conference on Computer Supported Education. Scitepress (2017)
2. Marks, M.: What is IT architecture. In: IT Architect Body of Knowledge (2016)

3. Scherer, S., Wimmer, M.: Analysis of enterprise architecture frameworks in the context of e-participation. In: Proceedings of the 12th Annual International Digital Government Research Conference: Digital Government Innovation in Challenging Times. ACM (2011)
4. Clements, P.: Certified software architects. IEEE J. Mag. (2010)
5. IEEE: Professional certification of software engineers: the CSDP program. IEEE J. Mag. (2005)
6. Markham, T.: Project based learning. In: Teacher Librarian. Information Age Publishing (2011)
7. Wankel, C.: Educating managers through real world projects. In: Research in Management Education and Development. Information Age Publishing (2005)
8. Kendall, K., Kendall, J.: Systems Analysis and Design, 9th edn. Pearson, New York (2014)
9. McCormick, M.: Expanding the College Classroom: Enhancing Engineering Education Through Project-Based Service-Learning. Tufts University, Medford (2008)
10. Harrison, R.: TOGAF 9.1 Certified Study Guide. Van Haren Publishing, Zaltbommel (2011)
11. Shuja, A.K., Krebs, J.: IBM Rational Unified Process Reference and Certification Guide: Solution Designer (RUP). IBM (2007)
12. Humphrey, W., Chick, T., Nichols, W., Pomeroy-Huffn, M.: Team Software Process Body of Knowledge. Pittsburg (2010)
13. Felder, R.M., Brent, R.: Designing and teaching courses to satisfy the ABET engineering criteria. J. Eng. Educ. **92**(1), 7–25 (2003)
14. Kalampokis, E., Tambouris, E., Zotou, M., Tarabanis, K.: The enterprise architecture competence framework. Int. J. Learn. Technol. **17**(1), 79–94 (2012)
15. International Association for Software Architects: Job description. In: IT Architect Body of Knowledge (2016)
16. The Open Group: TOGAF 9.1 - The Open Group Architecture Framework Version 9.1. The Open Group, San Francisco (2011)

piBook: Introducing Computational Thinking to Diversified Audiences

André Campos[1(✉)], Mário Rodrigues[2], Alberto Signoretti[3], and Marlene Amorim[4]

[1] DIMAp, Federal University of Rio Grande do Norte - UFRN, Natal, Brazil
andre@dimap.ufrn.br
[2] ESTGA/IEETA, University of Aveiro - UA, Aveiro, Portugal
mjrf@ua.pt
[3] DI, State University of Rio Grande do Norte - UERN, Natal, Brazil
albertosignoretti@uern.br
[4] GOVCOPP/DEGEIT, University of Aveiro - UA, Aveiro, Portugal
mamorim@ua.pt
http://www.ufrn.br/, https://www.ua.pt/, https://portal.uern.br/

Abstract. Information and communication technologies are reshaping the way we live and work. The expectation is that computational thinking will be a pervasive skill in (near-) future professions of ours' increasingly digitized and responsive economies. Although this idea is spread and well accepted, acquiring such skills often implies attending specialized courses. However, the basic concepts of computational thinking do not need to be a specialized skill learned disassociated from other school curricula. As it is more related with mental tools used in the process of reflecting and solving problems it can be learned by being applied to a large variety of topics.

This paper presents piBook, a tool designed to allow the acquisition of key computational thinking skills while working on topics such as history, biology, and mathematics, among other. By reaching diversified audiences piBook fosters the acquisition of those skills by future workers at large. It does so via the production of programmable interactive books, hence piBook, that make possible interactive storytelling using nonlinear narratives, by allowing the creation of textual games, interactive activities, tutorials and alike, therefore offering opportunities for new and engaging pedagogical methods.

Keywords: Computational thinking · Storytelling
Interactive activities

1 Introduction

In recent years several contributions have highlighted the importance of aligning the education of "digital natives" [1] with the development of digital skills and competences [2]. The increasing demands for the development of digital

P. Escudeiro et al. (Eds.): CSEDU 2017, CCIS 865, pp. 179–195, 2018.
https://doi.org/10.1007/978-3-319-94640-5_9

competences today goes far beyond a basic literacy on information and communication technologies. Digitalization is reaching industries and homes alike, leading to profound changes in the way individuals live and consume by replacing some human actions and fueling the debates about the roles and strengths of humans alongside technologies [3].

The agendas for social development are referring a need for higher-order skills for individuals to live and work in a digitalized and networked society [4]. However, the prevalent education and qualification models are still lagging behind these calls. Often, in education contexts, computers are still primarily used for information research, text editing and presentations. Moreover, while there are experiences of using computers as a motivational tool for learning, namely through the use of games and playful digital activities [5], often there is no direct stimulus for the students to learn about how games and applications are built.

Knowing how to use tools is the most basic relationship one can have with technology, which differs significantly from knowing how to apply concepts to construct them. In the current digital society, this ability will be increasingly appreciated in any career, as digital competences have been put forward as key for personal development, active citizenship, employment and inclusion [6]. Furthermore, knowing or identifying the logic behind a computer-based solution can help the student's autonomy to solve objective problems by developing the ability to think in a systematical and critical way [7].

Ten years after Jeanette Wing's influential article, where the term computational Thinking was coined [7], the idea has still not been widely adopted. Despite the growing interest in the subject, putting her ideas into practice is a complex process. Education institutions can be rather resistant to change, notably in countries with strong resistance to change or to provide more flexibility to their scholar curriculum [8]. As a consequence, several educational institutions that adopt computational thinking and correlated activities, usually do so through extracurricular activities, following the learn-to-code movement [9].

This movement has granted the support from many institutions and entities worldwide, acknowledging the stimulus that programming offers to logical thinking, creativity, reasoning and problem solving through abstractions and decompositions [10]. Therefore, it is critical to spend efforts in introducing computational thinking and, more specifically, programming logic in the early years of education.

This document is an extended version of [11] presented at CSEDU17, 9th International Conference on Computer Supported Education, and is structured in six sections. The current one exposes the motivation and goals of the work. The Sect. 2 presents the background and relevant related work to create digital non-linear narratives. Section 3 provides the piBook goals and main requirements, and Sect. 4 details the piBook system, by presenting its architectural elements and how programs are created on it. A discussion and a use case example already being put in place are the subjects of Sect. 5 and Sect. 6, the last one, provides some considerations about the developed tool as well as intended future work.

2 Background and Related Work

There are some platforms that already allow the creation of digital interactive stories as well as their publication in the form of books. In most of these platforms the narrative flows are defined using directed graphs and this way they make possible the creation of more than one linear sequence of a story. Alongside the definition of alternative story paths it is necessary to define how readers can select which alternative path will be followed. The mechanisms for selecting the story path often involve using some compute programming resources and concepts such as variables, conditionals, and loops. While some tools deal with this challenge through a purely visual approach, others allow authors to create a more complex logic by directly using programming languages.

StoryTec [12] is a storytelling platform composed of an authoring environment and a runtime engine. The authoring environment is based on a pluggable framework where different editors may be used to create the elements of a story. It was initially conceived with five components: a Story Editor, a Stage Editor, an Action Set Editor, a Property Editor, and an Asset Manager. Two components are directly related to the current work: the Story editor and the Action Set editor. The story editor provides an interactive 2D representation of the story graph, containing the scenes, the transitions between the scenes, and the story elements The Action Set editor is used to configure the story logic inside each scene made through a visual programming environment. The scene logic is described visually by a set of rules composed of conditions and actions. As it uses a visual approach it makes possible its usage by non-specialists due to the fact that no programming skills are required to define the story logic. Nevertheless, it restraints the ability to create rules for complex scenarios. The programming approach of this editor is similar to a flow diagram, as illustrated in Fig. 1.

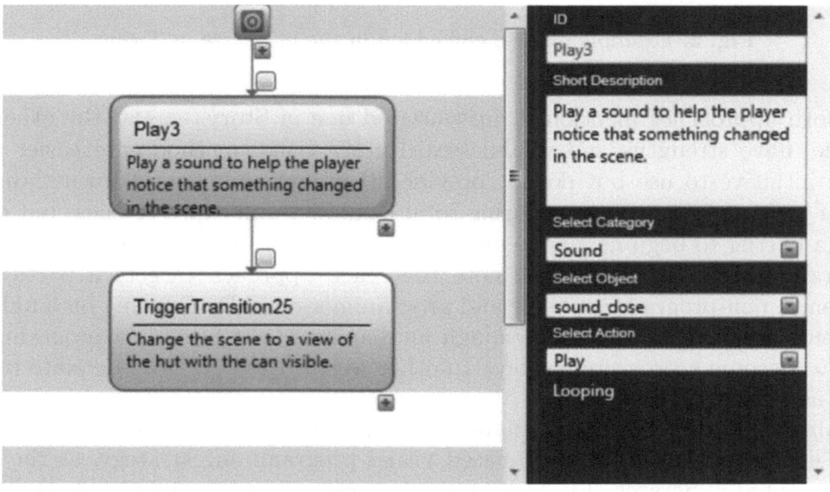

Fig. 1. The StoryTec action set editor for configuration of control flow [13].

Twine [14] is a more recent storytelling authoring tool. The non-linear structures of the story are created based on wiki systems. The user creates a text, which may have one or more wiki links to other texts, which by their turn may also connect to other ones, and so on and so forth. For increased usability, Twine provides a visualization tool where the user can see the overall story graph in a way similar to StoryTec. However, differently from StoryTec, it does not provide a visual editor for authoring the story logic. This is done using a textual programming language: Javascript. Each wiki text may have embedded a chunk of Javascript code in order to control, for instance, how many times the user has passed by that text or if a part of the text should be visible or not. This approach allows a very fine control but it requires previous knowledge of this specific programming language. Figure 2 illustrates the Twine approach to embed variables and coding instructions into a narrative text.

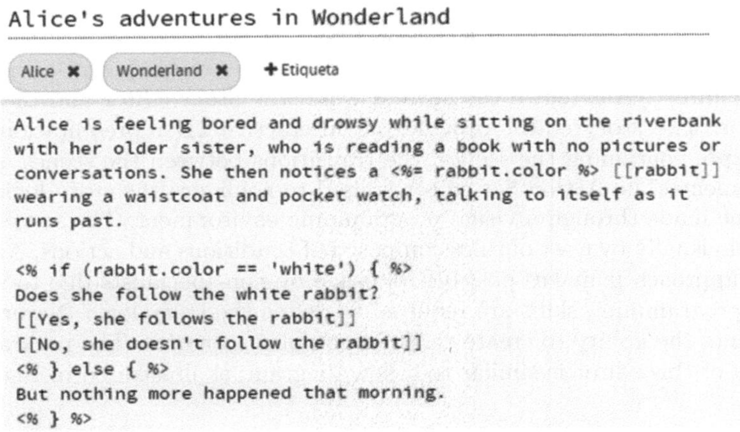

Fig. 2. Example of logic embedded in the narrative in Twine.

Both approaches mentioned, instantiated one in StoryTec and the other in Twine, have strengths and weaknesses. Purely visual methods are easier and more intuitive to use but do not provide all programming mechanisms, direct use of programming languages bring total flexibility and expressiveness but may pose a barrier to beginners or to authors that do not aspire to become computer programmers. It is worth then note that each approach targets a particular audience: non-programmer users and programmer ones. By focusing on a unique audience, they do not provide enough mechanisms to guide a non programmer user to become a programmer one. In other words, they are not adequate to be used as a learning tool.

Aiming at this learning guidance in programming skills, several tools have been constructed using a block-based visual programming strategy, as the one implemented in Scratch [15]. Indeed, the interest in block-based visual programming has grown in recent years, specially in the educational context, helping beginners to get involved in their first programming steps [16]. From a leaner perspective, the advantages of using block-based programming relies on the ability to use a visual language modeled for a specific domain, the possibility of gradually presenting parts of that language, and, finally, the capacity of not allowing syntax errors (only semantic ones) [16].

Because of the previously mentioned reasons, authoring applications using block-based programming interfaces, such as Scratch [15], AppIventor [17], and Code.org [18] have been widely used by educators to teach computer programming. However, concerning to the current work, although it is possible to create non-linear interactive stories with Scratch, AppInventor and similar applications, their visual languages do not target the specific purpose of creating non-linear interactive narratives. In fact, they can be categorized as general-purpose authoring tools. A tool targeting this particular application context may facilitate the authoring process, while helping teaching programming logic.

The present work correlates the three previously mentioned approaches in a unique learning platform. It provides a tool where the user can visually author a non-linear sequence through a graph-based flow, plus he can also program the story logic by using a block-based strategy or, when he becomes more proficient, a textual programming language.

3 Goals and Requirements

The pedagogical objective of the current work is to foster the development of computational problem-solving skills in the educational context by the challenge of authoring digital interactive storytelling. This objective has however a natural barrier: school teachers usually do not have previous background on computational thinking nor programming skills to set up a logic behind non-linear narratives. Taking into account this barrier, it is imperative to target different types of audience, from novice to expert users. So, the tool should be easy to use by newcomers (computer programming skills should not be required), but also expressive enough to computer programming experts. Besides that, as it is intended to be used in an educational context, it should also provide a smooth transition from the novice to the advanced one.

Considering novice users, they should be able to conceive non-linear narratives by visually creating states in a graph-based flow-oriented diagram. Each graph node is considered as state in the story, which can only go forward or backward according to the reader's choice. For intermediary users, they should be able to express more complex mechanisms by visually dragging and dropping programming blocks [16]. There should also exist the possibility of exploring further programming concepts useful for handling more complex reader interactions. Finally, as the intermediary users become more proficient in the concepts of programming blocks, they may turn into advanced users and change their programming environment to a textual programming language. At this stage, the tool should provide the possibility to fully customize the reader's interactive experience.

Besides the aforementioned objective, the following requirements were also established in order to set up a playful educational environment around the tool:

- Ability to collaboratively create the story contents, including the programs controlling the logic behind the story interactions;
- Ability to share the created story with other users (e.g. classmates and parents) and get feedback from them;
- Ability to publish a final version of the story (interactive digital book).

These items resume the scope of piBook. Nevertheless, it is worth to highlight that piBook has not been designed to be a self-guided learning tool. A self-guided or a self-discovery learning tool must follow a learning method and, for the moment, there is no particular methodological approach set up to piBook. Therefore, researchers and educators may explore the pedagogical possibilities (online and offline) and students are supposed to be oriented by them to use piBook as a way to put their skills and knowledge in practice.

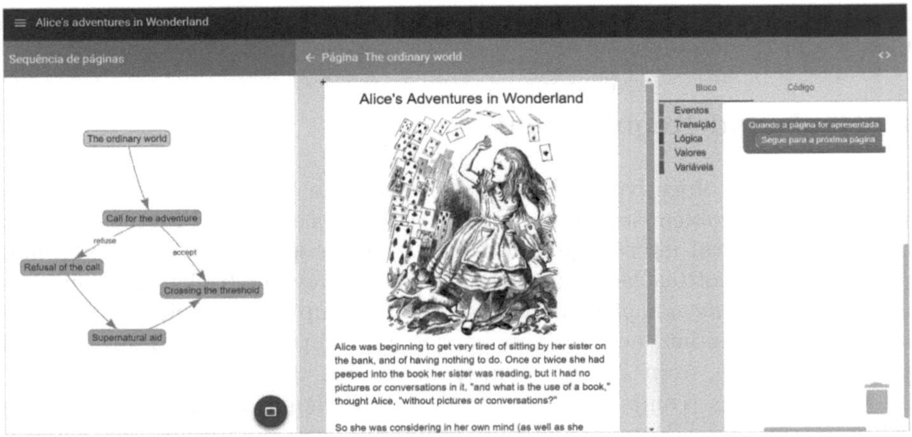

Fig. 3. Screenshot showing the page flow, gadgets composing the page content and its associated code (the user interface is in Portuguese).

4 piBook

piBook is an online application composed of two parts: an authoring platform and a running application. The first one is a web-based system where users may create interactive books for their audience, the readers. The second part is a mobile-based application able to load an interactive book description and execute it. This brief description of the platform focuses on the authoring tool. Figure 3 presents a screenshot of the authoring platform, showing a non-linear sequence of pages, a page being edited and its associated logical code (block-based mode).

For convenience, we refer hereafter the piBook authoring platform, the running application piBook tool, and the book authored by the application just as piBook.

A piBook is structured into several main elements. Some of them are metaphors from physical books or devices, such as sections, pages, and gadgets. Other come from general programming concepts, like code and data table. The diagram presented at Fig. 4 summarizes the its conceptual model, showing the relationship between a book, its sections, pages, tables, code, and gadgets.

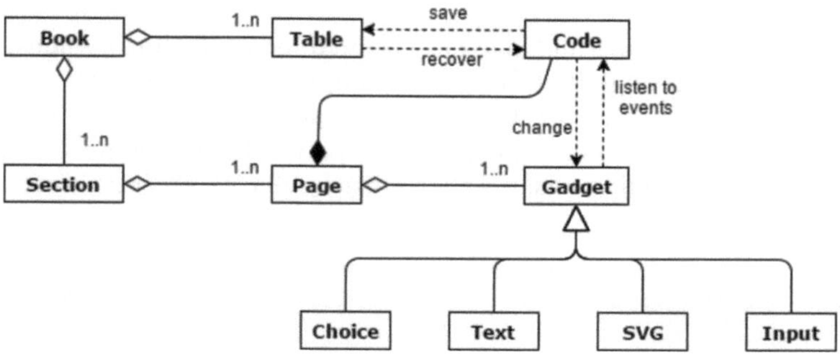

Fig. 4. piBook elements.

A book is structured as a collection of sections, as a way to provide either a sequence of a narrative, like book chapters, or to give a feedback of evolution in the activities, like game levels. Sections structure a set of related contents (pages) as a directed graph (left side of Fig. 3). So, the reader can follow a content sequence according to his interaction. In a non-linear narrative the reader may choose an option that drives the story's flow to a particular path in the directed graph. This visual feedback of the section graph facilitates the conception of non-linear stories. The author can have a glimpse on the overall section and when the flow changes.

Pages are nodes of the section graph. They are composed of gadgets, which are visual interactive elements that can be inserted on a page. Gadgets can be rich formatted texts, choice buttons, clickable SVG images, and textual inputs among other. Gadgets are then puzzle-block elements used to produce the interactive and non-interactive contents of a page. The central panel of screenshot of Fig. 3 illustrates the text gadget, where the user can inserted and format textual contents. Others gadgets may also be inserted to add interactivity to the page.

There are two types of pages in piBook, one aimed at the contents, a store plot for instance, and another for interaction, meaning brief interventions with the player. As such, there are also two rendering layers for presenting the gadgets during gameplay, one for each type of page. While there is always a content page rendered in the corresponding layer, the interaction layer is presented only when the game state reaches an interaction page, showing the interaction layer over the content one.

Each page has an associated programming code to provide reader interactions. The code handles page events like what to do when the book shows the current page or which actions to execute before showing the next page, as well as the events over gadgets on the page. They provide the logic behind the interactive book, by controlling the story plot according to the reader interaction, along with the control of animation, sounds, and other audiovisual effects of the gadgets. To help book authors with no or almost no programming experience, piBook provides a visual block-based programming environment, as illustrated in the right panel of Fig. 3. Experienced programmers can chose to write Javascript code.

Finally, piBook can save and load data from different reading sessions, i.e. in a persistent manner, through its tables. An example of the usefulness of persistent data is the possibility to record the reader's past choices to set up the context in a new reading session. This feature adds replay value to the book, especially in non-linear educational narratives that must be played several times.

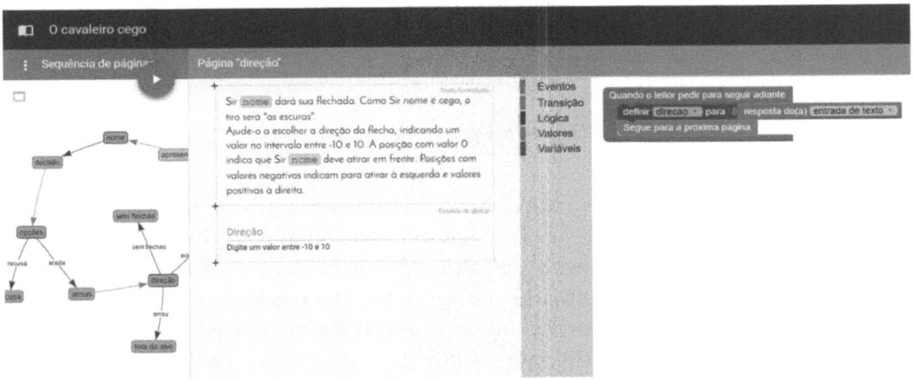

Fig. 5. Screenshot showing the page flow, different gadgets composing the page, text content with variables, and the page associated code.

Figure 5 shows another example of piBook illustrating the section page flow, through its directed graph, a page content with a rich text and an input gadget, and the block-based code associated with a page. In the example illustrated in the screenshot it is also possible to note the relation between the gadgets in the page and its associated code. In the rich text gadget there are two references to a variable named "name". For the book reader, this page is rendered with the variable value, normally acquired in previous pages. The figure also shows an input gadget that asks the reader to enter a number. With the provided block code, when the reader turns to the next page, the input value is set to a variable named "direction". This variable can then be used in the following pages either as data to control the logic of the story or as rendering information.

4.1 Defining Gadgets

The atomic element of piBook is the gadgets. They compose the book pages and provide the desired flexibility to allow a great variety of interactive forms in piBooks. They can assume the form of a rich formatted text, with embedded images and videos, a choice selection, a value input, a range definition, and a clickable image. For the moment, these are the existing gadgets in the platform, as illustrated in Fig. 6. However, many other gadgets may be included in the platform.

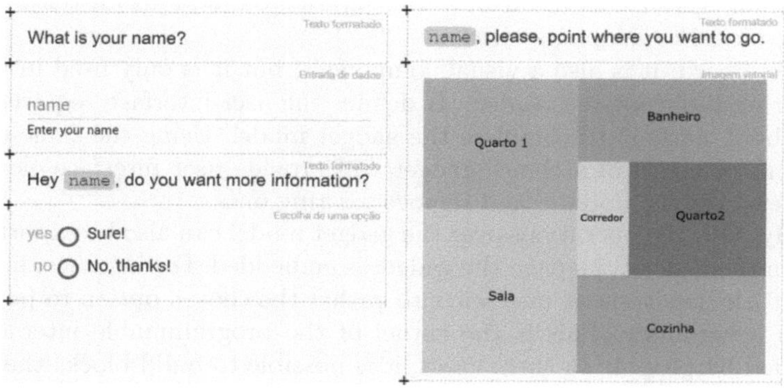

Fig. 6. Examples of interactive gadgets.

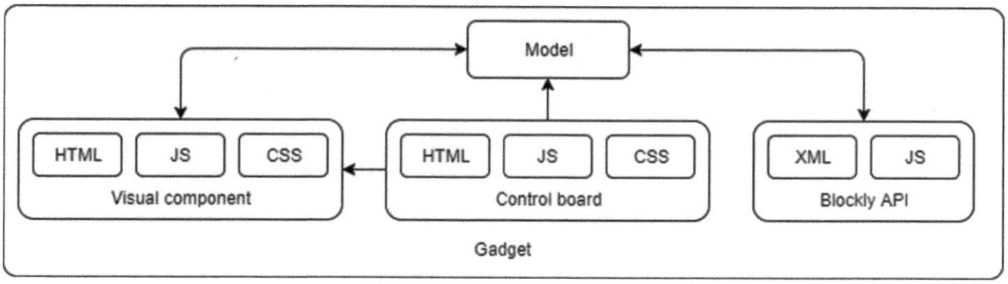

Fig. 7. Gadgets are defined by their visual component, a control board, a Blockly API, and a model.

For the moment, these are the existing gadgets in the platform. However, other ones can also be inserted through the definition of new gadget's components. To define a new gadget, it is necessary to specify the elements represented in Fig. 7, as described hereafter.

1. Model: it is the gadget's object data model. Any information concerning the gadget state should be represented in here. Choice gadgets, for instance, may be defined by an array of objects with the option statements and their corresponding values (used as an identifier for the user answer), as well as the operations over the array to add a new option, remove and updating existing ones;
2. Visual component: it is the component used to render the gadget in the book reader (how the user sees and interacts with the gadget when reading the book). The component is defined by its visual representation (HTML and CSS files) and its logical behavior (JS file). This component can change the model, for instance as result of a user interaction, and also listen to changes on the model to adapt its view;
3. Control board: it is also a visual component, but it is only used in the book authoring tool (not the reader). It defines the user interface required for the user (book author) to complete the gadget model. Using the same example, the control board of a choice gadget will provide user interface elements to add new options, update, and remove existing ones.
4. Blockly API: the operations over the gadget model can also be exported to be used in the logic of the page the gadget is embedded. For instance, in a choice gadget, the author user may want to gather the chosen option to perform an action accordingly. This is the kernel of the programmable interactiveness provided by piBook. In these cases, it is possible to build blocks that change the gadget model and blocks that answer for user interactions over the gadget. This is done by specifying an XML in Blockly format for each block and their associated code (template of code used when the block-based code is compiled to Javascript).

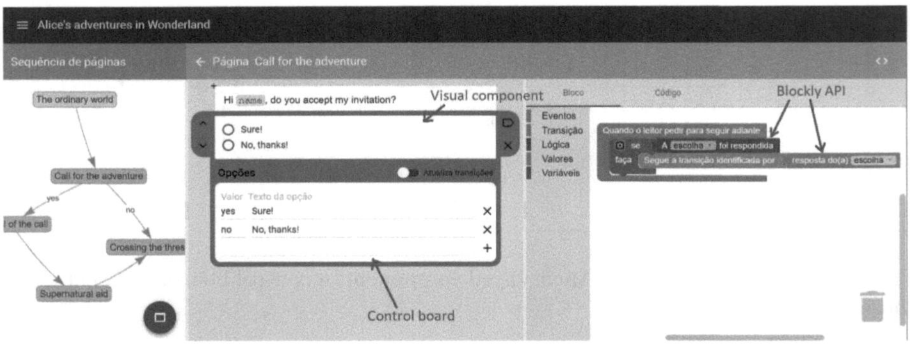

Fig. 8. The choice gadget.

```
function onNext() {
  if (page.get('choice').isAnswered) {
    next((page.get('choice').value));
  }
}
```

Fig. 9. Example of Javascript code generated from the blocks of Fig. 8.

Figure 8 illustrates the visual elements of the choice gadget. The visual component shows how the gadget will be rendered in the reader, but it also presented in the authoring tool to provide visual feedback of the page composition. When the gadget is selected, its control board in shown. So, its model can be modified by the user. The figure also illustrates the use of two blocks offered by the gadget API. The first one queries if an option was chosen by the book reader (user) and the second one retrieves the chosen answer. The code in the block (in Portuguese) is then compiled to the following Javascript code:

In the example illustrated in Fig. 8, there are two exit transitions from the page “Call for the adventure”, but just one should be performed. The page logic specified by the blocks (and compiled to Javascript code in Fig. 9) establishes that when the reader (user) requires the book's next page (the event ‘onNext’ is produced and captured by the ‘onNext()’ function), if there is an answer in the choice gadget, the book follows the transition specified by the value of the chosen answer. Case the user has chosen “Sure!”, the answer value is “yes” and the book will follow the transition labeled “yes” (in the graph flow). Case the user has chosen “No, thanks!”, the answer value is “no” and the book will follow the other transition.

This description illustrates how page code can interact with the gadgets in the page and how the sequence of pages can be programmed. Depending on how the programming blocks are combined, many other ways to handle the narrative flow can be created.

4.2 Content Representation

As previously mentioned, from the user perspective, piBook is an online application composed of two parts: an web-based authoring tool (book creator) and a mobile application (book reader). There is however a third component, a web server, to handle persistent data and to provide visible online data (published books). The server exposes a JSON-based REST API used by both the authoring tool and the mobile application to create, read, update or destroy book properties, sections, contents or logic specifications.

The authoring tool is a Single Page Application (SPA) composed of three main components: (1) a user dashboard, where the user can edit his authored books, create new ones and publish them; (2) a book editor, where the user can edit the book sections, their contents and logic; and (3) a data editor, represented by a spreadsheet where the user can collect data from book interactions and/or serve static data for his book.

```
{
  "id": "bookId",
  "info": {
    "published": false,
    "title": "Book title"
  },
  "gadgets": {
    "gadgetId": {
      "type": "text",
      "data": { },
      "label": "",
      "page": "pageId"
    }
  },
  "initialPage": "pageId",
  "pages": {
    "pageId": {
      "label": "Call for the adventure",
      "type": "content",
      "blockly": "<xml ...>...</xml>",
      "code": "function onNext() {...}\n",
      "codeMode": "block",
      "gadgets": [ "gadgetId" ]
    }
  },
  "transitions": {
    "transId": {
      "from": "pageId",
      "to": "pageId",
      "label": "a transition label"
    }
  }
```

Fig. 10. Extract code showing how a book is represented (JSON format).

The authoring tool, as well as the mobile application, consume data from the server in a specific format. The data format exchanged by server and applications induce the hierarchical structures of a piBook into sections, and the latter into a collection of gadgets and a page logic (blocks and Javascript code). Each gadget has its own data representation.

Figure 10 shows an extract of how a book is represented in the server side. Such format represents the book's contents in a static way. The data is then interpreted by the mobile reader to dynamically construct the interactive application.

5 Discussion and Use Case Example

The present work is complementary to the existing learn-to-code initiatives in extracurricular activities. However, differently from them, it considers that teaching programming logic and computational thinking does not necessarily have to be disconnected from the current existing school contents. In other words, it can be transversely used on diverse subjects, such as history, geography, science, literacy, mathematics, foreign language, among others. For this, it is necessary to embed the use of programming logic into the existing learning activities, so that it can be part of a teaching method.

A widely accepted "general purpose" teaching method is the use of storytelling. Digital interactive storytelling is a powerful teaching and learning method for engaging both teachers and students [19]. Several studies confirm its benefits in education, showing that the educational gains go beyond the novelty of the new technologies [20] or that it improves academic achievement, critical thinking, and learning motivation [21]. Storytelling can effectively be used in many different contexts and subjects. Besides playful learning capabilities, digital interactive storytelling can also be used as therapeutic support [22] which makes this technique particularly adequate on stressful learning environments.

A language teacher can, for instance, ask his/her students to create a non-linear narrative in order to improve their literacy skills [23], while a mathematics teacher may aim at developing the student's argumentative competences [24]. These examples show how flexible is the use of storytelling in the educational context.

The present work exploits the flexibility of the storytelling to promote computational thinking and programming skills in the existing scholar curriculum. The combination of text edition, non-linear page links, and the introduction of computer logic, makes possible to create contents that range from sequential immutable stories, to stories that can have alternative paths, and also stories that can take the form of a computer game. This flexibility and the way piBook was designed, being easy to use, makes it a suitable tool to conduct innovative learning experiences. Game creation usually requires technical expertise, making it difficult to produce new games around a particular subject or content. As a consequence, educators are often constrained to use already existing games. To create their own story, educators need an easy-to-use authoring tool that requires minimal effort or, at least, that the learning curve is as smooth as possible.

General purpose game authoring tools provide enough means for producing adventure games but also require expertise using the tools. This is due to their ability to create any game, and therefore they provide a significant number of options and possibilities, which creates a barrier for beginners. More straightforward and easy-to-use authoring tools targeted on education and interactive storytelling are more appropriate to a learning context.

A use case example on the usage of piBook as a digital interactive storytelling platform, where the story takes the form of a game is a project named Learning House, name translated from the Portuguese original "Casa do Aprender". Learning House aims at preparing students in Brazil for the national exam at the end of the high school named "Exame National do Ensino Médio (ENEM)". The project is developing a quiz-based interactive storytelling application based on piBook that takes the shape of an adventure game where the player is the protagonist. The story allows an immersion in a fictional world where the player has the role of an apprentice trying to find some pieces of book pages and rebuild four books lost. The plot takes place in a conventional home for better identification with the students' environment for increased immersion. The game progresses by exploring the virtual world, by talking with non-player characters, and by solving puzzles.

Learning House is an adventure game combining two sub-genres: point and click adventure and multiple-choice game. It is a point and click adventure game since players use their mouse to explore graphical scenes and interact with the virtual world. It is also a multiple-choice game as the player makes decisions in a non-linear story plot by using multiple-choice menus. It takes into account background states to support, for instance, inventory management and time tracking. Figure 11 presents a screen shot of one room of the house. At the left-hand side is visible the book graph that defines all admissible page transitions. At the right-hand side is visible "Quarto 1" where the action places are marked with a black circle. In this case they are: two beds, one larger an one smaller; one closet, one lamp at the bottom right corner, and one door.

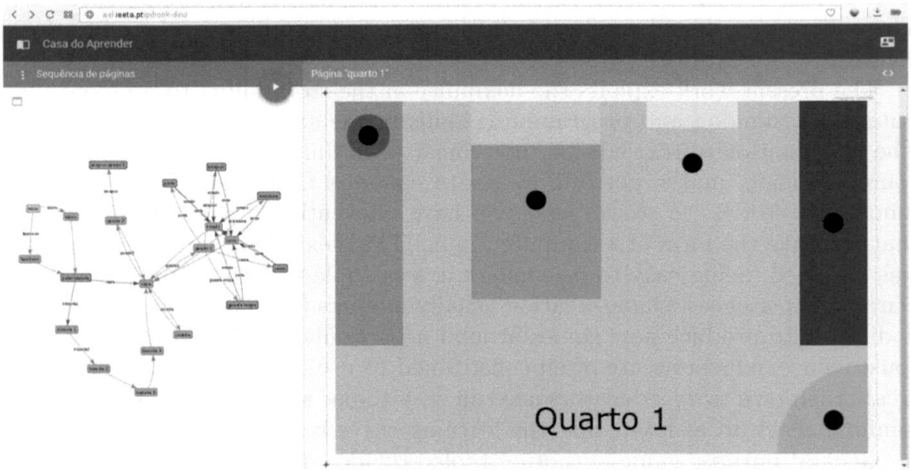

Fig. 11. Example of flow.

6 Conclusion

This paper introduced a tool, named piBook, that was developed with the purpose of assisting the introduction of programming logic in schools. The idea behind piBook is the intention to contribute to the development of learning experiences that promote the acquisition of competences on coding, in an engaging, flexible and creative manner. The paper offers a detailed description of ideas that framed the development of the tool, its key structuring elements, as well as the reasoning that supported the choices.

piBook supports the creation of interactive storytelling, using nonlinear narratives, an approach that grants flexibility in the learning process, therefore enabling the introduction of programming logic to diversified audiences, and allowing for its adoption in most of the subjects of a scholar curriculum, from history to sciences. This approach is aligned with the current concerns about the future of competences for work and life, where digital competences appear upfront as a basic literacy demand. Moreover the flexibility of piBook addresses also the concerns about the need for promoting education approaches that favor the integration of individuals with diversified backgrounds into active labor and engaging them in lifelong learning and re qualification efforts (e.g. young people, long term unemployed citizens, women, etc.).

The tool is not yet production-ready. To this date it is possible to specify interactive narratives in the flow-based programming mode, by writing formatted texts, options requests, and defining the logic to control the corresponding contents and interactions. Other elements, such as transitions to block and textual modes, are still in development. Usability tests in the flow-based mode are currently being conducted with the purpose of improving user experience.

piBook was conceived as a tool to support learning scenarios where students can apply previously acquired knowledge, in a given domain (e.g. history) and in this process develop their coding skills. Therefore, it was not developed with the purpose of being a self-guided learning tool, but rather as a tool to support the superior order learning of coding, wile students apply or create content. This approach allows for the utilization of piBook as a supporting mechanism that can be embedded in diverse teaching strategies. Yet, the preliminary experiences with the tool suggest that when combined with storytelling, piBook can be well suited for project-based learning initiatives (PBL) [25], where students are designated to author interactive contents for a specific subject and, for this, they must produce the logic behind the interactive activity. However specific methodological approaches for the utilization of piBook can be developed. In this context, usability tests with school teachers could offer rich context to identify adequate pedagogical approaches, that could be refined before the adoption for student use. Moreover, this would allow for pedagogical evaluations that could help to refine and improve the tool. For example, it is assumed that existence of different levels of programming modes facilitates project-based learning activities, since the same project can be assigned to a whole class, while each student may chose a personalized level according to his/her prior individual experience in programming. As such the future developments of the should bring together researchers from multidisciplinary perspectives, notably from education.

piBook, has the potential to meet very diverse teaching and learning styles, and reach very diversified audiences, notably individuals that are not familiarized are inclined to technology or programming learning paths. For these reasons, the tool offers a timely and relevant contribute for introducing key and advanced computer programming concepts, to a wide spectrum of audiences thus helping to qualify our societies for the future digital contexts.

References

1. Prensky, M.: H. sapiens digital: from digital immigrants and digital natives to digital wisdom. Innov. J. Online Educ. **5**(3), Art.1 (2009)
2. Leonard, L., Mokwele, T., Siebrits, A., Stoltenkamp, J.: 'Digital Natives' require basic digital literacy skills. In: The IAFOR International Conference on Technology in the Classroom. The International Academic Forum (2016)
3. Europeia, C.: New skills for new jobs: action now. A report by the expert group on new skills for new jobs prepared for the European commission (2010)
4. Forum, W.E.: The Future of Jobs: Employment, Skills and Workforce Strategy for the Fourth Industrial Revolution. World Economic Forum, Geneva (2016)
5. Felicia, P.: Game-Based Learning: Challenges and Opportunities, 1st unabridged edn. Cambridge Scholars Publishing, Newcastle upon Tyne (2014)
6. European Commission European Political Strategic Centre (EPSC): The future of work: skills and resilience for a world of change (2016)
7. Wing, J.M.: Computational thinking, **49**(3), 33–35 (2006)
8. Boyce, M.E.: Organizational learning is essential to achieving and sustaining change in higher education. Innovative High. Educ. **28**(2), 119–136 (2003)
9. Kafai, Y.B., Burke, Q.: Connected Code: Why Children Need to Learn Programming. MIT Press, Cambridge (2014)
10. Lye, S.Y., Koh, J.H.L.: Review on teaching and learning of computational thinking through programming: what is next for K-12? Comput. Hum. Behav. **41**, 51–61 (2014)
11. Campos, A., Signoretti, A., Rodrigues, M.: An interactive book authoring tool to introduce programming logic in schools. In: Proceedings of the 9th International Conference on Computer Supported Education, CSEDU, vol. 1, pp. 140–148, INSTICC, SciTePress (2017)
12. Gobel, S., Salvatore, L., Konrad, R.: StoryTec: A digital storytelling platform for the authoring and experiencing of interactive and non-linear stories. In: 2008 International Conference on Automated solutions for Cross Media Content and Multi-channel Distribution, AXMEDIS 2008, pp. 103–110 (2008)
13. Mehm, F., Göbel, S., Steinmetz, R.: Authoring of serious adventure games in StoryTec. In: Göbel, S., Müller, W., Urban, B., Wiemeyer, J. (eds.) Edutainment/GameDays -2012. LNCS, vol. 7516, pp. 144–154. Springer, Heidelberg (2012). https://doi.org/10.1007/978-3-642-33466-5_16
14. Hahn, R.: Collaborative creative writing in the L2 classroom using the software Twine. In: Proceedings of the 6th Future of Education International Conference, pp. 137–142. Pixel (2016)
15. Resnick, M., Maloney, J., Monroy-Hernández, A., Rusk, N., Eastmond, E., Brennan, K., Millner, A., Rosenbaum, E., Silver, J., Silverman, B., et al.: Scratch: programming for all. Commun. ACM **52**(11), 60–67 (2009)
16. Fraser, N.: Ten things we've learned from Blockly. In: 2015 IEEE Blocks and Beyond Workshop (Blocks and Beyond), pp. 49–50 (2015)

17. Wolber, D.: App inventor and real-world motivation. In: Proceedings of the 42nd ACM Technical Symposium on Computer Science Education, pp. 601–606. ACM (2011)
18. Partovi, H.: Transforming US education with computer science. In: Proceedings of the 45th ACM Technical Symposium on Computer Science Education, pp. 5–6. ACM (2014)
19. Robin, B.R.: Digital storytelling: a powerful technology tool for the 21st century classroom, **47**(3), 220–228
20. Campbell, T.A.: Digital storytelling in an elementary classroom: going beyond entertainment. Procedia-Soc. Behav. Sci. **69**, 385–393 (2012)
21. Yang, Y.-T.C., Wu, W.-C.I.: Digital storytelling for enhancing student academic achievement, critical thinking, and learning motivation: a year-long experimental study. Comput. Educ. **59**(2), 339–352 (2012)
22. Bergner, R.M.: Therapeutic storytelling revisited. Am. J. Psychother. **61**(2), 149 (2007)
23. Menezes, H.: Using digital storytelling to improve literacy skills. In: Proceedings of the International Conference on Cognition and Exploratory Learning in Digital Age - CELDA 2012, International Association for the Development of the Information Society, pp. 299–301 (2012)
24. Albano, G., Iacono, U.D., Mariotti, M.A.: Argumentation in mathematics: mediation by means of digital interactive storytelling. Form@re - Open J. per la formazione in rete **16**(1), 105–115 (2016)
25. Krajcik, J.S., Blumenfeld, P.C.: Project-based learning. In: Sawyer, R.K. (ed.) The Cambridge Handbook of the Learning Sciences, Chap. 19, pp. 317–334. Cambridge University Press, Cambridge (2006)

How Does the Learning Channel Affect Student Satisfaction in Hybrid Courses

Nestori Syynimaa[1,2,3(✉)]

[1] Faculty of Information Technology, University of Jyväskylä, Jyväskylä, Finland
nestori.syynimaa@gmail.com
[2] Gerenios Ltd, Tampere, Finland
[3] Sovelto Plc, Helsinki, Finland

Abstract. The traditional instructor-led classroom training has been a dominant training method for millennia. During the past few decades, the information and communications technology have evolved in giant leaps. This has brought new options for providing of and participating in training. Online participation has been found to be a cost-effective way to attend training using standard consumer technology. It allows people to attend to training regardless their physical location, allowing them to deal with the time and cost pressures typically faced in workplaces. But is online participation as effective as classroom training? Previous studies in the higher education sector have demonstrated that the student satisfaction and learning outcomes do not differ between online and classroom participants. However, little is known how does the learning channel affect commercial ICT-training, where typical courses are full-day instructor lead courses lasting one to four days. We studied student satisfaction of a commercial ICT-training provider, which provides hybrid courses having both online and classroom participants. As anticipated, the results show that online participants are not as satisfied with course arrangements as the classroom participants. The most surprising finding is that there is a small, but statistically significant, difference how participants perceive teacher's substance skills. This suggests that teachers might not be able to share their knowledge online as effectively as in the classroom. The results also provide some techniques and tools which could improve online participants' satisfaction.

Keywords: Learning channel · Online training · Online learning

1 Introduction

Information and communication technology (ICT) has evolved rapidly over the past few decades. Evolved ICT has provided new communication ways allowing people to be virtually present in meetings and similar events. In the education sector ICT will enable students to participate in the training using standard affordable consumer equipment. Typically, all that is needed is a computer with an internet connection and audio support. Modern laptops already have a built-in microphone, speakers, and a video camera, so the technology is no longer an excuse for not attending online courses.

P. Escudeiro et al. (Eds.): CSEDU 2017, CCIS 865, pp. 196–206, 2018.
https://doi.org/10.1007/978-3-319-94640-5_10

Interest towards participating in training using computers with audio and video has increased during the last few years. For instance, American community colleges have faced over 32% increase in distance learning in five years between 2008 and 2013 [1]. According to another recent report, the corporate e-learning will grow 13% per year [2]. In 2016, 77% of American companies were using online training tools [3].

There are many reasons for the increased interests towards the online training. For instance, work-related time and cost pressures have been found to such reasons [2]. Due to the latest recession in Europe, the number of workers has declined, leaving more jobs for those still working. Thus the workforce has more pressure to use their time wisely, so they prefer learning channels which does not require as much traveling. Travelling is costly so cost pressures also direct to seek alternative learning channels.

Due to increased interest towards various kinds of online training, it is fair to ask: are the new learning channels as good as the traditional ones? Johnson et al. [4] found no differences in *learning outcomes* between the classroom and online training. Similarly, Allen et al. [5] found no differences in *student satisfaction* between the classroom and online training. However, there has been some critique towards earlier studies conducted on the subject. Many of the studies have not ruled out other factors which may have affected the results [6]. Thus, many studies have failed to demonstrate what is the cause and what is the effect. For instance, some studies have compared two independent samples, one for online training and one for classroom training, but this kind of comparison does not rule out factors which are present only in a classroom or online training.

The aim of this paper is to study whether the used learning channel (i.e., online vs. classroom) effects the student satisfaction in commercial ICT-training. In the previous version of this paper, we found that the used learning channel did not affect student satisfaction [7].

1.1 Online Learning

Online learning is one of the learning methods used in various training settings. Learning methods can be categorized to four archetypes; traditional learning, e-learning, participatory learning, and facilitated learning community [8]. In this paper, we regard online learning as a technology supported traditional learning, where teaching occurs in the classroom and students are participating online using audio and video.

One concept closely involved to learning methods is Human Learning Interfaces (HLI). HLIs are the set of "interaction mechanisms that humans expose to the outside world, and that can be used to control, stimulate and facilitate their learning processes" [9, p. 1]. Humans learn, for instance, by interpreting observations they make by utilising their senses, such as seeing, hearing, and touching. Similarly, teachers are using their HLIs to observe and assess the students to find out whether the learning has occurred.

1.2 Challenges in Online Learning

Online learning limits the available senses to seeing and hearing, so the number available HLIs are reduced to two. This affects both learners and teachers. Learners may not be able to learn as effectively due to a limited number of HLIs. Depending on the used equipment, the seeing and hearing may also be reduced when compared to classroom training. For instance, if the camera is fixed to a certain point of the classroom, learners are not able to see the whole classroom. Also, the microphone may only capture sound near to it, so the learner may not hear everything happening in the classroom. For teachers, the effect is even bigger. Due to a limited number of available HLIs, the teacher is not able to assess effectively whether the learning has occurred. For instance, they cannot see learner's gestures or body language, which is an important communication method for humans [10]. Thus, teachers are not able to adjust their teaching to increase the learning same way they can do in the classroom.

2 Method

The data used in this paper was collected from a leading Finnish commercial ICT-trainer, *TrainingCorp*. *TrainingCorp* provides ICT-training to Finnish public and private sector organizations, and individual consumers. Training ranges from the end-user and ICT-specialist training to the CxO level management training. Typically the training is provided as full-day instructor lead courses (ILTs) with the length between 1 to 4 days. Since 2015 *TrainingCorp* has provided an online participation option, where learners participate in courses using either Microsoft Skype for Business (SfB) or Adobe Connect Pro (ACP). After each course, *TrainingCorp* collects feedback from all participants.

The data used in this paper was collected from the feedback database from the years 2015, 2016, and the first half of 2017. To increase the validity of the research, only the courses having *both* classroom and online participants were included in the sample. In this paper, we call this kind of courses a *hybrid course*.

2.1 Hybrid Course Classroom Setup

The hybrid course has both classroom (CR) and online (OL) participants. For classroom participants, the training experience is not different from a pure classroom training. The only difference is that there are a microphone and speakers in the classroom which allows online participants to hear the teaching and to speak. Typically a 360-degree camera is used, which allows online participants to see the whole classroom. The typical setup of a hybrid course is illustrated in Fig. 1. A 360-degree camera is located on the corner of teacher's desk, and two satellite microphones are used to maximize the coverage and sound quality.

The typical online participant's Skype for Business (SfB) view can be seen in Fig. 2. The teacher shares the computer screen to online participants, so they can see the same content that is presented to classroom participants. Usually, this is a powerpoint presentation or live demonstration. Teachers may also use an electronic whiteboard to illustrate or explain the taught content. Online participants can also see the list of other online participants, the 360-degree view of the classroom, and the person currently speaking. These help to follow the conversations taking place in the classroom.

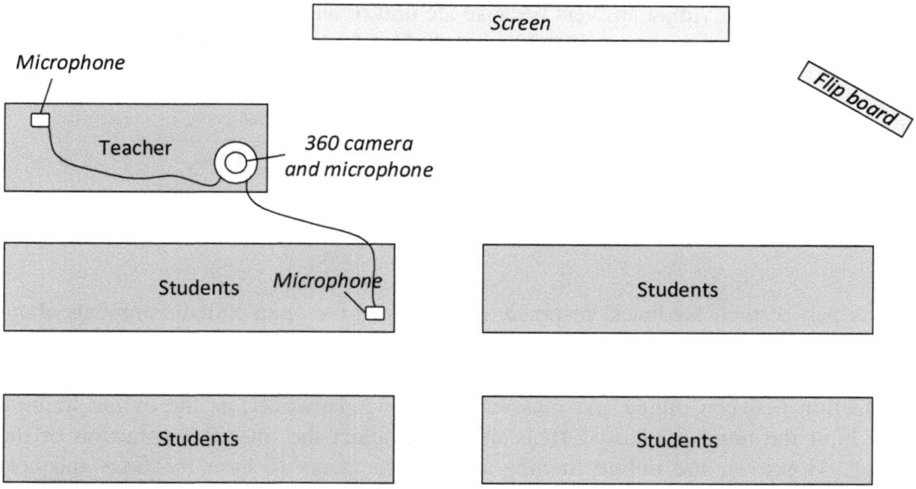

Fig. 1. Typical hybrid course classroom setup.

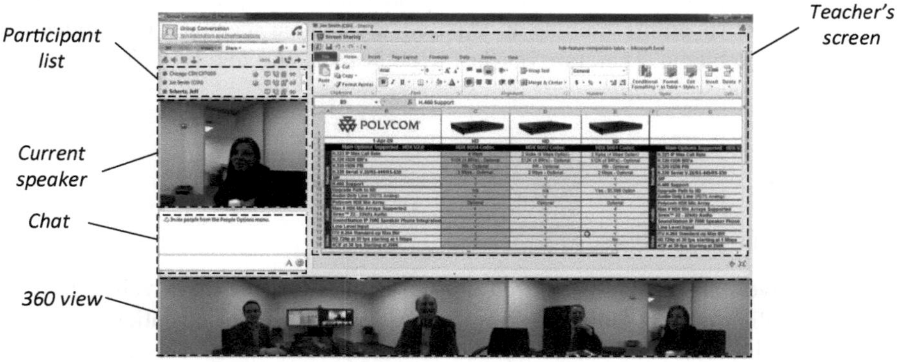

Fig. 2. Typical hybrid course online participant's view [adapted from 11].

2.2 Data Collection

In total, there were 80 hybrid courses between Jan 1st, 2015 and Jun 30th, 2017. The number of participants per year can be seen in Table 1. The feedback percentage for the classroom and online training were 69% and 71%, respectively. The total number of online participants was 163, which represents 22% of the total participants.

Available data variables are listed in Table 2. There are two nominal scale variables: *type* and *teacher*. The former variable refers to the training type (classroom or online) and the latter to the course teacher. The rest of the variables are interval scale variables containing average values calculated per course. The scale used in the feedback database is 1–5 where 5 is the highest value. Average values per course are used instead of individual answers because the unit of analysis is the course. The Type variable is used as a grouping variable and the last four as dependent variables.

Table 1. Hybrid course participants per year.

Training type	2015	2016	2017 H1	Total
Classroom (CR)	164 (79%)	179 (74%)	221 (80%)	564 (78%)
Online (OL)	43 (21%)	64 (26%)	56 (20%)	163 (22%)

As part of their feedback, respondents can also give open-ended comments about the course. These comments were also gathered for analysis.

As the previous studies suggest, there should be no differences in the perceived satisfaction between online and classroom training. However, as the online training does limit the number of used HLIs, it should affect the overall satisfaction of the course. Moreover, the online training helps participants to ease the time and cost pressures they are facing, which should affect the satisfaction. Therefore our first hypothesis is H_1: *learning channel affects the perceived overall satisfaction.* The training channel should be irrelevant regarding teacher's substance and teaching skills. Therefore our next hypotheses are H_2: *learning channel does not affect perceived teacher's substance skills* and H_3: *learning channel does not affect perceived teacher's teaching skills.* All online training is exposed to possible technical difficulties and unanticipated problems. Therefore our last hypothesis is H_4: *learning channel affects the perceived course arrangements.*

3 Results

3.1 Quantitative Analysis

The descriptive statistics presented in Table 3 indicates that the mean values for each variable are slightly lower in online training. Also, the standard deviation is roughly double in online training when compared to classroom training. This indicates that online participants perceive satisfaction more differently than the classroom participants. Next, we will test whether the differences between classroom and online training are statistically significant.

We are comparing two different groups of data so first we must test the normality of the dependent variables. We used Kolmogorov-Smirnov (Table 4) and Shapiro-Wilk tests (Table 5). Both test results indicate that that none of the variables are normally distributed (sig. < .050). Thus, we cannot compare differences between the classroom and online training using ANOVA. Therefore, we used a Kruskal-Wallis H test to find out possible differences.

The results of Kruskal-Wallis H tests can be seen in Table 6 and mean ranks in Table 7. The test showed that there was no statistically significant difference in the overall satisfaction (SA) between the classroom and online training, $\chi 2(2) = .665$, $p = 0.415$. Therefore we must reject the H_1 hypothesis. The test showed that there was

Table 2. Variables used.

Variable	Type
Type	Nominal
Teacher	Nominal
Overall satisfaction (SA)	Interval
Teacher's substance skills (SU)	Interval
Teacher's teaching skills (TE)	Interval
Course arrangements (AR)	Interval

Table 3. Descriptive statistics.

Variable	Type	Mean	Std. deviation
SA	CR	4.531	.3495
	OL	4.368	.6638
SU	CR	4.864	.1898
	OL	4.828	.3765
TE	CR	4.667	.3531
	OL	4.540	.5761
AR	CR	4.535	.3862
	OL	4.187	.8111

Table 4. Kolmogorov-Smirnov tests with lilliefors significance correction.

Variable	Type	Statistics	df	Sig.
SA	CR	.105	77	.036
	OL	.269	75	.000
SU	CR	.335	77	.000
	OL	.463	75	.000
TE	CR	.179	77	.001
	OL	.308	75	.000
AR	CR	.126	77	.004
	OL	.222	75	.000

Table 5. Shapiro-Wilk tests.

Variable	Type	Statistics	df	Sig.
SA	CR	.927	77	.000
	OL	.808	75	.000
SU	CR	.736	77	.000
	OL	.501	75	.000
TE	CR	.861	77	.000
	OL	.751	75	.000
AR	CR	.904	77	.000
	OL	.827	75	.000

a statistically significant difference in the teacher's substance skills (SU) between the classroom and online training, $\chi2(2) = 4.437$, $p = 0.035$, with a mean score of 72.24 for Classroom training and 84.76 for Online training. Therefore the H_2 hypothesis is rejected. The test showed that there was no statistically significant difference in the teacher's teaching skills (TE) between the classroom and online training, $\chi2(2) = .040$, $p = 0.841$. Therefore the H_3 hypothesis is not rejected. The test showed that there was a statistically significant difference in the course arrangements (AR) between the classroom and online training, $\chi2(2) = 6.389$, $p = 0.011$, with a mean score of 86.29 for Classroom training and 68.48 for Online training. Therefore the hypothesis H_4 is not rejected.

Table 6. Kruskal-Wallis H test (grouping by Type).

Variable	SA	SU	TE	AR
Chi-Square	.665	4.437	.040	6.389
df	1	1	1	1
Asymp. Sig.	.415	.035	.841	.011

Table 7. Kruskal-Wallis test mean ranks.

Variable	Type	N	Mean rank	N total
SA	CR	78	81,38	156
	OL	78	75,62	
SU	CR	78	72,24	156
	OL	78	84,76	
TE	CR	77	78,19	154
	OL	77	76,81	
AR	CR	78	86,29	154
	OL	76	68,48	

As anticipated, the results indicate that the used teaching channel does not affect perceived teacher's teaching skills. Also, as anticipated, the teaching channel affects satisfaction to course arrangements. However, it was not anticipated that the teaching channel had no effect on perceived overall satisfaction. The most interesting finding is that the teaching channel has an effect on the perceived teacher's substance skills. However, as the descriptive statistics in Table 3 shows, the difference between classroom and online training is small; 4.864 and 4.828, respectively.

3.2 Qualitative Analysis

In total, open-ended comments related to online participation were given for 32 courses. The quotes presented in this section are translations from the original feedbacks given in Finnish. The number after each quote refers to the feedback number.

Most comments were related to technical difficulties, i.e., audio and video connection. For instance, one online participant stated that "constant technical problems ruined the whole and I missed the most of the course" (31). Another one stated that "connection was okay for the first two days..on the third day there was some problems with the video.. the broadcast were cut at least for 30 min before it was fixed" (8). However, there were also opposite experiences. For instance, one online participant stated that "online possibility worked well for the course" (15). Another participant stated that "this was my first online participation and everything worked perfectly!" (30).

Besides the technical matters, there were some other issues mentioned by online participants. Many participants felt that they were not able to participate in discussions same way than the classroom participants. For instance, one online participant stated that "as an online participant, I was not given attention to" (3). Another participant shared similar experiences, such as, "dialogue and communication were limited" (35) and "I would have liked to hear what other participants said or asked.. as an online participant I totally missed this part" (29).

Another issue related to online participation was the usage of presentation techniques. Some participants were having problems to follow teaching when the teacher used for instance flip board or pointer. For instance, one participant suggested that teacher could have used "an electronic flip board so that online participants would also see the content" (13). Another participant suggested similarly that teacher could use "some drawing software instead of the flip board" (3).

Only two participants stated that having both online and classroom participants is not a good idea. The first participant (classroom) simply stated that "onsite and online participants at the same time is not the best option" (25). Another participant (online) argued that either online or classroom participants are always "suffering" (37) due to arrangements.

Some participants also shared the reasons why they participated online. One participant stated that "it would have been nice to be onsite, but at least this is cheaper" (2). Another participant emphasised that "online participation gives freedom to participate from wherever you like to" (28). Moreover, one participant stated that online participation is "a good alternative for traveling" (30). For one participant, the online participation "made it possible for me to participate in the training" (48).

4 Discussion

Our premise for the research was that the learning channel affects participants' satisfaction of the hybrid course. Online training limits the number of available HLIs, and therefore it was anticipated that there would be some effect on satisfaction. However, the data analysis provided only partial support for this. Thus, our findings are partly contradicting with previous studies. Allen et al. [5] found no differences in satisfaction between online and classroom students. What comes to overall satisfaction, our findings support these findings. Sun et al. [12] did not find any technological factor affecting satisfaction. Our results do not support these findings, as the learning channel affects the perceived satisfaction of course arrangements. Also, the learning channel does have a small but statistically significant effect on the perceived teacher's teaching skills, which is the most surprising finding. This suggests that teachers might not be able to share their expertise effectively to online participants. However, the difference between classroom and online participants, 4.4864 and 4.4828, respectively, is very small.

The open-ended feedbacks indicated some challenges in online participation. Biggest issues seem to be technical problems with video and audio. This is likely the reason for the lower course arrangement scores and is in line with previous findings; technical problems are frustrating students [12]. However, these issues were not faced by the whole class at the same time but by individual students. This may explain the high standard deviation (.8111) among online participants.

Some of the online participants felt that they did not receive enough attention from the teacher and that they were "outsiders". One reason for this might be teacher's repertoire of presentation techniques. Some online participants reported that they could not follow all teaching when the teacher used flip boards or pointers. Knipe and Lee [13] have noticed similar pedagogical challenges; online participants do not receive as much information and explanations from the teacher as the classroom participants do. This may very well explain the lower teacher's substance skills among online participants.

As suggested by Berger [2], participants indicated that online participation saves money regarding reduced traveling and saved time. It also gives the choice of freedom regarding from where to participate.

4.1 Limitations

In this research, we studied whether the used learning channel affects student satisfaction. As such, the results do not reveal any effects on actual learning outcomes. We used the data from a single ICT-training provider, which may limit the generalizability of our findings.

4.2 Contributions to Practice

As the findings revealed, the learning channel did not affect participants' overall satisfaction and teacher's teaching skill. The difference between perceived teacher's substance skills is so small that in practice it does not matter. Therefore, we would like to encourage training providers to consider offering more online participation options. At the same time, however, there are some issues which should be noticed and dealt with. First, the reliable internet connection and video conferencing equipment should be used and tested beforehand. Teachers should also familiarize themselves with the used technology. Second, teachers should give more attention to online participants to be able to share their expertise more effectively. This includes using appropriate teaching aids, such as electronic flip boards, and effective communication techniques, such as frequently asking questions.

4.3 Contributions to Science

The study partly contradicts with the findings of previous studies conducted in the higher education sector. As demonstrated, online participants are not as satisfied with course arrangements as the classroom participants. The most surprising finding was a little but the statistically significant difference in perceived teacher's substance skill.

4.4 Directions for Future Research

The findings pointed out some issues with used teaching aids, which may explain learning channel effects to perceived teacher's substance skills and course arrangements. The *TrainingCorp* used two different technical solutions to provide online training. The feedback data did not include information on which tool was used on each course. Thus, the first interesting area for future research would be to study whether the used solution affects satisfaction. The second interesting area would be to study which kind of teaching aids for classroom and online training do these solutions provide. The third interesting area would be to study how teachers feel teaching the classroom and online students at the same time. The fourth area of interest would be to find out which factors in hybrid courses are affecting the perceived teacher's substance skills. Finally, as indicated earlier, one should study whether the learning channel affects the actual learning outcomes.

Acknowledgements. The author would like to express his gratitude to *TrainingCorp* for providing access to the feedback data used in this study.

References

1. Lokken, F., Mullins, C.: ITC 2013 distance education survey results, in trends in eLearning: tracking the impact of eLearning at community colleges, Washington (2014)
2. Berger, R.: Corporate learning goes digital. How companies can benefit from online education. Roland Derber Strategy Consultants, Munich, 20 (2014)
3. Trainingmag: Training Industry Report 2016, Trainingmag (2016)
4. Johnson, S.D., et al.: Comparative analysis of learner satisfaction and learning outcomes in online and face-to-face learning environments. J. Interact. Learn. Res. **11**(1), 29–49 (2000)
5. Allen, M., et al.: Comparing student satisfaction with distance education to traditional classrooms in higher education: a meta-analysis. Am. J. Distance Educ. **16**(2), 83–97 (2002)
6. Merisotis, J.P., Phipps, R.A.: What's the difference?: outcomes of distance vs. traditional classroom-based learning. Change Mag. High. Learn. **31**(3), 12–17 (1999)
7. Syynimaa, N.: Does the learning channel really matter? Insights from commercial online ICT-training. In: 9th International Conference on Computer Supported Education (CSEDU 2017), April 21st–23rd 2017. INSTICC, Porto, Portugal (2017)
8. Leppänen, S.M., Syynimaa, N.: From learning 1.0 to learning 2.0: key concepts and enablers. In: 7th International Conference on Computer Supported Education (CSEDU 2015). INSTICC, Lisbon, Portugal (2015)
9. Koper, R.: Conditions for effective smart learning environments. Smart Learn. Environ. **1**(5), 1–17 (2014)

10. Roth, W.-M.: Gestures: their role in teaching and learning. Rev. Educ. Res. **71**(3), 365–392 (2001)
11. Schertz, J.: Updating the CX5000 and RoundTable firmware, 20th April 2017 (2012). http://blog.schertz.name/2012/02/update-cx5000-rt-firmware/
12. Sun, P.-C., et al.: What drives a successful e-Learning? An empirical investigation of the critical factors influencing learner satisfaction. Comput. Educ. **50**(4), 1183–1202 (2008)
13. Knipe, D., Lee, M.: The quality of teaching and learning via videoconferencing. Br. J. Educ. Technol. **33**(3), 301–311 (2002)

The Three Eras of Mobile Learning User Experience

Amir Dirin[1](✉) and Marko Nieminen[2]

[1] Business Information Technology, HAAGA-HELIA University of Applied Science, Helsinki, Finland
amir.dirin@haaga-helia.fi
[2] Department of Computer Science, Aalto University, Espoo, Finland
marko.nieminen@aalto.fi

Abstract. In this paper, we present how the design of mobile learning applications has undergone three different phases since the beginning of this millennium. Users' expectations and requirements on m-learning applications have continuously evolved and affected the applications through the different phases. Initially (era 1), the evolvement was a result of the advancement of mobile technologies, devices, and network services. However, technology is not the sole source of evolvement: users' changing expectations and cultural surroundings have an increasing impact on the utilisation of m-learning applications. During the second era focus shifted toward usability (efficiency, effectiveness, satisfaction). The emerging third era has focus on experiential factors which impact the sustainable use of a mobile learning application. The case examples in the paper demonstrate the transitions from technological era to usability era - and even further to user experience era with analyses on emotional, experiential, and engaging factors. The resulting three eras outlined in this paper help developers anticipating future demands with development activities focusing on emotions and engagement.

Keywords: Usability · User experience design · Mobile learning

1 Introduction

Knowledge and educational material has become widely available for anybody with access to internet and desire to pursue it. Wealth of material is available online, free of charge, at any time. Easy access to communication, information, and knowledge has also resulted in social and cultural changes: for instance, people rarely manage a day without a mobile phone or access to the Internet.

This easy access to knowledge creates additional and perhaps even surprising demands for the design of learning content and applications. Learning content and applications need to compete and stay up-to-date with other important and entertaining information and services.

Mobile learning aims to overcome the constraints of traditional educational settings where learning and teaching happen in classrooms behind closed doors. M-learning has been around for almost two decades, but so far it has failed to draw serious attention of

P. Escudeiro et al. (Eds.): CSEDU 2017, CCIS 865, pp. 207–220, 2018.
https://doi.org/10.1007/978-3-319-94640-5_11

educational institutes in comparison with e-learning. Utilizing smart devices for educational purposes is associated with several challenges including the usage of a small device with many limitations on display, keypad, and memory. Mobile learning applications also compete with students' time regarding other applications in the used device, including games.

There have been significant improvements in the technological capabilities of mobile devices during the last decade including mobile application development processes. New gadgets smartphones and tablets have been developed that are equipped with many advanced technologies and capabilities, including WIFI [1] and NFC [2]. Furthermore, these devices have become more intelligent than ever before due to the embedded sensors, camera, and high-quality audio and video equipment. The challenging drawbacks of these devices, namely the memory space and processing power, have been overcome in many ways. Network operators provide fast data connectivity to their subscribers at a relatively low cost.

Smartphone usage among youth is increasing [3] at the expense of PC usage [4]. Mobile applications including games, social networking, and professional tools, are proliferating in application stores. Mobile learning (m-learning) applications are competing for learners' time and attention, and they must meet learners' educational requirements while also encourage frequent use [5].

M-learning applications require careful design and development considerations as they deal with learning and learners alike. This is particularly true in formal learning settings where m-learning applications are meant to be used for long periods of time. In this respect, sustainability plays an important role. A contextual analysis of user's relation to m-learning applications is one way to address such challenges.

Mobile learning applications' usability has initially been applied in the form of usability inspections, although it was soon realized that this was not sufficient [6]. Therefore, alternative solutions, models, and frameworks have been proposed to anticipate these challenges. There have been significant methodological improvements, usability guidelines, and pedagogical development. Kukulska-Hulme [7] has emphasized that "for broad and long-term adoption the experience really matters".

Seong [5] formulates three usability evaluation categories for a mobile learning application, namely the user interface, the interaction, and the interface design. Furthermore, Seong [5] recommends ten usability guidelines to measure the mobile learning application's usability. Simultaneously, researchers have proposed a systematic mobile learning application design and development methodology in order to gain better usability and user experience (UX). This includes recommendations for the learner-centered design and development of m-learning applications [8–11].

In their literature review concerning mobile learning usability assessments, Navarro et al. [12] present an applied methodology for mobile learning usability assessments. Additionally, they recommend an evaluation framework for m-learning systems that consist of two parts: pedagogical usability and user interface usability. Their proposed set of guidelines for user interface design mainly focus on the usability of m-learning.

Yu and Kong [13] investigate the mobile web page interface design's impact on ease of use, interactivity, reading time, ease of learning, and perceived user-friendliness in order to predict the users' satisfaction with the mobile browsing experience. Their paper reveals the trend of using usability factors such as ease of use to achieve a better UX.

Their attempt to address UX indicates that usability is important in mobile learning, but not sufficient.

These types of frameworks and guidelines demonstrate that the usability of m-learning applications is still evolving and that the existing approaches are not sufficient to result in a successfully deployed and accepted mobile learning application.

There have been significant improvements in utilizing m-learning in the educational process during the last few years. This evolution is due to the advancement in wireless technology that enables one to send/receive various data type over the network. Similarity, the devices are also aligned with the network advancement and are capable of processing and presenting these data on the mobile devices. In the last few years, m-learning has evolved significantly from simple text -based contents to multi-media contents as adaptive, context-aware and ad hoc learning. However, mobile learning adaptation and popularity among users is far from e-learning counterpart. There are various reasons for the unpopularity such as the technological adaptations. Dillon and Morris [14] noted that users' acceptance of new technology depends on the user psychology, the design process of the information technology, and the users' perceived quality of the technology. This fact has already identified and aimed to ease the adaptation for example, Davis et al. [15, 16] TAM model which considers information technology contributions and adaptations as well as ease of use, usefulness, and enjoyment concept. Therefore, aforementioned shortcomings have been anticipated by researchers through development methodologies, usability guidelines, technological solutions, and user experience factors.

People's attentions and focus are extending from mobile devices to other "smart technologies" and gadgets, such as smartwatches. Chen et al. [17] present an interactive system that explores a design space of interactions between a smartphone and a smartwatch. Their design indicates that interaction and input media for gadgets are emerging based on device capabilities. A symphony of smart gadgets' emergence helps design mobile learning platforms more efficiently and effectively, for example by utilizing motion sensors in a smartwatch to detect the user's gestures as an input to the application [18].

2 Three Eras of User Experience

User experience (UX) has been considered to be an important element of a mobile application's success [19]. UX has become a viable supplement to traditional HCI design, which is indicated in recent practitioner discussions. UX design is a multidimensional phenomenon in which many factors influence success.

Despite the more than a decade-long [20] research and definition on user experience, the concept still suffers from vague and broad definition. This is, for instance, reflected in the 27 definitions of user experience reported as a result of the Dagstuhl Seminar on Demarcating User Experience [19] (see also http://www.allaboutux.org/ux-definitions). Application domain (e.g. m-learning) specific definitions of UX are even more scarce. However, Rusu et al. [21] recognize that there is a tendency to move from usability to user experience, although there is a lack of formal widely-accepted definition of UX among the CS communities.

The technological enablers to enhance mobile devices in education was raised already in early 2000. **The First Era** of mobile learning application design and development may be defined to have taken place during 2000–2006 [22, 23] and might be entitled as the *technical approach to UX* which still appears as the basis for much of the UX related discussion. Garrett's [22] model on UX is conceptual model of a development process to ensure the user's experience of a website. The model consists of five planes: the site objective, the requirements, interaction design, information design, and visual design.

Roto's [23] model on UX introduces human responses as part of mobile browsing user experience. The model identifies the different roles of mobile device, browser, connection, and site attributes which have an effect on mobile browsing experience.

The Second Era of mobile learning application design and development may be defined to be about *usability* (2006–2010). The era is characterised by the definition of usability that emphasizes user's satisfaction, application's efficiency, and effectiveness. The main transition during this period has been change of focus from beyond mere functionality to smooth usage and interaction between the user and the applications. During this period, alternative solutions, models, and frameworks were proposed to anticipate usability failures. Many researchers [7, 24, 25] have conducted literature reviews on m-learning state-of-the-art and usability. The design and development of m-learning applications increased in complexity, and usability inspections were presented as means to overcome the challenges. Literature reviews concerning publications on usability highlight this trend [7]. Seong [5] formulate three usability evaluation categories for an m-learning application: user interface, interaction, and interface design. They recommended ten usability guidelines to measure the usability of m-learning applications. Magal-Royo et al. [26] recommend criteria for mobile learning usability which is based on conventional usability methods. Aligned with this, Glavinic et al. [27] propose personalization as means to improve the usability and user experience of m-learning. Personalization relates to adjusting the capabilities of the mobile device, student's domain knowledge level, and interaction style and skills. Mostakhdemin-Hosseini [28] identifies satisfaction, efficiency, learnability, lack of errors, and memorability as relevant usability attributes to consider in the development of an m-learning application.

The previous two "conceptual eras of UX" are used to reflect the evolvement of m-learning applications over the last decade.

The Third Era of mobile learning user experience is described as the *experiential era*. (ISO, 2010) [30] defines user experience as "person's perceptions and responses that result from the use or anticipated use of a product, system or service". Nielsen and Norman [31] define user experience as simplicity of a product, which comes with elegance that users enjoy to own and enjoy to use. We characterize the third era for mobile learning as "human responses and emotions as UX". In this era developers aim at attaching users emotionally to the application to enable sustainable usage of the application.

The trend on m-learning user experience have focused exclusively on learners' experience after 2010. In 2009, Mostakhdemin-Hosseini [28] presented emotional factors such as funability and reliability which impact the learners' attitude on mobile learning application usage. Williams [32] examines m-learning effectiveness and students' acceptance of delivery of the learning through new paradigm and presents factors that influence user acceptance of m-learning application. The importance of user experience in e-learning platforms and educational media has been identified by several researchers [33, 34] including m-learning environments [35]. From the technical perspective, Yousafzai et al. [36] propose technical guidelines and taxonomy on m-learning environment to overcome the existing multimedia-enabled m-learning applications' constraints. The taxonomy addresses mobile device heterogeneity, network performance, and content heterogeneity.

Extending the focus from technical characteristics of m-learning, Ali and Arshad [37] propose an acceptance model that aims to affect the students' intention to adopt an m-learning application. They extend the Unified Theory of Acceptance and Use of Technology (UTAUT) model [38] with three supplementing factors: mobility, interactivity, and enjoyment. Badwelan et al. [39] reach even more toward non-technical characteristics in determining the factors that influence students' intentions to use m-learning. Their results show that the added UTAUT factors personal innovativeness, lecturer's influence, and self-management of the learner had a significant impact on students' intention to use m-learning. Dirin [40] identifies satisfaction, delightfulness, reliability, and adjustability as important UX factors for m-learning application sustainability in the attempts to move more towards non-technical and "beyond instrumental" [20] aspects of m-learning (Table 1).

Table 1. Overview of the three eras: the evolving m-learning user experience.

Era	Focus	Case application
Era 1 (utility/technical)	How to utilize mobile technology in educational institutes?	Java application
Era 2 (usability)	How to make m-learning applications effective and efficient which satisfy users' needs?	Adaptive m-learning application for driving school
Era 3 (experiential)	How to engage users emotionally with the m-learning applications to enable sustainable usage?	Business game

In the following sections, we analyse the impact of UX to m-learning applications in respective eras. The aim is to reflect on students' and teachers' evolving expectations towards future m-learning applications.

3 Samples on Evolving UX in M-Learning

The following three case applications demonstrate how user experience has evolved over time in m-learning. The analysis of these sample applications indicates how the users' expectations have changed from *instrumental* to *beyond instrumental* and *experiential* needs, as modelled by [20] over time.

3.1 Java Applet for a Java Course (UX Era 1)

The introduction of m-learning applications relates to the emergence and diffusion of mobile devices and applications in general. The Java-applet-based m-learning application (see Fig. 1) helped students to access the resources of a Java programming course including lecture notes, assignments, and other information such as feedback from a teacher using a Java-enabled mobile phone. Additionally, students could submit their laboratory and home assignments through the application if they had access to the network.

Fig. 1. The "Java Course" m-learning application [42].

The gathered requirements from teachers, courses assistants, and students indicate that users raised only functional demands and needs. For example, teachers and course assistants have concerned about the uploading course related materials while students were concerned about downloading materials. Or, Students asked for possible administrative features such as registering for a course.

The reliability of the application was the only user experience related requirement which highlighted by users for java m-learning application.

The screenshot (Fig. 1) presents an example of the application's user interface. The visual design of the java mobile learning application was restricted to the existing development environment (J2ME) on the phone. The user interface ("Main Menu") is divided into the following categories: presentation ("esitys"), activities ("toiminta"), communication ("yhteyden-pito"), and administration ("hallinto") according to the virtual course delivery model by Brusilovsky and Miller [43].

The application can be seen to conform to Garrett's [22] technology and process focused elements of user experience model. The design and development of the application was done by identifying the users' needs and defining the technical, structural, and functional requirements accordingly.

However, the development of this application reached towards the model presented by Roto [23]. The human response in relation to the application was evaluated through usability testing. There were many concerns raised by the users regarding connectivity, slow performance of the device, low memory, and short battery life. The slow data transfer connection and high data exchange cost were among major drawbacks in the application's usage. Connectivity was considered to impact content delivery, usability, and even support for offline usage. These were relevant concerns but the technology and the development environments at the time prevented the finding of a proper workaround to overcome the technical constraints.

3.2 Adaptive M-Learning Application (UX Era 2)

The adaptive m-learning application for driving licence candidates (see Fig. 2) was a joint project between Haaga-Helia University of Applied Sciences and Haaga Driving School in Helsinki. This application helps the driving school candidates to study and access the compulsory driving school theory lessons on their smartphones. Furthermore, the administration tool helps the instructors to trace students' theory progress and driving experiences.

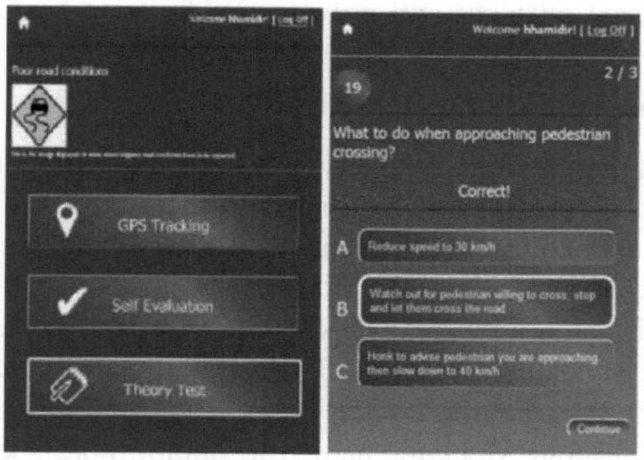

Fig. 2. The "Driving School" m-learning application.

The main goal of the project was to design a functional m-learning application as a proof of concept. The design, development, and assessment of this case study application is published in [44].

This m-learning application assists driving school students and instructors in their daily teaching and learning activities. The application helps the driving school candidates to study and access the compulsory driving school theory lessons on their smartphones. The administration tool helps the instructors to trace students' theory progress and driving experiences.

In contrast to the Java Applet mobile learning application, the user expectations for this application were much more than just the mere functionalities of the application or just extending the uses of the mobile devices. The users' needs and requirements of the potential application included many non-functional requirements which Hassenzahl and Tractinsky [20] refer to as "beyond instrumental" characteristics. The following are examples of non-functional requirements that users raised during the elicitation phase: (1) Customization of the potential application based on users' preferences. (2) The resources provided to users based on the context and user competences. (3) Instructors follow students' progress reliably. Figure 2 reveals that the above non-functional requirements were tackled through. (1) The user is able to customize application feel and look at any time. (2) Through color-coding, the adaptive m-learning application provides instance feedback to users on the context. (3) Instructors follow the students' progress through the color-coded interface.

The application was designed to allow users to combine external services to the application including, for instance, the search for information through their preferred internet search engine.

The responsive design of the application makes the mobile device adaptive to users' contextual requirements. This is an "affect mechanism" to depict the negative emotions. Furthermore, the application makes use of colors, visual symbols, and familiar icons to raise positive emotions during the use of the service.

This adaptive m-learning application also helped the user to receive feedback on learning instantly. During the driving experiment the application notifies the instructor on candidate's performance. Additionally, the application delivers pop-up messages as notifications on occurred mistakes and provides guidance to fix them.

3.3 Business Game Application (UX Era 3)

This mobile learning application helps users to become familiar with the complex premises and the offices in different buildings. In the "Business Game" (see Fig. 3) application [45] the user study was performed to learn about the target users' application preferences. The qualitative data from the user study was analyzed and categorized to produce the requirements. The designer focused on designing the product concept to be most appealing to users. User scenarios were applied and various application concepts were assessed by the users. The low-fidelity paper-based prototype created using Balsamiq Mockups helped to obtain more specific feedback from users.

Fig. 3. Sample of role character for the "Business Game" m-learning application [42].

Users' expectations on presenting the content as a game illustrate the "beyond instrumental" requirements. This non-functional requirement was raised in the concept design phase of the application. Furthermore, users' demand on having different game characters to play the game indicated that users strive for an emotional relation towards the application. Figure 3 presents sample of a character that we proposed in the business game application. Engagement with the application and communication with other peers are considered as important complementing non-functional requirements that reflect the "beyond instrumental" needs.

The desired increasing complexity in playing the game was raised by users in the usability test reflecting the hedonic aspects towards the application. Emotion appeared to provide a basis for the selection of the characters and affect was detected while analyzing achievements after playing each game. The "game appeal" appeared to increase learners' motivation to complete the game and go through the whole learning content.

4 Discussion

Over the years the users' requirements on m-learning has evolved. One may argue that the users' motivations to use the mobile devices for educational purposes has significantly changed. The users of the latest mobile learning applications have already learnt to use mobile devices for a multitude of purposes including the educational. Mobile learning applications are part of the large pool of high-quality services that contain educational elements and compete on users' time. Such services include using Google to search, online dictionaries, emails, instant messaging, and calendars.

The usability evaluation of the initial Java m-learning application (UX era 1) indicated that users do value high the utilization of their mobile device for educational purposes despite their initial mental model on m-learning as an "upgraded text messaging service". Students and teachers demands on mobile learning application (UX era 2) has changed from mere functional to more "usable" application. The more recent applications' (UX era 3) design and development reveals that students' demands and expectations were more than just "usable" consisting only of effective and efficient performance with the application. Users of the Java m-learning application desired to use their mobile devices solely for educational purposes which Hassenzahl and Tractinsky [20] present as "instrumental". In contrast, in the case of the driving school application, users mandated and required a usable mobile learning application which, according to ISO 9241, ends up being effective, efficient, and satisfying. Currently, as mobile applications have become an integrated part of learners' everyday lives, they expect m-learning applications that are not just convenient to use but intriguing and engaging.

In our case descriptions, the users in the first group (the "Java Course" m-learning application) did not have prior experience with mobile learning and, therefore, were eager to enhance the uses and functionality of the mobile device towards educational activities. In the "Java Course" m-learning application, the main requirements were focused on task-related and functional aspects. At the second era of mobile learning, however, users had already started using their mobile devices for a multitude of purposes including the educational process. The users at the second era expected good usability (efficiency, effectiveness, and satisfaction) for smooth and easy operation. During the third era users have started to consider "usable" as a "de-facto characteristic" for any mobile learning application. The work by Yu and Kong [13] justifies the importance of moving from usability and ease-of-use toward user experience and emotional engagement in "web browsing on a small screen". They demonstrate the importance of design in facilitating ease-of-use and ease-of-interactivity to achieve ease of reading and learning.

The latter case from "UX era 3" goes beyond the usability boundaries reaching towards the hedonic aspects indicated by Hassenzahl and Tractinsky [20]. The users of the recent m-learning applications emphasized the responsive and subjective experience on the use of the application. The feelings of joy and ownership affect users' emotional engagement with the application. The "beyond instrumental" and "experiential" requirements have become more important for m-learning application acceptance and continuing utilization.

In addition to technology, changes have also occurred in students' and teachers' social lives and cultural surroundings. Among the wide adoption of mobile devices people have become more connected through mobile messaging and social media. This has increased their dependency and emotional attachment on their mobile devices. As smartphones significantly impact learners' life, m-learning needs to be addressed as part of users' everyday activities. This implies a more holistic approach on the design and development of m-learning applications including contextual analyses (see e.g. [46]).

Alongside the maturing of mobile technology in general, users' attitudes and expectations regarding the m-learning applications' design and performance have also altered. Unlike the situation in 2003, smart devices are now equipped with extensive in-device applications to meet users' various daily needs. Additionally, millions of third-party applications are available for download in the different platform stores. Almost all these applications are competing for users', including students', time and dedication. These changes have resulted in additional expectations for m-learning applications' design, features, application performance, and user experience.

Aligned with the smart gadgets' technological advancement, many solutions aim at anticipating the technical changes. Mere technology-oriented solutions may not be sufficient to result in continuous usage of mobile learning application. Instead, the changing social and cultural surroundings provide a source of analysis for the "beyond instrumental" aspects that may be crucial for the acceptance of the applications. In 2004 the users only wanted to have the Java course content as an application on their mobile phones while in 2013, having only the content in the phone was not sufficient. Users demand the application to be fun to use, adaptable and adjustable to meet personal preferences.

As the focus of mobile learning application design appears to move from technical to experiential, the success of mobile learning applications depends on the "experiential design". In their recent research, Kuderna-Iulian et al. [47] recognize the importance of behavior and emotions in learning and the acceptance of a software product. Their multimodal monitoring tool for collecting emotional feedback through mobile devices' sensors provides interesting ways forward in analysing such impacts in using an m-learning application.

The technological developments have also had an impact on educational institutes' attitudes toward m-learning application utilization and, most of all, on students' expectations of m-learning applications' enhancement [48] of their educational process. Therefore, in contemporary educational institutes [49] with current social setups [50], m-learning applications have become a response to student and staff demands regarding their educational activities.

5 Conclusions

In this paper, we have analysed m-learning user experience evolution in three eras. The first era of user experience (2000–2006) focused on technical approaches, while in the second era (2006–2011), besides technical approaches, the focus shifted towards non-instrumental requirements. After 2010, technologies for mobile learning became mature and m-learning applications have started to compete on students' time with other entertainment applications in phone. Therefore, considerations on mobile learning user experience have become more important. The eras of the mobile user experiences are presented in the following timeframe figure (Fig. 4).

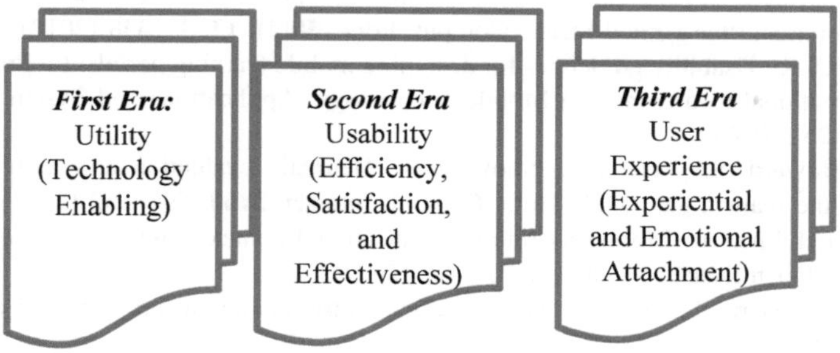

Fig. 4. The eras of mobile learning user experience.

A successful m-learning application is dependent on not only technological but especially design time and usage time factors such as support for wireless technologies, stakeholders' involvement in application development, and the context of use of the application. At the early phase of m-learning application design, elicitation of requirements typically focuses on functional and instrumental needs of users without deep analysis of the non-functional requirements arising from the everyday context-of-use. Application designers may apply traditional usability evaluations to assess m-learning applications, but findings about social behaviour and emotions in everyday situations supporting learning may remain uncovered.

Mobile learning applications need additional justification than just satisfying the practical needs impacting the effectiveness and efficiency of the application. User experience and emotional engagement play an important role in motivating users for continuing and sustainable usage of m-learning applications.

Proper addressing of user experience increases the possibilities for the m-learning applications to compete on students' time with other entertaining and engaging applications in their device. We suggest that special attention should be put to the "beyond instrumental" and "the experiential" aspects when designing engaging mobile learning applications for continuous and sustainable use.

Acknowledgements. Special thanks to students, educational institutes, and partners company who helped to design, develop, and utilize the applications presented in this paper.

References

1. Henry, P.S., Luo, H.: WiFi: what's next? IEEE Commun. Mag. **40**, 66–72 (2002)
2. Madlmayr, G., Langer, J., Scharinger, J.: Managing an NFC ecosystem. In: Proceedings - 7th International Conference on Mobile Business, ICMB 2008, Creativity and Convergence, pp. 95–101 (2008)
3. Lee, U., Lee, J., Ko, M., Lee, C., Kim, Y., Yang, S., Yatani, K., Gweon, G., Chung, K.-M., Song, J.: Hooked on smartphones: an exploratory study on smartphone overuse among college students. In: Proceedings of the SIGCHI Conference on Human Factors in Computing Systems, pp. 2327–2336 (2014)
4. Sung, E., Mayer, R.E.: Students' beliefs about mobile devices vs. desktop computers in South Korea and the United States. Comput. Educ. **59**(4), 1328–1338 (2012)
5. Seong, D.S.K.: Usability guidelines for designing mobile learning portals. In: Proceedings of 3rd International Conference on Mobile Technology, Applications and Systems - Mobility 2006, p. 25 (2006)
6. Po, S., Howard, S., Vetere, F., Skov, M.B.: Heuristic evaluation and mobile usability: bridging the realism gap. Mob. Hum.-Comput. Interact. **3160**, 591–592 (2004)
7. Kukulska-Hulme, A.: Mobile usability in educational contexts: what have we learnt? Int. Rev. Res. Open Distance Learn. **8**(2), 1–16 (2007)
8. Basaeed, E., Berri, J., Zemerly, M.J.: Learner-centric context-aware mobile learning. Eng. Educ. **2**(2), 30–33 (2007)
9. Low, L., Connell, M.O., Connellcitacteduau, M.O.: Learner-centric design of digital mobile learning. In: Framework, pp. 1–13 (2006)
10. Soloway, E., Guzdial, M., Hay, K.E.: Learner-centered design: the challenge for HCI in the 21st century. Interactions **1**, 36–48 (1994)
11. Wong, L.H.: A learner-centric view of mobile seamless learning. Br. J. Educ. Technol. **43** (1), E19–E23 (2012)
12. Navarro, C.X., Molina, A., Redondo, M.A., Reyes, J.-R.: Framework to evaluate m-learning systems: a technological and pedagogical approach. IEEE Revista Iberoamericana de Tecnologias del Aprendizaje **11**(1), 33–40 (2016)
13. Yu, N., Kong, J.: User experience with web browsing on small screens: experimental investigations of mobile-page interface design and homepage design for news websites. Inf. Sci. (NY) **330**, 427–443 (2016)
14. Dillon, A., Morris, M.G.: User acceptance of information technology: theories and models. Annu. Rev. Inf. Sci. Technol. **31**, 3–33 (1996)
15. Davis, F.D., Bagozzi, R.P., Warshaw, P.R.: User acceptance of computer technology: a comparison of two theoretical models. Manag. Sci. **35**(8), 982–1003 (1989)
16. Davis, F.D., Bagozzi, R.P., Warshaw, P.R.: Extrinsic and intrinsic motivation to use computers in the workplace. J. Appl. Soc. Psychol. **22**, 1111–1132 (1992)

17. Chen, X.A., Grossman, T., Wigdor, D.J., Fitzmaurice, G.: Duet: exploring joint interactions on a smart phone and a smart watch. In: Proceedings of 32nd Annual ACM Conference on Human Factors in Computing Systems - CHI 2014, pp. 159–168 (2014)
18. Gouthaman, S., Pandya, A.: Gesture detection system using smart watch based motion sensors. In: International Conference on Circuits, Systems, Communication and Information Technology Applications, pp. 311–316 (2014)
19. Roto, V., Law, E., Vermeeren, A., Hoonhout, J.: User experience white paper: bringing clarity to the concept of user experience. Dagstuhl Seminar on Demarcating User Experience, p. 12 (2010)
20. Hassenzahl, M., Tractinsky, N.: User experience - a research agenda. Behav. Inf. Technol. **25**(2), 91–97 (2006)
21. Rusu, C., Rusu, V., Roncagliolo, S., Carina, G.: Usability and user experience: what should we care about. Int. J. Inf. Technol. Syst. Approach **8**, 12 (2015)
22. Garrett, J.J.: The Elements of User Experience (2000). http://www.jjg.net/elements/pdf/elements.pdf. Accessed 22 June 2018
23. Roto, V.: Web browsing on mobile phones - characteristics of user experience. Dissertation (2006)
24. Deegan, R., Rothwell, P.: A classification of m-learning applications from a usability perspective. J. Res. Cent. Educ. Technol. **6**, 16–27 (2010)
25. Frohberg, D., Göth, C., Schwabe, G.: Mobile learning projects – a critical analysis of the state of the art. J. Comput. Assist. Learn. **25**(4), 307–331 (2009)
26. Magal-Royo, T., Peris-Fajarnes, G., Tortajada Montañana, I., Defez Garcia, B.: Evaluation methods on usability of m-learning environment. Int. J. Interact. Mob. Technol. **1**(1), 32–39 (2007)
27. Glavinic, V., Ljubic, S., Kukec, M.: A holistic approach to enhance universal usability in m-learning. In: Proceedings - The 2nd International Conference on Mobile Ubiquitous Computing, Systems, Services and Technologies, UBICOMM 2008, pp. 305–310 (2008)
28. Mostakhdemin-Hosseini, A.: Usability considerations of mobile learning applications. Int. J. Interact. Mob. Technol. **3**, 29–31 (2009)
29. ISO: Ergonomics of human-system interaction - Part 210: Human-centred design for interactive systems (ISO 9241-210:2010(E)), ISO, pp. 1–32 (2010)
30. ISO, ISO 9241 Part 210: Human-centred design for interactive systems in ISO 9241 Ergonomics of human system interaction (2010)
31. Nielsen J., Norman, D.: The definition of user experience. In: NNG Articles (2015)
32. Williams, P.W.: Assessing mobile learning effectiveness and acceptance. Ph.D., pp. 1–10 (2009)
33. Garaj, V.: M-learning in the education of multimedia technologists and designers at the university level: a user requirements study. IEEE Trans. Learn. Technol. **3**(1), 24–32 (2010)
34. Sutcliffe, A., Alrayes, A.: Investigating user experience in second life for collaborative learning. Int. J. Hum. Comput. Stud. **70**(7), 508–525 (2012)
35. Shen, R.: Constructing a user experience-based mobile learning environment: problems and solutions. Fernuniversitä, Hagen, Germany (2014)
36. Yousafzai, A., Chang, V., Gani, A., Noor, R.M.: Multimedia augmented m-learning: issues, trends and open challenges. Int. J. Inf. Manag. **36**(5), 784–792 (2016)
37. Ali, R.A., Arshad, M.R.M.: Perspectives of students' behavior towards mobile learning (m-learning) in Egypt: an extension of the UTAUT model. Eng. Technol. Appl. Sci. Res. **6** (4), 1109–1114 (2016)
38. Venkatesh, V., Morris, M.G., Davis, G.B., Davis, F.D.: User acceptance of information technology: toward a unified view. MIS Q. **27**(3), 425–478 (2003)

39. Badwelan, A., Drew, S., Bahaddad, A.A.: Towards acceptance m-learning approach in higher education in Saudi Arabia. Int. J. Bus. Manag. **11**(8), 12–30 (2016)
40. Dirin, A.: Toward enhancing user experience in mobile learning applications. Aalto University (2016)
41. Dirin, A., Laine, T.H., Nieminen, M.: Sustainable usage through emotional engagement: a user experience analysis of an adaptive driving school application. Cogn. Technol. Work **19**, 303–313 (2016)
42. Dirin, A., Nieminen, M.: User experience evolution of m-learning applications. In: 9th International Conference on Computer Supported Education, p. 9, 21–23 April 2017
43. Brusilovsky, P., Miller, P.: Course delivery system for virtual university. In: Access to Knowledge: New Information Technologies and the Emergence of the Virtual University, pp. 167–206 (2001)
44. Dirin, A., Casarini, M.: Adaptive m-learning application for driving licenses candidates based on UCD framework for m-learning application development. In: 6th International Conference on Computer Supported Education (2014)
45. Dirin, A., Vainio, V.: Case study: from requirements list to an educational game. In: 7th International Conference on Education and New Learning Technologies (2015)
46. Dirin, A., Nieminen, M.: mLUX: usability and user experience development framework for m-learning. Int. J. Interact. Mob. Technol. (iJIM) **9**, 37–51 (2015)
47. Kuderna-Iulian, B., Marcel, C., Mireca, V.: A multimodal affective monitoring tool for mobile learning. In: 14th RoEduNet International Conference – Networking in Education and Research (RoEduNet NER), pp. 34–38 (2015)
48. Dirin, A., Nieminen, M.: State-of-the-art of m-learning usability and user experience. In: Fourth International Conference on e-Learning (2014)
49. Collins, A., Halverson, R.: The second educational revolution: rethinking education in the age of technology. J. Comput. Assist. Learn. **26**, 18–27 (2010)
50. Vannoy, S.A., Palvia, P.: The social influence model of technology adoption. Commun. ACM **53**, 149 (2010)

Designing Engaging Learning Experiences in Programming

Chris Martin[1], Janet Hughes[2(✉)], and John Richards[3,4]

[1] Life Sciences - CITR, University of Dundee, Dundee, UK
c.j.martin@dundee.ac.uk
[2] School of Computing and Communications, The Open University, Edinburgh, UK
janet.hughes@open.ac.uk
[3] IBM T. J. Watson Research Center, Yorktown Heights, NY 10598, USA
ajtr@us.ibm.com
[4] University of Dundee, Dundee, UK

Abstract. In this paper we describe work to investigate the creation of engaging programming learning experiences. Background research informed the design of four fieldwork studies to explore how programming tasks could be framed to motivate learners. Our empirical findings from these four field studies are summarized here, with a particular focus upon one – Whack a Mole – which compared the use of a physical interface with the use of a screen-based equivalent interface to obtain insights into what made for an engaging learning experience. Emotions reported by two sets of participant undergraduate students were analyzed, identifying the links between the emotions experienced during programming and their origin. Evidence was collected of the very positive emotions experienced by learners programming with a physical interface (Arduino) in comparison with a similar program developed using a screen-based equivalent interface. A follow-up study provided further evidence of the motivation of personalized design of programming tangible physical artefacts. Collating all the evidence led to the design of a set of 'Learning Dimensions' which may provide educators with insights to support key design decisions for the creation of engaging programming learning experiences.

Keywords: Motivation · Programming · Learning Dimensions

1 Introduction: Motivating Learning

Motivation is defined in the Oxford English Dictionary as "a reason or reasons for acting in a particular way" [32]. If it changes desire into will and subsequent action, then it can be an important element to cultivate in the learner when designing an engaging learning experience. This paper is about creating a context for motivation and rich engagement with learning to program in particular.

The paper begins with a brief description of related literature, including work highlighted in detailed literature reviews on motivation and learning [9, 12]. Continuing with the theme of published literature relating to engaging learning experiences, Sect. 2 gives a

P. Escudeiro et al. (Eds.): CSEDU 2017, CCIS 865, pp. 221–245, 2018.
https://doi.org/10.1007/978-3-319-94640-5_12

review of a selection of studies relating to evidence of emotion generated by learning experiences. Section 3 introduces the main study of the paper, detailing the Whack a Mole study which compared the engagement resulting from screen-based programming work with that resulting from a matched piece of work that used a tangible physical artefact instead of a conventional screen. Sections 4–6 provide the study design, results and discussion. Section 7 then describes a follow-up study which further sets the learning of programming in the context of using tangible physical artefacts. All the lessons learned from the literature and the studies described here are then used to derive a set of Learning Dimensions, described in Sect. 8, which it is hoped will prove useful to educators seeking to design engaging learning experiences in programming.

1.1 Categories of Motivation

[33] described the ability to modify behavior through reinforcement in animal experiments. It was shown that if a reward was given in response to a desired behavior, this desired behavior by the animal was likely to recur. This reward is referred to as a task-extrinsic reward and its effect can be described as extrinsic motivation. Complementing this, [36] described a number of studies that demonstrate animal behaviors which were not purely functional but may be driven by intrinsic motivation, i.e. 'motivation from within' or to engage in an activity for its own sake without directly perceivable payoff to the participant.

[2] offer a good description of elements of task-extrinsic rewards and intrinsic motivation. The former may take any of the following forms: competition, evaluation, recognition and tangible incentives. Elements of the latter include self-determination, competence, task involvement, curiosity, enjoyment and interest, all of which are desirable behaviors for a learner engaged in an activity.

1.2 Extrinsic Motivation

[4] explored the effect of financial incentives on both central and peripheral learning tasks. An experimental group showed an increased performance (measured as time to complete a task) for the central task when offered an additional financial incentive. However, no improvement was observed with the peripheral task, suggesting that a financial reward narrows the focus of the participant and reduces the chances of incidental learning.

Extrinsic motivators are commonplace in education at all levels. Competency is typically measured with a summative assessment that results in a grade for the learner. This is an important aspect of assessment in education, though this risks fostering the type of motivation that encourages goal-oriented strategies in learners: [9] described extrinsic rewards as increasing speed and quantity of effort at a reduced quality. In addition to encouraging greater throughput of work at a reduced quality, extrinsic rewards increase focus at the expense of engagement in peripheral topics. In a learning situation, this is likely to foster shallow learning where the learner focuses only on activities that are clearly related to the examination at the end of the learning. From a review of 43 studies, [14] conclude that extrinsic rewards undermine intrinsic motivation where the reason for their delivery is poorly defined in the eyes of the recipient.

1.3 Intrinsic Motivation

[3] observed the effects of money, awards and verbal feedback on intrinsic motivation in kindergarten children engaged in a drawing activity. Only verbal feedback had a positive impact on the learner's motivation and time on task. [12] also found evidence that positive feedback can enhance intrinsic motivation. They also found that that tangible rewards undermined intrinsic motivation and were in some cases seen as methods of control that may forestall self-regulation. In a learning situation in particular, [10] robustly locate the importance of personalization and choice for increasing intrinsic motivation in learners. Their study of 72 fifth grade learners (10 to 11 year olds) found that there was a powerful learning benefit observed in the personalized choice condition. Learners displayed a deeper engagement as well as increased motivation.

In conclusion, intrinsic motivation is inarguably a desirable feature to encourage in any learning experience, with evidenced learning benefits described above. The role of extrinsic motivators is a little more uncertain: tangible rewards have been shown to narrow thinking and reduce the depth at which learners engage. However, positive feedback has been observed to enhance intrinsic motivation. For a review of motivation in a broad educational context, see [29], who identifies three over-arching themes in motivation in education. This work, however, focuses on motivation in computer science education, particularly with respect to programming. Understanding intrinsic incentives, and how they relate to the instructional paradigms, may give pointers to the design of engaging learning experiences. Understanding how to obtain evidence of engagement is a further challenge.

2 Evidence of Engagement in a Learning Experience

Anecdotal evidence from programmers will confirm that bugs are frustrating, finding and removing them is satisfying, and reaching a successful conclusion can lead to pride. In education in general, emotional response to learning with technology has been studied for some time, e.g. [23].

2.1 Emotion and Learning

D'Mello's review [13] of 24 studies noted that many learning contexts resulting in engagement had comparatively low reporting of negative emotions. [25] conducted a detailed literature review from 1974 through to 1990, which was later extended to 2002. It included studies attempting to establish links between emotion and learning and achievement. Their review highlighted a bias in the research towards test anxiety: in excess of 1200 studies were found in this area, with other emotions receiving single digit or tens of studies at most. This reveals that broader emotion in an education context was an understudied area. [25] proposed a set of nine emotions in an academic setting that are linked to achievement and learning. As well as anxiety, these include emotions that are positive and negative, and activating and deactivating: *enjoyment, hope, pride, relief, anger, hopelessness, shame*, and *boredom*. The validity of this set of emotions and their link to learning and achievement was established through a number of studies utilizing complementary research methods. Their findings imply students experience a wide range of emotions in an academic setting, with positive emotions represented in similar proportions to negative ones. Their findings also argue for emotion-oriented design of learning environments [25].

2.2 Emotion and Programming

Emotional response to *programming* has a more limited body of work in the literature, although some interesting work has been done [e.g. 6, 7, 15]. [7] sought to map the emotional states a novice experiences and their relative proportions, and explore the co-occurrence of emotional states and the relationship between interaction events. In addition, they mapped transitions between these states. Participants self-reported at a very high frequency, sampling every 15 s. Following a 30-min programming exercise, the participant was shown a web camera still of their face and the programming tool they were using at 100 random points in the session. At each of these points, they are asked to note their emotional state and asked optionally to note a second emotional state. In this study, a number of emotions were offered to participants to select from: *fear, sadness, disgust, flow/engaged, anger, confused, uncertain, surprise, natural, frustration, boredom, happiness, curiosity, anxiety*. This set has some overlap with the work of [25]. The approach offers a rich picture of the frequency of emotions, although it does not capture the strength of the emotion. For example, happiness could be mild in response to a small success or intense if a substantial challenge has been overcome. This is a result of the primary research aim being to identify frequency of emotional states and transitions, rather than their intensity. [7] also note the limitations of the approach and the accuracy of participant self-reporting. Reflecting upon this, it would be interesting to attempt to determine the repeat validity of participants' responses, by offering them a number of situations multiple times and assessing if they report the same emotion. The studies conducted by Bosch and colleagues may yet inform the design of affective programming learning environments that can make decisions based on the learner's emotional state.

2.3 Emotion and Programming Tangible Devices

[15] explored self-reporting of emotion in a study that evaluated two different approaches for students to self-report their affective state, in an attempt to help students self-regulate their emotions. The study used a computer-based widget and a tangible device called the Subtle Stone [1]. The Subtle Stone device had buttons and the ability to illuminate itself in a range of colors to represent different emotions. The study concluded that there was a preference among students for the Subtle Stone rather than the computer-based widget. It had a number of advantages: it was more visible and increased the students' awareness of their emotional state. It also provided a visible representation that other students could see and respond to. The Subtle Stone can be regarded as a physical application. It is a single unambiguous artefact; the interface only does one thing but seems to do it well. Where a desktop-based solution is used, this becomes yet another thing competing for attention on the same communication

channel as other interactions. In [15], a set of six emotional states were used: *enjoyment, pride, frustration, boredom, nervousness*, and *confidence*. In the desktop application, the intensity of each state was also captured. In both of the studies, a restricted set of emotions was appropriate because participants were required to report emotional state multiple times.

Robot Dance. "How do you teach a Robot to Dance" was developed as part of an outreach activity to engage and enthuse possible future computing students. The workshop, reported in [19, 22], was also designed to explore how working with physical robots can support introductory programming learning. Middle-school students were given the challenge of programming pre-fabricated Arduino-based differential drive robots to choreograph a robot dance. There were two constraints: the dance must last for exactly 20 s and the robot must not fall off the stage (a 1 square meter mat or equivalent table top for added suspense). Dance was partly chosen as a context that may make computer programming more appealing to female participants. This strategy (often seen in narrative tools as powerful) places a task in a context that has cultural relevance or 'coolness'. After the students have been given a relatively short development time of 10–15 min, they upload their final program and gather round the dance floor to watch each of the performances. [5] note that performance has a more wide-reaching motivational effect than competition in this area.

An increased understanding of the programming concepts of sequence and syntax was demonstrated by these learners when measured using a pre- and post-test approach. One aspect more directly related to programming motivation was having a performance opportunity for their work. The dance element of the workshop offered an open problem for which prior knowledge was largely irrelevant: the task was creative, subjective and without endpoint. This had a pitch-levelling effect: a number of teachers commenting that students who previously had been disinterested or failed to show aptitude for programming now had engaged in the workshop successfully.

Robot Dance in the Community. A follow-on workshop used a less constrained structure without the confines of a classroom, as described in [22]. Learners were given a greater degree of independence: the learning experience was organized to be drop-in, situated in a public shopping center. Following a brief introduction to Arduino, learners were given a skeleton program to extend and then were "walked-through" the program required to make the robot move forward a short distance. The challenge presented then was to create 20 s of dance moves. Participant observation recorded four different groupings: single child, child pairs, child parent pairs and multiple children and parents. All learners demonstrated an observable emotional response to the performance they had programmed. Irrespective of the small audience, learners showed an observable pride in their creation.

Robot Dance in the Community observations confirmed that programming has an emotional dimension. The main study described next (Sect. 3) investigated this further: it explored how to get a more detailed picture of the learner's emotional response to programming tasks. The Whack a Mole study used an alternative physical artefact for learners to work with and sampled emotion as an indicator of engagement. Details of the study and method are given next.

3 Whack a Mole Study Description

Whack a Mole is a simple game that challenges reaction time via the ability to respond speedily to a series of stimuli. In the simplest version, a light comes on at random and stays on until a corresponding button is pressed. This results in a 'playful interaction' although it lacks some of the key elements that make a game. For example, it lacks user feedback or performance tracking with respect to the performance of other players.

In the Arduino version devised for this study, each of four LEDs has a corresponding button. When the light comes on, the player must press the corresponding button to progress through the game (Fig. 1). Its screen-based equivalent had a programmable interface with representations of clickable 'buttons' and 'LEDs' that lit up (Fig. 2).

Whack a Mole involved two stages. In stage one, learners were given taught material via three specific worked examples. In stage two, learners had to demonstrate their understanding of the first stage taught material by applying it to a novel problem. A pilot version of this study performed with volunteer students identified potential problems. Firstly, if the learning material was delivered by the facilitator, there was potential for different aspects of the taught material to be emphasized with different groups. Secondly, there was a risk that the tuition would become a dialogue between the facilitator and the learner, resulting in different learner experiences. Given those insights, a set of learning materials was developed as a series of video tutorials to ensure that the tuition given to the learners was consistent across multiple deliveries.

3.1 Video Tutorials

A set of four 2–3 min video tutorials was produced. The single difference between the screen-based and physical artefact videos was in the part of the video that demonstrated a completed task. In the screen-based videos, the screen-based Whack a Mole system was shown to demonstrate the taught code working. In the physical artefact videos, this view changed to the physical game with LEDs, buttons and the visible Arduino.

Video 1 contained a brief introduction to the Arduino programming environment, which uses a C-style textual language. It outlined the workflow of programming Arduino: code, compile, upload, and test. It also explained where the learner's code should be placed, as in each case a minimal code skeleton is given. The final part described how to use the clickable documentation which included all the relevant Arduino functions required for the tasks together with a brief description of what each function did.

Video 2 walked the learner through the task of making a light blink (Fig. 3). This traditional starting point for Arduino is considered the equivalent of a `hello world` program: since Arduino has no straightforward method of displaying text, flashing an LED is the simplest program that does something observable. For both physical artefact and screen-based groups, this task introduces digital output that requires the defining of a pin as an output. This involves making a conceptual mapping between the electrical connections on the Arduino (numbered headers) where the component is physically or virtually inserted and the code that will control this pin and its attached component.

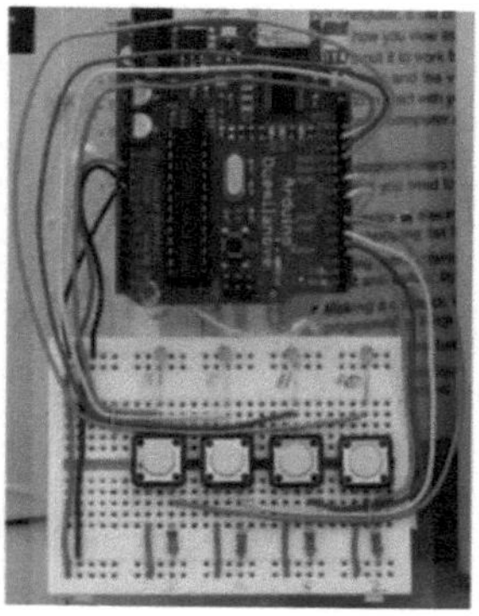

Fig. 1. Physical Whack a Mole interface [21].

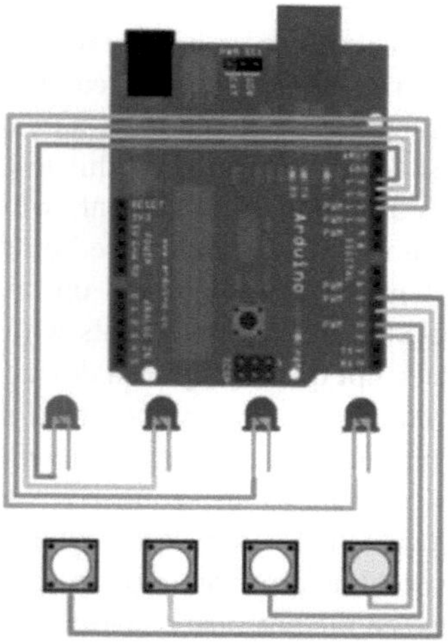

Fig. 2. Screen-based Whack a Mole interface [21].

The learner must then use the `digitalWrite()` function to change the state of this pin from high (5 volts) to low (ground). This exercise shows the learner how to use a variable as an abstraction device to store the pin number. For example, if an LED is connected to pin 13, declaring an integer variable called `led` and storing the value 13 allows the variable with a descriptive name to be used in place of 13. This clarifies the code: instead of modifying the state of a pin number directly, the variable name adds meaning to the functions with which it is used. An example is `digitalWrite(13, HIGH);` as contrasted with `digitalWrite(led,HIGH);`. To control the flow of execution, the `delay` function is used to introduce an interval between state changes. This example also gives learners the chance to become familiar with the structure of an Arduino sketch: the `setup()` function runs once to initialize the board and the `loop()` function iterates infinitely to carry out the interactions of the game.

```
int led = 13;
void setup(){
  pinMode(led,OUTPUT);
}
void loop(){
  digitalWrite(led, HIGH);
  delay(1000);
  digitalWrite(led, LOW);
  delay(1000);
}
```

Fig. 3. Code snippet for task 1 blink [21].

Video 2 also walked through the code for making a momentary light switch. This extended the previous example: the learner has to identify a pin to be used with the button as a digital input. The idea of using a variable to abstract the pin number is also used to reinforce the concept. The learner must use the `digitalRead()` function to retrieve pin state information. This requires understanding that a function may have a return type and at execution time, the function call can be resolved to return type. It is possible to treat the `digitalRead()` function as its return, which can be `HIGH` or `LOW`. When a variable is used for the pin number, this test the state of the component. Learners were then introduced to the `if` statement, which allows them to make a decision. In this case, they can make a decision based on the state of the button. If the button is pressed or `HIGH` then the LED is turned on or else the LED is turned off. Embedded in the `void loop()`, this action repeats whilst the Arduino has power.

Video 3 introduced the concept of an array as a device to simplify having multiple physical or virtual buttons and lights. Where before a single variable was used to abstract the button or LED pin, now an array can conveniently handle a collection of buttons or pins. Four physical buttons in sequence connect to consecutive digital general-purpose input/output pins that can become collected as an array of integers in the code. This required the use of an array notation to specify and initialize two arrays and form the association between the physical or virtual component, the IO pin and the code. The learners also had to use a fixed loop to iterate through the array, which is a typical strategy for combining arrays that are iterated together. This example highlights how the array index can link two concepts, in this case the buttons and the LEDs. When button `i` is pressed, LED `i` will be illuminated. This is a key concept for the second stage of the study, which required learners to demonstrate their understanding of the programming concepts taught via the video tutorial supported examples.

3.2 Whack a Mole Challenge

The challenge was for learners to devise an algorithm for a Whack a Mole game that (i) demonstrated understanding of the concepts that had been taught and (ii) used some additional features found in the documentation, such as the random function. Possible extensions were hinted at but not prescribed or described in detail. The code for the game (Fig. 4) consists of turning on a random light, waiting until the corresponding button is pressed and then picking another random light. Learners had to demonstrate the taught skills in context and integrate them into an application.

```
int[] button = {2,3,4,5};
int[] led = {13,12,11,10};
int turnOn=0;

void setup(){
  ...
  turnOn = random(4);
  digitalWrite(led[turnOn],HIGH);
}

void loop(){
  if(digitalRead(button[turnOn] ==
  HIGH){
    digitalWrite(led[turnOn],LOW);
    turnOn = random(4);
    digitalWrite(led[turnOn],HIGH);
  }
}
```

Fig. 4. Example code for Whack a Mole game [21].

Further examples of code extracts as provided in the various videos are provided in [21]. Ethical approval for the study design, which is described next, was given by the School's ethics committee.

4 Study Design

The Whack a Mole study ran as part of an undergraduate module in Physical Computing. This module is taught to Level 1 (first year) applied computing, computing science, product design and interaction design learners in the University of Dundee. The class was already organized into small practical groups of three or four. To optimize the staff to learner ratio, the class was arranged into two separate sittings. The two lab groups alternated between taught sessions and independent sessions. In one week, group A would have a taught lab session while group B would engage in an independent lab assignment. The following week, the sittings were reversed. Learners were assigned randomly to either group A or group B at the start of semester and these groupings were used in the delivery of the Whack a Mole study. In the first week of the study, Group A received the physical Whack a Mole intervention. This group had 22 participants of which 14 were male and 8 were female. The following week, the groups switched around, with Group B receiving the taught lab session. This group had 16 participants, 15 of whom were male. Two methods were designed to capture appropriate data. Firstly, a paper-based questionnaire was designed to test knowledge and understanding of arrays. Secondly, a method was devised and piloted to capture a learner's emotional response to programming. Both methods are described next.

4.1 Knowledge and Understanding

A paper-based questionnaire was designed to measure changes in knowledge and understanding of arrays. The first part contained four questions to test the learner's general level of knowledge of arrays, independently of any context or specific situation. The second part was designed to explore the learner's level of understanding of arrays, for instance asking the learner to "*describe in your own words (and pictures) what an array is in the context of computer programming*". Constructing a description of a concept and externalizing it in words and images requires a good understanding of the concept. It deliberately lacks a pre-defined framework into which learners could slot their knowledge. There also is no opportunity for learners to guess the answer. The third and final part of the questionnaire requires the learners to respond to three questions associated with given code snippets that demonstrate array use within a small program.

Before the lab teaching began, participants were given the questionnaire to complete independently under exam conditions. After completing the study, participants were asked to complete the post-test questionnaire. Participants were also given the emotions questionnaire (described next) and advised how to complete it.

4.2 Emotional Response

The method selected to measure emotion had to satisfy three criteria. Firstly, it had to enable learners to reflect on the emotions they experience as a result of learning to program. Whilst a record of a particular emotion is interesting, it is even more valuable to have the learner's explanation of the context of this emotion. Secondly, it had to be practical to deploy as part of a regular laboratory class activity that had a high volume of concurrent participants. Approaches such as that devised by [7] where participants review high volumes of still images to self-report emotion would not have been practicable. Finally, as this was an early stage in the exploration of emotional response to programming, it was considered premature to seek high volume time-series data such as would derive from automated facial recognition software. However, an interesting approach for future research would involve using that technology coupled with a reflective learner interview that discussed the emotions that had been captured.

The decision was made to design a post-test questionnaire that learners could fill out as a reflective process. The studies discussed earlier involve multiple sampling, identifying the points at which an emotion occurred and any transitional states. A high frequency of samples requires a small set of possible participant responses and ideally the reconciliation of similar emotions, such as *calm* and *content*. The approach taken in Whack a Mole is the opposite. As the response from the participant is sought once at the end of the study, a broader range of emotions can be included. The instrument is not designed to measure when the emotion occurred in relation to other emotions. Instead, it is designed to capture *why* a state of emotion occurred. With more time available and without repeat sampling fatigue, participants are able to respond to a larger range of emotions and offer contextual information about what they were doing and why the emotion occurred. Where similar emotions are present, this provides several opportunities for a subtly different trigger to elicit feedback from learners. For example, amusement, elation and pleasure all fall under the heading of *positive lively* but may be attributed to different activities. For these reasons, a new method to obtain emotion data was designed that was minimally disruptive for the learners. It was based on an ontology of emotional states: the Reflective Emotion Inventory.

The Reflective Emotion Inventory (REI) has been designed to capture emotional response in individuals. It is a reflective tool, designed to be delivered at the end of a session. It encourages learners to think back over their experience and indicate if they felt any of a range of emotions. The list of emotions used for the REI was derived from the HUMAINE project [28] which proposed a core of 48 different emotions arranged into 10 sub-categories (Table 1).

Table 1. HUMAINE emotion categories [28].

Negative	Positive
Negative and forceful: anger/annoyance/contempt/disgust/irritation	*Positive and lively:* amusement/delight/elation/excitement/ happiness/joy/pleasure
Negative and not in control: anxiety/embarrassment/fear/helplessness/power lessness/worry	*Caring:* Affection/empathy/friendliness/love
Negative thoughts: doubt/envy/frustration/guilt/shame	*Positive thoughts:* courage/hope/pride/satisfaction/trust
Negative and passive: boredom/despair/disappointment/hurt/sadness	*Quiet positive:* calm/content/relaxed/relieved/serene
Agitation: shock/stress/tension	*Reactive:* interested/politeness/surprise

The REI questionnaire captures three things (Table 2). (a) The learners are first invited to scan through the list of emotions and indicate if they have experienced any of them. (b) Learners can indicate the degree of arousal or intensity for each of the experienced emotions on a four-point unipolar Likert scale [11]. A unipolar Likert scale was selected for two reasons. Firstly, given that the REI contains many emotions, there was a preference for a unipolar scale because it is easier for users to respond to than a bipolar scale that places opposites at either end of the scale. Secondly, the REI is intended to be a reflective tool that captures emotions experienced over a period. It is therefore quite possible that opposing emotions will be experienced at different times throughout the event. (c) Learners can offer some contextual information in a free-text response space. The purpose of this is to describe why they experienced the given emotion. An example response might be: Annoyance, 3, "Getting the wires in the correct place".

Table 2. Components of reflective emotion inventory.

(a)	(b)	(c)
Which emotion has been experienced	Degree of intensity for each: 4-point Likert scale	Why and when was this emotion experienced

The two parts to the study thus captured change in knowledge and any emotional response to programming, in order to identify any difference between the two groups.

5 Results

5.1 Knowledge and Understanding

Table 3 presents descriptive statistics for test performance. The screen group scored a mean pre-test score of 76% and a mean post-test score of 79%. The physical artefact group scored a mean pre-test score of 57% and a mean post-test score of 61%.

Table 3. Screen-based and physical artefact group scores (%).

	Pre-test-Mean	SD	Post-test-Mean	SD	Sig. (2-tailed)
Screen	75.63	14.59	78.75	10.25	>0.05
Physical	57.27	20.74	60.90	19.50	>0.05

Each group had three distinct categories of learners. Some learners improved their performance, some showed no change and some performed worse in the post-test. The physical artefact group performed slightly better than the screen-based group across all aspects, with a greater percentage of the group improving and fewer reducing their pre- to post-test performance. No difference was statistically significant.

5.2 Emotional Response

Emotional response data was collected by the Reflective Emotion Inventory (REI) described in the study design. The results are presented at the level of 10 sub-categories, with the first five being negative and the latter five positive. The intensity scale for each emotion ranged from 0 to 3, where 0 indicated no emotion and 3 indicated the emotion occurred intensely. There is also a space for contextual response about when or why the emotion was experienced. Figure 5 gives the mean response from each sub-category of emotion for both groups.

Screen-Based Group. This group were less ready to offer free text comments to contextualize emotions than the physical artefact group. They expressed *negative forceful* emotions as the result of problems with the code: "code errors" or "sorting some issues with the program". Several participants intimated feeling envy when other

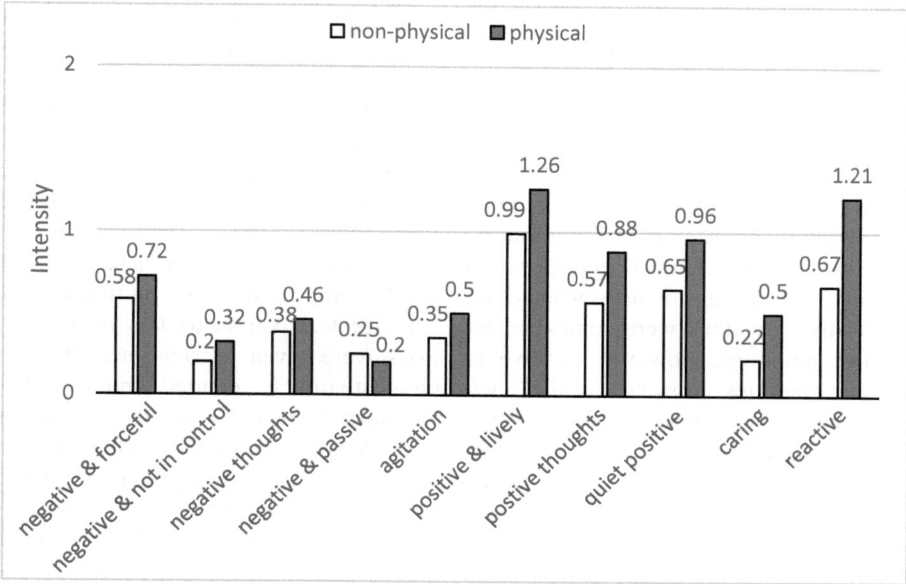

Fig. 5. Strength of emotional responses [21].

groups had their program working before they did. Several also expressed a feeling of friendliness as a result of working in a group. One group noted a feeling of worry "if they could complete the task on time" whereas other groups indicated a sense of boredom at being finished early. Positive emotions were largely because of task completion and "getting it working". This was recorded by many participants as feelings of amusement, joy and happiness. The contextualizing of positive emotions was as frequent as that of negative emotions. However, the reasons cited for a positive emotion were far less diverse.

Physical Artefact Group. This group offered comments for each sub-category of emotion. Negative emotions were attributed to a range of features of creating the game; one of the most frequently cited reasons was wiring. Responses include "when the wires fall out", which is a common problem if jumper wires are not cut long enough or well organized, and "getting the wires in the right places" (the pitch of the breadboards used is one hole every millimeter, which can be problematic). Specific components were mentioned, such as: "getting the LED the right way" and "wiring up resistors". LEDs have a polarity and require both the signal and ground voltage wires to be in the correct position. Resistors, on the other hand, do not have polarity but are very small, and placing them into breadboards can be problematic.

These type of difficulties were most common in the *negative forceful* category, with learners frequently associating these difficulties with feeling anger and annoyance. This category was the most strongly reported negative emotion in the physical artefact group. To a lesser extent, these difficulties also appeared under the *not in control* category, such as rage. Several participants cited negative thoughts related to whether their build would work or not. Also in the negative thoughts category, frustration was related to wiring-up of the build. Interestingly, frustration was also cited in response to poorly specified compiler errors. It is fair to say that the Arduino IDE provides much more novice-friendly compiler errors than some industry standard IDEs. Nonetheless, there are inevitably situations where there is disconnect between the error, the specific line of code and the description offered in the IDE. One or two of the learners expressed passive emotions, such as boredom, at being finished early. Being stressed was also noted by several individuals in response to the system as a whole (wires and code) not working, or being unsure as to whether they would complete the build on time or not.

Positive emotions were contextualized with free text comments less richly than negative emotions. However, positive emotions were given greater intensity than negative emotions. *Positive and lively* was the most strongly reported emotional category, particularly because of completing the build: "when it worked", and when engaging with their product: "playing the game". People also noted a feeling of happiness at getting their task completed. The second most strongly reported emotional category was *reactive*. This was noted as interest in "learning new things". One participant noted interest in the logic they had arrived at in developing the Whack a Mole algorithm.

Screen-Based Compared to Physical Artefact Group. When considering the screen-based group's emotional responses grouped together, there was a noticeable difference between the positive and negative emotions reported: positive emotions were experienced by all participants to a greater extent than negative emotions. However in the physical artefact group there was a difference in intensity of positive and negative emotional categories. With the exception of *caring,* all the positive emotions were more intensely experienced than the negative ones. This matched the rich contextual data offered by the physical artefact group. Where learners worked with the physical artefact, they had a strongly positive experience. Two of positive emotions reported by the physical artefact group are notably greater than that of the screen-based group: *positive & lively* and *reactive*. Reinforcing this, an observable difference was noted in the degree of engagement of different groups with the finished artefact. Several participants in the physical artefact group were seen taking pictures and videos to share on social media, indicating a degree of pride and a desire to share their work that was not observed in the screen-based group.

6 Discussion

6.1 Knowledge and Understanding

In both groups, around two-thirds of learners showed no change in knowledge or understanding about arrays and associated strategies. The most likely explanation for this is the fact that when both the screen-based and the physical artefact groups are ordered for performance, the top two-thirds of both groups had very high pre-test scores, leaving little room for improvement. It is therefore likely that this study took place too late in the teaching period and offered a substantially reduced opportunity for the interventions to create a change in knowledge and understanding. The groupings for this study also proved problematic. The pre-test data for the screen-based group showed a tight normal distribution centered on a very high mean. The physical artefact group had a slightly skewed distribution in pre- and post-tests, with several particularly weak scores. The two randomly allocated groups thus had different abilities or levels of experience. This may have reduced the sensitivity of the test to detect improvements between groups.

Alternatively, the lack of measured improvement in performance in the Whack a Mole study may also have related to the method of content delivery: video tutorials were used in preference to direct delivery by a tutor. This was in response to findings from previous studies (e.g. [19]) which contrasted the benefits and pitfalls of tightly delivered content versus a much looser learner-led approach. The intention was that the video tutorials would enable learners to control the pace of content delivery. While this was effective up to a point, it was susceptible to the same problem as giving someone a list of directions rather than a map: if they fail to act upon one of the directions, they can become lost. A list of directions also offers no contextual information for exploring different routes or other points of interest along the way. One of the key advantages of facilitating a session directly is the ability to identify and respond to spontaneous learning opportunities. The instructional videos served as narrow routes for learners to take. In addition, using video content to support delivery left the tutor far more removed from the process than when tight cycles of delivery and consolidation were used.

6.2 Emotional Response

Firstly, a low response was noted for the free text component of the REI. This is hardly surprising, given the additional effort required by learners to verbalize the contexts in which they felt a given emotion. Secondly, considering the two different groups, the REI did establish different responses from the two groups.

The screen-based group noted envy and friendliness. These emotions represent a competitive situation well, particularly if a tight group has formed which was keen to demonstrate its success relative to the other groups they are working with. The REI also established different emotions about completing the test on time. Differing rates of task completion is evidence that the screen-based group, despite having a high knowledge and understanding pre-test score, still contained a range of abilities.

The physical artefact group experienced almost all of the positive emotions with greater intensity than the negative ones. Most often, the anecdotal references to programming and emotion were focused on negative feelings. The free-text contextualization presented here shows that participants frequently experienced causes of irritation that are often reported in the literature, including obscure compiler and syntax errors. The physical elements mimic many areas of programming difficulty. Breadboarding with electrical components is an inherently finicky task requiring good eyesight and a steady hand. It also has many of the same problematic features as programming, such as error-prone nature, requiring high degree of detail, tracing of routes through a connected network and a one-to-many mapping from problem to solution. In programming, compiler error messages are offered to assist the learner.

Unfortunately, no such support exists when wiring breadboards. As a result, errors in electrical circuits are often very difficult to identify. It seems counter-intuitive therefore that combining programming and electrical prototyping activities could improve the emotional response to the programming experience. The dominance of positive emotions being reported suggests that this did happen in the Whack a Mole study. This suggests that creating a functioning physical game presented a challenge: completing the task generated an emotional response that outweighed the 'pain' endured in working through the task.

One possibility is that this resulted from the different bandwidth of interaction offered by the two systems. In the screen-based group, learners could only interact with a single device via its three components, namely the PC with its mouse, keyboard and screen. Using the physical system, learners interacted with **two** devices, namely the PC via its three components ***and*** with the Arduino via its buttons and LEDs. This may have contributed to the richer more positive emotional response from learners in the physical artefact group. Furthermore, a learner with a low ratio of negative emotions to positive emotions may signify someone who will do well in programming. The ability to take greater pleasure from the competed task than displeasure experienced by the challenges on the road to success may be an important attribute that resonates with Perkin's findings of movers and stoppers [26].

6.3 Whack a Mole Summary

The Whack a Mole study aimed to explore how learning with a physical device differed from learning with a screen-based equivalent. The original research question posed was: *how does working with a physical artefact as opposed to a screen-based artefact affect learning of computer programming*? There was no noticeable difference in learning effect measured between the two groups, indicating that the physical interface neither measurably contributed to nor hindered learning. The study also indicated that video-based teaching materials do not offer the opportunity for the interaction and subtle response that a tutor can provide in probing areas of difficulty for the learner. However, there was a difference in emotional response to the learning experiences. Both groups described a range of negative emotions with similar levels of strength and for similar reasons. Both groups also noted a similar range of positive emotions. However, the physical artefact group noted a greater intensity of positive emotions associated with the learning experience.

One of the main tenets of constructivism is that learners should engage in projects that are relevant to them and the world around them [35]. If this session were to be adapted to enable a greater degree of flexibility, for example allowing learners to design their own interface for the Whack a Mole game, there would be no additional programming overhead to create a physical game. All that would be required would be longer wires for the buttons and LEDs that could be embedded in any number of craft materials. For the same to be done with a screen-based solution, additional skills would need to be taught, adding to the complexity of the session.

Whack a Mole Limitations. One limitation of the study resulted from the composition of the screen-based and the physical artefact groups: different sizes, different academic abilities and with a non-ideal gender balance. A solution to the problem would be to administer the pre-test and then create groups based on the scores. In this case, that would have disrupted the established groups within the class. The sample size was small and the assessment instrument was new, neither of which allowed repetition and hence more formal statistical analysis of the responses.

One of the challenges with a pre/post-test methodology is pitching the test difficulty correctly to ensure maximum sensitivity to the phenomena being observed, which in this case related to knowledge and understanding of arrays. The pre-test knowledge results suggest that in many cases an understanding of arrays had developed prior to the study. As a result, for many of the learners the measure had limited sensitivity. Despite these difficulties, the Whack a Mole study offers some valuable insight into the differences observed in novice programmers working with screen-based and physical media.

Re-considering the literature, it is worth noting that the sample task learners engaged in for the study by [7] was a traditional CS1-style mathematics-based problem. Although this problem type is valid, it represents what [30] argue is a knowledge-driven approach to programming education. One can argue for an approach to programming education that is more stimulating and framed within a context of value to the learner. The results of this study suggest that the powerful affordances of physical computing, i.e. the ability to take intangible things and make them physical (such as when using an LED to indicate state) can lead to very positive emotions without jeopardizing learning. Despite its limitations, therefore, the study prompted further investigation of the effects of motivation upon learning to program. The follow-up study is described next.

7 Digital Makers Study Description

This follow-up field study included additional learner ownership, personalization and purpose. In the Robot Dance and Whack a Mole studies, learners had been constrained to solve a puzzle devised by the educator. In Digital Makers, design decisions were intended to make the product less constrained for the learners. This made it possible for learners to apply their newly acquired programming skills to solve a problem of their own. The Digital Makers study summarized here is reported fully in [20]. There were two stages to the study, which engaged 48 young learners (83% male) from across the country. In the morning, the learners had several iterations of short demonstrations of Arduino programming followed by enactment by learners to complete the following task: make an LED blink, using a potentiometer to control the blink rate and using a button to make the LED blink when pressed. Then, learners were guided through an idea-generation session.

7.1 Idea Generation

Equipped with post-its and marker pens, learners were asked to identify three things that make them excited and note them down concisely on the post-it wall. Learners were then encouraged to bring their post-its to the front and stick them on a predetermined part of the wall that was visible to the group throughout the day: the 'wall of situations'. The ideas gathered together on the wall served as an information radiator [31] for use later in the day. This process was repeated for things that make them cross and for things that make them stressed. The wall of situations served to identify physical app ideas to focus around later that day. Bringing all the ideas together allowed learners to react to each other's experiences and stimulated memories and new ideas.

The learners were finally guided through some additional Arduino output devices: servo, speaker and red green blue (RGB) LED. The final example the learners constructed was a red, green and blue color mixer. With a single RGB LED and three potentiometers, a physical color mixer was constructed. In a natural progression, the learners were shown how to group this now quite complex program into a single user-defined function and how to alter this so that the color of LED was specified by three parameters passed to the function. Extending this further and utilizing the random function and bringing in some sound with loudspeakers, playing beeps of a program-specified tone, the learners created a light and sound show.

7.2 App Generation

In the second stage, learners were given the chance to self-select groupings and build a physical app utilizing the morning's teaching. Groups revisited the post-it wall of situations that excite, irritate and stress them to pick several post-its they could relate to and expand upon them. Groups were given three hours to build a physical app based on one of the ideas from the selected post-its, with support available as required. The study ended with groups sharing their idea and resultant physical app with all other groups. Participants were asked then to complete the emotional response questionnaire.

7.3 Reported Emotions

The most striking result was that positive emotions were reported as being far more intensely experienced than negative emotions (Fig. 6). It is clear that the physical apps session evoked a rich emotional response from the participants. The contrast between the extent to which negative and positive emotions were experienced is strong. Negative emotions experienced do tie into many of the problems reported in the literature about novice programming. Interestingly, many of the error-prone features of coding do match with those of physical prototyping, with breadboarding being particularly error-prone. Nonetheless, the minor irritations of an error-prone medium were outweighed by the strength of the positive emotions that learners reported. Many positive emotions stem from a sense of overcoming challenges to produce something that works and it is important to note that each participant succeeded in producing something that he or she was able to present to the group. The strength with which learners expressed a sense of pride was further evidence of cultural impact: participants were very proud of their work.

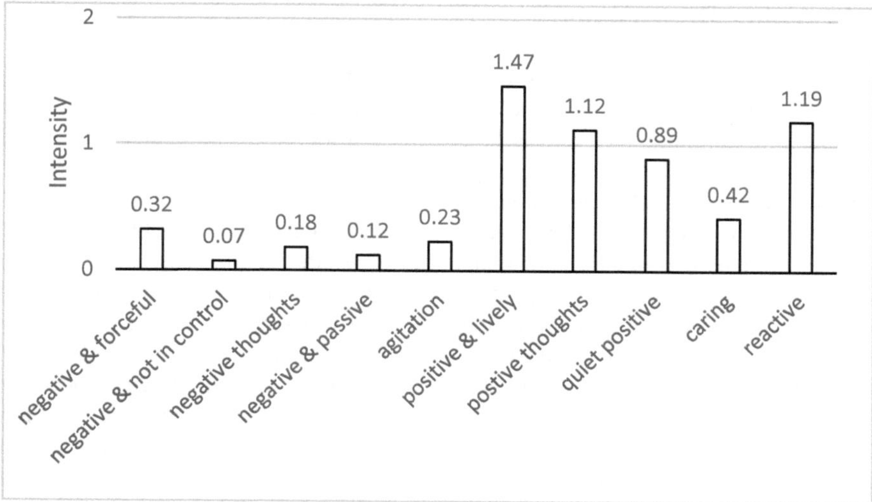

Fig. 6. Strength of emotional responses.

7.4 Digital Makers Summary

In summary, the Digital Makers study used ownership, personalization and purpose to create a highly engaging learning experience that resulted in strong positive emotional responses from learners. The ideas for physical apps reflected the culture the learners belong to: examples include notifications relating Facebook or personalizing their product by creating toys for younger siblings (police car with lights and sound). The complexity of the builds varied from relatively simple extensions of the demonstrations to complex compositions with multiple sensors and actuators. The only learners not to engage fully with the rich context were learners who had come to the session with an existing knowledge of Arduino and who had premeditated plans for what they wanted to explore. For these learners, the rich context was a distraction to their intentions.

The next section describes how insights generated from Whack a Mole and Digital Makers in particular were synthesized as a set of 'Learning Dimensions'. The Learning Dimensions follow the style that [16] proposed in their 'Cognitive Dimensions of Notations' framework, in which they outline a common vocabulary and reference point for the design and discussion of notations. The Learning Dimensions are a first attempt at capturing and describing key areas for design and decisions relating to learning experiences. They are not intended to be used formulaically, but rather to serve as a source of inspiration and information for educators who are designing or critically evaluating a learning experience.

8 Learning Dimensions

The Learning Dimensions (LDs) bring together findings from the literature and new empirical work that can guide the creation of engaging learning experiences for computer programming. The aim is to provide a resource for computer science educators that can be used either in the design of new learning experiences or as a reflective toolkit for the review and improvement of existing learning experiences. The Cognitive Dimensions framework by [16] has served as a very successful nucleus for a great deal of research relating to notations of many forms including code, sketching, algorithm visualization and musical staff notation. Cognitive Dimensions provided a much-needed common vocabulary that enabled researches to share and discuss insights. It is hoped that the LDs fulfil a similar role for educators in the design and evaluation of learning experiences. As a resource, the LDs are intended to be lightweight, accessible and easy to use. The intention of the LDs is not to present a new pedagogy or theory that tackles all or even most of the aspects of the creation of computer science learning experiences. Instead, the LDs are a set of insights and knowledge from which educators can select to add value and to make informed decisions about their practice. The eight LDs address three high-level aspects: (a) **design and delivery** of learning task, (b) **rhythm or tempo** of the learning experience and (c) **practicalities**. The first of these high-level aspects is described here (the remaining aspects and further detail of each learning dimension is reported in [22]). **Design and Delivery** describes learning dimensions that relate to the design of activities or tasks that make up a learning experience. It consists of four dimensions: Closed versus Open, Cultural Relevance, Recognition and Space to Play. *Closed versus Open* describes the relative merits of designing learning tasks with or without a lot of detail and structure. *Cultural relevance* describes the affordances presented by locating learning tasks within the learner's culture. *Recognition* describes opportunities that arise from enabling learners to share their work. *Space to Play* describes the impact of designing learning tasks that encourage iterative experimentation, for example with peers, and self-directed discovery of knowledge and skills.

8.1 Closed versus Open

LEGO Mindstorms [18] combined micro-controllers and programming with a very adaptable construction kit. The current generation of LEGO Mindstorms has a huge community to support its use. There are globally organized events such as RoboCup Junior (RCJ), in which teams of schoolchildren compete in three subject areas using robots almost exclusively developed using LEGO Mindstorms.

[27] presented empirical evidence for 'back door learning' taking place whilst young children compete in an RCJ event. Interviews with teams were followed up by a detailed case study with one team. Two topics that arose from their inductive analysis were motivation and evidence of learning. One frequently reported reason for being motivated was the 'openness' of the task. Although each event culminated in a competition that identified the best robots, there was no final definitive end point:

> *"you can always improve it and you never have it perfect" Participant* [27],

The *Closed versus Open* Learning Dimension encapsulates the extent to which these activities have a well-defined structure, route and end point. A good example of a closed problem is programming a robot to follow a line. The task defines the answer: there is little scope for the learner to take ownership. Towards the open end of the dimension would be a free choice activity where learners are able to demonstrate competency in a given skill through the creation of a piece of work that is not constrained by the educator, such as creating a robot dance.

8.2 Cultural Relevance

[10] robustly locate the importance of personalization and choice for increasing intrinsic motivation in learners. Their study engaged 72 fifth grade learners (10 to 11 year olds) who were randomly assigned to one of five groups, in a 2×2 factorial design with one control, with the first factor being personalization and the other factor being choice. They found that there was a powerful learning benefit observed in the personalized choice condition. Learners were observed to have not only increased motivation but also displayed a deeper engagement in the task.

Often part of a learning experience involves creating a product of some kind, such as code or a sketch. The *Cultural Relevance* dimension considers where this product sits within the learner's culture. It prompts consideration of whether or not the tasks they are asked to perform are authentic and relevant to their daily life experience. Ownership, personalization and purpose are key aspects of creating a learning experience that will have high cultural relevance for the learner. If the learning experience is divorced from the world the learner inhabits, the cultural relevance will be low.

8.3 Recognition

Many educational programming tools enable learners to contribute to vibrant online communities of learners [8]. Learners can be inspired and informed by the work of others and in equal measure provide the inspiration and support for those who follow them. There are significant motivational affordances to be found in sharing work and observing it being valued by a community of other learners. [27] noted a similar effect: a number of participants identified placing the task in a social context as a factor contributing to motivation. The ability to share ideas and the pride associated with demonstrating expertise was also reported to be important.

> *"It's interesting meeting new people and showing how good you can be"* [27].

It is typical for a learning experience to result in the generation of a product. It may be a program, a sketch or a concept. The *Recognition* dimension considers the potential for the learner to share the product of their learning. As early as nursery school, learners seek recognition from their teachers, peers and parents. A good example of this is pleasure gained from the displaying of work on the walls of the learning environment for all to see. In the Learning Dimensions context, a model of *recognition* has three parts: (a) mode of the interaction, (b) audience size, and (c) response or result. Each of these will have an effect on the learner's engagement and motivation.

8.4 Space to Play

The Contributing Student Pedagogy (CSP) [17] enabled learners to have a prominent role in their learning experiences. In CSP, learners co-create knowledge and understanding. This pedagogy moves beyond variations of peer-assisted learning, e.g. [34], and empowers learners to participate actively in all aspects of the learning. In this situation, the educator takes the role of a guide rather than that of a gatekeeper or provider of information. One advantage argued by its proponents is that it mirrors informal workplace learning, in which it is common for co-workers to support each other.

The *Space to Play* dimension seeks to break down the traditional view of a teacher-learner relationship. It encapsulates the extent to which a learning experience offers and encourages learners to explore independently, experiment and iterate over aspects of the learning experience. This idea is rooted in constructivist learning theory [24]: learning takes place best when learners engage in project work that results in an artefact that is relevant to the learners, as described in the *Cultural Relevance* learning dimension. *Space to Play*, however, addresses the fact that space and independence may be intimidating for certain learners. Furthermore, it acknowledges the tension between the learner as an individual and a need to cover a particular amount of content with a group of learners. Where space can be intimidating, direction, constraint and facilitation can be catalysts to creativity and learning.

9 Conclusions

One overarching theme that emerges from the literature is that learning is most fruitful in credible engaging learning experiences that place the learner at the center. Desirable features for education programming tools and learning experiences are increasingly being recognized as those relating to the motivation of the learner, such as personal, social and contextual elements, rather than purely technical elements. Examples include the capacity to tap into and contribute to a community of like-minded learners, and the ability rapidly to make a thing that the learner values. This section presents an overview of the field studies conducted by the authors to uncover and describe features that can stimulate engaging learning experiences in programming.

9.1 Engaging Learning Experiences Re-visited

Robot Dance explored supporting introductory programming learning with programmable robots. A small learning effect was measured as a result of the workshop. Learning in Robot dance was supported by the delivery of several small demonstrations followed by space for learners to experiment with the new skill. This ensured that new skills were always applied to avoid becoming inert [26]. Working towards a performance at the end of the session was a motivator for many of the learners: it showed the importance of recognition.

Robot Dance in the Community observed learners working with no structure imposed on how they arranged themselves. Learners were observed self-organizing into a number of differently groupings with evident emotional engagement in the task of programming the robot. The learners appeared to value the artefact they were working on and be highly motivated by taking control of this small object.

Whack a Mole explored the importance of working with a physical product as opposed to a screen-based simulation. Two similar groups of learners were exposed to identical learning tasks; one group produced a physical computing game while the other group programmed a screen-based equivalent. There was a significantly different emotional response, with physical artefact groups being more engaged with the task and experiencing a greater degree of positive affect.

Finally, Digital Makers explored a more sustained learning experience that afforded learners greater control over the product of their learning and the groups they worked in. There was empirical evidence that the majority of learners engaged deeply in the rich context in which the learning was situated. The emotional profile reported by the learners was similar to that of Whack a Mole. There was a more pronounced demonstration of positive emotions resulting from the physical computing programming.

9.2 Learning Dimensions

Learning Dimensions are distilled insights from existing literature and these four studies. The motivation was to support educators but also present a useful framework for researchers who seek to investigate the learning of programming. A subset of the Learning Dimensions is presented here as version one of an open set of key decision areas: *Closed versus Open, Cultural Relevance, Recognition, and Space to Play.* Future work is needed to provide additional research-driven detail to each of the Learning Dimensions and to identify additional Learning Dimensions.

The difficulties of learning to program have been studied for nearly 50 years and yet many challenges still remain. The essence of programming remains unchanged: it requires that the solution to a problem is described in sufficient detail, without ambiguity, such that a machine can follow the instructions. What has moved forward considerably is the set of tools used to support learning to program: educational tools have matured considerably as a result of the years of research and from the increased capacities of modern computers. It is now recognized that desirable features for education programming tools and learning experiences increasingly relate to the motivation of the learner, such as personal, social and contextual elements, rather than purely technical issues.

The work described here demonstrates that a physical interface can provide a more positive experience than a screen-based equivalent. Designers of learning experiences may wish to include consideration of this insight, and the others as summarized via the Learning Dimensions, when planning the introduction of new programming concepts or creating programming laboratory exercises and assessments. Creating an engaging learning experience is not a mechanical process that can be governed by a set of rules to be followed dutifully to guarantee consistent results. It requires reflection and consideration not just of what is to be learned but also of who is learning and how they can best be motivated to succeed.

References

1. Alsmeyer, M., Luckin, R., Good, J.: Developing a novel interface for capturing self reports of affect. In: CHI 2008 Extended Abstracts on Human Factors in Computing Systems, pp. 2883–2888. ACM (2008)
2. Amabile, T.M., Hill, K.G., Hennessey, B.A., Tighe, E.M.: The work preference inventory: assessing intrinsic and extrinsic motivational orientations. J. Pers. Soc. Psychol. **66**(5), 950–967 (1994)
3. Anderson, R., Manoogian, S.T., Reznick, J.S.: The undermining and enhancing of intrinsic motivation in preschool children. J. Pers. Soc. Psychol. **34**(5), 915–922 (1976)
4. Bahrick, H.P., Fitts, P.M., Rankin, R.E.: Effect of incentives upon reactions to peripheral stimuli. J. Exp. Psychol. **44**(6), 400–406 (1952)
5. Blank, D.S., Kumar, D.: Assessing the impact of using robots in education, or: how we learned to stop worrying and love the chaos. In: AAAI Spring Symposium: Educational Robotics and Beyond (2010)
6. Bosch, N., D'Mello, S.: The affective experience of novice computer programmers. Int. J. Artif. Intell. Educ. **27**(1), 181–206 (2015)
7. Bosch, N., D'Mello, S., Mills, C.: What emotions do novices experience during their first computer programming learning session? In: Lane, H.C., Yacef, K., Mostow, J., Pavlik, P. (eds.) AIED 2013. LNCS (LNAI), vol. 7926, pp. 11–20. Springer, Heidelberg (2013). https://doi.org/10.1007/978-3-642-39112-5_2
8. Brennan, K., Monroy-Hernández, A., Resnick, M.: Making projects, making friends: online community as catalyst for interactive media creation. New Dir. Youth Dev. **128**, 75–83 (2010)
9. Condry, J.: Enemies of exploration: self-initiated versus other-initiated learning. J. Pers. Soc. Psychol. **35**(7), 459–477 (1977)
10. Cordova, D.I., Lepper, M.R.: Intrinsic motivation and the process of learning: beneficial effects of contextualization, personalization, and choice. J. Educ. Psychol. **88**(4), 715–730 (1996)
11. Cummins, R.A., Gullone, E.: Why we should not use 5-point Likert scales: the case for subjective quality of life measurement. In: Proceedings, Second International Conference on Quality of Life in Cities, pp. 74–93 (2000)
12. Deci, E.L., Koestner, R., Ryan, R.M.: A meta-analytic review of experiments examining the effects of extrinsic rewards on intrinsic motivation. Psychol. Bull. **125**(6), 627–668 (1999)
13. D'Mello, S.: A selective meta-analysis on the relative incidence of discrete affective states during learning with technology. J. Educ. Psychol. **105**(4), 1082 (2013)
14. Eisenberger, R., Pierce, W.D., Cameron, J.: Effects of reward on intrinsic motivation – negative, neutral, and positive: Comment on Deci, Koestner, and Ryan. Psychol. Bull. **125** (6), 677–691 (1999)
15. Good, J., Rimmer, J., Harris, E., Balaam, M.: Self-reporting emotional experiences in computing lab sessions: an emotional regulation perspective. In: Proceedings of the 23rd Psychology of Programming Interest Group PPIG 2011 (2011)
16. Green, T.R.G., Petre, M.: Usability analysis of visual programming environments: a 'cognitive dimensions' framework. J. Vis. Lang. Comput. **7**(2), 131–174 (1996)
17. Hamer, J., Cutts, Q., Jackova, J., Luxton-Reilly, A., McCartney, R., Purchase, H., Riedesel, C., Saeli, M., Sanders, K., Sheard, J.: Contributing student pedagogy. ACM SIGCSE Bull. **40**(4), 194–212 (2008)
18. LEGO: LEGO mindstorms (2010). http://mindstorms.lego.com/en-us/default.aspx

19. Martin, C., Hughes, J.: Robot dance: edutainment or engaging learning. In: Proceedings of the 23rd Psychology of Programming Interest Group PPIG 2011 (2011)
20. Martin, C., Hughes, J.: Digital makers: ownership, personalisation and purpose. In: Proceedings of the 28th Psychology of Programming Interest Group PPIG 2017 (2017)
21. Martin, C., Hughes, J., Richards, J.: Learning experiences in programming: the motivating effect of a physical interface. In: Proceedings of the 9th International Conference on Computer Supported Education, pp. 162–172. SCITEPRESS (2017)
22. Martin, C., Hughes, J., Richards, J.: Learning dimensions: lessons from field studies. In: Proceedings of the 2017 ACM Conference on Innovation and Technology in Computer Science Education - ITiCSE 2017, pp. 299–304. ACM (2017)
23. Meyer, D.K., Turner, J.C.: Discovering emotion in classroom motivation research. Educ. Psychol. **37**(2), 107–114 (2002)
24. Papert, S., Harel, I.: Situating constructionism. Constructionism **36**, 1–11 (1991)
25. Pekrun, R., Goetz, T., Titz, W., Perry, R.P.: Academic emotions in students' self-regulated learning and achievement: a program of qualitative and quantitative research. Educ. Psychol. **37**(2), 91–105 (2002)
26. Perkins, D.N., Hancock, C., Hobbs, R., Martin, F., Simmons, R.: Conditions of learning in novice programmers. J. Educ. Comput. Res. **2**(1), 37–55 (1986)
27. Petre, M., Price, B.: Using robotics to motivate 'back door' learning. Educ. Inf. Technol. **9** (2), 147–158 (2004)
28. Petta, P., Pelachaud, C., Cowie, R.: Emotion-Oriented Systems. The Humaine Handbook. Springer, Heidelberg (2011). https://doi.org/10.1007/978-3-642-15184-2
29. Pintrich, P.R.: A motivational science perspective on the role of student motivation in learning and teaching contexts. J. Educ. Psychol. **95**(4), 667–686 (2003)
30. Robins, A., Rountree, J., Rountree, N.: Learning and teaching programming: a review and discussion. Comput. Sci. Educ. **13**(2), 137–172 (2003)
31. Sharp, H., Robinson, H., Petre, M.: The role of physical artefacts in agile software development: two complementary perspectives. Interact. Comput. **21**, 108–116 (2009)
32. Simpson, J.A., Weiner, E.S.: Oxford English Dictionary. Clarendon Press, Oxford (1989)
33. Skinner, B.F.: Science and Human Behavior. Simon and Schuster, New York (1953)
34. Topping, K., Ehly, S. (eds.): Peer-Assisted Learning. Routledge, Abingdon (1998)
35. Vygotsky, L.S.: Mind in Society: The Development of Higher Psychological Processes. Harvard University Press, Cambridge (1980)
36. White, R.W.: Motivation reconsidered: the concept of competence. Psychol. Rev. **66**(5), 297–333 (1959)

A Flipped Classroom Approach for Teaching a Master's Course on Artificial Intelligence

Robin T. Bye(✉)

Software and Intelligent Control Engineering Laboratory,
Department of ICT and Natural Sciences,
Faculty of Information Technology and Electrical Engineering,
NTNU—Norwegian University of Science and Technology,
Postboks 1517, 6025 Ålesund, Norway
robin.t.bye@ntnu.no
http://www.robinbye.com

Abstract. In this paper, I present a flipped classroom approach for teaching a master's course on artificial intelligence. Traditional lectures from the classroom are outsourced to an open online course that contains high quality video lectures, step-by-step tutorials and demonstrations of intelligent algorithms, and self-tests, quizzes, and multiple-choice questions. Moreover, selected problems, or coding challenges, are cherry-picked from a suitable game-like coding development platform that rids both students and the teacher of having to implement much of the fundamental boilerplate code required to generate a suitable simulation environment in which students can implement and test their algorithms. Using the resources of the online course and the coding platform thus free up much valuable time for active learning in the classroom. These learning activities are carefully chosen to align with the intended learning outcomes, curriculum, and assessment to allow for learning to be constructed by the students themselves under guidance by the teacher. Thus, I perceive the teacher's role as a facilitator for learning, much similar to that of a personal trainer or a coach. Emphasising problem-solving as key to achieving intended learning outcomes, the aim is to select problems that strike a balance between detailed step-by-step tutorials and highly open-ended problems. This paper consists of an overview of relevant literature, the course content and teaching methods, recent evaluation reports and a student evaluation survey, results from the final oral exams, and a discussion regarding some limiting frame factors, challenges with my approach, and future directions.

Keywords: Flipped classroom · E-learning · Active learning
Constructive alignment · Problem-solving · CodinGame · edX
C-4 dynamite for learning

This paper is an extended and revised version of a paper presented at the 9th International Conference on Computer Supported Education (CSEDU '17) in Porto, Portugal, April 2017 [13].

P. Escudeiro et al. (Eds.): CSEDU 2017, CCIS 865, pp. 246–276, 2018.
https://doi.org/10.1007/978-3-319-94640-5_13

1 Introduction

A simple definition of the flipped, or inverted, classroom teaching methodology is given as the act of swapping learning activities that traditionally have taken place in-class with learning activities that traditionally have taken place out-of-class [24]. However, this definition is somewhat limiting. As noted in a survey of research on flipped classroom by Bishop and Verleger [8], flipped classroom constitutes much more than a mere reordering of activities performed at home or in class. They give a more useful definition as the flipped classroom being "*an educational technique that consists of two parts: interactive group learning activities inside the classroom, and direct computer-based individual instruction outside the classroom.*" Furthermore, Bishop and Verleger [8] highlights that human interaction is the key component of the in-class activities, with a foundation in student-centred learning theories such as those of Piaget [31] and Vygotsky [43], where explicit instruction methods based on teacher-centred learning theories are outsourced to automated computer technology.

In similar vein, Abeysekera and Dawson [1] emphasise that in a flipped classroom, "*the information-transmission component of a traditional face-to-face lecture is moved out of class time* [... and replaced with] *active, collaborative tasks.*" By having students prepare for class by outside-class activities normally covered by traditional lectures, the teacher can free up valuable in-class time to student-centred learning activities. After class, students can continue working on in-class tasks they did not finish, explore some topics in more detail, revise material, and further consolidate knowledge [1].

But flipped classroom is not necessarily only about replacing traditional lectures outside of the classroom. Teachers can also take advantage of the existence of ready-made online material such as step-by-step tutorials, interactive web demonstrations, quizzes and tests, and coding platforms, to mention a few of the resources that teachers commonly spend much time preparing themselves. Thus, the teacher's focus can be shifted from the time-consuming task of making such resources from scratch themselves to selection and quality assurance ("cherry-picking") of online resources that the students can use for learning.

1.1 Active Learning

A common claim is that higher education is dominated by the *transmission method* of teaching, which can be popularly rephrased as *teaching by telling* (e.g., [39]). Synthesising research on the effectiveness of traditional lectures, Bligh [9] shows that they are not very effective for personal development, including skills or values, all of which are natural learning goals in higher education. Flipped classroom moves this one-way passive learning activity outside the classroom and replaces it with active learning, which can be defined as any teaching method that engages the students in the learning process [32]. However, as pointed out by Bishop and Verleger [8], this definition could in principle also include lectures where students reflect, take notes, and ask questions. Thus, to maintain a contrast with teacher-centred learning, it can be useful to separate lecture-based methods from traditional lectures and define active learning as students participating in the learning process, doing more than just passive listening [10]. In line with this, active learning is indeed an inseparable part of flipped classroom [37].

Several active learning paradigms can be identified (e.g., see [8]), for example *constructivism* and *collaborative learning*, which originate from the theory of cognitive conflict by Piaget [31]; *cooperative learning*, based on the theory of Vygotsky [43] on the zone of proximal development; *peer-assisted learning*, defined by Topping and Ehly [41] as "*the acquisition of knowledge and skill through active helping and supporting among status equals or matched companions*" and thus encompassing both the theoretical positions of constructivism and cooperative learning; and *peer-tutoring* (see [42], for a review). Yet another active learning method is *problem-based learning*, which has overlap with learning methods under the umbrella of peer-assisted learning but can also be undertaken individually [8].

There are several metastudies that show that active learning in science, technology, engineering, and mathematics (STEM) has several advantages regarding performance, ability to reproduce material, and motivation and engagement (e.g., [18,32,36,38]). In particular, cooperative learning strategies have been shown to be particularly effective for achieving deep learning (e.g., [12,17,23,40]).

1.2 Constructive Alignment

For the last decades, there has been a dramatic change in higher education worldwide, with many more students enrolling, from a wider diversity of background, and with a broader range of approaches to learning [5]. For example, at my own institution, about 50% of our students in the bachelor programmes of automation, computer, and power systems engineering have a background from vocational school [30]. This means that they often have strong practical skills and good self-discipline, especially if they have been in the work force for some years before entering university, but it also means that they sometimes lack academic skills.

Today's engineering students conceive learning as anything from simple memorisation of definitions, applying equations and procedures, or making sense of physical concepts and procedures, to seeing phenomena in the world in a new way or changing as a person [26]. The big variation among students in this taxonomy, ranging from *surface learning* (memorisation) to *deep learning* (learning associated with understanding and ultimately changing as a person), with an added category of *strategic learning*, in which students aim for good grades with minimal effort [15], has necessarily had an impact on how higher education is being taught [16].

It is well documented that students' *approaches to learning* has a significant effect on achieving learning outcomes outcomes (e.g., [19,27]). Therefore, many studies have tried to identify factors that promote deep learning (e.g., [28,33]). A popular answer for dealing with the challenges of today's diverse student mass is the theory of *constructive alignment* (CA) [6]. CA merges the constructivist view that students learn by doing with aligning the teacher, the students, the teaching context, the learning activities, and the learning outcomes [5]. This is achieved by the process of *working backwards* when designing a course, first starting with the *intended learning outcomes* (ILOs), then defining *assessment tasks* closely related to the ILOs, and finally choosing *teaching methods* and *learning activities* aligned with the ILOs and assessment tasks [5].

A particular concern of Biggs (e.g., [5–7]) is how the students' approaches to learning are strongly linked to the assessment tasks. Many students tend to be strategic in their approach to learning and are often mainly concerned with the level of their final grade, not learning per se. The result is an approach to learning where the exam (the assessment tasks) effectively defines the curriculum, since only those parts of the course that will affect their final grade will be prioritised. The answer in CA is to incorporate assessment tasks with grades well aligned with ILOs to ensure students achieve the latter.

1.3 Cognitive Load Theory

As noted in the literature review by my colleagues Schaathun and Schaathun [37], an active learning approach adopts the constructivist view that learners must construct their own knowledge. However, at the same time, in order to move new information from a working memory with very limited capacity into long-term memory, deep cognitive processing is required [4]. This process, referred to as *cognitive load theory* [14], represents a bottleneck in learning when too complex problems and information must be processed in too short a time. According to Sotto [39], a remedy suggested by several authors is to break problems into small, manageable exercises in order to reduce the cognitive load. In flipped classroom, where typically online video lectures and other resources are offered outside the classroom, students can manage this cognitive load by regulating pace and rewatching video lectures [1], as well as completing their other learning tasks in their own order of preference, with possible repetitions if necessary. They will also be better prepared when turning up in the classroom and getting help on difficulties they have experienced off campus.

1.4 The Teacher as a Facilitator for Learning

A key factor for success in CA is a teacher who is able to create a learning environment that facilitates learning activities that in turn make the students achieve the desired learning outcomes [7]. All teaching and learning components such as the curriculum and the ILOs, the teaching methods, and the assessment tasks must be aligned to each other. However, despite such measures being taken, it is commonly accepted that lack of *self-monitoring* and *self-regulation* among students will lead to poor academic results (e.g., [11,25]). Consequently, the learning environment itself is not sufficient to achieve ILOs, since students' individual skill in self-monitoring and self-regulation, that is, selecting and structuring the material to be learnt, will highly affect the learning outcomes [21].

Addressing this problem, Gynnild et al. [20] suggests that the teacher must adopt a role as a *facilitator for learning*, much similar to a personal trainer at the gym, guiding the trainee to do the right exercises, adjusting the "weights," or cognitive load, whilst encouraging and supporting the trainee, and eventually making the trainee self-monitored and self-regulated. In other words, the main job of the teacher is to guide the students along a path of learning, allowing for detours, and making sure that students achieve the intended learning outcomes at the end of the path, having walked themselves, and not having been lifted on the shoulders of the teacher.

Obviously, this is a bold ambition that can be challenging to achieve with large classes for which it is difficult to act as personal trainer and give individual advice and guidance. However, a flipped classroom approach may just be the tool that makes this possible, for example through systems that can automatically mark assignments and give immediate feedback on what the student struggles with, and suggest remedies such as topics to study more or exercises to be practiced.

1.5 Outline

In the following I first give an overview of a master's course on artificial intelligence (AI) in which I have employed several aspects of a flipped classroom approach in my own teaching (Sect. 2). Next, I present the teaching methods I have used (Sect. 3) and present a course evaluation that includes feedback from students in the autumn 2016 and spring 2017 cohorts (Sect. 4). Additionally, I present very recent results from an end-of-semester student evaluation survey of the 2017 cohort (Sect. 5) and final oral exam results from both cohorts (Sect. 6). Finally, I discuss some limiting frame factors and challenges to my approach, and point to possible future directions (Sect. 7).

2 Course Overview

The master's course *IE502014 Topics in Artificial Intelligence (TAI)* is a 7.5 credits (ECTS[1]) elective course (compulsory from 2018), which corresponds to a quarter of a full semester load. The course has been run with three different cohorts (autumn 2015 and 2016 and spring 2017) since the inauguration of a new master of science programme in simulation and visualization at NTNU in Ålesund autumn 2014. The course runs for 14 weeks during a semester, with all in-class activities confined to a single weekly teaching day, referred to as *workshops*. TAI provides an introduction to the field of AI and a number of selected topics therein relevant for solving real-world problems. The following key aspects are common across the topics being taught:

[1] European Credit Transfer and Accumulation System http://ec.europa.eu/education/lifelong-learning-policy/doc48_en.htm.

- *modelling* problems in suitable state space
- *design* and *implementation* of intelligent search, optimization, and classification algorithms
- *simulation* and *testing* of models and algorithms
- *visualization* and *analysis* of the results.

The ILOs of TAI are defined within the three categories of knowledge, skills, and general competence. Specifically, for each category as indication, students should upon completion of the course be able to

- *knowledge*
  - describe AI as the analysis and design of intelligent agents or systems
  - explain terms such as perception, planning, learning, and action as fundamental concepts in AI
- *skills*
  - define problems in suitable state space depending on choice of solution method
  - solve problems by means of search methods, evolutionary algorithms, swarm algorithms, neural networks, or other AI methods
- *general competence*
  - collect information from scientific publications and textbooks and reformulate the problem, choice of methods, and results in a short, concise manner
  - discuss and communicate advantages and limitations of AI as a science.

The course is split in two parts provided by two teachers. Part A, taught by me, gives an introduction to AI and revolves around solving problems by means of intelligent agents and the use of various search algorithms, including both uninformed and informed (heuristic) search, local search, and adversarial search. Part B, taught by my colleague Associate Professor Ibrahim A. Hameed, has a focus on optimisation and constraint satisfaction problems, and machine learning topics such as fuzzy expert systems, artificial neural networks (ANN), and hybrid intelligent systems. In this paper, the teaching methodology I apply for Part A is the most relevant but I may refer to Part B or the course as a whole where appropriate.

The main components of the course are as follows:

- course textbooks and scientific literature
- the learning management system (LMS) Fronter
- three mandatory assignments and a final oral exam
- online code development platforms
- massively open online courses (MOOCs)
- full-day in-class workshops.

In the following, I will present each of these components in turn.

2.1 Textbooks and Scientific Literature

The course relies heavily on the following textbooks:

- *Artificial Intelligence: A Modern Approach* (AIMA) [35]
- *Artificial Intelligence: A Guide to Intelligent Systems* (AIGIS) [29]
- *Learning for Data: A Short Course* (LFD) [2].

The course description gives the freedom to experiment with presenting different topics from the broad field of AI each time the course is run. However, all the three times we have run the course, the following ten topics from the textbooks have been studied (with some slight variation), where topics 1–5 constitute Part A, and topics 6–10 constitute Part B:

1. Introduction to AI (AIMA Chap. 1)
2. Intelligent Agents (AIMA Chap. 2)
3. Solving Problems by Searching (AIMA Chap. 3)
4. Beyond Classical Search (AIMA Chap. 4)
5. Adversarial Search (AIMA Chap. 5)
6. Constraint Satisfaction Problems (AIMA Chap. 6)
7. Fuzzy Expert Systems (AIGIS Chap. 2–4, case study Chap. 9)
8. Artificial Neural Networks for Pattern Recognition (AIGIS, Chap. 6, case studies Chap. 9)
9. Hybrid Intelligent Systems (AIGIS Chap. 8, case studies Chap. 9)
10. Nonlinear Transformation and Feature Extraction (LFD Chap. 3).

In addition, relevant scientific papers are provided to students on selected topics as case studies to provide insight into practical application and state-of-the-art in AI.

2.2 Fronter LMS

Until summer 2017, Fronter[2] is the official LMS in use at NTNU in Ålesund, after which all campuses of NTNU will use Blackboard.[3] Every course has its own virtual "room" in Fronter that enrolled students are required to use for accessing course material and receiving updated news messages. The course room for TAI contains a continuously updated Frontpage with a summary of all relevant information, including a welcome message; information about where to buy the course textbooks; and course material (course overview, oral exam information, assignment handouts, and workshop material). The Frontpage also contains internal hyperlinks to the course material (usually PDFs) contained in a well-structured Documents directory. Students can quickly and easily access the material from the Frontpage, which is important if using a smartphone or tablet, but can also choose to navigate the Documents directory for complete access to all material. Assignments are handed in through the Fronter submission system and detailed feedback on students' performance is also posted there. Using the Fronter news

[2] http://www.itslearning.eu/fronter.
[3] http://www.blackboard.com.

functionality, we inform students whenever new material is available or when already posted material has been updated.

The teachers have tried to encourage the Fronter *discussion forum* by posting answers to several questions that students ask in class or by email but there has been very little activity from students in the forum. According to the students, this is due to being on-campus and seeing each other steadily, thus reducing the need for an online forum. Still, the teachers find the forum functionality useful but then acting more as a knowledge bank of frequently asked questions (FAQs) with answers.

2.3 Assignments and Oral Exam

From experience with various coursework approaches at our department, we believe that compulsory coursework is very often required in order to make the students work steadily throughout the semester and be well prepared for the exam. Indeed, we have found that students' performance improved about one grade on average after making the coursework compulsory in some courses [30].

Three mandatory assignments must be passed for permission to enter the end-of-semester final oral exam. The assignments typically consist of both theoretical short answer questions and project-like programming (coding) exercises. Employing a grading scheme consisting of the letters A to F, where A is best and F is fail, a pass grade is awarded if the work has the quality of a C or better.

Whilst a requirement of C to pass the assignments may seem somewhat harsh, the reasoning behind this rule is to provide a strong incentive to students for studying hard before the exam. Furthermore, it should be noted that teachers tend to be somewhat lenient in grading, at least in borderline cases, and students usually are allowed at least one more attempt on an assignment they have failed.

The grades on the assignments do not contribute to the final grade, which is determined solely by a final individual oral exam. Students usually get 3–4 weeks to complete and submit their assignments on Fronter.

Individual assignment reports, as well as a laptop with computer code, can be brought to the exam to provide individual entry points of discussion. The oral exam is 25 min and students are examined by the course teachers.

2.4 Code Development Platforms

With a focus on *learning by doing* and practical application, TAI requires coded simulation environments in which students can implement, test, and analyze intelligent algorithms. However, developing such environments can be a time-consuming task and divert attention from the learning outcomes that we want the students to achieve. For the programming exercises for Part A, I have relied on two online websites that provide such simulation environments, namely *HackerRank*[4] and *CodinGame*.[5] Students have to register as users (free of charge) on both websites.

[4] https://www.hackerrank.com.

[5] https://www.codingame.com.

Using HackerRank and CodinGame removes the need for writing a lot of boilerplate code and simulation logic, leaving the students more time to focus on the design and implementation of the algorithms, and the teacher more time to do other more meaningful work. Both websites support more than 20 of the most common programming languages, provide discussion forums, blogs, and leaderboards (rankings), with CodinGame also providing entertaining game-like visualizations of the code execution, which is quite useful when testing an algorithm and for debugging purposes. They both provide fun and playful environments that act as a catalyst for learning where students can compete both against themselves and others in the quest of obtaining better scores.

2.5 Open Online Courses

With the advent of MOOCs, numerous online e-learning resources exist, often free of charge. Two of the leaders and pioneers in the field of MOOCs are Udacity[6] and edX.[7] Udacity was perhaps the very first MOOC and was born out of a experiment at Stanford University by famous AI researchers Sebastian Thrun and Peter Norvig, the latter of whom is also the director of research at Google and co-author of the AIMA course textbook [34]. They offered an online course called *Introduction to Artificial Intelligence* online for free and managed to achieve a simultaneous enrolment of more than 160,000 students in more than 190 countries. EdX was founded by the Massachusetts Institute of Technology (MIT) and Harvard University in May 2012 and provides courses from more than 60 universities, corporations and institutions.

We *encourage* students to enroll for free in one or more of the AI courses provided by Udacity, and *demand* that they enroll, also for free, in the edX course *CS188.1x Artificial Intelligence* prepared by staff at the University of California Berkeley. The courses that we recommend build heavily on the course textbook (AIMA) by Russell and Norvig [34] and other textbooks on AI and contain numerous interactive video lessons, self-tests such as quizzes and multiple-choice questions (MCQs), programming exercises, and other material that encourage active learning and are useful for TAI.

2.6 Workshops

All in-class learning activities in TAI take place in an ordinary flat classroom on a single weekday that typically begins at 8:15 and ends at 16:00. Calling this full day of teaching and learning activities a *workshop* is not unintentional but emphasises to students that they will be met by an active, collaborative, student-centred learning environment for constructing their own learning, in contrast with more teacher-centred learning environments.

---

[6] http://www.udacity.com.
[7] http://www.edx.org.

During the workshop, the teacher is neither required nor expected to be present at all times during the entire day but will have a detailed plan for the students to engage in learning activities (which will be discussed in the following chapter).

3 Teaching Methods

3.1 Information and Structure

Three important bits of information must be distributed to students before the very first workshop:

1. name of course textbooks and where to buy them
2. 10-page detailed course overview
3. description of first workshop and preparatory homework.

Naturally, many students fail to do this first homework and the workload of the workshop is therefore intentionally smaller than the remaining workshops to allow for this, with no homework reading, exercises, or video lectures.

Additionally, both teachers provided a detailed *list of potential oral exam questions* as early as possible in the semester. Posting such a list serves several purposes [30]: it reduces uncertainty and stress related to the exam but just as important, it provides students with *mental hooks* for constructing knowledge as they progress, since having read the questions will reduce the cognitive load when new material is introduced, and they will be able to more quickly putting new knowledge into context and storing it in long-term memory.

All of the above information is posted on Fronter in a highly structured way for easy and quick access, even when using smartphones and tablets. The course overview is rich in detail but is a document that we encourage students to refer back to regularly. It is useful for the students to have a schedule of when all the different topics will be introduced as well as assignment deadlines as early as possible so that students can plan their studies and reserve time for assignments. Introducing the teaching methodology with the emphasis on flipped classroom and active learning, with overarching ILOs and a well-defined main objective of the course, also provides a useful top-down view that guides the students during the course.

3.2 Workshops

Some time before each workshop (typically at least 4–5 days), a new workshop description is released on Fronter. Each workshop description contains details such as

- the date, classroom, start time, name of teacher;
- references to textbook chapters and online videos;
- the ILOs of that particular workshop;
- a rough schedule of tasks to be completed;

- details on each task; and
- and homework for the next workshop.

This homework consists of reading selected chapters and solving selected exercises in the textbook, as well as completing various tasks in the online edX course (see Sect. 3.3) or on the code development platforms (see Sect. 3.4).

Current Status. Every workshop begins with a short evaluation of the current status regarding problems students have faced in their homework, questions they may have, what they think about the teaching methods, and other things that come to mind. Typically, there will be some parts from the homework that students have struggled with and have questions about. Minor questions are answered immediately, however, if it is clear that a more thorough explanation is needed, the teacher writes down the questions or topics on a list and typically gives a *micro-lecture* on the various topics afterwards.

Next, students are given a number of active learning tasks, varying in size. For example, a two-minute task could be to discuss with another person in class the possible answers of a question I give them, whilst students can be working for up to several hours on larger exercises or assignments.

The teacher is not required to be available at all times. Indeed, it may be beneficial to leave the classroom at times, as internal discussion and group work seem to flourish with the teacher absent.

Self-tests. For *self-tests* (quizzes or MCQs), I usually ask everyone to do them individually, but encourage discussions with other students and myself. This has the advantage that those who prefer some time on their own to reflect on the answer get that, whereas those who prefer to interact with others in search of answers can do so. Afterwards, I ask students in turn for answers, and most importantly, the reasoning behind the answers. If the student's reasoning is weak, I ask for clarifications from the rest of the class, and finally, I often provide my own explanation, in different wording.

Digital self-tests has the advantage that *immediate feedback* is returned to the students. However, they also require questions to be unambiguously phrased. During a semester, there will very often be students who are dissatisfied with a question, claiming that another answer is more correct, or that there is no right answer. This should not be viewed as something unfortunate. Rather, it is a golden opportunity for discussion in class and a driver for deep learning. Students must have a thorough understanding of the topic of the question and be able to formulate to the teacher why they disagree with the question, and other students have to opportunity to delve into the discussion.

Oral Presentations. For *oral presentations*, students will generally be working in groups, which tend to lower the fear of presenting and generally improves the quality of both quiz answers and presentations. Each group will randomly be assigned a topic for the presentation, for example, a particular search algorithm.

Knowing that they will have to make a presentation in class but not knowing the topic beforehand likely acts as a catalyst for completing the homework in a serious manner. Also, making the presentation ad hoc in class and explaining the topic to others force the students to organise their knowledge and insight on the topics before turning up to class.

Naturally, the students' presentations will suffer from the short preparation time in the classroom. I therefore interrupt the presentations when needed and first ask the presenting students if they are able to clarify the issue at hand, and if not, I ask the class as a whole if someone can help out. Even if I get a good answer, I usually rephrase the answer with my own words and try to be as concise and precise as possible, and hopefully, both the presenters and the rest of the class get a much clearer picture of the particular issue.

Textbook Exercises. Another activity during workshops include discussing answers to *textbook exercises*. These exercises differ from typical online exercises and self-tests, as they often require more work and are more time-consuming; one often have to make an analysis of the problem first, and then provide a long and elaborate answer. It would therefore be a waste of time to do such exercises in class, and instead, students are given a short list of recommended textbook exercises to complete at home before each workshop. In class, answers to the exercises are walked through and discussed as needed.

Programming Exercises. Finally, being a course on topics in AI, writing computer code and implementing intelligent algorithms is an inherent and important part of the course. During workshops, on average, a large portion of the time is devoted to larger *programming exercises*, or *coding challenges*, contained in the assignments, or minor programming exercises that are solvable in a short period of time in class. More details on coding are provided in Sect. 3.4.

Competitions. To add some spice to the learning environment, I sometimes arrange for small informal *competitions* in the class, where the winner, or winning team, gets nothing more than pride and glory. Sometimes I split the class in groups and let each group work on the same problem for 10–15 min, say. The first team who submits a working solution gets a point. Points are then accumulated for various learning tasks during the day. The students tend to like this concept but it should not be overdone and detract from the learning process.

Discussions. *Discussions* are not a scheduled task in the workshop but rather something that happens ad hoc during the tasks mentioned above. Forcing students to discuss a topic is rarely very awarding. Instead, having outsourced the traditional lectures from the classroom provides more time to allow discussions to emerge as needed. This is extremely useful for deep learning, as it helps students learning by reducing the cognitive load, delving deeper into topics, and allowing time to organise and store new material in long-term memory. In addition, discussions will often sidetrack into related topics, evident of students looking at the world from a different perspective, discovering relationships across topics, and even changing as a person.

3.3 The Online AI Course

As mentioned earlier, all students in TAI are required to enrol in an online AI course offered by edX called *CS188.1x Artificial Intelligence*. This course has been archived since 2014, which means that no teaching staff maintain or are active in the course. Nevertheless, all the resources provided are available, free of charge, to edX users. In Part A of TAI, four of the five topics are covered by the edX course, with excellent video lectures, step-by-step tutorials, and quizzes. The video lectures come both in long and unedited versions and in short and condensed edited versions that are also interspersed with self-tests with immediate feedback, all easily accessible on portable devices such as mobiles and tablets. The voices in the videos are transcribed to text, which makes it easy for students to quickly browse through a video by scrolling through the text until a given point of interest.

Whereas some students favour watching the long videos in one go and then use the short, edited videos for repetition, others jump straight to the edited videos, especially if they have studied the textbook first. All the edX material is readily available via an edX app, which, when combined with the video format and interactive material, also make it easy for students to squeeze in short micro-sessions of homework during their day, e.g., when riding the bus to campus.

Figure 1 shows an example of the video user interface of the edX course, where users watch very short transcribed videos in sequence, interspersed with interactive quizzes and demos.

3.4 Coding Challenges

To construct knowledge, skills, and competence within the topics of TAI, students need to practice on modelling problems with relevance to the real-world, and be able to select or modify existing intelligent algorithms from the AI literature or devise new algorithms suitable to the level of abstraction in their models. The next step is to implement the algorithms and test them in a simulated environment, and perform an analysis of their behaviour, often requiring visualisations to understand what is going on. Doing this from scratch requires both skills and a lot of time, and henceforth we have outsourced this to two code development platforms, HackerRank and CodinGame, both of which provide excellent frameworks for students to focus on coding algorithms.

HackerRank. HackerRank provides numerous programming challenges in several domains and programming languages, including the domain most relevant for this course, namely AI. All challenges consist of a problem description and a code window in a web browser (see Fig. 2, top) where students can enter their

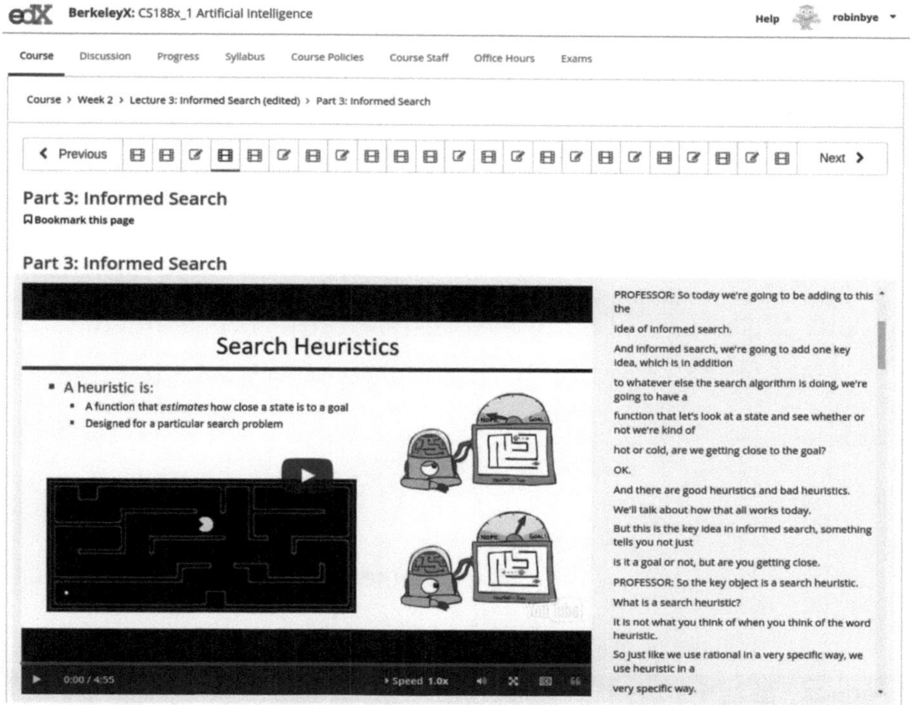

Fig. 1. Video interface for the edX course CS188.1x Artificial Intelligence.

programs, or they can use a plugin to enable writing their code locally in their own editor on their own computers. Programs are then tested on text input and must produce the correct text output. Sample stub code to get students started is provided in many cases.

For Part A of TAI, I cherry-pick exercises from relevant AI subdomains on HackerRank, including Graph Theory, A* Search, Bot Building, Alpha Beta Pruning, Combinatorial Search, and Games. An example exercise is BotClean Large,[8] in which students must program an *intelligent agent* (bot) to clean all the dirty cells in a 2D grid. After submitting their code, a simulation tests the bot of each student on a number of different scenarios and returns a score.

An example of input and output text formats for BotClean Large is shown in Fig. 2 (middle). For the input, the first line shows the coordinates ($x = 0$, $y = 0$) of the cleaning bot; the second line gives the dimensions of the 2D grid (5 rows × 5 columns); and the next 5 rows shows whether a cell in the maze is dirty (‘`d`’) or clean (‘`-`’), and whether the bot is in a particular (clean) cell (‘`b`’). For the output, the AI program must iteratively in an infinite loop return one

[8] https://www.hackerrank.com/challenges/botcleanlarge.

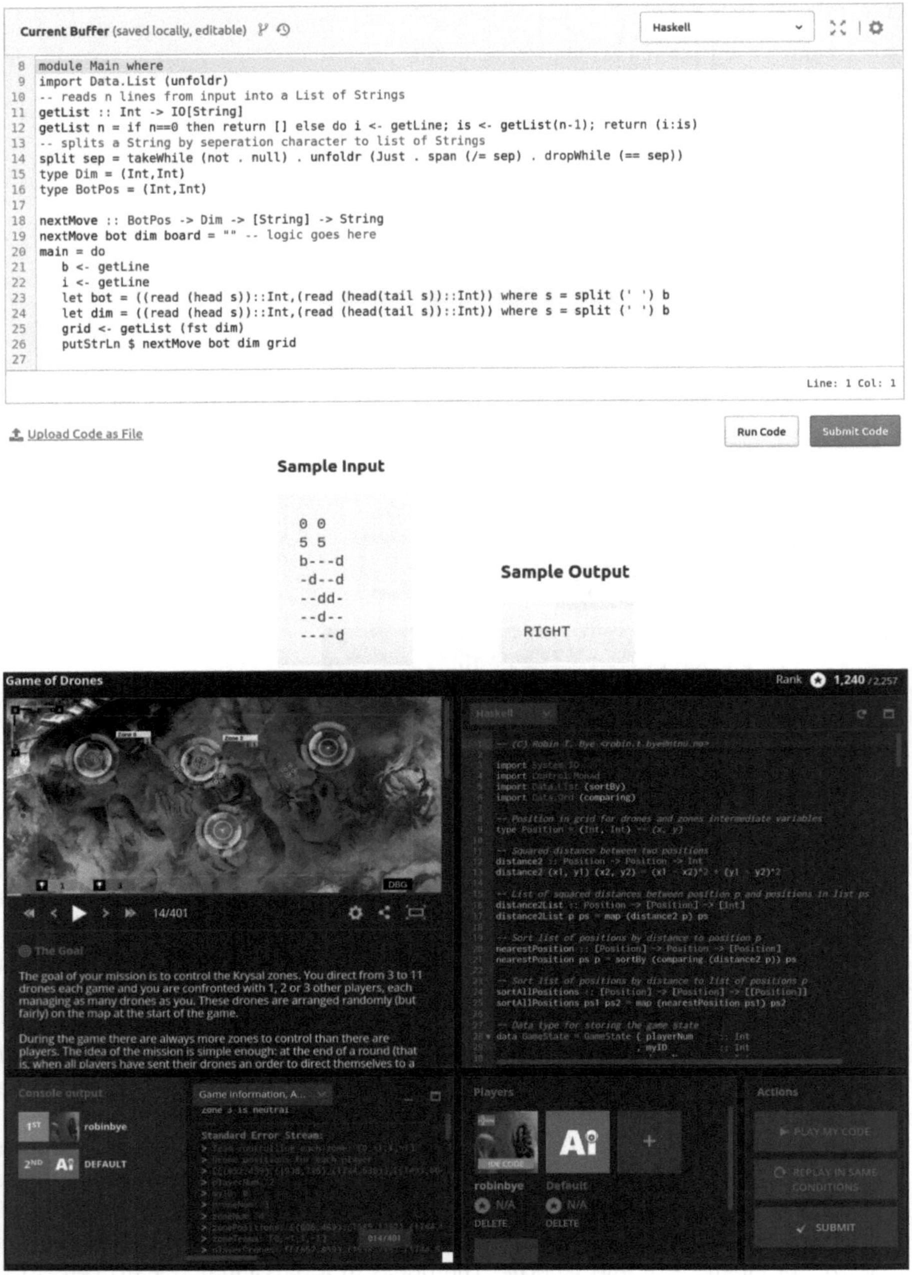

Fig. 2. HackerRank coding window (top) and sample input and output text for Bot-Clean Large challenge (middle), and example screenshot of CodinGame environment for Game of Drones challenge (bottom).

of the actions RIGHT, LEFT, UP, DOWN, or CLEAN, with the action RIGHT chosen in this particular case.

CodinGame. CodinGame works in a similar manner as HackerRank but also provides game-like 2D graphical feedback of the behaviour of the code. The stub code to get students started on a particular programming challenge is usually better than the one on HackerRank. Programming challenges are divided into single-player challenges (ranked Easy, Medium, or Hard) that can be found in the Training category, and larger, multiplayer games called Bot Programming, that can be found in the Multiplayer category (past contents) or Contests (currently running contests). One example of a multiplayer game is Game of Drones, in which students must control a fleet of drones and compete against other players (classmates, online players, or the default AI bot provided by CodinGame) with their own fleet of drones in a battle of controlling as many zones as possible in a large 2D grid.

The screenshot in Fig. 2 (bottom) shows an example of the CodinGame environment run in a web browser for Game of Drones. The top left window shows a graphical simulation of the game; the top right is the coding window; bottom left shows the console output; and bottom right shows which players are competing and has some buttons to for testing and submitting code.

Intelligent Agents. Both platforms have been designed in a similar manner where the user must input a computer program, commonly referred to as the AI, or *bot*, that reads data from standard input, does some processing, and then outputs a desired action to standard output. This loop repeats for a number of time steps until the simulation, or *game*, ends. Thus, the internals of the simulated environment behaves much like a black box to the bot, however, certain parameters in the environment are "sensed" and provided to the bot at each time step, and in addition, each coding challenge provides details of the model the simulated environment is based upon sufficient that a useful bot can be constructed. Hence, the coding challenges adopts the same paradigm as the course textbook, in which AI is centred around *intelligent agents* that *sense*, *plan*, and *act* [34].

Coding challenges typically revolve around certain themes in computer science and AI such as queues, lists, search algorithms, path planning, control, etc. Very often, each challenge comes in several versions, Easy, Medium, and Hard, in which the challenge becomes gradually more complex and difficult to solve. An example is the Mars Lander challenge on CodinGame, where students doing the Easy level must design an intelligent agent, first for controlling the landing of a spacecraft in the vertical dimension only, then, for the Medium and Hard levels, in two dimensions, which is exceedingly harder.

Design Process. When working on coding challenges, I emphasise the importance of thinking about the problem before jumping straight into coding.

Together with the students, we brainstorm various potential models of the problem to be solved, and discuss aspects such as levels of abstraction, and their advantages and limitations. The solution method to be used is dependent on the model, as an intelligent algorithm requires the problem to be represented by exactly those components that the algorithm was designed for. The students then run a number of tests on the coding platform to verify their design and receive automatic feedback on which tests were passed or failed.

In contrast with HackerRank, the CodinGame platform also provides *visualizations* of the simulated environment. This is very valuable to students in the iterative process of testing, debugging, refining, and analysing their algorithms, because visual feedback quickly can reveal problems in the execution of the algorithm.[9]

4 Course Evaluation

To conform with the requirement in NTNU's Quality System for Education that a *course evaluation* must submitted after every semester that a course is run, I have adopted a scheme where all students present during workshops (typically 7–8 students) belong to a so-called *reference group*. At the beginning of a workshop, we begin with a class discussion, or *status meeting*, about course-specific issues such as status, progression, problems, etc., as well as general issues about the master programme in general. These meetings, which are typically quite short (5–20 min) provide an important arena and opportunity for students to help the teacher adjust the course early before issues become too big to fix. Once or twice a semester, I ask the students to answer a detailed list of evaluation questions before coming to class, in order to get a more in-depth discussion. During the status meeting, the teacher takes notes, which form the basis of an end-of-semester course evaluation report by the teacher. Likewise, members of the reference group are required to write a short evaluation report on behalf of the students. Both reports are submitted to the university and are available to all staff and students.

In the sections below, I highlight some of the findings from my evaluation reports for the TAI courses that was run autumn 2016[10] and spring 2017.[11] I also present results from an end-of-semester student survey for the spring 2017 cohort.

4.1 Relevance

Students in both the 2016 and 2017 cohorts praised both this specific course on AI, as well as the master programme in simulation and visualization as a whole, for being highly relevant in today's society and job market. Specifically,

[9] For this reason, and other minor reasons, we have chosen to use the CodinGame platform exclusively starting from 2017.

[10] http://robinbye.com/files/reports/TAIevaluation16.pdf.

[11] http://robinbye.com/files/reports/TAIevaluation17.pdf.

they mentioned how many newly started technology companies of today both in Norway and internationally seem very focussed on incorporating AI and other themes of the master programme into their business models across a variety of domains. Students also gave the names of several companies that bear resemblances with the names of courses in the master programme to illustrate their point.

4.2 Workload

The 2016 cohort thought the overall workload was appropriate, although perhaps slightly bigger than in some other courses in the master programme. Some students thought the workload for the assignments was high but thought this was justified by the assignments being highly valuable. For example, one student stated that "*(...) the assignments were big but good. Even though this course had a high workload, in retrospect I would say that this was necessary, and the main reason I learnt so much.*"

Among the 2017 cohort, some students thought the overall workload was high and close to the limit of cognitive overload. Others agreed but underlined that this was counterbalanced by the assignments being highly valuable. In the beginning of Part A on search algorithms, some students said this part was a little overwhelming, and that it was difficult to know what was important in the AIMA textbook and the video lectures.

The teachers think both cohorts were faced with about the same workload in both Part A and Part B, thus the differences in perceived workload seem rooted in different expectations among the cohorts and not actual differences in workload.

4.3 Teaching Methods and Learning Environment

Both the 2016 and 2017 cohorts expressed enthusiasm for the workshop format and the elements of flipped classroom but for the 2017 cohort, especially in the beginning, this style of teaching was something they were not used to. The 2016 cohort suggested that when revising theory from homework, e.g., in a micro-lecture, it would be slightly better for the teacher to have slides than having to move back and forth in the online video lecture, whereas the 2017 cohort suggested that short revision/micro lectures on selected topics should still be prepared and provided in class and not only provided *ad hoc* on requests by students. This latter approach will of course require more work from the teachers, especially since it is difficult for the teacher beforehand to know which topics from the homework that will need a thorough treatment in class. However, it was pointed out by students that there exist a website[12] with the same online edX course material and maintained by the same edX teachers that also contains slides freely available to use. The teachers should therefore obtain copies of these

[12] http://ai.berkeley.edu.

slides and have them ready when questions regarding the online video lectures arise in class.

Both cohorts appreciated the fact that videos were available in both short and long versions, and different students sometimes favoured one over the other. The 2017 cohort also meant that the online video lectures provided a good "compression" and focus on key topics in the AIMA textbook.

In addition, students in both cohorts expressed that the interactive material was appropriate and useful, however, some of the interactive MCQs were not always well designed and could contain questions that were ambiguously phrased and therefore one could argue which answer was really the correct one.

Students critically challenging the course material such as online quizzes is very useful for both the teacher and for fellow students, as it triggers class discussion and deeper insight into the problem that is being studied. This is also an example of deep learning, commonly observed with skilled students, as more shallow surface learners will fail to note such ambiguities in the questions.

4.4 Assignments

Both the 2016 and 2017 cohorts thought the topics covered in assignments and the design of the problems to be solved were appropriate, although the workload was quite high. They also appreciated that assignments are first released as draft versions and then modified by the teacher and the students together through constructive class discussions.

Moreover, students were dissatisfied with the timing of deadlines of assignments across different courses run simultaneously and strongly suggested that all teachers across all courses speak together at the beginning of a semester and coordinate and spread out the deadlines for assignments more evenly.

In their student evaluation report, the 2017 cohort highlighted that the assignment feedback from the professors should be more oriented on code structure and implementation. Furthermore, after personal feedback of the assignments has been released on Fronter, they suggested that the teacher spend some time of the workshop on particular problems faced in the assignments, e.g., common errors or methodologies among the students.

The average quality of all assignments was generally very high. For Assignment 3 in the 2017 cohort, two students used Haskell and a genetic algorithm that they had learnt about in the course Functional Programming and Intelligent Algorithms run in parallel with Topics in AI. They expressed that learning functional programming and also to be able to use skills and knowledge across different courses was highly valuable.

4.5 Structure and Information

Both cohorts expressed satisfaction with the course structure and the continuous flow of information by means of Fronter but the 2017 cohort complained about the lack of compatibility and usefulness of the Fronter app for smartphones.

In their student evaluation report, the 2017 cohort wrote that "[the] *course material were* [sic] *perfectly organized in the combination of the textbooks and online recourses with detailed guidance by the professor*."

Furthermore, students found little use of the Fronter discussion forum, although both cohorts acknowledged that using the forum more as a *knowledge bank* of FAQs was useful.

4.6 Coding Platforms

There was mostly agreement in both cohorts that HackerRank should not be used, mainly because it is more difficult to use and lacks visualisations, in contrast with CodinGame. Students also thoroughly enjoyed the *gamification* part of CodinGame, where one achieves rating points and badges and therefore are continuously eager to improve.

In contrast with previous years, the 2017 cohort used the CodinGame platform exclusively. Some students said it was difficult to apply concepts from theory directly in the coding challenges. One student expressed a wish for the alternative platform HackerRank to be used because it contains many problems that are more directly related to the curriculum. Specifically, many HackerRank challenges forces the students to use a particular search algorithm to solve a problem, whereas CodinGame challenges are much more open-ended and can typically be solved by a black box, where it is entirely up to the students which algorithms or methods to put inside the black box. One student expressed concern with the heavy focus on programming in this course and in the master programme as a whole for students with little programming background.

Overall, students were generally pleased with using CodinGame and doing very practical problem-solving while having some fun. In their own evaluation report of the course, the 2017 cohort suggested that it could be advantageous to limit the freedom in solution methods to the search algorithms presented in class. Currently, students are instructed to solve selected CodinGame challenges any way they like, be it using search algorithms taught in the course or any other method. In particular, students suggested the possibility of solving much fewer coding challenges (e.g., just one) but solve it many different ways, using the search algorithms of Part A of the course. Students also emphasised that this would limit coding overhead related to implementing the necessary data structures and interfaces for several different coding challenges and "provide clearer opportunity to work with search algorithms intensively."

Contrasting the 2016 and 2017 cohorts, it seems clear that the 2017 cohort was slightly dissatisfied with the open-ended nature of the coding challenges and would like problems to be more tailored to the curriculum, possibly with more examples and step-by-step tutorials prepared by the teacher.

4.7 Alignment of Part A and Part B

As described previously, Part A and Part B of the course is taught by two different teachers. Especially the 2017 cohort expressed that the linkage between the two parts is too weak, with some students suggesting that the two parts co-exist almost as two smaller and separate courses that should be taught independently.

4.8 State-of-the-Art in AI

In their student evaluation report, the 2017 cohort suggested that it "*could be reasonable to have* [an] *optional lecture describing the state-of-the art solution in the AI.*" Moreover, they suggested that the proposed lecture could be student-organized, possibly with research results presentations.

4.9 Summary of Feedback

Throughout the course and in the weekly status meetings involving the entire class, students of both the 2016 and 2017 cohorts had very little negative concern about the course itself, be it teaching methods, workload, or curriculum. When they had concerns, this was mainly related to clashes of assignment deadlines across courses and suggestions to reduce workload or modify content of assignments. Interestingly, students were very eager to discuss issues of other courses and the master programme as a whole. We see this as a sign that this course provides a safe and relaxing learning environment, since students felt comfortable and very keen to share these details with the teachers.

Finally, almost all students told us that they were highly satisfied with the course, with two students expressing in writing that "*I also wish to express that this has been one of the best courses I have taken in higher education*" and "[t]*hank you for teaching one of the better courses if not the best course I've had in this master*[']*s program*[me]."

5 Student Evaluation Survey

The 11 students enrolled in the spring 2017 cohort were asked to complete an anonymous student evaluation survey about Part A of the course online, of which 8 responded (6 full-time students, 2 part-time students). The students were first asked to specify whether they had attended most classes or not, choosing one of the following three alternatives (answers as indicated):

1. Attended most classes: 7 students
2. Did not attend most classes due to work, children, or other reasons unrelated to the course: 0 students
3. Did not attend most classes due to own priorities/lack of usefulness: 1 student.

Then, for following set of 25 statements given by Table 1, the students were asked to indicate to which degree they agreed with the statements, categorising whether they strongly or partly agreed or disagreed, or were indifferent.

In addition, they were given the opportunity to elaborate on the statements and any other issues they wished to raise.

The results are summarised in Table 2, where the number n of student responses and the corresponding percentage is given for each statement and response category.

Table 1. Statements for student evaluation survey of Part A.

#	Statement
1	*I want more traditional lectures (typically slideshows)*
2	*I want more lectures where the teacher uses the blackboard*
3	*I want more active learning activities (e.g., exercises, discussion, quizzes, competitions, student presentations, practical coding assignments, etc.)*
4	*I want more flipped classroom and e-learning/web-based learning activities*
5	*I want more emphasis on practical application than theory*
6	*I want more problem-solving learning activities*
7	*I want more computer lab activities (coding exercises in the classroom)*
8	*The teacher calling the roll makes it more likely that I turn up to class*
9	*I want more compulsory assignments*
10	*I want more/better personal feedback on my progress*
11	*I want my final grade to be decided by an single final oral exam*
12	*I want my final grade to be decided by an single final written*
13	*I want my final grade to be composed of several grade components (e.g., computer labs, assignments, projects, mid-semester test, final exam)*
14	*I want digital exams to be employed*
15	*I want home exams to be employed*
16	*The workload was appropriate*
17	*The learning activities were appropriately aligned with the intended learning outcomes, course curriculum, and assessment*
18	*The teacher's role in this course as a facilitator/guide (e.g., cherry-picking suitable online material/resources) where I must do the hard work myself is a good model for learning*
19	*The grade I received on the final oral exam reflects my knowledge/skills/general competence in the course*
20	*This course is relevant in today's society and for this master programme*
21	*The structure, information, and quality of course material/resources were appropriate*
22	*Coding assignments should be less open-ended and more tailored to applying the search algorithms taught in the course*
23	*The course should have at least one overview lecture of current state-of-the-art*
24	*The course is suitable for off-campus study*
25	*Attending workshops was valuable for my learning*

5.1 Analysis of Survey

A thorough analysis of this survey is outside the scope of this paper. The following sections discusses briefly the most relevant findings.

Table 2. Results from student evaluation survey of Part A.

Statement	Strongly agree		Partly agree		Indifferent		Partly disagree		Strongly agree	
	n	%	n	%	n	%	n	%	n	%
1	1	12.5%	3	37.5%	1	12.5%	3	37.5%	0	0.0%
2	2	25.0%	3	37.5%	0	0.0%	3	37.5%	0	0.0%
3	2	25.0%	2	25.0%	1	12.5%	3	37.5%	0	0.0%
4	1	12.5%	1	12.5%	3	37.5%	2	25.0%	1	12.5%
5	4	50.0%	1	12.5%	3	37.5%	0	0.0%	0	0.0%
6	2	25.0%	6	75.0%	0	0.0%	0	0.0%	0	0.0%
7	2	25.0%	3	37.5%	0	0.0%	0	0.0%	3	37.5%
8	2	25.0%	1	12.5%	5	62.5%	0	0.0%	0	0.0%
9	0	0.0%	2	25.0%	1	12.5%	4	50.0%	1	12.5%
10	1	12.5%	2	25.0%	1	12.5%	2	25.0%	2	25.0%
11	1	12.5%	1	12.5%	2	25.0%	1	12.5%	3	37.5%
12	0	0.0%	1	12.5%	2	25.0%	3	37.5%	2	25.0%
13	4	50.0%	2	25.0%	1	12.5%	0	0.0%	1	12.5%
14	2	25.0%	1	12.5%	4	50.0%	0	0.0%	1	12.5%
15	0	0.0%	1	12.5%	3	37.5%	1	12.5%	3	37.5%
16	3	37.5%	2	25.0%	0	0.0%	3	37.5%	0	0.0%
17	1	12.5%	4	50.0%	2	25.0%	1	12.5%	0	0.0%
18	2	25.0%	2	25.0%	3	37.5%	1	12.5%	0	0.0%
19	4	50.0%	1	12.5%	0	0.0%	3	37.5%	0	0.0%
20	5	62.5%	0	0.0%	3	37.5%	0	0.0%	0	0.0%
21	4	50.0%	3	37.5%	1	12.5%	0	0.0%	0	0.0%
22	3	37.5%	3	37.5%	0	0.0%	1	12.5%	1	12.5%
23	2	25.0%	5	62.5%	1	12.5%	0	0.0%	0	0.0%
24	1	12.5%	3	37.5%	4	50.0%	0	0.0%	0	0.0%
25	1	12.5%	6	75.0%	0	0.0%	1	12.5%	0	0.0%

Flipped Classroom Approach. Statements 1–7 shows that the 2017 cohort appears somewhat split regarding the flipped classroom approach. Half the students (4) would like more traditional lectures (statement 1), whilst the other half is indifferent (1) or partly disagrees (3). On the other hand, regarding the following remedies in statements 2–7, which support (statements 3–7), or are not in conflict with (statement 2, using the blackboard), a flipped classroom approach, half or more wants more use of the respective approaches. Furthermore, 4 students agree and 2 students are indifferent to the teacher adopting a role as a facilitator for learning (statement 18), whilst the entire cohort agree (4) or are indifferent (4) to the course being suitable for off-campus study (statement 24).

Assignments, Feedback, Workload. Statement 9 shows that 5 of the students disagrees with having more compulsory assignments, whilst 1 is indifferent and 2 partly agree. An encouraging finding is that only 3 students want more/better personal feedback, whilst 4 disagrees. Finally, 6 students agree (2 disagree) that coding assignments should be less open-ended (statement 22), whilst the majority (5 agree, 3 disagree) that the course workload was appropriate (statement 16).

Exam Format. From statements 11–15, it appears the majority of students are not in favour of neither a single final oral or written exam (statements 11–12) deciding their final course grade, with 6 students being in favour of a composite grade consisting of several components (statement 13, e.g., lab work, assignments, projects, mid-semester test, final exam). This finding is supportive of the hypothesis of Biggs (e.g., [5–7]) and proponents of CA, who claim that students are strategic and mainly concernced about grades, therefore one should incorporate graded assessment tasks that are well aligned with ILOs. Moreover, the majority of students are in favour or indifferent to using more digital exams (statement 14), whilst they are against or indifferent to home exams (statement 15).

General Satisfaction. In general, the students appear satisfied with the course. All but one student agree or are indifferent to the learning activities being appropriately aligned with ILOs, curriculum, and assessment (statement 17). 5 students agree and 3 are indifferent to the course being relevant in today's society (statement 20). 7 students agree (1 partly disagrees) that attending workshops was valuable for their learning (statement 25).

6 Final Oral Exam Results

The grade distributions for the 2016 and 2017 cohorts are shown in Table 3 below: These are quite exceptional results, but not surprising based on the effort, interest, and enthusiasm experienced in class. The quality of the assignments handed in by students in both cohorts were very good or excellent and being closely aligned with the course curriculum have likely served as highly appropriate preparation for the exam.

Table 3. Results from final oral exam.

Grade	A	B	C	D	E	F	Absent
2016	5	2	-	-	-	-	-
2017	7	1	3	-	-	-	-

Notably, from Table 2, 5 students strongly agree with the grade they got, whereas 3 students partly disagree.

7 Discussion

In this paper I have presented a flipped classroom approach for teaching a master's course on AI. Whilst it is my clear impression that the course has been a great success, the reader should by no means believe that we have found the holy grail for teaching higher education courses, as reflected from the student evaluation survey and the evaluation reports by students and teacher presented above. Indeed, there are several limiting frame factors and challenges that must be overcome for flipped classroom to work as intended. Below I discuss some of these.

7.1 Teaching Methods and Learning Environment

This course, especially Part B on search algorithms, strongly emphasises active learning activities by outsourcing most of the theoretical foundation to online video lectures, textbooks, and scientific papers. The theory along with practical online interactive exercises such as MCQs, quizzes, and other forms of self-assessment are effectively outsourced as homework to be done before students arrive in class.

Whilst enforcing students to study the textbook and show up well prepared to class is not a new idea, my impression is that a flipped classroom strategy employing online video lectures and the interactive material increases the will of students to actually do their homework. For example, the video lectures in this course come both in long unedited versions and in short and condensed edited versions, all easily accessible on portable devices such as mobiles and tablets. The videos are also speech-to-text-annotated, which makes it easy for students to quickly browse through a video to a point of interest. The video format and interactive material also makes it easy for students to squeeze in short micro-sessions of homework, e.g., during a 15-min bus drive. When students face problems in the theory from their homework, the teacher can give a short micro-lecture on the topic.

By outsourcing traditional passive learning activities such as lectures, the time in the classroom during workshops (full days of teaching/learning activities) can be much more efficiently used for active learning activities, such as problem-solving, quizzes, informal competitions, exercises, discussion, and assignments and projects. Being a relatively small class, it is easy for the teacher to provide individual help to each student if necessary.

Importantly, the teacher is not necessarily present in the classroom the whole day, which have several advantages. For example, some students tend to be better at socialising and discussing topics when the teacher is not present, e.g., when working on a practical problem. In addition, the teacher can prepare topics or answers to questions raised in class whilst the students are working independently without supervision.

During workshops, students were active and eager to discuss topics but sometimes needed a bit of a push to get started on being active. Having outsourced valuable time for lectures also meant that the teacher has less pressure to avoid discussions or delving into sidetrack topics just because there was a pressing schedule to adhere to.

7.2 Frame Factors

The *number of students* in a class can be a limiting *frame factor* for achieving ILOs. In the course presented here, the 2015 and 2016 cohorts consisted of about 10 students, of which 2–3 quit early or never turned up, whereas 15 students were enrolled in 2017, of which 11 ended up doing the course. If the class had exceeded about 25 students, say (which is also the number of seats funded by the Ministry of Education), it may have been more difficult to achieve the same fruitful learning environment in the classroom. For larger classes, one would likely have to abandon flat classrooms and use large auditoriums. University management would typically see no problem in this and tell teachers to go ahead and do their traditional one-way lectures as usual, which is not desirable. Optionally, one could split such large cohorts into smaller groups, which would multiply the number of teachers required and associated costs. This begs the question why there is a transition in teaching methodology from classroom-style teaching (one teacher per class of 30 students, say) in lower education to auditorium-style lecture-based teaching in higher education, thus turning students into passive learners. Flipped classroom can still be useful for large classes, however, but may require much more effort in facilitating the in-class learning activities.

Another important frame factor is the *available online resources*. In TAI, we have been lucky to find both an edX course that is closely aligned with the topics in the course textbook for Part A, as well as the CodinGame platform that provides a high quality framework with a vast variety of AI coding challenges suitable for learning key aspects of the course, such a modelling problems, implementing intelligent algorithms, and perform testing and analysis.

Producing these online resources oneself with the same quality, as well as the material contained in textbooks, is an impossible task for the common teacher. Still, with *e-learning* as a buzz word nowadays, university management are very eager for teaching staff to make videos to put online. I think this approach is flawed, as it is extremely time-consuming to produce video lectures oneself of the desired quality, not to mention developing a suitable simulation environment for testing algorithms. Instead, teachers should act as *facilitators* and devote their time to finding such resources and tying them together in a didactically sound manner. For example, the teacher must take care in selecting the right coding challenges and guiding the students during problem-solving (see the next section).

7.3 Problem-Based versus Problem-Solving Learning

Problem-based learning is a hot topic of higher education and the interested reader may refer to our accompanying paper for reflections on many of its aspects [30]. Here, I refrain myself to a very important finding by Hattie and Goveia

[22], who upon examining 800 meta-analyses note that problem-based learning cannot be shown to have a positive effect on achieving ILOs! The reason for this, according to Sotto [39], is the distinction between *problem-based* and *problem-solving* learning. He argues that the problems handed to students must be carefully designed by the teacher so that students easily can progress and be able to practice and achieve the ILOs. Specifically, one should use a teaching approach that employs well-designed case studies and avoid problem-based and too student-centred learning, especially for larger problems and when there is no clear guidance towards how to solve them. Otherwise, students will get stuck or spend too much time on finding the necessary pieces to solve the puzzle by searching the Internet or studying textbooks.

Adopting this distinction of Sotto [39], I believe the focus on *problem-solving learning* is a major key to the success of this course. For example, the coding challenges on CodinGame are carefully selected and much attention is given during workshops on how to model the problems and how to select appropriate solution methods. Yet, there is still room for much improvement, since some students are dissatisfied with the selection of problems and would like problems to be less open-ended.

However, care must be taken to strike the *right balance*. If problems are too rigidly defined, with perhaps only one solution approach possible, as when instructing students to follow detailed step-by-step instructions, there is a danger that creativity is neglected and students only achieve surface learning [3]. Comparing with bachelor's courses, where such rigid schemes to some extent can even be desirable, master's courses should have a higher emphasis on being research-based and investigative in nature.

Hence, in TAI, we are still striving to find the right tradeoff between coding challenges being too rigid versus too open-ended. There are nearly always several paths for solving a given problem, and the teacher should often provide a simple outline of a solution as a starting point and then guide students towards improving the solution.

7.4 C-4 Dynamite for Learning

Central to my teaching approach is an emphasis on four axes of learning, **C-4**, that together are dynamite[13] for learning: *creativity*, *cooperation*, *competition*, and *challenge*.

First, the learning activities offered in the course should facilitate *creativity*. In a creative process, students model and design solutions to a wide variety of problems but are usually not restricted (much) on how to model the problem and which method to use.

Second, many *cooperative learning* activities are employed in class and students are encouraged to cooperate with each other also for individual work.

Third, as mentioned previously in Sect. 3.2, I sometimes run small, informal *competitions* in class as a driver for motivation. In addition, the CodinGame

[13] C-4 is also a common plastic explosive.

platform is inherently competitive, as users get rating points as they improve their solutions or solve more problems. Students therefore compete not only against others but also against themselves in a quest for better ratings.

Fourth, students should be encouraged to critically *challenge* all the concepts they are introduced to in the course and I have indeed found that students tend to do this more as the course progresses. Triggers for the students can be as minor as mistakes in the written formulations in quizzes, as discussed in Sect. 3.2, or discovering that a solution method has certain limitations that they first found out about when implementing it on CodinGame. For example, a given intelligent algorithm may not be able to provide a good answer in reasonable time and a particular CodinGame test might therefore fail.

Achieving all the C-4 components in a course is an ambitious task. Still, with the increasing availability of high-quality online resources in many fields of research and education, a flipped classroom approach to teaching clearly eases the burden of making this possible.

7.5 Future Work

Based partly on the work presented in this paper, a decision has been made to separate the topics of Part A and Part B of this course. Beginning 2018, Part A and Part B will form the basis of two new courses called *Artificial Intelligence* and *Machine Learning*, respectively. We will also address the issue of colliding assignment deadlines across courses run simultaneously during the same semester. Moreover, in line with theory of CA, it would be interesting to follow the students' advice and change the grading format from a single final oral exam to a composite grade, with assessment task distributed across the semester. Finally, at our department, we have begun to run educational seminars and roundtable discussions where teachers present their approaches to teaching and this course has been presented to both internal and external colleagues as a motivator for implementing flipped classroom themselves.

7.6 Conclusions

I have shown in this paper one way out of many that flipped classroom can be implemented in a master's course on AI. The key to success is to be able to facilitate learning by cherry-picking textbook chapters and relevant literature as well as suitable online resources such as video lectures, self-tests, and coding challenges. When such resources do not exist or lack in quality or theory, one can try to make one's own material, e.g., a compendium supplementary to the textbook, or one's own video lectures. However, this is a very time-consuming process if one wants to achieve the desired quality, and should be a last resort.

Whereas I favour a teaching approach that has much in common with CA, I emphasise that the right balance between too rigidly defined learning activities where students are being "spoonfed" and too vaguely defined problem-based learning activities must be found, so that the problems are investigative in nature with different possible paths towards solutions, yet at least one path must be reasonably easy for the students to find and follow. Compared to courses at the bachelor level, students of a master course like TAI must be trained in investigative and research-based methods, with higher demands on self-exploration. Offering a range of problems, where introductory step-by-step tutorials are used to introduce new material, and harder, more open-ended problems are presented subsequently, is likely a good approach.

Acknowledgements. The Software and Intelligent Control (SoftICE) Laboratory (http://softicelab.wordpress.com) is grateful for the financial support given by the Study Committee at NTNU in Ålesund through the educational research project *Research-Based and Innovation-Driven Learning (FILA)*, grant no. 70440500.

References

1. Abeysekera, L., Dawson, P.: Motivation and cognitive load in the flipped classroom: definition, rationale and a call for research. High. Educ. Res. Dev. **34**(1), 1–14 (2015)
2. Abu-Mostafa, Y.S., Magdon-Ismail, M., Lin, H.T.: Learning From Data: A Short Course. AMLBook (2012)
3. Andersen, H.L.: "Constructive alignment" og risikoen for en forsimplende universitetspædagogik. Dansk Universitetspædagogisk Tidsskrift **5**(9) (2010)
4. Anderson, J.R.: Cognitive Psychology and Its Implications, 8th edn. Worth Publishers, New York (2015)
5. Biggs, J., Tang, C.: Teaching for Quality Learning at University, 4th edn. McGraw Hill/Open University Press, New York (2011)
6. Biggs, J.: Enhancing teaching through constructive alignment. High. Educ. **32**, 347–364 (1996)
7. Biggs, J.: Aligning teaching for constructing learning. The Higher Education Academy, York, UK (2011). http://www.heacademy.ac.uk/assets/documents/resources/resourcedatabase/id477_aligning_teaching_for_constructing_learning.pdf. Accessed 27 Sept 2011
8. Bishop, J.L., Verleger, M.A.: The flipped classroom: a survey of the research. In: ASEE National Conference Proceedings, Atlanta, GA, vol. 30 (2013)
9. Bligh, D.A.: What's the Use of Lectures? Intellect Books (1998)
10. Bonwell, C.C., Eison, J.A.: Active learning: creating excitement in the classroom. 1991 ASHE-ERIC Higher Education Reports. ERIC (1991)
11. Borkowski, J., Thorpe, P.: Self-regulation and motivation: a life-span perspective on underachievement. In: Schunk, D., Zimmermann, B. (eds.) Self-regulation of Learning and Performance: Issues of Educational Applications, pp. 44–73. Erlbaum, Hillsdale (1994)
12. Bowen, C.W.: A quantitative literature review of cooperative learning effects on high school and college chemistry achievement. J. Chem. Educ. **77**(1), 116 (2000)
13. Bye, R.T.: The teacher as a facilitator for learning: flipped classroom in a master's course on artificial intelligence. In: Proceedings of the 9th International Conference on Computer Supported Education – Volume 1: CSEDU (CSEDU 2017), pp. 184–195. INSTICC, SCITEPRESS, April 2017. Selected for Extended Publication in Springer Book Series Communications in Computer and Information Science (CCIS)

14. Clark, R.C., Nguyen, F., Sweller, J.: Efficiency in Learning: Evidence-Based Guidelines to Manage Cognitive Load. Wiley, Hoboken (2011)
15. Entwistle, N., Ramsden, P.: Understanding Student Learning. Croom Helm, Beckenham (1983)
16. Felder, R.M., Brent, R.: Understanding student differences. J. Eng. Educ. **94**(1), 57–72 (2005)
17. Foldnes, N.: The flipped classroom and cooperative learning: evidence from a randomised experiment. Act. Learn. High Educ. **17**(1), 39–49 (2016)
18. Freeman, S., Eddy, S.L., McDonough, M., Smith, M.K., Okoroafor, N., Jordt, H., Wenderoth, M.P.: Active learning increases student performance in science, engineering, and mathematics. Proc. Nat. Acad. Sci. **111**(23), 8410–8415 (2014)
19. Gynnild, V.: Læringsorientert eller eksamensfokusert? Nærstudier av pedagogisk utviklingsarbeid i sivilingeniørstudiet. Ph.D. thesis, NTNU (2001)
20. Gynnild, V., Holstad, A., Myrhaug, D.: Teaching as coaching: a case study of awareness and learning in engineering education. Int. J. Sci. Educ. **29**(1), 1–17 (2007)
21. Gynnild, V., Holstad, A., Myrhaug, D.: Identifying and promoting self-regulated learning in higher education: roles and responsibilities of student tutors. Mentor. Tutoring: Partnersh. Learn. **16**(2), 147–161 (2008)
22. Hattie, J., Goveia, I.C.: Synlig læring: et sammendrag av mer enn 800 metaanalyser av skoleprestasjoner. Cappelen Damm akademisk (2013)
23. Johnson, D.W., Johnson, R.T., Smith, K.A.: Active Learning: Cooperation in the College Classroom. Interaction Book Co., Edina (1998)
24. Lage, M.J., Platt, G.J., Treglia, M.: Inverting the classroom: a gateway to creating an inclusive learning environment. J. Econ. Educ. **31**(1), 30–43 (2000)
25. Lan, W.: The effects of self-monitoring on students' course performance, use of learning strategies, attitude, self-judgment ability, and knowledge representation. J. Exp. Educ. **64**(2), 101–116 (1996)
26. Marshall, D., Summers, M., Woolnough, B.: Students' conceptions of learning in an engineering context. High. Educ. **38**(3), 291–309 (1999)
27. Marton, F.: Phenomenography – describing conceptions of the world around us. Instr. Sci. **10**, 177–200 (1981)
28. Marton, F., Booth, S.: Learning and Awareness. Lawrence Erlbaum, Mahwaw (1997)
29. Negnevitsky, M.: Artificial Intelligence: A Guide to Intelligent Systems. Addison Wesley, Boston (2005)
30. Osen, O.L., Bye, R.T.: Reflections on teaching electrical and computer engineering courses at the bachelor level. In: Proceedings of the 9th International Conference on Computer Supported Education – Volume 2: CSEDU (CSEDU 2017), pp. 57–68. INSTICC, SCITEPRESS, April 2017. Selected for Extended Publication in Springer Book Series Communications in Computer and Information Science (CCIS)
31. Piaget, J.: Six Psychological Studies. Tenzer, A. (Trans.) (1968)
32. Prince, M.J.: Does active learning work? A review of the research. J. Eng. Educ. **93**(3), 223–231 (2004)
33. Prosser, M., Trigwell, K.: Understanding Learning and Teaching: The Experience in Higher Education. Society for Research in Higher Education and/Open University Press, Buckingham (1999)
34. Russell, S., Norvig, P.: Artificial Intelligence: A Modern Approach. Pearson, Upper Saddle River (2010). 3rd (international) edn

35. Russell, S., Norvig, P.: Artificial Intelligence: A Modern Approach: Pearson New, 3rd edn. Pearson, Upper Saddle River (2013)
36. Schaathun, W.A., Schaathun, H.G., Bye, R.T.: Aktiv læring i mikrokontrollarar. Uniped **38**, 381–389 (2015). Special issue following MNT-konferansen, Bergen, Norway, 18–19 March 2015
37. Schaathun, H.G., Schaathun, W.A.: Learning mathematics through classroom interaction. In: The 18th SEFI Mathematics Working Group seminar on Mathematics in Engineering Education, pp. 155–161 (2016)
38. Schroeder, C., Scott, T.P., Tolson, H., Huang, T.Y., Lee, Y.H.: A meta-analysis of national research: effects of teaching strategies on student achievement in science in the United States. J. Res. Sci. Teach. **44**(10), 1436–1460 (2007)
39. Sotto, E.: When Teaching Becomes Learning: A Theory and Practice of Teaching. Bloomsbury Publishing, London (2007)
40. Springer, L., Stanne, M., Donovan, S.: Effects of small-group learning on undergraduates in science, mathematics, engineering and technology: a meta-analysis. Rev. Educ. Res. **69**(1), 21–52 (1999)
41. Topping, K., Ehly, S.: Peer-Assisted Learning. Routledge, Abingdon (1998)
42. Topping, K.J.: The effectiveness of peer tutoring in further and higher education: a typology and review of the literature. High. Educ. **32**(3), 321–345 (1996)
43. Vygotsky, L.: Mind in Society. Harvard University Press, London (1978)

Learning/Teaching Methodologies and Assessment

Computer Science in Online Gaming Communities

Lassi Haaranen(✉) and Rodrigo Duran

Department of Computer Science, Aalto University, Helsinki, Finland
{lassi.haaranen,rodrigo.duran}@aalto.fi

Abstract. The culture of playing video games has evolved rapidly in the past decade. Presently, there are many different types of online communities that have games or a particular game as their focus. Some games, in particular, can be used as a platform for introducing and discussing computer science concepts. We wanted to investigate how these online gaming communities and computer science are intertwined. We approached this by gathering user interaction data in two previous studies from which this article presents a more comprehensive synthesis. We found that the online gaming communities have rich interactions that relate to programming and computer science. Based on the qualitative analysis, we categorized these interactions in three themes: learning, programming experience, and community. In addition to the interaction analysis, we present four perspectives that we found particularly useful in analyzing these online communities: engagement, interactivity, exposure, and technical detail. We conclude that these communities and interactions within them can act as a form of outreach. Furthermore, they act as places where newcomers meet with more experienced programmers.

Keywords: Computer science education · Online communities
Informal learning · Collaborative learning · Game-based learning

1 Introduction

Within the past few years, the interest in computer science education has risen rapidly. One very visible and hotly debated side-effect of this is the one of whether computing education (computational thinking, algorithmic thinking, 21st-century skills, or other often used but rarely defined terms) should be something that is taught for all. And if so, how early should the education start. In some countries, such as Finland [3], this has lead to the inclusion of computer science topics being part of the official curriculum in elementary schools. In other parts of the world, this has lead organizations offering support in learning computer science and programming online, http://code.org perhaps being the best-known example.

However, in this article, we want to take a different perspective on computer science outreach and teaching programming by looking at what is happening

P. Escudeiro et al. (Eds.): CSEDU 2017, CCIS 865, pp. 279–299, 2018.
https://doi.org/10.1007/978-3-319-94640-5_14

outside of formal education and organizations facilitating outreach. We do this by looking at online gaming communities, places online where people come together to share their passion for playing games. In some cases these communities act as an informal outreach program and as a place to share programming knowledge, and more importantly, enthusiasm.

The reason why games and attracting new students to computer science is a particularly interesting topic to investigate is the fact that there's some prior tentative evidence that links playing games at an early age to interest in pursuing a degree in a related field [9]. We have also come to understand, that the computing education research community at large might not be aware of the various phenomenon that relates to gaming communities and learning to program. Due to this, we feel that this particular area has been lacking and this article seeks to remedy that as well.

In the past decade, playing games and gaming communities have risen to an all time high in popularity. This has reached the point where games and gaming is a massive cultural phenomenon. For instance, the revenue of gaming industry in 2013 was double the revenue of the film industry in that year [12]. It should be noted though, that the average age of people who play games has been steadily rising and it is most definitely not just a pastime for children, as perhaps some still view it to be. For example, industry research suggests that in the United States the average gamer is 35 years old [2]. The same report also noted, that in 65 per cent of households in the U.S. have at least one person that plays games for three or more hours per week.

This present research is a synthesis of two earlier studies on online gaming communities and how they are relevant in the context of learning computer science and programming. The first one of the previous studies is related to the gaming communities on YouTube in videos that feature games mixing computer science in some way. The other one previous study looked into the phenomena of live-streaming, having a person play a game or program, in front of a live audience sharing his or hers desktop as a video stream while providing live commentary to explain the process and entertain the community that is watching. The earlier studies are detailed more in the Sects. 3.1 and 3.2.

The overall goal of this research is twofold. Firstly, we wish to introduce these online gaming communities to the general computer science education research community, in the hopes that our work provides a spark for further investigation to this phenomenon, hopefully benefitting outreach activities in the future. The second, and more defined, goal of this research is to provide an insight into the interactions of users in these gaming communities that relate to computer science and programming. We approached this through analyzing chat logs and comments to videos that were originally gathered during the two previous studies. By looking at these two separate data sets as one combined data set we aim to provide a more robust and useful synthesis of the types of interactions that users have in these contexts.

The rest of this article is structured as follows. Next, in Sect. 2, we give background on how computer science and games are intertwined, especially focusing on the online gaming communities and how programming content is relevant to them. Then, in Sect. 3, we detail the parts of previous studies that are relevant to this article. In Sect. 4.2, we explain the methods used in this research. In the following Sect. 5, we go through the salient themes found in the interactions in these online gaming communities. In Sect. 6, we discuss our findings and provide a set of perspectives on online communities that might be relevant to further research. Finally, in Sect. 7, we conclude our work and discuss possible future directions for research.

2 Background

This section firstly gives a brief overview on how games and computer science are intertwined, then we focus on previous research conducted on online communities and learning. We also introduce different types of online communities that relate to playing video games and provide a categorization of various ways in which people watch other people play video games. We also explain how that is relevant to the current research.

2.1 Mixing Games and Computer Science

Programming and computer science can enrich playing games in various ways. Obvious examples of this are games where programming is one of the main activities within the game, like, for example, in Lightbot (https://lightbot.com/) where the player solves puzzles by programming a robot. However, there are other approaches to combining games and programming. In some games programming *supports gameplay* by allowing players to perform certain activities, such as controlling a character through programming, essentially automating an aspect of play that would be cumbersome, difficult, or tedious to do by the player herself. An example of this would be to use the macro commands available in the popoular massively multiplayer online role-playing game World of Warcraft to automate certain actions when particular conditions are met.

One other way that programming and games are typically intertwined is the culture and practice of modifying or modding a game. This typically happens through an API (Application Programming Interface) where the developer of a mod can access game data and state to create new and compelling experiences. A concrete example of this would be the kOS add-on for the game Kerbal Space Program (KSP). The main gameplay of KSP revolves around building spaceships and exploring a solar system that exists in the game. Once built, the spaceships are controlled manually. The kOS add-on implements a customized programming language for the game, making it possible for the players to write small programs to control their spaceships and automate various tasks (such as landing) in the game.

When it comes to formal education and computer science courses, four ways of utilizing computer games as part of the learning process has been described [17]. In the first approach, students create their own games in order to learn. Relatedly, in the second approach, they implement a critical part of a given game. In the third approach, students learn by implementing an agent to a game. This group is of particular interest given that this can be done in many of the current games meant for entertainment. In the last category, students learn by playing a serious game that has been designed to teach particular concepts.

2.2 Online Communities for Playing and Learning

As the popularity of playing games as a pastime has risen, watching other people play games has also become a popular activity as well. The following sections detail different motivations and reasons for watching other people play. With different reasons for watching other people play, there are also different forms of this media. While the distinctions are not always completely clear, we have identified three general categories of watching other people play digital games: let's plays, streaming, and esports.

Esports, playing digital games competitively and professionally, is an interesting and hugely popular category of watching people play. However, it is also the only category that has very little relevance to learning computer science or programming through games. Typically, games that are played competitively require a high level of mechanical and tactical skills in real time (e.g. League of Legends, Overwatch, etc.) as opposed to games which encourage building, creativity, and open 'sandbox' type games.

Youtube, Games, and Communities of Learning. *Let's plays* are a form content where one person records playing a game while narrating the events of the game at the same time. These recordings are typically split up into episodes and uploaded into popular video platforms such as YouTube. Some Let's Players focus on a particular game (e.g. Minecraft) or genre of games (e.g. strategy games) and others record and narrate a variety of games from different genres. Arguably the best known of these online personalities is Felix 'PewDiePie' Kjellberg, reaching an audience of 50 million subscribers in late 2016 (https://www.youtube.com/watch?v=7Vj5M0qKh8g).

Chau [1] noted that YouTube has a particularly low barrier to entry, consume and produce videos. He also categorized videos and one of the main categories was 'informal mentorship', manifested in the form of 'how-to' videos. Participating on these video platforms is inherently collaborative since videos can be added, commented upon, and spread easily in peer-groups.

Thus far, there has been little research on learning and YouTube videos, especially when it comes to computer science and learning to program. However, in the domain of medicine, Topps et al. studied releasing clinical training videos on YouTube instead of peer-reviewed services [16]. The number of views that their instructional videos gathered increased, but, as they point out, it is hard to assess what is the educational impact compared to previous services they used.

There is an overall culture of creating and sharing tutorial videos on YouTube focusing on wide range of topics. Perhaps due to the technical savviness of the creators, topics relating to computer science and programming are well represented in YouTube tutorials. Some research has also been conducted that look specifically into the programming tutorials on YouTube. For instance, Poché et al. [14] looked at how machine learning could be utilized in summarizing the comments that users left on tutorial videos. The goal of their work is that content creators (those who create and upload programming tutorials) could respond to feedback from their viewers faster and with less effort [14].

Live-Streaming Playing and Programming. Live-streaming video, or just streaming, is the act of playing a game whilst narrating the events live and interacting with the audience. The host of the stream, also known as a 'streamer', often has a webcam feed of his or her face to facilitate interactions with the audience. The members of the audience can either just watch the stream passively or participate in the stream via real-time discussion. Within the past years, streaming has become enormously popular.

Perhaps the best known and most popular service to facilitate streaming is Twitch.tv (http://twitch.tv). It first gained a great deal of media and audience attention during early 2014 with a stream called "Twitch Play Pokemon". In the streams, the participants were able to send commands and thus collaboratively control a game of Pokemon Red. It attracted 55 million viewers and 1.6 million participants [18]. Popular streams hosted by popular streamers on Twitch.tv typically reach audiences in tens of thousands and in 2015 Twitch.tv reported having 550,000 concurrent viewers (https://www.twitch.tv/year/2015). Earlier on Twitch.tv had focused solely on hosting streamers that stream gameplay. However, in 2015 they launched a new initiative called Twitch Creative (https://blog.twitch.tv/introducing-twitch-creative-fbfe23b4a114) which allows streams with creative content such as, for example, painting or programming.

Hamilton et al. [7] looked at live streams and the communities they form. They approached the streaming communities through Oldenburg [13] notions of third place. By third place, Oldenburg refers to *"public places that host the regular, voluntary, informal, and happily anticipated gatherings of individuals beyond the realms of home and work"*. The emphasized activity in a third place is the conversation. It happens in a live streaming in two distinct ways: the streamer interacts with the viewers (and they can interact back with the streamer) and the community of viewers have conversations amongst themselves. In these third places resides *regulars*, people who have visited that place often enough and participated in conversations long enough. They have a significant impact on the tone and style of conversations that occur, and, importantly, they also welcome and encourage the newcomers to the place, after all, they once were newcomers themselves.

Sjöblom and Hamari [15] investigated the motivations behind the act of watching other people play and participating in online communities on the Twitch.tv service. They employed the uses and gratifications theory and its five types of motivations: cognitive, affective, personal integrative, social integrative, tension release, and information seeking. Of these motivations, they found that tension release had the strongest effect on the number of hours watched. They also found that the information seeking was positively associated with the hours watched as well as on the choice in which streamer was watched.

Streams with programming and game development are particularly popular during Ludum Dare events. Ludum Dare is a game development competition where the participants have 48 h to develop a game to a particular theme that is announced at the start of the competition. Many of the participants choose to stream the process of creating their game on Twitch, e.g. Notch (the creator of Minecraft) has streamed his participation to Ludum Dare 22[1] in 2011.

Hamilton et al. [7] also reflected streaming through McLuhan's model [11] of hot and cool media. By hot media McLuhan refers to print, radio, movies etc. the idea being that they 'high definition', in other words, rich in sensory data. The opposite of this, cool media such as comics, writing letters, phone calls, etc. The key distinction being that cool media requires more participation whereas hot media fills the sense more fully and can be consumed more passively. YouTube videos with the comment section as well as live streams with real-time chat offer an interesting combination of the both. On one hand, it is completely possible to passively watch the streams or videos and only consume the available media. On the other hand, it is also possible to participate in the community more actively by either posting comments and thus participating in the discourse or by participating in the real-time discussions during the streams.

3 Previous Studies

This research is based on two earlier studies that looked at similar but distinct online gaming communities and how they relate to computer science and programming. Both of the data sets from the previous studies were analyzed together in this study to provide a more comprehensive picture of the phenomenon.

The first study [6], later referred to as `PS1`, focused on gaming videos on YouTube that featured programming in some way. Additionally, it focused on the discussions that viewers were having in the comment section.

The second study [5], `PS2`, was similarly looking at how a gaming related online community discussed programming and computer science, but in this case, the studied community was gathered around a live streamer who participated in Ludum Dare 37 rapid game development competition.

The following Sects. 3.1 (`PS1`) and 3.2 (`PS2`) describe these studies briefly, focusing on the data collection and the data sets that were used in this research. For a more detailed discussion on the topics, please refer to the original publications.

[1] Recording of the stream is available online at https://www.twitch.tv/videos/38122415.

3.1 PS1: YouTube Gaming Communities and Programming in Games

The first study [6] looked at the programming content available on the popular video sharing service YouTube. Two different data sets were collected for this study:

- A list of first 400 video titles found from https://gaming.youtube.com with the search term 'programming'. This section of Youtube is dedicated to content related to games, with the majority of content being let's play videos.
- Two of the videos in the previous list were selected for closer analysis. We downloaded comments related to these videos. This data set is comprised of 700 comments left to the videos (350 to each).

The first data set was used to investigate the different types of gaming videos that are related to programming. This data set is not used in this particular research but its purpose and main results are briefly introduced for completeness sake. We wrote a script that would fetch the first 400 video titles from a YouTube video search. Since we were interested in the videos that were aimed at the gaming community at large, we conducted a search with term 'programming' on YouTube's gaming section (https://gaming.youtube.com). We did not modify any of the default search parameters and selected the videos in the order of the appearance. Since the ranking algorithm on YouTube searches is unknown it is not possible to tell why the videos were ranked in the way that they were.

Five categories of gaming and programming related videos emerged from our grounded theory data analysis. The categories were: Games enhanced by programming, Game programming tutorial, Modding tutorials, Game programming discussion, and Other. Both authors classified the video titles independently using these categories. After individual coding agreement between coders was tested (Cohen's $\kappa = 0.619$) and disagreements were resolved through discussions. The results are briefly summarized in Table 1.

Table 1. The distribution of different types of gaming videos that relate to programming.

Category	#	%
Games enhanced by programming	38	9.50
Game programming tutorial	242	60.50
Modding tutorials	7	1.75
Game programming discussion	56	14.00
Other	57	14.25

The first category of 'games enhanced by programming' refers to games meant primarily for entertainment that features programming in some way, for example, where there is an API in the game through which the player is able to interact with the game world. From this category, we selected two videos for closer inspection. We selected these two based on the fact that they represented very different approaches to incorporating programming into games as well as the game in question is different. Again, we wrote a script that fetched us the first 350 comments for each video in the order that they appeared on the web page. The data set obtained from extracted comments served as one element for analysis in the combined analysis performed in the present study.

`[V1]`: **"BASIC Programming Language in Minecraft".** Is the first video and it features the author of the video describing how he built an interpreter for a BASIC language inside the game Minecraft. The video also includes a demonstration how this can be used to automate tasks within the game world by providing a small program in BASIC to an agent in the game world that then can execute commands. As of July 2017, the video has garnered close to 700,000 views, it has a running time of 13 min and 45 s and is available from the URL: https://www.youtube.com/watch?v=t4e7PjRygt0.

`[V2]`: **"Programming Rockets in Kerbal Space Program".** Is the second video and it features a game called Kerbal Space Program (KSP) and an add-on (a piece of user-created content for the game) called kOS. The main gameplay of KSP involves building rocket ships from available parts, launching those rockets, and exploring the fictional solar system in the game. The kOS add-on allows the player to write programs with an event based language created specifically for it with the purpose of controlling the space ships programmatically. Presently (July 2017), the video has 140,000 views, with duration of 8 min and 11 s, and it is available from the url https://www.youtube.com/watch?v=FPDPzsnlHOI.

Based on these two sets of comments we used a grounded theory approach to find themes that emerged from the data. We identified three main themes: programming languages, learning experience, and efficiency. These and the categories presented in the other previous study in the next section served as a basis for this research where we were interested in the commonalities and differences in the discussions.

3.2 PS2: Live-streaming Programming and Chat Communities

This study was concerned with live-streaming programming during a game programming competition held over a weekend [5]. The data set collected was chat log of about 200 people who participated in the conversation during three separe streams (lasting approximately 6, 12, and 14 h). The conversations were happening in a streamer's chat while the streamer was building a game for the competition during the weekend. Later on, the comments from this data set are marked with `[S1]`.

This data set comprised of approximately 39,000 comments. In the original research, these were filtered down to about 1300 comments by keywords that were selected based on the data. These comments were then analyzed and grouped based on themes emerging from the data. In this case, the emerged categories were: interest in programming, interaction with the streamer, questions and answers, and general computer science discussion. As with the study regarding YouTube and gaming communities in the previous section, these categories formed the initial basis for the current research.

4 Methods

In this section, we first briefly introduce the methodology of grounded theory in researching a new phenomenon. Then we describe how grounded theory was utilized in the current research based on the combined data sets that were gathered previously.

4.1 Grounded Theory in Computer Science Education Research

To provide meaningful descriptions of the textual data we gathered, the comments on YouTube videos and the discussion during the live stream, we adopted a grounded theory based approach. Grounded theory has roots in social sciences where it is commonly used to investigate new phenomena, and in this respect, it is a particularly well-suited approach for our purposes [4]. Kinnunen and Simon have written on the usage of grounded theory specifically from computer science education research perspective [8].

The process of grounded theory approach starts with an open coding of the data, where the researchers label the data with codes. Axial coding follows the initial open coding, where the codes are abstracted into groups and categories, extracting themes and emerging concepts of interest. These abstracted themes from the data are utilized in descriptive research, such as this one. After the analysis of the data grounded theory can also be utilized in hypothesis generations and suggesting preliminary models. In the current research, we did not proceed to do this but we aim to do so in future.

4.2 Analysis

The comment's data set from `PS1` was used in its original form. However, we refined our approach regarding the data set from `PS2`. Since the original sample consisted of 38694 user interactions on the IRC channel, we filtered the data using a set of defined keywords. The keywords were defined using an iterative process, first skimming through the original data set and selecting keywords related to programming languages, computer science concepts or topics of interest in the context of the stream. We added more keywords on every refinement step and compared the original data set with the filtered one until a saturation point was reached.

The final iteration of keywords consists of: program, debug, project, bug, code, coding, c#, c++, unity, javascript, python, loop, variable, function, recursi, implement, haskell, computer science, java, develop, experience, language, and class. It resulted in a 2079 comment data set. In some cases, stemming the keywords was used in order to increase the likelihood of relevant matches.

The authors carefully read the filtered data set and selected the most relevant comments, resulting in the final data set of 365 user interactions. Based on this data set, the authors performed separately the initial coding of the comments and later refined the codes through discussions. An axial coding was finally performed to list the emerged categories.

Since the categories coded in `PS1` and `PS2`, were slightly different from the categories that emerged from the current combined data set analysis, another iteration on coding was performed to extend and improve wording in order to accommodate codes from both analyses. The results of the analysis done on the combined data set is presented next, in Sect. 5.

5 Computer Science Discussions in Online Gaming Communities

On the previous studies `PS1` and `PS2` we analyzed the content and categorization of comments in online gaming communities. Each one of these studies followed a similar methodology and resulted in distinct but related categories. We reanalyzed the data from `[V1]`, `[V2]` and `[S1]` (see Sects. 3.1 and 3.2) to describe similarities and discrepancies between the online communities. It was possible to identify many different emergent themes related to computer science and programming with different levels of complexity and richness in the combined dataset. Looking at the interaction data regarding programming and computer science as a whole, we identified three main themes: **learning**, **programming experiences**, and **community**.

To illustrate the themes and categories, we present in the following sections some comments to exemplify the interactions and topics most relevant the discussion on the combined data set. Most of the selected comments came from `[S1]` since comments from that were more illustrative of the themes.

5.1 Learning

YouTube and Twitch are platforms with a large variety om content as well as audience. So, it is not surprising that some participants in the discussion were attracted to computer science and programming topics but had no previous experience in them. As such, learning was a dominant theme for them. The themes related to learning identified were: *desire to learn, poor self-efficacy, game development, resources to learn, what languages should I learn first?*, and *learning experiences.*

Desire to Learn was a sentiment that many participants expressed. It was possible to observe a very recurring theme in programming: the perceived complexity in learning and the rewards in doing so. Most users found the content both attractive and frightening *"I keep telling myself I want to learn programming. Watching this both inspires me and terrifies me"* `[S1]`, *"Now I feel stupid... This* *is insane!:D Wow"* [V1], and, in general, it was possible to observe that the positive perspective of learning to program surpasses the negative bias. Comments like: *"I am not a programmer, but I find it really interesting:D"* [S1], were more frequent in the discussions.

Poor Self-efficacy was less prevalent but was also expressed in comments like *"programming seems totally impossible to me"* [S1]. Sometimes feeling engaged and willing to learn is not enough, as illustrated by *"Meanwhile I'm 15 and I've tried to learn programming so many times with no success :/"* [S1], which was also present when self-directed learning methods were used *"The problem I'm having when programming is finding projects that fit my skill level, either I make them too easy or things come to a grinding halt"* [S1]. Some discussions show that not only young students express a desire to learn and face difficulties when doing it, but also older users as well *"I kind of wish I had learned to program and/or 3d model when I was younger. At 42 I've kinda lost the patience to learn it, though."* [S1].

Game Development as a context for programming might explain some of the interest in computer science and learning to code. As such, it could be a strong factor of attraction for younger students, as exemplified in *"[@user] ME TOO!! i was ±10 in that time, that's the reason i started coding... (and minecraft was the reason too but...)"* [S1], *"I pretty much got interested in programming because I wanted to make games. It ties the programming into something I'm interested in."* [S1], *"at least python is becoming more popular with the kids playing minecraft:)"* [S1] and *"Could try learning to mod the game; modding can range from needing almost no programming experience to advance programming, depending on how far you take it"* [V1].

Resources to Learn was a topic where many users sought advice. For example, a common question was about the best places to start learning to program *"I'm considering finally trying to learn programming languages and I have a slight question: would you recommend learning from internet courses, books or just wait until I could get into CS school?"* [S1]. Many times, especially during [S1], we observed the community providing answers to questions like these, such as *"You can watch video tutorials though this is the hardest way to learn programming"* [S1]).

What Languages Should I Learn First? was a really recurring theme during the discussions: *"Guys what to learn first: C# or Java?"* [S1]. Java, Python, and C# were the most cited ones *"I really like Python, but perhaps that's because it's easy. I kinda feel almost scummy using Python xD"* [S1], *"C# is an easy language to learn, you can pick up the important details in a few hours"* [S1]. Since the author was using a particular engine in C#, it is no surprise that it was also emphasized in the answers. Python, on the other hand, seems strongly identified with a "learning language".

Learning Experiences provided by more experienced users presented a different perspective on learning. Some users commented on the materials and methods used in learning to program *"[@user] I'm in high school and the closest thing to a coding class there is HTML which is just watching an online youtube course. Luckily I'm in PSEO so i can do coding there"* [S1]. Some participants had background in formal computer science education and commented on their studies, e.g. *"I'm doing CompSci at my university but I've been having a tough time dealing with depression and my workload simultaneously, but I know it's what I want to do so I've just got to stick it out and if need be retake a couple classes here and there"* [S1]. Other users presented their own opinion on how easy to learn a language is compared to another: *"C# is similar to Java, but easier in my mind."* [S1], *"I feel learning C++ first is a bad idea..."* [S1].

Given the anonymity provided by the platforms, it was very hard to extract any information or profile from the users. However, some of them claimed to very young and put a very strong opinion on how important it was to learn to program early *"im 13 and learning c# and uss unity and blender so I'm starting young but think I may be able to make it... and even better I find coding fun XD"* [S1]. Many schools and organizations are introducing programming to elementary or high school students, as was evident with comments like *"I can't program for **** but does scratch count?"* [S1] shows that some tools still lack authenticity in this audience perspective, or may be suited only to professionals *"Well, the main reason it was hard for me to get into programming was because the IDE was made for more experienced people and was packed with features"* [S1].

5.2 Programming Experience

In general, the learning theme was discussed by inexperienced users. More experienced users discussed topics related to their programming experience in more specific and technical details, such as *programming languages and paradigms, efficiency, debugging, and professional career.*

Programming Languages and Paradigms covered a broad range of topics. Some users discussed the application of some programming languages: *"[@user] you learn one, you know basically the other. C# has more application in gaming, Java in Apps, practically speaking"* [S1], *"pythons is great for machine learning"* [S1], and *"I just love the idea of kOS, and would gladly spend humongous amount of time playing with it...but, I also hate the programming language itself. It would be so awesome to see something like kOS which is using JavaScript/Python/Ruby/C# .. or any sensible programming language out there (thus object orientation would probably be very useful feature"* [V2].

In a lesser extent this discussion also involved preferred paradigms: *"I don't mind c# I'm just not a fan of object orientated programming"* [S1], *"OOP has uses for sure, I just would rather do procedural programming"* [S1] but this was less common.

Some topics of the discussion were more deep and advanced, for example *"[Streamer] A really really dumb question, but do you know how to keep an idle thread alive? ...”* [S1] and *“[user] I'm not sure exactly why you need this, but if you want to keep threads idle so they can quickly be reused consider using a ThreadPool if you are using c#”* [S1]. Code quality and readability aspects of coding were also a relevant and a recurrent topic in the discussion *“is there a reason his if - conditions are always verbose? (“== false” instead of ! isPlaying for example) is that a c# thing?”* [S1] and *“[user] He covers the boolean explicit thing in one of the videos, can be easy to miss the ! for false so explicit == true/false makes it human readable for no extra effort (and no difference to compiler down to machine code)”* [S1].

As one of the most cited and popular languages, Python had mixed opinions. For example, some users believed that Python is simple and suited for learning *“Python is a great introduction to programming I've found :)”* [S1], *“python is really good, lite and practical”* [S1], *“Yeah, a C or Python (maybe even Lua) version would have been nicer, but basic isn't hard to learn, it is very basic”* [V2], while others don't see Python as really authentic *“python is goofy, not sure how much I like it”* [S1] and *“I love Python as a ‘scrapbook’ language. When I just want to mess around with stuff or do maths that's a little more than my calculator is meant for.”* [S1]. Python's use of indentation for defining code blocks also received comments, *“Whenever I try to Python, I get about 80 errors from whitespacing wrong”* [S1].

Efficiency and optimization seemed to be one reason why some users disliked Python. Some users believe that true efficiency can only be achieved using very specific languages: *“C/C++ is the language you use if you are writing something that needs to be hardcore min/maxed or has never been done before”* [S1]. The efficiency theme itself was very present in the discussion, with some users discussing the pros and cons of automatic memory management *“[@user] imo the garbage collection is the very reason I wouldn't recommend it. If you can learn to code without it, your code will always naturally be more efficient”* [S1] and *“[user] Yes, even without 3rd party libraries like Qt or boost there are smart pointers built into the standard library since C++11 (and they are getting improvements every iteration). You decide the scope of your object (basically unique or shared) and its deleted when no longer referenced.”* [S1].

Others users discussed optimization techniques in algorithms: *“Instead of X-1 wouldn't 1/2 X be a better cutoff point for finding primes? (Since no number can be evenly divided by a number greater than 1/2 itself? That would save some cycles, especially as the numbers get higher”* [V1] and *“Yeah, computing the square root of something is usually ‘expensive’, but dividing by two is usually cheap. It'd be an easy optimization”* [V1].

Debugging was a theme only present in [S1], since the online interaction nature of the media allowed users to help the streamer to debug the application in real-time. Some aid came as simple reminders *“[@streamer] you need to assign the variable!”* [S1] or improving code structures *“ChangeValue() should be implemented as SetValue(name, GetValue(name)+val);” [S1]* and *“[streamer]* *using GetComponent() in your update loop is "bad", you should set a variable to the component in start instead and use that"* *[S1]*. Towards the end of the contest, users were presented with the source code and encouraged to help the streamer to find bugs in the game. Typically debugging is viewed as a difficult and tedious subject in formal education, but surprisingly there were positive comments about the topic, such as *"debugging is fun!"* `[S1]`.

Professional Career was a theme shared mostly by students doing undergraduate courses in computer science and professionals. Since the streamer itself is seen as a successful professional (also see the discussion related to streamer being a role model in the next Section), some questions were directed to him *"Hey [@streamer], this is pretty random, and unrelated to the stream but I just wanted to hear your thoughts on this, so I'm in my second year of Uni studying Computer Science, and I've decided to take a leave of absence and build on a portfolio instead"* `[S1]`, while others sought advice from professional users in the community about further job opportunities *"i'm also almost done with CS degree and found a lot of companies don't care if i have it or not they just want to see me be able to code"* `[S1]`.

5.3 Community

One of the key elements, especially pronounced in `[S1]`, was the strong sense of community and the presence of regulars. This interaction between inexperienced and experienced users made possible to not only discuss more complicated topics but also defined the community itself. The interactions were also present in the previous themes, but this theme specifically focuses on the strong sense of common place and a helpful and friendly environment, which is aligned with the third place definition of [13]. Since the streamer itself is a very important focal point of the community, the interaction between users and streamer helped to shape and define this relationship. In general, we identified the themes under the community category as: *encouraging to learn* and *author as a role model.*

Encouraging to Learn was a visible characteristic of the `[S1]` community. Rather than being a forum for just the experts, more experienced users embraced beginners and newcomers and, as presented in the previous sections, promptly helped and gave advice. This supportive attitude from users can be exemplified when a user commented *"I have zero experience programming but this is always fun to watch. Keep up the great work [streamer]:)"* `[S1]`, he promptly got replies like *"[@user] - Programming is one of the most rewarding things in my life. If you're enjoying this stream, you should try to dabble in the basics. I think you'll like that as well."* `[S1]`. On another moment, a user posted: *"Wish I knew programming. I think doing this even would be something fun."* `[S1]`, which was followed by many users supporting him, like in *"It's never too late to start, check out some basic Python tutorials, and you're going in a matter of minutes."* `[S1]`. Similarly, when a user showed poor self-efficacy *"Sorry. I have no idea about* *coding. And seeing [streamer] I think I never would understand it. I think it great but don't think I can ever do it"* [S1], the community replied *"[@user] nonsense, just takes time. You go do it"* [S1].

Author as a Role Model in the community's perspective shows that in some ways the engagement and attraction of the content are not only related to the topic but also to the author's persona. One of the themes in the discussion is how the author is often pictured as a wise expert *"I wish I were as good at programming as [streamer]"* [S1], but mostly his role is described as a motivator that presents the content in an alternative and more engaging format *"Your vids [videos on YouTube] helped me a lot with basic programming. Thanks man"* [S1], *"[streamer] thanks for getting me to enjoy programming again:)"* [S1]. Some users expressed their enjoyment in watching content specific videos from the streamer, illustrating that it can be a good source of technical information as well *"Hey [streamer], I really enjoyed watching your hell wars game from ludum dare 33, I learned a lot about c# delegates through it."* [S1] and *"[streamer] Your FPS Multiplayer tutorial was the one that opened the door to Unity3d programming for me. If I didn't find your channel I most likely would have never got into unity and the dev world. So thank you!!:)"* [S1].

Author's background attracted interest as well, mostly given the role model nature of the author. The majority of the users were interested in his education *"does [streamer] have a background in computer science?"* [S1] and what led him to develop games and work as a streamer of programming content *"[streamer] why you decided to be a game designer?"* [S1].

6 Discussion

In this section, we take a broader look at our findings and situate it to the context of formal education and outreach activities. We also introduce four perspectives that we devised and found particularly useful while discussing the interactions in the communities and these forms of media. Finally, we consider some of the limitations present in this research.

6.1 Relevance to Formal Education and Outreach

Since complete beginners who were interested in programming were present in [V1], [V2], and [S1], it is reasonable then to wonder if there actually were any learning gains. Based on the data we gathered it is hard to say what, if any, learning outcomes there might be from participating in these online communities. However, where the videos and streams seemed to be effective, based on the comments, was in introducing newcomers to programming and getting them interested in computer science and programming. Examples of this can be found in Sect. 5.1 "Desire to learn" as well as many participants in [S1] asking which programming language they should learn as their first one.

Particularly with [S1], it is also a factor that the community does include regulars who know how to program and some of whom are professionals in the software industry. They provide guidance to the newcomers with their perspectives on learning how to program, and perhaps more importantly, encourage newcomers and other members to go forward with their interest in programming. Also, the ability to watch someone working on a non-trivial project throughout the weekend offers a perspective on the world of software development that might otherwise be difficult to acquire to those not yet familiar with the field.

What is common to all [V1], [V2], and [S1] was the fact that many people were watching them because of the games involved in them or that they were already watching other content created by the same author. We suspect that this might have an impact on attracting future students to computer science since the context (e.g. the particular game featured) in which programming and computer science is discussed is already engaging to the viewers.

While [V1] and [V2] might work better in introducing new and interesting concepts from computer science to a wider audience, [S1] can function almost as a lecture. There is one central figure explaining the process and what is currently happening. And at the same time, the audience is free to talk with each other and ask the streamer questions without disturbing anyone else, something that would not be possible during a traditional lecture. Another key difference is, that unlike a professor in a lecture hall, the streamer is also an entertainer. Most of the popular streamers are doing it as their main source of income, which is heavily dependent on how many viewers they have and how the audience perceives the stream generally.

Overall, we can not make any claims regarding the actual learning outcomes from participating in these types of communities, though there is some indication for that. However, when it comes to exposure and getting people interested in computer science, we are more confident that for some individuals these types of media and communities might be quite significant. Even though it was not explored in this work, we feel that there is also plenty of unexplored potential in using these types of videos and streams within the context of formal education. And perhaps more importantly, using this type of media in planned outreach activities.

6.2 Perspectives on Online Gaming Communities and Computer Science Content in Them

Our investigation on Twitch streams and YouTube videos allowed us to better understand the nature of the relationships and interactions of users in these online communities. Although, most of the themes presented in Sect. 5 are relevant to both of them, some characteristics were more pronounced in the [S1] compared to [V1] and [V2]. In order to investigate the key elements that make these communities different, we used four dimensions that were useful in analyzing these differences using distinct forms of media. The perspectives we found most salient were: *engagement, interactivity, exposure*, and *technical detail.* We believe these to be of interest to CS researchers and that they can be useful in understanding the phenomena and how these platforms can be used to present programming concepts and introduce people to computer science. Next, we present in more detail these perspectives and discuss our views on them.

Engagement was more pronouncedly observed in [S1]. The topic itself was engaging for the participants in both videos, providing a mix of games and programming, themes that clearly attracted the audience. However, in [S1] the real-time interaction made participants immersed in the process, as illustrated in the debugging discussions. We see that this is connected to the ideas of situated learning and legitimate peripheral participation [10]. In [S1] some of the participants were actively contributing to the end product in a non-trivial and meaningful way through debugging and making helpful suggestions regarding the code. This type of participation was less evident in [V1] and [V2] since the final product had already been done and the engagement seemed to be more connected with the game and to the author of the video.

Interactivity was naturally affected by the platform design. While both platforms use a high fidelity (hot) media with videos, [S1] also offered a real-time chat that acted as a cool media for participants to have richer interactions. These characteristics had an impact on the relationships among the participants. The sense of community was more visible in [S1], the familiarity of the streamer and the real-time chat acted as a third place in Oldenburg's terminology [13] where regulars could be identified. These regulars not only acted as hubs of information about the streamer, the project, and general programming expertise but also welcomed and helped newcomers. Another important difference regarding interactivity was the asynchronous nature of [V1] and [V2] versus the real-time nature of [S1]. This characteristic seemed to also have an impact in how the community environment emerges and how it defines the relationship between from users to users, as well as, between the community and the streamer.

Exposure is the term we use to describe the potential reach of the platform as well as the diversity of the audience. The [V1] and [V2] videos have the potential to be viewed by more people due to the popularity of the platform and the particular games featured in the videos. Since the authors of [V1] and [V2] also create Let's Play videos, they end up attracting users to their programming videos as a byproduct. Due to the real-time nature of [S1], its exposure tends to be related to users knowing when the event will happen.

Technical Detail can be described as how deep the subject is discussed in the online community and it is intrinsically related to the target audience and content of the videos. The nature of the videos (games with programming versus game development) can be presented as one of the explanations for the differences in the audience that led to differences in technical details. For example, in the YouTube videos, even when discussing a topic that would mainly interest programmers (like compilers in [V1]), the level of the discussion is not intended as a guide on how to implement the presented feature, but rather to discuss it on a very general level. On [S1], the level of technical detail in the discussion is deeper with some coding details and advanced programming features. The community, in general, is heterogeneous, so experienced users and beginners are interacting within the same space allowing for a wider variance in complexity in the discussions.

Even though the applied methodology and the data itself don't allow us to make strong claims about the nature and profile of the people discussing in the comments and in the real-time chat, it was interesting to observe the interactions, such as the newcomers who got interested in programming because of games and experienced users encouraging them to learn to program.

6.3 Limitations

We sought to provide a comprehensive description of the computer science discussion happening in the online gaming communities. However, the context and users in these communities could not be investigated in detail. Given the anonymous and informal nature of the platforms, we can not verify the provided information about the users or if they are in fact expressing themselves truthfully.

The selection of these particular videos could also have an impact in the type of comments and topics discussed, impacting the ability to generalize from these results. However, this has a limited impact on the results, since our main goal was to provide an insight into the phenomena and show its existence to the research community. We acknowledge that the present study is only a starting point and further research is required to comprehend the phenomena.

7 Conclusions

We looked at two different types of online gaming communities and how they relate to learning computer science and programming. One of the investigated communities was formed around a particular live-streamer and streams over a weekend where he participated in a rapid game development competition ([S1]. The community interacted with the streamer and with each other through a real-time chat. The other type of community we looked at are the ones formed in YouTube's comment section on videos where games featured computer science concepts ([V1] and [V2]).

We collected the interactions in the chat from the live stream and comments from the YouTube videos and looked at common themes and topics that were discussed by the communities. Our first observation was that, indeed, the communities engage with the computer science topics and discuss them. Looking at these data sets we used a grounded theory approach to find emergent themes. We identified three major themes that were relevant to computer science and programming. The categories were: learning, programming experience, and community.

Under the *learning* theme, we observed a strong desire to start learning how to program as well as requests for resources and guidance on how to get started. *Programming experience* covers those discussions that more advanced programmers might have, for instance, discussions of particular programming languages or paradigms. The last category of *community* is mostly relevant to the live-stream. Real-time chat affords rich interaction and if the streams happen relatively frequently communities acting as a third place can be born. We observed positive environment that shared knowledge and encouraged learning to program. Another interesting observation regarding the community theme was the interest in the streamers background and how he was viewed as a role model.

We don't have the data to make any claims regarding actual learning outcomes in these communities regarding computer science. But what seems to evident based on the interactions within the communities is that this might have an impact on the interest of learning computer science. In a way, live streams and computer science content in gaming videos act as a form of outreach. The exposure, the community feeling, and the presence of newcomers attracted to programming by games create an engaging environment that for many is their first contact with programming. This is particularly encouraging since these communities have a positive outlook towards programming and computer science.

The phenomenon of mixing online gaming communities and computer science concepts is a new one, and as such it has not been researched. We have shown that the communities do discuss these concepts in various interesting ways and there is interest in learning how to program in people who have no previous experience with it. Furthermore, it seems that this might be an interesting avenue to pursue outreach activities in computer science. We hope that our research and our perspectives for online communities and programming is just a starting point for more research in the field.

7.1 Future Work

Tutorial videos, although acknowledged as a type of programming video by [6], was not investigated in detail by previous works and could provide more detail about the phenomena. It would be particularly interesting to check if the differences between `[V1]`, `[V2]` and `[S1]`, regarding the four discussed dimensions, are still relevant and useful with other types of programming video content. Also, other types of media such as online forums could be a compelling source of data for further analysis. Since we analyzed videos of games enhanced by programming or development videos of creating a game from scratch, it would be also important to analyze the modding (the act of creating modifications or additions to existing games, often requiring programming knowledge) scene to see how the differences in context affected users' interactions and perspectives.

There is also a gap in research on the topic of the profiles of the users interacting in these platforms. Collecting the data itself presents challenges not only due to the number of users but also because of the anonymous nature of the platforms. However, having a rich data set would allow future works to draw conclusions on the demographics and answer pertinent questions such as, What are the demographics of people watching this type of content? Are these communities really the first contact for many users with programming? What happens to these users later and do they pursue further studies related to computer science?

Acknowledgements. Rodrigo Duran was supported by CNPq-Brazil.

References

1. Chau, C.: Youtube as a participatory culture. New Dir. Youth Dev. **2010**(128), 65–74 (2010)
2. Entertainment Software Association: Essential facts about the computer and video game industry (2016). http://essentialfacts.theesa.com/Essential-Facts-2016.pdf. Accessed 15 May 2017
3. Finnish National Board of Education: The National Core Curriculum for Basic Education 2014. Finnish National Board of Education. Publications, 5 (2016)
4. Glaser, B.: Discovery of Grounded Theory: Strategies for Qualitative Research. Routledge, Abingdon (2017)
5. Haaranen, L.: Programming as a performance: live-streaming and its implications for computer science education. In: Proceedings of the 2017 ACM Conference on Innovation and Technology in Computer Science Education, ITiCSE 2017, pp. 353–358. ACM, New York (2017)
6. Haaranen, L., Duran, R.: Link between gaming communities in Youtube and computer science. In: Proceedings of the 9th International Conference on Computer Supported Education: CSEDU, vol. 2, pp. 17–24. INSTICC, ScitePress (2017)
7. Hamilton, W.A., Garretson, O., Kerne, A.: Streaming on twitch: fostering participatory communities of play within live mixed media. In: Proceedings of the 32nd Annual ACM Conference on Human Factors in Computing Systems, pp. 1315–1324. ACM (2014)
8. Kinnunen, P., Simon, B.: Building theory about computing education phenomena: a discussion of grounded theory. In Proceedings of the 10th Koli Calling International Conference on Computing Education Research, pp. 37–42. ACM (2010)
9. Knobelsdorf, M., Schulte, C.: Computer science in context: pathways to computer science. In: Proceedings of the Seventh Baltic Sea Conference on Computing Education Research, Koli Calling 2007, pp. 65–76. Australian Computer Society Inc., Darlinghurst (2007)
10. Lave, J., Wenger, E.: Situated Learning: Legitimate Peripheral Participation. Cambridge University Press, Cambridge (1991)
11. McLuhan, M.: Understanding Media: The Extensions of Man. MIT press, Cambridge (1994)
12. Mullich, D.: Who makes more money: hollywood or the video game industry? https://www.quora.com/Who-makes-more-money-Hollywood-or-the-video-game-industry. Accessed 07 Aug 2017
13. Oldenburg, R.: The Great Good Place: Cafes, Coffee Shops, Bookstores, Bars, Hair Salons, and Other Hangouts at the Heart of a Community. Da Capo Press, Cambridge (1999)

14. Poché, E., Jha, N., Williams, G., Staten, J., Vesper, M., Mahmoud, A.: Analyzing user comments on Youtube coding tutorial videos. In: Proceedings of the 25th International Conference on Program Comprehension, pp. 196–206. IEEE Press (2017)
15. Sjöblom, M., Hamari, J.: Why do people watch others play video games? an empirical study on the motivations of twitch users. Comput. Hum. Behav. **75**, 985–996 (2016)
16. Topps, D., Helmer, J., Ellaway, R.: Youtube as a platform for publishing clinical skills training videos. Acad. Med. **88**(2), 192–197 (2013)
17. Wallace, S.A., McCartney, R., Russell, I.: Games and machine learning: a powerful combination in an artificial intelligence course. Comput. Sci. Educ. **20**(1), 17–36 (2010)
18. Zhang, C., Liu, J.: On crowdsourced interactive live streaming: a twitch. TV-based measurement study. In: Proceedings of the 25th ACM Workshop on Network and Operating Systems Support for Digital Audio and Video, pp. 55–60. ACM (2015)

Uncovering Failures of Game Design for Educational Content (and How to Fix Them)

Kay Berkling[1(✉)], Heiko Faller[1], Micha Piertzik[1], Wolmet Barendregt[2], and Laura Benton[3]

[1] Computer Science, Cooperative State University of Baden Württemberg, Erzberger Str. 121, Karlsruhe, Germany
berkling@dhbw-karlsruhe.de, heiko_faller@t-online.de, official@piertzik.vip
[2] Divison of Learning Communication and ICT, University of Gothenburg, Forskningsgången 6, 412 96 Gothenburg, Sweden
wolmet.barendregt@ait.gu.se
[3] UCL Institute of Education, UCL Knowledge Lab, University College London, 23-29 Emerald Street, London WC1N 3QS, UK
l.benton@ucl.ac.uk

Abstract. More than 800 users from a cross-section of ages and gender were asked about the games they play and what motivates them to play these. The answers were cross-matched with game features. Based on this match and subjective answers of those surveyed, a pattern emerges for the essential ingredients of addictive games across these demographics, as well as an anti-pattern. With the derived pattern and anti-pattern several games and real-world scenarios can be designed and existing ones analyzed. Examples show how the pattern or anti-pattern can be applied and elucidate which key ingredients tend to be missing.

Keywords: Games · Content · Design · Addiction · Education Gamification · Analysis

1 Introduction

Playing games, pursuing a sport or enjoying a hobby can be both fun and addictive. In contrast to those contexts (that also often include learning) however, learning in the official context of school is often stressful or perceived as a duty. It is rare to find students who cannot wait to get up in the morning to continue their learning from the previous night, although this is more frequent in first grade than the later years. To improve the learning experience, researchers and educators have introduced games into the classroom in different ways: By using existing games in class or adding gamification mechanics to educational content. Not all educational or serious games show the desired effect of playfully or addictively engaging students to master perfection of a certain skill. In this paper, we

P. Escudeiro et al. (Eds.): CSEDU 2017, CCIS 865, pp. 300–324, 2018.
https://doi.org/10.1007/978-3-319-94640-5_15

build on previous work [3] that has derived pattern elements that appear in addictive mobile games in order to see how this knowledge about design can be incorporated into games with academic content; anti-pattern elements were established as a by-product of this process. For the purpose of self-containment, these findings are summarized here and then subsequently applied to several games and school environments for design and analysis. Comparing these along the pattern and anti-pattern elements, it can be shown that certain important aspects can easily be missed and offer a hint at how to improve the player experience.

In the following section, we briefly introduce the concepts and current understanding of games, gamification and motivation in the educational and demographic context, with a focus on literature overview papers.

Gamification. Gamification pertains to the analysis of mechanics that make games fun and then applying these to situations outside of gaming in order to recreate the feeling of fun or addiction to new applications such as learning or marketing or the solving of mundane tasks (rephrased from Oxford Dictionary).

According to [26], there have been a number of papers on various topics relating to gamification in education. Very few, however, deal with actual game design for experience, solution proposal, and validation with respect to mastering skills.

Dicheva [11] lists the papers that have studied various features in gamification usage for education. The most frequently studied mechanics in order of popularity are: "Status", "Social Engagement", "Freedom of Choice", "Freedom to Fail", "Rapid Feedback" and "Goals and Challenges". Researchers have studied gamification of educational material and shown that there is a strong interest in using game mechanics for education.

We believe that there remains a significant gap in actually designing and validating the use of games with educational content, going beyond gamification[1].

Games. Game-based learning (GBL) builds games or leverages existing games, such as *Civilization*, and re-uses them for an educational purpose, like economics or history [27,34]. Games are just starting to make a very slow move into schools [12,24]. The idea of using games in education is sometimes treated differently in the literature and called Educational Games or Serious Games (for example, [33]). These are designed specifically with educational content in mind. For the purpose of this paper, we prefer not to distinguish between games and serious games (this is not unusual and seems to agree with the findings in the literature overview on the subject [9]). According to Merriam Webster, a game is defined as: a) A form of competitive activity or sport played according to rules; b) An activity that one engages in for amusement; c) (adj) eager or willing to do something new or challenging. In this sense, there is no need to give a special name to a game that has educational content. The focus is instead on how the

[1] Academic or educational content for our purposes refers to content defined in the context of school.

content is designed as a game (for example pure game design [13], and its effect on children's learning outcome [29] and [5]).

Extrinsic vs Intrinsic. The difference between extrinsic and intrinsic motivation has been described extensively [23], as well as the negative effects of extrinsic motivators on intrinsic motivation and performance. Recently, Hanus [14] has shown the effects of gamification in the classroom in a longitudinal study:

- "Over time, gamified students were less motivated, empowered, and satisfied.
- Gamified courses negatively affected final exam grades through extrinsic motivation.
- Gamified systems strongly featuring rewards may have negative effects."

With "Educational" Games and gamification we often obtain, as a result, exactly this sort of extrinsic motivation by providing unrelated rewards. In contrast, popular games themselves seem to tend more towards the intrinsic motivation and working with the provided content to learn something. In this paper we would like to contribute towards moving education in the direction of understanding how to design and use games with educational content.

Demographic Dependence. Using game mechanics to design an addictive educational experience has been studied in detail. It is well known that personas, typical user profiles of a known demographic, are necessary for good design. Koivisto and Hamari [16] have shown that age and gender play a major role when designing gamification mechanics for their respective demographics. The work presented here incorporates demographics but looks at common themes across demographics for general audiences in education.

Relationship between Education and Games. Vallerand [32] explains in a very valuable summary the key to seeing education as a game: It is important to identify the intrinsic rewards relative to the culture and build game-like interactions on top of these by focusing on mechanics like "Freedom to Fail, Rapid Feedback, Progression and Storytelling" - note that these overlap with those studied in the gamification literature (Sect. 1). Stott [28] then makes the connection with existing terminology in education. "The Freedom to Fail" is analogous to formative assessment using "Rapid Feedback", "Progression" relates to scaffolded learning and "Storytelling" is equally recognized as a powerful tool in the classroom.

What we can learn about the current culture of games and what engages our time in gaming? The subject of this paper is a more detailed recipe-like mapping between these two areas.

Current Cultural Framework. The dynamics of change regarding which features in games are perceived as fun or addictive are not well studied. A similar approach to using design guidelines to create fun was developed by Malone and colleagues in the 1980s [18]. Based on his experience and analysis of games, he developed a taxonomy, a recipe to be used for game design. We will briefly compare our recipe to this taxonomy in Sect. 4.1. Some of these features in games may have universal appeal as they have remained constant over the years, while others might be dependent on current interests. This paper contributes to the general knowledge in the area by providing an updated analysis on what motivates gamers today.

The rest of the paper is organized as follows. Section 2 explains the framework that was developed through a detailed study of 27 popular mobile games. Based on this framework, a survey of over 800 participants was conducted and the results are described in more detail in Sect. 3. More details on this survey are given in [3] Sect. 4.1, which describes the resulting recipe or pattern that should guide successful game design. Section 4.2 specifies the corresponding anti-pattern. In the next two sections we will first show how the pattern or recipe can be used to design games (Sect. 5) and then demonstrate how the pattern can be used to analyze game environments in (Sect. 6). All examples contain educational content. Finally, Sect. 8 summarizes and proposes future work.

2 Analysis of Games

A list of popular mobile games from the Google Play Store charts as well as from the subjective experience of Bachelor students (two of the co-authors of this paper are Bachelor students with first-hand access to this information) is compiled. This list forms the basis of the questionnaire to analyze the features of these games in relation to the demographics of the players.

The list of games that are chosen for the study is as follows:

FIFA, Pineapple Pen, Block! Hexa Puzzle, Piano Tiles 2, Rolling Sky, Subway Surfers, Clash of Clans, Flippy Bottle Extreme, Color Switch, Roll the Ball, Temple Run, Pou, Hill Climbing Racing, Candy Crush, Angry Birds, Fruit Ninja, Geometry Dash, Cut the rope, 2048, Doodle Jump, Plants vs. Zombies, Jetpack Joyride, Stack, Dumb ways to die, Flappy Bird, Minesweeper, and Tetris.

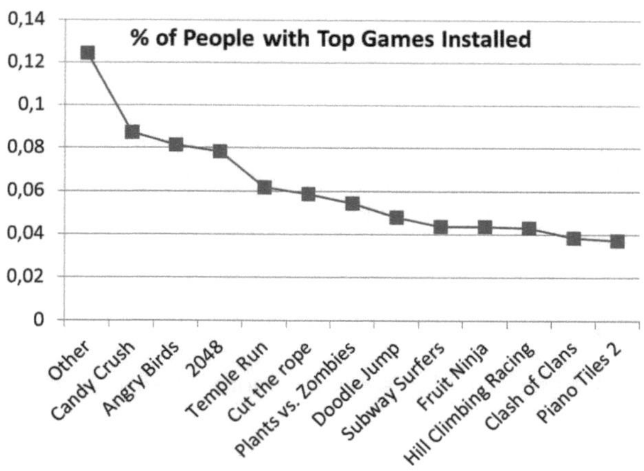

Fig. 1. Popularity of games. (See also [3])

Figure 1 depicts the distribution of users that selected this game as installed on their mobile device.

Four main categories of distinguishing features evolved out of an iterative analysis of the games list: Game-mode, Motivation, Emotion, Simplicity (as well as other features not categorized). These are each explained below (examples and feature assignment are given in [3]).

Game Mode. Games can be distinguished by game mode. These usually fall into one of these categories: Single level (Pineapple Pen), multiple level (Angry Birds), or storyline (Clash of Clans).

Motivation. Motivation for games are simple game mechanics that create extrinsic motivation such as listed below. We distinguish between rewards and currency that serves as a mechanism to acquire new tools to help the player progress. Goals define specific "tasks" that have to be accomplished irrespective of levels. Come-back motivations are types of appointments. High-score is a form of competition with self or others and a progress bar shows the path towards a goal or level.

Emotion. A major factor in games are emotions that can be supported with emotional faces, sound or graphics. Furthermore, fun, humor and spectacular death can support the creation of strong emotions for the player.

Simplicity. Simplification is important for on-boarding and ease of movement across levels of difficulty. It should be easy to start and proceed. The menu has to be quick, direct and easy to understand:

Other. Other factors that do not fit into the above categories have been determined as important aspects of a number of games that are currently popular: Their relation to reality, patterns that are learned to improve performance, social behavior (like feeding the animals in a friends' zoo) or competitions with self or others.

3 Survey: Design and Results

In order to gain a deeper understanding of how we can use games in education and generalize their design across populations, a survey reflecting current interests was conducted. The survey builds on the features that we have defined in the previous section.

3.1 Survey Construction

The survey includes the following sections (more detail is given in [3]):

- Demographic data
- Gaming Habits
- Games Installed and general Motivators
- Favorite Game and specific Motivators
- Emotions and their initiators

The evaluation of the survey should increase insight into the motivators based on three methods of eliciting information:

1. Installed games indicate interests indirectly though the framework,
2. Explicit motivation to play a favorite game, and
3. Indirect indicators of motivators that create a favorite emotion as a reason for playing.

These three insights allow us to understand how games can be designed with academic content.

3.2 Demographics of Participants

The survey, using Google forms, was announced via a Facebook games website and through university networks as well as employers. The result is a representative mix of people from industry and university, as well as a cross-section of different age groups and genders. Figure 2 depicts an overview of the population that answered the survey. In total 893 people responded to the survey within two weeks of posting it. Table 1 presents a breakdown of the respondents within each of the four categories of interest to us.

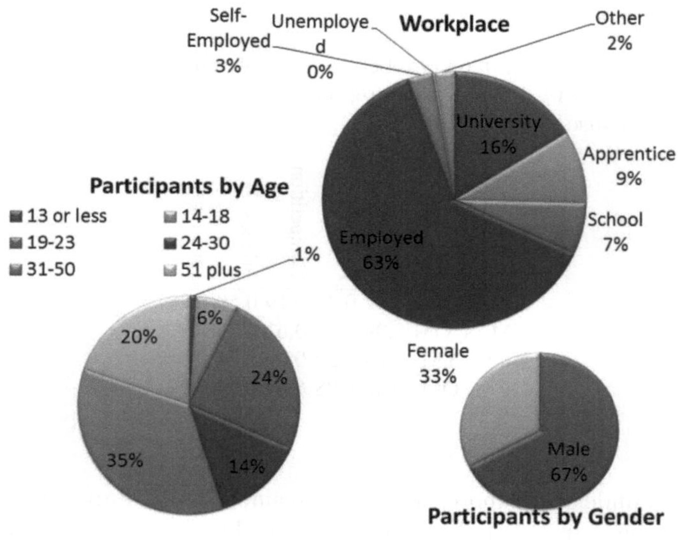

Fig. 2. Survey demographics. (See also [3]).

Table 1. Participant numbers by male/female and age bracket (<23 vs. >31). (See also [3]).

Subgroups	<23	>31
Male	173	347
Female	107	145

3.3 Results of Motivators in Favorite Game

Specific questions regarding motivators were asked within the context of the respondents favorite game. In particular distinguishing features of games were queried: Goals, Rewards, Competition, Friends, and Emotions. These points are compared across the four demographic groups defined above. Within the Likert scale from 1–6 (1=not at all and 6=very much), groups 1–3 and groups 5–6 are joined. The values in Table 2 represent the chance[2] that the resulting two queried subgroups respond differently to each motivator.

It shows that competition is of differing importance for males and females, regardless of age. Goals and Emotions have differing importance for younger vs. older males, Emotions differ also between younger males and females. Goals and Rewards are assimilated with age for both genders (see also [3]).

Table 2. Significance in differences between subgroups by % of chance that the two querried groups will differ in their reponse. (YM, YF, OM, OF = younger/older male/female) (See also [3]).

	Goals	Rewards	Competition	Friends	Emotions
YF vs. OF	0,47	0,32	0,19	0,50	0,28
YM vs. OM	0,99	0,73	0,61	0,75	0,99
YF vs. YM	0,84	0,37	0,99	0,84	0,96
OF vs. OM	0,02	0,08	0,89	0,74	0,22

In order to understand more closely which emotions are important when playing and how these are created, one question in the survey asks about emotions regarding a specific favorite game. Namely, which emotion is produced by the game and how this emotion is established. An interesting commonality is found here. Both genders and age groups play for fun and enjoyment, and each group has mostly minor differences in opinion on how this fun factor is established.

[2] This calculation is based on N-1 Chi-Square test as recommended by [10], using the 2-tailed p-value.

Namely excellent graphics, the ability to improve oneself and the increasing difficulty. The distribution is shown in Fig. 3. These results corroborates findings from game design and Psychology (for example, [8,17]).

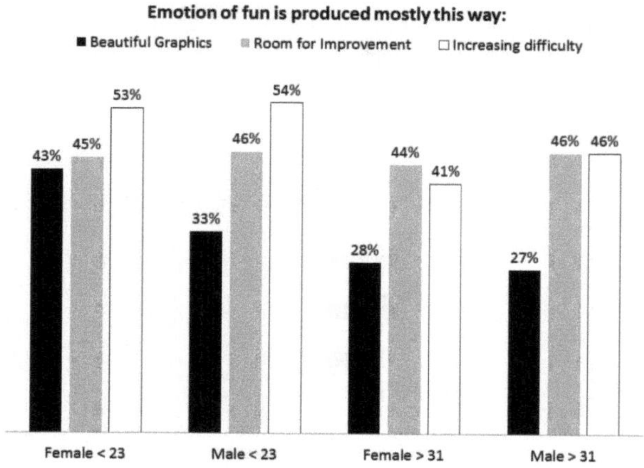

Fig. 3. Commonalities on most important emotion and how this emotion is created. (See also [3]).

3.4 Results of Motivators in General

Based on the installed games on people's mobile devices, we can establish a profile to describe which game features are favored as a function of gender or age. Equation 1 defines the cross product between the number of people within the subgroup who have installed a particular game on their mobile device with the feature vector (see [3]). This value represents a preference for a given motivator, or feature, with a particular group of respondents to the survey.

$$Value_{(Subgroup \wedge Feature)} \frac{\sum_i^{games}(X_i Y_i)}{\sum_i^{games} X_i \sum_i^{games} Y_i}, \tag{1}$$

where X is the vector of persons in a particular subgroup who have this game installed given the subgroup and Y is the analysis vector for a particular game feature across all games. This Vector has a 1 if the feature exists and a 0 if the feature does not exist (see also [3]).

The resulting values can then be compared across subgroups [3] and result in the following trends (among others):

- Differences between females and males get more pronounced as they get older.
- Males like faces, humor and a fun death.
- Older people need more goals.

- Females like a incentive to return.
- Females tend to be more interested in levels than males. This is less pronounced in younger ages.
- Some differences between gender are more pronounced in the older demographic.
- Figure 4 shows items that are most sensitive to gender specific demographics. Among these are also levels, rewards and competition that will be discussed in more detail later.

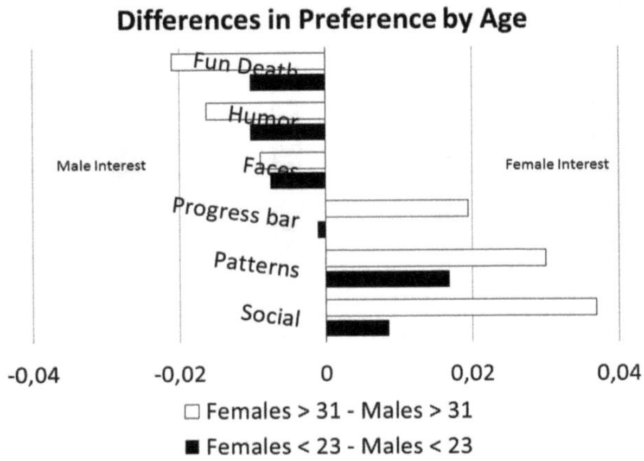

Fig. 4. Selected motivators showing differences in gender for younger and older demographic groups. The younger demographic tends to have less pronounced differences. (See also [3]).

Based on the feature preferences across the games we can establish that there are indeed differences when looking across all the various features that games have. While this information shows implicitly which features are preferred through the games that are installed, it is not guaranteed that all installed games become favorites. So, they do not necessarily represent a true picture of favorite games choices. However, they may serve as an indicator given the large set of data obtained from the survey. The next step is to compare features specific to favorite games.

3.5 Results of Direct Questions About General Motivators

Looking more specifically and detailed at the motivators of Levels, Rewards and Competition, questions were asked in reference to the respondent's favorite game. While levels seem to be favored in different ways by particular demographic groups, a more detailed examination shows commonalities. Figure 5 depicts the relative importance of levels in games for both males and females in general and in their favorite game. All demographics, whether in general or specific to their favorite game, favor levels.

The graph on the left hand side in Fig. 6 shows that there are different types of rewards. In general rewards may not be important to players (only 20% of players care about rewards that are not useful for advancement). However, looking in more detail at different types of rewards, there are differences. If the reward pertains to gaining more power or skills in the game, they are of interest to a larger number of people (about 60%) than simple rewards that do not help the player. This finding holds true across all demographics.

The graph on the right hand side in Fig. 6 depicts preferences for several different types of competitions that can be used in games. It shows that certain types of competition are more interesting than others. While there are gender differences, there is some agreement across demographics that competition with self is more preferred than global competition.

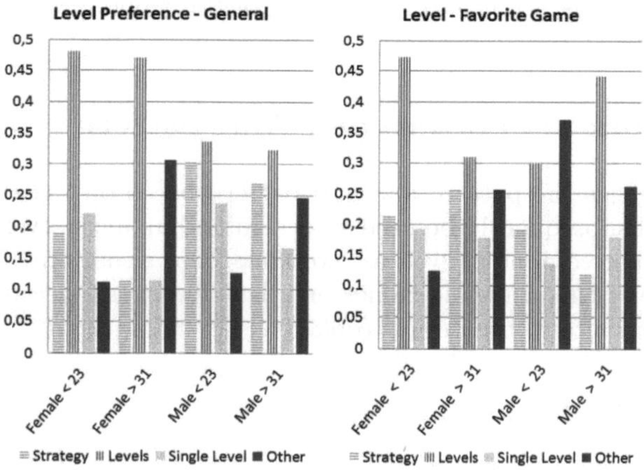

Fig. 5. How important are levels? (See also [3]).

3.6 Summary and Conclusion of Survey Results

Looking at implicit and explicit preferences in motivators, we have shown differences in demographic subgroups. But more importantly, we have gained insights into commonalities that are necessary to design a game for the general public regarding motivators for academic content learning. The survey shows how levels, competition and rewards have to be carefully used within a good design. With the gained knowledge, we can define anti-patterns, how not to use a game in the classroom or how to not design a game with academic content. Similarly, we can also define good practice on how to present content to users. Using this framework, we can now look at several games or gamified environments in order

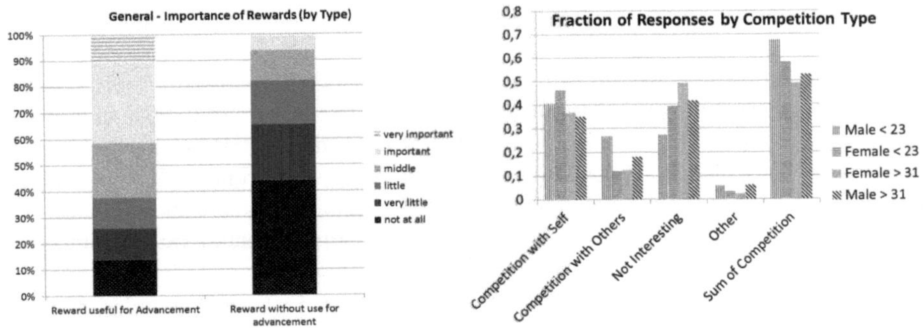

Fig. 6. Which types of competition are preferred? How important are rewards?

to see how they compare to universally addictive games. This in turn will help us to see which areas are typically not part of the game design and how they can be improved.

4 Framework for Pattern and Anti-pattern

This section defines the pattern and anti-pattern based on the study and findings. These will subsequently be used to design and analyze several games with academic learning content as well as two classroom situations. The goal is to see where some of the academic games may lack features that are important in games and contribute to the desire to play.

4.1 Pattern: Recipe for Good Design

Based on the findings of the 2016 survey on how games are played explicitly as well as implicitly, one can establish a checklist of important design elements when building a game around academic content for the general public, that is, they hold mostly true across the demographics that were polled. (Future research should focus on how well these generalize to younger children.)

In general, the following points are absolutely essential and can not be bypassed:

- Graphics (Consistent and Simple)
- Rewards (Must relate to capabilities)
- Increasing Difficulty
- Increased Knowledge (replay until expert)
- Easy to start and stop playing
- Competition with Self
- Leave out everything else

Design steps should include the usage of levels in the following way:

- Many Levels (Consistent and Simple)
- Frequent new elements
- Levels can be infinite (level-based improvements)
- Don't use single level

Pedagogical design, such as scope and sequence of content seems to be inherent to this recipe. When comparing to Malone's taxonomy of intrinsically motivating game design elements, some of his items (like social interaction) were not found to be generic for all players covered in the survey. Other elements were present, but in a slightly more explicit form. For example, while Malone's taxonomy mentions goals in general, the survey shows that goals in the form of levels and competition with oneself are especially motivating. Furthermore, in his taxonomy emotion plays an important role, while we break apart which components of the game create this emotion for the player. It was found that emotion can be created by self-improvement, graphics and increasing difficulty. While some of these items are also listed in Malone's taxonomy, the connection to the emotion is not explicitly drawn. There is a strong overlap however with Malone's taxonomy regarding the tight interconnection between the game design and the learning content that is apparent in our recipe. Curiosity, control and fantasy are equally important in both design proposals. This comparison can be an indication of the universality of some of these features to the human nature of play.

4.2 Anti-pattern

Game design can be done badly and it is of interest to define an anti-pattern, a pattern for bad design (when designed for a general population). The following checklist is generated from the survey results.

- Single Level (fits fewer demographics)
- Bad Graphics (Crowded, low quality (unless funny), unrelated to content): For example, too many icons, graphic elements and texts.
- No rewards or unrelated rewards (that do not contribute directly to increased skill)
- Little self-awareness of skill increase
- Too complex on-boarding or advancement
- Long units of play necessary
- No view of own high-score to compete with
- No replay of level - ie. no chance to improve
- Too much material at the same time (unleveled)
- Path too restrictive (no choices)

Levels can be designed badly as follows:

- Few levels
- Too many repetitions, no new elements
- No individual speed
- Competition with others
- No improvement in finished levels possible

5 Game Design

We look at two games that have been designed with these patterns in mind. In addition, a course designed in a school setting is described from the game point of view.

5.1 Software Engineering Classroom

In previous work, a Software Engineering course was gamified and then modified to improve student motivation in the classroom. The redesign was also based on student feedback and matches the pattern closely [6,7].

Students are asked to submit their homework not on a central platform that is chosen by the professor or the university but on a blog platform of their choice that they have designed and configured themselves. Rewards, ie. points are given for each submitted homework and relate directly to the final grade as well as the project. At the same time, these points show how much of the final project has been finished already. Each new homework builds on the previous knowledge. However, there are no unlocks of levels visible to the student. Students report that they find this course very challenging. The "progress bar" regarding the homework that has already been handed in shows how the students are moving through the material. Looking back on their semester, students agree that the things they were able to do after one year could not have been possible at the beginning. Nor could the last lesson have been taught in the first week. Student feedback regularly shows an improvement in the nine areas of learning. The change in self-evaluation of skills is shown in Fig. 7. Playing for short intervals is difficult in the context of a classroom but in a project-based course, there are always small tasks that can be approached in short time intervals. Students are expected or encouraged to hand in their assignments repeatedly until they are perfect. This is in contrast to traditional classrooms where the assignment ends after submission. The reviews are accomplished through peer reviewing [2]. There is little information in the course that does not pertain to the homework of the current level or week. Students can be observed to work on-task throughout class time.

If one can think of homework as a level, then there are 17 levels to be passed over the course of two semesters in order to submit the final project that consists of the combination of the 17 mastered levels. Each week, a new element is added to the previous knowledge and this has to be fulfilled by the end of the week for the assignment. Each homework is resubmitted until perfection. Peer review supports this process. The homework helps to distinguish the different tasks. Taking a brief look at the anti-pattern can help to review whether there are still remaining design flaws that are obvious. There is no single exam at the end of the course, which would be the equivalent of a single level game. Students are responsible for setting up their own blog and thereby also their own graphic interface configuration. In the past, bad learning platforms were one of the major complaints that students have had. This is no longer true for the current course design. Self-awareness of skill increase could probably be improved. However, the

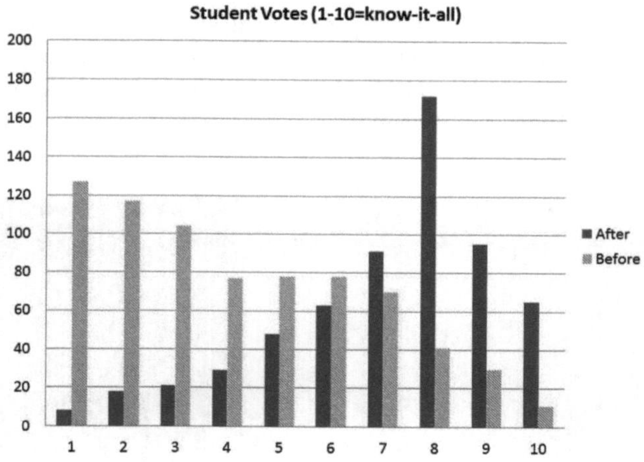

Fig. 7. Software engineering self evaluation on the nine skills on a scale from 1 (I know nothing) - 10 (I feel that I know this topic well). Answers are summed across all questions for each of three classrooms with an average of 25 students each, before and after the completion of the course.

progress bar supports visualization of progress, as does the growth of the blog length. On-boarding is easy, fast and satisfactory because it includes building their own platform and that is fun and easy. The first homework is easy and focuses on process over content as well as defining their own project. A unit of play is only one week (short in a school setting). You do not compete with others, only yourself. There is no leaderboard. Yet, there is some kind of peer pressure by seeing what others are accomplishing. At the same time, students are able to see their own score and improve it. They can replay any assignment (level) as often as they wish to gain the perfect grade, ie. the perfect project component to submit for a final grading at the end of the year. The final redesign of the course changed the overwhelming material presentation to a sequence of slowly presented units of information. The course gives some choices, like technology and project or tools to use, but there are no choices on methodology and homework assignment to reduce complexity.

5.2 Phontasia

Phontasia, shown in Fig. 8, is an iPad game (freely available via Appstore) that has educational content [4,5]. It has been successfully deployed in schools and has demonstrated an increase in skill level for the academic content presented within the game. The content of the game relates to phonics for German orthography and allows children to proceed from simple patterns to more complex patterns in the same way phonics does that for English. The game is set up as a magician's lab where the player mixes potions of letters into words. The potions become increasingly complex. Observation of game use has shown that it is highly addictive in addition to improving the skills. In fact, becoming expert at the skill is the central learning goal that children are pursuing because the skill is gained and the new level of difficulty is the reward, as new positions become available ("Tage" vs. "trage").

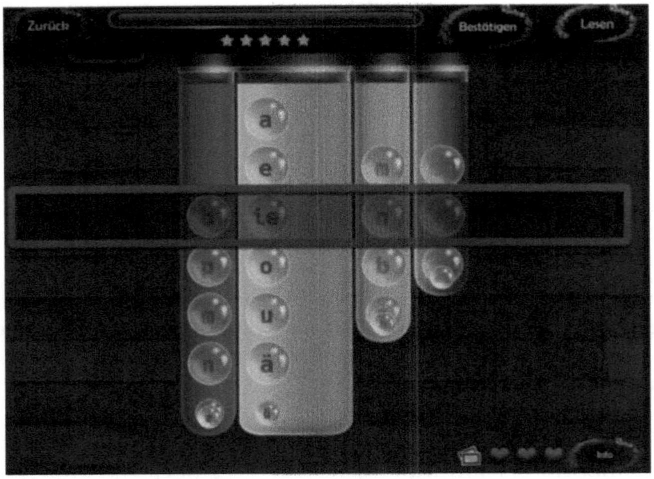

Fig. 8. Phontasia user interface (See also [3]).

Graphics are beautiful and supported with sounds that match the underlying theme and the task. There are negative rewards, a heart can be lost three times to catapult players back to the start (similar to the game of Ludo). The reward is indirect in that correctness of the work results in the ability to reach the next level. The next level has a larger number of potions resulting in new opportunities to explore and with that new difficulties and new potions to mix in. With this power comes difficulty of words to be spelled. The students learn to spell words that they had been previously denied because the necessary potions were not yet acquired. It is easy to start and stop playing at any time. Stopping in the middle of the most successful streak is even a good idea because kids cannot wait to come back and play again to prove they can reach the next level. There is intense competition with self in order to reach the next level, without losing a heart, faster than last time, improving automaticity and proficiency in the player (learner). Nothing else happens in this game except word spelling and the sounds of the magic mix.

There are 12 levels, a lot for a first or second grader. Each level adds only one small additional potion, offering new elements and challenges. They look and feel like rewards because the children can finally spell new words that they had been waiting for and were prevented from spelling previously (e.g. due to orthographic misconceptions by the player that result in learning). Each level can be played again. In fact, many children go back to replay the lower levels because they enjoy feeling comfortable with already mastered skills.

5.3 Drum Stix

Drum Stix is a game designed to teach rhythm. The game should have easy on-boarding and progression with constant improvement. Therefore, a complex original design idea was rejected for a simplified level design. Maximally simple and dedicated only to the content in question, the app is opened and a play button leads directly to the drums, which are the center of learning. In the first level, 2 drums are visible: 'Kick' and 'Snare'.

Each level consists of one task. A song is played in the background. Each drum is marked with a color and number. The progress-bar (for the song) indicates which drum should be played (Karaoke style). Missing a drum-beat results in a mark-down. Correct performance results in a mark-up of points. As the player repeats this rhythm, the karaoke support is removed. The level ends with the first mistake the user commits. As the levels ends, the user is shown his/her own current and his/her highest score. Played levels can be repeated any time, even as new levels open up.

Gamers can individually adjust the drums according to their needs. They can be placed differently or new drums can be purchased with the collected coins. In buying a new drum, the next level starts. Any open level can be played with the purchased drums. With the increasing number of drums, the game becomes more difficult. More coins can be won and bigger, additional instruments bought. Rhythms grow faster and more complex. While the first purchase is easy to obtain, further advancement is based on improved skill. There are a large number of levels and care will be taken to create fun graphics.

Figure 9 shows the design for DrumStix. It depicts drums and sounds that are falling from the top and need to be tapped in time as they hit the corresponding drums. The graphic to the right shows that the players earned points can be used to buy items that allow me to learn higher skills, in this case a new drum.

Fig. 9. Drumstix user interface. The left shows the current drumset and sounds moving down that should be hit as they hit the center of the drum. Points gained from playing can be used in the shop to buy new drums to open new rhythms for playing/learning. (See also [3]).

6 Game Analysis

In this section, we analyze existing learning environments. First, we take a look at the traditional school setting from the game point of view. Then we look at several games that have already been used in schools.

6.1 Generic Educational System

Analyzing the generic learning environments, that still pervade most of the education system, in terms of this anti-pattern one can see some design issues with regard to enjoying learning in schools or universities today. While schools have levels (first grade, second grade, ...), there is no individual speed. In fact, there often is competition with others and after a level is finished, no improvement is possible. A bad grade not only can not be improved, but can permanently hold students back in future levels.

While grades can be seen as rewards (for those who do well), they do not represent new tools for solving more complex problem sets. They may not even accurately reflect skills by themselves [25,30,31]. Students tend to have little knowledge of their own skills since there is no progress bar during the course of one class (with respect to skills - there are progress bars in terms of time and exam dates). The learning path is also very restricted with few electives and no control over the speed at which the content will be mastered.

Furthermore, the on-boarding process and further progression is not always easy, "I have no time to learn, I need to prepare for the exam next week" - is a typical anti-pattern in the game of learning.

Finally, the units of the game are often quite long, if we can measure them by time between exams. In school, there are weeks, at University there can be whole semesters between exams and level-unlocks. The number of levels with respect to the content are additionally too few. So learning, in our society has not yet matched the pattern of good game design for the general population. It remains to be proven quantitatively whether good game design in education improves the skills outcome.

6.2 Fingu - A Math Game

Fingu is an iPad game that has educational content and can be downloaded for free from the AppStore [1,15]. It has been tested in schools, and several schools, especially in Sweden, have downloaded the game. The content of the game relates to number sense, which is foundational to the development of arithmetic competence in addition and subtraction. According to Neuman [20], mastering elementary number concepts means understanding natural numbers in the range of one to ten as part-whole relations (e.g. 6 is constituted by 5 and 1, but also by 4 and 2 and so forth).

In Fingu one or two small moving sets of pieces of fruit are shown and the player has to determine how many pieces of fruit there are. Before time runs out the player has to place as many fingers on the screen as there are pieces of fruit.

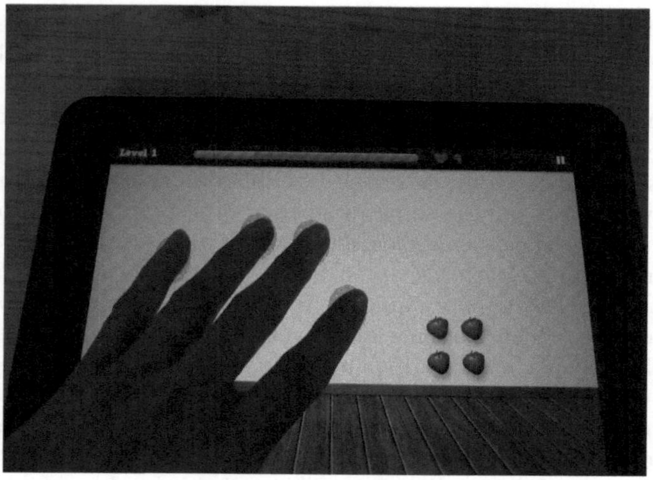

Fig. 10. Fingu user interface.

Figure 10, the sets are shown for a short time, but after they have disappeared the player gets some extra time to answer. Fingers can be placed anywhere on the screen. Once a finger is placed on the screen a timer is started to determine when the answer will be registered. The starting of this timer is made visible as a fingerprint. The fingerprints change color in order to indicate that a final answer has been registered. Before the answer is registered the player can (by default within part of a second) remove or add fingers and each change in finger configuration restarts the timer until a stable configuration is held down long enough.

There are 7 levels, and on each level there are a number of configurations of number patterns (10, 12 or 15), which are shown twice in random order. If the player answers correctly the first time a configuration is shown, the exposure time will be shorter as the configuration is shown the second time. On the first level the maximum total number of pieces of fruit is 5, on the second level 6 etc., to 10 pieces of fruit on level 6 and 7. On each level some new configurations are introduced as well. One proceeds to the next level by answering correctly to the most assignments. If the player gives an incorrect answer he/she will lose a heart. If the player runs out of time only half a heart is lost. When all the hearts are lost before the 20 assignments (24 or 30 for the higher levels) have been given, the player has to start all over at the same level. Players choose their personal character on the first screen and can continue playing on the levels that they have opened up.

Graphics are designed by a professional game design company (Image and Form in Gothenburg), and are supported with sounds that match the underlying theme and the task. There are negative rewards, a heart is lost when giving an incorrect answer, and half a heart is lost when not answering within the given time. If all hearts are lost, the player has to restart the level. There is a direct reward for answering correctly in the form of three funny characters that appear, or a negative reward in the form of a crying onion. There is also an indirect reward in that correctness of the work results in the ability to reach the next level. The next level has new configurations that are harder to master, but there is no increase in playing abilities. Each level offers new configurations, both in terms of new patterns for the same number of objects, and in terms of higher numbers of objects. The students learn to immediately see number patterns and add the numbers in to patterns up to higher sums, which also requires them to coordinate their fingers more quickly. It is easy to start and stop playing at any time. However, when stopping in the middle of a level, the level has to be replayed, unless the player has only paused the game. The user can compete with him/herself to reach the next level, and to play a level without losing any of the hearts. The number of hearts left is shown when completing the level. However, the number of hearts preserved on each level is only shown on an overview screen after finishing all levels, not in-between. This makes it hard for children to know how to improve themselves on a single level. Nothing else happens in this game except recognizing number patterns and addition of number patterns which have to be expressed by a number of fingers.

There are 7 levels, which is enough for a pre-school/first grade child. Each level adds either some patterns for previously encountered numbers, or patterns for new numbers. Although there are new elements on each level that make the assignment more challenging, there are no radically new kinds of challenges to look forward to. Each level can be played again, and many children go back to replay the lower levels because they enjoy feeling comfortable with already mastered skills.

Summing up, while Fingu has the potential to be addictive, the fact that the child is unable to see how well they did on each level before finishing all levels makes it less interesting to compete with oneself. Furthermore, the kind of challenge remains the same throughout the game; there are no real new kinds of challenges to look forward to. In combination with the fact that some children find the coordination of their fingers for the higher sums quite difficult, many children quit playing the game before reaching the highest level.

6.3 Teach Your Monster to Read - A Literacy Game

Teach Your Monster to Read (TYMTR[3]) is available both as a paid-for app (on iPhone, iPad, Android and Kindle) and can also be accessed for free via a website (note the version analysed was downloaded in July 2017 and there have subsequently been updates that have added additional features). It is designed to support the teaching of phonics and is specifically tailored to the government programme, Letters and Sounds, which is followed by the majority of primary schools in England. The game is predominantly aimed at young children learning

[3] https://www.teachyourmonstertoread.com/.

to read, it is split into 3 games (focused on letters/sounds, words, and simple sentences) and is intended to cover two years of learning.

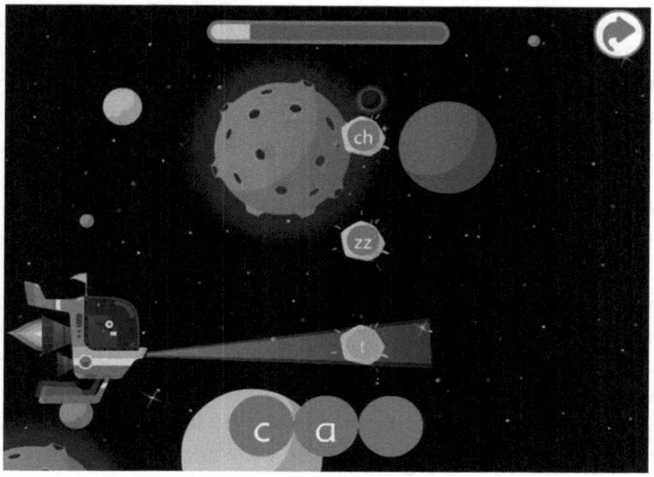

Fig. 11. Teach your monster to read.

In TYMTR the child gets to customize their own monster avatar. They then navigate a world in which they are tasked with completing various reading skill focused mini-games in order to help their monster. New content is introduced via teaching videos and the mini-games provide opportunities to both learn new content as well as practice previously learning concepts and develop their speed and accuracy in reading. As the player successfully completes mini-games further content is unlocked and when they leave the game their progress is saved within their own account. The game contains 47 levels (represented as planets grouped into galaxies), is designed to fit into short play sessions so it can be easily incorporated into lessons, and contains approximately 8 hours play.

Graphics are beautiful and supported by sounds, music and narrated content that match the underlying theme and the task (see Fig. 11). Within each mini-game the player is rewarded for correct answers through positive sound effects, character animations and sometimes praise. At the end of levels the player also gets the opportunity to collect stars as well as food that you can eat (but has no direct impact on the game so the reward does not fold back to new game capabilities). The progress bar also fills up, but the link between the achievement and the amount of progress made towards the goal is not very clear through this mechanism. The player is able to spend the stars on buying things for their avatar such as different clothing for your monster, which have no impact on game play. The player is also rewarded through advancements in the game narrative and the unlocking of new content within the game. Content is grouped, so a player works on multiple concepts (of similar difficulty) at the same time, for instance the graphemes s, a, t, p. The player has to demonstrate knowledge of all of these concept before they can move on. If a player struggles with a particular concept they encounter this more frequently within the games. Over the three games the player builds on their knowledge of reading letters, word and then simple sentences (one bit builds up to the next). Alongside this, the variety of game mechanics encourages players to develop reading skills such as blending and segmenting as well as explicitly practicing semi-decodable 'tricky' words. It is easy to start and stop playing at any time, with the progress saved within the game. However, when stopping in the middle of a level, the level has to be replayed. There is no competition with oneself built into the games, as allows the player to have an unlimited number of attempts to pass a level and the number of attempts (as well as the time taken) is not used to differentiate attempts at the same level. The narrative encourages the player to move on rather than go back to earlier games and the player practices previously learned content through it being presented in differently skinned mini-games, which avoids the game feeling repetitive. There are additional game elements designed around the core content which include a rich animated narrative, avatar customization as well as mini-games which involve solely collecting stars (and no learning) highlight that there are additional things happening around the core game focus.

There are 47 levels, which differentiate between learning and practice games. There are also variations across these levels in terms of the rewards gained and also different types of feedback for getting an answer incorrect. The game does not convince the player that new elements should be anticipated. They appear without any hype as the player progresses. None of the levels can be replayed. Once the player has progressed there is no way to go back, unless they reset the game completely to the starting point.

In summary, TYMTR mixes elements of consistency with new content, rewards, narrative elements and game types to maintain the child's engagement. It is easy to play for short periods and come back to the game, but the game encourages the player to continually progress forward through requiring the player to reach binary success criteria rather than encouraging them to return to earlier parts of the game to improve their accuracy. This may result in the potential of players becoming stuck at a certain level and not continuing with the game as they are no longer able to make progress. The additional elements external to the core game play, although engaging, may frustrate players looking to make quick progress through the games and also decreases the amount of learning time within any given play period.

7 Summary of Games Analysis and Design

This section compares the pattern and anti-pattern items for each of the games or school situations that were designed or analyzed in the previous sections. The goal is to see whether there are any commonalities of missing items that can then give a strong indication of how to improve these games with academic content. Table 3 shows the result for both pattern and anti-pattern items in the derived framework.

Table 3. Comparison of games and school for pattern and antipattern elements; X stands for element is present. (SE=Software Engineering).

		School SE	School classic	Writing phont.	Reading TYMTR	Rhythm drums.	Math fingu
Pattern desired features	Graphics	x	x	x	x	x	x
	Rewards (related to skill)	x		x		x	
	Increased difficulty	x	x	x	x	x	x
	Increased knowledge	x	x	x	x	x	x
	Easy start/stop			x	x	x	x
	Competition (self)	x		x		x	
	Nothing else	x		x		x	x
	Many levels	x		x	x	x	x
	Frequent new elements	x		x	x	x	
	Replay level (infinite)	x		x		x	x
Anti-pattern undesired features	Single level		x				
	Bad graphics						
	Unrelated awards		x		x		x
	Little self-awareness of skill		x		x		x
	Too complex onboarding						
	Long unit of play		x				
	No view on own high-score				x		x
	No replay of level		x		x		
	Too much unleveled material						
	Path without choice		x		x	x	
	Too much repetition		x				
	No individual speed	x	x				
	Competition with others		x				

It can be seen that aspects of learning and increasing difficulty are usually covered in the games we looked at. However, it is underestimated in the studied designs how important some other aspects are. Namely, the following points should be taken more strongly into account; they combine several features of the pattern/anti-pattern analysis:

1. Rewards should directly enable the student to apply the newly won "gadget" to learning new skills. (For example, a reward is a new drum that needs to be mastered in the new level.)
2. Students like to have the option to repeat a level and improve their skills, thereby competing with themselves. This encompasses the students knowledge about their own performance at any time in the game and the power to change it!

8 Conclusion and Future Work

This paper describes a design recipe and an anti-pattern for the design of motivational educational games. Both resulted from a survey among a large number of participants with different demographics. Although it was shown that demographics may differ in certain aspects of game features, there are nonetheless several very important commonalities. Those commonalities are that difficulty and the ability to improve support fun, that rewards should grant new abilities for learning and that competition is mostly relevant with respect to competing with oneself. We have shown how the use of levels is constructive for users. The paper also describes the application of the recipe during the design of a new game, and how both the recipe and the anti-pattern can be used to analyze and suggest improvements for several existing games from different domains. While there are other studies providing recipes for gamification [21] or blended learning [19], these are not based on large numbers of participants, nor are they focusing on generic vs. specific motivators as a function of demographics. These results have once more led the authors to believe that good game design principles are necessary to put the enjoyment back into learning while improving learner skills. The work described in this paper can inspire further research into how emotions are created in more detail by refining the questions in the survey. Furthermore, in order to show the relevance of game design for educational content, there must be more focus on measuring learning impact. According to the literature [9] few studies have measured both motivation and skill improvement, and many studies are performed in a specific environment without any quantitatively motivated framework and with a small number of participants. While there are some exeption (e.g. the study by Novak et al. [22]), more research effort is needed regarding generalizability and outcomes assessment.

References

1. Barendregt, W., Lindström, B., Rietz-Leppänen, E., Holgersson, I., Ottosson, T.: Development and evaluation of fingu: A mathematics ipad game using multi-touch interaction. In: Proceedings of the 11th international conference on interaction design and children. pp. 204–207. ACM (2012)
2. Berkling, K.: Connecting peer reviews with students' motivation - onboarding, motivation and blended learning. In: Helfert, M., Restivo, M.T., Zvacek, S., Uhomoibhi, J.O. (eds.) CSEDU 2015 - Proceedings of the 7th International Conference on Computer Supported Education, Volume 2, Lisbon, Portugal, 23–25 May, 2015. pp. 24–33. SciTePress (2015)
3. Berkling, K., Faller, H., Piertzik, M.: Avoiding failure in modern game design with academic content - A recipe, an anti-pattern and applications thereof. In: Escudeiro, P., Costagliola, G., Zvacek, S., Uhomoibhi, J.O., McLaren, B.M. (eds.) CSEDU 2017 - Proceedings of the 9th International Conference on Computer Supported Education, Volume 2, Porto, Portugal, April 21–23, 2017. pp. 25–36. SciTePress (2017)
4. Berkling, K., Pflaumer, N.: Phontasia - a phonics trainer for German spelling in primary education Singapore, September 19, 2014. In: Berkling, K., Giuliani, D., Potamianos, A. (eds.) The 4st Workshop on Child, Computer and Interaction, WOCCI 2014, Singapore, September 19, 2014. pp. 33–38. ISCA (2014), http://www.isca-speech.org/archive/wocci_2014/wc14_033.html
5. Berkling, K., Pflaumer, N., Lavalley, R.: German phonics game using speech synthesis - a longitudinal study about the effect on orthography skills Education, SLaTE 2015, Leipzig, Germany, September 4–5, 2015. In: Workshop on Speech and Language Technology in Education. SLaTE, vol. 6, pp. 167–172. ISCA(ISCA)

International Speech Communication Association (2015). http://www.isca-speech.org/archive/slate_2015/sl15_167.html
6. Berkling, K., Thomas, C.: Gamification of a software engineering course and a detailed analysis of the factors that lead to it's failure. In: Interactive Collaborative Learning (ICL), 2013 International Conference on. pp. 525–530. IEEE (2013)
7. Berkling, K., Zundel, A.: Change management: overcoming the challenges of introducing self-driven learning. iJEP **5**(4), 38–46 (2015). http://www.online-journals.org/index.php/i-jep/article/view/4945
8. Bianco, A.T., Higgins, E.T., Klem, A.: How fun/importance fit affects performance: relating implicit theories to instructions. Pers. Soci. Psychol. Bull. **29**(9), 1091–1103 (2003)
9. Boyle, E.A., Hainey, T., Connolly, T.M., Gray, G., Earp, J., Ott, M., Lim, T., Ninaus, M., Ribeiro, C., Pereira, J.: An update to the systematic literature review of empirical evidence of the impacts and outcomes of computer games and serious games. Comput. Educ. **94**, 178–192 (2016)
10. Campbell, I.: Chi-squared and Fisher-Irwin tests of two-by-two tables with small sample recommendations. Stat. Med. **26**(19), 3661–3675 (2007)
11. Dicheva, D., Dichev, C., Agre, G., Angelova, G.: Gamification in Education: a systematic mapping Study. J. Educ. Technol. Soc. **18**(3), 75–88 (2015)
12. Dickey, M.D.: K-12 teachers encounter digital games: a qualitative investigation of teachers' perceptions of the potential of digital games for K-12 education. Interact. Learn. Environ. **23**(4), 485–495 (2013)
13. Egenfeldt-Nielsen, S., Smith, J.H., Tosca, S.P.: Understanding video Games: The Essential Introduction, 3rd edn. Routledge, New York (2016)
14. Hanus, M.D., Fox, J.: Assessing the effects of gamification in the classroom: a longitudinal study on intrinsic motivation, social comparison, satisfaction, effort, and academic performance. Comput. Educ. **80**, 152–161 (2015)
15. Holgersson, I., Barendregt, W., Rietz, E., Ottosson, T., Lindström, B.: Can children enhance their arithmetic competence by playing a specially designed computer game? Cursiv, DK, 18, 177–188. Institut for Didaktik, Danmarks Pædagogiske Universitetsskole, Aarhus Universitet (2016)
16. Koivisto, J., Hamari, J.: Demographic differences in perceived benefits from gamification. Comput. Hum. Behav. **35**, 179–188 (2014)
17. Koster, R.: A Theory of Fun for Game Design, 2nd edn. O'Reilly Media Inc., Sebastopol (2014)
18. Malone, T.W., Lepper, M.R.: Making learning fun: a taxonomy of intrinsic motivations for learning. Aptitude Learn. Instr. **3**(1987), 223–253 (1987)
19. Naaji, A., Mustea, A., Holotescu, C., Herman, C.: How to mix the ingredients for a blended course recipe. BRAIN Broad Res. Artif. Intell. Neurosci. **6**(1–2), 106–116 (2015)
20. Neuman, D.: The Origin of Arithmetic Skills: A Phenomenographic Approach (1987)
21. Nicholson, S.: A RECIPE for meaningful gamification. In: Reiners, T., Wood, L.C. (eds.) Gamification in Education and Business, pp. 1–20. Springer, Cham (2015). https://doi.org/10.1007/978-3-319-10208-5_1
22. Novak, E., Johnson, T.E., Tenenbaum, G., Shute, V.J.: Effects of an instructional gaming characteristic on learning effectiveness, efficiency, and engagement: using a storyline for teaching basic statistical skills. Interact. Learn. Environ. **24**(3), 523–538 (2016)
23. Ryan, D.: Intrinsic and extrinsic motivations: classic definitions and new directions. Contemp. Educ. Psychol. **25**(1), 54–67 (2000)

24. Salen, K.: Quest to Learn: Developing the School for Digital Kids. The John D. and Catherine T. MacArthur Foundation reports on digital media and learning. MIT Press, Cambridge, Mass (2011)
25. Schuler, H., Funke, U., Baron-Boldt, J.: Predictive Validity of school grades-a meta-analysis. Appl. Psychol. **39**(1), 89–103 (1990)
26. de Sousa Borges, S., Durelli, V.H.S., Reis, H.M., Isotani, S.: A systematic mapping on gamification applied to education. In: Cho, Y., Shin, S.Y., Kim, S., Hung, C.C., Hong, J. (eds.) the 29th Annual ACM Symposium on Applied Computing, pp. 216–222 (2014)
27. Squire, K.: From content to context: videogames as designed experience. Educ. Researcher **35**(8), 19–29 (2006)
28. Stott, A., Neustaedter, C.: Analysis of gamification in education. Surrey, BC, Canada 8 (2013)
29. Suarez Caraballo, L.M.: Using online mathematics skills games to promote automaticity. Ph.D. thesis, Cleveland State University (01012014)
30. Trapmann, S., Hell, B., Hirn, J.O.W., Schuler, H.: Meta-analysis of the relationship between the big five and academic success at university. Zeitschrift für Psychologie/J. Psychol. **215**(2), 132–151 (2007)
31. Trapmann, S., Hell, B., Weigand, S., Schuler, H.: Die Validität von Schulnoten zur Vorhersage des Studienerfolgs - eine Metaanalyse 1Dieser Beitrag entstand im Kontext des Projekts "Eignungsdiagnostische Auswahl von Studierenden", das im Rahmen des Aktionsprogramms "StudierendenAuswahl" des Stifterverbands für die Deutsche Wissenschaft und der Landesstiftung Baden-Württemberg durchgeführt wird. Zeitschrift für Pädagogische Psychologie **21**(1), 11–27 (2007)
32. Vallerand, R.J., Gauvin, L.I., Halliwell, W.R.: Negative effects of competition on children's intrinsic motivation. J. Soc. Psychol. **126**(5), 649–656 (1986)
33. Vaz de Carvalho, C., Escudeiro, P., Coelho, A. (eds.): SGAMES 2016. LNICST, vol. 176. Springer, Cham (2017). https://doi.org/10.1007/978-3-319-51055-2
34. Wiggins, B.E.: An overview and study on the use of games, simulations, and gamification in higher education. Int. J. Game-Based Learn. **6**(1), 18–29 (2016)

Students' Perceptions on Co-creating Learning Material in Information Systems Education

Antonis Natsis[1(✉)], Pantelis M. Papadopoulos[1], and Nikolaus Obwegeser[2]

[1] Centre for Teaching Development and Digital Media, Aarhus University, Aarhus, Denmark
{anatsis,pmpapad}@tdm.au.dk
[2] Department of Management, Aarhus University, Aarhus, Denmark
nikolaus@mgmt.au.dk

Abstract. Following the increased interest in students becoming partners in teaching and learning in higher education settings, this study explores students' perceptions on a collaborative content generation activity, in which students assume also the role of peer-tutors. Students in an Information Systems course collaborated on domain topics, assigned to them by the teacher, and created learning material for their fellow students. In the peer-tutoring session following the creation of the learning material, students presented the topic in class and discussed it with their peers. Each peer tutoring session was assessed by the students as audience (students attending the student-tutoring sessions). The aim of the study is to explore students' perspectives on the collaborative content generation assignment. Our focus primarily is to examine how students' experiences regarding the collaboration were affected by learning strategies in self-regulation, peer learning, and help seeking. Results showed that students were more engaged in the course after participating in the co-creating learning material activity and also, four distinct patterns of collaboration were revealed by analyzing student activity. Even though students were in general satisfied with their collaboration, as they could suit the activity to their needs, those students who relied more on their group for help proved to be less satisfied by the communication among group members. In addition, the teacher and the audience evaluated positively the students' performance as peer-tutors. This paper is an extended version of [1], presented at the 9th International Conference on Computer Supported Education.

Keywords: Co-creation · Collaboration · Peer-tutoring · Learning strategies

1 Introduction

Lately research and practice on students being partners, producers and co-creators of their own learning has gained more ground among academics [2–4]. The educational benefits of co-creation can be of great value as it can adjust across different disciplines and institutions. It also provides collaborative opportunities among staff and students who may: (re)generate the content of courses; research learning and teaching;

P. Escudeiro et al. (Eds.): CSEDU 2017, CCIS 865, pp. 325–342, 2018.
https://doi.org/10.1007/978-3-319-94640-5_16

undertake disciplinary research; design assessments; assess course content and learning and teaching processes; and evaluate both their own and their peers' work [5].

On that ground, student generation of content can facilitate high levels of students' engagement and deep learning, leading eventually to enhanced conceptual understanding [6, 7]. Furthermore, when the generation of content is linked to research, then it can contribute to the integration of research and teaching which is a desired goal to be achieved in higher education. This link between research and teaching can promote learning [8] and an increasing number of studies conclude that students benefit in their learning process, when they actively participate in research activities and are instructed by active researchers [9–11].

Healy [9] proposed a generally accepted model on the different ways that research and teaching can be integrated in a course (Fig. 1). According to this model, the activities can be student- or teacher-focused while their emphasis could be on research content or on research processes and problems. When the activities are teacher-focused, students act as audience and learn through their teachers' personal research experience. When activities are student-focused, students act as participants and are actively engaged in writing and discussing research papers or they are asked to conduct their own research regarding a topic. Additionally, they can act as tutors for their peers by presenting and discussing with them the findings of their research. The types of research activities the students are engaged in depend on the domain [12] and it is possible that during a course, students deal with activities that fall into different categories (quadrants of Fig. 1).

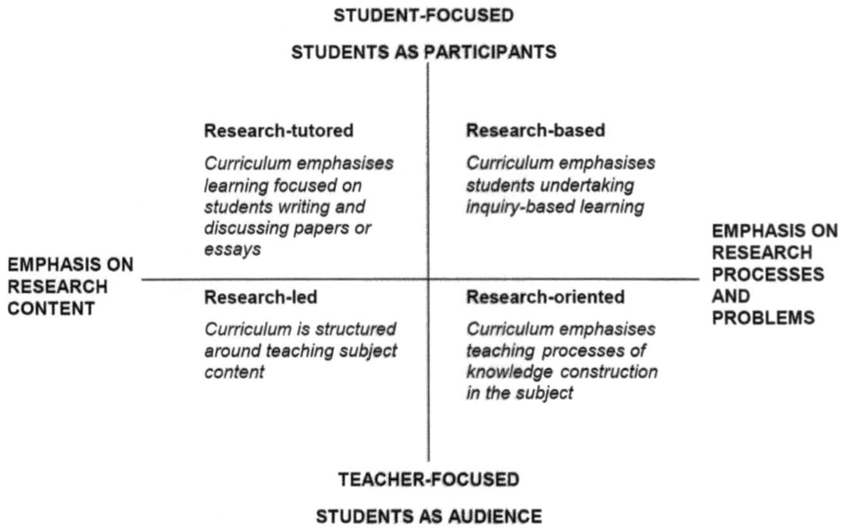

Fig. 1. Curriculum design and the research-teaching nexus [9].

When research and teaching are linked together, students either by acting as audience or participants have to deal with assignments which require the comprehension and processing of academic texts. Such tasks prove to be quite challenging and overwhelming for students who lack sufficient knowledge on their scientific domain and fail to apply appropriate reading strategies and so, they perform poorly in them [13, 14].

Students' processing of academic literature can be enhanced through collaborative learning [15, 16], as opposed to working individually. For a successful collaboration to be achieved, students should engage in explaining [17], questioning [18], or arguing [19] and through these activities, they can acquire both domain-specific knowledge and cross-domain skills such as collaboration, argumentation or peer-assessment skills [20].

In such collaborative settings, the learning outcomes can vary according to students' characteristics [19], among which the effective use of learning strategies is considered to be important [21]. The effective use of self-regulated learning (SRL), peer learning (PL) [22] and help seeking (HS) [23] strategies are considered to influence the success of collaborative learning. Self-regulated learning strategy has been extensively studied regarding individual learning, yet its impact on collaborative learning has been less investigated [24, 25].

Based on the above, this study aims to elicit students' perceptions on a collaborative content generation activity, in which students assume also the role of peer-tutors. More specifically, the following research questions (RQ) will be examined:

- RQ1: How do students as tutors (ST) assess the process of their collaboration in terms of communication, role assignment and contribution while creating learning material?
- RQ2: Does the use of different learning strategies influence students' assessment of the process of their collaboration?
- RQ3: Do students as tutors increase their engagement to the course?
- RQ4: How do students as audience (SA) assess the tutoring session produced by their peers?

To answer the aforementioned research questions, a survey was conducted on groups of first semester graduate students after they worked together in order to critically engage with scientific papers in the domain of Information Systems. Students had to create learning materials of different types (e.g., generating questions and answers based on the paper, summarizing the text etc.) representing the knowledge acquired from these papers. As a last step, in a peer-tutoring session following the creation of the learning material, student groups had to present and discuss the paper with their peers.

2 Method

2.1 Participants and Domain

The course "Information System Development and Implementation in a Business Context – ISDI" runs over the first semester of the "Master Degree Programme in Economics and Business Administration" in the Department of Management. In particular, it lasts 11 weeks and in total, 120 teaching hours. The course is taught in English and provides 10 ECTS credits. The aim of this course is to provide students with the necessary knowledge to develop and/or implement IS in organizational environments and to enable them comprehend the various challenges, risks and complexities that such development and/or implementation entails. At the end of this course, students will be able to describe, analyze, evaluate, reflect upon, and apply models of information systems development in a business context. Furthermore, through their engagement in the course activities, students are assumed to acquire cross-domain (general) skills like reading and analyzing original research papers, working effectively with others, writing and communicating clearly and organized and assessing their peers' work. The basic instruction form of the course is lectures held mainly by the teacher and during the lectures students present their work of the collaborative activities that they were engaged in with their peers.

Through the course, students are supposed to play two roles: as peer-tutors (students as tutors, ST) and as audience (students as audience, SA). As tutors, students are asked to collaborate in groups in order to produce a set of five deliverables based on a topic assigned by the teacher. On the other hand, students as audience need to provide feedback on the deliverables of their fellow students and evaluate the structure usefulness, and overall quality of the material produced. As audience, they are supposed to use this material to prepare themselves for the final exams. To score a grade in the final exams, students need to submit a group report and then, based on this report and the curriculum, each undertakes an oral examination.

Real-life context sets the background for this course and thus, the research-teaching nexus forms an integral part of the learning design. By playing both the roles as peer-tutors (students as tutors, ST) and as audience (students as audience, SA), students will experience the connection between research and learning in various ways (Table 1).

Table 1. Activities the students are engaged in during the course [1].

Research quadrant	Student activity
Research-led	Students learn about research findings through their teachers' own research activities
Research-tutored	Students work in groups of three or four. They are given a publication on a specific topic and are asked to prepare five different types of deliverables, including a presentation followed by a discussion session in front of their peers and their teacher
Research-oriented	Students have to critically reflect and discuss the research design and methods of seminal IS papers
Research-based	Students have to hand-in a group report a month before the final exam. The exam itself is conducted orally in a form similar to a thesis defense and is individual for each student. Each group of students can decide the actual topic and research design by themselves

The focus of the present study is on the research-tutored collaborative activity. In particular, students in groups analyze scientific literature and they are supposed to create a set of five deliverables that can be used as learning material by their fellow students. Their role as peer-tutors ends with the presentation of their assigned topic in the class. As audience, students need to provide feedback on the structure, usefulness, and overall quality of the material produced by the student-tutors. Students' research-oriented (discussion of research methodology), research-based (final report) and research-led (teacher's own research) activities complete the course canvas. However, analysis on student activity in these other quadrants span outside the limits of this study and will not be discussed.

In total, 65 first semester graduate students formed 18 groups. Seven of those groups consisted of three students and 11 groups consisted of four students. Regarding students' background, 34 of them were majoring on "Information Management", 28 on "Business Intelligence", while the rest were studying "Logistics and SCM" and "Technology Governance" programs. Finally, 13 students were international/exchange students.

2.2 Research Instruments

Three instruments were used for the purposes of the study: the Motivated Strategies for Learning Questionnaire (MSLQ) [26], the student-tutors' questionnaire, and the audience/teacher questionnaire.

With a view to measuring students' use of self-regulated learning (SRL), peer learning (PL), and help seeking (HS) strategies, the MSLQ was employed which is a comprehensive measurement instrument that can be used partially or entirely. Divided into two sections, this instrument includes 81 questions grouped in 15 scales. In this study, only three scales (i.e., SRL, PL, HS) were selected, because they were the ones that influenced more the collaborative activity. This version of the MSLQ included 19 closed-type questions (SRL: 12; PL: 3; HS: 4), each one using a 7-point Likert scale ranging from *"1: Not true at all"* to *"7: Very true"*.

To record students' attitudes and opinions on the collaborative activity, each of the students filled in individually the student-tutors (ST) questionnaire which was developed by the authors. The focus was to elicit students' perceptions of their collaboration in their group with aspects such as the volume and format of communication, role assignment, and their own contribution. A set of four closed-type questions, each one using a custom 5-point Likert scale, assessed both the volume and format of communication. A scale ranging from *"One of us was responsible for producing the final version"* to *"We worked together on the same parts producing together the final version"* evaluated the role assignment. A 5-point scale ranging from "Discussant" to "Leader" demonstrated the students' contribution to the creation of each deliverable, while a 5-point scale ranging from *"1: Not at all"* to *"5: Very much"* was used by the students to self-assess how much the other members of the group appreciated this contribution. Furthermore, a dichotomous item in the student-tutors (ST) questionnaire depicted students' general preference on collaborative/individual activities. Additionally, a set of five open-ended questions enabled students to elaborate on peer support, possible problems that had to be tackled during their collaborative assignment, and their satisfaction regarding the communication, collaboration and reaching consensus process. Finally, one question indicated students' opinion on how much working on the course assignments increased their engagement in the course and an open-ended question elicited students' comments and suggestions on the course assignments in general.

Regarding the audience/teacher questionnaire, both the students as audience (SA) and the teacher used it to evaluate the peer tutoring session based on a set of criteria: structure of the presentation, quality of material used, effectiveness of presentation as well as student-tutors' ability to respond to audience questions and provide clarifications on the presented topic. The audience/teacher questionnaire included six 5-point Likert scale questions and was used after each peer tutoring session.

2.3 Procedure

In the beginning of the course, students were asked to fill in the adjusted MSLQ instrument by providing their names in all instruments so that the researchers could follow their activity throughout the study. Students were aware of the research aspect of the course assignment and of the anonymity/protection of their identities and responses, as these would not be shared with their fellow students.

Groups of three to four members were then formed and each were assigned a course topic by the teacher. Each group received a seminal scientific paper on a course-related topic and had to create five deliverables:

- An annotated version of the paper, with comments and emphasized parts;
- A list of five highlights, providing a concise view of the paper;
- A list of five questions, along with their answers, that would cover the major issues discussed on the paper;
- A short summary of 200–300 words;
- A comprehensive presentation of the topic for the peer tutoring session that could use slides or any other material. The total duration of the presentation should not exceed 40 min, including a discussion session with the class audience and the teacher.

At the end of each peer tutoring session, all students had access to the deliverables as part of the course material. The teacher, with a view to ensuring homogeneity on learning materials and assisting the group who acted as peer-tutor provided detailed instructions and generic examples of how these deliverables should look like. In addition, access to a separate Google Drive folder was granted to each group and all the necessary assignment material, along with empty templates for the five deliverables was provided there. Google Drive tools were used on the ground that (a) students were familiar with these, (b) the tools allowed for real-time co-authoring, and (c) these tools provide a revision history log, offering the possibility of examining students' co-authoring activities during the semester. However, it should be noted that working online was only optional for the students (e.g., students could upload their deliverables after producing them offline or with other tools). Two weeks was the time allocated to each group to prepare its peer-tutoring session and present the topic in class.

Having as a goal the meaningful collaboration among students, general guidelines were given to them. More explicit instructions shaping the collaboration could have been more beneficial for some students, however, a high degree of self-regulation within the groups was purposefully allowed in order to understand emerging collaboration patterns and their relationship to different learning strategies. More specifically, students were encouraged to:

- Communicate as much as necessary and have all group members on the same page;
- Contribute to all group deliverables, even if it is on different levels;
- Reach a shared understanding, demonstrated by the ability to explain, analyze, argue, and answer questions on all deliverables;

At the end of each peer-tutoring session, student tutors (STs) filled in the student-tutor questionnaire while both the teacher and the students as audience (SA) evaluated the presentation, by using the SA/teacher instrument.

The assessment of the rest of the deliverables (i.e., annotated version, highlights, summary, questions & answers) is still ongoing and it will be the focus of a future study.

2.4 Data Analysis

A combination of quantitative and qualitative analysis of students' responses in the research instruments was carried out in order to address the research questions of the study. For all statistical analyses, a level of significance at .05 was chosen.

The sample was divided in low and high level MSLQ subscales (SRL, PL, HS), using the respective median as the cut-off point in order to explore whether students' learning strategies influenced students' assessment of group communication, role assignment, and contribution in the group work.

Independent-samples t-tests were conducted to compare the volume of communication, the role assignment among group members and their contribution in the deliverables' creation with High and Low groups of SRL, PL and HS. A series of Chi-square tests for independence was conducted aiming to investigate whether there is an association between the preference in individual or collaborative working and the MSLQ subscales.

The difference in students' knowledge before and after the presentations was examined through paired-samples t-tests.

3 Results

3.1 Students as Tutors (ST)

Students Use of Learning Strategies. The Cronbach's alpha coefficient for the self-regulated learning, peer learning and help seeking subscales of MSLQ were 0.82, 0.73, and 0.71, respectively, indicating satisfactory reliability. In general, the students scored (scale 1–7) rather high in the SRL (M = 4.36, SD = 0.93, min = 2.50, max = 6.50) and HS (M = 4.27, SD = 1.21, min = 1.50, max = 6.50) subscales, while they were split in PL (M = 3.96, SD = 1.35, min = 1.33, max = 6.67), with 22 students having a negative disposition towards peer learning.

The rather high score in the SRL strategy could be explained by the fact that the study sample consisted of graduate students who have developed the necessary skills and methods of setting goals, planning and monitoring their learning. Furthermore, from the difference in HS and PL strategies it seems that the students are keener on asking for help from their teacher instead of their peers.

RQ1: How do Students as Tutors (ST) Assess the Process of their Collaboration in Terms of Communication, Role Assignment and Contribution while Creating Learning Material? In order to answer the first research question, an analysis of student responses in the student-tutors (ST) questionnaire concerning the volume and format of communication, the role assignment and their contribution in the collaborative activity was conducted. Additionally, a qualitative analysis of student responses to the open-ended questions of the instruments was carried out. Finally, the revision history of their collaborative activities in Google Docs was examined.

Table 2 presents student responses in the questions regarding the volume and format of communication.

Table 2. Student responses in the student-tutor questionnaire, regarding the volume and format of communication.

Question	M	*SD*
Q1. How much communication happened in your group? *(1: A little; 5: A lot)*	4.28	*(0.71)*
Q2. How much of this communication was one-to-one (one member communicating directly with another member)? *(1: A little; 5: A lot)*	2.63	*(1.39)*
Q3. How much of this communication was one-to-many (one member communicating directly with two or more members)? *(1: A little; 5: A lot)*	4.00	*(1.21)*
Q4. What tools/methods did you use to communicate with the other group members? *(1:Rarely; 5: Very Often)*		
Chat, messaging (Facebook Messenger, SMS, etc.)	4.22	*(1.05)*
Email	1.31	*(0.78)*
Face-to-face meeting	4.15	*(0.82)*
Group posts (Facebook, Twitter, etc.)	2.13	*(1.51)*
Voice call (phone calls, etc.)	1.27	*(0.66)*
Video call (Skype, Google Hangouts, etc.)	1.45	*(0.98)*
Other	1.27	*(0.71)*

As it is shown from the table, there was high and effective communication among group members aiming to complete the assignment. Students opted for setting up meetings with all the group members in a synchronous manner either face-to-face or online, i.e. chatting mainly in Facebook.

In the open-ended part of the questionnaire, students had the opportunity to further elaborate whether they were satisfied with the communication among their group members. The members of the vast majority of the groups (15 groups) stated that they were very satisfied with the communication among their peers. They managed to communicate frequently and efficiently either face-to-face or online and they were able to ask and answer questions regarding their assignment. Some examples of students' comments denoting their satisfaction with the communication are the following:

"Yes, I think our communication was efficient."

"Yes, we had both face to face and virtual discussions."

"We discussed the topic whenever we met, in addition to the settled meetings. Thus, I would say I'm satisfied."

"Perfect. No issues what so ever."

In three of the groups, the main problem identified was the fact that one of the members in each group was not participating in the meetings and/or the discussions related to the assignment due to their busy program causing frustration and complaints by the rest of the members.

Regarding student assessment of role assignment and contribution, their responses in the relevant questions are depicted in Figs. 2 and 3, respectively. The main distinction regarding the role assignment is based on whether all members work together and equally contribute in the creation of the deliverables or one member of the group is responsible for producing the final version. In the latter case, the other members of the group provide different levels of feedback ranging from merely reading and approving the deliverable to providing detailed suggestions for the improvement of the final product. The way each group works affects the contribution of the members of the groups. For each of the deliverables the contribution of the members ranges from Discussant to Leader (Fig. 3).

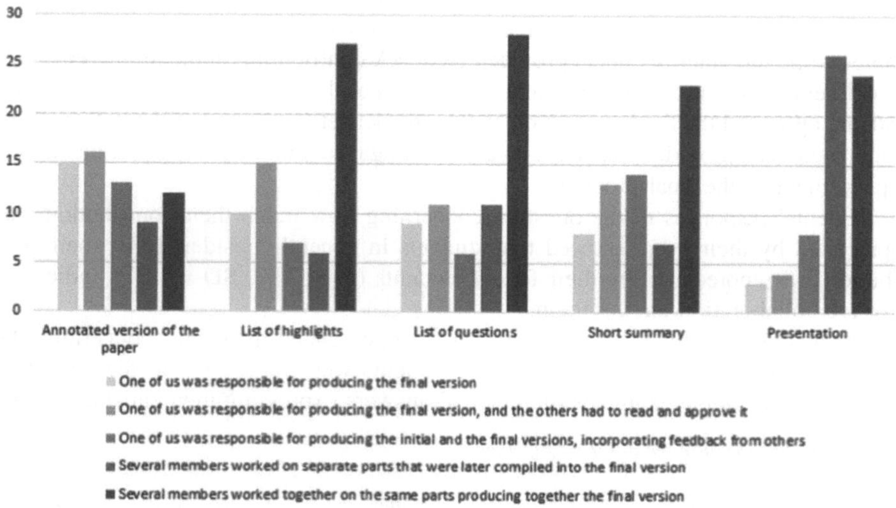

Fig. 2. Student responses (N = 65) in the student-tutor (ST) questionnaire regarding the role assignment (Q5. "For each of the learning artifacts, select the phrase that describes best the way your group worked.") [1].

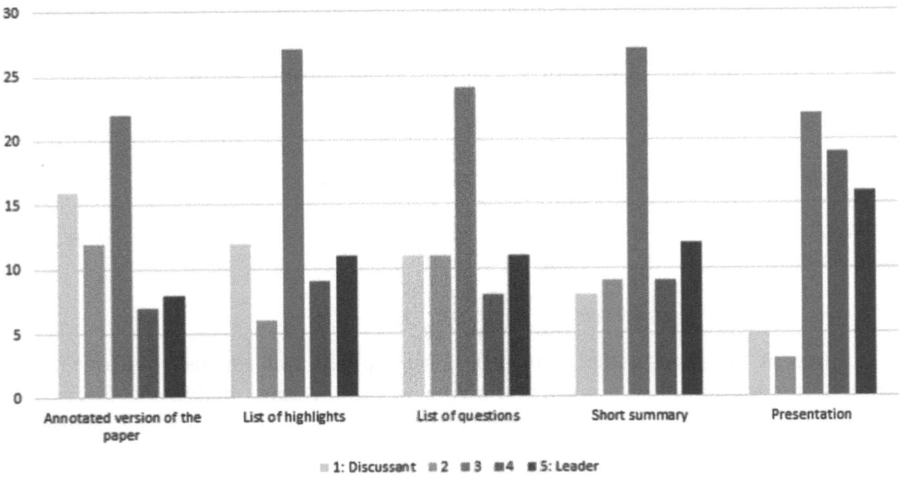

Fig. 3. Student responses (N = 65) in the student-tutor (ST) questionnaire regarding their contribution (Q6. "For each of the learning artifacts, select a value that describes best your level of responsibility.") [1].

Based on the figures, it is indicated that students collaborated most in the preparation of the presentation. Several members of the groups worked together and produced the final version of the presentation, even if in some groups a leader was set. To produce the list of highlights, the list of questions and answers and the short summary, students collaborated less while the annotated version of the paper was the deliverable that students collaborated the least. For these products, the majority of the groups set a member to be responsible for producing the initial and the final version of the deliverables while the other members provided feedback contributing in the improvement of the deliverable. In the case of the annotated version of the paper, the discussants mainly read and approved the final product created by the leader. In the rest of the deliverables, group members provided feedback and were engaged in discussions aiming in the improvement of the final products.

Students' responses to the question concerning how much their contribution was appreciated by their peers showed that students in general considered that their contribution was appreciated by their fellow students (M = 3.97, SD = 1.07), indicating effective collaboration among them.

The analysis of students' comments on the open-ended questions, concerning the way the groups worked, revealed that the students were satisfied with the way their groups worked. Some examples of students' answers expressing their satisfaction are:

"I'm satisfied because we did it all together."

"I was okay with the way we split the responsibilities and how we worked as a group on questions and summary."

"Yes, we scheduled a productive set of meetings and developed the deliverables fairly quickly."

"Very satisfied. We planned our time very well."

"Yes. We agreed on what we needed to create together, and which assignments we did individually."

"Yes, very satisfied. Everyone pulled the same workload and communication was fine."

"We managed to allocate the different tasks quite fast. After solving the different tasks, we reviewed and discussed each other's work, so I'm satisfied with the way we achieved our goal."

"We share work and meet online to discuss after we read what each other have written."

Furthermore, positive answers were also gathered in the questions regarding the support they gave or received and how easy it was to reach consensus. From students' responses, it can be concluded that they were engaged in transactive discussions and support each other when necessary. Some examples of students' answers in these questions are:

"We have collaborated really well, as all members came up with reasons for each statement we did not all agree on."

"We did work individually and then discussed - helping each other with concepts we didn't understand."

"Yes, I think we were good at reaching a consensus. We thought the article was really difficult, so we were good at helping each other out."

"Yes, we all benefited on each other thoughts to get a better understanding of our paper."

"We split out the work, then read and commented on each other's work. Furthermore, we added stuff if needed.

To investigate whether the communication and role assignment were perceived the same by all members of each group, the coefficient of variation (CV) for the questions Q1 and Q5 was computed and used as an indicator. If $CV < 0.3$, a group was classified as perceiving the same volume of communication and role assignment. Otherwise, when $CV \geq 0.3$, they had different perception. No differences were found regarding the perceived volume of communication between the members of all groups. In 10 groups, the perceived role assignment varied due to the fact that their members perceived the role assignment differently in the creation of the annotated version of the paper. Additionally, in three of these groups differences were found in the list of highlights, list of questions and short summary. Yet, there were no differences observed on the perceived role assignment for the presentation.

To explore the collaboration patterns that emerged in the groups, a comparative analysis of group member responses in questions Q5 and Q6 and their statements in the open-ended items of the student-tutor questionnaire indicated four distinct patterns (Table 3).

Three groups worked collaboratively, by having all members participating in the creation of all the deliverables equally, either together for all the different parts of the deliverable or in separate parts which they had to compile later in the final version after

Table 3. Patterns of collaboration among groups (N = 18) [1].

Pattern	Student participation	Number of Groups
Collaboration	Equal participation - group members worked together on the same parts producing together the final version	3
Mainly collaboration	Equal participation in most of the deliverables – in some deliverables one was responsible for the final product incorporating feedback from the other members	5
Mainly cooperation	Students split the work in most of the deliverables – one was responsible for the final product and the others had to provide feedback	8
Cooperation	Students split the work in all the deliverables – one was responsible for the final product and the others had only to approve it	2

reaching consensus. Five groups worked mainly collaboratively for the majority of the deliverables while in some other deliverables, one member had the leader role and was responsible for the final product incorporating feedback from the others. In the rest of the groups, members cooperated by splitting the workload and working individually (see [27] for a detailed discussion on the nature of collaboration).

Finally, we examined the revision history of Google Docs. Table 4 shows the average number of the different versions and edits for each of the deliverables. Students did not use Google Docs for the creation of the annotated version of the paper nor for the presentation.

Table 4. Average number of the different versions and edits for each of the deliverables created in Google Docs.

Deliverable	Versions	Total edits
Highlights	2,50	12,39
Summary	2,50	12,28
Five questions with their answers	2,56	10,72

The low number of different versions and total edits in students' deliverables suggests that the majority of groups completed the larger part of the assignment offline and used the Google Docs templates for minor edits or for submitting the final draft of their deliverables.

As far as the problems students had to resolve during their collaboration, in three groups the 'free riding' behavior of one of the members of the groups was observed. This behavior caused frustration and complaints from the other members of the groups. In four more groups students had difficulties in setting up meetings with all the members of the groups due to their busy program. Yet, the vast majority of the groups (11 groups) did not have any particular issues to resolve. Some examples of students' comments regarding the issues they had to solve during the collaborative activity are the following:

"There was some planning difficulties as we all had an exam the week before presenting."

"Yes we did, because it is very difficult to plan a meeting with four people with completely different calendars and plans."

"There was a little misfit in the amount of time that each one expected to spend."

"Time management was an issue."

"It was difficult finding time for meetings because of the fact that we were four people in the group. We had a couple of meetings with just three members present."

"There was a little misfit in the amount of time that each one expected to spend."

RQ2: Does the use of Different Learning Strategies Influence Students' Assessment of the Process of their Collaboration? T-test result analysis revealed that students with extreme values in the HS subscale had a significant difference on their perception of the volume of communication that occurred in their groups (HS_{High}: $M = 3.18$, $SD = 0.93$; HS_{Low}: $M = 3.86$, $SD = 0.98$; $t[63] = 2.57$, $p = 0.01$). Chi-squared tests for independence indicated a significant association between preference in group working (question Q7 in the ST questionnaire) and the students' score in the PL subscale ($\chi2(1, 65) = 6.78$, $p = 0.01$), as expected. Conversely, no significant association between Q7 and the use of SRL and HS strategies was found.

To explore the influence of students' learning strategies on the observed collaboration patterns (Table 3), the terms "Homogeneous" and "Heterogeneous" were used to describe each group. The coefficient of variation (CV) for the three MSLQ subscales was used as an indicator of homogeneity for the group. If $CV < 0.3$ for all three MSLQ subscales, a group was characterized as "Homogeneous", whereas when $CV \geq 0.3$ at least in one of the three subscales, it was perceived as "Heterogeneous". Based on the above, 10 groups were characterized as homogeneous and eight as heterogeneous. In particular, there were no discrepancies in the self-regulation subscale among the members of any of the groups. One group was characterized as "Heterogeneous" because of differences in HS and seven additional groups for differences in PL strategies (two of them also varied on the HS subscale). Nevertheless, no visible link between group homogeneity and collaboration patterns was observed, since the groups appeared equally distributed into the four observed patterns (Table 5).

Table 5. Patterns of collaboration among groups (N = 18) [1].

Pattern	Homogeneous groups	Heterogeneous groups
Collaboration	2	1
Mainly collaboration	3	2
Mainly cooperation	3	5
Cooperation	2	0

RQ3: Do Students as Tutors Increase their Engagement to the Course? Students' answers in the question regarding whether the assignments increased their engagement in the course were rather positive (M = 4.13, SD = .85). This finding was further supported by their answers in the open-ended question concerning students' comments on the course assignments. Some examples are:

> *"I like the idea about creating artifacts for the research papers. This was helpful when preparing for the exam and during the course."*

> *"The assignment has given a good basic "insight" into the course curriculum."*

> *"I like the course structure with student involvement during the semester (presentations) and the large report in the end of the semester."*

> *"The highlight notes and the summary was very helpful to get a quick understanding of the article. The presentation was also in some instances helpful."*

Of course, in their comments, students also stated the drawbacks of the procedure. They mostly focused on the heavy workload of the course in conjunction with the limited time they could spend in creating the deliverables.

3.2 Students as Audience (SA)

RQ4: How do Students as Audience (SA) Assess the Tutoring Session Produced by their Peers? The mean and standard deviation of the evaluation of the 18 peer-tutoring sessions by the teacher and the audience are shown in Table 6.

Table 6. Evaluation of student-tutor presentations (N = 18) by the audience and the teacher [1].

Questions	Audience		Teacher	
	M	*SD*	M	*SD*
Q1. What is your opinion about the organization/structure of the presentation? *(1: several issues on structure and/or time; 5: timely and well-organized)*	3,69	*(0,61)*	4,00	*(1,00)*
Q2. What do you think about the presentation material (slides)? *(1: too packed, boring, or confusing; 5: clear, easy to follow, and aesthetically nice)*	3,69	*(0,65)*	3,68	*(0,97)*
Q3. What is your opinion about the effectiveness of the presentation? Were the topics explained clearly? *(1: the paper was poorly outlined; 5: the main topics were clear and easy to understand)*	3,54	*(0,64)*	3,45	*(1,16)*
Q4. What is your opinion about the group's responses to audience questions? *(1: confusing or incomplete answers; 5: clear and correct answers)*	3,46	*(0,66)*	2,77	*(1,17)*
Q5. How knowledgeable were you on the topic, before the presentation? *(1: not at all; 5: very much)*	2,07	*(0,57)*	-	-
Q6. How knowledgeable do you feel on the topic, after the presentation? *(1: not at all; 5: very much)*	3,47	*(0,56)*	-	-

Throughout the semester, there was a variation in the audience population (approximately 50 on average each week) and the aggregated values refer to the overall structure and quality of all the ST presentations through the course timeline.

Based on Table 6, it can be seen that the structure, the quality, and the effectiveness of the student-produced presentations were evaluated positively by both the teacher and the audience. Such positive evaluation leads to the assumption that the group work led to well-structured and aesthetically pleasing presentations whose main topics were clear and easy to follow. Yet, both the teacher and the audience graded the discussion sessions, which followed the presentations, with the lowest scores, even though differences were found in the relevant scores. Such low scores could be explained by the poor preparation of students-tutors to respond efficiently to their peers' questions. However, there was a significant increase in audience knowledge during the student-tutor presentations for all presenting groups ($p < 0.05$), as it can be seen by a paired-sample t-test. In addition, both students and the teacher agreed in the ranking of the respective presentations in all the assessed factors, indicating students' ability to differentiate the quality of the different presentations accurately.

By analyzing students' comments in the open-ended questions regarding the activity, it was revealed that they had a positive attitude towards the deliverables, as they thought these were useful and helpful as preparation material for the exams.

4 Discussion

By analyzing the results, students' successful engagement in a collaborative content generation activity in the domain of Information Systems was evident. Their involvement in the collaborative activity and the peer-tutoring session also increased their engagement in the course. However, a poor use of the available digital tools, that could assist them when collaborating, was also evident. Due to such partial exploitation of these tools, students had to tackle with challenges in time management and primarily, with setting up meetings with all the members of the group. Overall, a general satisfaction from their collaboration was recorded, as there was adequate communication and contribution to the group deliverables by all members, although to a different extent. Finally, by reaching common consensus, they managed to present the topics in a clear and understandable way and answer questions on all the group deliverables.

As four collaboration patterns emerged, in most groups a student was leading the creation of each deliverable. The rest of the members either merely approved the already-made deliverable or provided constructive feedback and assisted in creating the final deliverable. However, all students collaborated the most when preparing the presentation, probably out of urge to respond well to their peers' questions during the discussion session, which followed the presentation.

The variance of group members regarding their self-regulated learning, peer learning and help seeking strategies did not have any impact on the collaboration patterns identified. Yet, the patterns may be affected by the fact that the students preferred to organize synchronous meetings either face-to-face or online in order to communicate and collaborate. This preference led to difficulties in finding common meeting hours for all the members and might have led to the patterns identified.

Students with higher scores on the help seeking scale were concerned of the communication among their group members, possibly due to their higher communication demands and their expectations for more support from their peers in the groups.

Students' self-assessment of group collaboration and their role during the activity were not influenced by self-regulated and peer learning strategies. Concerning the self-regulated learning strategy, few discrepancies were found among students, as they all had relatively high scores. Regarding the peer learning strategy, all students participated in a self-satisfying way, even the ones with extremely low scores on the peer learning scale, possibly due to the fact that there was no detailed collaboration script and so, they could adjust the activity to their abilities.

Students as audience evaluated their peers during the presentation and discussion sessions. There was common agreement in both the teacher and the audience that the presentations of the topics under study were of high quality. This leads to the assumption that students as tutors immersed themselves in the activity and collaborated efficiently with their peers. As a result all students as audience increased their knowledge of the topic under study after the presentation and discussion session with their peers.

5 Conclusions

Following the co-creation approach, in this study, students in small groups were asked to process academic papers and generate learning material in different forms that could be used by their fellow students. The assignment is concluded with a presentation and discussion session in front of their peers where the students assume the role of a tutor. This paper focuses primarily on students' perceptions of the assignment, while the possible learning gains will be examined after the analysis of students' performance in the exams.

Students assessed positively the assignment. It seems that the activity offered them the opportunity to apply and develop their skills in processing, presenting, and discussing academic work and fostered their engagement in the course, despite the heavy workload they faced. Additionally, the activity increased their engagement in the course despite the heavy workload they faced. The implication for designers and teachers is that student-academic staff partnership in content generation could be a valuable approach in higher education settings.

Our next step is to evaluate students' performance in the exams and examine whether the co-creation approach we followed led to deeper learning and enhanced conceptual understanding. Future research should focus in different contexts assuming different roles for the students involved in the co-creation process. Nevertheless, the current study provides a useful reference for further discussion regarding the co-creation process in higher education settings.

Acknowledgements. This work has been partially funded by a Starting Grant from AUFF (Aarhus Universitets Forskningsfond), titled "Innovative and Emerging Technologies in Education".

References

1. Natsis, A., Papadopoulos, P.M., Obwegeser, A.: Student groups as tutors in information systems education: students' perspectives on collaboration and outcomes. In: McLaren, B. M., Costagliola, G., Uhomoibhi, J., Escudeiro, P., Zvacek, S. (eds.), Proceedings of the 9th International Conference on Computer Supported Education – Volume 2: CSEDU 2017, pp. 37–45, Porto, Portugal (2017)
2. McCulloch, A.: The student as co-producer: learning from public administration about the student–university relationship. Stud. High. Educ. **34**(2), 171–183 (2009)
3. Bovill, C., Cook-Sather, A., Felten, P.: Students as co-creators of teaching approaches, course design, and curricula: implications for academic developers. Int. J. Acad. Dev. **16**(2), 133–145 (2011)
4. Deeley, S.J., Bovill, C.: Staff student partnership in assessment: enhancing assessment literacy through democratic practices. Assess. Eval. High. Educ. **42**(3), 463–477 (2017)
5. Bovill, C., Cook-Sather, A., Felten, P., Millard, L., Moore-Cherry, N.: Addressing potential challenges in co-creating learning and teaching: overcoming resistance, navigating institutional norms and ensuring inclusivity in student–staff partnerships. High. Educ. **71** (2), 195–208 (2016)
6. Draper, S.W.: Catalytic assessment: understanding how MCQs and EVS can foster deep learning. Br. J. Educ. Technol. **40**(2), 285–293 (2009)
7. Casey, M.M., Bates, S.P., Galloway, K.W., Galloway, R.K., Hardy, J.A., Kay, A.E., Kirsop, P., McQueen, H.A.: Scaffolding student engagement via online peer learning. Eur. J. Phys. **35**(4), 045002 (2014)
8. Brew, A.: Teaching and research: new relationships and their implications for inquiry-based teaching and learning in higher education. High. Educ. Res. Dev. **22**(1), 3–18 (2003)
9. Healey, M.: Linking research and teaching: exploring disciplinary spaces and the role of inquiry-based learning. In: Barnett, R. (ed.), Reshaping the University: New Relationships between Research, Scholarship and Teaching, pp. 67–78. McGraw Hill/Open University Press (2005)
10. Jenkins, A., Lindsay, R., Brew, A.: Reshaping Teaching in Higher Education: Linking Teaching with Research. Routledge, London (2003)
11. Obwegeser, N., Papadopoulos, P.M.: Integrating research and teaching in the IS classroom: benefits for teachers and students. J. Inf. Syst. Educ. **27**(4), 249–258 (2016)
12. Griffiths, R.: Knowledge production and the research–teaching nexus: the case of the built environment disciplines. Stud. High. Educ. **29**(6), 709–726 (2004)
13. Kolić-Vrhovec, S., Bajšanski, I., Zubković, B.R.: The role of reading strategies in scientific text comprehension and academic achievement of university students. Rev. Psychol. **18**(2), 81–90 (2011)
14. McNamara, D.S., Ozuru, Y., Best, R., O'Reilly, T.: The 4-pronged comprehension strategy framework. In: McNamara, D.S. (ed.), Reading Comprehension Strategies: Theories, Interventions, and Technologies, pp. 465–496. Lawrence Erlbaum Associates Publishers, Mahwah (2007)

15. Eryilmaz, E., Thoms, B., Mary, J., Kim, R., Canelon, J.: Task oriented reading of instructional materials and its relationship to message scores in online learning conversations. In: Paper Presented at the 2016 49th Hawaii International Conference on System Sciences (HICSS) (2016)
16. van der Pol, J., Admiraal, W., Simons, P.R.J.: The affordance of anchored discussion for the collaborative processing of academic texts. Int. J. Comput.-Support. Collab. Learn. **1**(3), 339–357 (2006)
17. Webb, N.M., Franke, M.L., De, T., Chan, A.G., Freund, D., Shein, P., Melkonian, D.K.: 'Explain to your partner': teachers' instructional practices and students' dialogue in small groups. Camb. J. Educ. **39**(1), 49–70 (2009)
18. King, A.: Transactive peer tutoring: distributing cognition and metacognition. Educ. Psychol. Rev. **10**(1), 57–74 (1998)
19. Noroozi, O., Weinberger, A., Biemans, H.J.A., Mulder, M., Chizari, M.: Argumentation-based computer supported collaborative learning (ABCSCL): a synthesis of 15 years of research. Educ. Res. Rev. **7**(2), 79–106 (2012)
20. Vogel, F., Wecker, C., Kollar, I., Fischer, F.: Socio-cognitive scaffolding with computer-supported collaboration scripts: a meta-analysis. Educ. Psychol. Rev. **29**(3), 477–511 (2016)
21. Solimeno, A., Mebane, M.E., Tomai, M., Francescato, D.: The influence of students and teachers characteristics on the efficacy of face-to-face and computer supported collaborative learning. Comput. Educ. **51**(1), 109–128 (2008)
22. Pifarre, M., Cobos, R.: Promoting metacognitive skills through peer scaffolding in a CSCL environment. Int. J. Comput.-Suppor. Collab. Learn. **5**(2), 237–253 (2010)
23. Kyza, E., Georgiou, Y., Hadjichambi, D., Hadjichambis, A.: Teacher framing, classroom collaboration scripts, and help-seeking and help-giving behaviors. In: Nikol Rummel, M.K., Nathan, M., Puntambekar, S. (eds.), To See the World and a Grain of Sand: Learning across Levels of Space, Time, and Scale: CSCL 2013 Conference Proceedings Volume 1-Full Papers & Symposia, pp. 272–279. International Society of the Learning Sciences (2013)
24. Dettori, G., Persico, D.: Detecting self-regulated learning in online communities by means of interaction analysis. IEEE Trans. Learn. Technol. **1**(1), 11–19 (2008)
25. Panadero, E., Kirschner, P.A., Järvelä, S., Malmberg, J., Järvenoja, H.: How individual self-regulation affects group regulation and performance: a shared regulation intervention. Small Group Res. **46**(4), 431–454 (2015)
26. Pintrich, P.R., Smith, D.A.F., Garcia, T., Mckeachie, W.J.: Reliability and predictive validity of the motivated strategies for learning questionnaire (MSLQ). Educ. Psychol. Meas. **53**(3), 801–813 (1993)
27. Dillenbourg, P.: What do you mean by 'collaborative learning'? In: Dillenbourg, P. (ed.), Collaborative-learning: Cognitive and Computational Approaches, pp. 1–19. Elsevier, Oxford (1999)

The Influence of First Year Behaviour in the Progressions of University Students

R. Campagni, D. Merlini(✉), and M. C. Verri

Dipartimento di Statistica, Informatica, Applicazioni,
Viale Morgagni 65, 50134 Florence, Italy
{renza.campagni,donatella.merlini,mariacecilia.verri}@unifi.it

Abstract. Advanced clustering techniques are used on educational data concerning various cohorts of university students. First, K-means analysis is used to classify students according to the results of the self assessment test and the first year performance. Then, the analysis concentrates on the subset of the data involving the cohorts of students for which the behavior during the first, second and third year of University is known. The results of the second and third year are analyzed and the students are re-assigned to the clusters obtained during the analysis of the first year. In this way, for each student we are able to obtain the sequence of traversed clusters during three years, based on the results achieved during the first. For the data set under analysis, this analysis highlights three groups of students strongly affected by the results of the first year: high achieving students who start high and maintain their performance over the time, medium-high achieving students throughout the entire course of study and, low achieving students unable to improve their performance who often abandon their studies. This kind of study can be used by the involved laurea degree to detect critical issues and undertake improvement strategies.

Keywords: Educational data mining · Clustering
Student progressions · Self assessment test

1 Introduction

Many fields and sectors, from economic and business activities to public administration, are involved with the growth of data in computer systems. For this reason it is important to develop new methodologies and technologies to manage and analyse all the information that can be derived from such big sources of data. For what concerns the field of education, EDM (Educational Data Mining) is a recent area of research that is designed to extract knowledge from data which are usually stored in the schools and universities databases for administrative purposes and that allows to understand and improve the performance of the student learning process (see [1,7–9] for recent surveys on the state of the art of educational data mining and on preprocessing educational data).

P. Escudeiro et al. (Eds.): CSEDU 2017, CCIS 865, pp. 343–362, 2018.
https://doi.org/10.1007/978-3-319-94640-5_17

The recent literature reveals that predicting performance at a university degree level has attracted considerable attention and interest. For example, [5,12,13] use regression and classification models to analyse how well indicators of undergraduate achievements and university performance characteristics can predict graduate-level performance; in [2], hierarchical cluster analysis is used to provide school leaders and researchers a method to make better informed decisions in schools earlier, using data already collected on students.

The present study uses data mining methods, in particular partitional clustering, to analyse the performance of students in the Computer Science laurea degree of the University of Florence (Italy), by using an explorative approach to mine information from students data. Two aspects of students performance are considered. First, we analyse the performance of students during their first year for six cohorts, starting from the academic year 2010–2011 up to 2015–2016. In particular, we combine results achieved by students in the courses of the first year with the results of a self-assessment test they are required to take before entering the university. This is done by clustering analysis using the `K`-means implementation of software `WEKA` (see [11]); the obtained results allows us to identify a few courses which can serve as indicators of good and low performance and to point out the influence of the self-assessment test in being successful in the first year exams.

Second, we concentrate on the first four cohorts of students and study their progressions during the first, second and third year of university. Three important groups of students have been identified: students who achieve quite high results during all the period under examination, medium-high achieving students who maintain a good profile throughout the entire course of study, low achieving students which often abandon their studies (see [3] for a similar study treated with a different approach). This analysis is done by clustering students of the first year according to the number of credits and the grades achieved during the first year, together with the result of the self-assessment test. Then we use this model to classify students during the other two years and thus identify the three typical behaviors. This second analysis is performed by using the *Cluster Assigner node* function of the software `KNIME` (see https://www.knime.org).

In Sect. 2 we introduce data used for the analysis and in particular we illustrate the operations performed on the original data to obtain the final data sets for the application of the appropriate algorithms. In Sects. 3 and 4 we explain the methodology and present the results obtained on a real case study. Finally, in Sect. 5 we present our conclusions.

This paper deepens and extends the analysis presented in [4] by adding the new cohort of students who started their career in the academic year 2015–16 and updating data to April 2017. The methodology applied to this enlarged data set confirms the results of [4] for the students of the Computer Science degree of the University of Florence in Italy. We wish to point out that all the figures and tables in Sects. 3 and 4 of the present paper although similar to those presented in [4], have been re-builded according to the enlarged data set corresponding to the cohorts 2010-15. Figures 10 and 11 are new and allow us to give a deeper inside of the problem analysed in the paper.

2 Data Sets for Analysis

In this section, we describe the data sets for our analysis referring to a laurea degree of the University of Florence, Italy; in particular we deal with data of the Computer Science degree of the Science School, under the Italian Ministerial Decree n. 270/2004. This academic degree is structured over three years and every academic year is organized with several courses, each course has assigned some credits (*CFU*) for an amount of 60 credits in each year.

Each student, before enrolling in the degree course, has to take an entrance test to self-evaluate his background in mathematics[1]. This test consists of 25 multiple choice questions (one correct answer out of four possible options) on mathematics arguments usually studied in high school: arithmetic, elementary algebra, equations, inequalities, elementary logic, combinatorics, functions, geometry, probability. Each correct answer counts as 1 point while a wrong or no given answer counts as 0 points: the test is passed with 12 points.

Data under analysis concern university students enrolled from academic year 2010–2011 (afterwards cohort 2010) up to 2015–2016 (afterwards cohort 2015), updated to 31th December 2017. We start with two different data sets: the first contains information about students and their school career before entering university, together with information on the entrance test; the second contains information about exams taken by students.

Table 1 illustrates an example of students data set after a preprocessing phase which allows us to integrate all the attributes related to students in a single table. Table 2 contains information about the exams given by the students, in particular the grade and the credits obtained. As often happens, we deal with data which need a preprocessing step to fix errors and to reorganize the data for the purposes of analysis, before applying the various analysis techniques, such that clustering, classification and several others (see [8] for a survey on preprocessing educational data). During this preprocessing phase we join Tables 1 and 2 and aggregate the data to obtain the productivity of the student in a year, in terms of credits and the average grade obtained in the corresponding exams.

At the end of this phase the resulting data set is organized as shown in Table 3, where, for example, the student identified by code 100 obtained a total of 24 credits in the first year (attribute `credits`) with a average grade of 25.5 (attribute `avggrade`); in the second year the same student obtained 60 credits with an average grade of 28. The attribute `test_grade` corresponds to the grade in the entrance test.

In this paper we present two different analyses based on two different data sets. The first analysis concerns the student productivity during the first year and considers all cohorts from 2010 to 2015. It is based on the data set related

[1] For more details, see http://www.scienze.unifi.it/upload/sub/testdiaccesso/syllabus-conoscenze-matematiche.pdf (in Italian).

Table 1. A sample of students data. The attributes in the table refer to the student identifier, `Student`, the grade obtained in the entrance test, varying in the range 0...25, `Test_grade`, the final grade obtained at the high school, varying in the range 60...100, `Hgrade`, and the typology of high school, `Hschool`. (Reprinted from [4]).

Student	Test_grade	Hgrade	Hschool
100	18	80	LS
200	22	100	IT
300	15	78	IT
400	24	100	LS
500	19	90	LC
⋮	⋮	⋮	⋮

Table 2. A sample of exams data. The attributes in the table refer to the student identifier, `Student`, the exam code, `Exam`, the exam date, `Date`, the grade obtained in the exam, varying in the range 18...30, `Grade`, and the corresponding number of credits, `Credits`. (Reprinted from [4]).

Student	Exam	Date	Grade	Credits
100	10	2011-01-14	24	12
100	20	2011-02-20	27	12
200	20	2011-02-20	21	12
⋮	⋮	⋮	⋮	⋮
300	10	2012-01-29	26	12
100	40	2012-02-15	26	6
⋮	⋮	⋮	⋮	⋮

Table 3. A sample of student productivity in the years. The attributes in the table refer to the student identifier, `Student`, the academic year under examination, `Year`, the number of credits achieved during the year, `Credits`, the average grade, varying in the range 18...30, `Avggrade`, and the grade obtained in the entrance test, varying in the range 0...25, `Test_grade`. (Reprinted from [4]).

Student	Year	Credits	Avggrade	Test_grade
100	2011	24	25.5	18
200	2011	12	21	22
⋮	⋮	⋮	⋮	⋮
300	2012	26	12	15
100	2012	60	28	18
⋮	⋮	⋮	⋮	⋮

to students who took at least an exam in their first year. The data set, analysed by the *K-means* implementation of the software WEKA, contains the detail about the grades obtained in each exam taken by students and is illustrated in Table 4.

The second analysis concerns the student productivity during the first three years; for each year we consider the credits and the average grade of exams and we analyse the way students behave in the different years in terms of the corresponding attributes. This analysis is based on students enrolled from 2010 up to 2013 and takes into account the entrance test and the examinations over the three years, as shown in Table 5. The indices I, II and III refer to the different years; the column names CreditsI, CreditsII, CreditsIII are for CreditsIgrade, CreditsIIgrade, CreditsIIIgrade, that is, they represent credits obtained in exams with grade. In particular we analyse how the career of the first year affects the entire career by using the *Cluster Assigner node* function of the software KNIME.

Table 4. A sample of data set for the analysis on first year. The attributes in the table refer to the student identifier, **Student**, the student cohort, **Cohort**, the number of credits corresponding to exams with a grade achieved during the year, **Credits_grade**, the average grade, varying in the range 18...30, **Avggrade**, the grade obtained in the entrance test, varying in the range 0...25, **Test_grade**, and the grade obtained in the *i*th exam, **exam_i**. (Reprinted from [4]).

Student	Cohort	Credits_grade	Avggrade	Test_grade	exam_1	...	exam_n
100	2010	60	26	18	27	...	24
200	2010	12	21	15	21	...	0
⋮	⋮	⋮	⋮	⋮	⋮	⋮	⋮
300	2011	12	26	12	26	...	0
⋮	⋮	⋮	⋮	⋮	⋮	⋮	⋮

3 Analysis of the First Year Productivity

In this section, we examine the first year *active* students of the six cohorts from 2010 up to 2015, for a total of 352 students. The term active refers to the fact that students under examination have given at least an exam within the month of December of the second year (for example, December 2011 for students of cohorts 2010). For some of these students, this fact corresponds to passing the English exam, which is a 3 CFU course without grade assignment. From our analysis are therefore excluded all the students that enroll at the Computer Science degree of the University of Florence and remain inactive within December of the next year: most of these students abandon their studies or make a different choice. However, among the active students just defined, there are some which are yet at risk of

Table 5. A sample of data set for the analysis on first three years. The attributes in the table refer to the student identifier, **Student**, the student cohort, **Cohort**, the number of credits corresponding to exams with a grade achieved during the I, II or III year, **CreditsI**, **CreditsII**, **CreditsIII**, the average grade, varying in the range 18..30, achieved during the I, II or III year, **AvggradeI**, **AvggradeII** and **AvggradeIII**, and the grade obtained in the entrance test, varying in the range 0...25, **Test**. (Reprinted from [4]).

Student	Cohort	CreditsI	CreditsII	CreditsIII	AvggradeI	AvggradeII	AvggradeIII	Test
100	2010	60	60	60	26	28	28	18
200	2010	12	36	48	21	23	25	15
⋮	⋮	⋮	⋮	⋮	⋮	⋮	⋮	⋮
300	2011	12	24	36	21	23	24	12
⋮	⋮	⋮	⋮	⋮	⋮	⋮	⋮	⋮

dropping out, due to the very low results during their first year. Understanding the productivity of first year students can point out these difficulties and gives an opportunity to improve the teaching and learning processes of the Laurea Degree. The data set we analyse is not big, however, as focused in [6], a data mining analysis is useful also in such small contexts. Moreover, the case study allows us to describe the methodology on a real situation.

In particular, we perform a cluster analysis by using the K-means implementation of the software WEKA. In our analysis we measure cluster validity with correlation, by using the concept of proximity and incidence matrices: in the proximity matrix $P = (P_{i,j})$, each element $P_{i,j}$ represents the Euclidean distance between elements i and j in the data set; in the incidence matrix $I = (I_{i,j})$, each element $I_{i,j}$ is 1 or 0 if the elements i and j belong to the same cluster or not. We then compute the Pearson's correlation, as defined in [10, p. 77], between the linear representation by rows of matrices P and I and we expect to find a negative value, where -1 means a perfect negative linear relationship.

We tried the K-means algorithm with several values of k and with $k = 3$ we obtained the cluster for the first year students of the six cohorts from 2010 up to 2015, illustrated in Fig. 1. As cluster attributes we used the number of credits corresponding to exams with a grade, attribute `credits_grade`, the average grade, attribute `avggrade`, and the grade of the self-assessment test, attribute `test_grade`.

The centroids of the cluster are illustrated in Table 6 and, in particular, cluster 0 corresponds to students that during the first year had success only with the exam of `English` and therefore have no credits and no grade in this clustering, cluster 1 identifies medium achieving students and, finally, cluster 2 identifies high achieving students. The clusters are characterized by colours red, blue and green in Fig. 1, respectively. The Pearson's correlation between the linear representation of the proximity and incidence matrices is -0.66, a good value of correlation.

Table 6. Centroids corresponding to Fig. 1 and corresponding to first year results of cohorts 2010–2015. The cluster 0 corresponds to students that during the first year had success only with the exam of `English` and therefore have no credits and no grade, cluster 1 identifies medium achieving students and, finally, cluster 2 identifies high achieving students.

Attribute	Full data (352)	Cluster_0 (37)	Cluster_1 (193)	Cluster_2 (122)
`credits_grade`	28.16	0	21.92	46.57
`avggrade`	22.73	0	24.46	26.88
`test_grade`	14.64	11.54	13.46	17.43

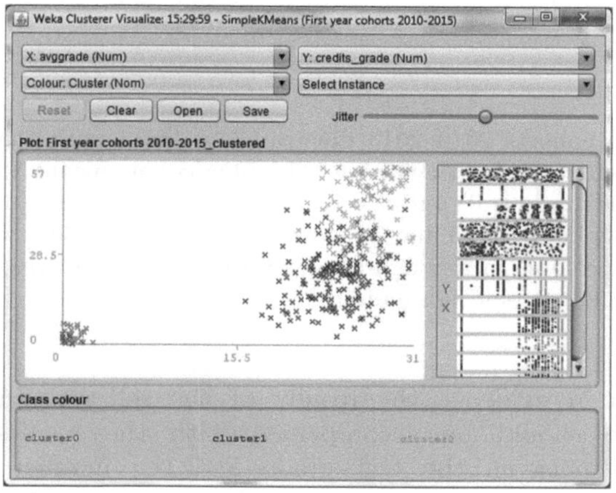

Fig. 1. Clusters for the first year students of cohorts 2010–2015 with respect to attributes `credits_grade`, attribute `avggrade`, and `test_grade` and their projection with respect to attributes `credits_grade` and `avggrade`. In red the students that during the first year had success only with the exam of `English` and therefore have no credits and no grade in this clustering; in blue medium achieving students and in green high achieving students. (For interpretation of the references to colours in this figure legend, the reader is referred to the electronic version of this article). (Color figure online)

The following Figs. 2, 3, 4, 5 and 6 illustrate the relation between the students in the cluster of Fig. 1 and the exams of the first year: Algorithms and Data Structures (`ADS`), Programming (`PRG`), Calculus (`CAL`), Architectures (`ARC`), Discrete mathematics and Logic (`DML`). In these figures, the blue colour means that the exam has not been given (the grade is 0) and the orange colour means that the exam has been passed with a grade between 18 and 30 (31 means 30 cum laude). As can be seen, there are some courses, such as `ADS`, organized in a such a way that most students in clusters 1 and 2 are able to give the corresponding exams, while there are two exams, `ARC` and `DML`, which are given mainly by students in cluster 2 and that therefore present some critical aspects.

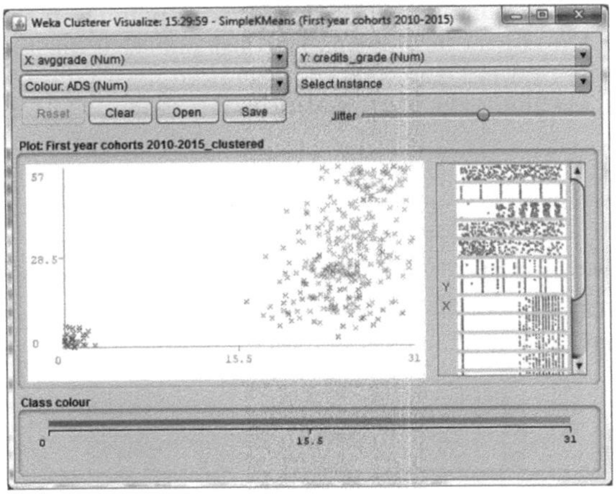

Fig. 2. Clusters of cohorts 2010–2015 illustrated in Fig. 1 with the Algorithms and Data Structures course, ADS, in evidence. The blue colour means that the exam has not been given (the grade is 0) and the orange colour means that the exam has been passed with a grade between 18 and 30 (31 means 30 cum laude). (For interpretation of the references to colours in this figure legend, the reader is referred to the electronic version of this article). (Color figure online)

Figure 7 puts in evidence the results of the self assessment test, however such figure should be accompanied with the results of the Pearson's correlation between the test grade and the number of credits and the average grade, respectively: for the six years 2010–15 the value corresponding to attributes **credits_grade** and **test_grade** shows a positive correlation of 0.44 while the value corresponding to attributes **avggrade** and **test_grade** shows a positive correlation of 0.35; a more detailed analysis, shows a particular positive correlation with the average grade of CAL and DML, that is, the mathematics courses of the first year. The self assessment test is mainly concerned with problems of logic, calculus, probability and the previous correlations between mathematics courses and the test are quite natural. These facts are summarized in Table 7 which shows the values of the correlation between each of the attributes **credits_grade**, **avggrade**, ADS, ARC, PRG, CAL, DML and the attribute **test_grade**, during the academic years from 2010 up to 2015, the four years 2010–13, which will be examined in the next section and, finally, the six years 2010–15.

For completeness, we computed also the Spearman and Kendall correlations between the same attributes as before and the test grade. The results are illustrated in Table 8 and reveal that the Kendall values are worse than Pearson values while the Spearman values are quite similar to Pearson values illustrated in Table 7.

A behavior similar to that illustrated in the previous figures, relative to cohorts 2010–2015 examined all together, can also be find on the single cohorts.

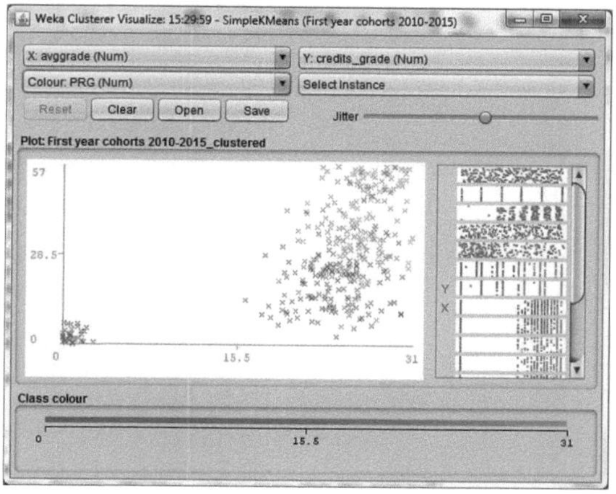

Fig. 3. Clusters of cohorts 2010–2015 illustrated in Fig. 1 with the Programming course, PRG, in evidence. The blue colour means that the exam has not been given (the grade is 0) and the orange colour means that the exam has been passed with a grade between 18 and 30 (31 means 30 cum laude). (For interpretation of the references to colours in this figure legend, the reader is referred to the electronic version of this article). (Color figure online)

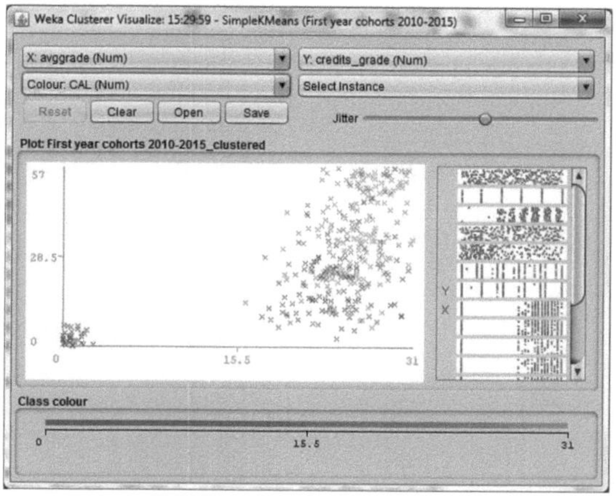

Fig. 4. Clusters of cohorts 2010–2015 illustrated in Fig. 1 with the Calculus course, CAL, in evidence. The blue colour means that the exam has not been given (the grade is 0) and the orange colour means that the exam has been passed with a grade between 18 and 30 (31 means 30 cum laude). (For interpretation of the references to colours in this figure legend, the reader is referred to the electronic version of this article). (Color figure online)

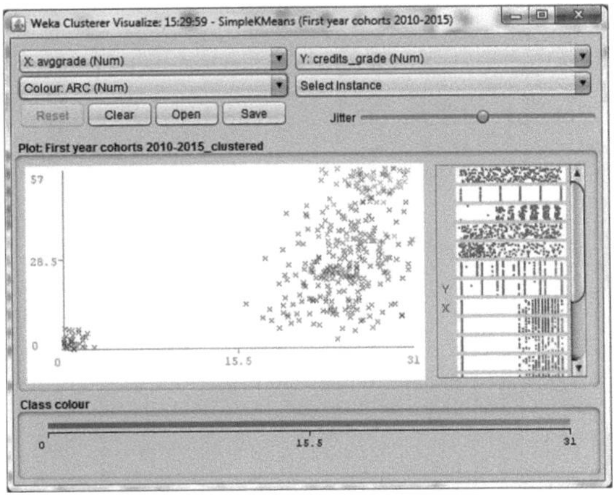

Fig. 5. Clusters of cohorts 2010–2015 illustrated in Fig. 1 with the Architectures course, `ARC`, in evidence. The blue colour means that the exam has not been given (the grade is 0) and the orange colour means that the exam has been passed with a grade between 18 and 30 (31 means 30 cum laude). (For interpretation of the references to colours in this figure legend, the reader is referred to the electronic version of this article). (Color figure online)

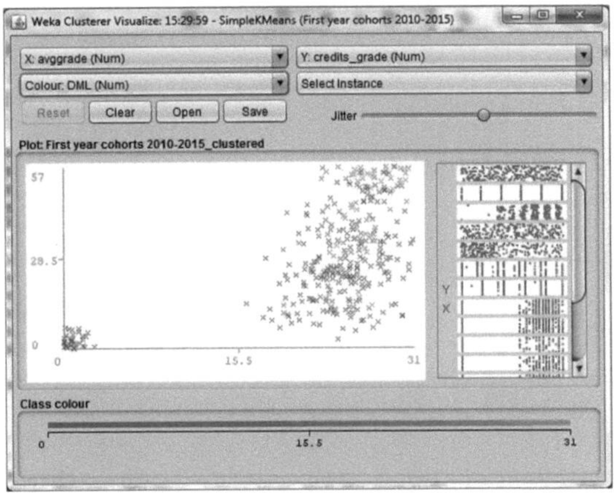

Fig. 6. Clusters of cohorts 2010–2015 illustrated in Fig. 1 with the Discrete mathematics and Logic course, `DML`, in evidence. The blue colour means that the exam has not been given (the grade is 0) and the orange colour means that the exam has been passed with a grade between 18 and 30 (31 means 30 cum laude). (For interpretation of the references to colours in this figure legend, the reader is referred to the electronic version of this article). (Color figure online)

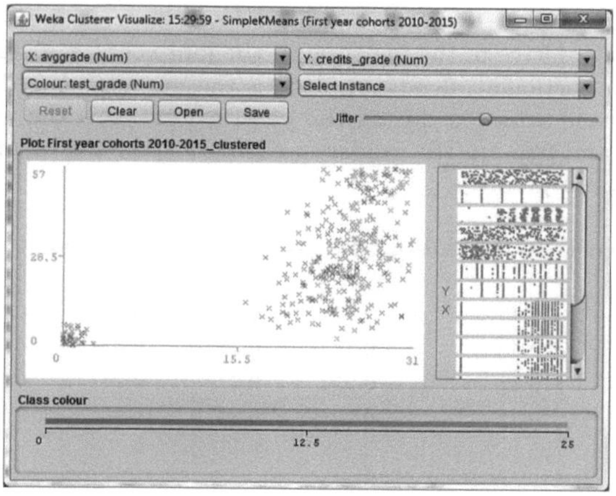

Fig. 7. Clusters of cohorts 2010–2015 illustrated in Fig. 1 with self assessment test in evidence. The blue colour means that the test has not been passed (the grade is 0) and the orange colour means that the test has been passed with the maximum grade 25. (For interpretation of the references to colours in this figure legend, the reader is referred to the electronic version of this article). (Color figure online)

The correlation values shown in Tables 7 and 8 have been computed with the R software (see https://www.r-project.org/).

Table 7. Pearson's correlation between various attributes and the test grade, `test`, relative to the first year of the cohorts 2010 up to 2015, of the four cohorts 2010–13 and of the six cohorts 2010–15. In particular, `Credits_grade` is the number of credits corresponding to exams with a grade achieved during the year, `Avggrade` is the average grade and `ADS`, `ARC`, `PRG`, `CAL` and `DML` are the grades in the corresponding exams (the grade is 0 if the exam is not been passed).

Cohort	Credits_grade/test	Avggrade/test	ADS/test	ARC/test	PRG/test	CAL/test	DML/test
2010	0.49	0.40	0.08	0.23	0.56	0.51	0.46
2011	0.12	0.14	−0.01	−0.02	−0.05	0.26	0.18
2012	0.39	0.42	0.25	0.26	0.27	0.30	0.42
2013	0.55	0.37	0.31	0.50	0.40	0.48	0.47
2014	0.61	0.40	0.39	0.37	0.56	0.55	0.53
2015	0.34	0.32	0.32	0.37	0.11	0.16	0.26
2010–13	0.42	0.35	0.21	0.31	0.30	0.37	0.41
2010–15	0.44	0.35	0.28	0.32	0.31	0.38	0.40

Table 8. Spearman (S) and Kendall (K) correlations between various attributes and the test grade, `test`, relative to the first year of the four cohorts 2010–13 and of the six cohorts 2010–15. In particular, `Credits_grade` is the number of credits corresponding to exams with a grade achieved during the year, `Avggrade` is the average grade and `ADS`, `ARC`, `PRG`, `CAL` and `DML` are the grades in the corresponding exams (the grade is 0 if the exam is not been passed).

Cohort	Credits_grade/test	Avggrade/test	ADS/test	ARC/test	PRG/test	CAL/test	DML/test
S 2010–13	0.39	0.43	0.33	0.29	0.31	0.41	0.40
S 2010–15	0.43	0.43	0.39	0.31	0.33	0.44	0.40
K 2010–13	0.30	0.32	0.25	0.23	0.24	0.32	0.33
K 2010–15	0.33	0.32	0.29	0.25	0.26	0.33	0.33

4 Analysis of the First Three Years Productivity

In this section we analyse the first four cohorts of students from 2010 up to 2013, for a total of 212 students, by studying their progressions during the first, second and third year of university. As in Sect. 3, we consider only active students during the first year, that is, students that have taken at least an exam in the same year. We point out that a student active in the first year can stop to be active during the second and/or third year, thus becoming inactive in that year. In particular, for the third year we consider exams and credits matured up to the end of April of the fourth year after enrollment; this date represents the end of the third academic year.

As already observed for the analysis of Sect. 3, the data set we study is not very big but we wish to underline the methodological approach that, as far as we know, is new. The analysis starts by clustering the results of students during their first year, obtaining a model that is the input for the next steps that classify students according to their results during the second and third years. This process allows us to analyse the way in which the student careers evolve over the three years and to understand how the performance during the first year affects the following ones. We developed a `KNIME` flow, illustrated in Fig. 8, that starts with the *K-means* node to analyse data of the first year and produces an output model; this model represents the input for a first *Cluster Assigner* node, that classifies students of the second year, and for a second *Cluster Assigner* node which classifies students of the third one. In the figure, these tree nodes are evidenced in green. As in the previous analysis, we applied the K-means algorithm with $k = 3$ and we considered the same cluster attributes, that is, `test_grade`, `credits_grade` and `avggrade`.

More precisely, the input to the `KNIME` flow consists of three data sets, evidenced in orange in Fig. 8; the input for the *K-means* node contains information about active students in the first year and concerns exams taken by students up to 31th December of the year following their enrollment. A sample of these data is illustrated in Table 9, where the attributes `creditsI_grade` and `avggradeI` contain respectively the credits and the average grade obtained

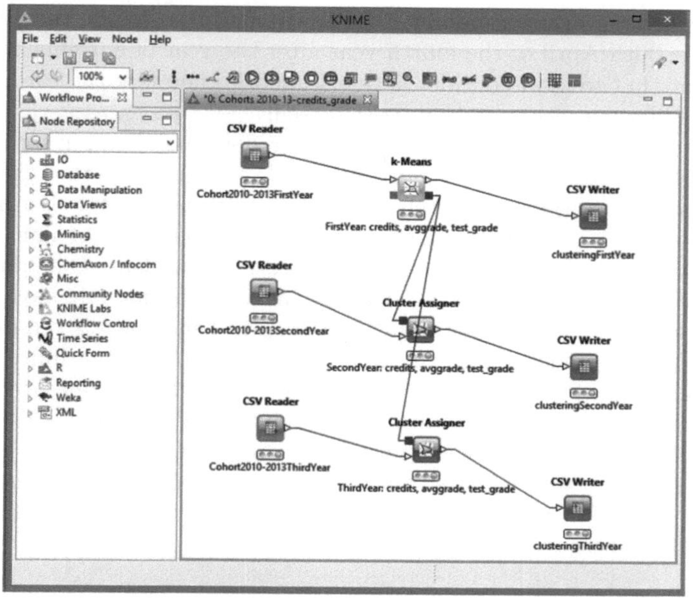

Fig. 8. The `KNIME` flow: the orange nodes are the input to the flow and contain information about active students in first, second and third year, respectively (see also Table 9); the first green node on the top is the *K-means* node where the clustering step is performed; the other green nodes are the *Cluster Assigner* nodes which classify students according to the previous clustering by using the results of second and third year; finally, the red nodes partition the students of each year according to the clustering (see also Table 11). (For interpretation of the references to colours in this figure legend, the reader is referred to the electronic version of this article). (Color figure online)

Table 9. A sample of input data set for the *K-means* node of Fig. 8. (Reprinted from [4]).

Student	Cohort	CreditsIgrade	AvggradeI	Test_grade	Hgrade	Hschool
100	2010	48	27	19	69	LS
200	2010	60	27	17	75	IT
⋮	⋮	⋮	⋮	⋮	⋮	⋮
300	2012	60	26	16	75	PS
⋮	⋮	⋮	⋮	⋮	⋮	⋮

from students in exams taken during their first year. The inputs for the first and second *Cluster Assigner* nodes are analogous; in this case we consider the attributes `creditsII_grade` and `avggradeII`, indicating the credits and the average grade obtained from students in exams taken in the second year, and the similar attributes corresponding to the exams taken in the third year, that is, up to the 30th April of the fourth year after the year of enrollment. We wish to point out that we still consider active students, therefore the cardinalities of these input files can decrease from year to year.

The result of the K-means step of the KNIME flow, expressed in terms of coordinates of the centroids, is showed in Table 10. We can observe that the attribute **credits_grade** separates very well the three centroids; cluster **Clu_High** identifies high achieving students, cluster **Clu_Medium** identifies medium achieving students and finally cluster **Clu_Low** corresponds to students that during their first year had success only with the exam of English and therefore have no credits and no grade in this clustering. This first step of this analysis required a pre-processing phase, evidenced by the value 25 relative to the attribute **avggrade** in the Clu_Low. In fact, since we want to use the model obtained by this clustering to classify students according to the results of the second and third year, since the English exam is the unique without a grade, we assigned an average **avggrade** value equal to 25 to all the students that took only the English exam during the first year. Otherwise, no active students would be assigned to that cluster in the subsequent steps of the analysis.

Table 10. Centroids resulting from the first step of the KNIME flow and corresponding to first year results of cohorts 2010–2014. The cluster **Clu_Low** corresponds to students that during their first year had success only with the exam of English and therefore have no credits and no grade in this clustering, the cluster **Clu_Medium** corresponds to medium achieving students and the cluster **Clu_High** identifies high achieving students. See Table 6 for the centroids of the analogous clusters on cohorts 2010–2015.

Attribute	Clu_Low (22)	Clu_Medium (91)	Clu_High (99)
credits_grade	0	18.46	44.10
avggrade	25	24.33	26.27
test_grade	11.63	13.81	15.64

Table 11 represents the output data set obtained from the clustering step, where the new attribute Clu_YearI indicates the cluster to which each student has been assigned: this data set corresponds to the first red node in Fig. 8, starting from above. The output data sets of the two *Cluster Assigner* nodes are similar and correspond to the other two red nodes, one for the second and one for the third year. This process is concluded by a last postprocessing phase which joins the previous data sets and produces a final output illustrated in Table 12: a triplet of cluster values is associated to each student, indicating the path followed over the three years under analysis. This path takes into account also the inactivity of students during a year. This data set is visualized in Fig. 9, where the green colour corresponds to high profile students, the yellow colour to medium profile students and the orange colour to low profile students; the blue colour represents inactive students. According to our definition of active students, a student can be inactive during the second year but become active again during the third. Figure 9 suggests that students inactive during the second year remain inactive also in the next year; moreover, students in the green cluster confirm their good trend in the subsequent years, students in the orange cluster tends to become inactive and, finally, some of the students in the yellow cluster move to the adjacent clusters, improving or getting worse. This hypothesis suggested by Fig. 9 is confirmed both by an analytic inspection of the data set and by a new clustering step performed on data organized as in Table 12. In fact, by using again the K-means implementation of `WEKA` with $k = 3$ and attributes `Clu_YearI`, `Clu_YearII` and `Clu_YearIII`, where nominal values `Clu_Low`, `Clu_Medium` and `Clu_High` have been transformed into the numeric values 0, 1 and 2 respectively, and the value -1 has been assigned to inactivity, we obtain the centroids illustrated in Table 13. With this choice of k, the Pearson's correlation between the linear representation of the proximity and incidence matrices gives the value -0.65, a quite good value.

Table 11. A sample of data set resulting from the *K-means* node of Fig. 8. (Reprinted from [4]).

Student	Cohort	CreditsIgrade	AvggradeI	Test_grade	Hgrade	Hschool	Clu_YearI
100	2010	48	27	19	69	LS	Clu_Medium
200	2010	60	27	17	75	IT	Clu_High
⋮	⋮	⋮	⋮	⋮	⋮	⋮	⋮
300	2011	0	0	12	65	IT	Clu_Low
400	2012	60	26	16	75	PS	Clu_High
⋮	⋮	⋮	⋮	⋮	⋮	⋮	⋮

Referring to the colours of Fig. 9, the cluster `Clu_Prog_Low` in Table 13 corresponds to students who started yellow or orange and became blu, the cluster `Clu_Prog_Medium` represents students starting as yellow and becoming green and, finally, cluster `Clu_Prog_High` represents the ever green students.

In other words, clusters `Clu_Prog_Low` represents students who started with low or medium results and were not be able to improve their performance often dropping out, cluster `Clu_Prog_Medium` represents the medium-high achieving students throughout the entire course of study and, finally, cluster `Clu_Prog_High` represents students who had overall very positive results during the three years.

The results of the clustering step in Table 10 are illustrated in Fig. 10; the colours have the same meaning as in Fig. 9. The first green histogram represents the students classified as high, the second yellow histogram represents students classified as medium and, finally, the third histogram corresponds to low students, during the first year of university. The Fig. 11 puts in evidence how students of the previous groups arrive to the third year, by using the same colours

Table 12. A sample of the final data set resulting from the KNIME flow and the post-processing phase. A triplet of cluster values is associated to each student, indicating the path followed over the three years under analysis. This path takes into account also the inactivity of students during a year, as in the case of student 400. For the clustering step in Table 13, nominal values **Clu_Low**, **Clu_Medium** and **Clu_High** are transformed into the numeric values 0, 1 and 2 and the value −1 is assigned to inactivity. (Reprinted from [4]).

Student	Cohort	...	...	Test_grade	Clu_YearI	Clu_YearII	Clu_YearIII
100	2010	...	...	19	Clu_Medium	Clu_Medium	Clu_High
200	2010	...	...	17	Clu_High	Clu_High	Clu_High
⋮	⋮	⋮	⋮	⋮	⋮	⋮	⋮
300	2011	...	...	12	Clu_Low	Clu_Medium	Clu_Medium
400	2012	...	...	16	Clu_High	*inactive*	Clu_High
⋮	⋮	⋮	⋮	⋮	⋮	⋮	⋮

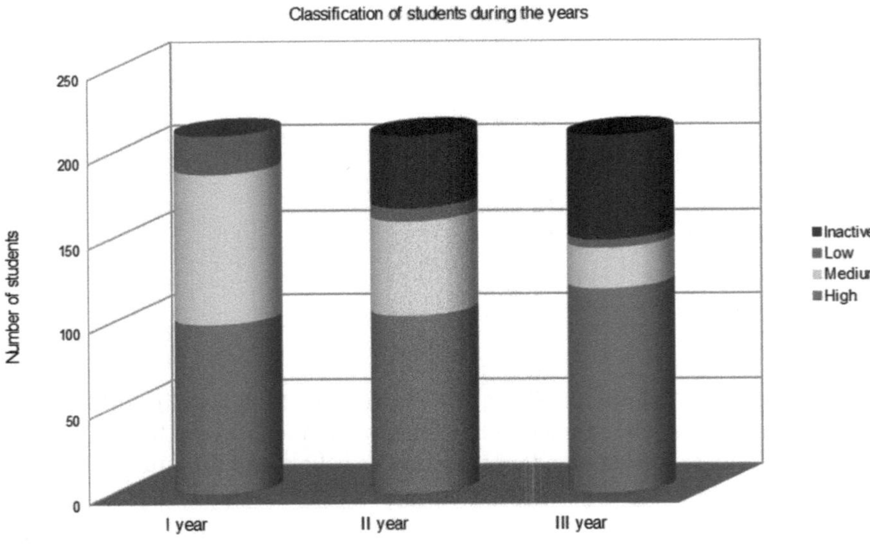

Fig. 9. A visualization of data corresponding to Table 12. The green colour corresponds to high profile students, the yellow colour to medium profile students and the orange colour to low profile students; the blue colour represents inactive students. (For interpretation of the references to colours in this figure legend, the reader is referred to the electronic version of this article). (Color figure online)

as before. For example, among the students who were green, many remained high, a small number became medium and the rest became low or inactive. Concerning the orange students who started low at the first year, we can observe

Table 13. Centroids resulting from the clustering step of data organized as in Table 12. By referring to Fig. 9, the cluster `Clu_Prog_Low` corresponds to students who started yellow or orange and became blue, the cluster `Clu_Prog_Medium` represents students starting as yellow and becoming green and, finally, cluster `Clu_Prog_High` represents the ever green students. (For interpretation of the references to colours in this figure legend, the reader is referred to the electronic version of this article).

Attribute	Full Data (212)	Clu_Prog_Low (66)	Clu_Prog_Medium (51)	Clu_Prog_High (95)
`Clu_YearI`	1.36	0.74	0.98	2
`Clu_YearII`	1.05	−0.29	1.41	1.78
`Clu_YearIII`	0.96	−0.88	1.74	1.82

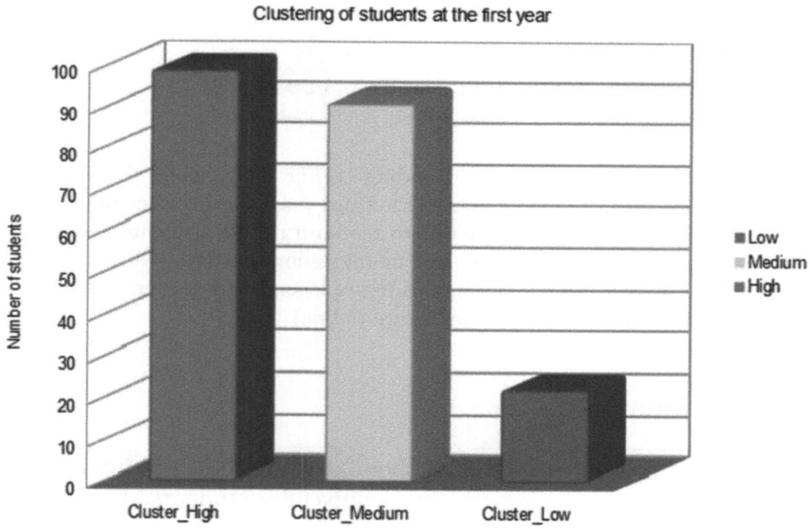

Fig. 10. A visualization of data corresponding to Table 10. The green colour corresponds to high profile students, the yellow colour to medium profile students and the orange colour to low profile students. This is the classification of students at the first year, corresponding to first cylinder in Fig. 9. (For interpretation of the references to colours in this figure legend, the reader is referred to the electronic version of this article). (Color figure online)

that almost all become inactive; the group in which there is a greater variability is that of students starting yellow and distributed at the third year over the four classes of students, becoming mainly green and blue.

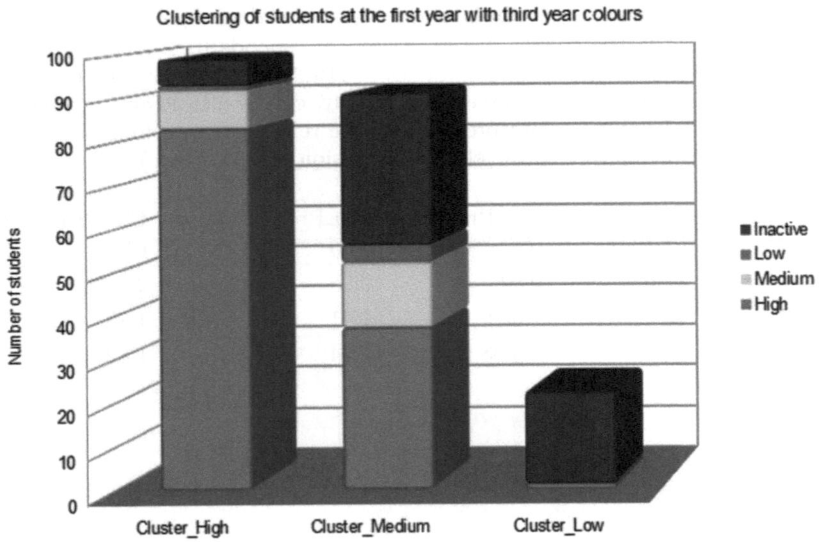

Fig. 11. A visualization of data corresponding to Fig. 10 by using the colours corresponding to the classification of students at the third year. The green colour corresponds to high profile students, the yellow colour to medium profile students and the orange colour to low profile students; the blue colour represents inactive students. (For interpretation of the references to colours in this figure legend, the reader is referred to the electronic version of this article). (Color figure online)

5 Conclusions

In this paper we have presented a methodology to study the influence of the first year behaviour in the progressions of university students. The analysis we propose is based on partitional clustering and first involves a data set containing information about various cohorts of students during their first year of university. Then the analysis concentrates on the subset of the data set corresponding to the students for which we know the results obtained during the second and third year also.

The first analysis is presented in Sect. 3 and can be summarized in the following steps:

1. we performed a preprocessing phase on students information to obtain data organized as in Table 4, relative to students results on first year;
2. we performed a clustering step to classify students according to the results of the self-assessment test and the university performance during the first year, by using K-means algorithm;
3. we deepened the analysis on the partition obtained at the previous step by exploring each exam dimension and by computing correlations between attributes.

For the cohorts 2010–2015 of students considered in this paper, the first analysis puts in evidence that the self assessment test is an important indicator to predict both the performance of the first year, in particular for what concerns mathematical courses, and the progress of the students career. On the other hand, courses of the first year in which students have more difficulties seem to give an important indication on the student success. The laurea degree course could use this information to support students having this kind of problems.

The second analysis is presented in Sect. 4 and can be summarized in the following steps:

1. we performed a preprocessing phase on students information to obtain data organized as in Table 5, relative to the results of students during their first, second and third year;
2. we performed a clustering step to classify students according to the results of the self-assessment test and the university performance during their first year, by using K-means algorithm (see Table 10);
3. we applied the model obtained at the previous step to the results of students during their second and third year and associated to each student the sequence of traversed clusters (see Table 12);
4. we performed a second clustering step according to the traversed clusters (see Table 13).
   Steps 2 and 3 were realized by a `Knime` flow.

For the cohorts 2010–2013 of students considered in this paper, the second analysis highlights three different trends strongly affected from the performance of the first year and suggests that supporting first year students seems to be a way to face the problem of inactive students and dropping out.

A practical implication of the results obtained from this research could be the introduction of tutors to support first year students, with special attention to the most critical courses. In particular, for the case study analyzed in this paper, the results illustrated in Fig. 11 suggest that we should pay attention to both low and medium students, since a large number of them become inactive.

Another aspect not to be underestimated concerns the orientation and information for incoming students: if it is true that the entrance test gives important information on the students progressions, then the laurea degree should try to make it clear to young people willing to join, what are the difficulties that they will encounter, in order to help them to make an informed choice.

We think that the proposed methodology could be possibly applied to similar university contexts to give suggestions for the definition of management strategies aiming to improve the students productivity. Of course, the conclusions could be different in other contexts, however, we wish to observe that the results obtained in this paper confirms the analysis obtained in paper [4] based on a smaller data set.

References

1. Baker, R.S.J.D.: Educational data mining: an advance for intelligent systems in education. IEEE Intell. Syst. **29**(3), 78–82 (2014)
2. Bower, A.J.: Analyzing the longitudinal K-12 grading histories of entire cohorts of students: grades, data driven decision making, dropping out and hierarchical cluster analysis. Pract. Assess. Res. Eval. **15**(7), 1–18 (2010)
3. Campagni, R., Merlini, D., Sprugnoli, R., Verri, M.C.: Data mining models for student careers. Expert Syst. Appl. **42**(13), 5508–5521 (2015)
4. Campagni, R., Merlini, D., Verri, M.C.: University student progressions and first year behaviour. In: Proceedings of CSEDU 2017 - the 9th International Conference on Computer Supported Education, vol. 2, pp. 46–56 (2017)
5. Kabakchieva, D., Stefanova, K., Kisimov, V.: Determining student profiles and predicting performance. In: Proceedings of EDM 2011, 4th International Conference on Educational Data Mining, Eindhoven, The Netherlands (2011)
6. Natek, S., Zwilling, M.: Student data mining solution-knowledge management system related to higher education institutions. Expert Syst. Appl. **41**, 6400–6407 (2014)
7. Peña-Ayala, A.: Educational data mining: a survey and a data mining-based analysis. Expert Syst. Appl. **41**, 1432–1462 (2014)
8. Romero, C., Romero, J.R., Ventura, S.: A survey on pre-processing educational data. In: Peña-Ayala, A. (ed.) Educational Data Mining. SCI, vol. 524, pp. 29–64. Springer, Cham (2014). https://doi.org/10.1007/978-3-319-02738-8_2
9. Romero, C., Ventura, S.: Data mining in education. Wiley Interdisc. Rev. Data Min. Knowl. Discov. **3**(1), 12–27 (2013)
10. Tan, P.N., Steinbach, M., Kumar, V.: Introduction to Data Mining. Addison-Wesley, Boston (2006)
11. Witten, I.H., Frank, E., Hall, M.A.: Data Mining: Practical Machine Learning Tools and Techniques, 3rd edn. Morgan Kaufmann, Burlington (2011)
12. Zimmermann, J., Brodersen, K.H., Heinimann, H.R., Buhmann, J.M.: A model-based approach to predicting graduate-level performance using indicators of undergraduate-level performance. J. Educ. Data Min. **7**(3), 151–176 (2015)
13. Zimmermann, J., Brodersen, K.H., Pellet, J.P., August, E., Buhmann, J.M.: Predicting graduate level performance from undergraduate achievements. In: Proceedings of EDM 2011, 4th International Conference on Educational Data Mining, Eindhoven, The Netherlands (2011)

Observations and Reflections on Teaching Electrical and Computer Engineering Courses

Ottar L. Osen(✉) and Robin T. Bye

Software and Intelligent Control Engineering Laboratory,
Department of ICT and Natural Sciences,
Faculty of Information Technology and Electrical Engineering,
NTNU—Norwegian University of Science and Technology,
Postboks 1517, 6025 Ålesund, Norway
{ottar.osen,robin.t.bye}@ntnu.no
http://softicelab.wordpress.com

Abstract. In this article, we make a number of observations and reflections based on our experience from many years of teaching courses in electrical and computer engineering bachelor programmes. We present important aspects of attendance, lectures, group work, and compulsory coursework, and how these can be addressed to improve student learning. Moreover, we discuss how to facilitate active learning activities, focussing on simple in-classroom activities and larger problem-based activities such as assignments, projects, and laboratory work, and highlight solving real-world problems by means of practical application of relevant theory as key to achieving intended learning outcomes. Our observations and reflections are then put into a theoretical context, including students' approaches of learning, constructive alignment, active learning, and problem-based versus problem-solving learning. Next, we present and discuss the results from two recent student evaluation surveys, one for senior (final-year) students and one for junior (first- and second-year) students, and draw some conclusions. Finally, we add some remarks regarding our findings and point to future work.

Keywords: Active learning · Problem-solving learning · Assessment Engineering pedagogy and didactics · Constructive alignment

1 Introduction

In this article, we make a number of observations and reflections based on our combined experiences from about 23 years of teaching (14 and 9 years for the first

O. L. Osen—This article is an extended and revised version of a paper presented at the 9th International Conference on Computer Supported Education (CSEDU '17) in Porto, Portugal, April 2017 [1].

P. Escudeiro et al. (Eds.): CSEDU 2017, CCIS 865, pp. 363–389, 2018.
https://doi.org/10.1007/978-3-319-94640-5_18

and second author, respectively) at NTNU—the Norwegian University of Science and Technology in Ålesund (formerly Aalesund University College (AAUC) before 1 January 2016). We have taught courses both in the computer, automation, and power systems bachelor programmes that we offer as well as in our master programmes in simulation and visualization and product and system design. The courses we have taught involve linear control theory and cybernetics; industrial control systems, microcontrollers, and instrumentation; artificial intelligence and intelligent systems; functional programming; and computer graphics, with aspects of modelling and simulation embedded in most of our courses. In line with the traditional role of university colleges in Norway, our teaching has always had a practical approach, focussing on the application of a sound theoretical foundation to solve real-world problems that face our students when they graduate and enter the work force. Hence, our department has always ensured that teaching and research activities are closely linked to local industrial partners.

When we present our observations and reflections below, we kindly ask the reader to please keep in mind the following:

- These are our subjective experiences, based on years of teaching activities, discussions among the faculty, and student feedback.
- Our experiences are naturally greatly influenced by factors such as personalities, education and work experience, authority, and likability (or lack of these).
- Our students are mostly young men in their early twenties from the town of Ålesund and the surrounding region.
- About 50% of our students have background from vocational school, thus with a tendency to be more practically than theoretically inclined.
- Our classes have usually had about 20–40 students, some as little as 8–12, which is quite different from larger classes of 100 or more students.

Whereas we are perfectly aware that what we present in this article does not generalise to all kinds of teachers, courses, and students, we hope that interested readers will be able to extract and adopt several of our ideas and approaches in their own teaching.

1.1 Outline

The remainder of this article consists of three main parts. In the first part (Sect. 2), we summarise a number of observations from our teaching experiences and reflect on these. In the second part (Sect. 3), we discuss our findings in relation to relevant pedagogical literature and theory. In the third part (Sect. 4), we include results from two recent student evaluation surveys. One survey was undertaken in January 2017 by final semester engineering students enrolled in computer, automation, and power systems bachelor programmes and the second was undertaken in June 2017 amongst the first- and second-year students from the same programmes at our institution. Finally, we summarise with some concluding remarks (Sect. 5).

2 Observations and Reflections

From working with students we have commonly observed that fairness is very important. Students react very negatively on anything that seems to be unfair or discriminating, that is, treating students differently. The studies are naturally the most important part of students' lives and the importance of a level playing field must not be underestimated. On the other hand, we have found that students easily adopt to rules and requirements set down for them as long as they make sense and are the same for everyone. Such rules and requirements can be related to achieving learning goals but also fair treatment.

We also believe that in an increasingly free society full of choices and distractions it may be beneficial for the students to have a highly structured learning environment. Many of the observations and pedagogical methods we present in this article may appear more appropriate for kids in school than students at the university level. However, we find that young adults, or most adults for that matter, share much of the same basic traits deep down. For example, whilst it is well known that kids love competitions and games, we also observe a positive change of atmosphere among students if we introduce a competition in the classroom, even if there is no reward.

In the following, we highlight some aspects of our teaching that we consider particularly important for our degree programmes, namely *attendance*, *lectures*, *group work*, *compulsory coursework*, *project-based learning*, *the bachelor thesis*, and *assessment*.

2.1 Attendance

Although our study programmes do not enforce *mandatory attendance*, we believe that in order to become a good engineer it is generally important to attend classes as much as possible, especially since many of the learning outcomes are related to practical skills (hands-on/laboratory work) and interpersonal skills. These skills are not learned in solitude at home or in a library. This of course demands that the classes we teach must be of sufficient quality and be perceived as useful and/or attractive to students.

Several studies suggest that there exists an inverse relationship between absenteeism (not attending classes) and learning (e.g., [2–4]). Moreover, enforcing a mandatory attendance policy can significantly reduce absenteeism and improve exam performance [5]. In addition to mandatory attendance, one way of improving attendance is to facilitate learning activities that complement the traditional lectures or that are sometimes missing or have limitations in courses offered online or at more traditional universities with larger classes and more theory-heavy degree programmes. Such learning activities may include good individual tutoring and feedback to each and every student, lectures on topics not covered in textbooks, laboratory work, group assignments and projects, all within an active learning environment. We observe that active learning gives us the opportunity to provide students with "*added value*" that can motivate the students to attend, and to attend in an active and constructive way.

Even though attendance is not mandatory we have often practised *calling the roll* before the class starts. Calling students' names can be done quite quickly and does not shorten the time available by any substantial amount, at least not for classes of up to 30–40 students, say. There are several benefits to this practice, for example, fewer students arrive late since they want to be present when their name is called, and also more students attend classes. We believe the reason for this is that the act of calling students' names creates social pressure to be present, whilst at the same time shows to students that the teacher care about whether they are present or not. Indeed, we have experienced students that have happened to be away from class due to a doctor's appointment or for other valid reasons send text messages to classmates for them to explain to the teacher their friend's absence. This can interpreted as a willingness from the students to obey to a social "rule" of attendance even if attendance is not mandatory.

It is our belief that this kind of *social contracts* between the teacher and the students and between students themselves can be a useful tool and may be further developed, since unspoken rules or norms are less subject to negative pressure or resistance when they are not formalised (mandatory) and therefore are acted upon on more of a subconscious level.

To summarise, we can improve attendance by using both carrot (added value) and stick (social contracts).

2.2 Lectures

Higher education is dominated by the *transmission method* of teaching, which can be popularly rephrased as *teaching by telling* (e.g., [6]) There is a common notion that active learning activities such as solving problems and working on projects are favourable to the *traditional lectures*. For example, according to Bligh [7], traditional lectures are not very effective for personal development, including skills or values, and deep learning, all of which are natural learning goals in higher education.

We have done some simple tests of how much students remember directly after a traditional lecture and admittedly been rather disappointed by the results. We believe the inactive and passive role of the students during a lecture is the reason for this and we welcome methods of activating the students in the classroom for example by means of "clickers," quizzes, competitions, discussions, and so on. However, there are situations when traditional lectures must be given, for example when the material is not covered by textbooks or online video lectures. In these situations, we often prefer *using the blackboard* and *writing by hand*. An advantage of this is that it encourages the students to be active and to take down the notes themselves simultaneously, since the students know they have ample time to write down whatever is being written on the blackboard. If the students also take notes by hand, which they commonly do in engineering courses since the material often covers mathematics and diagrams, the act of handwriting will trigger the brain to be more receptive to learning than from passive listening or writing on a computer [8].

In addition, the teacher will tend to be quite selective in what is being written and not overloading students with information. In order to move new information from a working memory with very limited capacity into long-term memory, deep cognitive processing is required [9]. This process is referred to as *cognitive load theory* [10] and represents a bottleneck in learning when too complex problems and information must be processed in too short a time.

Moreover, by using the blackboard, the teacher can display the thought process interactively, address questions with live written illustrations or examples, and easily improvise on the fly. Using slides, on the other hand, can often lead to a rigid display of a pre-made manuscript with little room for straying off the normal path, especially if the blackboard is hidden behind a projector screen, thus disallowing parallel use of the blackboard.

Lectures with slideshows often have the effect that students generally become passive listeners; they see no point in taking notes since the slides will usually be available electronically, and often there will not be enough time to copy down everything. To illustrate this point, we recap an experiment once done in class: After showing a slide with three main bullet points, each with three sub-bullet points (a fairly standard slide), the bullet points were read out loud and the students were given plenty of time to read the slide. Thereafter, the presentation was muted by showing the students a black slide and then they were asked to recreate the previous slide. In a class of about 30 students, nobody was able to do so.

Traditional lectures with computer-projected material do have their purpose though. Before teaching a new topic it can be useful to paint a backdrop for the students and put the topic into perspective. This usually requires textual information, pictures, videos, internet resources, or figures, diagrams or charts. However, the content that is presented simply serves as an introductory preparation for the students for storing the knowledge that will be presented to them afterwards in much more detail. The idea is that such a short keynote talk will give the students some mental hooks they can use for storing the details that follow. We have also found that students are more motivated and attentive if the lecture is closely connected to a problem to be solved in an assignment or an exercise.

As a precursor to giving a lecture, a useful approach is that of *delayed instruction*, where the teacher asks the students to start working on a problem and gives some individual assistance until at some stage most of the students realise that they need more knowledge to solve the problem. When the teacher then gives a lecture tailored to the problem at hand, the students will be attentive and motivated for learning the theory required for solving the problem. In contrast, starting a lecture by saying that the students will need this or that for their assignment does not yield the same effect. Delaying instruction has been found to be advantageous in a study where students outperformed their control group when they had first interacted in a collaborative problem-solving phase at the beginning of the learning process, with content-related instruction delayed until a subsequent phase [11].

Finally, we have found that it is a good idea to keep lectures short, or at least break up lectures regularly with active learning activities (variation) and breaks (time to digest).

2.3 Group Work

Project-based learning (see Sect. 2.5) is an important pedagogical tool that usually requires placing students together in suitable groups. Experience tells us that *group dynamics* can both bring the best or worst out of a group (see [12], for primer). Below we discuss our experiences on various aspects of constructing student groups for projects.

Size. How large a group should be depends of course on the estimated amount of work in the project (or assignments). According to the literature review of Pfaff and Huddleston [13], there is no clear evidence of an optimal group size for teamwork, with studies suggesting that either three, four, or five group members is the ideal. Larger groups tend to be less efficient, and thus emulate the Ringelmann effect[1].

In our case, for smaller assignments, groups of two can be sufficient, but normally we will aim for groups of four, and try to avoid groups with odd numbers. The reasoning behind this is that students working on a task in pairs are able to communicate efficiently and require both participants in the pair to be active. In groups of three, we have often observed that one member is less active than the other two and in the worst case, the third member becomes a mere observer, involuntarily or on purpose as a "free-rider."

Since oral communication only allows for the ideas of one participant to be shared, at any time a group of two is the most effective. However, a big drawback with groups of only two students is their limited capacity if the assignment is big and/or requires competence that may not be held among the group members. Hence, we generally favour groups of four. Finally, with four participants it is possible to make two subgroups that support each other and may re-arrange themselves depending on the tasks at hand and the competence within the group.

Selection of Group Members. In general, we favour *selecting groups randomly*. There are several reasons for this. If students are allowed to make groups by their own choice they will often assemble groups that follow existing social structures. As a result, the groups will often become rather homogeneous and strengthen these existing social bonds. The upside is that many of these *homogeneous groups* will have little internal friction and will not require time to socialise, since the students already know each other. The downside is that such homogeneous groups may lack the necessary diversity in competence to solve the problems they are facing. Furthermore, forming student groups at random

[1] A group effort in a rope-pulling task is inferior to the sum of individual performances; the discrepancy between potential and actual effort increases with size of group.

results in more *heterogeneous groups* and can help the teaching environment by widening the social networks in the class. It forces students to get to know each other when working on a common challenge and they therefore become less reluctant to ask questions in class and to interact. On the other hand, heterogenous groups can take longer to perceive and develop cooperative norms early in the groups' formation than more homogeneous groups [14].

We often experience some resistance from students when they are told they may not construct the groups themselves. This is not surprising, given that most people are resistant to changes and will feel more comfortable with people they know. Nevertheless, challenging this resistance is important in order to get optimal results.

We can attempt to improve the heterogeneity in the groups by not selecting the students 100% randomly, but instead also take into account their sex and background. For example, since we usually have very few female students, we generally prefer to make sure they are distributed evenly amongst the groups, unless there are good reasons not to. In a similar vein, the vast majority of students are native Norwegians, therefore, we try to distribute the non-natives evenly among the groups in order to improve integration. Finally, we often take into consideration that about half of our students have experience from vocational school. These students often have hands-on practical experience that can be very valuable in assignments with a large practical component.

By making sure there is a good mix in the groups, students with a more theoretical/academic background learn practical skills from their fellow students with a vocational background. Likewise the students with vocational background improve their methodological skills by learning from the more theoretical students. This way of grouping students may seem to require much work from the lecturer, however, by repeatedly pulling two names randomly from each of two lists of students (one for those who have vocational training and one for those without), we quickly get a set of possible groups, which then can be rearranged somewhat in order to get a better distribution of females and non-native Norwegians.

When presenting the groups to the students we do not mention such fine-tuning and instead emphasise that the groups have been put together randomly. We also remind them that working together in groups set down by others is something they must expect to do when they start working professionally and that cooperation skills will be beneficial for them in their future work. Finally, we randomly pick a group member to be the *leader of the group*. This person's responsibility is to make sure the group meets sufficiently often, that everyone contributes, and to report group malfunctioning to the teacher.

There are of course many social challenges that can arise in a class of students. We meet students that range from the extremely extrovert to the extremely introvert in addition to students that suffer from mental illnesses of various severity. Semi-random groups put down by the tutor can actively take these issues into consideration. Self-organised groups will, on the other hand, often enlarge these challenges since socially challenged students will be left out.

Although our primary goal is to educate the students in their area of study it falls within our contract with society to also develop the students' personalities in a direction that favours the community. Hence, we should help introverts to be more open and find ways to develop their interpersonal skills. Likewise it is also important to teach extroverts that a solution to a challenge may be found with an introvert that is reluctant to speak out in a group. Since universities commonly have health services that also cover mental health, we as teachers should not try to fill their place. Still, our support for students with mental health challenges is essential, but then as only a part of the total support programme.

2.4 Compulsory Coursework

From our experience with various approaches, we believe that *compulsory coursework* is very often required in order to make the students work steadily throughout the semester. Although our students are adults and should be able to take responsibility for their own learning, students, like the rest of us, are subject to conflicting interest and need to prioritise their time. Even with the best intentions in mind it is easy to push forward activities that have no deadline. Hence, compulsory coursework with hard deadlines help students prioritise. It should be kept in mind, however, that courses that do not have compulsory coursework quickly may be given lower priority by the students. We have found that students' performance improved about one grade on average after making the coursework compulsory in some courses.

The electronic learning management system Blackboard[2] is used at our institution for most teaching tasks, including handing in assignments, however, we have found it very effective to also ask the students to show the teacher their work in person, especially on more practical topics, for example where the students are required to write computer programs or otherwise use computers for their solutions. Much too often we have found that students split the work unequally to such an extent that some students have never had the actual computer program or design running on their own computers. By doing such quick *spot checks* we force the students to familiarise themselves with the problem and have an individually working solution they can understand and explain even if they have had a lot of help from fellow students. We have also noticed that the requirement of showing the coursework in person, even only a spot check, improves the quality of the work. It is probably easier to hand in a mediocre result in an electronic system than face to face with the teacher. This is probably especially true in cases such as ours, where coursework generally is not part of the final grading but only a prerequisite that must be passed to enter the exam.

When we design coursework, we believe it is good practice to start with simple questions and subproblems and proceed in a stepwise manner in order to guide the students' progress, in other words, making the assignments resemble step-by-step tutorials. There is a lot to be learnt from a well-formed question and even good students will not find this approach boring, they will just "climb

[2] http://www.blackboard.com.

the steps" faster. However, engineering problems in the real world do not come with detailed step-by-step instructions such as those describe above. Therefore, more research-based or investigative problems should not be completely avoided but build on and be carefully aligned with the less investigative problems. One approach that is quite investigative in nature is project-based learning, which we discuss below. Naturally, making good assignments is a lot of work but is probably even more important than making good lectures, since assignments may be re-used and consumed at any time, and especially as final preparations before final exam.

2.5 Project-Based Learning

A popular approach at all levels of schooling, including universities, is that of *project-based learning*, and a key ingredient in active learning. Below, we highlight two factors we have identified as important for success when adopting project-based learning, namely *project selection and ownership*, and *project planning*. Theory related to project-based learning is postponed to Sect. 3.

Project Selection and Ownership. In our courses, students usually get to choose between a *selection of assignments or projects*, and sometimes we even encourage them to participate in defining the problem, if possible. The goal of this approach is make students invest more time and effort into tasks of which they have *ownership*; they seem more reluctant to "lower the bar" if they have first put it high themselves. In other words, they are willing to suffer more from "self-inflicted pain" than from "pain" given to them by the teacher. Another important aspect is the fact that groups with different projects cannot easily copy material from each other and the uniqueness also strengthens the feeling of ownership.

Although this willingness to invest more time and effort into activities the students feel ownership to may be a result of pride, it may also be the result of a kind of "self-love." We believe people in general are less likely to blame themselves than others since blaming oneself is very tiresome in the long run and it is therefore easier to forgive oneselves. Hence, it is beneficial to avoid giving students opportunity to blame the teacher's poor assignment for their own lack of progress or success. Giving students ownership to the activity and giving a clear framework for execution helps in putting the responsibility for success firmly on the shoulders of the students themselves. With no scapegoat in sight the students will prefer to walk the extra mile rather than blame themselves and accept defeat.

We have seen many projects where the students have put the bar too high but instead of intervening, we have just anticipated that the students eventually will face the hard obstacles and lower the bar. To our surprise, quite often the students are able to deliver as they had planned in the beginning through massive team effort. As a teacher this may pose a dilemma since the students are putting more effort into the project than planned, and other teaching activities may suffer from it. In interviews after project hand-ins we have asked students whether we should have intervened, and the students seem to agree that although the load was heavy they felt they learnt so much from it and that they were able to prove to themselves that they are able to solve difficult tasks that is was worth the effort. Hopefully this self-confidence will help them not only in their studies but also in their postgraduate endeavours. However, there is of course a significant possibility of failure if projects are allowed to become to ambitious, which can have negative effects on learning and self-confidence. Hence, it is crucial to have close monitoring and follow-up of these projects in order to be able to intervene in time to secure "a soft landing" of the project. This can be done by the means of the teacher intervening and redefining the project goals into what we see as achievable for the group. The next section describes in more detail how the projects may be monitored in order to secure progress and awareness.

Project Planning. The process of *project planning* is important in order to make the students aware of time expenditure versus progress. Therefore, we prefer to let the students first make their *project plans* themselves before having to submit their plans to the teacher for approval. Students are faced with three requirements for their project plans: are that they should clearly present

- how different activities are relatively spaced out in time
- the size (duration and manhours) of each task and subtasks
- who is responsible for the tasks

Before approving the project plans, we make sure the plans are sufficiently detailed and that the students have taken into consideration constraints in both time and resources. Asking the students to make plans forces them to apply a common engineering approach of breaking the work down into manageable tasks, which is also important in order for them to understand the scope of the work ahead. Moreover, we insist on the *responsibility* for each task to be assigned to a single student. In addition, we usually recommend that one other student is assigned as a task assistant. This way, there is no doubt who is responsible for a particular task, while at the same time, the responsible student has another student to help out. This will prevent the many discussions and possible sources for misunderstandings that can arise when tasks are not completed on time. It also discourages "free-riders" by increasing each individual's *accountability* [15].

As the projects progress, we regularly ask the students to update their plans with task completeness given as a percentage. As a result, the students will immediately detect any lack of progress and see the need to take appropriate measures at a time when it is still possible to influence the result. In short, we want the students to panic well ahead of delivery date!

Further down the road, it is usually not necessary for the teacher to comment much on students' plan updates. Quite often the students will be behind schedule but it will be visible in their plans and the need to improve progress will be self-evident. Occasionally, we ask the students to present the updated plan to the teacher in person in order to "increase the pressure" and to verify their understanding of the project status.

Today, a wide range of planning and collaboration tools are available, many of them for free. We encourage the students to find one they prefer and in this way they also get useful insight into what kind of tools they may use in the future, both during study and in their professional life.

Finally, the teacher may use the project plan status as an important metric for follow-up of the students. As mentioned in the previous section this is crucial in order to make sure that the group learn as much as possible from the project, and that the difficulty level is adequate.

2.6 The Bachelor Thesis

At our university, bachelor students deliver a *bachelor thesis*, usually as a group, during their final semester. The workload is 20 ECST, where one full semester corresponds to 30 ECST. Hence, the students only have one 10 ECTS topic to study in parallel with the work on the thesis.

The bachelor thesis projects are often provided by the local industry and seen as being very positive by both the university and the students. The projects maintain the important cooperation between the university and the industry and the students appreciate the opportunity to get in touch with possible future employers. One of the key benefits from this arrangement is a two-way flow of information between the industry and the university. The university learns about the challenges the industry is facing, the industry learn about progress in science that are of relevance to them, and students get relevant and up to date challenges, thus representing a win-win situation for all involved.

Project planning and monitoring in bachelor thesis projects are mostly done as described before for smaller projects but it is important to emphasise the need of getting the projects on-track with milestones and deliveries from the very start. Otherwise, we have observed that students tend to believe they have a lot of time available and therefore will relax in the beginning of the project. We find it crucial that the students learn that projects depend on a constant effort and in this way differs from the typical home assignments and smaller projects they have delivered so many of before, with much of the work often performed very close to the deadline.

For the selection of group members for the bachelor thesis we allow the students to form groups themselves indirectly in a process where each student applies for the different projects they are interested in. Students will therefore often coordinate their order of preference of available projects. However, if two small groups favour the same project we might suggest merging the groups into one bigger group but out of respect for the fact that bachelor thesis is the students' most important work we are reluctant to enforce group memberships except making sure the groups are not too large.

As for defining the scope of the project the situation is often the same as for the smaller projects. The students may often influence the scope significantly since the problem definitions and assignments are usually rather open.

When we are to grade the bachelor theses we often find it hard to use the full span of grades as we usually do. It seems to us as the students put more effort into their bachelor theses than anything else. Hence, the quality of the theses as a whole is usually much higher than could be expected when we compare to other courses.

2.7 Assessment

Below, we reflect on various aspects of *oral and written exams*, *group exams*, and *exam preparation*.

Oral and Written Exams. A common perception among ourselves and our colleagues is that many students seem to dread *oral exams* out of (a sometimes unjustified) fear of performing worse than they think would have in *written exams*. On the contrary, however, many students may actually fare better at oral exams, for example if they have dyslexia or for other reasons struggle with written communication, or if the written exam is designed in a poor manner that prevents students from displaying their true knowledge, competence, and skills. Hence, both written and oral exams can be, or conceived to be, disadvantageous to some students and advantageous to others due to individual differences. Consequently, if limited to only these two means for evaluating students' performance, we believe a good mix of oral and written exams can be considered fair to the students. Still, a particular advantage of oral exams over written exams is that it is possible for the examiner to adjust the exam questions ad hoc, for example if a student is nervous. Therefore, a good oral examiner will be able to both uncover lack of knowledge and skill as well as providing an opportunity for students to show the opposite.

Group Exams. A drawback with project assignments is that it is difficult or impossible to grade the students individually based on a common written report. One approach to enable *individual grades* in *group exams* is to add an oral exam in addition to the report. By using the report as a starting point, it is possible to at obtain some variation in grades within the group, if appropriate. Whereas this approach is not perfect, at least it provides an opportunity to give a fairer reflection of the differences in skills and knowledge within the group.

We have also experimented with giving oral exams with the whole group present instead of each student individually. The students will typically sit in alphabetical order, be given individual questions one at the time, and may not speak out of order. A practical advantage of this approach is that the total examination time can be reduced compared with individual oral exams, since unanswered questions in a given context can immediately be passed on to the next student without repeating it and less time is used for bringing students in and out of the examination room.

In addition, another important advantage is that the examiner can more easily compare the students with each other, whilst at the same time, the students can observe for themselves who is able to provide the best answers. Students will therefore have a better understanding of why they deserve the grade they get.

We suspect this has the effect that individual students work harder (in group projects where they are assessed individually) because they will have the reward of a fair and better grade than fellow students who do not put in the same effort. Finally the teacher has the ability to ask questions about the project work in a way that will disclose students that have been passive during the semester. Different levels of commitment for the project is often observed by the teacher and the oral exam gives an opportunity to document this to the students and to the exam evaluator (usually an external examiner who has the final word on the grade) in a transparent way.

Exam Preparation. Common symptoms among students before exams include nervousness, anxiety, and stress. If students feel secure and good about themselves and have a feeling of being in control, they will likely be more prone to deeper learning and typically perform better at exam. To help students get into this positive state of mind, we attempt to *reduce uncertainty* about the exam procedure and content beforehand, typically by providing a well-defined curriculum for the course, run mock exams or practice presentation skills in class, and provide practical information about the exam.

We also have had good experience with giving the students a long *list of possible exam questions* to study before the exam, and try to provide the list as early as possible in the start of the semester. By making the list long and the questions rather open we can ensure that if the students are able to answer most of the questions adequately they will also have good coverage of the curriculum and have achieved most of the intended learning outcomes and hence will have better chances of obtaining a good grade.

Notably, having such a long list of questions is probably not of such big help to the students as they tend to believe it is. Rather, its main purpose it simply to help the students getting into a positive state of mind before the exam. Indeed, with a well-defined curriculum and list of intended learning outcomes and good supporting material such as a course textbook, students should be able to make such a list themselves, however, getting the list from the lecturer removes a lot of uncertainty and stress from the students. Feedback from our students have been unanimously positive and we have observed anxiety levels in the classroom go from high to low when the students learn that they will be provided a list of possible exam questions. Finally, we often offer a course revision workshop at the end of the semester, where students can obtain answers to questions that they may have accumulated during the semester and to topics they find difficult.

3 Relation to Theory

In the sections below, we highlight some pedagogical and didactical theory found in the literature that is relevant to the observations and reflections we have made so far.

3.1 Students' Approaches to Learning

It is well documented that *students' approaches to learning* has a significant effect on achieving learning outcomes (e.g., [16,17]). Many studies have tried to identify factors that promote *deep learning* (e.g., [18–20]), that is, learning associated with understanding, in contrast to *surface learning*, which is learning associated with the memorisation of facts and procedures, and with little or no understanding as a result [17]. In between deep and surface learning, Case and Marshall [21] also describe *procedural deep learning* and *procedural surface learning* as two learning approaches for student learning in engineering contexts. In addition to these learning approaches along an axis of deep and surface learning, a commonly observed third category of learning is so-called *strategic learning*, where students aim for good grades with minimal effort, ignoring whether they achieve the intended learning outcomes or not [22,23].

Students tend to have different conceptions of what learning means, and these conceptions can generally be categorised hierarchically along an axis from surface learning to deep learning. For example, according to Saeljo [24] and Marton et al. [25], students conceive learning as

1. increasing one's knowledge
2. memorising and reproducing
3. applying
4. understanding
5. seeing something in a different way
6. changing as a person

Similarly, and specific to engineering students, Marshall et al. [26] suggest the following categories of how students conceive learning:

1. memorising definitions, equations and procedures
2. applying equations and procedures
3. making sense of physical concepts and procedures
4. seeing phenomena in the world in a new way
5. changing as a person

Higher education institutions obviously have a duty to graduate highly qualified candidates and avoiding surface learning is a means towards this goal. However, according to Biggs and Tang [27], there has been a dramatic change in higher education worldwide, maybe due to the workplace increasingly requiring higher education degrees to qualify for jobs, with many more people enrolling at universities than before, from a wider diversity of background. This has resulted in a shift from perhaps more academically inclined students previously to students who may have a poorer background both academically, socioeconomically and perhaps also motivation-wise, where higher education studies are perhaps conceived more as a "necessary evil" in order to simply qualify for a job.

The big variation among students with respect to background leads to great differences in learning strategies and approaches to learning and has necessarily had an impact on how higher education is being taught [28]. At our institution, this change in students that we enrol has perhaps been less radical, since we have mainly been concerned with bachelor engineering programmes and "elite" students have generally favoured the bigger universities in Norway.[3] Therefore, we are perhaps better equipped with suitable actions to accommodate this new generation of students. Indeed, despite the fact that we also have some very talented students every year who approach their studies with learning strategies that favour deep learning, we believe many of the methods we have described previously are very useful for counteracting students with lesser motivation and weaker academic backgrounds.

Moreover, it is well known that lack of *self-monitoring* and *self-regulation* will lead to poor academic results [29,30]. One must therefore acknowledge the fact that the learning environment itself is not sufficient to achieve intended learning outcomes but is also dependent on the students' individual skill in selecting and structuring the material to be learnt [31]. *Formative assessment* and *feedback* are important tools to help students become self-regulated learners [32]. Also, the teacher must facilitate learning strategies that favour deep learning. One method for doing so consists of the teacher adopting a role as a *facilitator for learning*, adopting a role similar to a personal trainer at the gym or a coach [33,34].

In Sect. 2.5, we describe various aspects of project-based learning and how the teacher can use several means to facilitate deeper learning. We try to make the students adopt project ownership, whereby they become more willing to invest more time and effort on the tasks they must accomplish. This can help reducing a strategic learning strategy where students are not only doing the work to get a desired grade but because their pride is at stake, they actually want the project solution to become as good as possible. Likewise, for project planning, we require the students to presents plans that break down the work and include time, size, and responsibility for tasks. By doing so, the student are effectively self-monitoring and self-regulating themselves.

3.2 Constructive Alignment

According to Biggs and Tang [27], *constructive alignment* (CA) is a teaching strategy where components such as the teacher, the students, teaching context, learning activities, and learning outcomes must be aligned while maintaining the *constructivist view* that students learn by doing, commonly know as active learning, that is, any learning activity that actively involves the students in the learning process [35]. Specifically, when designing a particular course, one adopt a backward scheme, starting with the intended learning outcomes (what competence, skills, and experience students should have upon completion of the course), then define assessment tasks that closely relates to the intended learning outcomes, and then proceed to choosing teaching methods and learning activities aligned with the intended learning outcomes and assessment tasks [27].

[3] AAUC was a small university college before merging with NTNU to become Norway's biggest university.

We have perhaps not adopted a very rigid scheme based on CA for our teaching but it is clear that we emphasise active learning and constructivism and we are very careful in our choice of assignments and projects to ensure that a successful completion will lead to intended learning outcomes being achieved. For example, most of our courses involve compulsory coursework that is closely aligned with intended learning outcomes. By being compulsory and usually with a pass requirement for access to the final exam, students are forced to complete the assignments in a satisfactory manner and will achieve some intended learning outcomes while doing so. Also, in contrast with more rigid assignments where there often is only one correct answer to each problem, our projects are often open-ended, where many different approaches can lead to successful completion. This is in line with *research-based* or *problem-based teaching* and can be effective against too rigid implementations of CA where too much simplification and generalisation can in fact counteract deep learning and creativity [36].

3.3 Assessment

A very important aspect of teaching is the choice of *assessment* method. For example, according to proponents of CA, many students are mainly concerned with achieving grades, not learning. These students have a surface approach to learning, typically aiming for memorising and reproducing course curriculum, and essentially, the exam can be said to *define* the curriculum [27]. Therefore, in CA, one must align the exam, or rather, the set of components that make up a grade, such as laboratory exercises, assignments, projects, and oral and written exams, must all be designed in a manner that ensures that satisfactory completion also means that intended learning outcomes are achieved. It makes obvious sense to accept this premise at least to some extent, after all, who would want to be a passenger of an airplane where the pilot had only passed a big written exam, and not a variety of practical flight tests?

In our own teaching we have adopted similar means in a lighter manner, where components such as lab or project activities perhaps have not affected the final grade directly but at least usually required students both to show up and to complete the tasks at a pass grade level before being granted admission to a final exam.

3.4 Active Learning

As should be clear from our observations and reflections of teaching activities, we are proponents of *active learning*. There are several metastudies that show that active learning in science, technology, engineering, and mathematics (STEM) indeed has several advantages. Prince [35] found comprehensive support for core elements of active learning, for example that students being active during a lecture improve their ability to reproduce the material later and that they become more motivated and engaged. Likewise, Schroeder et al. [37] found that active learning improve students' performance, as did Freeman et al. [38].

Of particular importance are several studies on *cooperative learning* (e.g., [39–42]. These studies show that cooperative learning strategies are especially effective for deep learning. In our own teaching, cooperative learning is a core element, where students often work in groups not only on projects and large assignments but sometimes also in smaller exercises or quizzes that with great effect can be introduced to break up long lectures.

3.5 Problem-Based Versus Problem-Solving Learning

Summarising the results of 800 meta-analyses, Hattie and Goveia [43] points out the incredible fact that problem-based learning does not have a positive effect on achieving intended learning outcomes! Why is this so? Sotto [6] suggests that there is a distinction between *problem-based* and *problem-solving* learning. Specifically, Sotto argues that for learning to be successful, one must employ well-designed case studies and avoid problem-based and too student-centred learning. Specifically, a pitfall in problem-based learning activities is that the problem at hand is large (which is not by itself the problem) and there is no clear guidance towards how to solve it. Students end up spending too much time on searching the Internet or studying textbooks even for solving just small parts of the problem. Instead, Sotto [6] argues that the assignments given must be carefully designed in order for the students to quickly be able to practice the core knowledge and skillset selected by the teacher.

In our own teaching, we have at least tried to adhere to some of the suggestions of Sotto [6], for example by first providing an open-ended problem using a top-down approach but instead of leaving the students alone for an eternal chase of information, we usually interrupt with more information on the blackboard after some time and guide them towards a solution. Also, we sometimes use case studies where students work through detailed *step-by-step exercises*, carefully avoiding the risk of students spending too much time on any one step. Finally, we would like to emphasise the importance of *immediate feedback*, often easily achieved in lab work and programming assignments, as found in a pedagogical study on one of our courses [44].

4 Student Evaluation Surveys

In January 2017, all third-year students enrolled in their final sixth semester of the bachelor programmes in automation, power systems, and computer engineering were asked to complete an anonymous student evaluation survey online. Subsequently, in June 2017, the remaining cohorts of first- and second-year students who had just completed their second and fourth semester, respectively, were asked to complete the same survey. For simplicity in the following, we label the third-year students as *seniors*, and the first-year and second-year students as *juniors*. It should be noted that seniors at the time of their survey had completed all coursework of their degrees (except for a single 10 ECTS course), thus focusing most of their time in the final semester on their bachelor thesis (20 ECTS).

In contrast, juniors, especially first-years, had experienced a lot less courses at the time of their survey.

Out of approximately 70 seniors, we received a total of 31 responses, from 16, 3, and 12 automation, power systems, and computer engineering students, respectively. From the approximately 170 juniors (approximately 90 first-year and 80 second-year students), we received a total of 46 responses, from 28, 7, and 11 automation, power systems, and computer engineering students, respectively.

In both surveys, the students were asked to indicate to which degree they agreed with the statements in Table 1, categorising whether they strongly or partly agreed or disagreed, or were indifferent: In addition, they were given the opportunity to elaborate on the statements and any other issues they wished to raise.

Table 1. Statements for student evaluation surveys.

#	Statement
1	*I want more traditional lectures*
2	*I want more teaching using the blackboard*
3	*I want more active learning activities (exercises, quizzes, discussion, competitions, etc.)*
4	*I want more flipped classroom and elearning/online learning activities*
5	*I want more focus on practical application than theory*
6	*I want more problem-solving learning activities*
7	*I want more laboratory learning activities*
8	*Calling the roll makes it more likely that I will turn up in class*
9	*I want more mandatory coursework*
10	*I want more/better feedback on my work during the semester*
11	*I want my final grades to be fully decided by oral or written final exams*
12	*I want my final grades to be composed of several parts (e.g., lab, assignments, project, midsemester test, final exam)*
13	*I want more digital exams*
14	*I want more home exams*

The results are summarised in Table 2, where the number n of student responses and the corresponding percentage is given for each statement and response category. Below, we discuss answers relevant for the observations and reflections we have made above. Please note that in the text, all percentages without decimals have been rounded to the nearest integer.

4.1 Attendance

Only 10% of the seniors strongly or partly agreed that calling the roll would make it more likely that they would turn up to class (statement 8), whilst 20% were

Table 2. Student evaluation surveys for seniors and juniors.

Seniors	Strongly agree		Partly agree		Indifferent		Partly disagree		Strongly disagree	
Statement #	n	%	n	%	n	%	n	%	n	%
1	0	0.0%	3	9.7%	14	45.2%	10	32.3%	4	12.9%
2	1	3.2%	7	22.6%	12	38.7%	9	29.0%	2	6.5%
3	10	32.3%	12	38.7%	5	16.1%	4	12.9%	0	0.0%
4	6	19.4%	9	29.0%	9	29.0%	6	19.4%	1	3.2%
5	13	41.9%	14	45.2%	4	12.9%	0	0.0%	0	0.0%
6	12	38.7%	13	41.9%	6	19.4%	0	0.0%	0	0.0%
7	8	26.7%	14	46.7%	8	26.7%	0	0.0%	0	0.0%
8	2	6.5%	1	3.2%	6	19.4%	6	19.4%	16	51.6%
9	2	6.5%	8	25.8%	10	32.3%	8	25.8%	3	9.7%
10	22	71.0%	5	16.1%	2	6.5%	2	6.5%	0	0.0%
11	5	16.1%	11	35.5%	9	29.0%	5	16.1%	1	3.2%
12	7	22.6%	5	16.1%	8	25.8%	9	29.0%	2	6.5%
13	15	48.4%	9	29.0%	5	16.1%	2	6.5%	0	0.0%
14	2	6.5%	4	12.9%	15	48.4%	3	9.7%	7	22.6%
Juniors	Strongly agree		Partly agree		Indifferent		Partly disagree		Strongly disagree	
Statement #	n	%	n	%	n	%	n	%	n	%
1	1	2.2%	8	17.4%	23	50.0%	11	23.9%	3	6.5%
2	2	4.3%	10	21.7%	22	47.8%	8	17.4%	4	8.7%
3	12	26.1%	16	34.8%	13	28.3%	4	8.7%	1	2.2%
4	5	10.9%	14	30.4%	15	32.6%	8	17.4%	4	8.7%
5	19	41.3%	18	39.1%	7	15.2%	1	2.2%	1	2.2%
6	18	39.1%	21	45.7%	6	13.0%	0	0.0%	1	2.2%
7	9	19.6%	20	43.5%	13	28.3%	3	6.5%	1	2.2%
8	4	8.7%	2	4.3%	15	32.6%	10	21.7%	15	32.6%
9	0	0.0%	10	21.7%	22	47.8%	6	13.0%	8	17.4%
10	21	45.7%	13	28.3%	12	26.1%	0	0.0%	0	0.0%
11	10	21.7%	14	30.4%	8	17.4%	9	19.6%	5	10.9%
12	10	21.7%	13	28.3%	8	17.4%	9	19.6%	6	13.0%
13	20	43.5%	15	32.6%	9	19.6%	0	0.0%	2	4.3%
14	6	13.0%	10	21.7%	19	41.3%	4	8.7%	7	15.2%

Adapted from Osen and Bye [1].

indifferent. On the contrary, 19% partly disagreed and 52% strongly disagreed with this statement. Among the juniors, 13% strongly or partly agreed, 33% were indifferent, and 22% and 33% partly or strongly disagreed, respectively.

These results conflict with our observations that indeed more students do show up to class if the roll is called, despite attendance not being mandatory. We speculate that students in their responses may have wished to emphasise their own free will and autonomy in choosing whether to turn up to class, and from the results, this appears to be especially true for the seniors. In Sect. 2.1, we discuss how social contracts and unspoken rules and norms can emerge in the relation between teacher and students and among the students themselves, however, these mechanisms are acted upon more at a subconscious level than mandatory rules, and this may explain why the students fail to agree with the statement, as they may simply not be sufficiently self-aware to know whether they actually will yield to social pressure for turning up or not.

Another possible reason for this result is that the effect of calling the roll may not be as strong as we think it is. After all, we have only observed the effect across different cohorts, and not for the same cohort during a single semester. Thus, our impression that more students turn up to class when calling the roll may be due to variation across different cohorts. Moreover, we do not have accurate attendance numbers for all cohorts, thus our observations are more of a perceived kind than rigid studies.

4.2 Lectures

Statements 1 and 2 relate to whether students want more passive learning activities such as traditional lectures and using the blackboard, respectively. It is clear from the responses that seniors do not want more traditional lectures, with nobody strongly agreeing with statement 1, and only 10% partly agreeing, 45% being indifferent, and 33% and 13% partly og strongly disagreeing, respectively.

The juniors are more positive towards more traditional lectures than the seniors, although the average still wants less. Among the 46 juniors, only one student strongly agreed (2%), whereas about 17% partly agreed, 50% were indifferent, and about 24% and 7% partly or strongly disagreeing, respectively.

With respect to teaching using the blackboard (statement 2), seniors were mainly indifferent (9%), or partly agreed (23%) or disagreed (29%), whereas 3% strongly agreed, and 7% strongly disagree.

Juniors were even more indifferent (48%), and an equal number of students (12, or 26%) strongly or partly agreeing/disagreeing (although twice as many strongly disagreed rather than strongly agreed (8.7% vs 4.3%).

The results are in correspondence with our observation and reflections in Sect. 2.2. As teachers, we wish to emphasise active learning activities, yet, sometimes lectures or blackboard teaching are necessary. The students seem to think that we and the rest of our colleagues in the three study programmes employ about the right amount of blackboard teaching but should reduce the amount of traditional lectures.

4.3 Active Learning

Statements 3–7 relate to active learning activities and practical application versus theory. It is very clear from the responses that the students want more activities that facilitate active learning. For example, among seniors, nobody disagreed (partly or strongly) that they want more focus on practical application than theory (statement 5), more problem-solving (statement 6), or more lab work (statement 7). For juniors, only a single student (2%) strongly disagreed with each of statements 5–7, whilst only one (2%), zero (0%), and three (7%) students partly disagreed, respectively. On the contrary, a vast majority of both seniors and juniors strongly or partly agreed with statements 5–7.

Regarding more flipped classroom and elearning/online learning (statement 4), only one senior strongly disagreed, whereas six seniors (19%), partly disagreed. Among juniors, 9% strongly disagreed and 17% partly disagreed. Of the seniors, 19% strongly agreed and 11% of the juniors, whereas 30% of both the seniors and juniors partly agreed.

With respect to more active learning activities in general (statement 3), no seniors strongly disagreed and only 13% partly disagreed, whereas one junior strongly disagreed (2%) and 9% partly disagreed. Hence, in agreement with our own views, it seems very safe to conclude that most students want more active learning activities as described by statements 3–7, with a slightly smaller preference for flipped classroom (statement 4) when compared to statements 5–7 and active learning in general (statement 3).

4.4 Mandatory Coursework

Seniors were mainly indifferent (32%), or split between 26% partly agreeing/disagreeing, and 7% strongly agreeing and 10% strongly disagreeing to whether we should employ more mandatory coursework (statement 9). Juniors were even more indifferent (48%), although 17% strongly disagreed and 13% partly disagreed, whereas no junior strongly agreed with the statement, and 22% partly agreed. Hence, when contrasting seniors and juniors, the seniors were slightly opposed to having more mandatory coursework, whereas juniors were much more against the statement.

The result of the seniors is as expected and matches the student feedback we have got over the years, especially among the final-semester students. Many students know that they do not have the necessary motivation and willpower to do the necessary work unless they have mandatory coursework, whereas others, and often more academically skilled students, would like more freedom in their studies. The result of the juniors, however, is more skewed towards less use of mandatory coursework. We speculate that the reason for this is that it is easier to appreciate the hard work required for mandatory coursework in retrospect than being in the midst of it. At the time of the surveys, the seniors had only a single course left and were focusing on their bachelor theses, whilst the juniors were having three courses run in parallel and often several compulsory assignments within a short period of time.

4.5 Feedback to Students

An overwhelming majority of seniors (71% and 16% strongly or partly agred, respectively; 7% were indifferent or partly disagreed; and noone strongly disagreed) wants more/better individual feedback during the semester (statement

10). Of the juniors, 46% or 28% strongly or partly agreed, respectively, and the remaining 26% were all indifferent.

This statement was perhaps badly phrased, as almost nobody would ever say no to more of a given good, e.g., money. A better question would be whether students were *satisfied* with the amount and quality of individual feedback they have received during their studies, not if they wanted more feedback. In addition, students' answers to the statement act as an average of all the courses they have participated in. Hence, and as noted in the student comments, there may well be courses with sufficient levels of student feedback whilst other courses give far less feedback. Nevertheless, the result indicates that students are not satisfied with the current state of individual feedback provided in the courses we offer and our department will need to investigate this issue further.

That students are concerned with not getting enough individual feedback may also be an indicator of lack of self-monitoring and self-regulation skills, which to some extent can be mitigated by facilitating learning activities where students adopt ownership, such as projects or lab work.

4.6 Grades and Exams

Statements 11 and 12 relates to whether the final grade of a course should be fully decided by a single oral or written exam (statement 11) or be composed of several parts, such as lab work, assignments, projects, midsemester tests, and final exams (statement 12). The majority of seniors want a single final exam to be decisive for their grades (16% strongly agreed, 36% partly agreed, and 29% were indifferent). Interestingly, the majority of seniores also want their final grades to be composed of several parts (23% strongly agreed, 16% partly agreed, and 26% were indifferent) but with more disagreement (29% partly disagreed and 7% strongly disagreed) than for statement 11 (16% partly disagreed and 3% strongly disagreed).

For juniors, opinions appear to be more polarised, and fewer students were indifferent when compared with seniors. With respect to having a single final exam deciding the grade (statement 11), 17% were indifferent; 30% partly agreed and 20% partly disagreed; and 22% strongly agreed and 11% disagreed. Regarding composite grades (statement 12), the figures were approximately the same (17% were indifferent; 28% partly agreed and 20% partly disagreed; and 22% strongly agreed and 13% disagreed).

Hence, amongst both seniors and juniors, 50% either strongly or partly agreed with both statement 11 and statement 12, which are in conflict with each other.

Historically and currently, we almost exclusively use a single final exam to determine grades but in many courses we have mandatory coursework that must be passed for access to the exam. The results suggest students want both grading approaches and consequently, we should probably increase the number of courses where the final grade is composed of several parts to have a suitable mix.

Regarding digital exams (statement 13), a large majority of seniors wants more digital exams (48% strongly agreed, 29% partly agreed, 16% were indifferent, 7% partly disagreed, and nobody strongly disagreed), whereas the majority are indifferent (48%) or partly (10%) or strongly disagreed (23%) with wanting to have more home exams. Juniors are slightly less enthusiastic but still a large majority wants more digital exams (44% strongly agreed, 33% partly agreed, 20% were indifferent; nobody partly disagreed, and 4% strongly disagreed).

Digital exams have just recently started to take place but only in a few of our courses. Its usage will likely increase in the future, partly because of administrative pressure towards cost-saving measures and societal trends but also because of various advantages, especially in some courses where this kind of examination is suitable, such as programming-related courses.

With respect to more home exams (statement 14), many seniors were indifferent (48%) but 23% and 10% strongly or partly disagreed, respectively, whereas 7% strongly agreed, and 13% partly agreed. In contrast with seniors, juniors are more positive than negative towards adopting more home exams. 13% strongly agreed and 22% partly agreed; 41% were indifferent; and 9% and 15% partly or strongly disagreed, respectively.

Home exams have hardly ever been offered our courses, thus it is somewhat surprising to observe the seniors' resistance against a kind of examination that they have never experienced (at least not during their studies). There is currently no plan to begin to offer home exams in our courses as far as we know.

4.7 Summary and Conclusions

The views expressed by the students in the evaluation surveys can be summarized as follows:

- Students, especially seniors, are quite opposed to the idea that *calling the roll* (statement 8) will increase attendance. This finding is in contradiction with our own observations.
- Likewise, students are indifferent or opposed to having more *traditional lectures* (they want less on average), whilst they are indifferent and on average want neither less nor more teaching *using the blackboard.*
- Students clearly wants more *active learning activities*, especially more focus on practical application than theory, more problem-solving, and more lab work. They also want more flipped classroom, although to a smaller extent than for the abovementioned activities.
- Seniors are indifferent or slightly against more *mandatory coursework*, whereas juniors want less on average. We hypothesize that students are more appreciative of mandatory coursework and see its benefit when they are able to critically view back in retrospect in their final semester.
- Students, especially seniors, want more *individual feedback* during the semester. A possible reason may be that seniors have developed better skills for critical thinking than juniors and therefore have higher expectations regarding feedback from teachers.
- Students are split between having a *single final exam* (oral or written) deciding grades versus *composite grades*. They are positive to more *digital exams* but split towards *home exams* (juniors want more, seniors less).

If we as teachers were to act on the advice from students in our degree programmes, which is not necessarily obvious, since students do not have the same academic nor pedagogical insight as teachers, we should

- reduce the amount of traditional lectures (statement 1);
- continue using the blackboard as before (statement 2);
- use more active learning activities (statements 3–7);
- not call the roll (statement 8);
- keep the same amount of mandatory coursework (statement 9);
- strongly improve individual student feedback (statement 10);
- have a good mix of single final exams and composite grades (statements 11–12);
- use more digital exams (statement 13); and
- slowly introduce home exams and evaluate its effect (statement 14).

Notably, however, apart from calling the roll, student views are in accord with our own observations and reflections presented previously.

5 Final Remarks

Based on about 23 years of combined experience in teaching courses in computer and electrical engineering degree programmes, this article provides a summary of the most important observations and reflections we have made over the years. To nuance our findings, we present an overview of relevant literature, including topics such as students' approaches to learning, constructive alignment, assessment, active learning, and problem-based and problem-solving learning. Finally, we have tried to measure what students think about the learning environment that we currently provide, and how we examine students, through student evaluation surveys for our first-, second-, and final-year students of our engineering programmes in automation, power systems, and computer engineering.

There appears to be a trend in recent education literature suggesting that universities should shift their teaching from passive learning activities such as traditional lectures towards active learning activities involving more problem-solving, laboratory work, flipped classroom approaches, and practical real-world application, without sacrificing a solid theoretical foundation. We as teachers agree with these viewpoints, as do our students as evident from the evaluation surveys.

With respect to forms of examination, the surveys show that although many students want a single final exam grade (as of today), many students also want their grades to be composed of several parts, e.g., lab work, projects, mid-semester tests, and final exams. In line with proponents of CA, we have sympathy for the latter viewpoint since students tend to be more concerned with exam grades than with what they actually learn, and the non-final exam components provide an opportunity to offer formative assessment. Consequently, one should put much emphasis on aligning what the students should master after having completed a course (intended learning outcomes) with the means of examination, which may require grades to be composed of several subcomponents.

Our university has just recently begun to use digital exams, and only for a few of our courses. Both from the evaluation surveys and from our interactions with students it is clear that students are welcoming this new trend and want more digital exams, a change that is likely to be implemented over the next few years. We would like to point out that many of the great opportunities that come with digital exams, such as autograding, immediate feedback, variety of exam exercises, autogenerated problems, and storage and sharing of exams across campuses and institutions, to mention a few, are useful not only for exams but also during the semester as pedagogical tools.

In the foreseeable future, our aim is to undertake more studies on the various teaching methods and learning activities presented in this article, with a particular focus on studying whether the effects of our proposed methods are real and advantageous to the students. Performing student evaluation surveys is a challenging task, and we need to delve into the relevant research on this topic in order to design better surveys and collect more and better student evaluation data. Finally, we will continue to improve and facilitate an active learning environment, and in particular, we will investigate the possibility of adopting a flipped classroom approach in several of our bachelor courses similarly to what we have done for a master's course on artificial intelligence [34].

Acknowledgements. The Software and Intelligent Control (SoftICE) Laboratory is grateful for the financial support given by the Study Committee at NTNU in Ålesund through the educational research project *Research-Based and Innovation-Driven Learning (FILA)*, grant no. 70440500.

References

1. Osen, O.L., Bye, R.T.: Reflections on teaching electrical and computer engineering courses at the bachelor level. In: Proceedings of the 9th International Conference on Computer Supported Education - Volume 2: CSEDU (CSEDU 2017), pp. 57–68. INSTICC, SCITEPRESS (2017). Selected for Extended Publication in Springer Book Series Communications in Computer and Information Science (CCIS)
2. Durden, G.C., Ellis, L.V.: The effects of attendance on student learning in principles of economics. Am. Econ. Rev. **85**, 343–346 (1995)
3. Romer, D.: Do students go to class? Should they? J. Econ. Perspecti. **7**, 167–174 (1993)
4. Marburger, D.R.: Absenteeism and undergraduate exam performance. J. Econ. Educ. **32**, 99–109 (2001)
5. Marburger, D.R.: Does mandatory attendance improve student performance? J. Econ. Educ. **37**, 148–155 (2006)
6. Sotto, E.: When Teaching Becomes Learning: A Theory and Practice of Teaching. Bloomsbury Publishing, London (2007)
7. Bligh, D.A.: What's the Use of Lectures?. Intellect Books, Bristol (1998)
8. van der Meer, A.L., van der Weel, F.R.: Only three fingers write, but the whole brain works: a high-density EEG study showing advantages of drawing over typing for learning. Front. Psychol. **8**, 706 (2017)

9. Anderson, J.R.: Cognitive Psychology and Its Implications, 8th edn. Worth Publishers, New York (2015)
10. Clark, R.C., Nguyen, F., Sweller, J.: Efficiency in Learning: Evidence-Based Guidelines to Manage Cognitive Load. Wiley, Hoboken (2011)
11. Westermann, K., Rummel, N.: Delaying instruction: evidence from a study in a university relearning setting. Instr. Sci. **40**, 673–689 (2012)
12. Forsyth, D.R.: Group Dynamics. Cengage Learning, Boston (2009)
13. Pfaff, E., Huddleston, P.: Does it matter if I hate teamwork? What impacts student attitudes toward teamwork. J. Mark. Educ. **25**, 37–45 (2003)
14. Chatman, J.A., Flynn, F.J.: The influence of demographic heterogeneity on the emergence and consequences of cooperative norms in work teams. Acad. Manag. J. **44**, 956–974 (2001)
15. Joyce, W.B.: On the free-rider problem in cooperative learning. J. Educ. Bus. **74**, 271–274 (1999)
16. Gynnild, V.: Læringsorientert eller eksamensfokusert? Nærstudier av pedagogisk utviklingsarbeid i sivilingeniørstudiet. Ph.D. thesis, NTNU (2001)
17. Marton, F.: Phenomenography – describing conceptions of the world around us. Instr. Sci. **10**, 177–200 (1981)
18. Baeten, M., Kyndt, E., Struyven, K., Dochy, F.: Using student-centred learning environments to stimulate deep approaches to learning: factors encouraging or discouraging their effectiveness. Educ. Res. Rev. **5**, 243–260 (2010)
19. Marton, F., Booth, S.: Learning and Awareness. Lawrence Erlbaum, Mahwaw (1997)
20. Prosser, M., Trigwell, K.: Understanding Learning and Teaching: The Experience in Higher Education. Society for Research in Higher Education and/Open University Press, Buckingham (1999)
21. Case, J., Marshall, D.: Between deep and surface: procedural approaches to learning in engineering education contexts. Stud. High. Educ. **29**, 605–615 (2004)
22. Entwistle, N., Ramsden, P.: Understanding Student Learning. Croom Helm, Beckenham (1983)
23. Entwistle, N., Ramsden, P.: Understanding Student Learning (Routledge Revivals). Routledge, Abingdon (2015)
24. Saeljo, R.: Learning in the Learner's Perspective 1. Some Commonsense Conceptions. Report no 76, Institute of Education, University of Gothenburg (1979)
25. Marton, F., Dall'Alba, G., Beaty, E.: Conceptions of learning. Int. J. Sci. Educ. **16**, 457–474 (1993)
26. Marshall, D., Summers, M., Woolnough, B.: Students' conceptions of learning in an engineering context. High. Educ. **38**, 291–309 (1999)
27. Biggs, J., Tang, C.: Teaching for Quality Learning at University, 4th edn. McGraw Hill/Open University Press, New York (2011)
28. Felder, R.M., Brent, R.: Understanding student differences. J. Eng. Educ. **94**, 57–72 (2005)
29. Lan, W.: The effects of self-monitoring on students' course performance, use of learning strategies, attitude, self-judgment ability, and knowledge representation. J. Exp. Educ. **64**, 101–116 (1996)
30. Borkowski, J., Thorpe, P.: Self-regulation and motivation: a life-span perspective on underachievement. In: Schunk, D., Zimmermann, B. (eds.) Self-regulation of Learning and Performance: Issues of Educational Applications, pp. 44–73. Erlbaum, Hillsdale (1994)

31. Gynnild, V., Holstad, A., Myrhaug, D.: Identifying and promoting self-regulated learning in higher education: roles and responsibilities of student tutors. Mentor. Tutoring: Partnersh. Learn. **16**, 147–161 (2008)
32. Nicol, D.J., Macfarlane-Dick, D.: Formative assessment and self-regulated learning: a model and seven principles of good feedback practice. Stud. High. Educ. **31**, 199–218 (2006)
33. Gynnild, V., Holstad, A., Myrhaug, D.: Teaching as coaching: a case study of awareness and learning in engineering education. Int. J. Sci. Educ. **29**, 1–17 (2007)
34. Bye, R.T.: The teacher as a facilitator for learning: flipped classroom in a master's course on artificial intelligence. In: Proceedings of the 9th International Conference on Computer Supported Education – Volume 1: CSEDU, pp. 184–195. INSTICC, SCITEPRESS (2017)
35. Prince, M.J.: Does active learning work? A review of the research. J. Eng. Educ. **93**, 223–231 (2004)
36. Andersen, H.L.: "Constructive alignment" og risikoen for en forsimplende universitetspædagogik. Dansk Universitetspædagogisk Tidsskrift 5 (2010)
37. Schroeder, C., Scott, T.P., Tolson, H., Huang, T.Y., Lee, Y.H.: A meta-analysis of national research: effects of teaching strategies on student achievement in science in the United States. J. Res. Sci. Teach. **44**, 1436–1460 (2007)
38. Freeman, S., Eddy, S.L., McDonough, M., Smith, M.K., Okoroafor, N., Jordt, H., Wenderoth, M.P.: Active learning increases student performance in science, engineering, and mathematics. Proc. Nat. Acad. Sci. **111**, 8410–8415 (2014)
39. Foldnes, N.: The flipped classroom and cooperative learning: evidence from a randomised experiment. Act. Learn. High Educ. **17**, 39–49 (2016)
40. Bowen, C.W.: A quantitative literature review of cooperative learning effects on high school and college chemistry achievement. J. Chem. Educ. **77**, 116 (2000)
41. Johnson, D.W., Johnson, R.T., Smith, K.A.: Active Learning: Cooperation in the College Classroom. Interaction Book Co., Edina (1998)
42. Springer, L., Stanne, M., Donovan, S.: Effects of small-group learning on undergraduates in science, mathematics, engineering and technology: a meta-analysis. Rev. Educ. Res. **69**, 21–52 (1999)
43. Hattie, J., Goveia, I.C.: Synlig læring: et sammendrag av mer enn 800 metaanalyser av skoleprestasjoner. Cappelen Damm akademisk (2013)
44. Schaathun, W.A., Schaathun, H.G., Bye, R.T.: Aktiv læring i mikrokontrollarar. Uniped **38**, 381–389 (2015). Special issue following MNT-konferansen, Bergen, Norway, 18–19 March 2015

Computer-Assisted Method Based on Continuous Feedback to Improve the Academic Achievements of Engineering Students

Ana González-Marcos[1(✉)], Fernando Alba-Elías[1], and Joaquín Ordieres-Meré[2]

[1] Department of Mechanical Engineering, Universidad de La Rioja, c/ San José de Calasanz 31, 26004 Logroño, La Rioja, Spain
{ana.gonzalez,fernando.alba}@unirioja.es

[2] PMQ Research Group, ETSII, Universidad Politécnica de Madrid, José Gutiérrrez Abascal 2, 28006 Madrid, Spain
j.ordieres@upm.es

Abstract. This paper presents a computer-assisted method specifically designed to incorporate formative assessment into classroom practice. It is based on the following five key strategies. First, different written materials are provided to students to help clarify goals and success criteria. Second, students are involved in real-world engineering projects that are oriented to learning about project management. Thus, they adopt an active role during the learning process. Third, different types of feedback are implemented and provided several times during the project development in order to allow students to use the feedback to close their performance gap. Fourth, each student is assessed by all the other students of the project interacting with the student in question, i.e., peer-assessment is activated. Fifth, self-assessment is also considered. Data analysis from a specific academic course suggest that the proposed method has a positive impact on the academic achievements of engineering students.

Keywords: Assessment · Feedback · Project management
Higher education

1 Introduction

Improving the quality and efficiency of education and training is one of the strategic objectives stablished by the "Strategic framework for European cooperation in education and training ('ET 2020')" [11]. In this scenario, such quality is associated with the acquisition of competences that students will require in their professional careers [27]. The key is that these competences enable the task of learning, promoting knowledge, know-how, and knowing how to be, so that higher education plays a fundamental role in the effective preparation for a lifelong learning.

P. Escudeiro et al. (Eds.): CSEDU 2017, CCIS 865, pp. 390–403, 2018.
https://doi.org/10.1007/978-3-319-94640-5_19

From the teacher's point of view, helping students to the acquisition and development of competencies requires generating feedback on various areas or dimensions related to the process of knowledge construction, so that it can be used by these students to improve and transfer their learning in diverse contexts and situations [22,26].

In the specific case of teaching in higher education, this idea involves redefining the concept and value of assessment in the learning process. Thus, the assessment must now be considered as a learning situation in its own sense (*assessment for learning* or formative assessment), besides fulfilling its primary function of measuring students' learning at the end of a period of instruction (*assessment of learning* or summative assessment). From this conception, assessment has a key formative purpose [3,5,26] and the design of the learning process in the university classroom must be revised. In this sense, it should be remembered that what influence students most is not the teaching but the assessment [1,5,14,21,29].

Formative assessment is, without a doubt, a powerful tool to positively impact on students' learning and achievements. According to [6], there are five key strategies for implementing formative assessment:

1. Clarifying and sharing learning intentions and criteria for success;
2. Engineering effective classroom discussions and other learning tasks that elicit evidence of student understanding;
3. Providing feedback that moves learners forward;
4. Activating students as instructional resources for one another; and
5. Activating students as the owners of their own learning.

These strategies involve the three main actors in learning activities: teacher, peer, and learner. Furthermore, they are consistent with other studies that examine different mechanisms for providing formative assessment, such as feedback [22,28,30], self-assessment [22,24,25], and peer-assessment [15,22,33].

Aligned with the five strategies put forth by [6] and based on both the analytical method for measuring competence in project management proposed in [18] and the online assessment and feedback system presented in [19], this paper presents a model of formative assessment aimed at improving the quality of learning of competences in the field of engineering education. More specifically, a computer-assisted method based on continuous feedback is proposed.

The organization of the remainder paper is as follows: Sect. 2 is dedicated to briefly describe the key strategies that support the proposed model of formative assessment. Section 3 presents how the system is implemented. Section 4 provides the results observed in the academic course analyzed. Finally, Sect. 5 discusses some general conclusions and presents future work.

2 Key Strategies that Support the Proposed Model of Formative Assessment

As mentioned in the previous section, the proposed assessment and feedback system is based, on the one hand, on the analytical method for measuring competence in project management proposed in [18], which is focused on the methodology for gathering and integrating information about the individual performance of students in order to obtain numerical assessment values of each competence. On the other hand, the proposed system is based on the five key strategies identified by [6] for implementing formative assessment. How those strategies are implemented is explained below.

Key Strategy 1. Clarifying and Sharing Learning Intentions and Criteria for Success
A necessary condition for students to achieve learning goals is that they must know and understand those goals [26]. One way of clarifying goals, criteria and standards is to provide students with written documents containing statements that describe assessment criteria and/or the standards that define different levels of achievement [22]. Thus, the proposed learning experience contains the following materials:

- Assessment procedures and instruments. This document presents the competences to be assessed during the semester, the instruments (forms, audits, etc.) used to collect information, and how all this information is integrated to provide individual scores for the assessed competences. Furthermore, it explains how the feedback is provided.
- Specific procedure manuals that describe the responsibilities of each role, explain how to operate, how to do things, how to communicate mandatory information, etc.
- Quality criteria for management products. This document defines the requirements that the management products created during the project should fulfill.
- Quality criteria for management processes. This document provides the quality criteria for what is considered good practice standards.
- Assessment checklists and rubrics used to assess the project management competences.

The first module of the course is dedicated to explain the methodology that will be used during the semester, as well as to clarify goals and success criteria. In this way, students become familiar with the course objectives and requirements for success from the beginning of the semester, besides basic project management concepts or the use of the web-based learning environment.

Key Strategy 2. Engineering Effective Classroom Discussions and Other Learning Tasks that Elicit Evidence of Student Understanding
As part of the process of acquiring the skills needed to become project management professionals, a learning process should provide students with experiences that are similar to what they will encounter in the working world [17]. This is in line with the theory of situated learning [7,20], which is based on the proven idea that meaningful learning by the student cannot be considered outside an authentic context in which it occurs. Thus, students are involved in real-world engineering.

In essence, students are organized in project teams, so that each team is responsible for satisfying the needs and specifications requested by a client (teachers) in the agreed period of time and cost. These projects are oriented to learning about the professional project management methodology PRINCE2 TM(Project IN Controlled Environments) [23]. According to this methodology, a project is split into multiple phases or stages that do not overlap (Fig. 1). Between each phase the outcome of the prior phase is evaluated and it is considered if the plans for the upcoming phase might need to be modified.

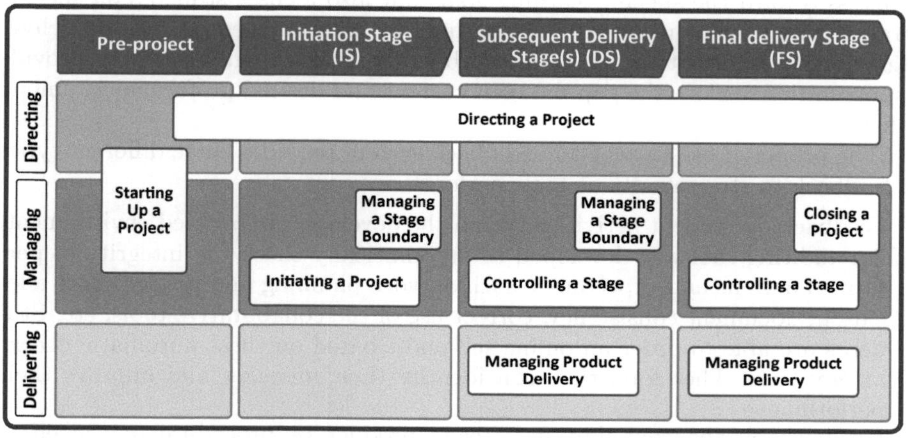

Fig. 1. The PRINCE2 process model (Source: [19]).

Students, as in professional projects, assume different roles with different responsibilities in the project team [23]:

- **EX:** Executive, which is ultimately responsible for the project. This role has the authority to direct the project within the requirements set by the Corporate.
- **PM:** Project Manager, with management responsibilities. On behalf of the EX, the PMs have the authority to run the project on a day-to-day basis.
- **TMg:** Team manager, which is responsible to ensure the production and delivery of those products defined by the PM team. A PM temporarily assigned as a TMg to manage Project Engineers (TM).
- **TM:** Team member, with engineering tasks development responsibilities.

In this way, students adopt an active role during the learning process and are able to put into practice different skills and competences that a project member should possess in the development of a project.

In summary, students are *situated* in a *project* development process that is interesting and useful to them and in which their individual differences are considered. Furthermore, *self-directed learning, learning by doing and a sense of responsibility are fostered.* A detailed description of the learning environment adopted can be found in [17].

Key Strategy 3. Providing Feedback that Moves Learners Forward
Within the literature there is general agreement that high quality feedback to students on their assessments is important and is of benefit to their future learning [30]. Feedback is not only regarded as crucial to improve knowledge and skill acquisition, i.e. achievement, but also depicted as a significant factor in motivating learning [28].

It is also recognized that effective feedback is not only based on monitoring progress toward the specific learning goals but also focuses students on specific strategies for improvement [9,16]. Consequently, effective feedback should deliver high quality information to students about their learning, as well as provide opportunities to close the gap between current and desired performance, among others [22].

The proposed assessment and feedback system provides three different types of feedback to students about their performance:

- Feedback on student activities within the developed web-based environment. An auditing tool was developed to automatically check the integrity of performed actions and procedures, such as work planning and proper effort allocation, document consistency, correct use of the collaborative tools, etc. Students are able to order an online self-audit based on these automatic checks at any time. Therefore, they can identify their mistakes and improve their performance.
- Feedback on the contribution of each product or procedure to the effort claimed by each student. Students can gather detailed –tabular and graphical– information about what product(s) and competence(s) affected their current scores. This information is provided at least three times during project execution (one per project life cycle phase).
- Lessons learned. Also conducted at the end of each project phase, a lessons learned review is provided to each project through the web-based environment. This report, which is based on actual project performing, identifies good and poor practices over the course of each project phase. Furthermore, each lessons learned report is analyzed in specific sessions to collectively discuss what is working and what is not working well. It is not possible to rebuild the already delivered and approved items, but this feedback provides advice on how to proceed and how to improve in the future.

Key Strategy 4. Activating Students as Instructional Resources for One Another
Peer-assessment can be defined as an arrangement in which individuals consider the amount, level, value, worth, quality, or success of the products or outcomes of learning of peers of similar status [32]. Although peers are not domain experts, the use of peer-assessment and feedback can be beneficial for learning, not only for the receiver but also for the peer assessor [4,15,31,32]. Furthermore, peer-assessment can be regarded as a form of collaborative learning [12,13].

In the proposed assessment system, each student is assessed by all the other students of the project interacting with the student in question for a given competence. The peer-assessment is carried out by means of different forms, by means of at least one piece of evidence clearly having those criteria determining the maximum degree of performance specified therein. Thus, the proposed system collects evidence-based opinions about the products being produced and how the team is managing the project.

Key Strategy 5. Activating Students as the Owners of Their Own Learning

Findings from research conducted on self-assessment [2,8,24,25] show that self-assessment contributes to higher student achievement and improved behavior. Since self-assessment requires students to reflect on their own work and judge the degree to which they have performed in relation to explicitly stated goals and criteria, they have the opportunity to identify strengths and weaknesses in their work [2] and, thus, what constitutes a good or poor piece of work.

Taking into account that self-assessment can have positive benefits for the students' learning process, the proposed assessment and feedback system also considers the opinions from those students who produce a product or are responsible for its process implementation.

In summary, the proposal described in this work gathers information from the three main actors in learning activities (teacher, peer, and learner) to assess each student's performance. Therefore, the proposed assessment and feedback system uses some kind of 360-degree overview of different activities inside the project. All the collected evidences are considered in a weighted integration to yield a numerical assessment score of each competence that is developed for each student [18].

3 Implementation of the Proposed Computer-Assisted Method Based on Continuous Feedback

The online assessment and feedback system was created by integrating information gathered from the following open source tools:

- A project and portfolio management software (http://www.project.net) that provides the necessary project management tools, as well as some collaborative tools such as blogs, document repository, etc. The lessons learned reports mentioned in Sect. 2 are provided through the project's blog of this web-based software.
- A survey collector (https://www.limesurvey.org) that contains the designed forms to conduct the proposed assessments. Teachers, learners and peers use the same assessing forms.

The developed assessment and feedback tool (P2ML) was designed to communicate with the aforementioned open source tools and to provide feedback as described in Sect. 2. The first type of feedback is based on student activities within the developed web-based environment. Figure 2 shows a partial view of the audit report about the integrity of performed actions and procedures that each student can order at any time. Text is displayed in red when the system identifies mistakes, inconsistencies or inappropriate behaviors.

Project Audit

Audit Date
2016-11-01 17:53:28

AUTOMATICALLY GATHERED DATA

Number of Project Members (PM and TM)
21

Current Stage (stage number)
DS: Delivery Stage (1)

Current Process
CS: Controlling a Stage

Process Start Date (creation date of the process)
2016-10-29 (2016-10-29 12:09:05)

Number of DS stages defined
1

ACTUAL STAGE DATA

Current phase correctly defined (name and progress reporting method)
YES

Number of summary tasks defined in current phase
5

Number of tasks defined in current phase (Number of delayed tasks)
30 (0)

Number of tasks defined in current phase that will NOT PRODUCE any deliverable (it should be 0)
1 (3.33%)

Number of tasks defined in current phase with no personal assignments (it should be 0)
1 (3.33%)

Number of milestones defined in current phase (Number of delayed milestones)
11 (0)

Number of deliverables defined in current phase
43

Number of management (mandatory minimum) / specialist deliverables correctly defined in current phase

Student Audit

Audited Student
[redacted]

AUTOMATICALLY GATHERED DATA

Number of assignments
18

Interrelated work (average number of TMs working together on those TM's assignments)
3.6

Assigned work at completion (hours)
34.9

Assigned work (hours)
17.5

Claimed work (hours)
20.8

Number of delayed tasks
0 (0%)

Number of total documents LINKED TO deliverables (Individual contribution percentage)
6 (83.33%)

Number of "COMPLETED" deliverables with LINKED documents
6

PNET MANAGEMENT ACTIVITY

Number of phases "created" (TOTAL: 3)
2 (66.7%)

Number of milestones "created" / "edited" (TOTAL: 18)
13 / 68

Number of tasks "created" (with work assignment) / "edited"
50 (39) / 406

Number of work assignments "created" / "edited"
0 / 73

Number of baselines "created" (TOTAL: 3)
3 (100%)

Number of deliverables "created" (TOTAL: 76)
56 (73.7%)

Fig. 2. Partial view of an audit report with data automatically gathered from a project (left) and a student (right). (Color figure online)

The second type of feedback is concerned with the contribution of each product or procedure to the effort claimed by each student. Detailed information about students' performance is updated at least at the end of each project phase. Thus, besides tabular information, different graphical views are provided to illustrate the performance evolution of each student:

- First, each student is able to identify what project management competences were developed during the project execution, as well as to compare his or her performance to the average of the students with the same role. In the case of the proposed system, the reference framework used as a reference for competences was the IPMA Competence Baseline (ICB) [10]. The IPMA Competence Baseline is the common framework document that all IPMA Member Associations and Certification Bodies abide by to ensure that consistent and harmonized standards are applied. Figure 3 illustrates the individual scores

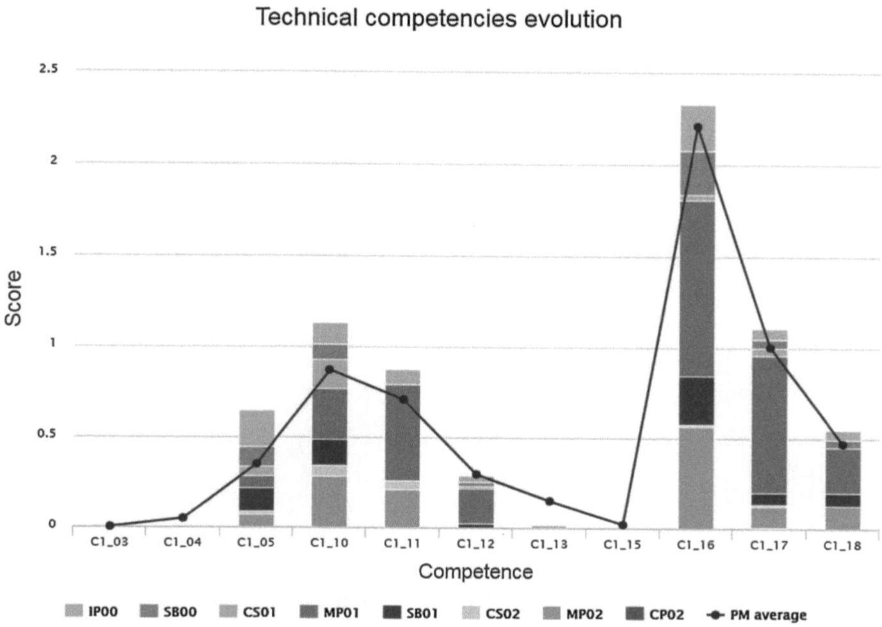

Competence	Description	Points
C1_03	PROJECT REQUIREMENTS & OBJECTIVES	0
C1_04	RISK & OPPORTUNITY	0
C1_05	QUALITY	0.6461
C1_10	SCOPE & DELIVERABLES	1.1285
C1_11	TIME & PROJECT PHASES	0.8769
C1_12	RESOURCES	0.2935
C1_13	COST & FINANCE	0.0202
C1_15	CHANGES	0
C1_16	CONTROL & REPORTS	2.3338
C1_17	INFORMATION & DOCUMENTATION	1.1102
C1_18	COMMUNICATION	0.5456

Fig. 3. Example of the *technical competences evolution* plot (top) and summarized tabular view (bottom) for a student who adopted the Project Manager (PM) role. (Color figure online)

evolution for each assessed competence for a student that adopted PM role. In this case, detailed information was also provided in tabular form (Fig. 3, bottom). Finally, competence information was provided for each PRINCE2 process.

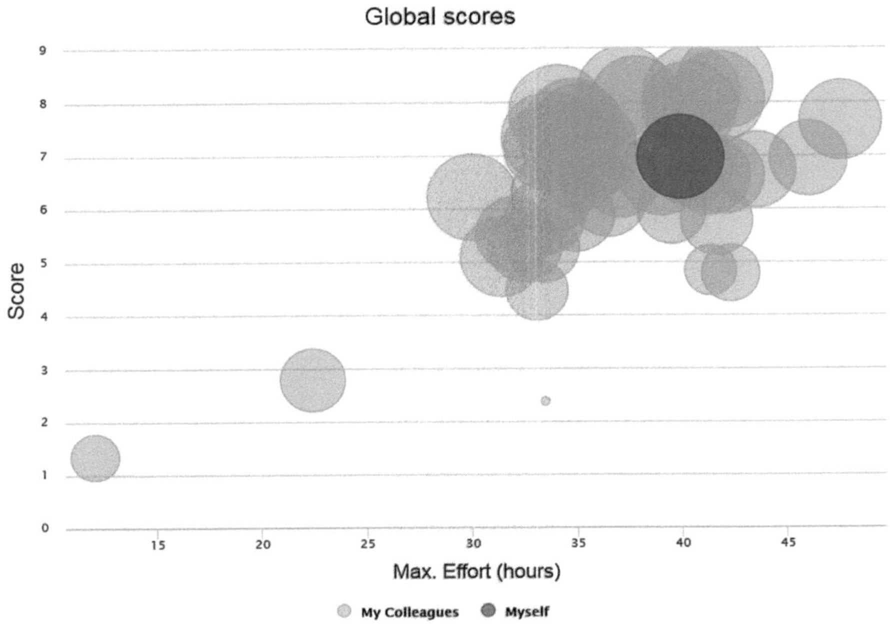

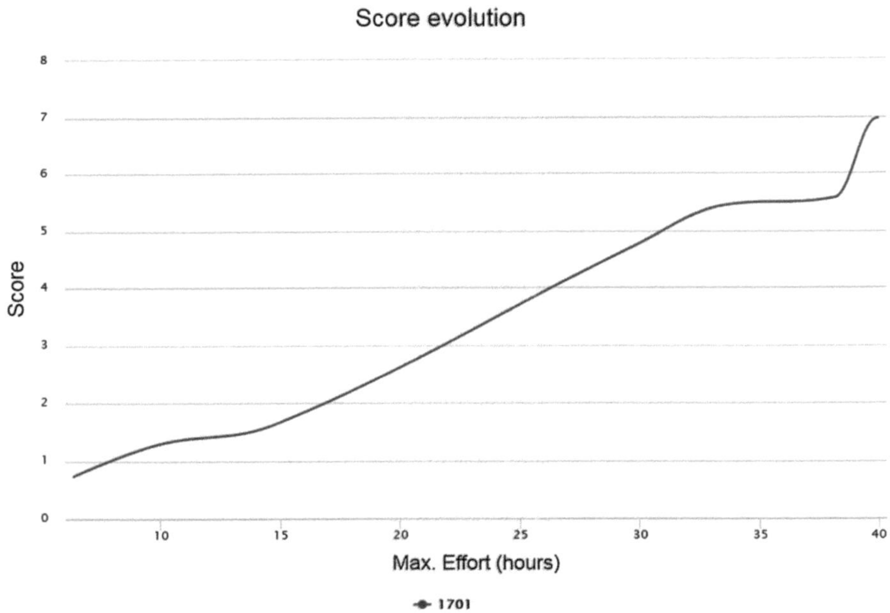

Fig. 4. *Global scores* screen (top) and *learning curve* (bottom) for the same student shown in Fig. 3. (Color figure online)

- In addition to competence assessment details, the online system also provides a unique, numerical, global score for each student. For example, Fig. 4 shows the global score obtained by the same student showed in Fig. 3 (red circle) against the effort claimed by he or she. The size of the circle is related to the efficiency of the student, i.e., it indicates how well a student was able to finish their assignments within the adequate time. This plot also allows students to anonymously compare their performance to that of the other students.
- Finally, the system provides the learning curve through project execution for each student. Figure 4 illustrates the learning curve for the same student shown in Fig. 3. In this case, detailed information was also provided for each PRINCE2 process. This plot represents the increase (or decrease) of learning (global score) with experience (claimed effort).

Furthermore, teachers are provided with different views that allow them to analyze individual and project team results during project execution. For example, Fig. 5 illustrates students evolution during the final project stage.

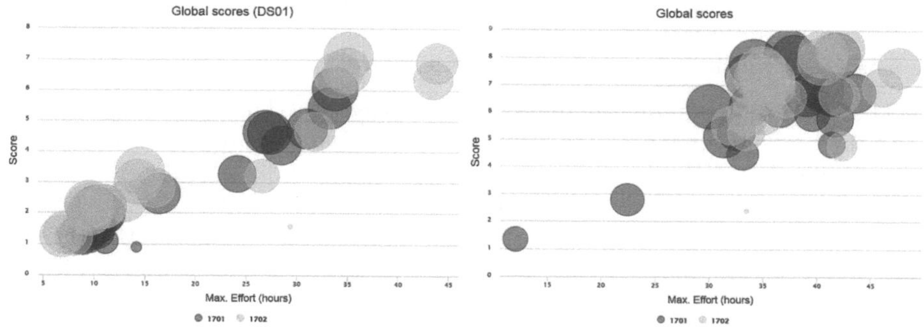

Fig. 5. *Global scores* screen views available for teachers: (left) students' scores after the second project stage and (right) students' scores after the final project stage. (Color figure online)

4 Results and Discussion

The participants in this study were 42 engineering students from the University of La Rioja (UR). These engineering students were either undergraduates in their fourth year (26 students) or first-year master's degree students (16 students) who were enrolled in project management courses scheduled for the fall semester.

First, students' academic performance was analyzed using descriptive statistics. Since the system provides information at least three times during the execution of a project, one per project life cycle phase (or stage), this analysis is performed at the end of each executed stage (IS00, DS01 and FS02). Table 1 shows the descriptive information of efficiency scores for each project stage according to the degree program in which students are enrolled. In this work, the efficiency is defined as the ability to accomplish high quality tasks (project products, management activities, etc.) within the adequate time and effort. These results indicated an improvement in students performance with every stage, i.e., after each assessment and feedback.

Table 1. Descriptive statistics of efficiency for each project stage according to the degree program in which students are enrolled.

Stage	M.Sc. students		B.Sc. students	
	Mean	SD	Mean	SD
IS00	52.88	14.41	-	-
DS01	61.90	8.63	60.91	11.22
FS02	67.75	7.95	67.18	8.31

The distribution of the efficiency scores of students through the project execution is presented in Fig. 6. Data analysis was carried out by means of boxplots because they are a way of summarizing a distribution. A boxplot (also known as a box and whisker plot) is interpreted as follows:

- The box itself contains the middle 50% of the data. The upper edge (hinge) of the box indicates the 75th percentile of the data set, and the lower hinge indicates the 25th percentile.
- The line in the box indicates the median value of the data.
- The ends of the horizontal lines or *whiskers* indicate the minimum and maximum data values.

Figure 6 illustrates the continuous and global improvement in students performance with every stage. Since the feedback was provided at the end of each project stage, these results suggest that the proposed combination of different types of feedback has a positive impact on both master and undergraduate students' performance.

As shown in Table 1 and Fig. 6, the results obtained for the students at the end of the second stage (DS01) were superior to the ones obtained by them at the end of the first stage (IS00). In the same way, the results obtained by the students at the end of the third stage (FS02) were also higher than the ones obtained at the end of the second stage (DS01). To ascertain whether the performance results observed after each project stage differ significantly, the non-parametric Wilcoxon signed-rank test was employed because a normal distribution cannot be assumed. The level of significance (alpha) was determined to be 0.05. All the differences observed where significant in the corresponding Wilcoxon signed-rank test (Table 2). This fact, seems to corroborate the hypothesis that the proposed assessment and feedback system is useful for the students to improve their performance in project management.

In summary, tracking students performance by means of the provided numerical and graphical information enables each student to identify strengths and

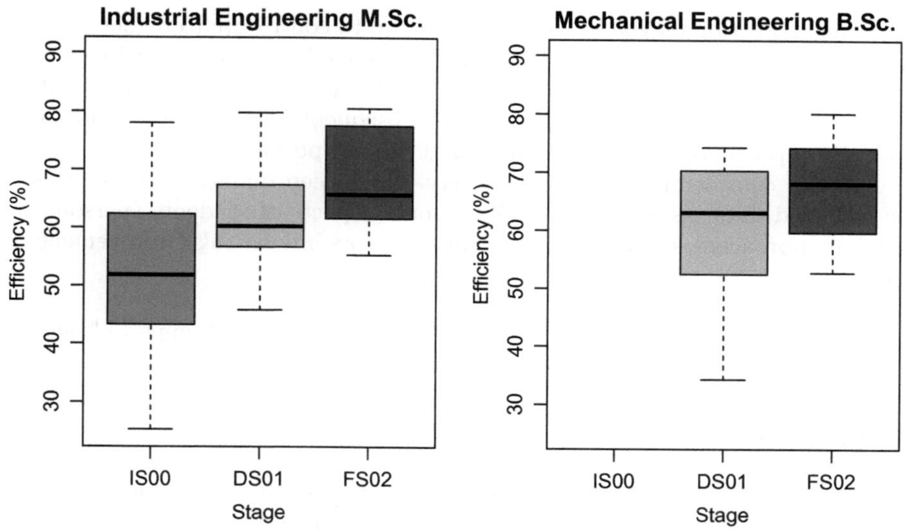

Fig. 6. Evolution of students' performance during the course based on the degree program in which students are enrolled.

Table 2. Comparison of students' performance between consecutive project stages according to the degree program in which students are enrolled.

Stage	M.Sc. students		B.Sc. students	
	Z	*p*	Z	*p*
DS01 - IS00	6.154	$<0.001^{***}$	-	-
FS02 - DS01	5.712	$<0.001^{***}$	5.841	$<0.001^{***}$

$^{***}p < 0.001$, $^{**}p < 0.01$, $^{*}p < 0.05$

weaknesses in his or her work. On the other hand, the lessons learned reports, which identify what is considered as good and poor practices, provide advice on how to proceed in the future. Thus, students have the opportunity to close the gap between current and desired performance on a stage per stage basis, at least.

5 Conclusions

The proposed assessment and feedback system was demonstrated to be useful for improving the academic performance of engineering students in the field of project management. Based on five key strategies for implementing formative assessment, the developed computer-assisted method provides learners with opportunities to put into practice different skills and competences that a project member should possess in the development of a project. Furthermore, structured opportunities for self-assessment and peer-assessment are created in order to encourage reflection on the learning process and to contribute to higher achievements and improved behaviors. Finally, the provided continuous feedback combined with a three-stage development of the learning process (project) allows students to use this information to make subsequent improvements and so, to close the gap between current learning and desired performance.

Authors consider it necessary to carry out a deep quantitative analysis of the collected data, as well as to analyze some aspects of students (personality, learning approaches, etc.), to better identify factors influencing improvements in students' performance.

Acknowledgements. The authors wish to recognise the financial support of the University of La Rioja through grant EGI16/11.

References

1. Andersson, C., Palm, T.: The impact of formative assessment on student achievement: a study of the effects of changes to classroom practice after a comprehensive professional development programme. Learn. Instr. **49**, 92–102 (2017)
2. Andrade, H., Du, Y.: Student responses to criteria-referenced self-assessment. Assess. Eval. High. Educ. **32**(2), 159–181 (2007)
3. Bennett, R.E.: Formative assessment: a critical review. Assess. Educ.: Princ. Policy Pract. **18**, 5–25 (2011)
4. van den Berg, I., Admiraal, W., Pilot, A.: Design principles and outcomes of peer assessment in higher education. Stud. High. Educ. **31**(3), 341–356 (2006)
5. Black, P., Wiliam, D.: Assessment and classroom learning. Assess. Educ.: Princ. Policy Pract. **5**(1), 7–74 (1998)
6. Black, P., Wiliam, D.: Developing the theory of formative assessment. Educ. Assess. Eval. Account. **21**(1), 5–13 (2009)
7. Bodner, G.M., Orgill, M.: Theoretical Frameworks for Research in Chemistry/Science Education. Prentice Hall, Upper Saddle River (2007)
8. Boud, D.: Enhancing Learning Through Self-assessment. Kogan Page, London (1995)
9. Brookhart, S.M., Moss, C.M., Long, B.A.: Teacher inquiry into formative assessment practices in remedial reading classrooms. Assess. Educ.: Princ. Policy Pract. **17**(1), 41–58 (2010)
10. Caupin, G., Knoepfel, H., Koch, G., Pannenbcker, K., Perez-Polo, F., Seabury, C.: IPMA Competence Baseline, version 3. International Project Management Association (2006)
11. European Council: Council conclusions of 12 May 2009 on a strategic framework for European cooperation in education and training, 'ET 2020'. Official Journal of the European Union (2009/C 119/02) (2009)
12. Falchikov, N.: Learning Together. RoutledgeFalmer, London (2001)
13. van Gennip, N.A., Segers, M.S., Tillema, H.H.: Peer assessment as a collaborative learning activity: the role of interpersonal variables and conceptions. Learn. Instr. **20**(4), 280–290 (2010). Unravelling Peer Assessment
14. Gibbs, G., Simpson, C.: Conditions under which assessment supports students learning. Learn. Teach. High. Educ. **1**, 3–31 (2004)
15. Gielen, S., Peeters, E., Dochy, F., Onghena, P., Struyven, K.: Improving the effectiveness of peer feedback for learning. Learn. Instr. **20**(4), 304–315 (2010)

16. Gikandi, J.W., Morrow, D., Davis, N.E.: Online formative assessment in higher education: a review of the literature. Comput. Educ. **57**(4), 2333–2351 (2011)
17. González-Marcos, A., Alba-Elías, F., Navaridas-Nalda, F., Ordieres-Meré, J.: Student evaluation of a virtual experience for project management learning: an empirical study for learning improvement. Comput. Educ. **102**, 172–187 (2016)
18. González-Marcos, A., Alba-Elías, F., Ordieres-Meré, J.: An analytical method for measuring competence in project management. Br. J. Educ. Technol. **47**(6), 1324–1329 (2015)
19. González-Marcos, A., Alba-Elías, F., Ordieres-Meré, J.: An online assessment and feedback approach in project management learning. In: Proceedings of the 9th International Conference on Computer Supported Education, CSEDU 2017, vol. 2, pp. 69–77 (2017)
20. McLellan, H.: Situated Learning Perspectives. Educational Technology Publications, Englewood Cliffs (1996)
21. Miller, C.M.L., Parlett, M.R.: Up to the Mark: A Study of the Examination Game. Society for Research into Higher Education, London (1974)
22. Nicol, D.J., Macfarlane-Dick, D.: Formative assessment and self-regulated learning: a model and seven principles of good feedback practice. Stud. High. Educ. **31**(2), 199–218 (2006)
23. Office of Government Commerce: Managing Successful Projects with PRINCE2(^{TM}). Office of Government Commerce (2009)
24. Panadero, E., Alonso-Tapia, J., Huertas, J.A.: Rubrics vs. self-assessment scripts: effects on first year university students' self-regulation and performance. Infancia y Aprendizaje **37**(1), 149–183 (2014)
25. Ross, J.: The reliability, validity, and utility of self-assessment. Pract. Assess. Res. Eval. **11**(10), 1–13 (2006)
26. Sadler, D.R.: Formative assessment: revisiting the territory. Assess. Educ. **5**(1), 77–84 (1998)
27. Seidel, T.: Implementing competence assessment in university education. A comment on using the collegiate learning assessment as a prototype. Empir. Res. Vocat. Educ. Train. **4**(1), 91–94 (2012)
28. Shute, V.J.: Focus on formative feedback. Rev. Educ. Res. **78228173**(1), 153–189 (2008)
29. Snyder, B.R.: The Hidden Curriculum. MIT Press, Cambridge (1971)
30. Strudwick, R., Day, J.: Developing effective assignment feedback for an interprofessional learning module-an action research project. Nurse Educ. Today **35**(9), 974–980 (2015)
31. Tenório, T., Bittencourt, I.I., Isotani, S., Silva, A.P.: Does peer assessment in online learning environments work? A systematic review of the literature. Comput. Hum. Behav. **64**, 94–107 (2016)
32. Topping, K.: Peer assessment between students in colleges and universities. Rev. Educ. Res. **68**(3), 249–276 (1998)
33. van Zundert, M., Sluijsmans, D., van Merrinboer, J.: Effective peer assessment processes: research findings and future directions. Learn. Instr. **20**(4), 270–279 (2010)

Social Context and Learning Environments

The Network Structure of Interactions in Online Social Learning Environments

M. E. Sousa-Vieira(✉), J. C. López-Ardao, and M. Fernández-Veiga

Department of Telematics Engineering, University of Vigo, Vigo, Spain
{estela,jardao,mveiga}@det.uvigo.es

Abstract. The widespread use of computing and communications technologies has also arrived at the education field, an area where general and custom-designed online social networking software platforms are being increasingly employed in formal course offerings at all education levels. Despite the widespread use of open online social networks (OSN), the relationship between the social ties among students and their academic performance is not yet well understood. In this chapter, we report on a longitudinal experiment with a purpose-specific OSN run at the graduate level and apply a structural analysis of the students' network. We show that some of the basic structural properties in these networks (e.g., centrality, community structure, reciprocity, egonetworks) are correlated with the final outcome and grades of the students. Thus, social network analysis during the instruction period can be effectively used to classify, rank and identify types of students according to the intensity, quality and engagement into the OSN. These features and the network structure are plausible variables to predict their ultimate academic achievements, too. Our analysis contributes to the understanding of the role of social learning among highly educated students.

Keywords: Online social networks · Collaborative learning
Social networks analysis

1 Introduction

Information technology is also changing the ways we learn. The widespread use of computing and communications technologies has enabled the formation of personal communications or online social networks (OSNs), and it is behind the popularity of social networks oriented to learn. Social learning emphasizes the role of knowledge gained informally through social relationships (real or virtual), regardless these taking place between peers or with experts [10,26]. In social learning, the building of skills draws strongly on collective work and information exchange [5].

A properly designed software platform which integrates contents, users and educational experiences is key for the effectiveness of any social learning environment (SLE). The popular learning management systems (LMSs), e.g., Moodle,

P. Escudeiro et al. (Eds.): CSEDU 2017, CCIS 865, pp. 407–431, 2018.
https://doi.org/10.1007/978-3-319-94640-5_20

Claroline, Blackboard, cannot offer full functionality for embedding OSN features like direct interaction among the students, a reputation system, or the creation of informal learning activities. Consequently, some genuine SLEs have been recently developed [20,23,25], with a focus on collaborative work. Since these kind of learning platforms collect a detailed record of each student's activity, a growing body of research aims to understand to what extent the social interactions among the students reinforce their learning process or improve the quality of the learning outcomes.

This type of data has been used to analyze the individual behavior of users, potentially for identifying the behavior patterns that lead to success in learning [14,15]. In other studies, the datasets are mined to quantify how the information flow shapes the learning results, e.g., to discover the most influential students or to find out how collaboration among groups of students arise, and the impact of relationships on learners' performance. In other words, whether the structure of the community to which a student belongs while he/she is engaged in the SLE has any substantial correlation on his/her performance. Uncovering relationships between social behavior and performance would allow the enhancement of community detection algorithms [8] with predictors of success, by identifying early what communities exhibit good behavioral dynamics. Thus, mathematical techniques from the field of social network analysis (SNA) [27] are being increasingly applied to disentangle the relationships taking place among social actors in a SLE, and for understanding the distinctive patterns arising from these interactions [13].

1.1 Related Work

In the past years, a significant research effort has focused on understanding how the interpersonal interactions in OSNs shape, reinforce and enhance the learning process.

In [19], authors consider three aspects of asynchronous learning networks: design, quality of the resulting knowledge construction process and role and power network structures, concluding that a well-designed asynchronous learning network develops significant role and power structures that lead the knowledge construction process to high phases of critical thinking. The aim of the study proposed in [3] is to empirically investigate the relationships between communication styles, social networks and learning performance in a learning community. The results show that both individual and structural factors significantly affect the way the learners develop collaborative learning social networks whose properties largely influence learners' performance. In [6], authors explore the relationships between a student's position in the social learning network and their sense of community. The findings suggest that the position is indicative of both their degree of perceived sense of community and of the nature of the academic and social support the student requires for future progression through the course. The study proposed in [11] addresses learning communities from a social network perspective, including what relations are evident in these communities, how media affect online relationships formation and what benefits can arise from successfully maintaining learning networks. The work described in [2] analyses two distributed social learning networks in order to understand how characteristics of the social structure can enhance students' success, while in [12], authors study the influence of social networks, motivation, social integration and prior performance on learning, proposing degree centrality as a key predictor for students learning. More recently, a theoretical model is developed in [4] to investigate the association between social network properties, content richness in academic learning discourse and performance, concluding that these factors cannot be discounted in the learning process and must be accounted for in the learning design. Other works [9] have investigated the relationship between social network indices, creative performance and flow in blended teams. The results indicate that social network indices, in particular those measuring centralization and neighbors interactions, can offer valuable insight into the creative collaboration process. Related to the role of course facilitators, the study proposed in [21] shows that the teaching function becomes distributed among influential actors in the network, both human and technological, but the official course teachers preserve a high level of influence over the flow of information in the investigated course. Finally, the aim of the study proposed in [7] is to empirically examine various categories of social network sites use, showing that there are significant positive relationships between them and students learning.

1.2 Contributions

In the past decade, SNA techniques and tools have been extensively applied to a variety of data sets collected through different learning environments (LMS, SLEs, MOOCs, etc.) with the aim of understanding how social relationships drive the flow of information among students and scholars. Our previous work [24] is inscribed within this area of research, but pays detailed attention to the characterization of *informal* learning activities. To this end, we use our custom software platform, SocialWire, for discovering what factors or variables have measurable correlation with the performance of the students: his/her level of participation in the system, his/her position (importance) inside the network graph or his/her neighborhood. The dataset was collected along three consecutive editions of an undergraduate course on computer networks, and our findings showed that the structural properties most correlated to the final academic results are robust measures of centrality (degree and eigenvector), which are already detectable since the first weeks of the course.

This chapter reviews and extends some of the results previously reported in [22,24], where we measured the extent and strength of social relations in a online social network used among college students. Here, we address a more comprehensive analysis of the network structure of interactions, performing a thorough study of the connection network(s) among the students, and asking whether these structures have a measurable impact on their final academic performance. The dataset is also bigger and more diverse, compared to our prior works, since we collected more data from courses at the master level and enlarged the measurements to comprise a period of three academic years. Overall, as the chapter discusses, we have found that, in addition to the quantity of interactions among participants, successful prediction of performance is possible when the quality of interactions can also be observed, or inferred on the basis of the network structure.

The rest of the paper is organized as follows. In Sect. 2 we give an overview of the core social engine, and describe the general principles of our learning-enhanced social platform. The methodology employed in the master level course is reported in Sect. 3. Section 4 contains the main results of the data mining applied to the datasets, including the new analyses conducted for quantifying the correlations between structural organization and students' performance. Finally, some concluding remarks and guidelines for further work are included in Sect. 5.

2 The Learning Platform

SocialWire [23] is a SLE purposely designed to provide a complete networked learning paradigm, including features not available in other SLEs. By design, SocialWire uses games and social meritocracy as conducting threads. The software is based on ELGG, a popular engine for developing OSNs, and allows the creation, assessment and reporting of a range of collaborative activities based on social interactions among the students, offering a reward mechanism by means of ranking and reputation.

The platform was developed upon four building blocks:

1. The online social network. SocialWire leverages on the core of ELGG for reusing the fundamental elements of a generic OSN. Every group (classroom group) defined in the system has its own wall to maintain open communication among all its members. The group can also use common tools in the social web for its virtual classroom activities: classroom blog, collaborative publishing and document editing, creation of web pages, social tagging, files repositories with hierarchical structure (including a viewer for images, audio, video and the usual document formats), and event calendars. All the activity unfolded in the classroom gets eventually reflected on the public wall, so it can be commented, highlighted or voted. Sharing videos, uploading a file, save and send a link are extremely simple actions which the user can invoke through an user interface deliberately similar to a typical OSN user interface. The user-friendliness is higher, as a bonus, and the learning curve of the platform itself is greatly softened.
2. The formal learning processes. To furnish SocialWire with the usual features of a LMS, custom software modules were developed that extend the bare OSN based on ELGG. Specifically, there exist modules for proposing and submitting tasks (either online or offline), for the creation and assessment of quizzes and questionnaires, for the creation and processing of forms or polls, for building an e-portfolio, for designing rubrics for evaluation, and more. Another software module gives the teachers the possibility of structuring the learning units in their courses, for instance weekly, monthly, by topic,... and adding to each unit as many resources as they like.

3. The informal learning processes. SocialWire brings forth the possibility of carrying out other sort of activities requiring a higher degree of social interaction. This is done by means of the questions and contests modules. Besides the usual grading procedure used in formal courses (on a numeric scale or by discrete levels), in SocialWire the students can receive "points" or "marks" for their works. The points accumulated along the course determine their position in the students' ranking. This ranking serves primarily to send signals to the students about their relative performance, in a way that directly stimulates comparisons and that automatically conveys the meaning of social reputation.
4. The collaborative work processes. Most of the popular software platforms for collaborative work fail to give real, effective support for working with true and smooth collaboration. First, the users are not given a virtual workspace where direct communication and sharing between colleagues can happen, so they must resort to external programs to solve this (or in extreme cases, physical meetings). Secondly, teachers are not provided with the opportunity to manage, coordinate, assess, evaluate, share or communicate with the workgroups. SocialWire does permit subgroups, i.e., smaller groups within an existing group. The instructors are in charge of deciding how many groups will be created, their sizes and their membership policies, if any is due. Every activity supported by SocialWire can be assigned to a group or to an individual, and in the former case any group member is entitled to participate in the role of group's representative. Additionally, every subgroup is internally a group and has a private space so that their members and the instructors can communicate.

3 Applying the Methodology: The Datasets

3.1 Environment

As explained in the previous section, SocialWire provides a social networking platform for interaction between teachers and learners. The platform has been conceived as a complementary tool to a traditional course offering, so it provides two of the different learning modes typically found in standard MOOCs: video lectures/talks, assessments (in form of quizzes, homework and exams), and social networking. SocialWire supports the last two modes, while the lectures are still held face-to-face in real classrooms.

The SocialWire platform has been used to teach one master level course over three consecutive academic years, 2014/15, 2015/16 and 2016/17. This is an advanced graduate course within the scope of the underlying technologies in computer networks, continuing and intensifying the introductory concepts studied in the undergraduate subjects. In the first and second editions 16 students followed the course. All had studied at least a subject in the degree following a methodology similar to the one described in this paper. As to the students' background, 9 in the first edition and 7 in the second held an undergraduate degree related to computer networks. In the last edition 24 students followed the course,

4 had not studied the degree in our school and the other 20 had studied at least a subject in the degree following a methodology similar to the one described in this paper. From this 20 students, 7 held an undergraduate degree related to computer networks. We remark that, although the students' community is quite small, it is possible to gather a significant amount of information to infer their statistical behavior, since the average level of participation into the online social environment is high. As a matter of fact, the reduced size of the target group has been beneficial for the experiment, for most of the students have already built strong collaboration ties personally outside the OSN.

The course has a weekly schedule that lasts 14 weeks. The activities are organized as follows. *Lectures/recitations* mix the exposition of the ideas, concepts, techniques and algorithms belonging to the lessons of the course with the resolution of problems and theoretical questions in the classroom. *Laboratory sessions*, in small study groups, are complementary sessions where the students design and analyze different network scenarios and with different protocols, using the GNS3 emulator. Finally, *online activities* (in the form questions, tasks, tests, etc.), are done in the virtual classroom. Students and teachers belong to a single group in SocialWire, wherein general communication about the topics covered takes place.

To encourage networked learning activities and collaborative work, the teachers planned different activities in SocialWire whereby the students may gain points (the resulting ranking is made public to the group):

- Collaborative answering of questions. This activity consists in posing and solving any question, doubt or problem about the subject. The students send their questions, and so do the instructors occasionally. From the questions posed by the students, each question aligned to the course objectives and not repeated receives some points. The answers to any question (not absolutely correct, since the effort to participate and try to answer is also valuable) get also some points, depending on their quality and completeness and the difficulty of the underlying question. Correct answers are clearly marked, so that there is no misunderstanding.
- Tasks previous to the laboratory sessions. By means of this activity the teachers successfully encourage the students to prepare the material covered in the laboratory sessions in advance.
- Tests previous to the partial exams.

Face-to-face interaction (in the classroom and in the laboratory session) is still the bulk of the course, for a total of 40 h. But the social networking activities occupy a significant fraction of the independent study time (an average of 10 h). More importantly, there is actually a connection between the more formal face-to-face learning activities and the online tasks, in that many discussions and homework problems start in the classroom but take place further through the online platform, and are finished there.

In the three academic years, the weight of the continuous assessment path was 50%, and the remaining 50% is awarded as the result of a final exam held on two different dates (January and July, non-exclusive). The 50% in the continuous assessment is split into a 40% from two partial exams (thus, each one contributes a 20% of the final grade) and a 10% of the final grade comes out from the game points gathered by engaging in the social activities commented above, to increase the level of participation. While it is true that one point in the final grade might seem a too scarce pay off for the best student, we believe it is important that the full score is easily achievable by a significant fraction of the class. Thus, in order to convert the point marks into a grade, if P_{av} and P_{med} are the average and median number of game points per student and P_{max} is the maximum, we compute $M = \min\{P_{\text{av}}, P_{\text{med}}, P_{\text{max}}/2\}$. In the conversion scale, M represents 0.5 grade points, and every student having at least $2M$ game points gets the full 1 grade possible with this part. In doing so, we try to preserve the incentive-driven effect whereby the average-performing student is still engaged and the best students attain fair pay offs.

3.2 Anatomy of the Dataset

The questions and answers game has been active along three consecutive academic years. In the first edition of the course along the term the students submitted 43 questions and 40 answers to the platform. The quality of the answers was remarkable, all got some game points and 18 were highlighted by the teachers. Moreover, the teachers submitted 1 question, answered successfully by 8 students. In the second edition of the course the students submitted 35 questions and 36 answers worthy of game points, from which 6 were highlighted by the teachers. In this case, the teachers submitted 3 questions along the term, answered successfully by 8, 12 and 14 students, respectively. Finally, in the third edition of the course the students submitted 11 questions and 25 answers worthy of game points, from which 4 were highlighted by the teachers. Moreover, the teachers submitted 1 question, answered successfully by 6 students. It is important to highlight that in the first and second editions each student had to post at least two questions, but in the last edition the participation in this game was non-mandatory.

As we can see in Figs. 1(a) and (b) in the first and second editions the activity is more concentrated around the second midterm exam date (at the end of November) and one week before the final exam (January 20 and December 17, respectively). Nevertheless, as we can see in Fig. 1(c) in the last edition the activity is only concentrated in the two weeks before the second partial exam date.

In our datasets we recorded all the events taking place within the game: users who post questions, users who answer each question and the valuations they received. With these data points, we build social graphs where two nodes (i.e., students) are connected by an edge if one has given an answer to a question posted by the other (notice that these graphs are directed, since it is important to know who made the question and who is answering it).

In Figs. 2, 3 and 4 every node is a student identified by his/her position in the ranking of game points (the node with label 0 represents the teachers). The light green points correspond to students that accomplished the subject in January,

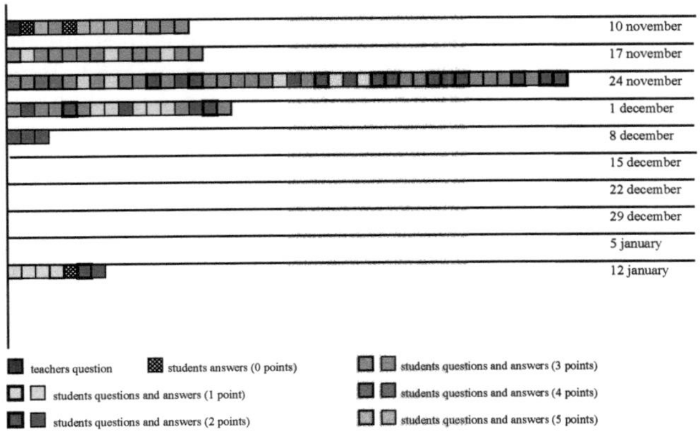

(a) First edition

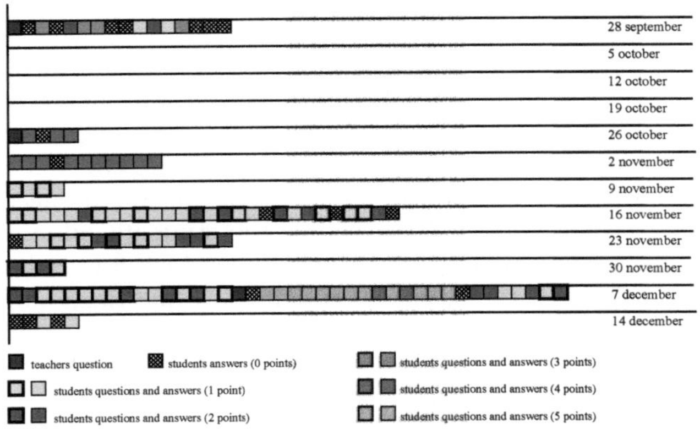

(b) Second edition

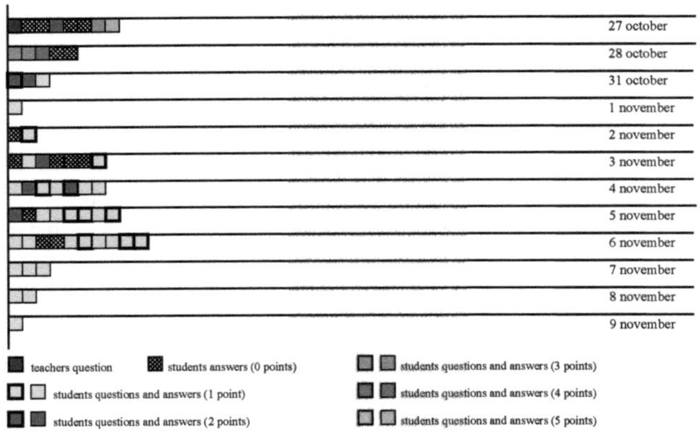

(c) Third edition

Fig. 1. Activity in the questions and answers game in the three edition of the course. Reprinted from [22].

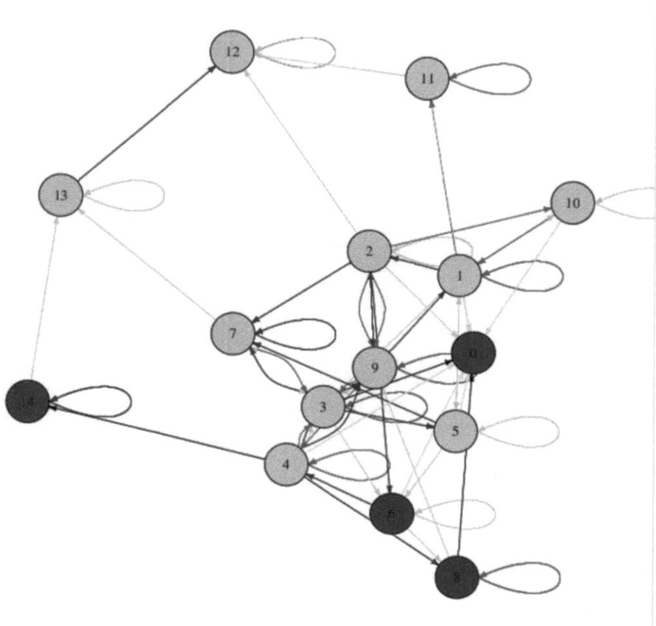

Fig. 2. Interactions in the questions and answers game in the first edition of the course. Original figure from [22]. (Color figure online)

the dark green is for students who passed in July, and the grey points are for students who dropped off the course or failed the subject in the end. The color in the answers (edges) serves to classify them on the basis of the points received (black means 0 points, blue 1 point, red 2 points, pink 3 points, orange 4 points and yellow 5 points).

In the graph of the first edition of the course we can see that 14 of the 16 students followed the continuous assessment path and took part in this activity. All of them finally passed the course, 11 in January and 3 in July (only one of them, node 6, with prior exposure to computer networks). Moreover, of the two students not engaged in continuous assessment (neither of them with a computer networks background) only one finally succeeded in the course.

In this edition, among the most active students in this game are those who reach the highest positions in the ranking, a fact suggesting that they were competent in solving the rest of the online activities proposed along the academic year. In the graphs, nodes 6 and 8 correspond to students with medium or high performance in the online activities, having average grades in the midterms but who had to improve their grade in the finals in order to pass.

In the second edition of the course, all the students participated in this activity, and all but one were able to pass, 12 in the first call and 3 in the second one (again only one of them, node 13, with a computer networks background).

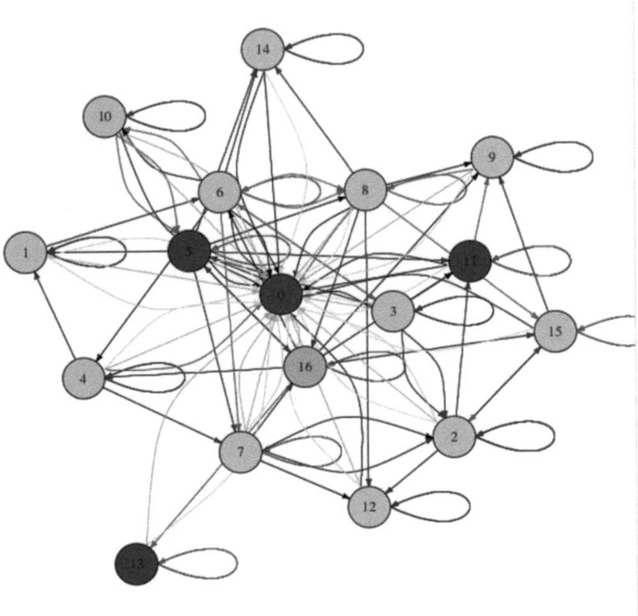

Fig. 3. Interactions in the questions and answers game in the second edition of the course. Original figure from [22]. (Color figure online)

Node 16 is a student without previous specialization in computer networking who, despite outstanding at this game, did not complete the remaining online activities, so ended up relegated to the last position in the ranking.

In the third edition, although 22 of the 24 students enrolled in the course followed the continuous assessment path, only 16 took part in this activity. All but two were able to pass, 9 in January and 5 in July (neither of them with a computer networks background). Moreover, of the 8 students not engaged in the game (only one with a computer networks background) 3 that had participated in some of the other activities of the continuous assessment path finally passed the course. From the 4 students that have not studied the degree in our school only one, node 10, participated actively in this game and in the course in general.

Finally, in Figs. 5(a) and (b) we can see that in the first edition of the course the students in the lowest positions of the ranking concentrate the activity in two weeks (two days in some cases). The horizontal axis in these figures is the week number, and the vertical axis shows the accumulated number of game points earned by each student, earned in the game of questions-and-answers, as well as in all the other online activities. This fact suggests a non-steady study of the subject along the term. The same pattern is observed in students 5, 11 and 13 in the second edition. All of them passed the subject in July. Figure 5(c) shows the activity per student in the game in the third edition of the course. We can see that in this edition several students concentrated the activity in one or two days, but with good contributions, due to its short duration and non-mandatory nature.

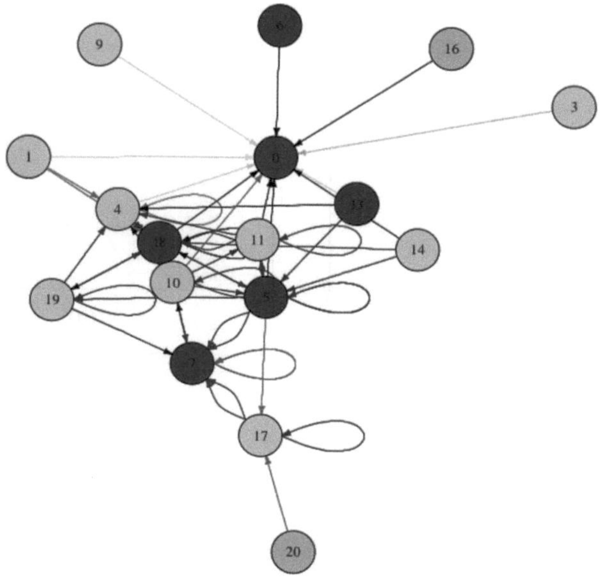

Fig. 4. Interactions in the questions and answers game in the third edition of the course. (Color figure online)

4 Structural Analysis of the Social Network

In this section we apply SNA techniques and tools to mine the data collected. As we explained in the previous section, we model the social relationships taking place in the questions and answers game as directed simple graphs, and aim to explain the basic structural properties of such graphs as consequences of the social interactions among its agents. Formally, a graph (N, g) consists of a set of nodes $N = \{1, 2, \ldots, n\}$ and a square matrix g, the adjacency matrix, where g_{ij} represents the relation between nodes i and j. The neighborhood of a node i is the set of nodes that i is linked to, $N_i(g) = \{j : g_{ij} = 1 \text{ and/or } g_{ji} = 1\}$. The degree of a node $d_i(g)$ is the number of links that involve that node. For undirected graphs, $d_i(g) = \#N_i(g)$. In directed graphs, the in-degree $d_i^{in} = \#\{j : g_{ji} = 1\}$ and the out-degree $d_i^{out} = \#\{j : g_{ij} = 1\}$ count how many edges finish (respectively, start) at that node.

4.1 Graph-Level Measures

In social network analysis, the static or dynamic structural characteristics of the graph reveal key aspects of the collective and individual behavior of the agents. Let us briefly report some of the typical descriptive measures of a graph [16], and their values in our dataset.

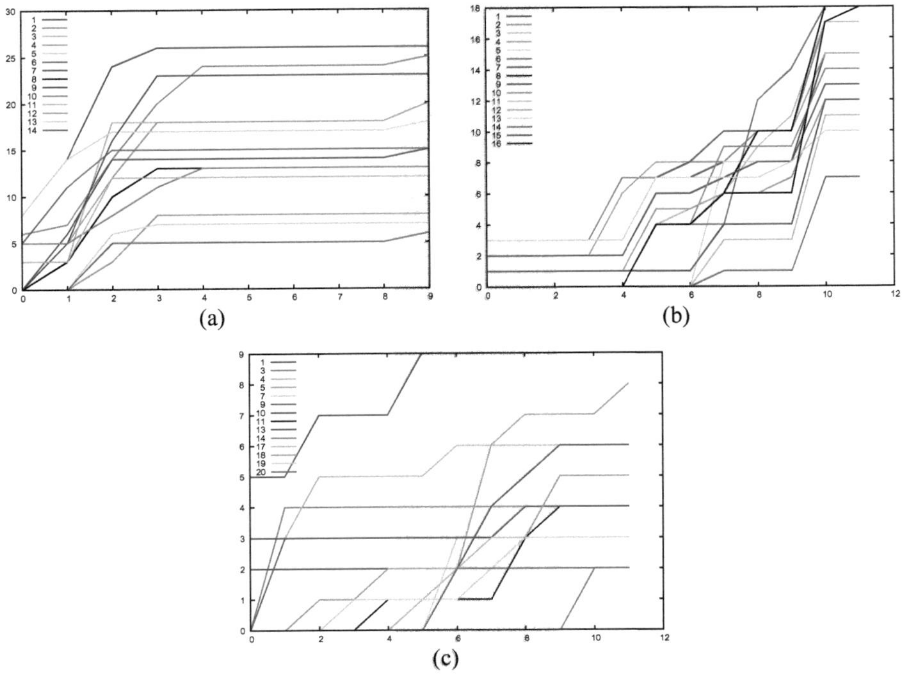

Fig. 5. Activity per student in the questions and answers game.

Density. The density of a graph keeps track of the relative fraction of edges that exist (compared to the maximum $\frac{n(n-1)}{2}$ of a complete simple graph with n nodes). It is simply the ratio between the number of edges and the total number of possible edges, with values ranging from 0 (sparsest) to 1 (densest). Our dataset is dynamic, i.e., the social graph starts empty and the links are established as a result of the information exchanges between pairs of agents. In Table 1 we show that the graph density values and other descriptive structural figures of the three editions of the course are moderate. This is due to the nature of the links: only a part of the students provide answers to each question.

Global Centrality. Global centrality is a graph-level measure that gives an idea about the dependency of the graph on the activity of a small group of nodes. Its normalized values range from 0 (even distribution of activity) to 1 (the most centralized graph). It is based on the underlying node-level centrality measures. Many different measures of centrality have been developed, that capture different features of nodes's position in a graph, the following ones being some of the most commonly used [1]:

- Degree centrality: measures how connected a node is, computing the (normalized) count of neighbors to a node.

Table 1. Summary of basic structural parameters of the social networks.

			2014/15	2015/16	2016/17
Density		Answers	0.2197	0.1916	0.2501
		Questions and answers	0.4561	0.3375	0.3333
Degree	In-degree		0.3431	0.1511	0.5207
	Out-degree	Answers	0.3431	0.3644	0.3223
		Questions and answers	0.3901	0.3291	0.3939
Eigenvector	Directed	Answers	0.6614	0.5602	0.5328
		Questions and answers	0.8493	0.7847	0.5931
	Undirected	Answers	0.6079	0.4758	0.5955
		Questions and answers	0.7895	0.4862	0.6271
Reciprocity			0.2585	0.1304	0.5227
Transitivity		Global	0.3278	0.3156	0.4285
		Average	0.3131	0.3415	0.4845
Number of cliques		Size			
		2	29	38	24
		3	12	19	14
		4	1	2	2
Assortativity	Degree		0.1121	−0.4153	−0.1564
	Nominal (computer networks background)		−0.1594	−0.1135	−0.0565

- Betweenness centrality: tries to capture the importance of a node in terms of its role in connecting other nodes, computing the ratio between the number of shortest paths that a node lies on and the total number of possible shortest paths between two nodes.
- Closeness centrality: measures how easily a node can reach other nodes, computing the inverse of the average length of the shortest paths to all the other nodes in the graph.
- Eigenvector centrality: a measure based on the premise that a node's importance is determined by how important or influential its neighbors are. The scores arise from a reciprocal process in which the centrality of each node is proportional to the sum of the centralities of the nodes it is connected.

In our context, degree and eigenvector centralities seem good indicators of the students' activity. Nevertheless, closeness and betweenness centralities turn out to be inconsequential for our purposes, since in the underlying graph the exchange of information is always direct, without relays or intermediate nodes, between the source agent and the destination agent.

For the case of degree centrality, we consider separately the in-degree centrality (the number of answers a student receives), and two measures of the out-degree centrality: the number of answers given by a student and the number of questions proposed and answers given by a student. The results in Table 1 show that the out-degree centrality values are moderate and similar in the three datasets, but the in-degree centrality is smaller in the second dataset, indicating a more homogeneous distribution of the questions submitted and the answers received by the participants.

For the eigenvector centrality, we have tested different configurations of the graph built up from the datasets. In the first, we remove the edges corresponding to questions posted by the student, and revert the direction of the edges which model the answers. So, in this case, an edge from node a to node b means that student b has answered a question raised by a. We apply this edge reversal operation to measure the centrality of the students who answer some question, not those who make the questions, because the eigenvector centrality measure is sensitive to the in-degrees of nodes. Further, to understand the effect of mutual interaction, we also consider an undirected version of the latter graph. In the second configuration, we include explicitly the questions posed by each student in the graph, by adding a self-edge in such cases. Again, both the directed and the undirected versions of this graph have been used to analyze the datasets.

The results in Table 1 show larger values of the eigenvector centrality (for the directed as well as for the undirected graphs) when the self-edges are considered, which is reasonable. The normalized centrality values are noticeable and higher in the first edition, a hint of stronger centralization in the network, meaning that not all nodes act as sources of information in the same way.

4.2 Individual Centralities

Due to the fact that global centralities can hide some characteristics of the graphs, it can be interesting to graphically analyze the distribution of the participation of the students in each graph. In Fig. 6 we depict histograms of the individual out-degree and directed eigenvector centralities, including the self-edges corresponding to the questions posed by each student, which are good indicators of the student's activity. Notice that the tail of the empirical distribution accumulates a non-neglibible probability. This is consistent with the view that some students concentrate a significant part of the activity of the graph.

4.3 Collaboration Among Groups of Students

The social networking component of SocialWire opens the door to collaboration among groups of students. Therefore, we focus now on the discovery of structural properties in the graph that reveal some form of collaboration. Specifically, we analyze the coefficients of reciprocity, transitivity and assortativity (or homophyly).

Reciprocity. Reciprocity accounts for the number of mutual exchanges of information in the graph, happening in the form of request-response pattern. In mutual collaboration either part poses a question and receives at least one answer from the other part. In other words, this entails the existence of the edges (a, b) and (b, a) simultaneously.

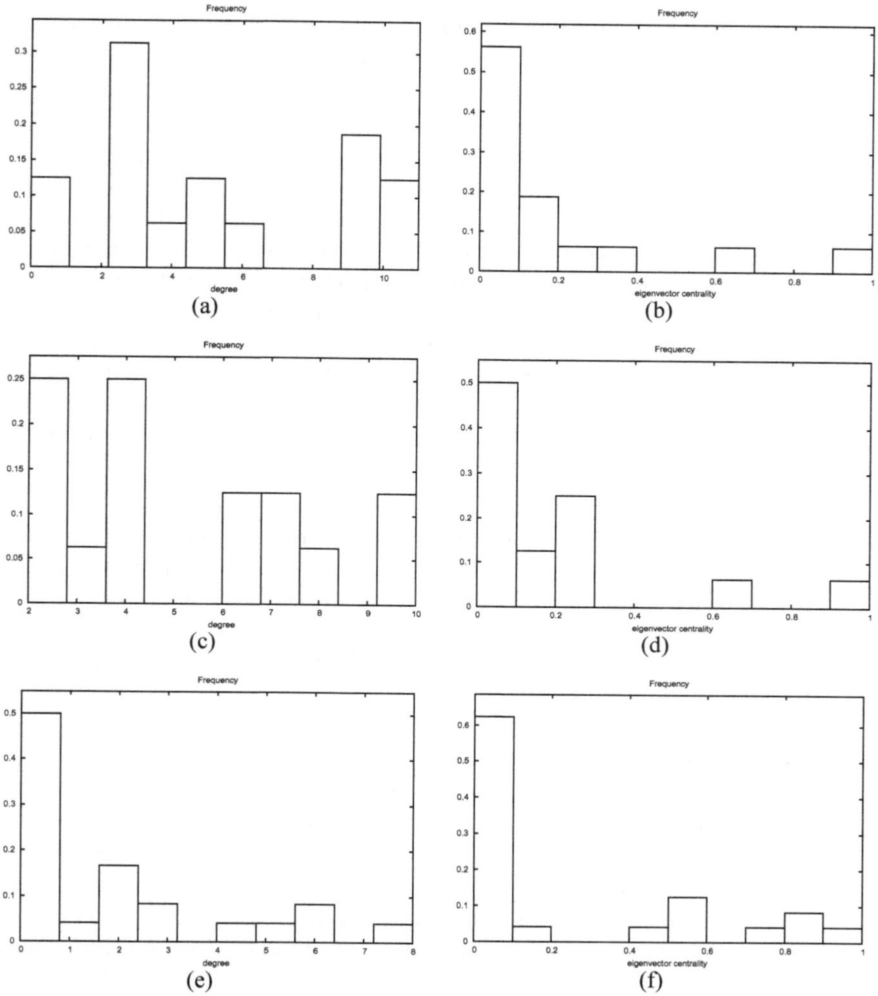

Fig. 6. Degree and eigenvector centralities' distribution in the first (top), second (middle), and third (bottom) editions of the course.

In our setting, reciprocity can be used to assess the degree of mutual collaboration or trust between two given students who have discovered each other either randomly or by a previous request-response exchange. Table 1 also lists the average reciprocity in the networks. The small values obtained in the first and second datasets suggest that in these social environment mutual collaboration is rare. This is not surprising, after all, since this is a not iterative activity more effective in the formation of communities (three or more students) than in encouraging strong mutual relationships. In the last dataset the higher value obtained is due to the decrease in the number of questions in that edition of the course, that makes mutual collaboration more likely.

Transitivity. A broader form of collaboration is transitivity (the fraction of closed loops with three nodes in the graph, sometimes also called the clustering coefficient). We were also interested in detecting whether transitivity is significant in the student network. Thus, the standard transitivity coefficient has been computed for the three datasets, both the global transitivity coefficient and the average value of the local (individual) transitivity coefficients of the nodes. The results obtained are shown in Table 1 again, and confirm that transitivity is noticeable. However, this is not entirely unexpected, since the social network fosters direct relationships between the participants. There is no benefit in acquiring or propagating information through a third party, and the data are consistent with this observation. Consequently, both average and global transitivity are quite high.

Cliques. A clique is a maximal completely connected subgraph of a given graph. So, a clique represents a strongly tied subcommunity where each member interacts with any other member. 3-cliques are the transitivity relations discussed in the last paragraph. Given the nature of our datasets, though 3-cliques are likely, larger cliques seem less probable. Table 1 lists the number of cliques in the graphs by their size.

Assortativity. The assortativity coefficient measures the level of homophyly of the graph, based on some labeling assigned to the nodes. It is positive if similar nodes tend to connect to each other, and negative otherwise.

As we can see in Table 1 we have measured the degree assortativity and the case of nominal assortativity where each student is labeled according the computer networks background. For the nominal assortativity we have obtained low values, many of them negative, suggesting randomness in the relationships. For the degree assortativity, the high negative value of the second edition of the course suggests relationships between the less and the most active students, as it is desirable.

4.4 Local Neighborhood and Students' Performance

Another interesting measure is to find out to what extent the social peers (i.e., his/her neighborhood in the social graph) influence the student's performance at the end of the course. A reasonable conjecture would suggest that information exchange with other good students improves the insights and the learning pace gained by the followers, but this should be confirmed by the data, especially after having checked that the assortativity in the graph is low.

To that end, because the small sample sizes are not suitable to obtain accurate enough correlation measures, we have represented the students' performance vs. the average performance of their neighborhood.

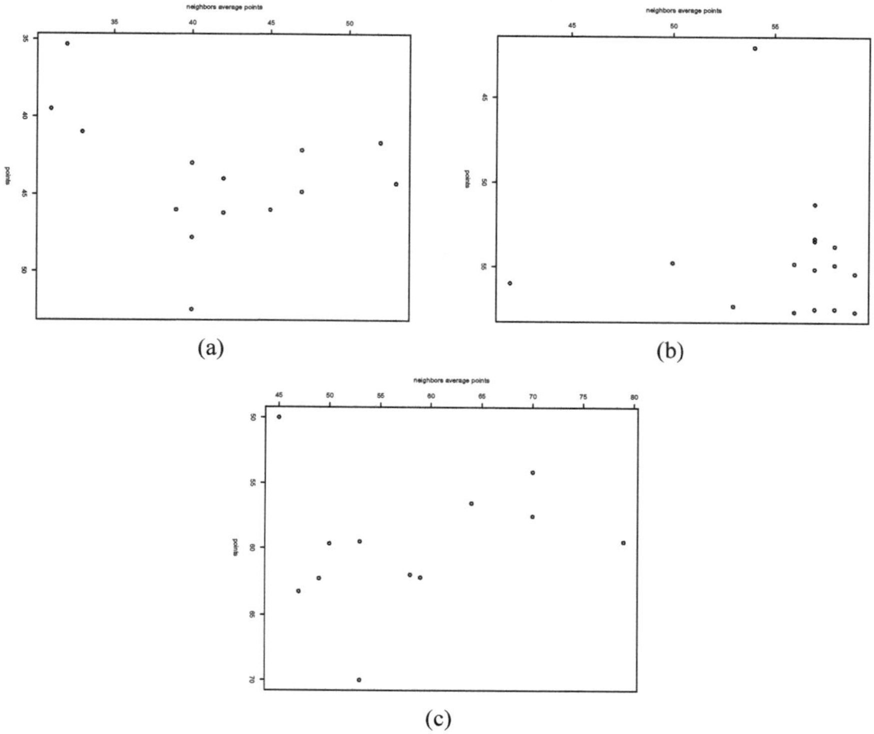

Fig. 7. Neighborhood composition vs. students' performance (points) (first edition -top left- second edition -top right- third edition -bottom-).

As we can see in Figs. 7 and 8, there is no clear evidence that a student's performance has a significant influence on that of their neighbors. This is partly because the dataset is small, but the main reason is the design of the assessment: the main part of the final grade still comes from traditional evaluation activities, not from the online participation.

Finally, Figs. 9, 10 and 11 show the egonetworks of some of the students of each edition that are representative of different patterns of activity. We see that in the first edition good students tend to show denser egonetworks. Nevertheless, in the second edition, the egonetworks are always quite dense for the reason that the relationships between the less and the more active students are more likely. The egonetworks of the third edition are the result of the non-mandatory nature of the activity.

In Fig. 9, node 1 is the most active students in the online activities and node 5 corresponds to the student with higher final grade in the subject. Nodes 6 and 7 are in the middle of the ranking (both with the same number of points): the first one is a student with a computer networks background that passed in July, whereas the second one is a student without previous specialization in computer

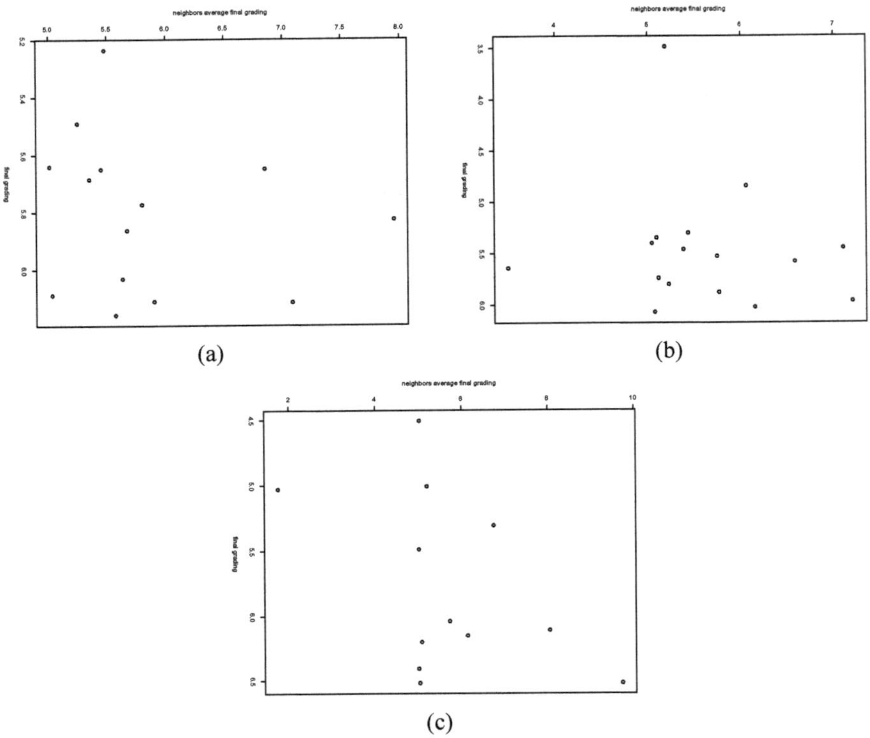

Fig. 8. Neighborhood composition vs. students' performance (final grading) (first edition -top left- second edition -top right- third edition -bottom-).

networking that passed in January due to the fact that he obtained better results in the middle and final exams. Node 11 is a good student with computer networks background and medium performance in the online activities. Finally, node 14 represents the less active student in the online activities of those that followed the continuous assessment in this edition.

In Fig. 10, node 1 is the student with more points and higher final grade in the subject, and node 6 is the second high performing student. Nodes 5 and 13 are two of the student that concentrate the activity in few days: the first one is a student without previous specialization in computer networks, whereas the second one is a student with a computer networks background. Both passed the subject in July. Node 15 is a good student with computer networks background and medium performance in the online activities. Finally, node 16 is the student who, despite outstanding at this game, did not complete the remaining online activities, so ended up relegated to the last position in the ranking.

In Fig. 11, node 1 is the student with more points and second final grade in the subject. Node 5, without a computer networks background, is the most active student in the questions and answers game. In the middle of the ranking

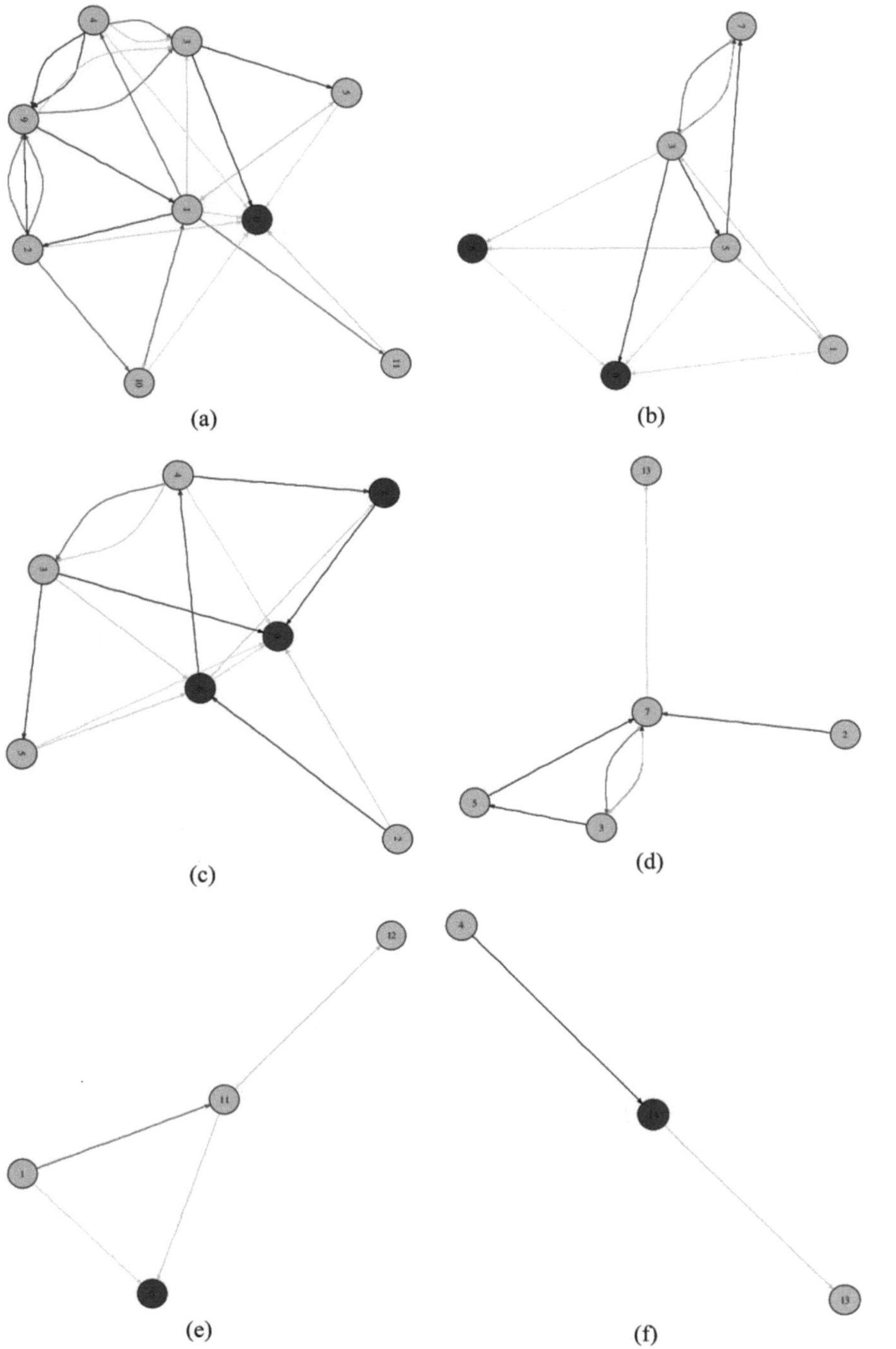

Fig. 9. Egonetworks in the first edition of the course (nodes 1, 5, 6, 7, 11 and 14).

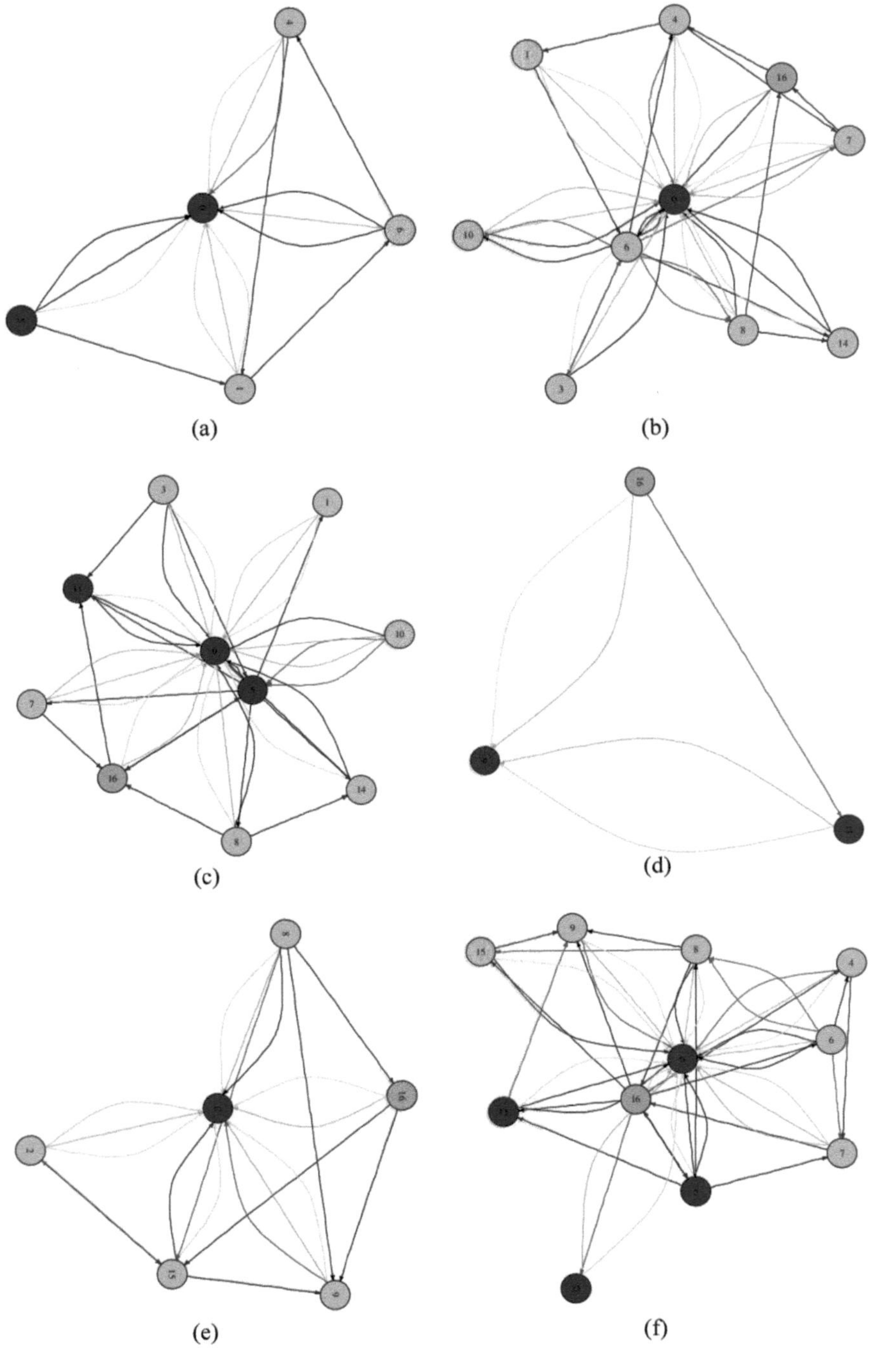

Fig. 10. Egonetworks in the second edition of the course (nodes 1, 6, 5, 13, 15 and 16).

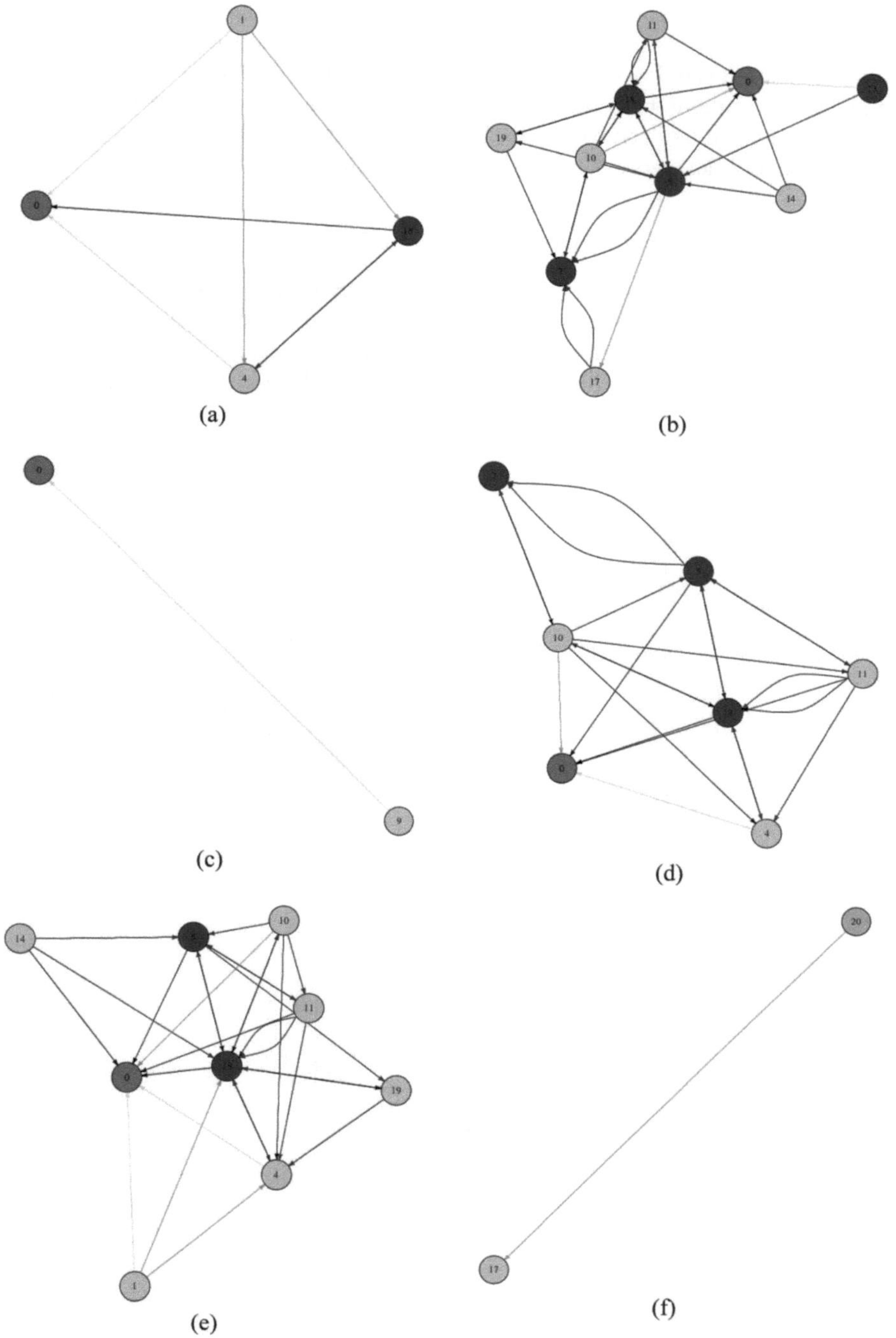

Fig. 11. Egonetworks in the third edition of the course (nodes 1, 5, 9, 10, 18 and 20).

are node 9, that is a good student with computer networks background but low performance in the online activities and node 10, that is the only student that have not studied the degree in our school that participated actively in this game. Node 18 is a student that outstands at the game but with low performance in the remaining online activities. Finally, node 20, with previous specialization in computer networks, represents the less active student in this activity.

4.5 Community Structure

The analysis of the community structure in the network uncovers a great amount of information about the patterns of collaboration in the group. Nevertheless, the reliable detection of the community structure in untagged graphs is a well-known hard statistical problem, which has been addressed through varied approaches in

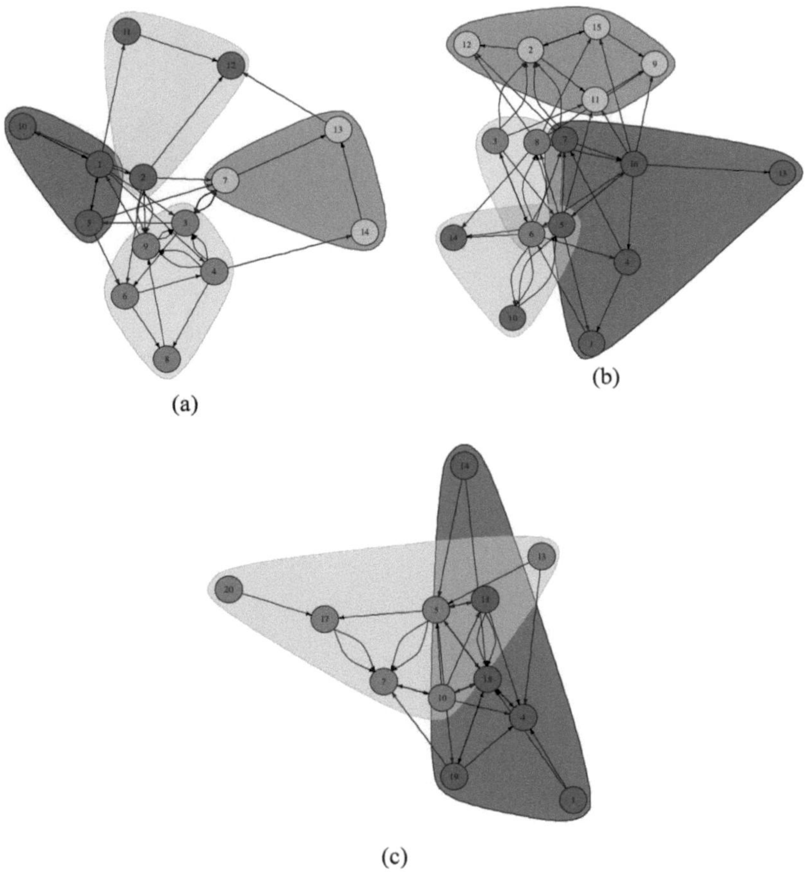

Fig. 12. Community structure in the students' network (first edition -top left- second edition -top right- third edition -bottom-).

the specialized literature (see [8], e.g.). In this chapter, we apply three common community detection algorithms (robust and fast) to discover the division of nodes into communities: leading eigenvector [1], spinglass [18] and walktrap [17].

We have obtained the best results in terms of modularity [1] with the leading eigenvector (modularity ≈0.27) and walktrap (modularity ≈0.25), whereas a lower modularity value was attained with spinglass (≈0.13). In fact, despite the seemingly low values of modularity, the two former algorithms were quite effective in identifying correctly the true underlying communities active in the questions and answers game. Graphically, a depiction of those communities can be seen in Fig. 12 (leading eigenvector), where one can easily recognize, except in the last academic year, four almost-disjoint communities of students. This reflects reality remarkably well, in that some of those communities correspond the possible tracks of specialisation followed by the students in their second year of the programme. Note also the connections between communities, in other words, the fact that some nodes belong to two neighbor, overlapping communities, which indicates that groups of strong collaboration are typically not closed. Instead, some nodes (students) act as bridges between those loosely related groups, allowing a faster propagation of information across de class.

5 Conclusions

In this chapter, we have reviewed the extent to what structural properties of networks can help to explain, and ultimately predict, the behavior and performance of students in online social learning environments, especially the ones which integrate support for informal learning activities. Provided these informal activities are well designed to capture the students' interest and engage them in participation, the structure itself of the collaboration networks reflects and contains useful, statistically significant information to identify the leaders (in terms of reputation), the communities, and a strong correlation between network position or activity and the academic performance of students. The presence of structure and correlations can greatly help the instructor in several respects: (i) to aid in the design of better informal activities for improving or accelerating the acquisition of knowledge; (ii) to identify at early stages students performing poorly, compared to their classmates; (iii) to identify at early stages those students performing over the average, possibly the leaders in their (sub)groups; (iv) to clarify the substructure of communities within the class, and detect isolated or closed subgroups. Our observational study extends over three consecutive years and, even though limited in size, gives enough support to the use of standard social network analysis techniques in this sort of learning systems.

As a summary, we have found that quality participation in the online activities appears to be highly correlated with the final outcome of the course. Therefore, social learning environments must include tools for recognizing and, especially, *rewarding* valuable participants in the designed online activities. Accordingly, a sound reputation and ranking system that overarches the online learning activities would play a key role in the prediction of success and failure of the students. Secondly, or results suggest that good students tend to show denser egonetworks, that is, they are likely to engage in richer interaction patterns with their classmates, both as a consequence of their high reputation and of the positive feedback of becoming leaders in their respective local communities. Therefore, the discovery of different patterns in egonetworks, even in the midst of the academic term, can be a strong sign of outstanding learners and leaders from the perspective of information flow within the whole network. Out third main observation in this study is that, although the communities that arise in the social network are mixed in academic performance (a fact largely due to the type of activities scheduled), not only the public ranking system enables the group to identify quickly and effectively the best students, but also can mark them properly as authoritative sources of information. The application of standard techniques for community detection, e.g., those based on modularity, can easily discover, according to our experiments, the subgroups and communities that are taking place in the class. And these communities happen to be important in two respects. On one side, for identifying the leaders in each community. On the other side, community detection is an extremely useful tool to check whether the communities are isolated or connected through bridges, namely students which are active in two or more groups. Bridge "nodes" break closed groups, so they are essential as facilitators of the flow of information issued by the leaders toward other distant receivers. Since in social network analysis and general learning theory it is also well known that non-closedness of the networks is a necessary condition for herding and reaching consensus, this type of community detection provides fundamental insight into the propagation of knowledge.

As a general conclusion, we believe that these findings may contribute to a better understanding of the learning experience and possibly to devise more effective designs of the academic activities. We have shown that with the application of well chosen techniques for the analysis of the network structure of interactions, the dynamics of learning within the students can be revealed easily and be used to optimize the design of the course and for classifying in advance the achievements of students with reasonable accuracy.

References

1. Barabasi, A.-L.: Network Science. Cambridge University Press, Cambridge (2016)
2. Cadima, R., Ojeda, J., Monguet, J.: Social networks and performance in distributed learning communities. Educ. Technol. Soc. **15**(4), 296–304 (2012)
3. Cho, H., Gay, G., Davidson, B., Ingraffea, A.: Social networks, communication styles and learning performance in a CSCL community. Comput. Educ. **49**(2), 309–329 (2007)
4. Chung, K., Paredes, W.: Towards a social networks model for online learning and performance. Educ. Technol. Soc. **18**(3), 240–253 (2015)
5. Cross, J.: Informal learning: rediscovering the natural pathways that inspire innovation and performance. Pfeiffer, San Francisco (2006)
6. Dawson, S.: A study of the relationship between student social networks and sense of community. Educ. Technol. Soc. **11**(3), 224–238 (2008)

7. Eid, M., Al-Jabri, I.: Social networking, knowledge sharing and student learning: the case of university students. Comput. Educ. **99**, 14–27 (2016)
8. Fortunato, S.: Community detection in graphs. Phys. Rep. **486**(3), 75–174 (2010)
9. Gaggioli, A., Mazzoni, E., Milani, L., Riva, G.: The creative link: investigating the relationship between social network indices, creative performance and flow in blended teams. Comput. Hum. Behav. **42**(1), 157–166 (2015)
10. Hart, J.: Social Learning Handbook. Centre for Learning and Performance Technologies, Bath (2011)
11. Haythornthwaite, C.: Learning relations and networks in web-based communities. J. Web Based Commun. **4**(2), 140–158 (2008)
12. Hommes, J., Rienties, B., Grave, W., Bos, G., Schuwirth, L., Scherpbier, A.: Visualising the invisible: a network approach to reveal the informal social side of student learning. Adv. Health Sci. Educ. **17**(5), 743–757 (2012)
13. Laat, M., Lally, V., Lipponen, L., Simons, R.: Investigating patterns of interaction in networked learning and computer-supported collaborative learning: a role for social network analysis. Int. J. Comput.-Support. Collab. Learn. **2**(1), 87–103 (2007)
14. Lykourentzou, I., Giannoukos, I., Nikolopoulos, V., Mpardis, G., Loumos, V.: Dropout prediction in e-learning courses through the combination of machine learning techniques. Comput. Educ. **53**(3), 950–965 (2009)
15. Macfadyen, L., Dawson, S.: Mining LMS data to develop an "early warning system" for educators: a proof of concept. Comput. Educ. **54**(2), 588–599 (2010)
16. Newman, M.: Networks: An introduction. Oxford University Press, Oxford (2010)
17. Pons, P., Latapy, M.: Computing communities in large networks using random walks. J. Graph Algorithms Appl. **10**(2), 191–218 (2006)
18. Reichardt, J., Bornholdt, S.: Statistical mechanics of community detection. Phys. Rev. E **74**(1), 016110 (2006)
19. Reuven, A., Zippy, E., Gilad, R., Aviva, G.: Network analysis of knowledge construction in asynchronous learning networks. J. Asynchronous Learn. Netw. **7**(3), 1–23 (2003)
20. Rodrigues, J., Sabino, F., Zhou, L.: Enhancing e-learning experience with online social networks. IET Commun. **5**(8), 1147–1154 (2011)
21. Skrypnyk, O., Joksimovic, S., Kovanovic, V., Gasevic, D., Dawson, S.: Roles of course facilitators, learners and technology in the flow of information of a cMOOC. Int. Rev. Res. Online Distance Learn. **16**(3), 743–757 (2015)
22. Sousa, M., López, J., Fernández, M.: Characterizing social interactions in online social networks: the case of university students. In: Proceedings of the 9th International Conference on Computer Supported Education (CSEDU 2017), vol. 2, pp. 188–199 (2017)
23. Sousa, M., López, J., Fernández, M., Rodríguez, M., Herrería, S.: An open-source platform for using gamification and social learning methodologies in engineering education: design and experience. Comput. Appl. Eng. Educ. **24**(5), 813–826 (2016)
24. Sousa, M., López, J., Fernández, M., Rodríguez, M., López, C.: Mining relations in learning-oriented social networks. Comput. Appl. Eng. Educ. **25**(5), 769–784 (2017)
25. Thoms, B.: A dynamic social feedback system to support learning and social interaction in higher education. IEEE Trans. Learn. Technol. **4**(4), 340–352 (2011)
26. Vassileva, J.: Toward social learning environments. IEEE Trans. Learn. Technol. **1**(4), 199–214 (2008)
27. Wasserman, S., Faust, K.: Social Networks Analysis: Methods and Applications. Cambridge University Press, Cambridge (1997)

From Idea to Product – Participation of Users in the Development Process of a Multimedia Platform for Parental Involvement in Kindergarten

Dionisia Laranjeiro[1(✉)], Maria João Antunes[2], and Paula Santos[1]

[1] CIDTFF, Department of Education and Psychology, University of Aveiro, Aveiro, Portugal
{dionisia.mendonca,psantos}@ua.pt

[2] CIC.Digital/Digimedia, Department of Communication and Arts, University of Aveiro, Aveiro, Portugal
mariajoao@ua.pt

Abstract. Parental involvement in kindergarten has been pointed out as an important factor in cognitive development, child behavior and school adaptation. In kindergarten, parents can get involved in various ways. Web technologies can facilitate two types of parental involvement: communication with the early childhood educator, to learn more about child's learning process in kindergarten, and home-based educational activities, using digital educational content. In this sense, the research team set up a design research, aimed to develop a multimedia platform that promotes communication and resource sharing among educators, parents and children, to facilitate parental involvement in learning. This article presents the development of the platform, from the preliminary studies to the evaluation of the functional prototype, with the participation of parents and educators in all phases of the development process.

Keywords: Parental involvement · Multimedia platform
Prototype development · Learning process in kindergarten

1 Introduction

Parental involvement (PI) is a very broad issue that implies the participation of parents in children's formal learning process, taking part in school-related activities [1]. Studies suggest that PI is a multidimensional construct and different types of PI may provide diverse results. Epstein [2] developed a theory and framework with six types of PI: parenting (e.g. parents offer a supportive environment and conditions to learn), communication (e.g. exchange information with school), volunteering (e.g. fundraising, helping in classroom), learning at home (e.g. help with homework, develop educational

From the article presented at the 9th International Conference on Computer Supported Education [42].

P. Escudeiro et al. (Eds.): CSEDU 2017, CCIS 865, pp. 432–456, 2018.
https://doi.org/10.1007/978-3-319-94640-5_21

activities), decision-making (parents' participation in school decisions), and collaboration with the community. This framework is largely accepted and used by schools to promote family-school partnerships. Hoover-Dempsey and Sandler [3] present another theoretical model for PI, focused on "why" and "how" parents get involved in their children's learning. They also consider involvement activities at home, involvement activities at school, parent/teacher/school communications, but they add another form of involvement, which is values, goals, expectations and aspirations parents communicate to their children, thus influencing attitudes and behaviors toward school. In Early Childhood Education (ECE), the Harvard Family Research Project distinguishes three processes of PI related to young children's outcomes: parenting, consisting of attitudes, values and practices in education (including parent-child relationship and child-centered activities); home-school relationships, comprehending formal and informal connections between parents and kindergarten (e.g. communication with the educator about their children's achievements and behavior, participation in the classroom, volunteer to solve a problem or organise an event); responsibility for learning, that refers to activities parents can do with children to promote learning skills (e.g. reading or cooking with the child, visiting museums or libraries, talking with the child about school) [4].

There are several studies that recognize the importance of PI for the success of children's learning, pointing it as an important factor in the development of skills and the results achieved [2, 5]. It's associated with higher grades and test scores, better attendance and more homework done, better grades and fewer placements in special education [6]. PI has a significant effect on child's adaptation to school and success in learning, regardless of other factors, such as social class [7]. Involvement at home plays an important role in student achievement and positive attitudes toward school [8]. Expectations that parents transmit to their children about what they academically aspire to them have strong influence on their success [9]. Also, communication between parents and children is a key factor to help them succeed in study. With regard to preschool children, PI also has an impact on general development, cognitive development and school readiness [10]. Positive relationships between educators and parents have an effect on children's social skills [11]. Some studies have found a positive relationship between PI in kindergarten and the performance of children in reading and mathematics [12]. An essential element for PI is school-family communication. Effective communication is associated with academic success [13]. When parents communicate constructively with teachers and participate in school activities, they have a greater understanding of what their children should learn and how they can improve their formal education at home [14]. Parent collaboration in school community is also related to better results and better student behavior [2]. Success at a later stage of life, particularly in employment, is established in the preschool years, which are the basis for acquiring study and work skills. This requires strong partnerships between agencies, families and children [15].

The importance of PI is recognized in governmental guidelines for ECE in several countries [16]. The No Child Left Behind Act (NCLB), implemented in USA Schools, recognizes that PI is part of children's academic success and should be integrated into school curricula [17]. Other countries implemented programs valuing parent's role in children's education, such as "Children's Plan" in UK and the "Schooling Strategy" in

New Zealand" [18]. In Portugal, the Ministry of Education published the "Curriculum Guidelines for Pre-school education", an official document with a set of principles for kindergarten educators. Throughout the document, there are numerous references to PI, referring the need to establish bilateral and positive communication, promote good relationships and encourage the participation of families in the educational process [19]. However, PI has logistical, emotional or cultural constraints. Barriers to PI can be categorized in four areas: family factors, child factors, teacher-parent factors and society factors [18]. Family factors include parent's beliefs about PI (the role they think they should have in their child's education), parent's perception of invitations from school (if the school is welcoming to PI), parent's life context (work, family, health, schedules); class, ethnicity and gender. Factors related to the child are: age (PI decreases as children grow up), learning difficulties/disabilities as well as gifts and talents (sometimes bring disagreement between parents and school, parents lose confidence and reduce PI), behavioral problems (possibly make parents reluctant to go to school). Parent-teacher factors may be different goals and attitudes about PI, having major repercussion in the way PI is perceived and implemented. Society factors include historical (school culture based on formality and inflexibility), demographical (changes in family structure), political (lack of legislation about PI) and economic factors (little money assigned to PI initiatives). The report *Learning in families* [20] presents results of a survey to parents of pre-school and elementary school children, identifying barriers to PI in ECE and indicating lack of time as the most important. Other barriers encountered were costs associated to transportation or babysitting, and difficulties in communicating with teachers [13, 20]. A study conducted at 1205 kindergartens, to ascertain PI over the years, has shown that the quality of interaction between parents and educators decreases, although participation in home-based activities is consistent over time. It suggests that activities requiring physical presence in school are more difficult to maintain [21].

Today, we witness the use of technology in everyday life, for a variety of purposes, from work to entertainment, communication and personal organization. Technological tools, such as websites, social networks, blogs or e-mail, create new channels of communication and information sharing, and can improve the relationship between educators and parents. The importance of technology for PI in learning is mentioned by several authors [22–24].

Some studies corroborate that technology represents an opportunity for increasing communication between parents and schools, as well as PI. In USA, a large-scale study intended to examine the usage and benefits of Internet-based communication between parents and school. The study involved 14.387 teenagers, 88% of participant's parents and 99% of their school administrators. Parents completed questionnaires about parental involvement and Internet-based family-school communication. School administrators' questionnaire asked whether teachers used Internet to communicate with parents. Students completed achievement tests in 10th and 12th grades. Results show that Internet-based family–school communication is associated with higher achievement and higher educational expectations, and students from all backgrounds benefit equally from Internet-based family-school communication. These findings suggest that Internet is an opportunity for promoting family-school communication [23]. In a case study involving two elementary schools, students, teachers and parents, Grant [22] found that there was a discontinuity between what children learn at home with parents, and what they learn in schools. Parents, teachers and children considered that the use of technologies for school-family communication could play a positive role by making communication more direct and timely. Blanchard [25] examined four projects of introduction of technologies in schools, reaching conclusions in the area of PI and school-family connection. She pointed out some advantages. Technology can help establish a two-way connection by making parents aware of the academic reality of the school and teachers' can better understand families' responsibilities. Technological tools can promote conversations within families on school issues. Technology can involve families difficult to reach. Technology can extend learning opportunities from school to home, for example, guiding parents to act as instructors and help homework. The use of technology also motivates children to learn. Technology can help reduce costs involved in educating children. Lunts [13] describes how different technologies can be used in PI. One suggested is e-mail, because the teacher can easily reach all parents, who can respond at a convenient time. Web sites function as information broadcasters and link to families and communities, informing about the curricula and course objectives. A classroom website can complement instruction and communication with parents, display students' projects, assign homework and suggest tips for parents to help. Chat rooms/videoconferencing are an opportunity for interaction in real time, between parents and the teachers. Olmsted study's [24] purpose was to determine whether technologies facilitate parent-teacher communication and parent involvement. Data were collected through surveys and semi-structured focus group interviews. She concludes that online textbooks, links to educational websites and teacher websites provide resources to parents to engage in their children's learning at home. Blogs, wikis, and e-mail provide two-way communication between school and home. Voice-calling systems keep parents contactable. Institutional websites spread important news and events about the school. Teachers' websites provide parents with homework assignments and class news. Parent portals allow parents to access students' courses, homework assignments, grades, attendance, and allow parents to directly communicate with teachers. Text messaging, instant messaging and social networks can also be used to keep parents informed about school. Virtual Learning Environment (VLE) software provides group discussion, chat, scheduling and collaboration tools, that can be used for PI and reduce barriers such as different schedules of teachers and parents [26].

Horizon Report Europe [27], which examines trends and challenges of technology in education, point to social networks as a fast trend to accelerate the adoption of technologies in schools, as they provide dialogue between students, teachers, parents and institutions, helping parents to stay informed and giving feedback to teachers. On the other hand, children grow up well acquainted with technologies such as computers, Internet, videogames, tablets and mobile phones, using them to play, learn and communicate. Digital educational resources can be part of learning activities promoted by parents or educators, and can be shared between them, using online tools.

2 Methodology

Given the relevance of the theme and verifying the existence of specific needs at this target audience, the research team decided to develop and evaluate a multimedia platform, using design research methodology, to answer the question: what are the functionalities, contents and dynamics that a multimedia platform must have to promote PI in learning of children attending kindergarten?

The term *design research* covers a group of research methodologies based on design and development, with some variations [28]. So, it's pertinent to highlight some specific characteristics of this methodology: it includes activities of analysis, design of educational prototype, evaluation and revision [29]; scientific knowledge influences development, which is then tested in the field, bringing empirical data to improve the product and validate knowledge; the development process is interactive and iterative, as it reaches a satisfactory approximation of the ideal intervention; it allows to exploit the potential of ICT, in order to solve a real problem in education [30]; It is based on rigorous and reflective research to build knowledge and principles that can guide future developments and studies [31]; The user is involved in the entire process, from preliminary studies to evaluation, in order to obtain a higher quality intervention [32]. This type of research can bring specific knowledge to a context, but be transferable and relevant to other learning environments [33]. This research is being carried out by the authors (research team from the University of Aveiro), in collaboration with the multimedia company Criamagin® (development team), four educators and 84 parents of three kindergartens in Aveiro (target audience). In this way, the target audience is integrated into the project in all phases: collaborating in the preliminary study, that will help to define the functional specifications of the platform; using the prototype and participating in tests and improvements; contributing to a final study on the impact of the platform on PI in the learning process of children attending the involved kindergartens.

Several authors present models for the operationalization of design research. Although the models vary in detail, they have similarities, synthesized by Plomp [34] in three stages: preliminary studies, development and evaluation. For this study, the model was adapted as follows: Stage I - Preliminary studies, consisting of literature review and search for state-of-art platforms, characterization of participants, survey the needs of educators and parents. Stage II - Iterative development of the platform, consisting of cycles of analysis, design, evaluation and revision of the prototype, until reaching the final product, involving the target audience in all process. Three development cycles are planned: First cycle - functional specifications, paper prototype and usability tests; Second cycle - functional prototype, pilot implementation in kindergartens and use by educators and parents, for tests and evaluation; Third cycle - final product, use in kindergartens. Stage III - Final evaluation of the impact of the product on PI in children's learning. This moment helps to verify the success of the product, i.e., to ascertain the practical results and contributions to the theory, as well as, suggestions for future studies.

Design research uses mixed methods to collect data, analyze and refine the intervention [35]. Thus, a combination of different forms of data collection is used in this study, such as inquiries (interviews, focus groups and questionnaires), observation, usability tests, e-mailing and meetings with the users, access to platform content and statistical data. Content analysis and descriptive statistical analysis were used to analyze data. Next sections present the results of preliminary studies, the first cycle of development and the beginning of the second cycle of development.

3 Preliminary Studies

This research involves four classrooms of three kindergartens, with the participation of four educators and 84 parents. Preliminary studies started with a questionnaire to parents (responses = 59) and interviews to the four educators to include both perspectives and needs in a platform that should improve communication and promote PI in learning. Also, the search for existing platforms helped to identify their main features and to understand market trends. A literature review was done to find out research about PI with technological tools, to predict good practices and learn from projects already implemented.

The questionnaire to parents was divided into three parts: The first one was aimed at characterizing the parents' technological affinity; at the second part, it was intended to identify the characteristics a platform should have in order to promote their involvement in their children's learning process – most important features and contents, dynamics that must be provided, presentation, update frequency, access permissions, devices used; the third part focused on the collection of personal data, needed for contextualizing the responses.

Results of parent's questionnaires showed that they have access to technology (Internet, computer and mobile phone) and most parents use it every day. They have reasonable to good knowledge about different Internet services (e-mail, social networks, web search). Most parents perform technological activities with their children (filming, show photos, playing games and apps). Their children access technology at home, being the tablet their preferred device. Parents value some features: news and events calendar, photo and videos gallery of children's projects and private messaging with the educator. The greater advantage of the platform is to access updated information on the work carried out at kindergarten. A general concern is the protection of personal information, in particular, sharing photos where children are identified. For the assessment of educators' needs, semi-structured interviews with the four educators participating in the research were carried out, to find out how they use technology in activities with children, to communicate with parents, and to understand educators' perceptions about the use of the platform - advantages and disadvantages, the devices to use, frequency of use, contents to share, tools and dynamics that the platform should contemplate. Since they will play the main role in the dynamization of the platform, it was essential to understand what could lead to its adhesion and use. Results of interviews with educators indicate that the platform must gather official information of kindergarten and direct contacts of parents. Also, it should integrate specific areas, such as child/group history, activities being developed, suggestions of activities to do with children and links to educational resources. The biggest advantages are celerity and automation of communication; promotion of parent's feedback; separation of professional contact from personal social networks. The constraints are lack of time for maintenance and parent's fear about privacy issues. Educators use the computer and the mobile phone for different purposes, and associate the execution of long tasks to the computer and immediate tasks to the phone, reason why the platform must be adaptable to different devices, to have a more effective use. There were few allusions to the use of the platform by children and there is no mention of the impact or benefit that a platform for PI can bring to children's learning, which seems to reveal that the educators are looking for a tool focused on communication and information sharing among adults.

Another preliminary study was the web-search for state-of-art platforms, with the objective of knowing the variety of platforms for PI in the national and international market, identifying the features they offer, innovations, trends and good practices, as well as weaknesses that can be suppressed. Search was done using Google, blogs, digital magazines and websites of technologies in education, and resulted in a set of sites that offer platforms, reviews, experts opinions and links for download.

This study revealed the existence of a considerable set of platforms that facilitate communication between schools and parents, such as Classdojo, Classmessenger, SimplyCircle, FreshGrade, Edmodo, ParentSquare, MyChild, Weduc[1]. The most common features are: private groups, with the possibility of associating teachers, students and parents, individual/group messaging; image gallery; and events calendar. Some platforms have social network components (e.g. like, share, comment), others have Virtual Learning Environment components (e.g. creation of tasks, students' monitoring). Two platforms allow the customization by the institution (e.g. logo, colors). There was only one platform specifically developed for ECE, and it focus on disseminating information (events that happened or that are planned), but lack the provision of strategies or suggestions that parents can explore at home, contributing more actively to their child's learning.

Literature review presents some research projects which promoted PI in kindergarten through technological tools. Some results are: active participation and higher feedback from parents; awareness about the work developed in kindergarten; improvement of relationships between parents and educators; parents' ability to extend home learning based on the information shared; reading comments with children contributed to collaborative and constructive learning [36–39]. A detailed presentation of the preliminary studies, methodological decisions and a critical discussion of the results found at this stage, can be consulted in Laranjeiro, Antunes and Santos [40].

4 First Cycle of Development

4.1 Conceptual Structure

Based on the contributions of the preliminary studies, the II Stage of research started. In the first cycle of development, the functional specifications of the platform were

[1] Platforms Webpages: www.classdojo.com, www.classmessenger.com, www.remind.com, www.simplycircle.com, www.freshgrade.com, www.edmodo.com, www.parentsquare.com, www.mychild.pt, www.weduc.com.

defined. These resulted in a paper prototype, subjected to usability tests for formative evaluation.

Functional specifications are detailed descriptions of the functionalities that will be included in the platform, to meet the needs of the users and the objectives of the product [41]. This is an essential document for teamwork as it is a starting point for a joint understanding of the product. Until the specifications are written, there are many development possibilities, derived from brainstorming sessions, team opinions and user surveys. Functional specifications must clearly limit the scope of the project, defining what will be done and what will not be done, and set priorities (most important features first) and responsibilities in development (who must deliver what). Functional specifications were written following three principles: specific, objective and positive description (say what the system should do, instead of focusing on what should not happen), avoiding misinterpretation [41]. The definition of functional specifications allowed the organization of the conceptual structure of the platform, that is presented in an architecture diagram (Fig. 1), a flowchart showing the organization and interconnection of different areas [41]. The unit of the diagram is the node, which corresponds to a sort of information. The structure is hierarchical, composed of categories and subcategories, forming a navigation that is consistent and easy to learn by the user. Starting from the homepage, it is divided into four main nodes. Within each node, specific contents and functionalities are presented. The diagram shows the nomenclature used in buttons and menus.

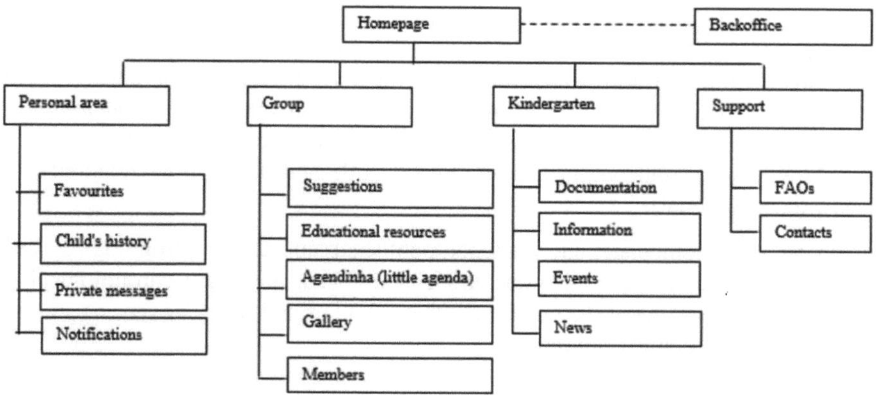

Fig. 1. Architecture diagram [42].

4.2 Functional Specifications

The platform is divided into four areas, defined by the type of information, level of privacy and access permissions. In the personal area, there are functionalities and contents available to each user, individually and privately – access to child's history, private messages service, favorites and notifications. In the group area, content is published and shared by all members of the group, educator and parents – suggestions, educational resources, *agendinha*, gallery, members. In the kindergarten area, the educator provides institutional information to parents – documentation, information, events and news. The support is an area where users can contact the development and research team, as well as find more information about the project. The functional specifications are presented below, briefly, for the understanding of each functionality, layout and navigation of the platform.

General specifications - the left side menu appears in all pages, giving access to three areas (personal, group, kindergarten). Each area contains submenu buttons, using the nomenclature defined in the architecture diagram. The logo of the project is placed in the header. Group name and user's photo must always be present, in an upper area of the site. In the central block, below the heading, is placed the writing area, where users can write posts. Below the writing area, posts of group members appear in chronological order. Group members can comment a post. On the right-side menu, there are news of the institution, calendar of events and support area.

Writing area - in all pages there is a writing area, where users can write posts, to share contents with other group members. Users can choose where they want to publish the post, selecting the corresponding tab - messages, *agendinha*, activities, educational resources. By default, the 'messages' tab is selected. Messages composed in this tab will appear at homepage. If users want to choose another area to write, they must change the tab. If they choose 'Educational Resources' tab, they can insert links to web pages, apps, educational games and other resources that will appear in Educational Resources Area. In each post, they must include title, link, description (required) and images (optional). If they choose the 'Activities' tab, they will insert content in the 'Suggestions' area. Here, they can choose typology: Books and stories; Songs, Handcrafts, Games and playtime, Outdoors, Other. Each contribution consists of title and description (required), link and images (optional). If they choose *Agendinha* tab, they can insert events, using subcategories - exhibitions, cinema, theatre, music and other shows. Each contribution is composed by title and description (required), link, images, date (optional).

Homepage - at homepage, all contents published appear in chronological order, regardless of the area where they are associated. Thus, there is a chronological presentation of all posts, but at the same time, there is an organization by type: *Agendinha*, suggestions, educational resources.

Next, the descriptions of the main features are presented. In the group area, there are the following nodes: Gallery, Educational Resources, Suggestions, *Agendinha*, Members.

Gallery - area where parents and educators can share photos, videos and audio files. Possibility of creating albums within the gallery, associating name, description and date, for organization of contents. Upload of contents into an album and possibility of editing description. Chronological listing of albums and contents. Ability to comment and reply to comments about a content.

Educational resources - area where users can see the list of links inserted by group members. The list appears divided by typologies (websites, apps, games, others).

Within each typology, links appear from the most recent to the oldest. Possibility for each member to mark a link as favorite. Ability to comment and answer to comments on each item.

Suggestions - area where users can see all suggestions of activities inserted by group members. The list appears divided by typologies: Books and stories; Songs, Handicrafts, Games and playtime, Outdoors, Other. Activities appear from the most recent to the oldest. Possibility for each member to mark an activity as favorite. Ability to comment and answer to comments on each content.

Agendinha - area where users can see all events inserted by group members. The list appears divided by typologies: exhibitions, cinema, theatre, music and other shows. Events appear from the most recent to the oldest. Possibility for each member to mark an event as favorite. Ability to comment and answer to comments on each item.

Members - area presenting the list of group members, with photograph and name. Photos connect to the public profile page, which displays personal information - photography, name, publications on the platform and direct connection to private messaging.

In the kindergarten area, there are the following nodes: Events, News, Information and Documentation.

Events - kindergarten calendar, where educators can highlight activities already done or to be carried out in the future, for example, Mother's Day, Christmas. Each contribution consists of a title, a description, date (required) and images (optional). This functionality is visible to all members, but only available for editing by educators, who have permissions to insert, edit and delete events.

News - news are composed of title, text (required) and image (optional). They serve to communicate official information from the kindergarten. News are listed from the most recent to the oldest. This functionality is visible to all members, but only available for editing by educators.

Information - area where educators can upload temporary files (.pdf or .jpg) to parents, such as weekly menu and weekly planning. Possibility of associating title and description to the file. List from the most recent to the oldest. This functionality is visible to all members, but only available for editing by educators.

Documentation - area where educators can upload files (.pdf or.jpg) to parents, such as regulations, school calendar, pedagogical plan, other. Possibility of associating title and description to the file. List from the most recent to the oldest. This functionality is visible to all members, but only available for editing by educators.

In the personal area, there are the following nodes: Events, News, Information and Documentation.

Private Messages - area where private messages can be read and written. Ability to create message and choose the recipients from the list of group members - educator, member, several members or the whole group. Ability to respond to a message.

Favorites – accessing this area, users can view all the posts they saved as favorites, listed and divided by categories - *agendinha*, educational resources, suggestions.

Notifications - users can receive notifications by e-mail. They can customize notifications by frequency - choosing to receive a daily or weekly summary; members - receiving notifications from the educator, a specific member or all members; and areas - choosing to receive notifications about events, educational resources, suggestions or messages. In the personal area, users can see and delete notifications. Unread notifications are written in bold, to be distinguished from the others.

Child's History - in this private area, parents have access to information sent by the educator about their child - images, files (e.g., pdf document with annual evaluation), or text messages. The information is stored in chronological order, constituting a portfolio or history of the child, related to his/her development and achievements in kindergarten. When accessing the child's history area, the educator has a drop-down menu to choose the parent and, after this step, share private information about the child.

In addition to the personal area, group area and kindergarten area, the support area offers information to users, providing explanations about the portal, how it works, what functionalities are available, how to participate, conditions of use. It also has a form to contact the development team, addressing suggestions, debug and help.

For managing information, users and accesses to the platform, it is planned to develop a Backoffice. In addition to the profile of educator and the profile of parent, there is a third profile, the administrator's, that belongs to the development team of Criamagin, responsible for managing the platform. The administrator has got access to the Backoffice, to monitor platform data, access usage statistics and manage rooms and users. The administrator creates access to the members of kindergarten, which means creating groups, registering users with e-mails (previously provided by the kindergarten), and associating users to a created group. Users receive an e-mail confirming registration, with instructions to enter and start using the platform.

4.3 Paper Prototype and Usability Tests

With the definition of the functional specifications and the architecture diagram, a paper prototype of the platform was elaborated (Fig. 2), to test the usability and the overall design with the user, at an initial phase of development. Usability is formally defined in standard ISO 9241, as the ability of a product to be used with effectiveness, efficiency and satisfaction by specific users to achieve their objectives in a given context [43]. It is a quality attribute that measures whether the interface is easy to learn and use, whether the features are easy to remember, the type and number of user errors, and speed of task execution [44].

A paper prototype is a recommended technique for making usability studies, in the beginning of the development, because its implementation is fast and economic. It allows the team to gather data about usability, at a very early stage of a project, and to improve the user experience. At this stage, it is still possible to change the approach to the problem, change the set of resources specified for development, and even change the interface architecture. These changes are no longer feasible in terms of costs and deadlines when the product is tested at a later stage of development [45].

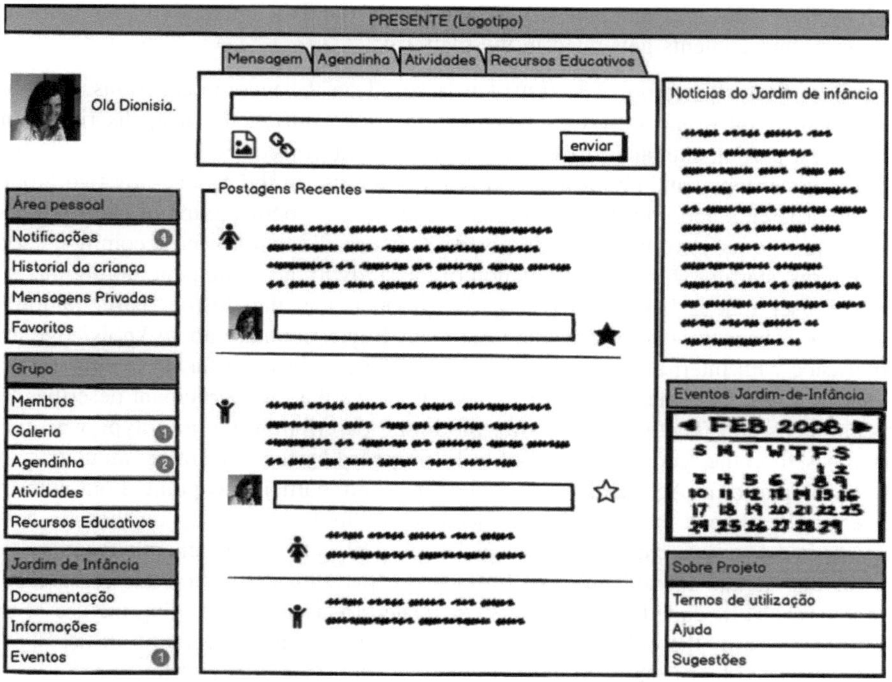

Fig. 2. Paper prototype [42]

At this global design definition phase, the topics to be evaluated with the user are Relevance (to verify if there is the need for the platform - content validity), Consistency (to check it's properly planned or structured - construct validity) and Practicality (to check if users expect to use the product in the context for which it was created) [32]. This constitutes a formative evaluation that is a systematical procedure, including planning tests, data collection and analysis, and report). The study of usability in the global design phase doesn't focus on graphic or layout, but test general understanding, navigation, concepts, buttons and menus nomenclature, contents associated to each area, choices to display information on each page, identification of missing features and resources [45]. For these tests, there is no need to have all functionalities implemented, but an horizontal representation, a first level that presents the features and allows the users to perform/simulate tasks [46]. A balanced usability test can be performed with five potential users. Five users discover 80% of the problems, including in this percentage the biggest problems. The fifth user typically observes the same results and does not add much new information. In case there are different categories of users, for example, teachers and students, it is advisable to test with three potential users of each group [47].

The paper prototype was created to be tested with users. It was necessary to simulate the main areas of the platform and create a fictional room, with members of both profiles (educators and parents), to better understand the interactivity, navigability, dynamics and contents generated in the platform.

Usability Tests Planning. The test plan is based on the recommendations of Rubin and Chisnell [46], and describes what will be done during the test, discriminating objectives, participants and procedures. Usability test objectives are: to probe the relevance, consistency and practicality expected of the use of the product, by two groups of users (parents and educators); to understand whether both groups of users can use the product equally well; to identify obstacles to use. Tests followed a common set of procedures, starting with the presentation of the study to the participant, noting that it's not the user that is being tested, but the product, and that his/her participation is important. Then, the participant filled out a small questionnaire about knowledge and experience with Internet communication tools. The usability test had two parts. First, a "walk through" [48] the paper screens, which means that the participant describes the screen, areas and functionalities. After the initial description, the prototype was evaluated based on the accomplishment of tasks proposed by the moderator, simulating the use of the platform. According to the question asked, participants pointed out with the finger and explained the procedure to accomplish the task. As they finished the task, they moved forward, changing the page of the prototype. Researchers encourage the use of the "Think aloud" protocol [49] by the participant, to facilitate researcher's annotations. Tests ended with an interview related to attitudes regarding the use of the platform, to know the opinion and perceive the interest and expectation of users.

Eight individual tests were carried out with four educators and four parents, representing both groups of the platform users. The instruments were pre-tested with a parent from another kindergarten.

With these tests, researchers intended to collect two types of data: performance data, that includes errors, omissions and completed tasks, understanding of the structure and navigation; preference data, in particular, the ease of use and learning, nomenclature, perceived utility, expectations. The results of the paper prototype usability tests are presented below, suggesting changes and improvements to implement in the functional prototype.

Usability Tests Results. The usability assessment was done with four educators (E1 to E4) and four parents (P1 to P4). According to the data collected through the questionnaire, all of them use Internet services every day, but have different levels of participation in social networks, from observation (e.g., P2 and P3 only read posts) to full social interaction (e.g., P4 and E4 read/write/answer posts, share images/videos; belong to Groups; use instant messaging). These profiles represent most of the parents involved in the project and, at the same time, reveal a level of technological affinity needed to understand, test and critically evaluate the platform.

Initial Considerations. After ended the questionnaire, participants described the main screen, on paper, pointing out the defined areas, giving suggestions and expressing doubts. This part of the test served to verify the general understanding of the platform and hear the first opinions of the eight participants. All participants understood the general layout, identifying the menu area, the writing area, and the body of the site, where users' posts appear, as well as the division of the menu into three sub-levels (personal, group and kindergarten). Some considerations were retained for possible implementation in the second cycle of development. E1 thinks that the tabs above the writing area are confusing, as well as the use of the word 'Messages'. She was unsure if it was related to private messages or messages to the homepage. She suggested to put the writing area of each section only in that section, that is, if the user is at the homepage, his posts appear only there. The tabs were not understood by P2, who described it as buttons to change pages. E3 asked if 'Child's History' is only accessible to the child's parents, showing concern about privacy. She also suggested that parents could share with the educator what their children do at home, in this private area. P3 noticed that the posts did not have date and time details. Three parents asked about the possibility of blocking members.

Results of Tests with Tasks List. After the initial description, the moderator applied a tasks list, which users performed sequentially, simulating the action on the paper prototype, pointing the finger and changing the page to move forward.

Table 1 presents the tasks questions associated to functionality and the participants who could successfully complete the task (x). For those who did not understand the task or performed it with error, that space remains in blank. Visually, the table gives an overview of the functionalities best understood and the ones that caused major errors.

Analyzing the table, tasks that caused major problems are associated with the areas: edit profile, educational resources, activities, information, and favorites. Participants' comments were considered for revision of the prototype in the second cycle of development. In task two, E1 said that "Edit profile" should be written next to the photo. Three parents said there should be a button in the personal area to edit the profile. In task four, P4 pointed out that a submit button is missing. He asked if he should just press the ENTER key. In task six, E4 found an error. The structure did not have a back button. Without it, he gets stuck in private messages. He also suggested that it should be possible to send private messages to multiple members at the same time. In task eight, E4 didn't identify the news because he was looking for a button named news. Task 11 was not achieved by any participant due to the nomenclature educational resources. Four participants suggested changing the name to links, useful links, or interesting links. Likewise, in task 12, none of the participants understood what were suggestions of activities, confusing the purpose of this area (sharing stories, songs, arts and crafts…), with educational resources (links to websites, apps, videos) and activities done in the kindergarten classroom. E1 said she did not agree on the division by typology, because the activities they do aren't confined (a book becomes a theatre, a song, a drawing), so they shouldn't be labeled in one category inside the platform. E3 has proposed taking out the word Suggestions because what makes sense is to share activities that they are doing at school or at home. P3 has identified another error: a link to return to homepage is missing. Task 13 was well understood, although P4 confused *agendinha* with events. Three participants considered that *agendinha* and events could be together. Two educators did not like the term *agendinha* (little agenda), it should be agenda, because they don't like to infantilize the language with children. E1 thinks that, like in resources and activities, it shouldn't be divided into categories, because it is one more step. She thinks it is simpler, just entering the event and describe what it is. Task 15 caused errors and several considerations. Three participants feel that

Table 1. Tasks and performance of the users [42].

Task	Functionality	E1	E2	E3	E4	P1	P2	P3	P4
1 - Who is the user who owns this page?	Profile	x		x		x	x	x	x
2 - Imagine this is your personal page. How can you change your profile info?	Edit profile	x		x				x	x
3 - Do you think there's new information you haven't seen yet? Where can you check?	Notifications	x	x	x	x	x	x	x	x
4 - Imagine you want to comment on the second post. What should you do?	Comment	x	x	x	x	x	x	x	x
5 - Now you want to add a photo and insert a comment to share with the group	Write post	x	x	x	x	x	x	x	x
6 - Send a private message to the educator	Send messages	x	x	x	x	x	x	x	x
7 - Do you have unread messages? From who?	Received msg.	x	x	x	x	x	x	x	x
8 - Access the news from kindergarten	News	x	x	x		x	x	x	x
9 - Add the news to favorites	Add favorites	x	x	x	x	x	x	x	x
10 - Access photos about outdoor activities	Gallery	x	x	x	x	x		x	x
11 - Share with other parents a site with funny activities	Educational resources								
12 - Check for interesting book suggestions to read	Suggestions								x

(*continued*)

Table 1. (*continued*)

Task	Functionality	E1	E2	E3	E4	P1	P2	P3	P4
13 - Share, with the other parents, information about a play that will happen at the Congress Centre	*Agendinha*	x	x	x	x	x	x	x	
14 - Check the date of Kindergarten's party	Events	x	x	x	x	x	x	x	x
15 - Check the menu and weekly activity plan of the kindergarten classroom	Information	x							x
16 - Open the rules of kindergarten to check the periods in which it closes	Documentation	x	x	x	x	x	x	x	x
17 - See the profile of the mother Anna	Members	x	x	x	x	x	x	x	x
18 - You want to do an educational activity with your child/class. Show some contents you've saved	See favorites	x	x	x					x
19 - See information the educator shared with you about your child's development	Child's history	x	x	x	x	x	x	x	x

there is no distinction between documentation and information. Three participants see no advantage in having this area, as information can be published in activities or news. E2 thinks information should disappear and be replaced by two new buttons, one for menus and another for planning. Educators and parents agree that menus are important to get parents to consult the platform. Task 18 also caused some errors. Participants were not considering favorites as a tool to save posts (links, events, photos) to show to their children, but for their own use. However, once they understood it, the possibility was very well accepted.

Final Interview. Finally, an interview was made to understand the attitude towards the platform, perceive interest and expectation of use by the participants, either parents or educators. Everyone considered the platform intuitive, easy to learn and use. Three participants mentioned that the kind of interaction is familiar. All educators said they will use the tool to communicate with parents privately and share information with everyone. All parents said they will use the platform to communicate with the educator, but only two considered sharing information with other parents. All educators think they will use the platform to develop learning activities with children in the classroom. Regarding parents, two of them said they will use it to do activities with their child. P2 said it depends on available content and P3 said she does not know, due to lack of time. Regarding the frequency of consultation and participation in the platform, responses varied, with educators tending to consider daily use and parents considering weekly use. Two participants mentioned that they will probably use the platform more if they can access it by a mobile phone.

4.4 Evaluation Moment – End of First Cycle of Development

The evaluation with users of the paper prototype served to ascertain the relevance of the content, platform consistency and expected practicality, helping to predict the use of the platform by educators and parents. It allowed the research team to check the overall understanding of the platform by both profiles and to identify some improvements and changes to the initial prototype. It also allowed to identify attitudes towards the use of the platform.

Thus, regarding the performance of the users, most of the functionalities were well identified. There were mistakes and doubts that happened, recurrently, in same tasks: Change Profile, Educational Resources, Suggestions, Information and Favorites. Some navigation failures were identified, such as lack of back button. From this evaluation, it was decided to proceed with some changes: Add new buttons - edit profile, return to homepage, send comments, back in private messages; Rename 'Educational resources' to 'Educational links'; Remove Information area and create Menu area; Writing area will have no tabs; Join Events and Agenda, instead of being a calendar, it will be a chronology of posts where, both parents and educators, can post events of general interest or events related to kindergarten; Activities will be an area to share comments and photos about classroom projects; Educational Links, Activities and Agenda will not have subdivisions, since it is an extra step and it is not valued.

Regarding the user's attitude toward the platform, answers to the interview indicate that users value the platform and intend to use it. Educators want to have an active role, with a daily use for sharing photographs and comments on the activities they do with the children, while parents point to a weekly use, more directed towards communicating with the educator than for sharing with other parents or carrying out educational activities with children. Access through mobile devices seems to be a condition for more frequent use.

To conclude, tests on the paper prototype have identified small changes that could also be implemented at a later stage of development, such as back buttons or nomenclature. However, this evaluation led to rethinking areas of the platform that would be difficult to change later, due to complexity, development time and costs. As these changes were identified at this stage, they will optimize the programming work of the functional prototype and allow the inclusion of functionalities according to user's suggestions, such as: join agenda and events, writing area without tabs; Links and activities chronologically available, without subdivisions. This evaluation ended the first cycle of development, with important information to be included in the planning of the next development tasks.

5 Second Cycle of Development

5.1 Programming the Functional Prototype

The Second Cycle of Development took place between July and December 2016. Between July and September, the functional prototype was programmed. In October, the platform began to be used in kindergarten rooms for testing and improvement. The research team wanted to launch the functional prototype (Fig. 3) on the 15th September, to present it to parents and educators at the beginning of the school year at kindergartens. Having a small team and short development time, it was necessary to define priorities and choose the features to develop for the launch.

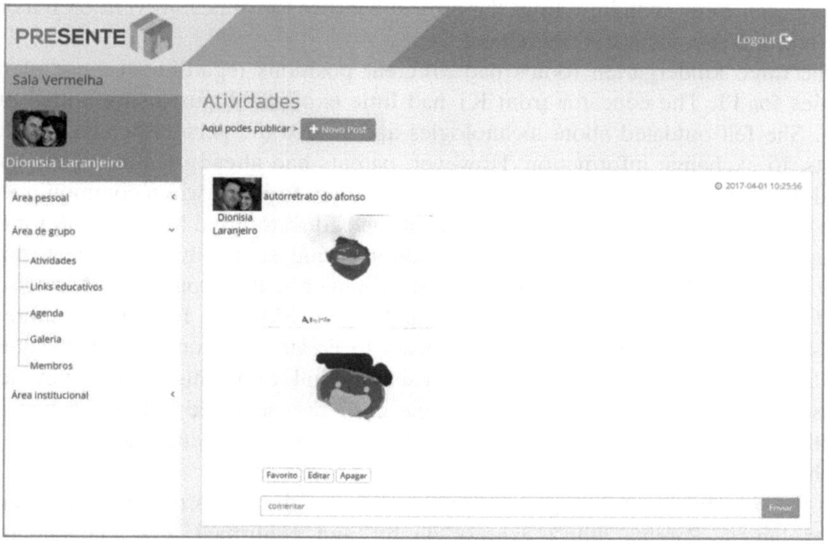

Fig. 3. Functional prototype [42].

Thus, it was decided to have a version that included a Backoffice, for the creation of virtual groups and users, and a Frontoffice, with selected functionalities that could promote more participation of users. In Backoffice, it was developed: a managing system of private groups, to list, create, edit and delete virtual rooms for kindergartens; a managing system for users, to list, create, edit and delete users, associate profile (educator or parent) and associate group. Since the platform contains personal data of children, users only access the information of the classroom attended by their children, with their login identification. At Frontoffice, it was privileged the development of the following functionalities: (i) Personal area - Child's history, to share private information between parents and educators; Favorites, to save posts of greater interest; Notifications, to inform when there is new information and encourage the consultation of information; Profile, to edit personal information, change password and profile image. (ii) Group area - sharing activities, allowing the inclusion of text and image in the post, events, allowing the inclusion of date, place and extra information, and educational links, allowing the introduction of weblinks, description and title. All members of the room can participate and see the posts in the group area. (iii) Kindergarten - news, area where the educator can share news from kindergarten with parents of the group. Other functionalities and system security measures will be implemented at the third cycle of development.

5.2 The Start of the Pilot Project

The pilot project started in two kindergarten rooms (K1 and K2), with presentation of the platform in the start-up meetings of the school year. The third kindergarten room (K3) started later, in an interim meeting, in November. The participants of the fourth Kindergarten room withdrew from the project because the educator went on maternity leave and the substitute did not adhere.

The three kindergarten rooms had different positions regarding the use of technologies for PI. The educator from K1 had little experience, just using e-mail punctually. She felt outdated about technologies and valued the personal contact with the parents, to exchange information. However, parents had already requested the use of digital media to follow the work done in kindergarten. In K2, it was a common practice to use digital media to engage parents. Parents and educator used Messenger® for daily messages (e.g. remember to give a medication, bring something to school), private group of Facebook® (to share activities of the room or visits abroad), file sharing in the Cloud (sending photos every month) and even Skype® for videoconferences home-kindergarten. In K3, the educator used to create a bimonthly e-newsletter, in HTML, that she published online and then sent the link to parents. In the e-newsletter, she used to share photos and activities done in kindergarten, educational suggestions and other interesting subjects. Parents liked to receive the newsletter, however, it was a task that occupied the educator a lot of time.

In the presentation meetings, all functionalities of the platform were demonstrated and explained. Parents didn't express doubts and confirmed they understood the structure, navigation and functionalities. In K2, one parent said she understood but she needed to try at home, and maybe then she could have new doubts. Another parent agreed. The researcher encouraged parents to contact her by e-mail, to clarify doubts, report errors or give suggestions, that may promote the improvement of the platform. In K1, parents asked about safety measures. They wanted to know who could access the information about the classroom, showing concern about sharing pictures or personal information of their child's development. This was a recurrent theme in K3. A parent, that was a computer security expert, pointed to a series of measures needed to ensure information security. At the end, they signed an informed consent and gave their e-mail address. The intention was to collect parents' and educators' e-mails, to create virtual rooms and logins for all users, so that they had the opportunity to use the platform during one school year.

To create user accounts at the Platform Backoffice, the administrator only needs a valid e-mail, the profile of the user (educator or parent) and the kindergarten room to associate the user. A hidden password is automatically created and the login information is sent to the e-mail associated to the account.

Virtual rooms for K1 (with 23 users) and K2 (with 23 users) were created in October and started being used by parents and educators of both kindergartens. The research team could monitor the use of the platform through a web statistic program, observation of content posted by users on the platform, contact with the educators (emails, phone calls and meetings) and parents (e-mails).

5.3 Data Collection for Platform Improvement

The collected data refers to the period between October and December 2016, ending the Second Cycle of development.

Web Statistics of the Platform. Statistical data on the number of hits, visits and page views per month were collected through Webalizer, a program provided by the hosting service. The following table shows the evolution of accesses during the first three months of use (Table 2).

Table 2. Web statistics from October 2016 to December 2016.

Month	Daily average			Monthly totals		
	Hits	Pages	Visits	Hits	Pages	Visits
Oct	112	50	9	3473	1558	286
Nov	278	86	16	8348	2603	487
Dec	72	26	10	2254	817	320
	154	**54**	**11.6**	**14075**	**4978**	**1093**

Considering that the total number of users in this period was 46 (2 educators and 44 parents), it was verified that there was a high volume of visits to the platform during the first month (286 visits), having almost doubled in the second month (487 visits). In the third month, the values dropped (320 visits), but remained above the first month. Altogether, during the first three months of use, there were 1093 visits with 4978 page views and an average of 11.6 visits per day.

Content Posted on the Platform. Contrasting with good access numbers, the participation in the first three months was short. In K1, the educator shared six events (related to activities in the library, amusement parks, cinema, among others), six activities (three posts to encourage parents to participate, others to report on activities developed with children), one link to an article on education. Regarding the parents' participation in the platform, there was a parent who published two articles on education, in the links area. There was another parent who made a comment to wish the group members a good weekend. Without accessing the content of the personal area, it was possible to verify that there was one private message between a parent and the educator. In K2, the educator shared eight events (activities taking place in kindergarten, theatre, solidarity, etc.), one activity (English activity performed with children), and one link to a video with English music to teach the lyrics. In this case, the educator complemented the information transmitted in the activities, with links to explore at home. During this period, there was no participation of parents in the platform, in the areas of activities, links, events, comments or private messages. However, eight parents have changed their profile information (name, photo). No educator shared any news in the kindergarten area.

Contact with the Educators. Both educators were disappointed with the lack of participation of the parents. But they were motivated by the high number of visits that the web statistics showed, which could mean that parents assumed a passive role, but they were accessing the platform to see the information. Both educators reported some errors and gave suggestions for the third cycle of development. The errors that the K1 educator identified were that she couldn't comment, edit or delete a post that she had already published. As suggestions for improvements, the educator thinks that events should have the possibility of adding images and should not be obligatory to fill date and time fields, as these are not always known with precision. She suggested that in the description field of the event, each user could fill in with the data they have. She asked if it was possible to share videos, either. It would be a good functionality for parents. She also suggested that the next functionalities to be developed should be sending of notifications by email and the implementation of galleries with pictures from children's projects, two triggers to promote parent's participation in the platform. K2 educator reported the same errors, but added a problem in inserting profile image. The platform sometimes failed to insert the image. When it did, the image was inserted upside down. Also, she couldn't add posts to favorites. She mentioned that some parents had not received the e-mail with the access data (login and password), so they did not use the platform. As suggestions for improvements, the educator considers it very important to receive notifications when there is new content in the platform and, also, the adaptation to the mobile phone, which at this stage was not yet fully developed.

Contact with the Parents. During this period, the support had received three e-mail messages from parents reporting that they didn't receive the e-mail with access information to login in the platform. The access data was resent to these users. One parent sent an e-mail suggesting that navigation between menus and content should take fewer steps. For example, when he was in the group area and wanted to see news of the institution, he had to open the Kindergarten menu and choose the submenu news. He thinks the submenu structure should always be open, so that navigation becomes more immediate. Another parent requested a meeting to discuss the platform's security issues. He found two points to improve. The first is that the platform should be on an HTTPS secure domain so that if users are accessing through a public Wi-Fi network, the data is encrypted and is not easily intercepted by strangers. The second is that the platform shouldn't allow for infinite login attempts. After three attempts and errors, the platform should block that IP's access for 15 min.

5.4 Evaluation Moment – End of the Second Cycle of Development

The use of the functional prototype in the Second Cycle of Development was intended to collect data for improvements and corrections to be included in the final version of the platform. The collected data allowed to understand the functionalities that should be implemented in the last development cycle and, at the same time, it gave an overview of the use by the educators and the parents. In terms of improvements to be implemented in the third development cycle, it is considered:

Correction of Errors: fix the errors of edit, change and comment posts; correction of the problem of uploading the profile images (it is necessary to put a limit of Kb to upload the images); fix the Favourites feature.

Priority Implementation of Features in Response to user Suggestions: notifications, image gallery, recover password, improvements in events area.

Implementation of Security Measures: HTTPS and IP blocking for continued attempts to access.

Implementation of the Remaining Functionalities to Complete the Platform: private message and child's history, members' page, documentation and menus in kindergarten area.

Regarding the use of the platform in this period, educators shared varied content (activities, links, events), however, with a small amount of posts. This may be due to the parents not giving feed-back or the platform still have some errors that make it difficult to use more frequently. Parents reported errors and submitted suggestions for improvements to the support e-mail. Web Statistics show that there was an average of 364 accesses per month to the platform, which suggests that parents accessed without participating. As an explanation, it may be due to the need to adapt to a new form of communication or because the parents take the platform as a unilateral means of communication, to receive information about what is going on in kindergarten, rather than to communicate with the educator or with other parents.

6 Final Considerations

The development of a platform for PI in kindergarten must consider the needs, motivations and expectations of parents and educators, both in planning, use and evaluation. In this sense, the research team involved, from the beginning, four kindergarten groups with four educators and 84 parents, who participated in the whole process. In preliminary studies, numerous possibilities of development were presented to parents and educators. Results of this stage helped define the functional specifications and the architecture diagram. This led to the creation of a paper prototype that was tested in the First Development Cycle, with parents and educators. Usability tests allowed to redirect, simplify, and even eliminate previously specified functionalities. In the Second Cycle of Development, the use of the platform by two groups allowed the identification of some errors and to understand the most important and prior functionalities, as well as the tendencies of use by educators and parents. Thus, parents take a passive role, based on viewing the content of the platform, while the educators share information, but are waiting for parents to respond.

These data will also be important for the third cycle of development, not only in the implementation of corrections, but also to find ways to stimulate and promote parental participation in the platform, so that communication flows both ways and can have more impact in the PI in children's learning process.

Acknowledgements. This article reports research developed within the PhD Program Technology Enhanced Learning and Societal Challenges, funded by Fundação para a Ciência e Tecnologia, FCT I. P. – Portugal, under contract # PD/00173/2014. The first author has a grant from the Foundation for Science and Technology (FCT) and the European Social Fund (ESF) under the III Community Support Framework (SFRH/BDE/95701/2013).

References

1. Laranjeiro, D., Antunes, M.J., Santos, P.: Plataforma tecnológica para o envolvimento parental na aprendizagem das crianças que frequentam o jardim-de-infância - Estudo exploratório sobre as necessidades dos pais. In: TIC Educ. 2016 - Digit. Technol. Futur. Sch. (Artigos selecionados), pp. 366–386 (2016)
2. Epstein, J.: School/family/community partnerships: caring for the children we share. Phi Delta Kappan **76**, 701 (1995)
3. Hoover-Dempsey, K., Sandler, H.: Why do parents become involved in their chidren's education? Rev. Educ. Res. **67**, 3–42 (1997)
4. Weiss, H., Caspe, M., Lopez, M.E.: Family involvement in early childhood education. Harv. Fam. Res. Proj. **1**, 1–8 (2006)
5. Harris, A., Goodall, J.: Do parents know they matter? Engaging all parents in learning. Educ. Res. **50**, 277–289 (2008). https://doi.org/10.1080/00131880802309424
6. Henderson, A., Berla, N.: A new generation of evidence: the family is critical to student achievement. National Committee for Citizens in Education (1994)
7. Desforges, C., Abouchaar, A.: The impact of parental involvement, parental support and family education on pupil achievements and adjustment: a literature review. Nottingham (2003)
8. Melhuish, E.C., Phan, M.B., Sylva, K., et al.: Effects of the home learning environment and preschool center experience upon literacy and numeracy development in early primary school. J. Soc. Issues **64**, 95–114 (2008)
9. Fan, X., Chen, M.: Parental involvement and students' academic achievement: a meta-analysis. Educ. Psychol. Rev. **13**, 1–22 (2001)
10. Hilado, A.V., Kallemeyn, L., Phillips, L.: Examining understandings of parent involvement in early childhood programs. Early Child. Res. Pract. **15** (2013)
11. Diamond, K.E., Justice, L.M., Siegler, R.S., Snyder, P.A.: Synthesis of IES Research on Early Intervention and Early Childhood Education. NCESR 2013-3001, p. 6 (2013)
12. Sonnenschein, S., Stapleton, L.M., Metzger, S.R.: What parents know about how well their children are doing in school. J. Educ. Res. **107**, 152–162 (2014). https://doi.org/10.1080/00220671.2013.788987
13. Lunts, E.: Parental involvement in children's education: connecting family and school by using telecommunication technologies. Meridian: Middle Sch. Comput. Technol. J. **6**, 1–8 (2003)
14. Stevenson, D.L., Baker, D.P.: The family-school relation and the child's school performance. Child Dev. **58**, 1348–1357 (1987)

15. Plowman, L., Stevenson, O., McPake, J., et al.: Parents, pre-schoolers and learning with technology at home: some implications for policy. J. Comput. Assist. Learn. **27**, 361–371 (2011). https://doi.org/10.1111/j.1365-2729.2011.00432.x
16. European Commission/EACEA/Eurydice/Eurostat: Key Data on Early Childhood Education and Care in Europe. Luxenbourg (2014)
17. Downer, J., Myers, S.: Application of a developmental/ecological model of family/school partnerships. In: Handbook of School-Family Partnerships, pp. 3–29. Routledge, Taylor & Francis (2010)
18. Hornby, G.: Parental Involvement in Childhood Education: Building Effective School-Family Partnerships. Springer, Heidelberg (2011). https://doi.org/10.1007/978-1-4419-8379-4
19. Silva, I.L., Marques, L., Mata, L., Rosa, M.: Orientações Curriculares para a Educação Pré-Escolar. Ministério da Educação/Direção-Geral da Educação, Lisboa (2016)
20. Grant, L.: Learning in Families: a review of research evidence and the current landscape of Learning in Families with digital technologies. Bristol (2009)
21. Izzo, C.V., Weissberg, R.P., Kasprow, W.J., Fendrich, M.: A longitudinal assessment of teacher perceptions of parent involvement in children's education and school performance. Am. J. Community Psychol. **27**, 817–839 (1999). https://doi.org/10.1023/A:1022262625984
22. Grant, L.: "I'm a completely different person at home": using digital technologies to connect learning between home and school. J. Comput. Assist. Learn. **27**, 292–302 (2011). https://doi.org/10.1111/j.1365-2729.2011.00433.x
23. Bouffard, S.: Tapping into technology: the role of the internet in family – school communication. Fam. Involv. Res. Proj. 1–5 (2008)
24. Olmstead, C.: Using technology to increase parent involvement in schools. TechTrends **57** (6), 28–37 (2013). https://doi.org/10.1007/s11528-013-0699-0
25. Blanchard, J.: The Family-School connection and technology. In: Proceedings of the Families, Technology, and Education Conference Chicago, pp. 235–245 (1998)
26. Carlson, C.: Future directions in family-school partnerships. In: Christenson, S., Reschly, A. (eds.) Handbook of School-Family Partnerships, pp. 407–419. Routledge (2010)
27. The New Media Consortium: Horizon Report Europe > 2014 Schools Edition (2014)
28. van den Akker, J., Gravemeijer, K., McKenney, S., Nieveen, N.: Educational Design Research. Routledge, London (2006)
29. Coutinho, C.P.: Aspectos metodológicos da investigação em tecnologia educativa em Portugal (1985–2000). Para um balanço da Investig. em Educ. 1960 a 2005 Teor. e práticas actas do Colóquio da AFIRSE (2006)
30. van den Akker, J.: Principles and methods of development research. In: van den Akker, J., Branch, R.M., Gustafson, K., Nieveen, N., Plomp, T. (eds.) Design Approaches and Tools in Education and Training, pp. 1–14. Springer, Dordrecht (1999). https://doi.org/10.1007/978-94-011-4255-7_1
31. Reeves, T.C.: Enhancing the worth of instructional technology research through "Design Experiments" and other development research strategies. In: International Perspectives on Instructional Technology Research for the 21st Century, vol. 27, pp. 1–15 (2000)
32. Nieveen, N., Folmer, E.: Formative evaluation in educational design research. In: Educational Design Research, pp. 152–169 (2013)
33. Richey, R.C., Klein, J.D., Nelson, W.A.: Developmental research: studies of instructional design and development. In: Handbook of Research for Educational Communications and Technology, pp. 1099–1130 (2008)
34. Plomp, T.: Educational design research: an introduction. In: Educational Design Research. Netherlands Institute for Curriculum Development, Enschede, pp. 10–51 (2013)
35. The Design-Based Research Collective: Design-based research: an emerging paradigm for educational inquiry. Educ. Res. **32**, 5–8 (2003)

36. Hong, S.B., Trepanier-Street, M.: Technology: a tool for knowledge construction in a reggio emilia inspired teacher education program. Early Child Educ. J. **32**, 87–94 (2004). https://doi.org/10.1007/s10643-004-7971-z
37. Faria, Á., Ramos, A.: Redes sociais no jardim de infância para aprender e partilhar com a família e a comunidade. In: XI Congr. Int. Galego-Portugués Psicopedag. Universidade da Coruña, pp. 3–13 (2011)
38. Knauf, H.: Interlaced social worlds: exploring the use of social media in the kindergarten the kindergarten. Early Years (2016). https://doi.org/10.1080/09575146.2016.1147424
39. Näsänen, J., Oulasvirta, A., Lehmuskallio, A.: Mobile media in the social fabric of a kindergarten. In: Proceedings of the SIGCHI Conference on Human Factors in Computing Systems, pp. 2167–2176 (2009)
40. Laranjeiro, D., Antunes, M.J., Santos, P.: Development of a multimedia platform for parental involvement in learning of children attending kindergarten - Preliminary Studies. In: INTED2017 Proceedings Valencia, pp. 3157–3166 (2017)
41. Garrett, J.J.: The Elements of User Experience: User-Centered Design for the Web and Beyond, 2nd edn (2011). https://doi.org/10.1145/889692.889709
42. Laranjeiro, D., Antunes, M.J., Santos, P.: Multimedia platform development for parental involvement in learning of children attending kindergarten - iterative cicles of development. In: CSEDU - 9th International Conference on Computer Supported Education, pp. 208–219 (2017)
43. ISO: ISO 9241-11 Ergonomic requirements for office work with visual display terminals (VDTs) - Part 11: Guidance on usability (1998)
44. Berns, T.: Usability and user-centred design, a necessity for efficient e-learning! Int. J. Comput Internet Manag. **12**, 20–25 (2004)
45. Nielsen, J.: Paper Prototyping: Getting User Data Before You Code. Nielsen Norman Group (2003). https://www.nngroup.com/articles/paper-prototyping/
46. Rubin, J., Chisnell, D.: Handbook of Usability Testing: How to Plan, Design, and Conduct Effective Tests, 2nd edn. Wiley, Indianopolis (2008)
47. Nielsen, J., Sova, D.: 234 Tips and Tricks for Recruiting Users as Participants in Usability Studies. Nielsen Norman Group (2003). www.nngroup.com/reports/how-to-recruit-participants-usability-studies
48. Wharton, C., Rieman, J., Lewis, C., Polson, P.: The Cognitive Walkthrough Method: A Practioner's Guide, Boulder, Colorado (1994)
49. van Someren, M.W., Barnard, Y.F., Sandberg, J.A.C.: The think aloud method- a practical guide to modelling cognitive processes (1994)

Adapting Enterprise Social Media for Informal Learning in the Workplace: Using Incremental and Iterative Design Methods to Favor Sustainable Uses

Christine Michel[1(✉)], Carine Touré[1,3], and Jean-Charles Marty[2]

[1] INSA de Lyon, Univ Lyon, CNRS, LIRIS, UMR 5205, 69621 Villeurbanne, France
{christine.michel, carine-edith.toure}@liris.cnrs.fr

[2] Université de Savoie Mont-Blanc, CNRS, LIRIS, UMR 5205, 69621 Villeurbanne, France
jean-charles.marty@liris.cnrs.fr

[3] Société du Canal de Provence, Le Tolonet, France

Abstract. Informal Learning in the Workplace (ILW) is ensured by the everyday work activities in which workers are engaged. It accounts for over 75% of learning in the workplace. Enterprise Social Media (ESM) are increasingly used to promote informal learning environments. In this paper, we discuss the principles and features of social media, and present to what extent they promote informal learning in the workplace. We propose also a user-centred design methodology to redesign a traditional knowledge-sharing tool with social features. We then present an implementation, in a real context, of the methodology. It shows that ESM are appropriate to promote ILW. Three adaptations must nevertheless be carried out: (1) Base the design on a precise and relatively exhaustive informational corpus and contextualize the access in the form of community of practice structured according to collaborative spaces; (2) Add indicators of judgment on the operational quality of information and the informational capital built, and (3) Define forms of moderation and control consistent with the hierarchical structures of the company. Our analysis also shows that an incremental and iterative approach of user-centered design had to be implemented to define how to adapt the design and to accompany change.

Keywords: Lifelong learning · Informal learning · Knowledge-sharing tools Enterprise social media · User-centered design · Adult learner

1 Introduction

Lifelong learning is an approach to education that has been addressed since the 1970s to provide the skills and knowledge needed to succeed in a rapidly changing world [1]. It includes formal, non-formal and informal learning [2]. Unlike informal learning, formal and non-formal learning are structured with tools or training sequence. The latter occurs during daily experiences, while working or interacting with other people. It is characterized by the merger of learning with the everyday work activities in which

P. Escudeiro et al. (Eds.): CSEDU 2017, CCIS 865, pp. 457–476, 2018.
https://doi.org/10.1007/978-3-319-94640-5_22

workers are engaged [3] and is motivated by personal needs. Informal learning is of central importance for enterprise since it accounts for over 75 per cent of learning in the workplace [4]. It is the most important way to acquire and develop skills required in professional contexts.

The Knowledge Management (KM) research field promotes the management and maintenance of knowledge sharing in the workplace. Three generations of technologies were privileged for informal learning [5, 6]. Two main strategies can be identified to manage knowledge: valuation of informational capital and valuation of human capital with collaboration [5, 7].

The first generation considers that workers can continuously learn and be able identify solutions to problems they can meet during working activities. They have to look for information on processes and know-how related to their activity. To support them, enterprises produce relatively exhaustive information corpuses on working activity and make them accessible. Despite their exhaustiveness, these knowledge databases remained most of the time unused because they were maladjusted to collaborators needs and characteristics; particularly regarding information access and training [8, 9]. Moreover, access tools to this information are not dedicated to learning process. Indeed, Graesser [9] recommended to privilege training objectives based on auto-regulation and meta-cognition; and by this way help learners to "learn how to learn". He describes [10] various principles based on fun, feedback or control to support learning.

The second generation focus was on expertise sharing and identification of experts able to provide useful information to collaborators. Communities of practice (CoP) were commonly adopted by enterprises to help practitioners express, share and exploit their knowledge [7, 11]. Direct interaction between peers was recognized to facilitate knowledge transfer and improve information quality [12]. However, the lack of information completeness, accuracy in identification and recommendation of expert, privacy protection and control revealed some limits [5]. CoPs have remained hardly ever used.

The third generation combines principles of both first and second generations. It is characterized by collaborative information spaces merging information repositories, communication and collaboration processes. Many enterprises chose to implement enterprise social media (ESM) to improve organizational performance, especially in the knowledge sharing context [13]. They integrate management of working activity, knowledge management strategies and social aspects promoting interactivity between peers [14–16]. ESM foster informational and social capital valuation; they are particularly well adapted to find and interact with collaborators, receive and seek for help [5]. They are also easier to manipulate, more attractive and interactive than traditional collaborative environments. They fulfill users' needs for usefulness and gratification [17]. Indeed, they allow the recognition of each one in the contributions made and permit social connections materialized by simple actions as following a post or as commenting. Nevertheless, the free access to information, contribution and cooperation features has opened the door to misuse leading to a lack of efficiency in the exploitation of information resources or a feeling of harassment [18].

Our objective is to study to what extent ESM are actually adequate tools to implement informal learning strategies. More specifically, we will study what social features are the most effective to match learning objectives stated by Graesser and how to make them coherent with the objectives and practices of the organization and collaborators. The long-term objective is to favor a sustainable use. To answer these questions, we present in the next section ESM characteristics and how they can significantly support informal learning in the workplace. We also present a user-centered, incremental and iterative design methodology which aims to effectively implement knowledge-sharing artefacts according to users' requirements. By including workers in the design process of their knowledge-sharing platform, our objective is to capture their contextual needs and improve their engagement in effective usage. We argue that a user-centred approach allows proper adjustment of the social features to the context and users, and so mitigates the risks of misuse. We implemented these propositions in a real context to evaluate their accuracy and refine them. This study is presented in the fourth section of the paper. A first version of this work has been previously published [19]. This paper extends it and provides the reader with new information about the experimental study: the results of the first design cycle has been strengthened and an analysis of the use, obtained from the connection's tracks (logs) recorded during 2 years, extends the evaluation.

2 Using ESM for Informal Learning

2.1 Pros

ESM features promote construction and identification of relevant information. Comments within social media are an emblematic form of expression and a communication tool for users to effectively judge the quality of information and easily participate to content construction. Indeed, information captured within informal learning tools evolves and may become rapidly outdated. Comments have the advantage that workers can communicate and participate online to the construction of the knowledge corpus [20], they reduce the risk of forgetting or losing practice. Appreciations left by users provide us with an additional way to evaluate information quality and to promote information submission. They can be formalized as in some wikis where content posted can be qualified with completeness and readability indicators. These indicators allow collaborators to form their opinion on the content and better understand how they can participate to its refinement. This feedback helps authors to be aware of the usefulness of their publications [21] and helps to build their reputation. Moreover, wikis frequently use these features to support collaborative innovation, problem resolution and more generally help organizations improve their business processes [18].

ESM provide visibility and persistence of several communicative actions like download, content publication, identification of what others do, status update, profile creation (possibilities to highlight particular aspects of themselves), connecting with or following people [15, 22]. They expand (and precise) the range of people, networks and contexts from which people can learn across the organization.

Making communicative activities visible also allows self-regulation. Notifications, number of appreciations, new submissions, etc. help identify what and how others do, evaluate what one's do and adjust one's own behavior. It promotes meta-cognition and meta-knowledge (learn how to learn) [23]. This awareness thus becomes an intrinsic motivator to construct one's own numerical identity through indicators [24]. Being involved in a group helps collaborators develop meta-social knowledge and facilitates their ability to collaborate and coordinate [25], particularly within CoPs.

2.2 Cons

Janssen *et al.* [25] identifies two groups of risks linked to the problems of acceptance and to the use of ESM and quality of content published by collaborators.

The acceptance and the ability to use play a basic role on the initial and continuous use of technologies. The process of acceptance begins with the construction of initial beliefs towards the information system. They are generated by external stimuli such as system quality, service quality, knowledge quality or information quality [26–29]. These beliefs are moderated by personal factors like age, previous experience or service quality [30]. They also influence the ease of use of the system. Indeed, an efficient use may require high levels of literacy and technical proficiency in seeking for information, evaluating its usefulness and truthfulness or connecting with remote people or computers [31, 18]. Contextual characteristics of collaborators are most of the time not considered during the design process [3]. To develop meta-social skills and improve communication as proposed by Graesser [10], users need clear learning objectives and awareness on peers feedback and information quality. They also need recognition of what they do (improvement of professional reputation, acknowledgement from community, being informed that their actions are appreciated by others) [12]. Moreover, policies and structure of governance (i.e. monitoring, control or filtering of system accesses) have to be established as well as management campaign of training) [18]. These solutions are money and time consuming, especially for limited IT budgets and companies that seek rapid and simple collaborative solutions. After this initial cycle of use, the user acquires an experience that helps him to construct new beliefs and experience confirming or refuting the previous ones; this impacts his attitude towards the system (satisfaction or dissatisfaction) and his intention to use the system [32, 33].

The second group of risks concerns the validity and quality of information created and published. Despite the fact that published content is most the time not anonymous within ESM, it can be useless for informal learning since information is often poorly detailed and proofread, particularly if knowledge objects manipulated are of technical nature. Within social media, posts are very often brief and people give generic information without giving details. This may be suitable for updates, but not for the construction of the core information corpus. Moreover, people may engage in informal behavior when using social media. Activities like using improper language, publishing information that is confidential, using incomplete information or using ratings or comments to harass colleagues may be common. The ability to discern the quality of the accessible information is mostly incumbent upon users and they have little control in these environments, which is one principle of social media [18, 33]. These risks may negatively affect the social and learning environment and call into question the expected learning processes.

2.3 Summary and Proposition

ESM appear to be suitable to support informal learning in the workplace. They supply functionalities that promote and facilitate collaboration, knowledge sharing, user motivation and visibility, and information persistence. They also propose reflexive indicators that facilitate the analysis and coordination of collective activities, social connection and learning. These characteristics position workers and their needs at the heart of the learning environment, making ESM appropriate tools to support informal learning in the workplace. However, their use may be inefficient due to the profile of workers, who are adult learners and need to be aware of the value of their participation in the learning group: they seek concrete personal and professional feedback, usefulness and gratification. Moreover, the quality of information published may be problematic regarding learning strategies.

To reduce the risks related to information quality, we believe that it is important to base the learning environment on a precise and exhaustive information corpus. This informational architecture which is most of the time already formalized into information systems can then be enriched with collaborative characteristics. Literature review showed that indexation and structuration of information have to be reviewed to facilitate contextual access. A search engine and indexation tags are fundamental elements to guaranty a transversal access to information.

Activity's contextual aspect such as the one proposed by CoPs can be reproduced with structured wikis according to enterprise's working communities. Various elements have to be considered to guaranty quality and trustworthiness of published content; and also facilitate contribution: select useful information, organize it according to specific template files, and organize validation according to hierarchical decision-making structures of the community.

As regards to learning support, literature review showed three additional characteristics of ESM to promote users' engagement: visibility and reflexivity. Comments and appreciations (*e.g.* "Likes") can be considered as tools for expression and communication, allowing collaborators to provide feedback and participate to construction of contents. These features allow them to be involved into the co-construction of knowledge and maintain an updated available information which is important for the quality of learning processes. Awareness indicators like notifications (of new submissions, who and when, number of comments) promote the construction of meta-cognitive skills for self-regulation and stimulate participation. Indicators of information quality facilitate identification of useful content and collaboration by a critical analysis of items to be added to update and improve contents.

Finally, to minimize risks of misuse of the environment, we propose to use a user-centered, incremental and iterative design methodology. This methodology allows to identify characteristics and preferences of users and to design a contextually adapted environment. The incremental and iterative nature of the approach also makes it possible to accompany the change associated with the introduction of a new information system and thus to positively influence its acceptance and its initial and continuous use. Indeed, since informal learning is inherent in the employee's will and not stimulated by accompanying strategies, this characteristic appears fundamental. Analysis of core acceptance of technology models in the workplace showed that the acceptance model can be represented with a spiral (see Fig. 1) structured with conditions of use. Every loop builds an artifact increasingly adapted to users' needs and behavior. We posit that the sustainability of our process can be effectively ensured by providing users with an artifact matching their profile and needs at each stage of this cycle.

We implemented our methodology in a real context. The objective was to identify the most adapted ESM features that promote informal learning, to assess the feasibility of the methodology and to identify a structuring order of the various items which have to be considered at each stage. We present the results of this experimentation in the next section.

3 Implementation

3.1 Context and Constitution of the Working Group

The *Société du Canal de Provence* (SCP) is located in the south of France and specializes in services related to the treatment and distribution of water for companies, farmers and communities. The intervention territory is divided into ten geographic areas called Operating Centres (OC). Each OC corresponds to a community of practice in which we find three positions: the Operator (O), the Coordinator Technician (CT) (an operator who also has the role of manager of the community), and the Support and Customer Relationship Technician (SCRT). They are the responsible people for the maintenance of hydraulic infrastructures (canals, pumping stations, water purification stations, etc.). The operators need a wealth of knowledge about their work: there is a lot of (sometimes dynamic) information to learn and knowledge sharing is especially important.

To assist them, SCP produced in 1996 a knowledge book about the processes and hydraulics infrastructures. This information was accessible through a tool named ALEX (*Aide à L'EXploitation*). It gathered information from returns on experience sheets developed in HTML format, and stored it within a directory on a dedicated server in each OC. Throughout its twenty years of existence, it was hardly ever used even though collaborators agreed with the learning environment principle. One main reason was because accessibility to information was not adapted. ALEX was a typical sample of traditional KM strategies based on knowledge books and produced in the 1990's. It is an appropriate context to work on means capable of supporting lifelong learning.

Four OCs were selected by the responsible person for the project to act as pilot OCs. Eleven employees coming from those OCs were invited to freely participate in the working group. They were chosen according to their experience and various positions, thus being representative of various trades within the company, and according to their use of the previous version of the knowledge book. The focus groups were moderated by ourselves and by a member of the working group (a board member, responsible for the ALEX project). We count in total twelve sessions conducted on a two years period. The first year consisted in formalizing the basic users' needs. Six meetings, separated by about two to three weeks, allowed us to propose a solution increasingly refined until a last version fully usable in the work context. The platform

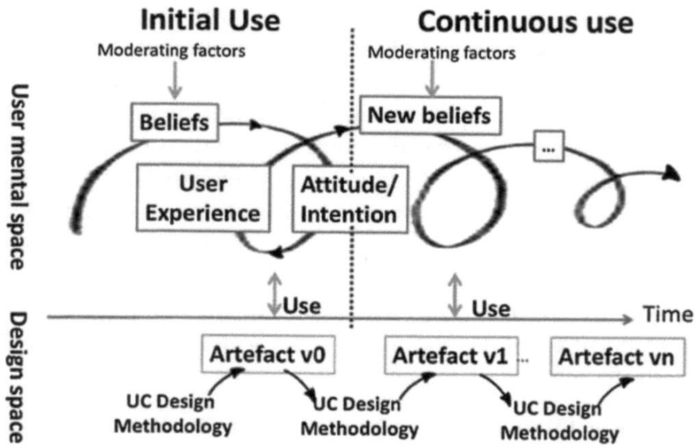

Fig. 1. Incremental and iterative design of information systems for informal learning [19].

was made available to users for three months. At the end of this first year, a debriefing meeting was held on the eligibility of the proposed solution and a new analysis and design cycle was initiated. It took seven months and six working sessions.

3.2 The First Design Cycle

Need Analysis. The first focus group was dedicated to need analysis. The main requirement that emerged from this meeting was to propose easier ways to search for, submit and access knowledge. The study of the initial system showed that the information filled in on business procedures was generally of good quality, which is fine since we haven't had to rework on the formalization of the knowledge itself. Users' needs collected during this focus group can be summarized as follows: workers wish to have an accessible platform from both the office and the outside (web platform), that is easy to learn but effective (casual and responsive functionalities), which reduces the time for entering information (content easily updatable), facilitates data search (a good search engine) and allows exchanges between employees (with a social area). Our proposition of implementing an ESN therefore was well accepted since it met the needs.

Design of the Information Structure. The following focus groups were dedicated to the design of the information structure. It consists of designing patterns of interaction and structuring information models that are familiar to users and their work context. We discussed interaction patterns adapted to the system (information reading, submission, navigation and search). The discussions allowed us to identify the general structure of navigation and organization of the information of the website and the methods of structuring knowledge and know-how. To facilitate information reading and search, we organized the ESN like a community of practice structured according to collaborative spaces dedicated to each OC. Indeed, each OC has dedicated team work, equipment and operations. These operations done by the collaborators on infrastructures are described in experience sheets, with descriptions of equipment, operating instructions, processes and alarms. This resulted in the definition of eleven types of sheets. Each sheet is presented as a form formatted according to its type-specific metadata (type of equipment for equipment sheets or instruction name for operating instruction sheets), by cons, the content of fields is open written as shown on Fig. 2. Experience sheets have been classified and indexed in accordance with their type and relevance with the working needs of OC. For the submission, a simplified numerical space reproducing a word processor office suite and various document templates were designed. To facilitate the navigation between the different tools and thus their accessibility from every workstation and in mobility, a work of harmonization of the architecture of the various IS was carried out to integrate Alex with the other IS and with the intranet of the company.

System Policies. The following focus groups was dedicated to the system policies. Four user roles were proposed to control submissions and guaranty information quality – the reader, the contributor, the validator and the manager. The working group was in charge of attributing the different roles. For example, the validator roles were attributed to CTs who are responsible for each OC while the manager roles were attributed to ALEX project responsible person. Employees, depending on the role they have in the system, are more or less involved in the animation of the platform and content validation. These roles helped develop access features according to system security levels and promote empowerment of actors.

The group decided that the submission of experience sheet should be made by the contributor under moderation of the validator or the administrator. It is done using forms with large areas of open writing because the activity is too complex to be defined by a structure; employees without any role distinction communicate by comments left on the sheets. These comments serve to convey the appreciation of the reader regarding the record, as its content is a good idea to generalize or if there is a need for additional information; research content is natural language or keywords; photos of the galleries will be indexed according to the operating structures and equipment in order to facilitate research.

Skeleton and Visual Design. Lasts focus groups were dedicated to skeleton and visual design. This phase was animated by discussions based on a proposal of a skeleton made with a content management system (CMS) named Drupal[1]. The use of a CMS allowed us to accelerate the development and modifications of the prototype according to the users' feedback.

At the end of this design cycle, we delivered a new version of ALEX. The new ALEX (see Fig. 3) is a collaborative corporate wiki organized according to the different OCs. The refined platform proposes three main functionalities: (1) online submission and edition of an experience sheet using online media (pictures, documents, video); (2) a search engine for natural language and keywords to tag information and a carousel for the visualization of pictures; and (3) a contribution validation workflow. The proposed features fulfil the need for visibility, collaboration, information persistence

[1] www.drupal.org.

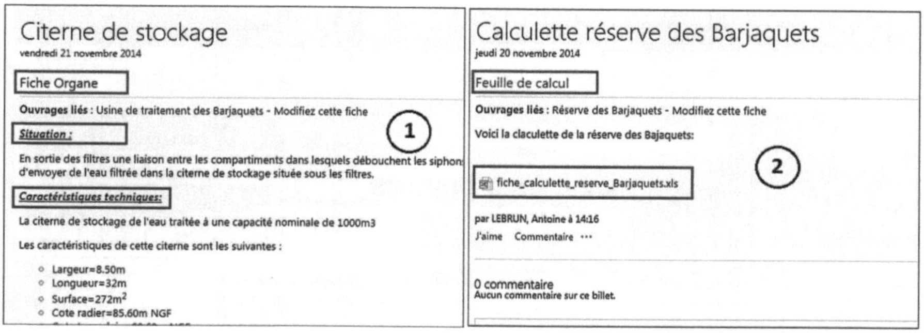

Fig. 2. View of two types of sheets. Form 1 is an equipment sheet and form 2 a worksheet. Organization of the content depends on the type: equipment sheets are arranged in predefined paragraphs while a worksheet contains an attached file with a free content textbox.

and knowledge sharing. This refinement corresponds to the first occurrence in our continual improvement process presented in Fig. 1.

After a three months use, an evaluation was conducted and showed that this new version of ALEX match the basic users' expectations but lacked attractive items to guaranty a long-term usage [34]. The second design cycle allowed us to work on these elements.

3.3 The Second Design Cycle

Discussions were about design of items for stimulation, control and monitoring of activity. They revealed two emerging groups of needs for readers/contributors and for validators/managers. The first ones were sensitive to the addition of social features and activity indicators (comments, ratings, notifications…) while the latter expressed expectations about monitoring activity via an activity dashboard. We present in the following subsection results related to social features, since the dashboard is still being developed currently.

Comments and Appreciations. Discussions on comments and appreciation were based on mockups presenting interactions that mimic what is commonly done in Web 2.0 knowledge construction tools like blogs or wikis: comments and "Likes" counting number of positive appreciations.

All the participants agreed with the idea of using comments as they are simpler means of communication than emails. They also make the sheets interactive, as they can be seen as an 'annotation tool'. However, they noted that contributors must be informed when a new comment is added on their experience sheet. Moreover, unlike comments left within classic social networks, SCP collaborators asked for moderation and archiving of comments to improve their readability and to control potential excess or harassment in relation to co-workers. Validators (collaborators with enough expertise who are in charge of electronic validation of experience sheets) will manage and ensure that propositions made within comments are effectively taken into account for the improvement of sheets. They are also in charge of archiving comments.

Fig. 3. View of ALEX: an OC front page. Boxes 1 and 2 show different types of browsing, with tabs at the top or with a menu on the side. Box 3 presents a slideshow of pictures posted in the OC library. In box 4, we placed the submission options. Box 5 shows the research form.

The 'Like' functionality gave rise to much discussion. Some participants had concerns about the real meaning of the term 'like', potential abuse (if a 'Like' is just given by affinity and does not reflect the quality of a contribution) and the negative impact it could have on contributors' motivation if they do not receive any. Some participants thus asked for clarification by relabeling the functionality to 'useful sheet'. Others were very enthusiastic about it as they are already familiar in other social networks and consider it as 'playful' in a professional context. During the next session, where the resulting feature was shown to users, they finally argued that the 'Like' functionality, in the context of SCP, is not a key motivator for contribution but rather signifies the reactivity of other collaborators and the awareness of their feedback, the feeling of being in a human community that works. Ultimately, they agreed to consider 'Likes' as assessments of the sheet's content usefulness expressed by readers and to leave the term 'like' as is. Some adaptations have however been requested: replace the raised thumb by a smiling emoticon, and initiate discussions, among collaborators, on this social functionality to prevent the risks of misunderstandings and abuse.

Activity Indicators. Several pieces of information were proposed as representative of reflexive indicators: notifications of new publications, authors and date of submission, last sheets read, view of contribution status, number of comments received on a sheet. The view of publications and number of comments did not trigger any discussion as they have been already discussed in previous sessions (see Fig. 4 zone 3, 4). Notifications of new contributions published or consulted were mentioned to facilitate the identification of recent information and the interests of other collaborators. The identification of the actors, such as the last contributor or the last reader, was deemed useful for initiating direct discussions between colleagues. However, the identification of the successive contributors was not considered necessary, a validated form being considered as a collective work. The status of publications (pending, rejected, and accepted) has emerged due to the expressed need to know if and when the validator has taken into account a contribution. Finally, by considering possible use cases, the discussions revealed two ways of presenting these indicators: in a personal page linked to profiles (see Fig. 4 zone 6 for access) and on OCs front pages. The first page was seen as a way for each collaborator to follow his/her own activity and see its scope within the organization. The second was seen as a means for identifying the dynamics of a community, updated or useful information and thus initiating discussions among colleagues (see Fig. 5 zone 1).

Information Quality Indicators. Three indicators were proposed to express information quality: readability, completeness with respect to the concept described and relevance [35]. The objective is to inform the user of the reading effort necessary to realize the information presented in real situations of work or problem solving. There was general support for the use of such indicators. Discussions focused on evaluation scales, how values were allocated, and the names of indicators. To describe readability, participants proposed a 4 levels scale: operational (the information on the sheet is immediately or quickly exploitable, such as alarms records specifically describing each step to perform a corrective maintenance operation); support (can be used in case of emergency but requires more analysis for information appropriation); acquisition (general information to train the reader); and sharing (information that needs further work). An agreement was reached on the term 'presentation level' to name the indicator. Completeness was found useful using the name 'Level of coverage'. The evaluation scale of this indicator is on three levels: weak, medium and good. This indicator was not deemed appropriate, as content is relevant if accepted for publication by the validator. As with the readability indicator, the completeness assessment of the sheet is made by the validators. The participants did not deem it useful to depict this indicator with an icon (stars, lights …) and preferred the indications to be directly written in the header of each content form (see Fig. 4 zone 1).

4 Evaluation

4.1 Methodology

Two evaluations have been conducted. After four months of uses, a qualitative evaluation has first been done to measure the design quality and the potential learning effectiveness. We have also collected the track of ALEX's uses during more than two years from the end of the first cycle. This quantitative evaluation has been conducted to measure coworkers real uses.

Qualitative Evaluation. Criteria for design quality are deriving from uses success factors identified in the TAM, UTAUT and ISSM models of technology acceptance [26, 30]: Use (Use), Usefulness (Usef), Satisfaction (Sat), Perceived benefit (Ben), Usage intention (UI). Indeed, successful use of the tool is related to positive satisfaction, attitude and intention; this is why we focus on these criteria. We measured learning effectiveness according to users' statements on impact on use, work habits and performance (IOU&W).

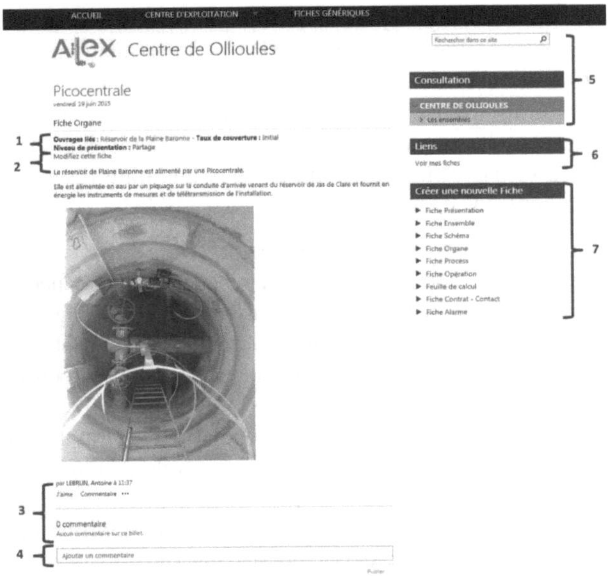

Fig. 4. View page of a content form [19].

Fig. 5. An OC front page with contributors' names in zone 1 (* names were modified).

ALEX with social functionalities was made available for four months. Ten collaborators have been interviewed about their uses and positions about new social functionalities. A first group (group 1) was composed by five of them (named P1 to P5) that had participated to the design working group, while a second group (group 2) was composed by five other people (named P6 to P10) who were not involved at all in ALEX design. Interviews were individual and lasted one hour per person. During the interview, an interface of ALEX was available to help participants to contextualise and refine their appreciations. The interviews were anonymously recorded and manually encoded to identify the parts of sentences, called utterances, corresponding to the different criteria. A positive (+), neutral (=) or negative (-) polarity was assigned to each selected utterance. An utterance was considered as neutral when participants said that they did not know how to answer a question or when it was not possible to detect a polarity in the given answer. We analysed participants' appreciations according to the number of statements and polarity on each criteria and compare the two groups to measure if the working group proposition are shared with the other collaborators.

Quantitative Evaluation. We have collected the log tracks of ALEX uses during two years and a half. Tracks, collected in 2014 have been produced by the 4 OC test using the first version of the platform Alex (with navigation function and roles). Tracks, collected in 2015 and 2016 correspond to the uses made on the platform Alex "version 2" (with social functionalities). Alex was opened to only 4 OC test in 2015 and to all of them in 2016. We mainly analyzed the way of building new knowledge by measuring what actions were performed to produce experience sheet, who were the actors involved and how they collaborate.

4.2 Results

General Results. 111 utterances (n = 111) were collected. Table 1 describes their distribution according to the six criteria and the three polarities in frequency and percentage. We note that appreciations are globally positive (60.2%). Only 11.3% are negative and 28.5% are neutral. Usefulness is the most expressed statement (40) and is globally positive (52.5%) even if one third of the participants don't have an accurate point of view about it (32.5%). Satisfaction and impact on work and performance are the most positive criteria (with respectively 90% and 72.7%). A third of the participants (35.7%) express positive statements about usage intention while nearly half of them (42.8%) have no real idea of the kind of usage they can introduce. Statements about real uses are diverse. Half of the participants express positive uses (50%) but a third of them (31.3%) didn't use Alex. Comments of participants related to each criteria are presented in the third part of this section and are useful to refine and understand these results.

Group Answers Comparison. Table 2 shows the distribution of positive, negative and neutral responses among people from groups 1 and 2. People in group 2 express more satisfaction than in group 1. This corroborates the fact that we succeeded in transcribing future users' needs. This is the same for usefulness, benefits and usage intention, for which we collected more positive appreciations from the participants who were not involved in the design. This may be related to the surprise effect and let's expect a motivating effect for further use. The negative appreciations about usefulness in group 1 were given by participant P4 concerning quality indicators. This can be explained by the position of the participant (engineer) and his seniority. He stated that *"engineers use ALEX only in specific maintenance operation periods"*. As he is an expert, quality indicators do not have particular usefulness for him.

Comments of Participants Related to Each Criteria. The participants provided us with very valuable comments. A more complete transcription of these interviews can be found in [36]. Here, we give the most salient comments.

Table 1. Distribution of utterances according to criteria (frequency) and polarities (percentage) [19].

	Use	Usef	Sat	Ben	IOU&W	UI	Means
n	*16*	*40*	*20*	*10*	*11*	*14*	
+ (%)	50	52.5	90	60	72.7	35.7	60.2
− (%)	31.3	15	0	0	0	21.4	11.3
= (%)	18.7	32.5	10	40	27.3	42.9	28.5

Table 2. Group 1 and 2 comparison [19].

		Use	Usef	Sat	Ben	IOU&W	UI	Means
Group 1	+ (%)	50	52.5	90	60	72.7	35.7	60.2
	− (%)	31.3	15	0	0	0	21.4	11.3
	= (%)	18.7	32.5	10	40	27.3	42.9	28.5
Group 2	+ (%)	50	52.5	90	60	72.7	35.7	60.2
	− (%)	31.3	15	0	0	0	21.4	11.3
	= (%)	18.7	32.5	10	40	27.3	42.9	28.5

Usefulness. Six out of ten participants explicitly found comments functions useful: four from group 2 and two from group 1. Three out of ten participants explicitly found indicators useful. One relates that: "*... in the previous version of ALEX, we couldn't really rely on sheets during maintenance operations... as the information evolves rapidly, when someone notices a mistake or something else... it was discussed face to face with the person supposed to operate the sheet's modifications ... which was done... or not... for me, comments are a feature more rewarding than oral exchanges, comments come from everyone... a trace of their viewpoint is kept, less chance of forgetting or losing information as was common in previous versions*". Indeed, having up-to-date information is an important part of information quality, positively related to an effective use of the platform [26] by two participants from group 2 and one from group 1. *Concerning 'Likes', three out of ten participants explicitly found this functionality useful: one from group 2 and two from group 1. One participant qualified as "sympathetic" the idea of adding this social functionality and highlighted "a lack of communication and social components in the previous version of ALEX".*

User Satisfaction and Benefits. Participant generally find the platform more modern and satisfactory overall; they did not find many negative aspects. Participant P1 said that ALEX was "*a renovated tool, similar to those findable in the internet market, more playful and pleasant*", while participant P4 argued that Alex was "*more user-friendly*". They express benefits to use new 'comment' and 'Like' functionalities. Participant P5 employed the phrases "*peers' acknowledgment and feeling useful*". Participant P3 said: "*...as it is now easier to use, we have more time to submit and seek for information... I am personally satisfied to participate in the building of the tool... inter alia to help the new colleagues integrating in the company... but I would like to be aware of my exact role in the tool and also have a kind of acknowledgements from the company...*" In these words, we identify the belief of social influence which arises from the use of the tool and motivates users. This is an interesting finding, as intrinsic benefits like reputation, joy and knowledge growth positively leverage continued use of knowledge-sharing tools [37].

Impact on Use and on Performance. At the time of the interviews, most participants did not mention any significant increase of ALEX use compared with how they used the previous versions. Four out of ten participants were frequent users (from twice a week to every day, according to the working tasks to perform), while the remainder used it once a month or less. When asked why, most of them answered that they had enough experience and knowledge of the hydraulics infrastructures. They also justified this by the fact that they were rarely confronted with difficult or atypical issues they didn't already know how to deal with, or needed more frequent connection to ALEX. Nevertheless, three participants argued that ALEX had been "*a time saver to access unknown intervention venues*" and useful to "*get information about the components of my new OC*", or to assist him "*during a drain, a common maintenance operation*" in water infrastructures. The two first ones were new to the OC, and the last one had a complex maintenance operation to perform.

Usage Intention. About half of the participants expressed usage intention linked with information seeking. Few of them plan to submit and collaborate on ALEX's content. However, the score 42.9% of neutral appreciation rate (see Table 1) can be explained be the youth of the project and the particular conditions of the context. For example, participant P2 was about to leave SCP (termination of his contract). He nevertheless participated in the evaluation and specified that "*ALEX usage perspectives are positive ... under the conditions of a general advertisement campaign within the company...*". Participant P1 also stressed the positive effect of the user-centred design approach on workers' involvement and on sustainability of the new ALEX: "*... everyone participated in the refinement of the tool, the result satisfied more people and strengthened the project... everyone sees more clearly its real interest, which was not necessarily the case before, so I think it will be continuously used ...*".

Use Analyses. During the 2.5 years of the project, 2095 experience sheets were produced. Figure 6 shows the evolution: 279 sheets were produced in 2014, 379 sheets were produced in 2015 and 1437 in 2016. The small progress in 2015 seems to be linked with the addition of the social functionality, while the big progress in 2016 seems to be linked with a communication campaign and the access of the platform to everyone in the company.

7867 actions of experience sheets manipulation were recorded. Figure 7 describes the types of users who realized these actions. Half of the actions (46%) are made by readers and correspond to consultations and comments. The other half is realized by validators, contributors and administrators. They correspond mainly to reading, creation, update or validation. Most of the actions are made by the validators (26%) and the administrator (21%). The contributors intervene only weakly (7%). Validators and administrators are the main producers of new sheets. These creations correspond to the transfer of the experience sheets (coming from the native version of ALEX) to the new platform. Validators and contributors attempt mainly to update theses sheets or to create new ones.

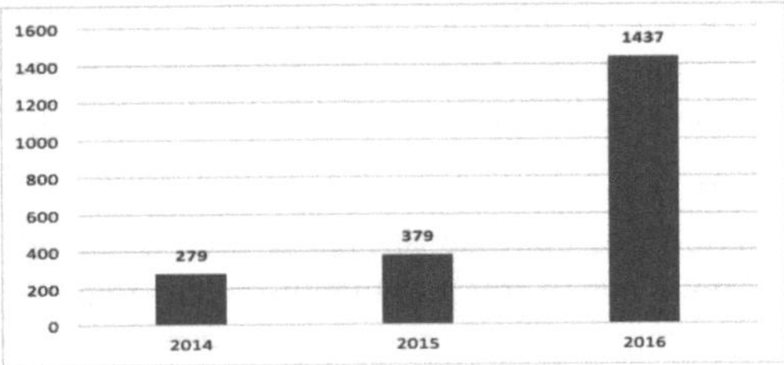

Fig. 6. Number of experience sheet produced each year.

Figure 8 presents the number of collaborations committed to the production of sheets. We observe an increasing, but homogeneous, volume of sheets (238, 303, 387) produced every year by a single author. In 2016, a big quantity of sheets (1029) was produced further by a collaboration between two actors. Collaborations between more authors remain marginal, but increase gradually. The unique author should have been the administrator who directly transferred and validated the sheets contained in the original platform. Sheets produced by 2 collaborators correspond either, to updates done by the validators of the sheets transferred by the administrator, or to the creation of new sheets by the contributors then updated by validator. The interactions between more users correspond to the integration of the comments, left by the readers, and treated by the contributor or the validator. Thus, the comment process is not usual, but increases gradually.

5 Discussions and Conclusion

In this paper, we proposed to address the lack of acceptance and usage with which companies may be confronted when they use traditional KMS for informal learning. We argued that ESM present functionalities that can improve the meta-social level of traditional KMS, making them better tools for self-regulation and learning. Our objective was to identify: which principles and functionalities of social media can be adapted to support informal learning in the workplace, and which method can be used to identify the adaptation that fit collaborators requirements and prevent risks of misuse that are inherent in the use of common ESM.

Our analysis showed that ESM are appropriate to support informal learning strategies in the workplace. Indeed, social features like comments, appreciations, activity indicators are adapted to stimulate use behaviors and support learning, particularly meta-cognitive aspects. Three adaptations must nevertheless be carried out: (1) Base the design on a precise and relatively exhaustive informational corpus of the procedures and know-how already formalized in the company and contextualize the access in the form of community of practice structured according to collaborative spaces; (2) Add indicators of judgment on the operational quality of information and the informational capital built, and (3) Define forms of moderation and control consistent with the hierarchical structures of the company.

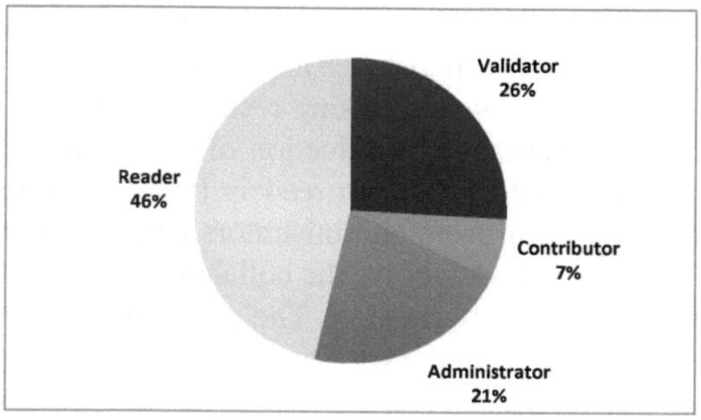

Fig. 7. Percentage of action on the platform by role.

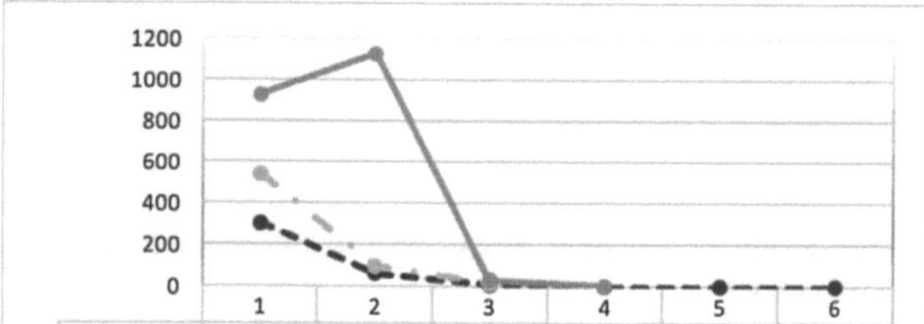

	1	2	3	4	5	6
2016	387	1029	18	3		
2014	238	35	6			
2015	303	64	9	1	1	1

Fig. 8. Number of experience sheet produced by 1, 2, 3… collaborators each year.

Our analysis also showed that an incremental and iterative approaches of user-centered design are useful to define how to adapt the design and to accompany change. Indeed, the discussions between the collaborators during the focus groups allowed to make design choices shared by all. During the first cycle, for example, they agreed on the information architecture to be used, the specification of the system policies (the users' roles and the processes of information validation). During the second cycle, they found issues about the uses of likes and comments as well as about the publication of activity indicators.

The reinforcement of the design work on information architectures should be done. Evaluation shows that information seeking is a massive use intention. It thus could be useful to refine this work for proposing information search recommendation based on users' tracks. On the other hand, the need to adapt forms of moderation and control to the hierarchical structures of the company questions us. This principle is coherent with learning objectives since it creates some forms of mediation but is less so if one considers the principles of social media which consist in smoothing these forms of hierarchies to highlight the speech of each moderated by the collective. We wonder whether it is realistic to add this additional work load. Its implication is indeed critical to guarantee this type of functioning. In addition, we are wondering whether these requirements are indeed sustainable over the long term or whether they are an acceptance step in the design cycle as a form of temporary guaranty that should fall after the use of this type of platform all over the company.

The evaluation conducted shows promising results about uses. The uses observed are balanced between consultation and production of information. Currently, the production of information does not come from readers (via comments) or from contributors (by new sheet creation) but from administrators and validators. The preliminary existence of many experience sheets allows the collaborators to have a rich platform in terms of quantity and quality of information. The proposed organization seems to be adapted to update and refine existing experience sheets. The creation of new sheets remains difficult, but we have observed some sign of new collaborations. A longer study will allow us to see if communities of practice are really growing. On this basis, our next objectives will be to observe the long-term acceptability of the principles to the whole organization, the informal learning effects and answer more general questions about the forms of moderation.

References

1. Sharples, M.: The design of personal mobile technologies for lifelong learning. Comput. Educ. **34**, 177–193 (2000)
2. Commission of the European Communities: A Memorandum on Lifelong Learning (2000)
3. Longmore, B.: Work-based learning: bridging knowledge and action in the workplace. Action Learn. Res. Pract. **8**, 79–82 (2011)
4. Bancheva, E., Ivanova, M.: Informal learning in the workplace. In: Private World(s): Gender and Informal Learning of Adults, pp. 157–182 (2015)
5. Ackerman, M.S., Dachtera, J., Pipek, V., Wulf, V.: Sharing knowledge and expertise: the CSCW view of knowledge management. Comput. Support. Coop. Work CSCW. **22**, 531–573 (2013)
6. Hahn, J., Subramani, M.R.: A framework for knowledge management systems: issues and challenges for theory and practice. In: ICIS 2000 Proceedings of the Twenty First International Conference on Information Systems, pp. 302–312 (1999)
7. Wenger, E.: Communities of Practice - A Brief Introduction (2006)
8. Hager, P.: Lifelong learning in the workplace? Challenges and issues. J. Workplace Learn. **16**, 22–32 (2004)
9. Graesser, A.C.: 25 Principles of Learning (2009)
10. Graesser, A.C.: CE corner: improving learning. Monit. Psychol. **42**, 54–60 (2011)
11. Pettenati, M., Ranieri, M.: Innovative approaches for learning and knowledge sharing. In: Tomodaki, E., Scott, P. (eds.) Innovative Approaches for Learning and Knowledge Sharing, EC-TEL 2006 Workshops Proceedings, pp. 345–355 (2006)
12. Wang, S., Noe, R.A.: Knowledge sharing: a review and directions for future research. Hum. Resour. Manag. Rev. **20**, 115–131 (2010)
13. Ellison, N.B., Gibbs, J.L., Weber, M.S.: The use of enterprise social network sites for knowledge sharing in distributed organizations: the role of organizational affordances. Am. Behav. Sci. **59**, 103–123 (2015)
14. Dennerlein, S., et al.: KnowBrain: an online social knowledge repository for informal workplace learning. In: Conole, G., Klobučar, T., Rensing, C., Konert, J., Lavoué, É. (eds.) EC-TEL 2015. LNCS, vol. 9307, pp. 509–512. Springer, Cham (2015). https://doi.org/10.1007/978-3-319-24258-3_48

15. Leonardi, P.M., Huysman, M., Steinfield, C.: Enterprise social media: definition, history, and prospects for the study of social technologies in organizations. J. Comput.-Mediat. Commun. **19**, 1–19 (2013)
16. Riemer, K., Scifleet, P.: Enterprise social networking in knowledge-intensive work practices: a case study in a professional service firm. In: 23rd Australasian Conference on Information Systems, pp. 1–12 (2012)
17. Ersoy, M., Güneyli, A.: Social networking as a tool for lifelong learning with orthopedically impaired learners. Educ. Technol. Soc. **19**, 41–52 (2016)
18. Turban, E., Bolloju, N., Liang, T.-P.: Enterprise social networking: opportunities, adoption, and risk mitigation. J. Organ. Comput. Electron. Commer. **21**, 202–220 (2011)
19. Touré, C., Michel, C., Marty, J.-C.: How to promote informal learning in the workplace? The need for incremental design methods. In: Escudeiro, P., Costagliola, G., Zvacek, S., Uhomoibhi, J., McLaren, B.M. (eds.) Proceedings of the 9th International Conference on Computer Supported Education (CSEDU 2017), Porto (Portugal), pp. 220–229 (2017)
20. Kaplan, A.M., Haenlein, M.: Users of the world, unite! The challenges and opportunities of Social Media. Bus. Horiz. **53**, 59–68 (2010)
21. Kietzmann, J.H., Hermkens, K., McCarthy, I.P., Silvestre, B.S.: Social media? Get serious! Understanding the functional building blocks of social media. Bus. Horiz. **54**, 241–251 (2011)
22. Stocker, A., Müller, J.: Exploring factual and perceived use and benefits of a web 2.0-based knowledge management application: the siemens case references+. In: Proceedings of the 13th International Conference on Knowledge Management and Knowledge Technologies (2013)
23. Schön, D.A.: Educating the Reflective Practitioner: Towards a New Design for Teaching and Learning in the Professions. Jossey-Bass Publishers, San Francisco (1987)
24. Zhao, X., Salehi, N., Naranjit, S., Alwaalan, S.: The many faces of Facebook: experiencing social media as performance, exhibition, and personal archive. In: Proceedings of the CHI 2013 Conference, Paris, pp. 1–10 (2013)
25. Janssen, J., Erkens, G., Kirschner, P.: Group awareness tools: it's what you do with it that matters. Comput. Hum. Behav. **27**, 1046–1058 (2011)
26. DeLone, W.H., McLean, E.R.: The DeLone and McLean model of information systems success: a ten-year update. J. Manag. Inf. Syst. **19**, 9–30 (2003)
27. Kulkarni, U., Ravindran, S., Freeze, R.: A knowledge management success model: theoretical development and empirical validation. J. Manag. Ldots. **23**, 309–347 (2007)
28. Jennex, M.E., Olfman, L.: A model of knowledge management success. Int. J. Knowl. Manag. **2**, 51–68 (2006)
29. Venkatesh, V., Morris, M.G., Hall, M., Davis, G.B., Davis, F.D., Walton, S.M.: User acceptance of information technology: toward a unified view. MIS Q. **27**, 425–478 (2003)
30. Venkatesh, V., Thong, J.Y.L., Xu, X.: Consumer acceptance and use of information technology: extending the unified theory of acceptance and use of technology. MIS Q. **36**, 157–178 (2012)
31. Benson, A.D., Johnson, S.D., Kuchinke, K.P.: The use of technology in the digital workplace: a framework for human resource development. Adv. Dev. Hum. Resour. **4**, 392–404 (2002)
32. Bhattacherjee, A., Limayem, M., Cheung, C.M.K.: User switching of information technology: A theoretical synthesis and empirical test. Inf. Manag. **49**, 327–333 (2012)
33. Bhattacherjee, A.: Understanding information systems continuance: an expectation-confirmation model. MIS Q. **25**, 351–370 (2001)

34. Touré, C.E., Michel, C., Marty, J.-C.: Refinement of knowledge sharing platforms to promote effective use. In: 11th IEEE International Conference on Signal Image Technology and Internet based systems, Bangkok, pp. 1–8 (2015)
35. Lee, Y.W., Strong, D.M., Kahn, B.K., Wang, R.Y.: AIMQ: a methodology for information quality assessment. Inf. Manag. **40**, 133–146 (2002)
36. Touré, C., Michel, C., Marty, J.-C.: Towards extending traditional informal learning tools in the workplace with social functionalities. Int. J. Learn. Technol. **12**, 119–150 (2017)
37. He, W., Wei, K.-K.: What drives continued knowledge sharing? An investigation of knowledge-contribution and -seeking beliefs. Decis. Support Syst. **46**, 826–838 (2009)

Author Index